The Incest Theme in Literature and Legend

Translated by GREGORY C. RICHTER

With an Introductory Essay by Peter L. Rudnytsky

Otto Rank

The Incest Theme in Literature and Legend

Fundamentals of a Psychology of Literary Creation

The Johns Hopkins University Press
Baltimore and London

Originally published as *Das Inzest-Motiv in Dichtung und Sage* in 1912 by Franz Deuticke, Leipzig and Vienna.

Printed in the United States of America

The Johns Hopkins University Press
701 West 40th Street, Baltimore, Maryland 21211-2190
The Johns Hopkins Press, Ltd., London

The paper used in this book meets the minimum requirements of American National Standard for Information Sciences—Permanence of Paper for Printed Library Materials, ANSI Z39.48–1984.

Rank, Otto, 1884–1939.
[Inzest-Motiv in Dichtung und Sage. English]
The incest theme in literature and legend : fundamentals of a psychology of literary creation / Otto Rank ; translated by Gregory C. Richter ; with an introductory essay by Peter Rudnytsky.
p. cm.
Translation of: Das Inzest-Motiv in Dichtung und Sage.
Includes bibliographical references and index.
ISBN 0-8018-4176-3 (alk. paper)
1. Incest in literature. 2. Psychoanalysis. 3. Creation (Literary, artistic, etc.) I. Title.
PN56.I55R313 1992
809'.93353—dc20 91-19851

Nowhere is the ailing psyche of an author so clearly revealed as in his own protagonists, whom he always tarnishes, against his will, with the secret defects of his own character.

JEAN PAUL

Contents

PART II

The Relationship between Siblings

Introductory Essay

PETER L. RUDNYTSKY

The first three meetings of the Psychological Wednesday Society for which minutes are extant took place on October 10, October 17, and October 24, 1906. Viennese physicians and other intellectuals interested in Freud's ideas had begun gathering for weekly discussions in his apartment at Berggasse 19 as early as 1902, but not until 1906, with Otto Rank's appointment as salaried secretary to the group—an appointment that lasted until 1915, when World War I intervened—were the proceedings recorded in writing.

Rank's function at these October 1906 meetings was pivotal in two respects, for he not only transcribed them but also read the paper that was discussed. His three-part presentation, "The Incest Drama and Its Complications," outlined the ideas that he fully elaborated in his 1912 magnum opus, *Das Inzest-Motiv in Dichtung und Sage: Grundzüge einer Psychologie des dichterischen Schaffens* [The incest theme in literature and legend: Fundamentals of a psychology of literary creation], which appears here for the first time in an English translation.

Beyond Rank's double function as speaker and reporter, it is symbolically appropriate that the minutes of the Psychological Wednesday Society should begin with a sketch of *The Incest Theme*. During 1906–12 the psychoanalytic movement grew to maturity. The group to which Rank delivered his ideas was renamed in 1908 the Vienna Psychoanalytic Society; in 1910 it ceased meeting in Freud's apartment. Also in 1910, in the aftermath of the Nuremberg Congress, the International Psychoanalytic Association was founded, with Jung as president. After the Nuremberg Congress adjourned, Freud wrote to Ferenczi: "With the Nuremberg *Reichstag* closes the childhood of our movement; that is my impression. I hope now for a rich and fair time of youth" (Jones 1955, 70–71).

By existing in preliminary and final form at either end of the period 1906–12, Rank's work frames the years in question. The historical significance of *The Incest Theme* is inseparable from its theoretical concern with incest. As Rank summarizes his main thesis, "The incest fantasy is not simply the 'nuclear complex of neurosis' " that "dominates the unconscious psychic life of normals, determining their social and erotic orientation in life," but is also "of primary importance in the psychic life of the author" (1912b, 12). During 1906 to 1912 the Oedipus complex emerged as the touchstone of psychoanalytic truth.

The story of Freud's discovery of the Oedipus complex has often been told; here only one point solicits attention. In a valuable study, John Forrester (1980, 84–96) has documented how Freud gradually consolidated the concept of the Oedipus complex, which integrated such disparate themes as infantile sexuality, children's sexual researches, generational conflict, the family romance, Jung's idea of a "complex" derived from word association experiments, and the triangular relation between a child and its parents into a single theoretical whole. The term itself first surfaced in Freud's paper, "A Special Type of Choice of Object Made by Men" (1910). Challenging traditional accounts of Freud's career, Forrester argues that "Freud did *not* discover the Oedipus complex *as such* during his self-analysis. . . . Rather, he discovered Oedipal impulses. If we mean by the Oedipus complex the nucleus or core of a neurosis, then it seems clear that Freud did not establish this until the period 1908–10" (1980, 232 n. 19).

Building on Forrester's work, John Kerr (1988, 25–30) has charted the evolution of Freud's belief in a "nuclear complex" (*Kernkomplex*) of the neuroses. As Kerr shows, it was again only gradually that the "nuclear complex" became synonymous with the Oedipus complex, so that Freud could declare in *Totem and Taboo,* "We have arrived at the point of regarding a child's relation to his parents, dominated as it is by incestuous longings, as the nuclear complex of neurosis" (1912–13, 17). Kerr points out that the first reference to the term "nuclear complex" in the Freud-Jung correspondence, in Freud's letter of December 11, 1908, occurs in connection not with Oedipus, but with an altogether different notion of a "poisoning complex": "I am so obsessed by the idea of a nuclear complex in neuroses such as is at the heart of the case of Little Herbert [Hans] that I cannot make any headway. A recent observation tempted me to trace the poisoning complex, when it is present, back to the infant's interpretation of the mother's morning sickness" (McGuire 1974, 186). Kerr links Freud's interest in this developmental aspect of the poisoning complex—the bewildered child's inference that sexual intercourse makes people sick—to his deeply held belief that libido would prove to be a toxic chemical process in the brain.

The inquiries of Forrester and Kerr usefully complicate oedipal-centered narratives of Freud's intellectual development—such as my own in *Freud and Oedipus* (Rudnytsky 1987)—but they do not undermine them. In his *Autobiographical Study,* Freud states that "the ubiquity of [the Oedipus complex] gradually dawned on me" (1925, 63), and the labors of the revisionist historians simply substantiate this retrospective realization.

Moreover, although Freud's arrival at his 1910 formulation of the Oedipus complex was indeed gradual, a chain of references to Oedipus in his writings beginning with the section "Typical Dreams" in *The Interpretation of Dreams*—itself a recasting of the insight expressed in his October 15, 1897, letter to Fliess—shows that a conjunction between the ideas of Oedipus and incest was well established in his mind. In *Three Essays on the Theory of Sexuality,* Freud affirms: "Among these [infantile] tendencies the first place is taken with uniform frequency by the child's sexual impulses towards his parents, which are as a rule already differentiated owing to the attraction of the opposite sex—the son being drawn towards his mother and the daughter towards her father." A footnote directs the reader "to my remarks in *The Interpretation of Dreams* on the inevitability of fate in the fable of Oedipus" (1905, 227). Alluding to the foregoing passage, Freud writes in the case of Little Hans: "In his attitude toward his father and mother Hans confirms in the most concrete and uncompromising manner what I have said in my *Interpretation of Dreams* and my *Three Essays* with regard to the sexual relations of a child to his parents. Hans really was a little Oedipus who wanted to have his father 'out of the way,' to get rid of him, so that he might be alone with his beautiful mother and sleep with her" (1909a, 111). In the case of the Rat Man, although he does not mention Oedipus, Freud defines *"the nuclear complex of the neuroses"* as "the complex which comprises the child's earliest impulses, alike tender and hostile, towards its parents and brothers and sisters" (1909b, 208). He remarks of his obsessive patient: "There can be no question that there was something in the sphere of sexuality that stood between the father and son, and that the father had come into some sort of opposition to the son's prematurely developed erotic life. Several years after his father's death, the first time he experienced the pleasurable sensations of copulation, an idea sprang into his mind: 'This is glorious! One might murder one's father for this!'" (1909b, 201).

When one reads these excerpts from Freud's writings between 1905 and 1909, it becomes evident that the Oedipus myth never had a serious rival as an explanatory paradigm. The passages from the two case histories directly refute Forrester's contention that in 1909 "Freud and his co-workers were not particularly concerned with the triadic relation of father, mother, and child" (1980, 89). With commendable honesty, Kerr concedes that the poisoning complex "was not destined for great things in the evolution of psychoanalysis" and that it "was one of the few ideas that Freud seems simply to have discarded altogether" (1988, 28–29).

As Freud's letter to Fliess of October 15, 1897, attests, Oedipus inheres in the very origins of psychoanalysis: "A single idea of general value dawned on me. I have found, in my own case too, being in love with my mother and jealousy of my father, and I now consider it a universal event in early childhood. . . . If this is so, we can understand the gripping power of *Oedipus Rex*" (Masson 1985, 272). He rephrases the same idea less personally in *The Interpretation of Dreams:* "It is the fate of all of us, perhaps, to direct our first sexual impulse towards our mother and our first hatred and our first murderous wish against our father" (Freud 1900, 262). In both the letter to Fliess and *The Interpretation of Dreams,* his exegeses of *Oedipus the King* and *Hamlet* follow. Already in the letter to Fliess, Freud asserts the oedipal paradigm to be his "single idea of general value" and a "universal event." Thus, when in 1910 he formulates the Oedipus complex and in 1912 equates it with the nuclear complex, Freud is simply restating at higher levels of theoretical abstraction the basic contention he had proposed to Fliess in the wake of his abandonment of the seduction theory and then advanced publicly in *The Interpretation of Dreams*. In psychoanalytic terms, Freud's progression from the letter to Fliess to *Totem and Taboo* is one of *deferred action,* in which the later moment completes the meaning of the earlier moment but the two cannot be understood independently of one another.

As I have shown elsewhere, the chain of "supplements" in Freud's identification with Oedipus begins before the letter to Fliess and continues after *Totem and Taboo;* its origins lie in his family constellation, in which his father was a generation older than his mother (Rudnytsky 1987, 3–17). Nonetheless, these are the two decisive moments. Consequently, Freud's abandonment of the seduction theory in September 1897, which led immediately to his reorientation toward infantile sexual fantasy and invocation of Oedipus, retains its standing as a turning point of his thought, and no account of his career can be accepted that loses sight of this benchmark.

Freud's engagement with the Oedipus myth forms the backdrop to Rank's achievement in *The Incest Theme*. Rank's progression from his 1906 presentations to the Vienna Psychoanalytic Society to his 1912 publication of the completed work parallels Freud's intellectual development and forms an integral subplot to the history of psychoanalysis during this period. In his comments on Rank's first talk, Freud criticized the lack of clarity in his organization and proposed: "Oedipus should be presented as the core [*Kern*] and model; then the one tried and tested method of presentation would be on the one hand to group the material around this core, and on the other hand, by developing a series, to follow the theme from its core to its furthest ramifications" (Nunberg and Federn 1962, 10). In the first recorded meeting of the Vienna Psychoanalytic Society, Freud heralds his search for a nuclear complex, and he does so in connection with Oedipus.[1] That Rank took Freud's strictures to heart is clear from *The Incest Theme*, not only in the passage I have already quoted but also in the conclusion, where he reaffirms that "the incest complex with all its diversity, opposing aspects, and derivatives represents the nuclear complex of neuroses and of the literary creative drive as well" (Rank 1912b, 570).

Rank's relationship to Freud is triangulated by Jung, who in 1912 published *Wandlungen und Symbole der Libido* (Transformations and symbols of the libido), translated into English in 1916 as *Psychology of the Unconscious*. Not only were *Transformations and Symbols* and *The Incest Theme* published in the same year, but the two works mirror one another in that they approach the problems of incest and libido from antithetical vantage points. Jung's work announces his dissatisfaction with Freud's system; Rank's champions Freudian orthodoxy. As Jung wrote to Freud on August 2, 1912, upon receiving Rank's book: "It is a very distinguished piece of work and will make a big impression. But, as you know, I am not in agreement with his theoretical position on the incest problem. The salient fact is simply the regressive movement of the libido and not the mother" (McGuire 1974, 512).

The doubling between Jung and Rank is redoubled, since both published revised editions of their landmark books. The second edition of *The Incest Theme* appeared in 1926; the second edition of Jung's treatise, reti-

1. The English edition of the minutes ascribes to Eduard Hitschmann the comment that Rank's paper is "no more than a rather superfluous extension of Freud's discovery of the Oedipus complex" (Nunberg and Federn 1962, 9). This is an anachronistic mistranslation, since Freud did not coin the term Oedipus complex until 1909. In the German text, Hitschmann refers simply to "der von Freud aufgedeckten Tatsache (Ödipus)" (the fact uncovered by Freud [Oedipus]; Nunberg and Federn 1976, 9).

tled *Symbols of Transformation*, appeared in 1952. Both later editions reflect changes in their authors' relationship to Freud.[2] A distillation of Jung's mature thought, *Symbols of Transformation* is implacably antipsychoanalytic. By contrast, the second edition of *The Incest Theme* stems from the period between 1924 and 1927, when Rank had broken personally with Freud over the crisis precipitated by *The Trauma of Birth* (1924) but still continued to regard himself as a psychoanalyst.[3] Thus, whereas in Jung's case the first edition is transitional and the second definitive, for Rank the reverse is true. Still, the appearance of revised editions testifies to the importance both authors attached to the works in question, and a properly historical reading would require a scrutiny of the disparities between the two versions.

Jung's modifications cannot be considered here, and even Rank's can be only cursorily assessed. But it surely bears mentioning that both occurrences of the phrase "nuclear complex" I have cited from the 1912 edition of *The Incest Theme* (13, 681) are eliminated in the 1926 edition (19, 623). In *The Trauma of Birth*, by contrast, Rank speaks of the disturbance of the "blessed peace" the fetus enjoys in its mother's womb by the paternal phallus during intercourse as the "nuclear complex of the neuroses," of which the later Oedipus complex is merely the "psychosexual elaboration" (1924, 194). He thereby displaces Freud's oedipal paradigm from its place of theoretical primacy in favor of the prenatal period. The notion of the birth trauma receives only two passing glances in the 1926 *Incest Theme*. First, Rank claims to have shown by it that the child's "original bodily relationship to the mother" is the "deepest biological source" of its love for its parents (1926, 35; cf. 1912a, 27; 1912b, 23). Second, Rank writes of Cronus's castration of his father Uranus during intercourse that "besides the sexual rivalry over the mother, we must discern as well its previous infantile stage, namely separation, or, if one may so call it, 'castration' from the mother, whose root I have shown to be the actual separation from the mother in birth" (1926, 277–78; cf. 1912a, 287; 1912b, 231–32). By treating castration as a form of separation, the second passage makes clear the

2. In addition to the 1926 edition of the *Incest Theme*, a further revised French translation of the work appeared in 1934. The Otto Rank collection in Columbia University's Butler Library contains a final, shorter German manuscript version, as well as an English translation by George Wilbur, entitled *The Incest-Motif in Poetry and Saga: An Anthropological Study of Literature*. I have been unable to consult either the French translation or the final unpublished German version.

3. Elsewhere I have examined Rank's relationship to Freud in detail and proposed that this three-year interval between Rank's militant psychoanalytic and antipsychoanalytic periods contains his richest thought, in which he anticipates contemporary object relations theory (Rudnytsky 1991, 31–69). On Rank's life and work as a whole, see the biographies by Jessie Taft (1958) and E. James Lieberman (1985) and the study by Esther Menaker (1982).

radical shift from oedipal to preoedipal levels of analysis that characterizes Rank's 1924–27 period.

The intertwining of the fates of Rank and Jung culminates in their roles as psychoanalytic apostates. In the *New Introductory Lectures* Freud contemplates the schisms that have taken place in psychoanalysis: "Suppose, for instance, that an analyst attaches little value to the influence of the patient's personal past and looks for the causation of neuroses exclusively in present-day motives and in expectations of the future. . . . We for our part will then say: 'This may be a school of wisdom; but it is no longer analysis.' Or someone else may arrive at the view that the experience of anxiety at birth sows the seed of all later neurotic disturbances" (1933, 143). These unnamed heresies are transparently those of Jung and Rank. Although they "start from diametrically opposed premisses," Freud adds, they share the characteristic that "each of them takes hold of one fragment out of the wealth of themes in psycho-analysis and makes itself independent on the basis of this seizure" (143–44).

Freud seeks to exonerate himself of responsibility for the ruptures in the psychoanalytic movement by claiming that they were simply a series of partings that became inevitable when theoretical differences exceeded tolerable limits. To the extent that "strong emotional factors" were involved, Freud imputes them exclusively to his opponents, who (apart from Wilhelm Stekel) "excluded themselves" because they found it difficult "to fit themselves in with others or to subordinate themselves" (1933, 143–44). Freud's polemic is a rhetorical tour de force, but it serves a defensive function, and his anonymous portraits of Jung and Rank show for whom he reserved his greatest scorn.

Freud's assimilation of Jung and Rank as dissidents was taken over by Ernest Jones in his biography of Freud. Indeed, Jones maintains that this parallel is in one important respect unfair to Jung: "The outstanding difference between the two cases is of course that Jung was not afflicted by any of the mental trouble that wrecked Rank and so was able to pursue an unusually productive and fruitful life" (1955, 77). Jones's depiction of Rank is prejudiced in the extreme, for there is no evidence that he suffered from any serious mental illness, and he retained the productivity of genius until his death in 1939 at age fifty-five.

Despite Jones's animus, however, his assimilation of Rank to Jung ironically finds vindication in the intellectual realm. As I have contended elsewhere, although Rank's early thought was antithetical to Jung's, by the end of his career Rank espoused Jungian views (Rudnytsky 1991, 48–50). As late as *The Trauma of Birth,* Rank attacked Jung for slighting sexuality (1924, 27), citing the passage in *Transformations and Symbols* where Jung asserts of the longing to return to the mother's womb: "It is not incestuous cohabitation which is desired, but the rebirth. . . . Thus the libido becomes *spiritualized in an imperceptible manner*" (1912, 251). Six years later, however, Rank affirms in *Psychology and the Soul:* "Symbolic and anxiety dreams . . . can be understood only in relation to that 'unconscious' which never becomes conscious, and which Jung has properly called 'collective' because of its identity with the spiritual. The typical sexual symbols of serpent, mouse, and bird originally had spiritual meanings" (1930, 126). In keeping with his conversion to a "collective" unconscious with "spiritual" meanings, Rank in *Art and Artist* scores Freud's "concrete" view of the mother and the birth trauma, which he now disdains "only as typical and ideological," and approvingly quotes *Transformations and Symbols* on "the symbolic significance of the mother" (1932, 378). Thus, in his final phase, Rank repudiates psychoanalysis and his own earlier work in *The Incest Theme* and endorses Jung's critique that "the salient fact is simply the regressive movement of the libido and not the mother."

Like Jung, Adler mediated between Rank and Freud. But unlike Jung, who lived in Zurich, Adler was part of Freud's circle in Vienna, to which Rank also belonged. In an excellent study, Paul E. Stepansky has warned against reading Adler's place in the early history of psychoanalysis from the retrospective standpoint of his 1911 break with Freud. Rather, during 1906 to 1910 Adler was a leading member of the Vienna Psychoanalytic Society, whose "emphasis on the psychological repercussions of organ inferiority was neither exceptional nor controversial" and whose contributions "were generally welcomed for the clarifying connections they provided between clinical medicine and psychoanalysis" (Stepansky 1983, 104). Since Adler's views remained largely unchanged during the years of his association with Freud, Stepansky persuasively suggests that the reasons for his ouster in 1911 were not intellectual but political. After the Nuremberg Congress and the founding of the International Psychoanalytic Association, Freud's heightened emphasis on ideological purity in the psychoanalytic movement and his confidence that its future rested with Jung caused him to become intolerant of diversity among his Viennese followers and to "reinterpret the status of his own prior reservations about Adler's theories with a view to ending Adler's active collaboration" (136).

Stepansky (1983, 91–92) adduces as the best example of Adler's respected position during the earlier, open-ended years of the Vienna Psychoanalytic Society Rank's attempt on March 4, 1908, to prove that "the inferiority of Schiller's eyes" was "one of the roots of his Tell figure by referring to the myth of the blind archer and to some characteristic passages in the Wilhelm Tell drama" (Nunberg and Federn 1962, 341). Strikingly, several members of the group who later sided with Adler against

Freud found the greatest fault with Rank's presentation. Stekel complained that "the continuous recourse to the doctrine of inferiority has by now become painful"; Eduard Hitschmann concurred that Rank's explanation was "paradoxical and forced," with inferiority "dragged in by the hair." Freud, in contrast, came to Rank's defense and pronounced his exegesis "a particularly beautiful mythological confirmation of Adler's principle and secure as are few interpretations" (341–43).

Like Rank's three-part 1906 paper, his presentation in 1908 shows *The Incest Theme* in the making. His Adlerian reading of *Wilhelm Tell* was incorporated into the published text (Rank 1912b, 88–91). Rank adroitly argues that the theme of blindness is displaced from the shooter Tell to his son Walter, who refuses to be blindfolded, although Tell himself is overcome with dizziness at the moment of shooting. He augments biographical evidence of defects in Schiller's eyesight with the etymological detail that the name Schiller, given to the poet's ancestors, is derived from the verb *schielen* ("to squint"). Here Rank's 1912 edition reflects the ecumenical spirit that prevailed through 1910 in the discussions of the Vienna Psychoanalytic Society. Elsewhere, however, Rank shows his Freudian colors by discounting an Adlerian explanation of sibling love in Shelley and Byron in terms of "male protest" (1912b, 447). This polemic was deleted from the 1926 edition of *The Incest Theme* (514), when Rank no longer had reason to cast himself as Freud's disciple.

Stepansky's analysis reveals that the politicization of the international psychoanalytic movement "provided a structural foundation for the crystallization of rival 'Freudian' and 'Adlerian' conflict groups within the Viennese psychoanalytic community" and that Adler's ensuing departure from the group "was the product of a premeditated assault engineered entirely by Freud" (1983, 144, 146). Its upshot is to expose as disingenuous Freud's intertwined claims in the *New Introductory Lectures* that the rifts in the psychoanalytic movement were intellectual in origin, that his opponents' decisions to depart were voluntary, and that he himself had no responsibility for what occurred. On the contrary, as Stepansky points out, the pattern detectable in Freud's dealings with Adler emerges even more distinctly in his relationship with Jung. From his first letters, Jung openly acknowledged his reservations about Freud's theory of sexuality. Freud, keen to secure Jung as a convert and then to anoint him as his heir apparent, did not accept these qualms at face value, but rather "resorted to the wish-fulfilling prophecy that Jung's theoretical timidity would inevitably yield to the input of additional clinical experience" (Stepansky 1983, 177). Only after the rift between the two men became irrevocable did Jung's expanded definition of libido as general psychic energy, which followed consistently from his original premises and appealed to Freud's own analysis of paranoia in the Schreber case, retroactively receive its "deviant" stamp (177–78).

The same pattern of emotional reversal surfaces for a final time in Freud's rupture with Rank. As I have documented elsewhere, to grasp the crisis surrounding *The Trauma of Birth* it is necessary to realize that Rank, like Jung a decade earlier, had reason to regard himself as Freud's probable heir (Rudnytsky 1991, 37–39). In a letter of August 4, 1922, Freud regrets that he has not encouraged Rank to study medicine, for he then would not "be in doubt as to whom I would leave the leading role in the psychoanalytic movement. As it now stands I cannot help but wish that Abraham's clarity and accuracy could be merged with Ferenczi's endowments and to it be given Jones's untiring pen" (Taft 1958, 77–78). Although Freud's tone is rueful, such praise sparked Rank's ambition, which burst into flame at the news of Freud's cancer in spring 1923. Rank initially regarded *The Trauma of Birth* as a capstone to the psychoanalytic edifice, with which he simultaneously consummated Freud's ideas and established his own claim to the throne. Only when Freud, heeding the warnings of Abraham and Jones—the conservative members of his inner circle—refused to bestow his unqualified approbation did Rank manifest the negative side of his ambivalence and construe his innovation as a birth trauma heralding his own intellectual independence.

Like his predecessors in Freud's disfavor, Rank doubtless had his personal failings and must be apportioned some of the blame for the painful quarrels that took place. As in the cases of Adler and Jung, moreover, Rank's secession from Freud was in part a political drama in which many of the elements were beyond Freud's control. But the litany of defections and broken friendships—including that with Fliess in the 1890s—mandates the conclusion that their ultimate cause lies in Freud's early experiences and their effects on his unconscious mind (Rudnytsky 1987, 18–53). Hence Peter Gay's contention that Freud "was not the victim of some obscure repetition compulsion" (1988, 242) must be dismissed as an unwarranted idealization, in the same vein as Freud's apologia in the *New Introductory Lectures* and no more convincing. The triumph of psychoanalysis was also its tragedy.

In *On the History of the Psycho-Analytic Movement,* Freud wrote that "among the strictly scientific applications of analysis to literature Rank's exhaustive work on the theme of incest easily takes the first place" (1914, 37). This judgment remains true today. In its encyclopedic erudition, interpretative brilliance, and theoretical cogency *The Incest Theme in Litera-*

ture and Legend is the greatest and most important single work of psychoanalytic literary criticism.

Rank's book belongs to the first great efflorescence of psychoanalytic theory, before the turn toward analysis of the ego that Freud initiated in "On Narcissism" (1914). It thus culminates the already substantial body of psychoanalytic writings on art and literature that had appeared by 1912. These include above all Freud's *Delusions and Dreams in Jensen's "Gradiva"* (1907), "Creative Writers and Day-Dreaming" (1908), and *Leonardo da Vinci and a Memory of His Childhood* (1910) as well as the earlier publications by Rank himself—*The Artist* (1907), *The Myth of the Birth of the Hero* (1909), and *The Lohengrin Legend* (1911). (*The Artist* was the manuscript that, in 1905, had provided the basis of Rank's introduction to Freud; *The Lohengrin Legend* was Rank's Ph.D. dissertation at the University of Vienna, the first at any university to employ a psychoanalytic method.) Other major works of applied analysis cited by Rank in *The Incest Theme* include Karl Abraham's *Dreams and Myths* (1909), Ernest Jones's *The Problem of "Hamlet" and the Oedipus Complex* (1911), and the "pathographies" by Isidor Sadger.[4] Although Rank affirms in his preface that the "main content" (1912b, 1) of *The Incest Theme* was already extant by the time of his presentations to the Vienna Psychoanalytic Society in 1906, the numerous references to later sources make it clear that he must have been revising the book until the last minute and that much of it was in fact written after that date.

Both psychoanalysis and literary criticism have undergone profound evolution in the eight decades since Rank published his work. Object relations, Lacanianism, reader-response criticism, feminism, and deconstruction are only some of the movements to have changed the face of psychoanalytic and literary studies in the intervening years. But if these later developments point up limitations in Rank's perspective, or at least raise questions different from the ones he addressed, his work remains a classic because it articulates with superlative rigor and consistency a theoretical position that will always have to be taken into account when literary issues are debated.

Rank's guiding premise is that since literary works are "the completely personal, uniquely determined achievements of individual psyches" (1912b, 3), it is legitimate to approach literature in biographical terms.

4. Sadger's *From the Love-life of Nicholas Lenau* (1909), the monographs by Jones and Abraham, Freud's studies of Jensen and Leonardo, and Rank's *Myth of the Birth of the Hero* all originally appeared in Freud's series Schriften zur Angewandten Seelenkunde (Essays in applied psychology). Sadger also wrote pathographies of Conrad Ferdinand Meyer (1908) and Heinrich von Kleist (1909).

Rank admits that his focus is less on literary history than on the psychology of creativity, although he hopes to afford insight into the works he discusses. In thus framing the problem, Rank adopts a position complementary to that of René Wellek and Austin Warren, who, despite their new critical preference for a purely "intrinsic" mode of literary analysis, concede that "there is use in biographical study" if one bears in mind that "a work of art may rather embody the 'dream' of an author than his actual life, or it may be the 'mask,' the 'anti-self' behind which his real person is hiding, or it may be a picture of the life from which the author wants to escape" (1942, 78–79). By stressing the elements of fantasy, disguise, and frustration embodied in the work of art, moreover, Wellek and Warren actually corroborate the psychoanalytic tenets put forward by Freud in "Creative Writers and Day-Dreaming" and expanded by Rank.

In his introduction, Rank places Freud's understanding of literature in a historical context. Rank aligns Freud with Aristotle through the idea of catharsis (1912b, 5–6), citing Jakob Bernays's medical interpretation of the *Poetics* and an 1897 paper by Alfred Freiherr von Berger comparing Breuer and Freud's "cathartic method" of therapy in *Studies on Hysteria* (1895) to the cathartic effects of drama.[5] From the ancient distinction between imitation and inspiration, Rank passes to Nietzsche's opposition between the Apollonian and Dionysian elements in tragedy and to the psychology of literary creation advanced in 1887 by Wilhelm Dilthey. Rank lauds Dilthey as having been the first "to derive for modern man a usable poetics—not through abstraction from exemplary works but from the universally relevant laws of literary creativity" (1912b, 7). He sees Dilthey's project as brought to completion by his own investigation, which unprecedentedly points out "based on our increased knowledge of the unconscious—both the underlying content of the author's fantasies, or at least of a group of them, and the mechanism of their inception and artistic transformation" (8). Since Dilthey is the founder of modern hermeneutics, Rank's sketch of the intellectual antecedents of psychoanalysis brings these two modes of self-reflective inquiry into direct conjunction.

Rank's is primarily a psychology of literary creation, not literary effect. Unlike contemporary reader-response critics, he does not suppose that the work is an invention of the reader or substitute his own private associations for an analysis of the text. The role of the author is not symmetrical with that of the reader, since he (Rank's examples are almost exclusively male), as the maker of the text, stands in a privileged relation to it. Yet Rank

5. Although Rank does not say so, Jakob Bernays was the uncle of Freud's wife, Martha. His medical exegesis of catharsis in the *Poetics* contested the moral interpretation of Lessing. In addition to Berger, the comparison between Aristotle and Freud was drawn by Hermann Bahr in his *Dialog vom Tragischen* (Dialogue on the tragic, 1904). See Worbs (1983, 320–33).

recognizes that Aristotle's doctrine of catharsis focuses on audience response, and he too does not neglect issues of reception. Rank contends that the literary work arouses in its reader or spectator a milder version of the same emotions that animated its creator:

> In the gratified spectator of a work of art, who thus "likes" the work, the same psychic impulses that drove its creator to artistic production are gratified much as in the experience of the creative artist himself. The only difference is that the artist must expend on his own the psychic energy providing these impulses with a means of expression, whereas the spectator, who has stronger (normal) inhibitions opposing these impulses, escapes the need to expend this psychic energy, since this has been done by the creative artist. (1912b, 119–20)

Between the artist and the spectator, there is "a single chain characterized by the same unconscious impulses" (120). Rank notes that the correlation between the dynamics of creation and response is exemplified by translations and adaptations, in which the author, himself a reader, is drawn to his material out of psychological motives and then reshapes it in an individually determined way.

In common with Freud's other early followers, Rank takes for granted the universality of the findings of psychoanalysis. The artifacts of disparate periods and cultures exhibit the same patterns because the complexes that give rise to them "are a component of the basically uniform development of all human beings" (1912b, 14). What Rank says of Schiller's *Don Carlos* can be extended to virtually all literary works: "Thus, given our psychological interpretation, the characters can be reduced to only three—the playwright-hero and his parents in their various attitudes and multiple relationships with the son" (49). A corollary is that "the political drama is a continuous facade for the incest drama" (63). Rank's beliefs in an essential human nature and the priority of psychological over political meanings are unpopular in many quarters today, but they are far from having been discredited. Jung too emphasizes that "the human mind possesses general and typical modes of functioning" that "can easily produce in the most widely differing individuals ideas or combinations of ideas that are practically identical" (1952, 313). But whereas Jung explains this uniformity by a wholly mystical and collective theory of archetypes, Rank appeals to conditions of infancy and parent-child relationships that are empirically verifiable and grounded in individual experience.

Despite his concentration on typically recurring patterns, Rank possesses a model of historical change. Already in *The Interpretation of Dreams* Freud had contrasted *Oedipus the King*, where "the child's wishful phantasy that underlies it is brought out into the open," with *Hamlet*, where "it remains repressed" and "we only learn of its existence from its inhibiting consequences," and accounted for this difference by "the secular advance of repression in the emotional life of mankind" (1900, 264). This theory of advancing repression is endorsed by Rank in *The Incest Theme,* and he adds *Don Carlos,* where the stepmother replaces the mother as the object of the son's desire and the father remains alive to bar their union, as a third to the series begun by *Oedipus* and *Hamlet* (1912b, 30–50).[6] Rank compares this continuous heightening of repression in culture as a whole with that in an individual writer, where in the composition of a given work "from the first outline to the final version, the same gradual weakening and disguising of certain sexual themes is observed that we pointed out earlier in the discussion of general psychic development" (54).

As a theory of history, this model of increasing attenuation of an originally unrepressed incest fantasy leaves much to be desired. When, in discussing the three-generational sequence of filial rebellion among the Greek gods recounted in Hesiod's *Theogony,* Rank asserts that "the progress of sexual repression . . . can be fully equated with general cultural progress" (1912b, 230), it is not necessary to be a Marxist to agree that too many important social and economic factors are being overlooked. Moreover, Freud's assumption that *Oedipus the King* depicts the fantasies of incest and patricide in unrepressed form is highly suspect, since Oedipus commits these deeds unwittingly (Rudnytsky 1987, 271). As Rank points out, "even the first coherent mythological forms must be characterized by repression," and such a preliminary stage can only be said to exist in a "psychological sense" (1912b, 132–33).[7] Despite its conceptual limitations, however, Rank's schema proves to be of great heuristic value when applied to literature.

6. From the standpoint of what Freud later called the negative Oedipus complex—the son's love for the father and aggression against the mother—Rank also sees in the matricidal fate of Orestes "a Hamlet drama more perfect in some respects than Shakespeare's," with again the difference that Aeschylus's hero "is able to carry out what Hamlet hardly even dares to contemplate" (1912b, 266).

7. Freud's belief that the Oedipus myth depicts its underlying fantasies in undisguised form explains why he placed his discussion of it in the chapter titled "Typical Dreams" in *The Interpretation of Dreams,* but it created a stumbling block for his early expositors. To the question why dreams of incest and patricide should be exempted from the distortions of censorship, Abraham unconvincingly answers that since "we believe ourselves to be further removed from such wishes than from all others," the censorship is "unprepared for such enormities," and he bewilderingly adds that the Oedipus legend is "very poor in symbolic means of expression" (1909, 161). Rank grants that patricidal wishes are disguised both in dreams and in myths, but he claims that incest dreams are often undisguised because they are orgasmic, and hence "the tension of the current libido eliminates all defenses without hesitation" (1912b, 210). This too raises more questions than it answers. Are all incestuous dreams orgasmic? Are all orgasmic dreams incestuous? Are all orgasmic dreams undistorted?

Rank devises brilliant classificatory typologies throughout *The Incest Theme*. He juxtaposes the "Carlos schema," in which the son passionately but hopelessly loves his stepmother, with the "Phaedra schema," in which the stepmother is spurned by the son she desires (1912b, 93). (A subcategory of the Phaedra schema is the Potiphar theme—the false accusation of the son by the father's wife—which "seeks to realize the son's incest fantasy without reproach, while on the other hand expressing the fear that the father's suspicions may have been aroused" [127].) Schiller's play thus culminates the progression both from *Oedipus* to *Hamlet* and from Euripides' *Hippolytus* to Racine's *Phaedra,* since Carlos, like Hippolytus, dies through his father's wish and there is likewise an advance in repression from Euripides to Racine (124). Schiller, moreover, translated *Phaedra* into German (119). The thematic connection between Sophocles and Shakespeare had been canonized by Freud and Jones, but Rank is the first to integrate that between Euripides and Racine, which involves direct literary influence, into a psychoanalytic framework.

Rank's original presentations to the Vienna Psychoanalytic Society treated the incestuous relationship between siblings separately from that between parents and children, and this organizational principle is preserved in the book. Its model lies in *The Interpretation of Dreams,* where, in his discussion of typical dreams, Freud first takes up "the child's death-wishes against his brothers and sisters" before turning to "dreams of the death of parents" (1900, 255–56). In 1912 Rank assumes that the sibling complex "belongs to a later developmental stage and falls victim to a later layer of repression" than the parental complex, and that it can be classified as a "subcategory" of the latter (1912b, 365). By the 1926 version, however, Rank regards sibling relationships as belonging to a "pre-Oedipus situation"—a term of his own devising—in which an elder child's newly arrived brother or sister plays the role of "disturbing third" in competition for the mother's attentions even before the father gains this significance (407). Rank's comments on Eteocles and Polynices, the reciprocally fratricidal sons of Oedipus, exemplify the modification in his views between 1912 and 1926. Whereas in 1912 Rank wrote that it was inevitable that one should find this "second level of the incest complex" in the Oedipus legend (1912b, 487; cf. 1912a, 586), in 1926 he changed "second level" to "prior stage" (460).

One of Rank's classifications for sibling incest is the "ancestress schema," in which the protagonist combines hatred toward his father with love for his sister, although the identity of these characters is initially unknown (1912b, 405). Rank names this configuration after *Die Ahnfrau* (The ancestress), the first play by the nineteenth-century Austrian dramatist Franz Grillparzer. Rank's biographical analysis of the play turns on the argument that Grillparzer, who had no sister, defended himself against his incestuous desire for his mother by reversing his actual situation and creating a drama in which there is a real sister but an imaginary mother (the specter of the ancestress), although the images of the two women are confounded by the characters in the play, as in Grillparzer's own fantasy (385). In thus granting priority to fantasy over fact, Rank anticipated Wellek and Warren's recognition that "a work of art may rather embody the 'dream' of an author than his actual life" (78).

Rank's discussion of Grillparzer has ramifications for the history of psychoanalysis. Both in his October 15, 1897, letter to Fliess and in *The Interpretation of Dreams,* Freud cites Grillparzer's *Ancestress* as an example of the modern "tragedy of fate" that fails to move its audience in the way that *Oedipus* and *Hamlet* continue to do. *The Ancestress* was thus for Freud a defective counterpart to what *Don Carlos* became for Rank—a work to be set beside those of Sophocles and Shakespeare. Rank does not allude to Freud's low opinion of *The Ancestress,* but he surely would have been aware of it. (He notes that Grillparzer always objected to the appellation "tragedy of fate" [1912b, 388].) Since Rank is at pains to show that tragedies of fate—not merely Grillparzer's play, but the entire nineteenth-century genre (503–13)—are structured by incestuous fantasies and defenses, his analysis of *The Ancestress* in *The Incest Theme* is implicitly an exercise in rehabilitation that mitigates Freud's disparagement.

Rank's chapter on Grillparzer concludes with an excursus concerning the playwright's insane younger brother Karl, who pled guilty in a Vienna court to a murder he did not commit (1912b, 398–404). Franz Grillparzer wrote an official report that clarified his own role in his brother's behavior. In Rank's psychoanalytic interpretation, Karl's chief symptom, the fear that Franz would meet with an accident, concealed his repressed wishes for Franz's death and led him, out of unconsciously justified feelings of self-reproach, to confess to murdering a journeyman who reminded him of his brother. The case of Karl Grillparzer resembles that recounted by Freud in *The Interpretation of Dreams* of a young obsessional neurotic who was unable to leave his room for fear he would kill everyone he met (1900, 260). As I have previously argued, this patient is one of two with whom Freud crucially identified in the course of his discovery of the Oedipus complex (Rudnytsky 1987, 65–75). Thus Rank's discussion of Grillparzer in *The Incest Theme* tacitly comments on biographical as well as literary aspects of Freud's engagement with the Oedipus myth. That Freud was impressed by Rank's analysis of Karl Grillparzer, which points to the connection between insanity and artistic creativity within a single family, is evident from the minutes of the Vienna Psychoanalytic Society, where he is quoted as having singled it out for "special praise" (Nunberg and Federn 1962, 19).[8]

Both in plots structured by parental and by sibling incest, Rank distinguishes between *rivalry,* in which two men compete for one woman, and *double love,* in which a man vacillates between two women (1912b, 83, 418). (This alternative could also be contemplated from the female point of view.) Invoking Aristotle on the power of recognition scenes among family members in tragedy, Rank further contrasts those plots, like that of *Oedipus,* in which incest is committed by family members who are unaware of their relationship (or who discover their kinship in time to avoid consummation), with others in which the presumed blood relationship proves false, thus allowing the lovers to seal their heretofore forbidden union. Rank observes that this latter type of plot "demonstrates a more complete wish fulfillment, less oppressed by guilt" than the former, since "the mechanism of the discovery of kinship, which originally served for defense, is used for the purpose of enacting incest in a disguised manner" (427).

All these typologies corroborate Rank's hypothesis that the universal impulses of mental life give rise to "peculiar formations of compromise whose ingenuity is exhausted in a few stereotypical forms" (1912b, 489). Although Rank notes influence whenever it occurs, his emphasis is the reverse of most literary historians', who seek to explain a writer's use of a given topic by pointing to its conventionality. For Rank, the subjective *motives* for this choice are rather the issue, since the writer "deals with given material not through external borrowing or adoption, but from a deep psychic need" (571). Among other "stereotypical forms" Rank discerns, which reflect a compromise between wish and defense, are those of lovers who die together, viewed as "a symbolic expression of sexual union influenced by defense mechanisms grappling with unconscious guilt" (102), and reciprocal murder—such as that between Eteocles and Polynices—where "fulfillment of the wish for the brother's murder" is again fused with a defense through "the receipt of the same punishment" (487).

Rank's anatomy of literary structures is empirically grounded, and even a reader not convinced by his psychoanalytic explanations can profit from much of it. On the other hand, his thought constitutes a coherent system, and it gains considerable strength from the inferences and extrapolations that Rank's theoretical foundation permits him to make. For example, Rank suggests that whenever an episode in a myth appears to be

8. The editors of the minutes mistakenly assume that Freud commends Rank's analysis of Franz Grillparzer, not that of his insane brother Karl.

weakly motivated, there must be a repressed meaning to be sought elsewhere in the narrative (1912b, 257). Yet another methodological principle—tied to his notion of advancing repression in human history—is that fragments and first drafts are more illuminating psychologically than final versions, since in them the artist's underlying fantasy "is expressed in a much less disguised, more complete manner" (481). Above all, by presenting the Oedipus paradigm as the "core and model," as Freud recommended, Rank is able to situate the entire panorama of world literature in relation to it. This capacity for logical subordination forms a further crucial contrast between Rank's psychoanalytic perspective and Jung's analytical psychology, which, in addition to ignoring individual determinants, discerns analogies between various myths of rebirth but has no means of deriving one manifestation from any other.

Rank's range of reference in *The Incest Theme* is so vast as to defy summation. It includes folktales and accounts of crimes culled from the popular press as well as more elevated literary sources, but his greatest emphasis falls on classical mythology, the Bible, Shakespeare, Schiller, Goethe, Grillparzer, and Byron. An excellent specimen of Rank's interpretative technique is his analysis of the story of Jacob in Genesis (1912b, 239–43). Focusing on Jacob's dream of wrestling with a mysterious stranger, who blesses him and gives him the name Israel, Rank notes elements in the dream that refer to Jacob's relationship with his brother Esau, with whom he had struggled even in the womb, and with his father Isaac, who had blessed him and asked his name, and he argues that the unknown figure in the dream "comprises brother, father, and God, all of whom are to forgive Jacob and sanction his deeds" (242).

Although incest themes proliferate in the Judeo-Christian tradition as well as in classical myths, Rank remarks that the heightened degree of instinctual repression in Christianity "could only be maintained at the cost of a fantasy life pouring forth in the most voluptuous degree" (1912b, 271). Hence the medieval tales of saints and martyrs reveal an admixture of sadistic and masochistic elements largely absent in antiquity. Like the pagan gods, who are permitted to gratify the desires that individuals must renounce (223), the Christian heroes and heroines show the forbidden impulses of the populace in projected form, but with an exaggerated emphasis on "punishment and forgiveness" that allows the repentant sinner "to receive correspondingly greater divine grace" (272). Rank interprets the Griselda legend, familiar to English readers from Chaucer's "Clerk's Tale," as expressing the fantasy of "the father's marriage with his own daughter, which in attested versions has been reduced to a pseudomarriage with the rationalized purpose of testing the fidelity of the first wife, whom he then, as though in the daughter's place, also marries a second time" (308).

The Griselda legend, like that of Apollonius of Tyre, used by Shakespeare in *Pericles,* is one of father-daughter incest. (Rank notes the presence of this pattern also in *The Winter's Tale* [1912b, 310–11].) By contemporary feminist standards, Rank's attitude toward this second great constellation of cross-generational incest themes is at once benighted and enlightened. When he observes that "just as the fantasy creations of the mother complex are presented from the son's perspective, . . . the fantasy substitutes created by the father-daughter complex are not presented from the perspective of the young child, the daughter, as one would expect from analogy, but are instead dealt with mainly from the standpoint of the father," Rank seems on the one hand deplorably to take this disparity for granted as inevitable. "Just as the man is the active partner in wooing and in procreation, so too the development of myths and religions, as well as artistic activity, is intended to gratify and justify male sexual fantasies" (300).

On the other hand, if Rank's diagnosis is regarded as not prescriptive but descriptive, he can be credited with having drawn attention to an empirically irrefutable and ideologically conditioned imbalance in the relations between the sexes. A far greater proportion of Western literature has been written by men, and hence reflects masculine fantasies, than one might expect given that girls and boys are born in roughly equal numbers and lead comparably active imaginative lives. Rank's most objectionably chauvinistic sentence, which refers to women as "less favored by nature and life" than men (1912b, 300), is deleted in the 1926 version (337; cf. 1912a, 368). Moreover, despite his psychoanalytic attention to fantasy, Rank does not shrink from the realities of sexual abuse and rape, pointing out that "incest between fathers and daughters (often stepdaughters), especially rape of the daughter, is among the most frequent sexual crimes" (1912b, 301).

As in his discussion of mother-son incest, Rank finds "a continually increasing repression of the attraction between father and daughter, expressed in the increasing obscurity and delicacy with which this relationship is depicted" (1912b, 330). Rank takes as his father-daughter equivalent to *Don Carlos*—a work in which the core fantasy has been thoroughly disguised—Ibsen's *Rosmersholm* (329–30). Rank's analysis of the incest theme in *Rosmersholm* was borrowed, with due acknowledgment, by Freud in "Some Character-Types Met with in Psycho-Analytic Work" (1916).

In assessing *The Incest Theme* from a feminist standpoint, it cannot be overlooked that virtually all the authors Rank discusses are male. The travails of Schiller's sister Christophine are examined at some length (1912b, 478–81), but the only female writer mentioned even perfunctorily is Karoline von Günderode, a playwright who died in 1806 at the age of twenty-six (532–33). Were *The Incest Theme* to be rewritten today, it would surely be necessary to expand Rank's canon to include more female authors and to study them with a psychoanalytic psychology that does not presuppose masculine criteria. Although Rank's work can be criticized for its androcentric bias, it would be a churlish feminism indeed that did not profit from his dissection of the Western patriarchal tradition or that assumed women lack incest fantasies because Oedipus is a male hero.

The Incest Theme contains several important contradictions in its argument. In the first place, Rank affirms that "the experiences of the playwright must be considered in an analysis of his works just as the experiences of the neurotic must be considered in the corresponding investigation" (1912b, 70). As we have seen, however, Rank qualifies this emphasis by insisting that "it is psychologically misguided to look for actual experiences in the author's life as parallels to his literary themes, because the themes are the products of fantasy activity, for which actual experiences are only raw material, subject to the most extreme modifications" (94).

Rank's juxtaposition of the artist and the neurotic points to a second contradiction, more profound than that concerning fantasy and experience. On the one hand, he rejects Stekel's equation of art and neurosis: "Instead, we should at least attempt to bear in mind the only thing that is actually clear in this connection—that the creative artist's achievement, which has a liberating effect for him while being highly valued by society, will always distinguish him from the uncreative neurotic so clearly that the distinction can never be blurred, despite the extreme similarity of the preconditions for creativity and neurosis" (1912b, 393). On the other hand, Rank elsewhere blurs the distinction that he here draws so sharply: "In incest dramas, [an artist's] symptoms reveal that he has been unable to deal successfully, once and for all, with his incestuous impulses. In life, therefore, he nearly always loves 'unhappily' " (513). Far from epitomizing psychic health, "the writer expresses all the possibilities of his own being, lying within him, through a sort of neurotic turning away from life" (571).

Rank's third contradiction touches his model of progressing sexual repression. Although his theory seems to require the opposite, Rank admits that "modern literature tends most strongly to the undisguised depiction of sexual, especially incestuous, themes" (1912b, 549). The explanation is bewildering. Repression has indeed advanced, but so has consciousness, and the impulses now being expressed in art are under the control of consciousness and hence still repressed, although no longer disguised.

These inconsistencies are of qualitatively different orders. That concerning fantasy and experience is the least unsettling, since a psychoanalytic awareness of the power of fantasy does not preclude attentiveness to actual experiences; the influence of a writer's inner and outer worlds on the creative process is not called into doubt. That concerning art and neurosis is the least resolvable. Rank here addresses a problem that has been debated from the time of Plato and Aristotle to that of Edmund Wilson and Lionel Trilling, and to which no solution can be found. Art is at once indubitably a sign of mental health and as closely allied to disease as Milton's poetry is to his blindness or the bow of Philoctetes to his festering wound. Rank's self-contradiction on this point reflects his complexity as a thinker. That concerning sexuality in modern literature is the most damaging. As I have already noted, Freud and Rank's theory of cultural progress is subverted by the presence of repression in *Oedipus the King,* and Rank's confusion in trying to explain how sexual explicitness can coexist with heightened consciousness delivers the coup de grace to all but the most allegorical uses of this schema.

Rank's theory of history reflects the underlying ambivalence in his attitude toward art. In coming to praise creativity, Rank actually buries it. He concludes *The Incest Theme,* as he did *The Artist,* by exhorting that "the artist, with this increased need for repression, must learn to master himself consciously, thereby teaching us to pass beyond him" (1912b, 573). The artist, in short, must become a psychoanalyst. When this happens, contemporary literature, which "clings with remarkable conservatism to the tragic conflicts and solutions of Sophoclean Athens, will free itself from these primitive complexes as soon as the requisite spheres of consciousness are attained" (573).

The fallacy in Rank's assumption that creativity could ever be rendered obsolete by consciousness was pinpointed by Adolf Häutler in the discussion after his third presentation in 1906 to the Vienna Psychoanalytic Society. Häutler objected: "So much will never become conscious as to impair a normal individual's power of imagination. Much will always remain obscure in the human mind, hence one of the driving forces of creative writing will never cease to exist; such an end could only come if all sexual energies were obliterated" (Nunberg and Federn 1962, 23). As Häutler's critique indicates, Rank's prediction of the end of art is a utopian fantasy that is defeated by the logic of his own psychoanalytic position. Despite the allowances that must be made for cultural diversity, human beings cannot overcome their "primitive complexes," and the "tragic conflicts and solutions of Sophoclean Athens" continue to resonate even in our postmodern era.

Rank's psychoanalytic vision belongs to the romantic tradition. Art is not a "psychic luxury" but arises from a "tormented drive for psychic self-preservation, which can be achieved only with the help of the colossal compensations of fantasy" (1912b, 540). Although Rank recognizes "how much more value is associated with the 'how' in art (technique and depiction) than with the 'what' (the material)" (541), he ultimately reduces the mystery of creative talent to an overly exuberant fantasy life produced by premature sexual arousal. "In the final analysis, what the author has in common with the neurotic is an abnormally strong sex drive, precociously demanding activation and fantasy activity, as well as the powerful inhibitions necessary to keep the sex drive in check, which constitute the feeling of guilt" (397).[9] (This passage was deleted from the 1926 edition [1912a, 485; 1926, 543].) Rank makes his priorities clear with respect to form and content: "If one hears again and again that powerful repressed complexes, no matter how strong, do not make an artist in the absence of technical talent, there is even more truth in the reverse of this statement: an individual gifted with technical ability, no matter how perfect, will remain nothing but a craftsman unless he has psychological struggles to deal with through his technical ability" (1912b, 570).

How much of Rank's psychoanalytic theory of art continues to hold good today? To all but the most formalist literary critics, his basic assumption that there is a relation between a writer's life and work will be self-evident. Psychoanalytic criticism is always implicitly a form of biographical criticism, although it is of course possible to interpret works of literature and art psychoanalytically (or to study the dynamics of aesthetic response) without reference to the author's life, just as it is possible to have a biographical criticism that is not psychoanalytic.[10] Rank's further contention that "compared with childhood experiences and impressions and their unconscious traces and emotional effects, which no one has previously considered, all subsequent experiences are relevant only insofar as they awaken and revitalize those childhood experiences" (1912b, 106) also commands assent. The shaping influence of early childhood experiences remains a cornerstone of psychoanalytic thought, however unpalatable this idea may seem to others.

No less incontestable within a psychoanalytic framework is Rank's claim, also forcefully advanced in *The Myth of the Birth of the Hero*, that

9. Rank here foreshadows his classification of individuals into normal, neurotic, and artistic types in *Art and Artist* and other postpsychoanalytic works. He writes in the final sentence of *The Incest Theme:* "The normal person is able to master these [infantile complexes] with relative ease; the neurotic fails but under favorable conditions can learn to master them consciously with the help of psychoanalysis; the artist, under favorable conditions, deals with them through unconscious abreaction" (1912b, 573).

10. For a systematic review and critique of psychoanalytic approaches to art, see Spitz (1985). In a later essay, Spitz (1991) points out that in *Art and Artist* Rank assails any attempt to explain an artist's work biographically.

myths are *projective* phenomena, whose meaning must be sought not in the heavens but in the psyches of their human creators: "If one conceives of Oedipus as a sun-hero who murders his father, darkness, and shares his bed with his mother, the dawn, from whose womb he sprang, this explanation will perhaps suffice if one has modest expectations." However, Rank continues, "these conceptions of incest with the mother and the murder of the father arise from human life" and "the myth could never have developed from celestial observation without there being a corresponding psychic conception" (1912b, 224). Although not written with Jung in mind, Rank's critique of those who accept the astral explanations of myth at face value tellingly refutes his position in *Transformations and Symbols*. That Rank later in life came to share Jung's point of view is an irony that does not diminish the cogency of his argument or its exemplarity as a formulation of the psychoanalytic case.

Rank requires modification in light of contemporary psychoanalysis above all in his exclusive emphasis on the sexual roots of artistic creation. For Rank, as for Freud in "Creative Writers and Day-Dreaming," the artist is someone "disappointed by [erotic] experience and by reality in general," who then in fantasy "creates for himself the experiences that reality has denied him and that, in a deeper sense, it can in no way provide" (1912b, 71). The paradigm for art, even before the daydream, is thus *masturbation:* "From these masturbation fantasies and their forbidden objects, and from intense self-reproach and self-punishment, a broad path leads to artistic fantasy activity" (236). As is inevitable given its date of composition, Rank's model of the mind in *The Incest Theme* presupposes Freud's theory of the drives. From this standpoint, he maintains that "the tragic conflicts [the writer] continually attempts to resolve in his works simply correspond to his inner conflict between drive and repression" (571).

Elsewhere (Rudnytsky 1991) I have expatiated on my reasons for concluding that it is necessary to abandon Freud's drive theory in favor of a theory of object relations, whose intellectual architect is W. R. D. Fairbairn and whose best-known proponent is D. W. Winnicott. In brief, the crucial point is that the greatest need of human beings is not for sex but for *attachment,* and hence Freud's essentially solipsistic model of behavior as motivated by the desire to reduce instinctual tensions must give way to one that places object-seeking in the forefront. The consequences of this recasting of psychoanalytic theory for the understanding of art are spelled out by Winnicott in *Playing and Reality* (1971). The nub of the matter is that the prototype for art is no longer masturbation but *play.* This play takes place in a *potential space* between child and mother that is neither purely internal nor external and becomes filled with *transitional objects* that are symbols of both separation and union. Play differs from masturbation precisely in that it entails a suspension of somatic urges, which terminate the activity if they become too insistent. Winnicott provides a psychoanalytic account of art that respects its integrity as an autonomous human activity and does not reduce it to a sublimation of sexual drives.

There are, then, two psychoanalytic paradigms for art—the classic one of masturbation and the contemporary one of play. Both drive and object relations theorists agree that the origins of art lie in early childhood. But whether their outlooks are ultimately compatible or contradictory remains an open question. On this score, as on others, to read *The Incest Theme* is to embark on a voyage of discovery.

References

Abraham, Karl. 1909 (1955). *Dreams and myths: A study in folk-psychology.* In *Clinical papers and essays on psycho-analysis,* ed. H. Abraham, trans. H. Abraham and D. R. Ellison, 2:153–209. New York: Basic Books.

Forrester, John. 1980. *Language and the origins of psychoanalysis.* New York: Columbia University Press.

Freud, Sigmund. 1900 (1953–74). *The interpretation of dreams.* In *The standard edition of the complete psychological works,* 24 vols., ed. and trans. J. Strachey et al., vols. 4 and 5. London: Hogarth Press.

———. 1905. *Three essays on the theory of sexuality.* In *Standard edition,* 7:125–245.

———. 1909a. *Analysis of a phobia in a five-year-old boy.* In *Standard edition,* 10:5–149.

———. 1909b. *Notes upon a case of obsessional neurosis.* In *Standard edition,* 10:155–249.

———. 1912–13. *Totem and taboo.* In *Standard edition,* 13:1–161.

———. 1914. *On the history of the psycho-analytic movement.* In *Standard edition,* 14:7–66.

———. 1925. *An autobiographical study.* In *Standard edition,* 20:7–74.

———. 1933. *New introductory lectures on psycho-analysis.* In *Standard edition,* 22:7–192.

Gay, Peter. 1988. *Freud: A life for our time.* New York: Norton.

Jones, Ernest. 1955. *The life and work of Sigmund Freud.* Vol. 2. New York: Basic Books.

Jung, Carl G. 1912 (1947). *Wandlungen und Symbole der Libido.* Trans. B. Hinkle as *Psychology of the unconscious.* New York: Dodd, Mead.

———. 1952 (1976). *Symbols of transformation.* Trans. R. F. C. Hull. Princeton: Princeton University Press.

Kerr, John. 1988. The devil's elixirs, Jung's "theology," and the dissolution of Freud's "poisoning complex." In *The persistence of myth: Psychoanalytic and structuralist perspectives,* ed. P. L. Rudnytsky, 1–33. New York: Guilford.

Lieberman, E. James. 1985. *Acts of will: The life and work of Otto Rank.* New York: Free Press.

McGuire, William, ed. 1974. *The Freud/Jung letters: The correspondence between Sigmund Freud and C. G. Jung.* Trans. Ralph Manheim and R. F. C. Hull. Princeton: Princeton University Press.

Masson, Jeffrey M., ed. 1985. *The complete letters of Sigmund Freud to Wilhelm Fliess, 1887–1904.* Cambridge: Harvard University Press.

Menaker, Esther. 1982. *Otto Rank: A rediscovered legacy.* New York: Columbia University Press.

Nunberg, Herman, and Ernst Federn, eds. 1962. *Minutes of the Vienna Psychoanalytic Society.* Vol. 1. *1906–1908.* Trans. M. Nunberg. New York: International Universities Press.

———. 1976. *Protokolle der Wiener Psychoanalytischen Vereinigung, 1906–08.* Vol. 1. Frankfurt: Fischer.

Rank, Otto. 1912a. *Das Inzest-Motiv in Dichtung und Sage: Grundzüge einer Psychologie des dichterischen Schaffens.* Leipzig: Deuticke.

———. 1912b (1991). *The incest theme in literature and legend.* Trans. G. C. Richter. Baltimore: Johns Hopkins University Press.

———. 1924 (1929). *The trauma of birth.* New York: Harcourt, Brace.

———. 1926. *Das Inzest-Motiv in Dichtung und Sage: Grundzüge einer Psychologie des dichterischen Schaffens.* 2d ed. Leipzig: Deuticke.

———. 1930 (1961). *Psychology and the soul.* Trans. W. D. Turner. New York: Barnes.

———. 1932. *Art and artist.* New York: Knopf.

Rudnytsky, Peter L. 1987. *Freud and Oedipus.* New York: Columbia University Press.

———. 1991. *The psychoanalytic vocation: Rank, Winnicott, and the legacy of Freud.* New Haven: Yale University Press.

Spitz, Ellen H. 1985. *Art and psyche: A study in psychoanalysis and aesthetics.* New Haven: Yale University Press.

———. 1991. Conflict and creativity: Reflections on Otto Rank's psychology of art. In *Image and insight: Essays in psychoanalysis and the arts,* 235–49. New York: Columbia University Press.

Stepansky, Paul E. 1983. *In Freud's shadow: Adler in context.* Hillsdale, N.J.: Analytic Press.

Taft, Jessie. 1958. *Otto Rank: A biographical study.* New York: Julian Press.

Wellek, René, and Austin Warren. 1942 (1970). *Theory of literature.* Harmondsworth, Eng.: Penguin Books.

Winnicott, D. W. 1971. *Playing and reality.* New York: Basic Books.

Worbs, Michael. 1983. *Nervenkunst: Literatur und Psychoanalyse im Wien der Jahrhundertwende.* Frankfurt: Europäische Verlagsanstalt.

Translator's Note

Otto Rank's place in the history of psychoanalysis is an important one, secured in part by his later works, chief among them *Das Trauma der Geburt* (1924), translated as *The Trauma of Birth* (1929), and *Technik der Psychoanalyse* (1926–31), volumes two and three translated as *Will Therapy* (1936). Yet it is not his later writings alone that are of significance and interest. From his early days as a devout Freudian to his ultimate rejection of much of Freud's thought, he underwent a great deal of intellectual growth and change. If we wish to understand the development of Rank's thought, a knowledge of his early works, many still unavailable in English, is essential. This is particularly true of his greatest early work, *Das Inzest-Motiv in Dichtung und Sage,* an exhaustive wedding of literary criticism and psychoanalysis spanning the entire course of Western literature, from the Greeks to the twentieth century, and treating as well the mythological traditions of non-Western cultures. A 1934 French translation exists, but an English-language version is overdue, especially in view of the current interest in the subject of incest.

Das Inzest-Motiv initially appeared in print in 1912 (Leipzig and Vienna: Deuticke), but internal evidence suggests that the work progressed in stages, the last one being in the period just before publication. Various technical terms—*Infantilismus* and *Abreaktion*, for instance—are used in the Conclusion and nowhere else in the book. Moreover, Rank indicates in his Preface that the volume was largely complete by 1906, making it a very early work indeed and therefore likely to provide insight into his earliest psychoanalytical thought.

For this reason I have chosen to translate the first edition, rather than the revised edition of 1926. Although changes in the 1926 edition (Leipzig and Vienna: Deuticke) were not as extensive as one might expect—Rank did not attempt to bring the work completely into line with his current ideas—his thinking had by then evolved substantially. All this is neatly illustrated by the dedication of the two editions. The first is inscribed, "To my honored teacher, Professor Dr. Sigmund Freud." The second edition carries no dedication at all.

Rank was not a consistently lucid writer, even setting aside such technical problems as misspellings or errors in verb agreement and sequence of tenses. Like many of his contemporaries writing in German, he demonstrated a special fondness for sentences of Gargantuan proportions. Too often his convoluted constructions are difficult to follow, the antecedents of relative pronouns ambiguous. Here, gender helps to an extent, but literal translation into English would in some cases produce constructions even more impenetrable than those already present. Moreover, paragraph divisions are frequently absent for pages at a time. Rather than being slavishly bound to the structure of the original, I have generally kept in mind the needs and convenience of English-language readers.

Like other scholars of his day, Rank was conversant with several *Kultursprachen* in addition to German. He included in the text untranslated material in classical Greek, Latin, Old French, modern French, Italian, and Spanish, apparently in the sanguine expectation that his readers could cope. All such passages appear in this edition in English, but I have included the original as well when it seems of literary or linguistic significance. In general, translations of psychoanalytical and literary excerpts are my own; when this is not the case, sources are duly acknowledged. In biblical citations I have employed the New World translation throughout. Perversely, Rank quotes German translations of Shakespeare, Shelley, Byron, and others, making necessary a painstaking search for the original sources in English. Similarly, he presents all excerpts from Ibsen in German translation; since it is these renderings (most likely authorized by Ibsen) that underlie Rank's analysis, I have chosen to translate them directly in lieu of consulting English or Norwegian versions.

The bibliographical information Rank provides is more a challenging puzzle than a useful resource, but through library research and inspection of the 1926 edition, I have been able to locate nearly complete references for most of the works he cites. These are listed in the References appended to the translation and are generally referred to in the text by author and year only. References that I could not locate have been retained in the text as they appear in the 1912 edition.

Like his contemporaries, again, Rank was wont to write essay-length footnotes, whose basic function was to supplement voluminous previous examples of a given point. I have translated footnotes only when direct reference is made to them in the main body of the text. Within the text I have enclosed Rank's notes in angle brackets ⟨ ⟩, while my own clarifications are enclosed in square brackets [ ].

Let me briefly discuss some of the issues that arose and the choices I made in translating. My aim has been to translate German psychoanalytical terms using their standard English equivalents. For example, *veredelt* has been rendered "sublimated," even though a more literal English version would be "ennobled," which might better suggest the highly positive sense Rank clearly associated with the German word. In *Freud and Man's Soul,* Bruno Bettelheim (1983) said of the standard translations of Freud, by James Strachey and others, that "many . . . native German-speakers . . . are quite dissatisfied with the way Freud's works have been rendered in English." He argues convincingly that *Verteidigung* should be translated not "defense" but "parry"; that *Verdrängung* should be translated not "repression" but "repulsion"; and that *Seele* should be rendered not "psyche" but "soul." In deference to the weight of tradition, I have retained the forms first cited, but readers are nonetheless encouraged to refer to Bettelheim for an enlightening discussion of these and other terms in the psychoanalytical usage of Freud and his circle.

A crucial difficulty for the translator of Rank is that the semantic scope of key terms may be wider in German than in their English equivalents. Rank uses both *Neigung* and *erotische Neigung* in the same context, so that both must be translated "erotic affection." (The claim that men feel affection toward their mothers is hardly controversial; the claim that they feel erotic affection calls for elaboration.) Elsewhere the term *Neigung* appears to signify simply "affection," "attraction," or "inclination." Similarly, *Zwang* has been translated in various ways. I render *Zwangsneurose* as "obsessional neurosis," but *Zwangsvorstellung* as "obsessive fear" or simply "hallucination," and *Zwangshandlung* as "compulsive act." Finally, *Familienroman* may be translated "family romance," "family novel," or even "family complex." Often, eschewing scientific precision, Rank varies his terminology, using two words in what is apparently the same sense. A single English translation, however, seems most desirable. For instance, Rank uses *Inzest* and *Blutschande* in what are apparently equivalent contexts; both are translated here as "incest." Further, the "dampening" by the unconscious of one concept to another, less offensive one is referred to at times as *Abschwächung* and at times as *Abmilderung*.

Anthropological and literary terms present their own difficulties. I have chosen to translate *Naturvolk*, for example, as "primitive society" and *Kulturvolk* as "civilized society," though cogent arguments for other renderings could certainly be made. Similarly, it seemed necessary to translate the all-encompassing term *Dichter* sometimes as "playwright" and sometimes as "author," "poet," or simply "writer," depending on context.

Rank, I should emphasize, was a writer of immense diversity, and one may be alternately pleased and appalled by what he has to say. Playing the etymologist, for example, Rank claims that Electra's name derives from the Greek *a-léktron*, "without a bed," whereas the name is simply a form of the Greek word for "amber." Enlightening, clever, and eloquent passages abound, too. Particularly noteworthy in this respect is the discussion in chapter 12 in which Rank argues that incest myths are not a human reflection of the divine but rather "a divine reflection of humanity." Given its vast coverage, this book will have something profitable to offer scholars in a number of disciplines. For a complete Otto Rank bibliography, see *The Don Juan Legend*, translated and edited by David G. Winter (1975).

Thanks are due Patrick Lecaque and Maren Partenheimer, who assisted with the translation of brief passages in Old French and German, respectively. I am grateful to Alice M. Bennett, my manuscript editor, for her patience, her high standards of scholarship, and her expert stylistic improvements of the text. Any errors are of course my own. This translation project was made possible in part through the granting of research time by the Division of Language and Literature, Northeast Missouri State University. Very special thanks are due Robert Bates Graber, who read the entire manuscript and provided numerous valuable suggestions. His keen insights into Rank's psychology proved invaluable, and without his support the translation project would not have been possible.

The Incest Theme in Literature and Legend

Author's Preface

The main content and major points of this work already existed in autumn 1906, when it was brought to the attention of the intimate circle that has since become known as the Vienna Psychoanalytic Society. That the work is only now being published is due more to my own inhibitions than to any other problem. The conclusions, though nearly always based on numerous and solid results of psychoanalysis, were often so surprising, and at times astonishing, that it seemed desirable to produce a series of preliminary works as a broad psychological/theoretical background to this volume. Since then, developments in psychoanalysis applied to the most varied areas of creativity have been rich and fruitful beyond expectation. This recent research, found in the various psychoanalytic journals, now seems capable of giving solid support to this book, while certain aspects of recent research are themselves confirmed by this volume. The task of bringing the whole work up to the level of our current knowledge seemed impracticable. In a few sections, especially some pertaining to mythology and modern literature, I attempted revisions, sometimes at the cost of disrupting the unity of the presentation. At least in the footnotes, however, I have systematically taken the copious recent literature into consideration.

Vienna, Spring 1912

Author's Introduction

The unconscious, united with the consciously contemplated, makes the great author.

SCHILLER

In this book an attempt will be made, based on a narrowly defined set of data, to gain insight into the process of literary creation. This attempt will proceed from a completely new theoretical foundation and will utilize unusual perspectives. As the title page indicates, the book is not a literary/historical investigation, but instead emphasizes psychological problems; it is only through an investigation of literary works and biographical information that the psychology of authors is revealed. Yet it is to be expected that illuminating the psychology of individual authors and their works will also cast light on the historical development of literature, which of course consists only of a succession of authors, each developing individually. Major emphasis will be placed on the psychological analysis of drama—initially, within the sphere of a single theme (with many ramifications) and without detriment to other modes of analysis. Dramatic works will be analyzed with reference to the psyches of their creators; they will be treated as the completely personal, uniquely determined achievements of individual psyches. Thus we shall be examining most closely not literary works, but the authors who produce them; we shall be engaged not with the history of literature and art, but with the psychology of the author. Of course this shift from an exterior perspective to an interior one does not imply the rejection or disparagement of other research methods; indeed, it has become possible only through an examination of the previously available data and their scholarly analysis. However, it illustrates dramatically the extent to which our method differs from others.

This special approach to the consideration of art, with all its consequences, has become possible only through the accomplishments of a school of psychology that has nothing in common with earlier models except the name. This psychology, founded by Sigmund Freud and further developed by numerous pupils and adherents, forms the basis of the current investigation. We have attempted to organize the volume so that a knowledge of this psychology is not absolutely essential. Still, familiarity with this psychology is in no way superfluous. If the largely internal, psychological analysis of so basic a social product as art seems to produce many astonishing perspectives and conclusions, familiarity with Freud's psychology, itself new and unique, will certainly not diminish this impression. Freud's psychology, which penetrates the dark depths of the unconscious, leads us to our elemental drives—to the very roots of human behavior and thought. These revelations by no means confirm the generally accepted assumption of the nobility of man's nature and the divinity of the creative artist. It has been said that hunger and love, interpreted in the widest possible sense, rule the world. This telling maxim seems to apply not least to authors. And if we regard erotic and egotistical drives not as irrelevant, superfluous elements, but as determining factors in the creative process—as decisive in the creation and formation of a work of art—this conclusion is perhaps much better suited to increase our respect for the power of nature, which allows the sublime flowering of literature, so valuable to all of humanity, to proceed from such primitive, instinctual roots.

In the following investigations, we will attempt to illustrate how this occurs. Of course, when dealing for the first time with such a complex topic, and one with so many ramifications, one cannot expect a simple solution to all the problems that present themselves. Instead, given the vast extent of the data, one must be content with a few rough schemas and incomplete attempts at solving a few major problems. Therefore the individual chapters represent only more or less independent aspects of the immense theme and are intended only to suggest various methods one will need to apply in any specialized investigation if one wishes to come to grips with the diversity and complexity of the topic. It remains for such specialized investigations to demonstrate in each case the details of the connection between the deepest elemental drives of the creative process, yet to be discovered, and the apparent psychological state of each author. In this investigation, which deals mainly with basic conclusions—with the establishment of the typical—this can be attempted only in a few cases. That many of the conclusions seem so astonishing can be attributed, to a large degree, to this unavoidable deficiency. One would be well advised not to reject these conclusions out of hand, but to assume that there are comprehensible intermediate steps leading from the seemingly strange, unconscious roots we have posited to conscious thought, though these steps cannot always be dealt with in this study.

Through its psychological perspective, this investigation adopts a unique position. Attempts by literary critics to understand works of literature have not been lacking. However, given their point of departure, their scholarly methods, and not least of all a certain practical orientation, these efforts are quite distinct from this undertaking. The first scholarly essay of this type was of course that by Aristotle, who presented certain technical rules of literary production in his *Poetics*, which survives only in fragments. Since Aristotle considered all artistic activity the result of an inborn imitative drive, the creative aspect of art remained a problem for him, and he was unable to proceed to a psychological investigation of the nature of creativity. Thus Aristotle's aim was to produce a theory of form and, based on that, a technique of literary production; these he deduced from popular literary works of his day and his impressions of them. Aristotle's success in solving the problem is illustrated by the persistent and determining influence that this oldest theory of poetics, though sometimes misunderstood, has exercised on all subsequent literature, aesthetics, and criticism. Our high estimation of Aristotle's formal poetics, though that theory has long since been superseded, can perhaps be attributed to the fact that we find in the *Poetics* fundamental insights into the nature of the literary art that are not of merely historical interest but can only now be fully appreciated, given the illumination of our current knowledge.

Now more than ever we are convinced of the deep psychological truth of the Aristotelian doctrine of catharsis. According to this doctrine, the spectators of a tragic drama are pleasurably freed, through fear (shock) and pity (compassion), from these very emotions. (Whether this entails becoming truly free of these emotions or simply purging them remains a debatable point.) The notion of catharsis, according to Jakob Bernays, was originally borrowed from medicine (where it signifies the expulsion of a sickness-inducing agent from the body), and it is only through a medical achievement of our own time that this notion has attained its full psychological significance. Breuer and Freud (1909) characterize psychotherapy, which frees the emotions from repression, as "cathartic," and in a noteworthy article Baron Alfred Berger (1897) convincingly adduces the cathartic treatment of hysteria in explaining the cathartic effects of drama. But we must disregard here the highly significant topic of the effects of art—a topic so rich in its various insights—and return to artistic activity, where, as Kant said so well, the essence of aesthetic expression reveals itself in intensified form. Aristotle extends this law of catharsis to the author, though weakly and as if unintentionally, when he says that those personae who portray emotions are most convincing when they arise from the emotional world of the author himself (*Poetics*, chap. 17). He adds that literature is therefore the means of expression of the especially talented or of those whose inner life is especially intense: the first can imitate with facility, while the latter are capable of ecstasy. In this remark we find the double origin of literature, already hinted at in Homeric poetry; we find the psychological distinction between inspiration and conscious imitation—a distinction that has become the basis of all subsequent investigations of artistic creativity and that echoes in Friedrich Nietzsche's distinction between the Apollonian and Dionysian elements in artistic creativity.

Although Aristotle progresses no further than these beginnings in understanding the psychology of the process of artistic creation, we are in no position to blame him, for it was not until modern times that the first conscious discussion of the psychology of literary production appeared—that attempted by Wilhelm Dilthey (1887, 303 ff.). He begins by demonstrating the strong influence of Aristotle's poetics in all periods of literary production through the second half of the eighteenth century (Boileau, Gottsched, and Lessing). He then follows the development of recent aesthetics from its origins in the Scottish school, which placed the source of all literature in the imagination of the author, to the systematic German aesthetics, which emphasizes the creative force in man and indeed in all of nature. Correctly appreciating the true significance of Aristotle's poetics for the lifework of the two great national poets of Germany, Dilthey comes to the conclusion that every historical period must create its own historically conditioned aesthetics through lively interaction with the literary creations of its own authors: "The Aristotelian principle of imitation was objective; . . . since more recent discussions have concerned themselves with the subjective abilities of the human spirit and emphasized the independent power of these abilities to transform sensual experience, the principle of imitation could no longer be retained in aesthetics" (Dilthey 1887, 320). "Poetics found its basis first in the exemplary literature from which it abstracted, and later in some metaphysical conception of beauty; now it must seek its basis in the psyche" (335). In contrast to Aristotle, Dilthey now sets out to derive for modern man a usable poetics—not through abstraction from exemplary works, but from the universally relevant laws of literary creativity. "The foundations of such a theory must lie in the analysis of creative ability, the inner processes of which determine the nature of literature. The imagination of the author in its relation to the world of experience forms the necessary foundation for any theory that seeks to explain the rich world of literature in its varied forms" (311).

Dilthey achieves his two goals—the establishment of psychological foundations and of an interpretive theory based on them—as successfully as possible, given the means available under the psychological theory he assumes. However, this psychology does significantly restrict him—at decisive points he stops short of a complete analysis. In one section of his article Dilthey discusses "the imagination of the author in its relation to dreaming, insanity, and other states that differ from the normal waking state" (Dilthey 1887, 350 ff.) and declares in conclusion that the visions of the dreamer, the madman, or the artist cannot be explained by contemporary psychology, which assumes ideas as fixed entities (351). He correctly adds that every idea in the psyche is really a process (352). According to Dilthey, there are several ways "the creative experience of the author resembles the delusions, dreams, and fantasy images of other mental states" (350): in all these states there arise images that transcend experience; these situations, images, and processes are experienced with hallucinatory intensity; finally the individual ego is capable of transforming itself into that of the protagonist. Dilthey is no doubt correct in considering this function of the author to be "dependent on the greater energy of certain psychic processes," but this does not really transcend Aristotle's claim that literature is the means of expression of those whose inner life is especially intense (*Poetics*, chap. 17).

Otto Behagel, the well-known Germanist, basing his work largely on that of Dilthey, makes a significant step forward in his address, *Bewusstes und Unbewusstes im dichterischen Schaffen* [The conscious and the unconscious in literary production] (1907). Based on the personal declarations of several authors, he makes the following important statements: "The psychic state from which literature arises—the state in which literary production takes place—is a state of excitation. . . . And it is by no means a coincidence that the author is so inclined to play with erotic images" (Behagel 1907, 5). "The power of fantasy is the source of all artistic creativity" (8). "The roots of literary creativity lie in the mysterious depths of the unconscious" (4). "For this is the nature of the genesis of literary works: dreamlike, obeying dark drives, the images arise" (21). "Thus, this state is closely related to dreaming" (16) but also shows "nearly the character of hallucination" (43, n. 94). In the author, however, we note also the role of thought and conscious effort (17). These, "in the case of the author, complement the unconscious process in three ways: by completing and assisting the unconscious; by selecting and organizing unconscious ideas; and by tempering and pacifying the unconscious" (24).

Our seemingly isolated research fits into place in this sketchily drawn history of the scientific investigation of the literary creative process. This is the first investigation to point out—based on our increased knowledge of the unconscious—both the underlying content of the author's fantasies, or at least of a group of them, and the mechanism of their inception and artistic transformation, as well as reasons for the especially intense feelings associated with them, which will become clear when we discuss the origin of these fantasies. If the unconscious sources and erotic associations of these fantasies are placed at the center of attention in this study, this is due not to a tendentious overestimation of their importance, but rather to the nature of things. Thanks to an extremely extensive series of detailed biographical, historical, and aesthetic investigations, the conscious and "asexual" contribution of the psyche in the creation of artistic works is better known to us than it deserves to be, given its true importance. The justification for establishing the true contribution of the unconscious/erotic component lies not merely in the need to expand our knowledge or to provide a balance in our treatment of the two components, but in the realization that the unconscious/erotic component is the more important one, essential to deeper understanding and psychological investigation.

The idea that it is the unconscious combined with the conscious that makes the author has been expressed in various forms by almost all productive writers. And though the vast majority consider the unconscious to be the decisive and meaningful component, they also emphasize its incomprehensibility. Thus, for example, Paul Heyse (1900, 346) says in his *Jugenderinnerungen und Bekenntnisse* [Memoirs and confessions of youth]: "The crucial portion of all artistic creativity occurs in a mysterious, unconscious state of excitation closely related to the actual dreaming state. The somnambulant creations of fantasy usually bear the character of dreams in that they lack any clear connection with one another and must be organized and purged of random elements by reason and artistic circumspection if they are to achieve legitimacy in the light of day."

In his essay "Aus einer Seelenlehre des Künstlers" [Aspects of the psychology of the artist] (1899a), Klages makes similar points: "A sound or a beam of light, upon entering his consciousness, suffices to produce in his unconscious an ambiguous play of dark feelings and associations in which he becomes deaf and blind to the details of everyday reality, so counterproductive to art. This unconscious selection, already complete when the creative process begins, is the main thing. Later, during the actual creation of a work of art, the analytical activity of the conscious mind fills in the details."

In his fascinating essay "Wie dichtet man aus der 'blauen Luft'?" [Poetic inspiration "out of the blue"], the Swiss Carl Spitteler, equally eminent as a poet and as a critic of his own works, writes in a similar vein. In literary creativity he sees three distinct personifications: the poet, who passively yields to his unconscious forces; the artist, who sifts, organizes, and combines the wealth of unregulated and inconsistent fantasies and images thus brought to light; and finally the author, who so to speak clothes the material in its final, conventionalized shell. Spitteler says that these important "unconscious (or at least passive) states and events of the psyche . . . can hardly be described and certainly cannot be explained. First it would be necessary to explain the human psyche and life and the whole world." Convincingly, and as if speaking of dreams, he says: "The state of susceptibility to images, which the artist takes over from the poet, is characterized by an abundance of individual, momentary impressions—interrelated, it is true, but without transitions and without logical connection. For fantasy gives us no relationships. Thus, assisted by poetic logic, the artist must establish a sensible and continual plot progression, always moving toward the conclusion." And in stating that the unconsciously inspired poet recognizes no contradictions—these are dealt with by the artist—Spitteler makes a direct comparison with dreams. While dreaming, he claims, one is uncritical; their internal contradictions become apparent only when the dreams are retold. It cannot be emphasized enough here that, in the spirit of Spitteler's remarks, we will be considering almost exclusively processes that occur on this deepest psychic level of the poet's mind, so rich in contradictions, shocking material, and apparent inconsistencies. Only occasionally will we be able to cast a glance at the artist or at the author. We are fully aware that the entire ability to give form to the material, and the necessary technique, lie within the working domain of the artist; the giving of form is related to the problem of the aesthetic impression (which we also choose to disregard), since the poet's fantasies must be so clothed that the spectator is able to experience them pleasurably. We certainly do not underestimate the value of giving form, for we recognize that it is in the course of this process that the moment occurs when the work of art truly emerges as such. For like the author, we are all able to fantasize; this explains art's power to affect us. This is revealed in dreams, the unconscious of the neurotic, and still more in so-called daydreams. Owing to their egoistic and erotic nature, though, these are limited to the individual producing them.

In a few unfortunately isolated investigations, Freud (1909d, 1911, 1912a, 55 ff., 1912b) achieved some initial insights into the transformation of these socially unacceptable images—which we have learned to recognize and understand in neurosis, in dreams, and in egoistic daydreams—into works of art, enjoyable and highly esteemed by society. He recognized several conditions under which a socially effective work of art may arise from self-centered daydreams and, it seems to me, equated these conditions with the author's unconscious technical ability, which is not significantly influenced by his aesthetic, intellectual, and critical capacities. From his daydream fantasies, the author must strip away what is purely personal. To present his fantasies to his audience, he must be able to distance them appropriately from the unconscious, yet without freeing them fully from it, which would impair their effectiveness. The form must engage the intellect of the audience and must also be perceived as pleasurable; the form must appear to justify this sensation of pleasure, though it arises almost exclusively from the unconscious sources of gratification of repressed fantasies. Unknown to him, these repressed fantasies also constitute the main source of creative energy in the author. Of all the complicated processes involved in literary production—all the more complex owing to the involvement of purely intellectual faculties—we can pursue here only the daydream, with its unconscious fantasies demanding form and life during their transformation into gratifying literary works.

Although Arthur Schopenhauer, with keen intuition, recognized the role of daydreams in literary production and Freud, proceeding from children's play, recognized it as the basic raw material of prose, perhaps no one has more thoroughly and accurately portrayed daydreams as a source of literary creativity, especially with reference to prose, than the prolific and popular English novelist Anthony Trollope in his *Autobiography* (1980, 1:42–43):

> I will mention here another habit that had grown upon me from still earlier years, which I myself often regarded with dismay when I thought of the hours devoted to it, but which, I suppose, must have tended to make me what I have been. As a boy, even as a child, I was thrown much upon myself. I have explained, when speaking of my school-days, how it came to pass that other boys would not play with me. I was therefore alone, and had to form my plays within myself. Play of some kind was necessary to me then, as it has always been. Study was not my bent, and I could not please myself by being all idle. Thus it came to pass that I was always going about with some castle in the air firmly built within my mind. Nor were these efforts in architecture spasmodic, or subject to constant change from day to day. For weeks, for months, if I remember rightly, from year to year, I would carry on the same tale, binding myself down to certain laws, to certain proportions, and proprieties, and unities. Nothing impossible was ever introduced, nor even anything which, from outward circumstances, would seem to be violently improbable. I myself was of course my own hero. Such is a necessity of castle-building. But I never became a king, or a duke, much less when my height and personal appearance were fixed could I be an Antinous, or six feet high. I never was a learned man, nor even a philosopher. But I was a very clever person, and beautiful young women used to be fond of me. And I strove to be kind of heart, and open

> of hand, and noble in thought, despising mean things; and altogether I was a very much better fellow than I have ever succeeded in being since. This had been the occupation of my life for six or seven years before I went to the Post Office, and was by no means abandoned when I commenced my work. There can, I imagine, hardly be a more dangerous mental practice; but I have often doubted whether, had it not been my practice, I should ever have written a novel. I learned in this way to maintain an interest in a fictitious story, to dwell on a work created by my own imagination, and to live in a world altogether outside the world of my own material life. In after years I have done the same, with this difference, that I have discarded the hero of my early dreams and have been able to lay my own identity aside.

Although investigations of dreaming, fantasy, and erotic experience have been frequently and persuasively suggested as models and sources for our research, we are setting out upon new paths; despite hints from ancient and modern authors and thinkers, the necessary methods were not previously available. Of course the influence of sexuality upon fantasy, briefly mentioned by Behagel, has been emphasized by a series of important researchers beginning with Löwenfeld (1911, 186 ff.). But with its full consideration of all the sources, manifestations, and consequences of the sexual drives considered in their biological aspect, especially the unconscious ones, psychoanalytical research has made the first strides toward a deeper understanding of the relation of sexuality to fantasy. Today we already recognize the very intimate and significant relation between unconscious fantasies which are directly involved in the development of the literary products of fantasy and those forms of imagination that in an earlier stage of life lead the sexually and intellectually precocious individual first to autoerotic gratification, then to autoerotic fantasies involving beloved persons, and finally to the transition to a normal love life. With the supersession of autoeroticism and the achievement of heterosexual orientation, these fantasies are repressed into the unconscious, where under appropriate conditions they can manifest their effects in the genesis of dreams, in the development of symptoms, and as the creative element in artistic production. In connection with our topic, we must assign great importance to the way these first and most persistent erotic fantasies of early childhood and puberty take as the goal of their gratification parents and siblings—those persons most loved by the child but forbidden by the culture as sexual objects.

The same holds true for the relation of literary production to our dream creations and to the hallucinatory visions of the deranged. That all these processes are related and have a common origin has been expressed since ancient times by authors themselves, by philosophers, and not least by laymen. Still, insightful though the observation is, it has remained, as for example even in Nietzsche's *Geburt der Tragödie* [Birth of tragedy], until now only an attractive simile. Based on our deeper psychoanalytical insights into psychic mechanisms and into the development of dreams, symptoms, and delusions, it has become possible to take this parallel between dream and art seriously and to hope that, based on our knowledge of related phenomena, we will be able to penetrate the secret of unconscious artistic production. However, the often misused comparison of the work of art and the dream, based only on certain formal similarities, is now deprived of its poetic veil. The relation of the dream to the work of art, especially the drama, goes beyond external similarities; it arises from the deep psychological identity of both processes, whose psychic stimulus, basic content, and—important—mechanisms of formation and development belong to the unconscious. Given the unconscious content, tendency, and origin of dreams and neuroses, we can be sure that the artist too creates for himself in his work a partially disguised fulfillment of his most secret desires and that, like the dreamer and the neurotic, he too is driven irresistibly by his infantile drives and erotic fixations, long repressed but still highly active in his unconscious. Since we must acknowledge unconscious sexual impulses as the common source of the normal, neurotic, and artistic activities of the psyche—dreams being the normal activity—it would be a mistake to assume that our unexpected and surprising conclusions relate only to the data that form the basis of the following investigations. As long as similar treatments of other artistic data remain unavailable, we must assume that the validity of our conclusions is not limited to the data at hand. These data have been selected and narrowly specified mainly because through other channels of psychological investigation the incest theme, its meaning, and its essence are already so comprehensible and familiar to us that we can hope, based on this knowledge, not only to penetrate with a high degree of certainty the structure of the psychic life of the artist, but also to confirm and unify retroactively the knowledge already obtained.

This expectation is supported in that the psychoanalytical investigations of Freud and his school have shown more and more convincingly that the incest fantasy is not simply the "nuclear complex of neurosis" and, as research of the Zurich school seems to indicate, of several psychoses (Freud's *paraphrenia* = Emil Kraepelin's *dementia praecox*). Instead, these investigations have shown that it also dominates the unconscious psychic life of normals, determining their social and erotic orientation in life. Our investigation will lead us to recognize that the incest fantasy is of primary importance in the psychic life of the author. This work has its deeper justification in that it is precisely based upon the incest theme that the "fundamentals of a psychology of literary creation" can be developed; in connection with the incest theme, we shall attempt to demonstrate paradigmatically how the process of literary production characteristically resembles and differs from normal dreaming and from neurosis. One purely external indication of the importance of the incest complex in the psychic life of the author is that nearly all major authors in world literature have handled the topic with a willingness lacking in the neurotic. This will be amply confirmed by the abundance of our data. Owing only to a number of typical and easily recognized disguises and to the transformation of the infantile/pleasurable into the tragic/guilty, the relevant passages seem to approach neurotic repression and are not perceived as shocking. However, it is in neurosis that we have observed the greatest distortions of the original infantile psychic configuration. Therefore, in addition to the obvious incest dreams of normal adults, experienced with revulsion and disgust, we have been obliged to recognize an even larger number of disguised incest dreams (which may be termed "hypocritical"). Similarly, in addition to the many obvious incest fantasies and those partially veiled in a literary guise, we must acknowledge the existence of a still greater number of more or less distorted incest fantasies. But were we to include these in the discussion, we would need to expand our research significantly and would probably find it necessary to include most of our classical literature and belles lettres, as well as most folktales, sagas, and myths. This is inappropriate for a preliminary investigation and must be relegated to specialized monographs based on as wide a range of data as is our own investigation.

In keeping with the general purpose of the volume—to establish a basic outline—we have limited the investigation to the manifestations of the incest theme in its various guises and derivative forms, still in need of conclusive identification. The ubiquity of the incest theme among the major authors of world literature has become apparent, as has the continual recurrence of certain typical patterns within this theme. It is also important to point out that it is by no means necessary to attribute these typical, recurring forms and motives in literature to conscious borrowing or imitation, or to literary influences, as was previously supposed. Indeed, it seems that they can be attributed mainly to a common psychic configuration shared by the various authors and resulting in a certain uniformity in their output, external influences merely serving to intensify this result. In explaining the existence of such regularly recurring motives not attributable to literary influence, critics have considered it sufficient to invoke the vague notion of "literary common ground"; they have made no attempt to associate the common source of these related literary achievements with the psychic life of the authors themselves. This investigation, however, will attempt to do so. We will try to demonstrate that certain typical patterns in literature arise from shared psychic complexes, evinced with special intensity in all authors but shared in a weaker form by the literarily unproductive (as shown by their strong response to literature). After all, these complexes are a component of the basically uniform development of all human beings.

Thus our investigation proceeds from a consideration of the nature of the literary art and its effects to an investigation of the psyche of the author, and then to expanded insights into the psychic life of human beings in general and into the development of this psychic life. Yet one may object that we are proceeding in a roundabout way. One may question our justification for making inferences regarding the psychic life of the author based on literary materials and for asserting that certain motives and themes have been preferentially taken up and treated as effective and indispensable dramatic material, theatrically "tried and true," by dramatists of all times. Still, one must recognize that through allusion to its generality and its universal effects, the problem has only been transferred from the realm of individual psychology to that of mass psychology, thereby becoming slightly more inaccessible still. To attempt to dispel these objections through polemics would be as dull as it would be ineffective. Below, we shall attempt not only to demonstrate with examples the usefulness of our framework in achieving a deeper understanding of literary works, but also to prove in each individual case that our framework is justified—except when this seems unnecessary given the general psychological preliminaries that underlie our work, whose acceptance is the necessary precondition for their true appreciation.

Since we are basing our investigation on analytical/determinist psychoanalysis, we shall not debate whether we are justified in inferring from the content of literary works the existence of certain emotions and fantasy images active in the psyche of the author. The results of research on dreams and neurosis entitle and even force us to deny the existence of "chance" or "superficial explanations" in the psyche, or in nature in general, and to see every psychic event as the result—rule governed and strictly determined by biological processes—of the total psychic configuration. Within this framework, we are compelled to accept the view that literary works are the symptomatic expressions of corresponding emotions in the psyche, and that to achieve a psychological understanding of these works we must investigate their connections with these emotions. The naive claim that the author can use only those themes that enable him to portray emotional conflict and tragic complications, and thus necessarily chooses these themes, collapses in the face of the justified rejoinder: Why, then, is it necessary for him to seek out and present tragic actions, otherwise avoided whenever possible, and why must he do so with such characteristic and inexorable determination, if not because the tragic involvement and guilt in his own psyche seek resolution and release? Many of the greatest authors have openly stated that the great author writes, basically, only as a means of inner release, and for his own enjoyment. Thus Schiller writes to Goethe (August 17, 1797) that "it is definitely true that one only writes and philosophizes for oneself." Goethe repeatedly expressed similar sentiments: "And so began that inclination from which I have never been able to diverge—the inclination to transform whatever gladdened or tormented or otherwise occupied me into an image, a poem, and to come to terms with myself about it in order to improve my understanding of the externals and to pacify myself inwardly. This talent was probably more useful to me than it ever was to anyone else, for my nature continually cast me from one extreme to the other. Therefore, all the things that have become known about me are simply fragments of a great confession." And responding to Schiller (March 3, 1799) he uses words similar to Schiller's own: "In creating literary works, one satisfies most of all oneself; as a result, one can better relate to others."

Another apparently justified objection could be raised against our conception of the deepest sources of literary creativity when we make the psychologically justifiable assumption that the psychic life of the author can be inferred from his works: one could object that it will be all too easy to find the ultimate sources of artistic creativity in the erotic and to find the conditions for the unfolding of literary talent in specific excesses in psychosexual development if one considers only works that deal with so thoroughly sexual/pathological a theme as the erotic attraction of blood relatives for one another. However, we must emphasize that our investigation will actually seek to rid the literary expression of incestuous feelings of its pathological character and to conceptualize it as the manifestation of common, unconscious human emotions. In connection with this, we should point out that in all of world literature it would be impossible to find a single genuine author in whose works the theme of passionate love and its distortions, with all their relationships and variations, is not dominant. For it is precisely the frequency with which incestuous relationships have been selected as the topic of dramatic works that has helped to justify the conception of the erotic sources of literary creativity. It must remain for future investigations to provide a wider foundation for this model by analyzing other typical themes in dramatic literature.

The most serious objection that can be raised against our investigation concerns the "misuse" of authors and their works for such research. One might inquire why the very depths of authors' psyches should be illuminated, given that biographical research has already rooted up the most intimate details of the lives of these defenseless research subjects. And even if one admits the possible theoretical value of such psychic analyses, one might object that identifying the ultimate sources of literary creativity will impair the aesthetic enjoyment of literary works and make literary production itself impossible.

Concerning the first objection, we will surely be permitted to mention the deepened insights into the nature of works of art and artistic production that present themselves within such a framework and that in themselves seem sufficient as a scientific justification for it. But the results of our investigation include more than these discoveries concerning previously mysterious processes. Ultimately, these discoveries contribute to the investigation of human psychic life in general, which more than any other natural phenomenon is worthy of the research so long neglected. But as we now understand, the investigation of the normal psyche must be based on the observation of the abnormal psyche—either inferior or superior to the norm—since in the case of the normal person we lack access and, more significantly, occasion to delve into the depths of psychic processes. Occasion for such research is provided by the psychoneurotic, who, as a consequence of his so-called immature psychic life, cannot function in society; access is provided by the artist, to whom a god has granted the ability to relate his sufferings through his creations. From our knowledge of these two rather extreme psychic manifestations, and from appropriately focused observation of normal psychic processes, we can construct a picture of normal psychic development and of the average psychic life. In conducting this research, we are especially surprised by the clear correspondences between the statements and psychic processes of the neurotic and those of the author, indicating that it is only slight differences that determine whether the psychic configuration will develop according to one pattern or the other. In our further efforts to determine specifically these points of difference, we come to the unexpected conclusion that the so-called normal psyche also shows all the initial signs of both pathological and superior development and that it can only be certain dynamic (quantitative) factors that determine the character of the psyche. Thus, though apparently by sidetracks and detours, we are actually proceeding on the only possible path leading to an understanding of the normal psyche and hence to a correct analysis of deviant psychic processes.

If our undertaking now seems justified in more than one respect by its conclusions, we also can show that there have been erroneous attempts to attribute to our undertaking certain consequences for which it is not responsible. It has been objected that through such fundamental analyses as those we are attempting in our study of authors' psychic life and works, all finer structural distinctions—and most significantly the aesthetic enjoyment of literature—will be sacrificed. This objection is perhaps justified to a certain extent, but in a quite different and much deeper sense than it can possibly be meant to imply.

Our whole psychic life, and consequently our whole cultural life, depends unmistakably on the progressive expansion of consciousness, which is synonymous with continually increasing control over unconscious drives and emotions. This process is subject to the biologically determined repression of culturally unutilizable drives; this repression is intensified by cultural demands and would soon lead to generalized neurosis if the sublimation of drives and the expansion of consciousness, proceeding parallel to the repression, did not maintain equilibrium. The decisive effect of these "sexual repressions" upon the manifestations of artistic creativity will be revealed very clearly through our method of literary analysis. Like an X-ray image of the many-faceted course of development described by literary history, an analogous course of development subject to psychic factors will become apparent. As predicted by the principle of the repression of drives, this course of development reveals a gradual tendency toward the neurotic organization of the fantasy life and also, in compensation, toward higher achievement in the realm of conscious intellectual activity. Since it arises from the cultural sublimation of repressed drives, artistic activity may appear to be only a passing symptom in the course of general mental development, adapting itself to progressing mental development through its own shifting manifestations.

However, in this developing series of literary manifestations there still are limits on the ability of expressive artistic forms to transform themselves. These limits are not quantitative—for new possibilities of course present themselves at each stage—but are of a qualitative nature. As poets themselves agree almost unanimously, the ability to produce and enjoy art is connected with an extremely high degree of unconscious mental activity, and also with a certain degree of conscious thought that cannot be exceeded without danger to the artistic effect. To call forth the literary effects it is true art's function to produce, the problems addressed must be expressed in disguise, as of course occurs through the author's unconscious creative energy. Contrary to what one might believe, the effect suffers in no way when these problems remain unperceived. Quite the reverse, it is precisely their perception that is detrimental to the effect. Translated into the language of our psychology, this means that the author's unconscious fantasies should not be brought to such conscious awareness that the spectator completely understands the source of the powerful effects of the work. But the author cannot do without those unconscious abilities that we are learning to recognize as the basis of all artistic creativity. For some time during the process of repressing drives, as the author approaches neurosis, artistic creativity still flourishes without harm to the artistic effect. Owing to its basically unconscious nature, though, artistic creativity is incapable of adapting itself permanently to progressive changes in the conscious. As several examples in our contemporary dramatic literature suggest, the ability to create universally effective works of art will first be extinguished. Then, presumably, the general public will lose its ability to appreciate and enjoy artistic works. Thus Klages asks (1899b): "Is our art perhaps after all the sad sunset glow over the day of mankind, coming to an end? Is reason the hostile power capable of extinguishing the fire of the will? Will all passions finally end in a fanaticism of recognition, and will that itself end in apathetic omniscience?" If the prophecy of such a calm future sounds depressing, one should note that we are dealing not with the sudden disappearance of all artistic endeavor from our contemporary culture, but with the gradual replacement of certain artistic tendencies and interests by others, bringing with them a new culture with its own intellectual and affective pursuits, uplifting and gratifying in equal measure.

If such cultural/historical considerations do not seem comforting, however, these speculations concerning the ultimate goal of the development of art will at least counter the objection that our methods of considering art are deleterious to aesthetic enjoyment. Once the advancement of consciousness has been recognized as a psychic principle in the development of culture, and once one has seen how, under the influence of this advancement, certain unconscious abilities and affects are gradually and independently transformed and become extinct, one will not be able to blame the modest efforts of one individual or even the more significant influence of a whole school for such fundamental shifts in the mental life of man. And though the demise of our traditional forms of art is unavoidable, given the advancement of consciousness, it is comforting to know that our modest efforts to investigate these two processes and their mutual relationship, far from being able to solve the conflict between them, are themselves a consequence of that conflict.

PART I

The Relationship between Parents and Children

1 The Origins of the Incest Fantasy in the Individual

If the savage were left to his own devices . . . combining the infant's small measure of reason with the power of the passions of a man of thirty years, he would break his father's neck and dishonor his mother.

DIDEROT, *Rameau's Nephew*

In *Traumdeutung* [The interpretation of dreams] (1900), Sigmund Freud revealed for the first time the sexual nature of the child's relationship to its parents: he described the child's early erotic affection for the parent of the opposite sex and the resulting jealous aversion to the same-sex parent. Further, he applied these findings in his analysis of both typical adult dreams: incestuous emotions in the child's psyche, later repressed into the unconscious, are gratified in dreams of the death of the father and of sexual union with the mother. From the frequent occurrence of these two dreams among adults, and based on the psychological laws governing the development of dreams, one must conclude that most people experience these incestuous feelings in childhood. "For psychoneurotics, this supposition has been confirmed beyond the shadow of a doubt through previously completed investigations" (Freud 1900, 182). Freud says further:

> In my already extensive experience, parents play the main role in the infantile psyche of all later psychoneurotics; being in love with one parent and hating the other are basic components of our psychological fabric. These components emerge in childhood and are highly significant in the development of later neurosis. In this respect, however, I do not believe that psy-

> choneurotics differ greatly from normal children, or that they exhibit behavior unique to psychoneurotics. It is far more probable, as is also suggested by limited observation of normal children, that psychoneurotics merely exhibit to a greater degree those feelings of love and hate toward parents that occur with lesser intensity in the psyche of most children. (180)

This supposition of Freud's, expressed over a decade ago, has since been dramatically confirmed through further research. Freud himself had the opportunity to test the correctness of his insight into child psychology on an actual child. "In his relationship with his father and mother," says Freud, "Hans confirms most clearly and directly the claims concerning the child's sexual relationship with his parents that I expounded in *The Interpretation of Dreams* and in *Theory of Sexuality* [1905]. He is really a young Oedipus who wishes to see his father 'removed' so he can be alone with his beautiful mother; so he can sleep with her" (Freud 1909a, 84). Further, the analysis of young Hans's phobia fully confirms Freud's insights into the development of these infantile wishes—incomprehensible as they are to the mature mind—gained through his analysis of dreams. Most important, confirmation is provided for Freud's insight into the development of the "criminal" death wish felt toward the same-sex parent. In *The Interpretation of Dreams,* it is stated that "the child's conception of 'being dead' and our conception of the idea have very little in common except the word itself. . . . For the child, 'being dead' . . . is synonymous with 'being away'—with ceasing to disturb the living. The child is not concerned with how this absence arises, be it through traveling away, alienation, or death" (Freud 1900, 179). "If the young boy can sleep with his mother as soon as the father travels away but must return to the children's room—to a much less pleasing person—when the father returns, it will be easy for the boy to develop the wish that his father would always be absent so that the boy can keep his place near his beloved, beautiful mother. Of course, one means of attaining this goal is for the father to be dead. This the boy has learned from experience: 'dead' people, like his grandfather, for example, are always absent, and never return" (Freud 1900, 182). Further, young Hans "developed this wish during a summer vacation, when the alternating presence and absence of his father made clear the conditions on which the desired intimacy with the mother hinged. At this point, the wish that his father 'travel away' sufficed. . . . Later, probably first in Vienna, where he could no longer count on his father's traveling away, he progressed to the wish that his father would always be away—that he would be 'dead' " (Freud 1909a, 84).

In analyzing the child's feelings of jealousy toward the same-sex parent, we must be careful not to attribute to the child the thoughts and feelings of an adult. And to understand the child's loving relationship toward the parent of the opposite sex, we must disregard the familiar association of sexual desire with a specific goal. Although the child's state of being in love evinces almost all the psychic characteristics of the adult state, the utmost subtlety is necessary in trying to understand it. In the child's state, crucially, the conscious aspect—which through its predominance characterizes the adult state—is lacking. The child's erotic inclination toward the father or mother is unconscious, hidden beneath the child's love for the parent, which is clearly permitted and encouraged. Viewed in this light, the child's state of being in love seems neither strange nor repulsive, though it may indeed appear so when we attempt consciously to understand its unconscious erotic components. One must always remember that in our investigations, like the author himself, we must always exaggerate and coarsen the actual state of affairs in order to make it perceptible and comprehensible at all. One must remember that we are carrying out a sort of psychic microscopy. We must never forget to place the disproportionately enlarged details within the total framework of psychic activity. A large part of the distaste many readers will feel toward our revelations arises because, within the framework of this volume, this reduction to true proportions is not always possible. Therefore we may appear to be overestimating the importance of one psychic complex.

Freud (1909c) discussed the surprising origins of the child's state of being in love with the parent of the opposite sex rather discreetly:

> I have learned to consider such unconscious feelings of love by the daughter toward the father, or by the son toward the mother, evinced by their abnormal consequences, as a renewal of infantile emotional stirrings. We must suppose that this early erotic affection of the daughter for the father, or of the son for the mother, probably evinced by some clear trace in most persons, is present from the very beginning to a higher degree in those children constitutionally predisposed to neurosis and hungry for love. Then certain influences I shall not discuss here begin to play a role, firmly establishing or even intensifying these rudimentary feelings of love to the extent that even during childhood or at the time of puberty a state arises that can be equated with sexual attraction and that like sexual attraction, is subordinate to the libido. This probably occurs at the time of the precocious appearance of true genital sensations, either spontaneously or due to temptation and masturbation.

In submitting the relationship between parents and children to psychological analysis, one has the impression that in a very large number of cases it is the parents themselves who unintentionally encourage and fix their children in an Oedipal orientation, previously perhaps only a tenuous one, through excessive coddling and obvious preferential treatment. Indeed, when one sees how the young father treats his young daughter with all the tenderness characteristic of adult love life, and how the mother unambiguously treats her son as though he were her lover—though the sexual goal is repressed—even into the years of sexual maturity, one must comment that the expressed incest complex of the child generally corresponds to an incest complex on the part of the parents as well. This is clearly indicated by observing the behavior of parents toward their children, as described by Freud (1900, 182): "Sexual selection is generally observed in the parents themselves. Natural inclination ensures that a man is affectionate toward his little daughters and that a woman has a similar relationship with her son. . . . The child notices this preferential treatment very well and bears a grudge against the parent who opposes this state of affairs. Thus the child follows his own sexual drive and, if he chooses between the two parents accordingly, further stimulates the signals emanating from them." It can escape no unprejudiced observer that the love and hate a child expresses toward parents are returned by them in like manner. Just as the child's feelings of love or hate may vary—depending on the child's psychic constitution and on environment influences—from slight preference or disinclination to erotic love or deadly hatred in extreme cases, so too can the behavior of parents be intensified or mitigated. Just as the child's awakening erotic feelings are normally directed toward the parent of the opposite sex, so the ungratified or waning erotic feelings of the respective parent center on the child, from whom both revival and gratification of erotic feelings are hoped for. And just as the child's first hostile impulses are directed toward the same-sex parent, so it is natural that that parent should develop an antipathy toward the child who is attempting to steal the other parent's love. It is clearly feelings of jealousy concerning the child's young, developing sexuality that lead to parents' animosity toward their same-sex children—sometimes unconscious and sometimes conscious.

The child's jealousy concerning the parent's adult sexuality produces hatred toward the same-sex parent. The great role played in human sexual life by this sexual jealousy, arising from the relation between parents and children, is well known. One can easily see that adult jealousy, characterized by hatred toward a same-sex, preferred, envied competitor, has as one of its deepest sources the sexual jealousy the child feels toward parents and preferred siblings. These relationships are further complicated because an intense emotional involvement between two people is seldom characterized by positive feelings only. Instead, in any great love there is in general a light subcurrent of unconscious antipathy, often evinced by a reaction of exaggerated hate (emotional transformation) in response to a strong repressed attraction. Such a psychic orientation, characterized by Bleuler as "ambivalent," is especially clear in the exaggerated emotional outbursts of psychoneurotics. Such an "ambivalent" orientation is observed in Freud's female patient who professes such affection for her mother that she wishes to be with her all the time and anxiously rushes home from wherever she has been to be sure nothing has happened to her. Analysis reveals that this apparently very loving relationship can be attributed to the patient's childhood wish for her mother's death, which the patient now fears could be realized.

Thus the psychological aspects of the relationship of parents and children, and of relationships of any two people in general, are not always simple. Instead of the generally acknowledged attraction between parents and children of opposite sex, hatred can also make a surprisingly sudden appearance. This unexpected result can be explained by conclusions of Freud's neuropsychology indicating that every psychic occurrence may arise in one of two ways: either directly or through reaction. Although the origin is in most cases unclear, the emotion of hate reveals its source to the more or less skilled observer through direct signs and, more important, through its consequences. Psychoanalysis easily reveals in all cases that behind such obvious feelings of aversion or hate there is an original feeling of love; the observed hatred is only a way to combat (by repression) these feelings of love. Results of psychoanalysis compel us to conclude not only that love and hate are very closely related psychologically, but that they are in fact the same emotion. The inner content varies only to the extent that the same feelings occur sometimes with positive and sometimes with negative manifestations. Jealousy is a bridge to such a shift of value. Thus we can easily understand that as the son matures, the mother's erotic affection for him steadily increases, but that the son's attraction to the mother diminishes in the same proportion as she grows older; the son's love affairs or marriage plans dash the mother's unconscious hopes. The mother's intense objections to her son's marriage plans, which develop, as one might fear, into objections against the future daughter-in-law personally, have their origin in her love for her own child, whose "unfaithfulness" is never forgiven and whose wedded life is now tainted by her hatred arising from repressed feelings of love. (Similar conditions hold for the father-daughter relationship.) This perception of the child's married life as "unfaithfulness" toward the parent arises in its turn from the childhood imagination, which upon becoming aware of sexual intercourse, perceives it as unfaithfulness toward the child.

This ambivalence in our emotional orientation, from which we cannot free ourselves our whole life long, is first and most intensely expressed in our relationship with our parents, both of whom, after all, we originally love. If, as a consequence of the Oedipus complex, the previously latent aversion to the same-sex parent becomes manifest, the conflicting emotions that then arise must lead to the first "psychic conflicts of childhood" (cf. Jung 1909). In these conflicts, as isolated analyses of children have revealed, all the components that will later lead to neurosis are already present.

Probably certain children are constitutionally predisposed to the precocious development of true genital sensations, which may develop in response to parental affection and are observed in clearly expressed childhood Oedipus complexes. "In the sexual constitution of young Hans, the genital zone had always been the one erogenous zone most strongly associated with pleasure" (Freud 1909a, 81). The further destiny of the libido, and therefore of the entire person, depends on the subsequent development of the genital zone and of its relationship to the other erogenous zones. Hans's case illustrates how precocious emphasis on and manipulation of the genital zone can lead to an increase in fantasy activity and to the precocious choice of a sexual goal, which must first be the mother; fixation of these incestuous tendencies can lead to mental breakdown through neurosis. However, Hans also shows the beginnings of normal sexual activity in his relationship with female playmates, onto whom he projects his feelings for his mother. Freud also indicates how this early emphasis on the genital zone, as important as it is for the later development of a normal sexual life, can instead lead through gradual stages to a great "perversion"—homosexuality (Freud 1909a, 82).

Between all these possible outcomes lies one that concerns us in our investigation. This is a solution to the conflict that permits the individual to escape true incestuous activity, neurosis, and perversion and leads to the equilibrium of a relatively normal psychosexual development by dealing with incestuous feelings through fantasy. Those individuals whom I characterized as "creative artists" in an earlier work (Rank 1907) are able to make use of this solution. I characterized them as those who can compensate for the disturbances in their psychosexual development through fantasy activity, though it is below the level of the consciousness. Such fantasy activity gratifies the infantile emotions still active in the unconscious of these artists while also gratifying the long-repressed infantile wishes of normal adults. I consider the category "creative artist" to include the musician, the visual artist, the philosopher, the founder of religions, and the mythmaker. Most important though, it is the author, especially the playwright, who reveals to us his innermost emotions in but slightly altered guise through the medium of language. He thereby awakens our own feelings, identical to his but less intense, to a short, illusory life. It has always been authors who have provided the deepest insights into the human psyche, and through the analysis of a modern work, Freud has been able to show how these unconscious psychic experiences of the author, made palpable through his presentation, correspond to the statements obtained through conscious, scientific, psychological investigation (Freud 1907a). Although it is unconscious representation and not conscious analysis that the author uses to free himself from psychic conflicts, his knowledge of the psyche and his ready willingness (one might almost say shamelessness) in revealing it should be appreciated. In this way certain modern authors have more or less consciously recognized and presented their incestuous feelings.

Stendhal, with intimate knowledge of all human passions, writes in his *Confessions of an Egoist:* "I was always in love with my mother. I always wanted to kiss my mother and wished that clothes did not exist. She loved me passionately and often embraced me in her arms. I kissed her with such fervor that she was to an extent obliged to withdraw. I despised my father when he approached and interrupted our kisses. I always wished to kiss her on the breast. One must realize that I lost her when I was hardly seven years old. She died in the blossom and beauty of her youth. Thus I lost forty-five years ago what I loved more than anything on earth." Similarly, Charles Baudelaire writes (*Letters: 1841–1866,* Bruns ed., 204): "What is it that the child loves so passionately in his mother, his nurse, his favorite sister? Is it only the being who feeds, combs, washes, and cradles him? It is also the tenderness and the sensual pleasure. Without the woman's knowledge, this tenderness is revealed to the child through all of her feminine charm." Also August Strindberg, who is not highly regarded as a psychologist, states again and again that to a man, every woman is a mother *in nuce*. And very recently, Peter Rosegger has clearly conceded the generality of incestuous tendencies in arguing against the opinion that absolutely no friendship can exist between a man and a woman unless sexuality is also involved: "Clearly, there are many friendships in which it is involved, consciously or unconsciously. I would also admit that in the love between mother and son there is a bit of the sexual—unconscious, of course. After all, a mother loves her son quite differently than she loves her daughter."

Of course most authors are not so frank, and cannot be so. These feelings remain unconscious. They find their artistic expression in literary works, where they appear more or less clearly according to the degree of their repression. Just as the psychologist coarsens unconscious emotions by the very act of bringing them to light, conquering unconscious conflicts through art also coarsens them, despite the subtle and varied means available to the author. Indeed, as we will show, these dramatic means of expression, analogous to the mechanisms of dreaming and neurosis, lead the author to render his material so tangibly that we see the most secret impulses of the psyche, slumbering deep in the unconscious, brought to life as in a dream. This playing out of unconscious stirrings, which is also characteristic of dreaming, forms the basis of the liberating effect of literature, both in the author and in his audience. Still, in literature as in dreaming, this tendency to play out repressed drives leads to a corresponding obfuscation of those drives. This sometimes goes so far that their original character becomes almost unrecognizable and is revealed only in a few small details.

It is not our intention to delve into such deeply buried incest fantasies, however, nor will we concentrate on the conscious declarations of authors, like those presented above, concerning the existence of such impulses. Instead, we wish to reveal the persistent and determinate effects that these impulses, present in all persons during childhood and later repressed into the unconscious, have on the life and creativity of the artist. Indeed, we shall attempt to demonstrate that a certain degree of repression of these impulses, unsuccessful in comparison with the repression that occurs in normal development, is necessary for the later highly valuable sublimation, and thus for the unfolding of literary talent. For in normal development all these numerous infantile sexual impulses undergo a complete transformation toward what is accepted and encouraged by the culture, so that they lose their original character almost completely. Yet deeper psychological analysis regularly succeeds in revealing this original character. Freud illustrates the definite influence the incest complex has upon the subsequent normal sexual life of the adult. "Even the individual who has successfully avoided the incestuous fixation of the libido is not completely removed from the influences of the incest complex. A clear aftereffect of this developmental stage is observed when a man's first serious love centers on a mature woman, and when a young woman's first serious love centers on an older male authority figure. The older individual reactivates in the younger one the image of the mother or father. In fact, the selection of a sexual goal probably proceeds largely based on the parental models. The man especially looks for the image of his mother, which has obsessed him since early childhood" (1905, 68).

Freud (1910) has recently analyzed the conditions and certain obvious characteristics of a love life dominated by affection toward the mother as a "special type of choice of object made by men." After our previous discussion, it will not be a surprise that all these special characteristics, exhibited in individual cases in the actual love life of individuals under the influence of the incest complex, are found once again in the magnificent creations of the author's fantasy, and in sharpest detail. The author is by no means obliged to take the real situation into account, to reduce his still-active infantile wishes to the dimensions of the attainable, or to deprive himself of their complete fulfillment in his fantasy. In this respect, however, the psychoneurotic is hampered by the strong defense mechanisms that arise against these desires—desires intensified during the process of sexual maturation and therefore felt to be objectionable. This conflict finally leads to neurosis. Only in the course of normal development can one erase the memory of these infantile wishes and bring them, still intensely active, into harmony with the opportunities for gratification offered by the culture. That this is almost never completely successful is demonstrated by the dreams of normals, in which the old childhood wishes sometimes appear, seeking gratification, behind the insufficiently gratified wishes of the present.

Just as Freud has explained the individual's dreams as the delayed and disguised realization of infantile wishes, he has taught us to conceive of the phenomenon of dreaming as a reactivation of the infantile psyche of mankind: "What once occupied the individual in a waking state, when his psychic life was still young and inefficient, has now been banished to the nightly life of dreams. . . . To dream is to enter the infantile psyche, now superseded" (Freud 1900, 349). And it cannot be doubted that in the incestuous dreams of modern man, the ancient family incest, which surely existed at one time, lives again. Thus Westermarck (1909, 45) writes: "As is the case with other animals, there must have been a time among the ancestors of man when relationship by blood was no hindrance to sexual intercourse." Children often assume that mother and father must always have been related, and this conceptualization appears as an erroneous infantile "theory of procreation" in the incest fantasies of the individual. Again, though, the history of the evolution of human sexuality gives this conceptualization some justification, while this naive assumption on the child's part attempts, as it were, to justify incestuous feelings.

It must remain for other investigators to uncover the phylogenetic, developmental history of incestuous tendencies. In our investigation, we cannot concern ourselves with their origin and developmental history. Instead, we shall take it as our point of departure that these incestuous feelings do exist in the unconscious mind of all modern humans, as has been proved by the investigations of Freud, and within a narrowly defined sphere we shall investigate their effects. Freud's interpretation of this problem differs from all others mainly in two aspects. According to Näcke (1902, 106), "it is being more and more recognized that love toward spouses, parents, children, and siblings, and even friendship and love of one's fellowman, arose without exception from sexual love." This might appear to be a phylogenetic confirmation of Freud's interpretation. But such observations should not be confused with Freud's interpretation itself. Instead, based on his psychological investigations, Freud has come to the conclusion that the so-called forms of asexual love are still derived even today from sexual stirrings experienced in the development of all individuals—that these relationships are nurtured by sexual feelings and cannot exist without unconscious erotic undertones. The difference between normal love for relatives and incestuous love for them lies only in the original intensity of the sexual drive and in how far the individual is able to sublimate it and give it a culturally acceptable form. This indeed deepens the problem. The second aspect of Freud's interpretation, which follows as a logical consequence, is the decisive influence on the individual's psychic life attributable to incestuous feelings. One can fully appreciate this only if one considers the many components of the incest complex, which, as revealed by psychological investigation, involves not only all the erotic relationships but also opposing emotions such as hatred of the father. Within this framework, the logical consequence of our psychological insights, we can now briefly present our interpretation of the developmental history of incestuous feelings.

After the previous discussion, the act of incest itself should require no special explanation. It is the direct realization of an incest wish that has remained alive since childhood and has been intensified during adult sexual life. In primitive circumstances incest not only is possible, as Westermarck indicates, but is from a purely psychological point of view the most natural form of sexual intercourse. The riddles that occupy psychologists, cultural historians, and ethnographers equally begin with the notion of aversion to incest, which must be a consequence of higher civilization and especially of the establishment of family life. To this day, the old opinion stubbornly persists that aversion to incest, as well as the specific prohibition against it, arises from a natural drive that functions to maintain the health of the species. Yet objective observers of the facts have declared that this interpretation cannot be maintained. After critically reviewing all the information, Marcuse comes to the following conclusions: "First, that aversion to incest cannot be a human instinct based on phylogenetic inheritance; and second, that if such an instinct existed, it could not have been produced by any natural drive to maintain the health of the species" (Marcuse 1908, 143). The first conclusion follows from the frequency of actual incestuous relationships in ancient and modern times and from the quite varied ways incest is dealt with in custom, tradition, and law in different societies. The second conclusion follows "from the observation that the species does not seem to be threatened in any way at all by sexual intercourse between close relatives" (141).

In our skeptical attitude toward earlier theories we are justified by the numerous known cases from all historical periods of incest in violation of the prohibition, by those instances that must have escaped our knowledge, by the marriages of relatives that have been permitted and even encouraged among certain peoples in all historical periods, and by the fact that these marriages have had no harmful effects on later generations. Abraham comes closer to a new and useful interpretation of the problem in his short but very notable article "Die Stellung der Verwandtenehe in der Psychologie der Neurosen" [The place of marriage among relatives in the psychology of neuroses] (1909). He shows that the traditional belief that marriage among blood relatives produces nervous and psychic disorders in the offspring does not take sufficient note of the complexity of the situation. "That incest and nervous or psychic disturbances coincide in many families cannot be doubted. But we cannot conclude that the two factors must necessarily stand in the simple relation of cause and effect. Rather, one must ask whether there is some specific reason for the frequent occurrence in certain families of marriages between relatives, and whether there is not a predisposition in neuropathological families for marriage among family members." And on the basis of solid results of the psychology of neurosis, Abraham assumes "that in those cases when relatives are brought together through mutual attraction only, the ability to extend erotic affection to unfamiliar persons is insufficient, while the degree of attraction to members of the family exceeds the norm."

The great revulsion with which most persons react to the act or even the idea of incest clearly expresses disapproval of this behavior, observed not only in neurotics. This strongly emphasized disgust, which is the crux of the theory of phylogenetic aversion to incest, leads the psychologist to a conclusion that directly contradicts that theory, seemingly developed to justify the behavior of the human race—to the conclusion that incestuous impulses and thoughts were in earlier times very much associated with pleasure, both ontogenetically and phylogenetically, and that they later became subject to repression, which implies a transformation of emotion (Freud 1900, 375). In contrast to the popular theories, it must be strongly emphasized that aversion to the act of incest can by no means be a phylogenetically inherited instinct and that the positive inclination to incest, rather, is far more likely to be instinctive. This is clearly demonstrated by the psychoanalysis of neurotics, who, unable to dissociate their infantile libido from their closest relatives, illustrate for us an aspect of prehistoric sexual behavior that most persons supersede only at the cost of an exaggerated aversion to incest. When the process of repression, presumably organic in origin, is already under way in most individuals, there results an expressed constraint on sexual relations between blood relatives—mainly for social and economic reasons. Then, in individuals who remain in a developmentally primitive stage, and in later cultural periods, the strength of this constraint artificially accelerates and intensifies the process of repression (originally brought about by natural laws of development) or brands as undesirables and criminals those who attempt incestuous acts.

It is only through their particular elaboration in the individual that phylogenetically inherited tendencies toward incest achieve their individual character. If they are subsequently reinforced, allowing them to be retained with high intensity up to the age of sexual maturity, these tendencies can in constitutionally predisposed individuals lead to actual acts of incest, branded by our culture as perverse and criminal. When repressed and psychically transformed, though—as in normal individuals—these impulses become unconscious, occasionally revealing themselves in dreams. If this subsequent repression fails to occur or is incomplete, given an especially intensive expression of these tendencies and early fixation, the continuing conflict between these impulses and diametrically opposed ones may lead to serious disturbances in psychosexual development. Under especially favorable conditions, when compensation is made for incomplete repression and thus results in sublimation, these impulses lead to achievements we admire as the highest creations of the human spirit.

2 *Types of Incest Drama* (Oedipus, Hamlet, Don Carlos): *The Mechanisms of Artistic Creativity*

The genesis of a work of art is the genesis of art, and he who wishes to know, for example, how the human spirit came upon tragedy would have had valuable information if Shakespeare had told us how he came upon Hamlet or Lear.

HEBBEL

In its naive mode of thinking, ancient Greece has given us a body of legend that, with its mythological images of the killing of the father and of sexual relations with the mother, shows us in full detail the child's incestuous wishes brought to realization. The content of this mythological material is so similar to the incestuous dreams many people experience today that one must come to the following undeniable conclusion: the psychic forces that produce myth are the same as those that produce dreams; moreover, the psychic processes associated with these forces are closely related as well. Based upon this realization, and in connection with the interpretation of dreams, Freud was able to determine the psychological source of the Oedipus legend: "The Oedipus legend is the reaction of the imagination to two typical dreams (of the death of the father and of sexual relations with the mother), and just as adults associate these dreams with feelings of revulsion, so must the legend incorporate elements of horror and self-punishment" (Freud 1909f, 185 ff.).

In a later cultural period, when these childhood love fantasies have receded into the psyche of a myth-creating people and remain alive in only a few individuals (including creative artists), the author, motivated by powerful unconscious memories, seizes upon the legendary material in order to reshape it with his own means and to free himself, in so doing, from impulses that cry out for gratification and from the painful defense mechanisms with which they are associated—in short, to free himself from his deepest psychic conflicts. Such a close connection between the material attracting his artistic interest and the content of his deepest fantasies, a connection never realized by the creative artist, can now be proclaimed in advance as a result of the detailed analyses below. Thus we shall have an explanation for why the incest theme has been so popular among the most important authors of all times. The regular appearance of the childhood incest fantasy, its content—soon felt to be distasteful (leading to the repression of the fantasy)—and finally the powerful aftereffects of the fantasy that rise from the unconscious to play a role in the emotional and fantasy life of the adult all lead us to see that the universal dramatic effectiveness of the incest theme is quite understandable.

The decisive way these erotic fantasies, present in childhood and subsequently repressed to an insufficient degree, influence the selection of artistic material and especially its treatment can be instructively demonstrated by a brief comparison of various characteristic manifestations of the incest theme. Such an analysis leads not only to insight into the actual process of literary creation, but also to the realization that these mechanisms, in the process of cultural development, are subject to certain regular modifications comprehensible only in light of the repression of precocious drives and fantasies that with ever greater intensity continually progresses within the human psyche. Corresponding to an initial stage in the course of this repression, in the dramatic manifestation of the incest theme passed down to us in *Oedipus the King* by the Attic tragedian Sophocles, the fulfillment of the erotic wish appears undisguised. To give a typical example of the effects of progressing repression, let us consider this incest drama, created from naive mythological material, in connection with two other dramatic creations that belong to vastly different cultural periods but, as we will see, arise from the same unconscious source in the psychic life of their authors.

The legend, which Sophocles followed rather closely in his dramatization, relates that Oedipus, the son of Laius, king of Thebes, and of his wife, Jocasta, was exposed immediately after birth because an oracle had revealed to the father, eager for offspring, that he was destined to be killed by his son. The infant, once exposed, is rescued by shepherds and grows up as a prince at another court until, unsure of his origin, he consults the oracle and is advised to avoid his homeland lest he become his father's murderer and his mother's husband. Upon leaving his new home, he encounters King Laius, his unrecognized father, and kills him. Then he arrives in Thebes, solves the riddle of the sphinx that is bringing doom to the city, and is rewarded by the Thebans with the remuneration reserved for the liberator of the city: he is made king and receives the hand of his mother, Jocasta, in marriage. For a long time he reigns peacefully and with honor, and he has two sons and two daughters by his mother. Then a plague breaks out in the city, and the Thebans, inquiring of the oracle how they can be freed from the plague, are informed by messengers that the plague will cease as soon as Laius's murderer is banished from the land. The Sophoclean drama begins with the Thebans awaiting the arrival of the messengers [i.e., Creon]. According to Freud,

> the action of the drama consists precisely in the gradual and artistically intensified revelation, reminiscent of a psychoanalytical investigation, that Oedipus himself is the murderer of Laius but is also his son and the son of Jocasta. Overwhelmed by the terrible act he has unwittingly committed, Oedipus blinds himself and leaves his homeland. . . . His fate seems so pertinent to us precisely because it could have been our own. . . . Perhaps we all associated our first sexual impulses with our mother and our first feelings of hate and violence with our father. Our dreams convince us of this. King Oedipus, who has killed his father and married his mother, is nothing but the fulfillment of our childhood wishes. . . . In the presence of the person for whom this prehistoric infantile wish has been fulfilled, however, we feel the revulsion with which these wishes have come to be associated in our innermost being. (Freud 1909f, 182)

Two thousand years later this general human theme, though in a different guise, offered another great playwright the material for a drama: William Shakespeare's *Hamlet.* Freud has also provided the key to the only correct interpretation of this work. With impetuous passion, Hamlet stabs the listener behind the curtain and sends his two friends to the death intended for Hamlet himself: "Hamlet can accomplish everything but the revenge upon the man who has killed his father and taken his father's place beside his mother—the man who shows him the realization of his repressed childhood wishes. The revulsion that should drive him to revenge is replaced by self-reproach, by pangs of conscience that suggest to him that he is literally no better than the sinner he must punish. Thus I have expressed consciously what remains in Hamlet's unconscious" (Freud 1909f, 183). The relation of *Hamlet* to the Oedipus legend thus becomes obvious. That such an interpretation is necessary demonstrates the diametrically opposed influence of a powerful tendency for repression. "In the altered treatment of the theme in question, the differences in the psychic life of the two temporally disjunct periods and the continual progress of repression in human emotional life are revealed. In *Oedipus* the underlying fantasy wish of the child is brought to light and realized, as might occur in a dream. In *Hamlet* it remains repressed; reminiscent of the situation with a neurotic, we learn of its existence only through the inhibitory effects its produces" (Freud 1909f, 183).

And once more, two thousand years after Sophocles, this typical theme appears in Johann Friedrich Schiller's *Don Carlos*. Here again, the increasing degree of sexual repression in the human psyche is revealed by the way the material is treated. The incest fantasy is realized in *Oedipus,* and the son lovingly embraces the mother (though he does not know it). In *Hamlet,* owing to greater repression, only the reverse side of love for the mother appears—jealous hatred. In *Don Carlos* the rejection of the incest wish has gone so far that it is no longer even the actual mother the son desires, but rather the stepmother—a woman who only bears the name Mother; she is no blood relative, but is nevertheless the father's wife. In *Oedipus,* that the son considers his mother a stranger makes a sexual relationship possible. In *Don Carlos* this remains impossible even though the mother is not a blood relative—even though the obstacle is no longer present—since the internal mechanisms against incest have become too powerful within the playwright. With Sophocles, incest is unconsciously justified because the wish for the realization of this fantasy produces in the legend a delay in the revelation that the two characters are related. With Schiller, the rejection of the distasteful impulse brings about the demotion of the relationship from mother to stepmother.

The increasing repression is illustrated still more clearly in the varying treatment of the relationship with the father. In *Oedipus* the son's erotic inclination toward his mother is associated with only minor inhibitions; the son removes the physical obstacle to the realization of his love fantasy without hesitation. At the beginning of the tragedy he not only has killed his father long ago but has also forgotten (repressed) this event, since in response to mechanisms opposing the impulse to kill the father, he considers his father a stranger. In *Hamlet,* however, the father has been dead only a short time; his memory lives on in the son with such overwhelming force that it appears as a "ghost," separating mother and son (act 3, scene 4). Hamlet does not possess his mother, nor is he his father's killer. As though effecting a compromise between the vehement insistency of these wishes and the powerful impulses opposing them, he permits both wishes to be realized by the "uncle." In *Don Carlos,* erotic inclination toward the natural mother is disguised as a loving relationship with a woman who is half mother to the son (as the father's spouse) and half his lover (his former fiancée). Similarly, in *Hamlet,* hateful jealousy of the real father is disguised as justified hatred of the "uncle-father" (2.2). The drama itself can be analyzed to demonstrate that the powerful emotions of jealousy and hatred Hamlet feels are actually directed toward his true father and that their deflection to a substitute, the "uncle," serves to disguise and justify them. We need only remove the ghost episodes from the drama to recognize the underlying schema of the son jealous of the father because of his own love for the mother. According to this schema, King Claudius appears as the true father, toward whom the son's hatred is directed. Such frankness, however, is counteracted by the playwright's tendency for repression. Therefore the competitor for the love of the mother is demoted to stepfather (cf. the stepmother in *Don Carlos*). In this sense, King Claudius is half father to Hamlet (and as such his competitor and enemy) and half murderer of Hamlet's true father (thus representing Hamlet in his relationship to his mother). He is the embodiment of Hamlet's wishes. In the Sophoclean drama, the son truly kills the father, whereas in Shakespeare's play the father appears half dead (as a "ghost"). That is, he is nothing but the powerful, unconscious desire of the son, who wishes for his father's death and lets him appear dead while he himself lives hidden behind the mask of the stepfather. It is only in this guise that the son can kill the father (cf. Oedipus, who can kill his father because he does not know him). In Schiller's tragedy, finally, the father is still alive and physically places himself between the loving mother and son (*Don Carlos,* final scene: "The king stands between them").

Thus *Oedipus* and *Don Carlos* represent two poles in the process of repression within the psyche. As effective and highly valued works of art, they embody both the psyche of the playwrights and the innermost feelings of their times. In *Oedipus,* the true father is long since dead and forgotten, while the beloved mother is married to the unrecognized son. Thus both of the child's wishes are completely fulfilled, and in the dimensions of adult love life. In *Don Carlos,* by contrast, not only do these two wishes remain unfulfilled, but the plot is rife with exaggerated reactions to such an outcome—defensive measures to combat the now feared realization of these wishes. The actual mother has long been dead (she died bearing the son). The actual father is a priori the son's bitter enemy and mistrustful competitor. This shows how strong the inner defense mechanisms combating these wishes have become. In the stepmother theme and in the theme of the father's exaggerated hatred of the son (*Don Carlos*), we recognize two variations of the originally positive incest wish (*Oedipus*). The stepmother theme reveals not only the progression of repression but also a possible means of realizing the incest wish. The theme of the father's hatred indicates the direction of the repression. This process aims first to still the son's undesirable impulses of hatred toward his father. Subsequently, though, it directs these impulses against the son himself as a form of compensatory justice—as the father's punishment of the son. (Don Carlos dies at the command of his father.)

If the Carlos material in Schiller's drama has become the antithesis of the Oedipus fable, we find in Shakespeare's *Hamlet* the turning point in this process. Here, first of all, the repression is achieved only halfway. Only one of the wishes, the wish for the father's death, finds partial fulfillment. The erotic inclination toward the mother is almost completely repressed and disguised by opposite emotions, as is clearly seen in Hamlet's sexual abstinence (with regard to Ophelia). But the original love for the mother is still suggested in isolated incidents. This is especially true in the great fourth scene of the third act, where Hamlet vehemently rebukes his mother, clearly suggesting the jealousy of one rejected. In bidding farewell to his mother, he admonishes her: "Good-night: but go not to mine uncle's bed." It is important to note that he reproaches her nearly exclusively on account of her hasty second marriage, and not because of her implied shared guilt for or acceptance of the murder. It almost seems he is simply annoyed with his mother for engaging in her marital duties, thus robbing the son of his unconscious hopes for her love. Just as the erotic affection for the mother is expressed less naively than in *Oedipus,* the same is true of the wish for the father's removal. It finds gratification only behind a double disguise created by powerful defense mechanisms. The playwright lets Claudius, the king's brother, murder the king, thus apparently removing the need for Hamlet to experience the painful desire to murder his father. But the son's jealous hatred, actually meant for the father, is simply redirected in all its force against the substitute father, the stepfather. When directed toward this person, not only can the son's inimical feelings be expressed more clearly, but they are justified because the father's murder has been carried out by this straw man. Indeed, the son's duty to avenge the father's death is motivated by noble emotions. Here, then, defenses against the son's unbearable hatred of the father have led to a transformation of this impulse; to the extent that the defenses have not led to neurosis, this transformation can be classified as successful sublimation. The impulse of hatred, originally directed toward the father, is displaced to the murderer—the stepfather. The son's great enmity toward this person supposedly arises from the son's great love for the father, whose death ineluctably cries out for vengeance.

However, the son is still unable to murder this second person because he sees in him, according to Freud's solution of the Hamlet problem, the realization of his own repressed wishes. The son also cannot carry out vengeance on his father's murderer, his uncle and stepfather, because that person is a second father to him. Here we are reminded of the image of the hydra. In the place of the father, who has been removed, a demoted image of the father appears (cf. also the ghost). The father's brother becomes a new father—a man who has the same claims on the mother as the father did. On the one hand, it is as though nothing has changed for the son through the death of the old king. On the other hand, it seems that what has happened is superfluous and without purpose, for when he thinks of the dead father (the ghost) and the still living father, the son is hindered in the loving relationship that in *Oedipus* is made possible by the naive removal of the father. That the central emotional element in *Hamlet* is the wish for the father's removal—associated with the incest complex—is illustrated by a little-noticed detail: the disguised murder of the father. Just as Hamlet has displaced his murderous impulse from the father to the stepfather, he now redirects it from his uncle, in whom he now sees only the equivalent of his father, to Polonius, who like the father attempts to place himself between Hamlet and his mother. But even this third, unrelated incarnation of the father can be killed only by a Hamlet unaware of what he is doing, and in an assumed guise. That the unintended death blow suffered by the eavesdropper behind the curtain has for Hamlet the meaning of patricide is revealed after the fact by Hamlet's calm question: "Is't not the king?" (the father). Here again, Hamlet's powerful hatred of his competitor for his mother's love comes to the fore. The realization that in his delusion he has killed the innocent Polonius nullifies the effects of this brief gratification of his hatred for his competitor, leaving the emotion to burn again in full flame. Unconsciously, Hamlet also sees through the self-deception he carries out in replacing the father with Claudius and Polonius: the "ghost" of the murdered father still torments him until in the end he openly kills with his own hand the spouse of his mother, his (step)father. Simultaneously, though, he also destroys the image of the realization of his own wishes for the removal of his father and for possession of his mother. Thus he has nothing left to hope for, and "the rest is silence."

No one who has learned through the study of unconscious psychic processes never to underestimate the meaning of even the most seemingly obvious psychic events will object to the multifaceted nature of this interpretation, the important points of which will be further supported below. Instead, he will find the analysis quite lacking in detail. However, the playwright's creations resemble the images of dreams and the symptoms of psychoneurosis so closely that he will be convinced beyond doubt of the close relation of the drives behind these psychic activities and even of the relation of the mechanisms. Still, this mention of the relation between literary creations, dream images, and the symptoms of psychoneurosis does not imply that the creative artist is a neurotic, which would contradict our theoretical perspective. It implies instead that psychologically he bears a close relation to the neurotic, as is only too often demonstrated by reality. This corresponds thoroughly to our framework and to our expectations. The creative artist is not led by supernatural powers. Instead, his creations are closely related both to the productions of the neurotic and also to the psychic creations of the normal person. The most important of these is the dream. We would have no occasion or procedure for research on the psychic creations of normals had not both been provided us by the psychic creations of the demented, which exceed what is normal in sharpness and clarity. But the boundaries here, as elsewhere in nature, cannot be drawn with precision. Mixed forms are so frequent and numerous that such a distinction would have only theoretical meaning. Practically speaking the author, while dreaming in a normal fashion, will also exhibit several neurotic traits that will be more fully characterized below. It is fine, gradual distinctions that are significant, not broad categories.

Our attempt to describe the psychological position of the author, which for the time being seems to vacillate between that of the dreamer and that of the neurotic, seems at first to have the opposite effect: the boundaries between normal, pathological, and highly valued psychic activity are obliterated. Most important, though, two psychic mechanisms, repression and condensation, seem most significant in characterizing the psychic activity of the creative artist. Freud discussed these in *The Interpretation of Dreams* and showed them to be of practical value in treating neurotic symptoms.

Thus far, we have avoided using these terms and have employed a more figurative means of expression intended to correspond to a literary viewpoint. (The process of cultural repression is not to be confused with the mechanisms of repression in the individual.) However, we need only translate our comparisons into the language of our psychological insights to see the substantial contribution of these mechanisms to literary creativity. The distinction between "blood relatives" and "unrelated persons," which we have invoked in our psychological interpretations as though merely playing with the words, is nothing but a figurative representation of the process of repression that occurs as the author deals with incestuous impulses. And the normal repression of the child's erotically colored inclination toward the mother can best be seen if we deliberately make use of the intuitive literary image: erotically speaking, the mother must become unrelated to her son (*Oedipus, Don Carlos*), and the son must learn to associate his erotic feelings with unrelated women, behind whom remains, as authors unashamedly reveal, the image of the mother. The literary representation also shows us this mechanism of repression in progress. In a manner of speaking, we experience along with the protagonist the transformation of blood relatives into unrelated persons, but we also recognize how repression is apparently circumvented in undisguised incestuous dreams; we realize that total failure to repress incestuous impulses will lead to neurosis.

With increasing repression, a second psychic process arises, and a knowledge of it is extremely important to understanding literary production. It corresponds to long-known laws of the psychology of consciousness: directly similar thoughts and series of mental images are closely associated not only with each other, but also with opposing thoughts and images. It now appears that similar laws hold for unconscious psychic processes as well: those thoughts that have been repressed into the unconscious are intensified in the presence of similar thoughts and are united with opposing thoughts, developing into mixed conceptions. If a comparison is made with the process of dreaming, which has become familiar to us, we can easily see that this condensation of unconscious impulses plays a substantial role in the creation of dramatic works. To characterize this psychic activity for the time being, it will suffice to bring into conscious psychological recognition the contrasts that arose in the analysis of the emotions underlying dramatic characters. It seemed that individual dramatic characters (especially the stepmother in *Don Carlos* and the stepfather in *Hamlet*) were the result of a compromise between various trains of thought—usually two opposing ones. We spoke of this situation figuratively by stating that the two "halves" of the character represented different ideas. This analysis assumes that the dramatic character arose through the joining and blending of various thoughts and images. In his analysis of the development of dreams and of jokes, however, Freud described this process as condensation. He also demonstrated the role of this process in the development of psychoneurotic symptoms, which according to Freud's research always constitute the result of a compromise between two opposing psychic motives (1909f, 351).

In our efforts thus far to understand the psychic processes of the author, we have been able to devote special analysis only to those mechanisms whose smooth operation leads to normal psychic function and whose occasional failure to operate smoothly causes psychoneurotic disturbances. But further investigation of the nature of the act of creativity will help us understand mechanisms that differ characteristically from those employed by the conscious mind. Those mechanisms not only are involved in literary creativity, but also determine certain pathological processes. Thus far, in accordance with our psychological framework, we have analyzed dramatic works from the egocentric point of view of the playwright—and thus from the point of view of the child's emotional life—by associating the playwright with his protagonist without comment. If systematically pursued, this procedure, justified by the results obtained above, will provide new insights into the secret of the creation of literary works. One will easily recognize that the regular transformations in the behavior of the parents that we observed in the three exemplary works do not correspond to a depiction of reality or to actual historical events. Rather, one has the impression that the behavior of the parents in the dramas discussed is emphasized more or less depending on the psychic needs of the protagonist. It is only intuitively, based on his own unconscious childhood impressions and the emotional and fantasy life that later develops, that the playwright shapes, in a biased manner, the relationship of protagonist and parents. From his egocentric perspective, he exaggerates the relationship to justify and gratify his feelings about his own parents or to condemn these feelings through repression and to punish himself.

This biased strategy in the development of the dramatis personae, central to the playwright's talent for characterization, achieves new psychological significance if one brings into the discussion a similar but thus far untreated insight. In the past, in the critical analysis of dramatic works and their creators, since the dramatis personae are perceived as real persons in the playwright's fantasy and even more so by the audience, the principal mistake has been to regard the characters as real and to evaluate their behavior according to the standards of real life. If one stops to consider that the dramatis personae are to be regarded as psychic reflections of certain emotions in the playwright, however, as was demonstrated in our three exemplary dramas through the behavior of the parents, one gains a new basis for evaluating the playwright and his works. This personal component in the formation and characterization of the dramatis personae, based on the playwright's own psychic tendencies, interacts in an apparently random way with the historical details of the plot. The reason is clear: the historical details are nothing but a mold into which the playwright pours his emotional conflicts. Thus the behavior of a dramatic character may appear incomprehensible or even impossible from the perspective of real life yet may be completely comprehensible and justified from a psychological perspective. The most extreme forms of this biased mode of characterization reveal to us another highly significant mechanism of creative talent at work: certain emotions of the playwright are projected outward and are embodied as dramatic characters that serve the protagonist as external driving or inhibiting forces. We notice also that this mechanism of projection, which we will discuss with reference to our three exemplary dramas, stands in a certain opposition to the mechanism of repression. Just as certain psychic complexes are dealt with inwardly, in the unconscious, they also find a route outward through the process of projection. But though repression is basically connected with the condemnation of a thought, projection generally establishes a sort of justification for that thought.

Just as the repressed complexes continue to undergo condensation in the unconscious, their projection outward splits dramatic characters into their elements—usually mutually opposing ones. Here again, it is evident that this splitting acts in contrast to or as a compensation for the process of condensation; the mixed complexes are once again segmented into their components. The facts will become clearer if we refer once again to the image we used above when we said that the two "halves" of a dramatic character represent opposing tendencies. In the playwright's unconscious, these two impulses exist toward the same person (ambivalence) and thus are synthesized, or condensed, despite their opposition. Similarly, through the mechanism of projection, these impulses once again appear separately, in the person of one dramatic character each. In the two fathers of the Oedipus fable (Laius and Polybus) and in the two fathers of the Hamlet story (the old king and Claudius), we therefore recognize impulses that have become independent of the son's original, unified perception of the father—originally synthesized in its turn, though, from independent impulses: the noble, irreproachable father, as the admiring child sees him, is contrasted with the deeply hated father, as the jealous youth perceives him. Here one sees clearly how this split allows the uninhibited gratification of the condemned impulse. In *Der Mythus von der Geburt des Helden* [The myth of the birth of the hero] (Rank 1909), it is shown that this mechanism of projection and splitting (analysis) especially characterizes the creation of myths but is also dominant in certain types of dementia. As various analyses have shown, the projection outward of one's own psychic perceptions plays a central role in the creation of illusory images in the paranoiac, and Freud hints that the splitting of unified complexes into their elements leads to dementia praecox [schizophrenia]. Just as the literary mechanisms of repression and condensation characterize both normal psychic experience and the development of neurotic symptoms, the literary mechanisms of projection and splitting are for the most part characteristic of psychosis.

We are now in a position to extend our psychological characterization of the artist, whom we have claimed stands psychologically between the normal dreamer and the psychopath, by stating that the process of literary production evinces the use of the two normal dream mechanisms [repression and condensation] and the two pathological mechanisms [projection and splitting]. But we also understand why the use of these clearly opposing mechanisms is necessary. Within the psyche of the author, the two dream mechanisms process the material in the unique manner that confuses us in neurosis, alienates us in dreams, annoys us in daily life, and amuses us in jokes—and that we admire in literature. The two pathological mechanisms, however, are crucial to literary creativity in that they project outward the material that has been internally processed, on the one hand providing therapeutic release for the author and on the other hand making the material socially acceptable. In contrast to the author there stand the, so to speak, asocial dreamer, whose "projections" are played out within, and the antisocial paranoiac, who confuses them with reality. Practically, though, these oppositions cannot be strictly maintained; in the author, further, we must assume some sort of internal dream process as a preliminary stage of creativity. Yet our estimation of his achievements grows in proportion to his ability to present us with a second reality. Among authors, the playwright, who is supported by the actor, is best able to accomplish this end. Almost in the manner of the paranoiac, he watches his inner impulses act and speak—personified as dramatic characters. It is his special talent for psychic projection that distinguishes the playwright from the poet, who must use other devices to give form to these fantasies and to achieve therapeutic release.

Thus the specific talent of the playwright bears an extremely close relation to the fantasy activity that produces myths, and this accounts for the frequent adoption of mythic material as a background for dramatic action (cf. *Oedipus* and *Hamlet*). The playwright need only restructure the myth—maintained through the generations with a constant orientation by a majority with a constant psychic framework, for example, the Oedipus legend—in terms of his own (incest) complex; just like a myth-creating people, he finds in the myth a justification for those emotions that are oppressing him. However, whereas the makers of myths significantly simplify the material the individual playwright, if he wishes to express the framework of his own complexes, must permit the material to diffuse according to the various aspects of his own psychic orientation. One could compare a myth to a stone in a stream, worn down as it is constantly carried along, while the body of material presented in dramatic form could be compared to volcanic rock, congealed and unabraded. The myth receives its typical form only after a long process of formation, whereas in literary works one strives to keep the original content as pure and unadulterated as possible. Here we cannot investigate the extent to which certain special psychic mechanisms are dominant in the various literary genres (including myths and folktales) or the extent to which certain tendencies in the author himself, associated with his psychic abilities and personal fate, will incline or induce him to choose a given genre. We are principally concerned with dramatic works, which are most closely related to our dreams and to certain constructs and processes of dementia. But as the dramatic genre gradually evolves through time, it is unmistakably clear that the originally dreamlike character of literary productions, still clear in myths, takes on a more and more neurotic form. Suspecting a connection between this development and the advancing process of repression in society, we are justified at this time in pursuing the developmental history of the dramatic genre based on our three exemplary works before attempting a synthesis.

We began our investigation with incestuous dreams and recognized the dramatic treatment of certain typical themes as a sort of sublimated expression of the infantile emotions that underlie these dream images. That this literary treatment of incestuous tendencies can, from a psychological point of view, be viewed as a continuation of the process of repression of dream-producing mechanisms is confirmed by playwrights themselves, those most profound of unconscious psychologists; they often refer to this connection, which they themselves feel deeply. In almost all literary works dealing with incest, we observe more or less obvious traces of the original association with dreams, as well as the unmistakable signs of the process of repression as it approaches neurosis. In his interpretation of the Oedipus legend, Freud (1909f, 182) refers to this circumstance: "That the Oedipus legend sprang from prehistoric dream material dealing with the painful disturbance that arises in the relationship with the parents at the first sexual feelings is unmistakably clear from a hint in the text of the Sophoclean tragedy itself. Jocasta comforts Oedipus, who has not yet discovered the truth but is disturbed by the memory of the oracle's words, by mentioning a dream dreamed by many persons, yet in Jocasta's opinion a meaningless one: 'For many men have seen themselves joined with the mother in dreams. But he who disregards all of this bears life's burden lightly.'"

In *Hamlet* also, dreams are discussed, but their content is not approached as directly as in *Oedipus*. Instead, Hamlet sighs: "Were it not that I have bad dreams" (2.2). He too tries to take the content of these dreams lightly, to resist them, to consider them meaningless: "A dream itself is but a shadow." But Carlos is greatly oppressed by his dreams: "Like furies from hell, the most terrible dreams pursue me."

Unlike Oedipus, Carlos can no longer be comforted by his mother's telling him his dreams are meaningless. Instead, "she reveals in all clarity that which should have been kept from Carlos forever" (1.5). With the whole weight of her moral defenses, she depicts for him the realization of his dream wishes:

> *Queen:* You place your hopes in me, your mother? (She observes him for a long while, penetratingly, and then says seriously and with dignity:) Why not? Oh, the newly elected king can do more than that. . . . He can even take the dead man's mummy from its resting place in the Escorial into the sunlight and strew his desecrated dust to the four winds—who would stop him?—and then at last, as a worthy finale—
>
> *Carlos:* In God's name, do not say it.
>
> *Queen:* At last wed his own mother [i.e., stepmother].
>
> *Carlos:* Cursed son!

If one compares this almost neurotic fantasy—which underlyingly toys with the idea of patricide and of replacing the father in his relationship with the mother—with Jocasta's naive assessment of dreams, one will best be able to recognize the advancement of repression and the tendency toward neurosis. This characteristic distinction can be observed in the whole tone and execution of the drama.

Already in *Oedipus,* this still almost completely dreamlike presentation of the incest theme, one finds the beginnings of the outward projection of inner psychic processes and of their personification as independent dramatic characters. The role that in the Sophoclean drama falls to the blind prophet Teiresias and the whole way he reluctantly reveals his prophecy, at first indignantly rejected by Oedipus, create the impression that in this mythic figure the playwright too has only personified the unconscious childhood emotions of the protagonist, which gradually become conscious despite his active defense mechanisms.

The projection mechanism in action is seen still more clearly in Shakespeare's drama, and the key to its meaning in the context of our investigations is provided in the ghost of Hamlet's father. It has been said that Shakespeare was naive enough to believe in ghosts. Yet Shakespeare clearly shows that he gives no credence to such superstitions. Demonstrating subtle psychological understanding, he depicts the ghost of Hamlet's father as the personification of an inner voice within the son, driving him to expel the stepfather—or as we might say more correctly based on our interpretation, the father. The emphatic defense against this undesirable impulse, as well as the need for its objective motivation and justification, causes it to be projected outward, creating a personification as an outer driving force. This personification of an unbearable impulse is complicated in *Hamlet* through the increased need for further justification of Hamlet's inimical feelings toward his father, which still oppress the son's psyche, though in disguised form. Thus, as we mentioned above, the murderous impulse is displaced toward the "uncle," so that it is the ghost of the murdered father himself who drives the son to kill his mother's spouse (the stepfather).

But the literary mechanism of projection is not capable of dealing with such a complex justifying fantasy: the defense is not completely successful, and the personification remains only half accomplished. Instead of a flesh-and-blood character, only a "ghost" arises to encourage the son's thoughts of revenge. However, this failure of literary projection provides deeper insights into the complicated psychic processes of the playwright—through the phantom, as it were. We recognize in the ghost of Hamlet's father the personification of Hamlet's hatred of his competitor for his mother's love. This special form of repression not only illustrates the wish for the father's death through his representation as a ghost but also sanctions this undesirable impulse by establishing the noble theme of vengeance. Thus jealous animosity toward the true father can easily be hidden behind the well-motivated need for retaliation against the stepfather; that Shakespeare derives the son's hatred of the preferred competitor for the mother's affection from effusive love for the father is completely in keeping with our analysis. According to proven results of psychoanalytic research, we are justified in suspecting that such effusive emotions are a reaction to originally opposite emotions, repressed because they are intolerable. If normal love for the father and the consequent noble need to take revenge on his murderer were Hamlet's basic driving force, the protagonist's behavior would still be incomprehensible. The forces that inhibit Hamlet in carrying out his revenge remain unclear unless one assumes that repressed feelings of an opposite nature, as discussed above, are also in effect. Further, specific meaningful elements also lose their significance if one refuses to accept this psychologically well founded interpretation. Hamlet's comments would not seem fully motivated when, prepared as he is for the appearance of his father's ghost, he nevertheless resists it in terror, crying: "Angels and ministers of grace defend us" (1.4). This reaction seems appropriate, however, if one considers the hateful thoughts that underlie the noble motive and if one looks on the appearance of the ghost less as an incitement to revenge than as an awakening to consciousness of the intolerable complex of hatred toward the father.

In Schiller's *Don Carlos,* finally, corresponding to the playwright's inner conflict—which reminds one of the "split personality" of the psychotic—the two main characters appear as fragments of the whole, each corresponding to one of the opposing conceptions or emotional orientations of the poet. Carlos and Posa represent the "two souls" in Schiller's breast. Posa is the virtuous son, asexual with respect to his mother—the personified rejection of the incestuous impulse. The loving, desiring son, possessed by passionate erotic feelings for the mother, is personified in Carlos. This split is paralleled by an analogous split in the character of the mother. Her motherly, asexual nature is personified in the noble, pure queen (*Princess:* "She is like a saint in heaven"). Her passion for the son is personified in the princess herself. The princess of Eboli is clearly characterized as a "mother" in that she gives herself to the king/father (whereas Elisabeth, the pure mother, withholds herself from him). Simultaneously, though, she is branded a whore, and thus the idea appears once again, as suggested in Hamlet's relationship to Gertrude, that by giving herself to the father, the mother debases herself in her son's eyes. On the other hand, to the unsuccessfully loving son, the mother must of course seem so sublime and unapproachably pure that he dares not associate her with sexual pleasure, not even of the conjugal sort, but instead pictures her as a saint.

In the fantasies of normal as well as neurotic persons, Freud (1910) frequently noted this apparently contradictory and ambiguous estimation of the mother, a remnant of the child's relationship with the parents. As we shall observe, this orientation is the one regularly observed in literary fantasies as well. In *Hamlet* too, the mother is portrayed as a despicable fornicator (Gertrude), while the virginally pure Ophelia, chaste and unapproachable, stands in contrast to her. Once again the mother nature of Ophelia is indicated by the way Hamlet confuses and identifies her father, whom he has stabbed through the curtain, with his own father (*Hamlet:* "Is't not the king?") and by the way he identifies Ophelia with his mother, Gertrude, by saying the same thing to both of them. To Ophelia he says, "Get thee to a nunn'ry. Why wouldst thou be a breeder of sinners?" And to Gertrude he says, "Go not to mine uncle's bed. . . . Refrain tonight." On the basis of this partial reverse projection of individual characters as psychic currents within the playwright, we understand Hamlet's otherwise obscure behavior toward Ophelia, as well as the similarly indecisive behavior of Prince Carlos in his double relation to the queen and to the princess of Eboli, as expressions of the unceasing conflict between incestuous attraction toward the mother and defense against this impulse. We can clearly see that the consciously perceived and contrasting dramatic characters (cf. Laertes, chap. 6 below) correspond to unconscious conflicts.

Under such an analysis, the result of psychological consideration of the act of literary creation, not only can many otherwise incomprehensible actions of the dramatic characters be explained, but a portion of the secret of dramatic form is revealed to us. We recognize in Schiller's *Don Carlos,* with its succession of dialogues, the outward projection of the conflict between distinct psychic tendencies belonging to the incest complex. This projection of various psychic states in the various scenes is extremely similar to the way the paranoiac projects changes in his inner being. In this sense, through reverse projection, one could analyze each scene in terms of the corresponding psychic tendency in the playwright, thus establishing the psychological skeleton behind the flesh and blood of the dramatic work. For now the highly instructive pursuit of these relationships must be left to the readers, who will themselves find their natural boundaries. To help achieve an understanding of all the characters, though, we can now point out the various disjunct images of the father in *Don Carlos.* His severity and unwavering strictness, as well as his hatred for his son, are symbolized by Duke Alba (*King:* "Do I not know that Alba is brooding over revenge?"), while Domingo expresses the father's doubt and his jealous suspicion. In Philip himself is personified the purely sexual relationship of the father with the mother (the queen): "My sword—and Duke Alba—can defend my people; my wife's love can be defended only by this eye. . . .

Whatever the king has, he has from fortune: Elisabeth is the king's. Here I am mortal."

In Count Lerma, finally, we see the personification of the fatherly, gentle impulses of the father toward the son. Thus, given our psychological interpretation, the characters can first be reduced to only three—the playwright/hero and his parents in their various attitudes and multiple relationships. Ultimately, though, the parents too are seen as the personification of psychic tendencies within the playwright—as the conflict of opposing psychic tendencies and of outward conditions.

It seems to be no coincidence that it was the appearance of the ghost in *Hamlet* that provided the most important insight into the mechanism of literary projection. This appearance of the father as a ghost obviously recalls the dream image of the father's death, and below we will fully demonstrate that the ghost is in fact the literary incarnation of the same unconscious psychic impulses that appear in the dream of the father's death (cf. chap. 6, "Shakespeare's Father Complex"). In this context it seems important to note that in *Don Carlos*, too, the ghost appears episodically, and that the protagonist takes on the form of his grandfather, who wanders about as a ghost, in order to penetrate at night into his mother's bedchamber, where he is surprised by the jealous father. The same situation is found in Shakespeare's *Hamlet*, where the ghost of the father also appears in the mother's bedchamber during the son's absence (3.4).

In Schiller, however, with the advancement of repression, the son's sinful wish for the death of the father is carried out, like a punishment, upon the son himself. In *Hamlet* the ghost of the murdered father appears as the son's accuser and the mother's defender, whereas in *Don Carlos* the son appears disguised as a ghost, as if in anticipation of his impending death, with which the father punishes him. On the other hand, the mask the son dons during his visit with his mother clearly expresses his wish to take the place of the father (grandfather) beside the mother, a fantasy realized in *Hamlet* in the form of the "uncle." The typical association of the ghost's appearance with the mother's bedchamber, filled with associations as it is, not only unites all the components of the incest complex in an ingenious literary expression of compromise, but also provides an important etiological explanation. Just as the ghostly apparition of the father presupposes not only the realization of the death wish but also the immortality of this hatred, the role the father plays as the vexing impediment in the childhood love relationship with the mother indicates the likewise undying pangs of conscience and self-reproach that torment the son on account of this hatred. This perception of the father as an impediment is characteristic of the child's mode of thought and reveals the infantile nature of this whole fantasy, while the place of action, the mother's bedchamber, points unmistakably to the real experiences that underlie this perception. Just as the ghostly apparition reminds one of the dream image of the father's death, the son's visit to the mother's bedchamber can be seen as a dampened act of incest impeded by the appearance of the father. Thus we see in the ghost theme and in its place of action the literary expression of the emotional complexes that underlie both incest dreams. To establish these unexpected relationships, one can cite a prosaic fact, but one that has been demonstrated through psychoanalysis: the fear of ghosts in children who later become neurotic is almost always revealed to be a consequence of the repression of certain incestuous fantasies associated with the parents' habit of assuring themselves, before retiring, that the child, who usually sleeps in the same room and has become a prejudiced witness of their conjugal intimacies, is really asleep. Usually dressed only in nightshirts, they approach the child's bed (Freud 1909f, 109).

The unsuccessful forms of projection, to which category we can now assign ghostly apparitions, indicate that literary fantasy is associated in origin and character with dreams. Similarly, the completely successful personification of psychic tendencies as dramatic characters who produce in the spectator the impression of real persons is related to certain pathological images in which an individual sees his deepest wishes and fears realized and acted out by other persons. The most characteristic element of the literary creative force, however, is that in the true author, as a consequence of the unique development of his drives and psychic life, certain general human psychic conflicts can reveal themselves, as it were, in a socially valuable form. This form enables not only the author himself, but also most normal persons, to gratify in a psychically hygienic and therefore socially approved and highly valuable manner those repressed emotions that the dreamer sometimes lives out in his inner life and that the paranoiac, assisted by his delusion, can only partially master. During the evolution of this culturally valuable means of gratifying rejected emotions, we believe it will be possible to observe a gradual development away from the original dream character and toward a constantly more neurotic form. As the most general and most important result of this investigation, let us emphasize that the same primitive sexual wishes that in gray prehistoric times were actually realized made their way into undisguised dreams and naive myths when the possibility of real gratification was no longer available. From there, in constantly more disguised (repressed) form, they can be followed in the most important works of art of three cultural periods until they achieve an almost pathological, neurotic form and are rejected. Thus literary production gradually shifts from its dreamlike tendency of release for repressed emotions toward neurotic inhibition of those emotions.

3 *Schiller's Incest Fantasy: The Psychology of Outlines and Fragments*

The son loves his mother. The customs of the world,
The order of nature and Rome's laws
Condemn this passion. My demand
Offends terribly my father's rights.

SCHILLER, *Don Carlos*

With growing cultural repression of purely incestuous impulses and wishes, it becomes increasingly difficult to detect these ever more hidden and subtle tendencies in the author as they are symptomatically expressed in his works. Whereas in the interpretation of *Oedipus* the role of incest is clear from the dramatic material itself, in the case of *Don Carlos* this interpretation may seem forced, and further proof may be desired. Most crucially, it is to be expected that such an important psychic complex, which we see expressed in its literary form in incest drama, should characterize a whole range of artistic creations by the author in question. One will also be correct in assuming that many of the author's casual remarks should be filled with references to this theme, which has occupied the depths of his psyche since earliest childhood. The hypothesis that these fundamental psychic impulses should be constantly expressed in all the artistic works of the authors we are considering is confirmed to an unexpected degree through a psychological investigation of the evolution of their works; one must return to the individual fantasies that seek artistic expression in literature. If we pursue these fantasies through their development in earliest childhood, their intense repression, occurring soon thereafter, their reawakening during puberty, their attempted realization in real life, and their complete transformation into artistic themes—all in connection with an author whose works are completely familiar to us and whose life and artistic development are clear to see—we will receive a strong impression of the crucial influence of the incest complex on artistic creation. We will also gain deeper insight into the ways artistic production relates, on the one hand, to the impressions real life has made on the author and, on the other hand, to the actions through which he has expressed himself in real life. We will see how artistic production, decisively influenced by these factors, becomes the idealized fulfillment of unfulfilled reality.

The interpretation of *Don Carlos* as an incest drama, sketched out in the preceding chapter, may seem improbable owing to certain observations, the most important being that in this work, besides the incestuous family drama, there is a powerful political drama that comes to the fore. However, from Schiller's letters, from the first outline of *Don Carlos,* and from the first version of the first three acts, published in *Rheinische Thalia,* it is clear that Schiller was initially interested only in the family drama, especially in the infante's love for his stepmother. Thus he writes (June 7, 1784) to Dalberg, who initially suggested the Don Carlos material to him: "*Carlos* will by no means be a political play. Instead, it will actually be a family portrait in a royal house; the terrible situation of a father so unhappily jealous of his own son and the even more terrible situation of a son who, though heir to the greatest kingdom on earth, loves without hope and is finally sacrificed, should, I believe, certainly be interesting. I shall, however, carefully avoid anything that would offend the sensibilities." In fact, in the first sketch of *Don Carlos,* composed in Bauerbach in 1783, the political drama still has no significance. The central theme is the infante's passion for his stepmother, as is shown in an abridged version of the first outline, published recently in the centenary edition of Schiller's works (4:292 ff.).

Act 1. The plot thickens.
- A. The prince loves the queen, as demonstrated by:
  1. His attentiveness.

  . . . .
- B. This love has its impediments and seems to be dangerous for him, as demonstrated by:
  1. Carlos's strong passion and audaciousness.
  2. His father's deep affect, suspicion, inclination to jealousy, and vindictiveness.

Act 2. The plot thickens.
- A. Carlos's love grows. Causes:
  1. The impediments themselves.
  2. The queen's love for the prince. This is expressed and motivated:

a) By her affectionate nature, which lacks an object.
   (1) Philip's age.
   (2) The duties of her class.
b) By her initial positive impression of and affection for the prince. She enjoys recalling these pleasant memories.
c) By her remarks in the presence of the prince. Internal suffering. Fear. Devotion. Confusion.
d) Certain sparks of jealousy concerning Carlos's relationship with the princess of Eboli.

. . . .

f) Certain confidential remarks from a conversation with the marquis and in a scene with Carlos.

B. The impediments and dangers grow.

Act 3. Apparent conclusion, which complicates all aspects of the plot.

A. The dangers begin to realize themselves.
   1. The king suspects the truth and becomes intensely jealous.
   2. Don Carlos embitters the king still further.
   3. The queen seems to justify the suspicion.
   4. All forces combine to inculpate the prince and the queen.
   5. The king determines that his son must die.

B. The prince seems to escape from all danger.

. . . .

   3. The prince and the queen conquer their inhibitions.

. . . .

Act 4. Conclusion and catastrophe.

A. Stirrings of fatherly love, pity, etc., seem to improve the prince's situation.
B. The queen's passion worsens the situation, causing the prince's doom.

If one compares this first sketch of *Don Carlos* with the source from which Schiller derived the material, Saint-Réal's *Tale of Don Carlos,* it is immediately evident that the original core of the drama concerns only the relationship of mother, son, and father, thus showing that the literary work, though it does become more complex, actually began with the simple relationships to which we reduced it in the preceding chapter. In the original version, which omits all court cabals, political intrigues, imperialistic ideas, and the whole set of characters associated therewith, the personal roots of the work in the psychic life of its creator are clearly revealed. In this outline the incestuous elements, especially the queen's erotic affection for the prince, are more obvious than in the first version of the work or in the final version, where these strong impulses are to a great extent disguised and placed in the background. However, it is very obvious that Schiller did not simply intensify or emphasize incestuous elements from Saint-Réal's novel in his own version. Indeed, Schiller himself first introduced into the plot the whole steamy atmosphere of incest, which is completely absent in Saint-Réal's work. Characteristic of this "incestuous" conception of the plot, not even hinted at in Schiller's source, are the incestuous fantasy the queen relates to the prince (cf. chap. 2) and the father's similar fantasy concerning incest between his son and the (step)mother. Philip says to Lerma (3.2): "Your hair is silver gray and still you do not blush to believe in your wife's fidelity? Go home, then! You will find her in your son's incestuous embrace." But immediately thereafter follows Philip's rejection of these fears, actually his personal fears. He says to Lerma: "You look at me meaningfully? Since my hair too is silver gray? Wretched one, come to your senses! Queens do not stain their honor. You are a dead man if you doubt."

In Saint-Réal's novel, Prince Carlos is passionately in love with the young wife of an aging man. That this man is the prince's father and the mightiest ruler of Christendom is only an undesirable complication for the lover, but a very desirable complication for Saint-Réal, a French historical writer fascinated by the external play of intrigue. That the queen is the prince's stepmother is not considered by any of his characters. As we must assume from Schiller's own incest complex, however, this is the aspect that first interested Schiller in the material and in its characteristic conception and restructuring. That the very word "stepmother," used not even once by Saint-Réal, played an important role in this respect will not surprise anyone who understands the tendency of the unconscious mind to associate the deepest and strongest emotional complexes with their most ordinary external connections. It is no coincidence that we have played with words in the same way as a bridge to the analysis of these associations (cf. also the opposition of physical vs. nominal mother in chap. 2). It is Schiller's initially handling the relationship of the infante to Elisabeth like the relationship of a son to the physical mother that directly confirms our earlier suppositions and fully justifies our procedure: "In *Thalia*, the incestuous character of the relationship is emphasized by Schiller intentionally and to an inappropriate degree, as though love for the actual mother were involved" (Minor 1890, 2:540).

In the composition of an individual work, then, from the first outline to the final version, the same gradual weakening and disguising of certain sexual themes is observed that we pointed out earlier in the discussion of general psychic development. The consideration of these processes of repression in the individual is essential for a deeper, detailed psychological investigation and is extremely fruitful in many respects. It indicates to us especially that the heavy emphasis on political activity in the final version, which once again assimilates the work to its source, arises from a tendency to disguise undesirable elements in the underlying incestuous family drama that provides the psychic energy for the creation of the literary work. This tendency operates for the purpose of distracting the conscious interest from the taboo sexual theme. Of course this gradual dampening of the sexual theme occurs first of all within the author himself, enabling him to present without reproach or inhibition the material chosen from erotic themes and formed by unconscious sexual drives. But it also serves to distract the viewer. Still, in so doing, it preserves the truly powerful (unconscious) effect of the actually erotic drama upon the viewer. In addition, we notice that even the most seemingly obvious similarity between the final form of a dramatic work and its source, such as seems to hold in the case of Schiller's *Don Carlos,* is not always attributable to the simple assimilation of the material appropriate for "dramatization." Instead, the internal developmental history of Schiller's play shows us that between the material that served the author as a model and its dramatic representation, accurate even in the small details, there exist preliminary psychic phases of production in which the personal complexes of the author obstinately attempt to permeate the whole plot, while a certain psychic shame (the repressive tendency) seeks to obliterate the contribution of his own erotic fantasies. Strange as it may seem, these processes, which appear to delay and frustrate production, are essential prerequisites to the actual act of creation. Beginning with those areas determined by the unconscious selection of the material, the author's erotic complexes permeate and fill the whole plot, only to flow away again under the influence of a countertendency (the repressive tendency). It is only in this way that one can understand the author's interest, which extends equally to all details and which we must suppose to be derived from erotic sources and to be very intense indeed, considering the psychic and purely technical problems to be surmounted and the enormous creative effort required. Thus what we perceive from the author's subjective point of view as a necessary condition of production is seen from the spectator's point of view as one of the technical artistic devices that, by distracting the viewer's interest from content to form, make personal complexes and fantasies of the author suitable for presentation and enjoyment by the viewer. Schiller himself has described this process, which we have recognized as the dissolution of personally colored fantasy elements, as "the destruction of content through form," and in a similar sense Spitteler has also noted the necessary "artistic neutralization of a literary theme" (1906).

That the incestuous character is emphasized much more strongly in the original outline, and even in the first version of *Don Carlos* in *Rheinische Thalia,* than in the final version of the drama is explained through the influence of a repressive tendency that arises to combat the emergence of certain intense erotic complexes in the author and strictly censors objectionable text, but that strives to maintain in the plot that erotic material necessary for its structure. In the powerful emergence of the erotic incest complex, which brings about the selection and incestuous interpretation of much more innocent material and also leads to the subsequent repressive tendency, we observe—based upon demonstrated conclusions of the psychology of neurosis—a mirror image or, more accurately, a reactivation of corresponding infantile processes. We must therefore assume that Schiller felt an early, highly intense love toward his mother that, though soon repressed, was able to find a largely distorted but nevertheless highly gratifying expression in literary creativity. Thanks to a fragment preserved in Schiller's estate, we can demonstrate the complete and undisguised literary expression of this tendency and thus also confirm, as it were experimentally, the foregoing hypotheses. The fragment, a partial sketch of a drama called *Agrippina,* enables us to cast some light on the psychology of unfinished literary works as well.

These uncompleted passages never went beyond the initial stage of composition. Just as we observed a clearer trace of repressed impulses and fantasies in the outline than in the completed work, a similar generalization must hold for fragments. In fact, they prove even more useful than outlines, since they clearly demonstrate which problems led to the cessation of the artistic process of sublimation. Although in fragments, too, the degree of immediacy and the spontaneous manner of conception initially diminish psychological censorship and permit a freer expression of repressed fantasies, psychological compensation for this freedom is provided when dealing with certain themes in that the work remains unfinished. The psychic inhibitions, although they may not prohibit the freer expression of individual repressed impulses, nevertheless act together to inhibit the creative process in toto. Thus we notice that the two processes discussed above—the unconscious permeation of the plot with personal erotic complexes and the repressive wave that artistically sublimates this raw material—affect fragmentary works too, but in an even more intense manner. In this case erotic fantasy life emerges so strongly that the repressive tendency necessary to hold it within bounds actually brings the whole stream of creativity to a standstill. The *Agrippina* fragment, which will serve as further evidence of Schiller's incestuous feelings, confirms especially well our conception of the powerful emergence of the erotic incest complex and of its repression. First, though, let us recount in brief the historical background necessary for understanding the incomplete Schiller fragment. We will also present the historical report of Agrippina's incest that the author consulted.

The Roman emperor Claudius (c. A.D. 41–54) had two children by his wife, Messalina—a daughter, Octavia, and a son, Britannicus. After having Messalina killed, Claudius married his niece Agrippina, who already had a son, Lucius Domitius, later known as Nero, from her first marriage to Ahenobarbus. Claudius adopted Nero, named him heir to the throne, and married him to Octavia (Nero's stepsister) at Agrippina's urging. When Claudius began to regret the adoption, Agrippina is supposed to have poisoned him, whereupon Nero ascended the throne. The following details concerning Nero's relationship with his mother are taken from the reports of Tacitus and Suetonius. It has been proved that Schiller made use of Tacitus. We do not know whether he also used Suetonius, but one suspects so, given Schiller's conscientiousness in studying sources and his comprehensive historical knowledge.

Tacitus reports (*Annales*, 14.2) on the incestuous relationship between Nero and his mother, Agrippina:

> Cluvius relates that Agrippina, desiring to maintain power, went so far as to present herself frequently, in broad daylight, bejeweled and ready to commit incest, to Nero, himself aglow with wine. He also reports that when friends and relatives realized that her lusty kisses and fondling were the prelude to incest, Seneca (Nero's teacher) sought another woman to protect Nero from the advances of Agrippina. He is supposed to have sent Akte to him. Akte, worried by the danger she was in and by Nero's bad reputation, was compelled to inform Nero that the incestuous relationship was public knowledge, since his mother openly bragged about it, and that the soldiers would not tolerate the leadership of a sinful prince. Fabius Rusticus relates that the incestuous relationship was not Agrippina's wish, but that of Nero, and that it was thwarted only by the same freedwoman [Akte]. But other sources agree with Cluvius's report, and general opinion inclines in that direction.

In *De Nerone* (chap. 28), however, Suetonius also reports that it is Nero who encouraged his mother to commit incest: "No one doubts that he wanted to sleep with his mother, nor that this was prevented only by her enemies, who did not want to let this wanton and unrestrained woman increase her power in this way, too—especially given that he included among his sexual partners a young woman who is said to have looked very much like his mother. We are also assured that even earlier, whenever he was carried together with his mother in a sedan chair, he carried out upon her his unbridled lusts—as revealed by the stains on his clothing."

Later, when Nero began to fear the influence of his mother, he is supposed to have decided she must die. Under the pretense of a feast, he took her to Baiae: "There he accompanied her out after the meal, firmly pressing his mouth upon her eyes and breasts, either because he wanted to play out his dissimulation to the hilt or because his final glance of his mother, walking to her death, filled him with remorse, despite his brutality" (Tacitus, *Annales,* 14.4). Though this plot proved unsuccessful, he did have his mother murdered and then spread the rumor that she had stabbed herself out of fear of punishment for plotting to murder him. Suetonius further reports: "Other frightful things are also reported by reputable writers. He is said to have hastened to see his mother's body and to have touched the various parts of her body, finding fault with some and praising others, and becoming thirsty, to have drunk wine while doing so" (chap. 34). Tacitus (*Annales,* 14.9) regards it as uncertain whether Nero viewed his mother's body and praised her figure. But Xiphilinus reports that he gazed at her nude body and said, among other shocking things, "I did not know I had such a beautiful mother."

This short report of historical events, which will give only an impression of the material with which Schiller intended to occupy himself, is all the more necessary since the fragment itself, as we mentioned, is highly incomplete. Here, though, are the portions of Schiller's fragment relevant to the present discussion. "It is not without difficulty that Nero has his mother killed; his remorse is not caused by remaining love, for he never felt love for her. It is simply the ineradicable voice of nature, which he finds difficult to silence. This voice of nature is so universal . . . that even a Nero must experience a violent crisis in conquering it; and he fails to conquer it, but must circumvent it." Schiller also makes the marginal notation: "Indeed, in the drama matters go so far that his mother wins him over once again. . . . She has shown herself capable of every crime, since she has already attempted adultery, incest (having married her uncle), and murder. . . . A secret encounter between Nero and his mother gives her hope that she will win him over again, or that he will not kill her after all. . . . Agrippina attempts to arouse her son's lust—to the extent that this can be done without harm to the tragic dignity of the drama. This is, of course, more suggested than spoken."

As one can see from the portions of the fragment just presented, Schiller motivates the mother's unusual attempt to seduce her son neither as a pathological exaggeration of normal motherly love (as Lohenstein attempts to do in his *Agrippina,* at least by suggestion) nor as a reflection of her ambitious desire to obtain influence over her son, but as a means of saving her own life. Consistent with this motivation, Schiller had to choose the version in which Agrippina is the instigator. However, he probably preferred this version mainly because it provided a means of expression for the rejection of his own repressed erotic affection for his mother ("he never felt love for her") while also fulfilling in an exaggerated manner the wish of every rejected lover that the beloved reciprocate.

Despite the attenuations and psychological disguises that distinguish Schiller's sketch from the historical documents, the playwright was not successful in coming to grips with the portion of the undisguised material that he found offensive. It seems to have been the tragic element, but most of all the quite undisguised representation of actual incest with the mother, that drew him to the material: this is of deep psychological significance. It was also this incest material that impeded his completing the drama when defensive mechanisms came into play. Schiller consciously motivated his decision to abandon the project with the excuse that the theme could not be given sufficient tragic dignity.

Approximately a century before Schiller it was still thought possible to do so, as is demonstrated by Caspar von Lohenstein's tragedy *Agrippina*. Lohenstein paid close attention to the historical sources; in his tragedy, too, it is the mother who is the seducer. A scene in the third act, which takes place in the emperor's bedchamber, contains a seduction by the mother of her son that borders on the limits of what can be presented. This scene is worthy of notice because of the unconscious naïveté by which she associates this love with the first sexual stirrings of childhood:

> *Agrippina:* My child, my sweet light, why do you deprive me of the riper fruits of half-tasted pleasure? Oh! Love's final purpose will refresh us! Sweetness itself bids us come to this purple bed.
>
> *Nero:* Yes, Mother, were it not the very womb that bore me.
>
> *Agrippina:* The breasts you so often kissed have nursed you: What difference do breast and womb make now? . . . Should a mother be ashamed to love her son? The breast that flowed for you with both milk and love . . . who could love the mother's breast more than her own child does?
>
> *Nero:* Yes, but one must be sure that poisonous lust does not flow there too.
>
> *Agrippina:* Where the suns of love shine follow also the shadows of lust. . . . Why should it be cursed as a crime if a gracious son seeks the womb of his mother, the wellspring of his birth, if he seeks the fruits of love and renewal for his tedious life?

We should mention that the story of Nero, that trove of incestuous cruelty, tempted playwrights of all subsequent periods. In addition to the dramas already named, let us mention briefly Jean Racine's *Britannicus* (1669) since fragments of Schiller's attempted translation of this work have been found in Schiller's estate. This drama, which portrays Nero's murder of his stepbrother Britannicus, will concern us further in chapter 21, since it motivates the murder through jealousy and rivalry over a woman. Nero's love for his mother, consistent with Racine's more refined sense of propriety, is only suggested (5.3):

> *Agrippina:* Nero gave me all too certain pledges of his fidelity. Oh, if you could have seen the tenderness with which he renewed his vows to me! How he held me wrapped in his embrace! His arm, enveloping me, could not let me go when we parted; his love, reflected in his eyes and brow, agreeably engaged in smaller secrets.

Excepting the clear but incomplete expression of Schiller's erotic love for his mother in *Agrippina* and the disguised, but no less convincing, hints of the same in *Don Carlos,* there is in Schiller's works no direct indication of his passion for his mother. This leads one to assume strong repression and other means of dealing with this impulse, which must originally have been very strong. In his dramatic works, however, heavy emphasis is placed with noticeable frequency on the conflict between father and son. In the three consecutive versions of *Don Carlos,* as the incestuous character of the relationship of the queen and the infante is dampened, one notices growing emphasis on Don Carlos's relationship with his father. Although in the outline it is the queen's erotic affection for the son that is emphasized, beside which the king's jealous suspicions seem subordinate, in the two later versions it is the king's hatred that is emphasized. This inversely proportional relation between the emphasis placed on motherly love and on the father's hatred in the various versions of the drama indicates an especially strong association between these two emotions. It seems that the gradual repression into the unconscious of erotic love for the mother also leads, in compensation, to increasing aversion toward the father. This process of replacing a repressed impulse by a usually opposite or otherwise closely related, exaggerated conscious idea is well known in the psychology of neurosis as a "mechanism of intensification of reaction" (Freud 1909c, 47). We must also assume that this mechanism, clearly active in the gradual evolution of *Don Carlos,* is a reactivation of corresponding infantile processes. Intense affection for the mother necessarily leads to a certain jealous animosity toward the father, whom she prefers, and the repression of the incestuous passion is brought about as much by inner developmental factors as by the external hindrances that for the child are personified in the father. Thus the father, as inhibitor of the son's first erotic interest toward the mother, provides the initial trigger for its repression, but he simultaneously draws upon himself the son's hatred, fed by jealousy. Indeed, it seems that it is through the intensification of reaction associated with repressed love for the mother that the son's existing disinclination toward the father, who is preferred by the mother, acquires the exaggerated and undying character of deadly hatred. For according to an observation by Freud (1909b), even the source from which the enmity toward the father derives its persistent character has the nature of sensual desire.

To the extent that it continually reminds the son of the impediment to the realization of his incest fantasy, excessive emphasis on hatred toward the father is a defense against the repressed incest wish. On the other hand, by substituting apparently asexual, ambiguous content for sexual content, it allows for a socially more acceptable result: repressed erotic emotions are diverted, appearing as increased feelings of antipathy toward the father. This explains excessive hatred toward the father as a symptom of the repression of intense erotic love for the mother, a connection highly apparent in the still relatively uncomplicated psyche of the child and expressly emphasized by Freud (1909a, 102): "Further, it cannot be denied that in Hans the complex of hatred toward the father masks the complex of eroticism toward the mother."

This hatred of the father, incomprehensible unless we consider its mother-related etiology, now requires a certain justification. This is often provided through a theme that further obscures the role of the mother complex—a theme that is characteristic of the neurotic orientation, but that also appears in normal childhood development and has a large role in the creation of drama. This peculiar motivation of hatred toward the father arises through the projection mechanism, the meaning and nature of which we are already familiar with. It has already been emphasized that in his fantasies the child "corrects" the relationship between the parents in a biased way, according to his own sentiments, without regard to whether his assumptions correspond to the facts. Such a correspondence is irrelevant to psychic effectiveness, for in psychic processes reality and fantasy appear at first to be equally valued. Actually, fantasy is valued more. Analytical investigation of psychoneuroses has revealed that it is not actual experiences but rather the fantasies associated with them that have the deepest and most lasting psychic effects. Just as the child establishes in his mind the relationships that correspond to his own wishes, the neurotic produces everything necessary for the formation of his symptoms; in a similar way, the artist creates the psychic conditions for justifying or condemning his emotions. In the case of the neurotic, the psychoanalytic method provides us with insight into this mechanism. The young man experiences strong disinclination toward his father. Since he does not realize that the deepest source of this emotion, inexplicable in its intensity, is his erotic inclination toward his mother (having repressed this), he finds no plausible justification for this exaggerated hatred. Therefore he projects it onto his father: that is, he lives with the firm conviction that his father bears hostile feelings toward him. (This is a mechanism characteristic of both normal and abnormal psychic function.) In this way he can justify to himself and to those around him his own aversion toward his father, which arises from sources unknown to him. This theme of supposed hatred by the father is of great significance in *Don Carlos*. The prince's disinclination toward his royal father is repeatedly motivated by allusions to the father's hatred toward his son and heir:

> *Carlos:* Hate me no more. I will love you like a child, I will love you intensely, but hate me no more.

Of course it is easy for the playwright to realize this fantasy of the hating father within the bounds of normal emotion. (In the paranoiac, owing to the distortion of emotions, this fantasy appears in the form of a persecution complex.) And the same mechanism that makes possible the necessary projection activity in the normal person has, as we already know, an important role in the creation of drama. The playwright projects hatred of the father, which has become incomprehensible following the repression of erotic love for the mother, so as to create an image of the hating father. In concerning itself with the full intensity of such feelings by the father and their justified reciprocation by the son, the playwright's fantasy, usually functioning through the association and intensification of emotions already present, knows no bounds (cf. the theme of the tyrannical father, below).

In the father, who harbors inimical feelings of jealousy toward his son, the same mechanism effects the reverse projection of his disinclination toward his son, which also expresses itself in a typical form: the fear of retribution. But this is due not only to the actual situation in question, for like every anxiety, it is the result of a repression. Because of this unconscious complex, when he has become a father himself, the son, who has felt inimical feelings toward his father and has had to repress them, will fear the same behavior from his own son. This typical repressed form of hatred toward the father was also utilized by Schiller in *Don Carlos*. In the first version (*Rheinische Thalia*), the great colloquy between father and son (2.2) did not close, as it does in the version familiar to us, with the prince's resigned words: "I now abandon my pursuits." Instead, the prince mounts a final attack on his father's heart:

> *Carlos:* In a dream, not long ago, I saw the [last] emperor's will and testament smoldering in a bonfire.
> *Philip* (with a start): What do you mean to say?
> *Carlos:* How much must be lacking in such a son, it seems to me, when he becomes a father.
> *Philip* (covers his face and pounds his breast): Too heavily, O God! Thy hand lies too heavily upon me. My son, my own son—ghastly trial—is the servant of thy wrath.

If in this first version Philip still perceives his son's hatred as a just retribution for his behavior toward his own father, and if Schiller's feelings here are still unambiguously on the side of the son, in the final version the echo of these feelings, arising directly from anxiety concerning the son's revenge, allows one to detect a slight inclination on Schiller's part toward more fatherly emotions. Lerma (the personification of fatherly emotions) says to the infante: "Undertake no bloody act against your father. No, nothing bloody, my prince. Philip II forced your grandfather from the throne. This same Philip trembles today fearing his own son."

As will be discussed below, Schiller's shifting perspective, which sides sometimes with the father and sometimes with the son, develops because various portions and drafts of *Don Carlos* were completed during different stages of his emotional life. We will observe a similar ambiguity of feeling in Shakespeare's psychic life. The myth of Cronus, which will be discussed below (chap. 9), expresses this fear of retribution very clearly, and in an especially characteristic manner. In mythology this fear is regularly aired in the oracular prediction of the death of the usually royal father at the hand of his own son.

Thence arises another motivation of hatred toward the father, which in literature is observed with surprising frequency in the son's impetuous demands concerning inheritance and succession, stubbornly opposed by the father. This motive, which emphasizes the revolutionary side of hostility toward the father, is revealed by psychoanalysis to be a displacement from the sexual sphere to a less objectionable social or political sphere. In this sense it is no coincidence that all the literary works discussed thus far, and most of those to be discussed, take place in royal houses. This enables the playwright to associate the conflict between father and son, which has its roots in unconscious sexual life, with the political conflict between ruler and successor and in this way to motivate in a conventional way the hatred on both sides, as happens often enough in life. The son's wish to expel the father and to replace him is a disguised expression of the same wishes concerning the mother. This is particularly clear in *Oedipus;* Oedipus simultaneously receives his mother's hand and his father's realm. In *Hamlet* the theme of succession to the throne already receives much greater emphasis than the erotic theme of rivalry over the mother, and in *Don Carlos* the sexual theme is almost completely obscured by the political theme. In the theme of succession to the throne thus utilized, we recognize one of the trains of thought that in *Don Carlos* causes a drama of political intrigue to be substituted for an erotic family drama. That the political drama is a continuous facade for the incest drama is characteristically reflected in a motive relevant in the development of the dramatic plot. The marquis de Posa, as a confidant of the king, effects a shift in the king's suspicions of his son from the sexual to the political sphere by pretending that the prince's dealings with his [step]mother are directed only toward the liberation of the Netherlands (4.2). Actually, Posa is only deflecting the king's suspicions back to the political sphere, for the first warning about his son he received from Duke Alba concerned political ambitions. Only later do the king's suspicions grow (3.3):

> *King* (to the duke): You have warned me of his ambition. Is it only his ambition, only this, that I should fear?

As the first version reveals, however, these fluctuating suspicions have their psychological point of departure in sexual feelings—incest-based hatred between father and son—that are conventionally disguised as political rivalry. We already know that Schiller introduced the political conflict into the drama only later, at first with secondary significance. A passage from the Bauerbach manuscript demonstrates how he still subordinated it to the erotic theme.

> Act 4: A new danger threatens Don Carlos.
> A. The king discovers a rebellion planned by Don Carlos.
> B. This further arouses his jealousy.
> C. Both forces combine to bring about the prince's downfall.

Here, in connection with the theme of succession to the throne, we can also explain the theme of the rebellious son and of his sympathy with the revolutionaries as a typical disguise for hostility toward the father, who is perceived as tyrannical. For both father and son, these themes provide justification, welcome to conscious thought, for the mutual antipathy whose deep source, competition for the affections of the mother, is unconscious.

That hatred toward the father, which characterizes these two political themes, originates in competition for the mother is clearly revealed in two strictly erotic themes that also deserve to be emphasized as typical of the incest complex. The first of these is the theme of abduction of the betrothed by the father, which plays an important role in *Don Carlos:*

> *Carlos:* You were mine, promised to me in the sight of the world by two great thrones, granted to me by heaven and nature, and Philip, Philip has stolen you from me.
> *Queen:* He is your father.
> *Carlos:* And your husband.

Repeatedly this theme functions as an unconscious expression of the mother's unattainability for the son. Translated into conscious terms, it corresponds to the thought that the father has taken the mother (represented by the betrothed) from the son. Now we also recognize how the playwright's attempt to realize this logically impracticable thought can bring about the transformation of the mother into the stepmother: the stepmother can very easily be presented as a mother whom the father has indeed taken from the son. Further, despite the historical model, it is worthy of note that in the first version of *Don Carlos* Schiller, influenced by the incestuous elements, had in mind an intensification of this theme. At one point the princess of Eboli remarks to Don Carlos: "And if you were to decide upon a partition? One throne, I should think, would be more than enough for one young woman. What more does she want, the emperor's proud daughter?" Here Schiller makes the marginal notation: "An Austrian princess and niece (incest!) of Philip II who had been promised to the infante, Don Carlos, but who became Philip's fourth wife after the death of Carlos and of Queen Elisabeth; thus through a trick of fate, this king married both princesses intended for his son."

Thus the theme of abduction of the betrothed by the father gives us the key to a deeper understanding of the son's impetuous demands regarding his inheritance (the theme of succession to the throne), which are unconsciously associated in the son's mind with the betrothed—the mother—whom he feels has been unjustly withheld from him. Further, corresponding to the theme of the rebellious son who wishes to snatch his inheritance and absolute royal power from his father with force is another fantasy concerning the reconquest of the mother and her rescue from the supposed violence of the father. This fantasy, also typical of the incest complex, that the mother must be unhappy at the father's side—that she longs passionately to be rescued by her son—is also suggested in *Don Carlos* (1.5):

Queen: Who claims my fate at Philip's side would be a bitter one?
Carlos: My heart, which ardently feels how enviable your fate would be with me.

We shall return later to the rescue fantasy, which according to Freud is significant in human sexual life, and which plays an immense role in mythical and literary fantasy creations.

The noticeable regularity with which the strained relations between father and son are transported into the political sphere cannot be due only to some conventional motivation for this enmity, basing it on the son's impetuous demands regarding his inheritance and on the father's rejection of these demands. In different social circumstances, similar situations could not easily be observed or created. If one wishes to appreciate and understand this typically recurring conception of the father as a powerful, tyrannical master in its full significance for literary production, one must search for its root, which has been acted on by its own conditioning factors in the history of cultural development. In a literary/historical sense, the regular representation of the hated and feared father as a man who stands in a powerful position with respect to his son—as a ruler does with respect to his subjects—can be explained through the development of the institution of the kingdom from patriarchy within the family. As the family began to dissolve into the state, the king became for his people what the husband and father had been within the household: the ruler and the strong protector. Among the many derivations for "king" and "queen" in Sanskrit noted by Müller (1869, 2:20), one is simple: "father" and "mother." "Sanskrit *ganaka* means 'father,' from the Sanskrit root *gan*, 'to procreate'; it occurs also as the name of a famous king in the *Veda*. This is cognate with the Old High German *chuning* and English *king*. In Sanskrit, 'mother' is *gani* or *ganî*, cognate with Greek *gyné*, Gothic *quinô*, Slavic *žena*, English *queen*. Originally, then, 'queen' meant 'mother' or 'mistress,' and we see once again how the language of family life gradually became the political language of the oldest Indo-European state, and how the brotherhood of the family became the *phratría* of the state." This conception and designation of the royal ruler as the father of his subjects is still customary in smaller states (cf. German *Landesvater*, "sovereign"), where the relationship of the ruler to the people is a much closer one than in large confederations. Yet even the peoples of the mighty Russian empire call their emperor "little father," and the ruling sovereign of the Catholic church is called "holy father" by the faithful. The Latin for "pope" is *papa*. Thus, once again, he is designated in the same way children address their fathers.

Those who are familiar with the psychology of unconscious psychic processes will not find it strange that this conception of the father as an absolute and feared ruler, which arises from the child's respect for the father and the overestimation of his greatness and might, incomparable and unique for the child, is still evinced in the dreams of adults, in which, according to Freud, the emperor and empress (king and queen) almost always represent the dreamer's parents. The paranoiac's delusions of grandeur, in which the patient's supposed royal or divine descent is central, can also regularly be explained in this manner, since this explanation reveals to us the individual determinacy of mythical fantasy activity. From the psychological standpoint, we can now easily see that this substitution of a king for the father, arising from feelings of respect, must be made useful for the purpose of repressing the rejected and intolerable impulses that arise when jealous sexual envy and its own incipient repression obscure the childlike relationship with the father, transforming feelings of respect into feelings of contempt. This may lead to various results. The son may displace his feelings for the father to the real king, becoming a revolutionary or an anarchist. Or he may not respond actively but may instead displace the whole relationship into the passive domain, leaving the infantile relationship with the father largely intact: in his paranoiac delusions, he may place himself in the position of the king (the father) in order to flee from the persecution and prejudice supposedly perpetrated against him by the king. Or he may sublimate the whole process in literary or mythical fantasy, dissociating the role of his own father from that of a royal, tyrannical father and setting up the tyrant as a substitute for his own father (as does the anarchist). Thus he is able to express freely his hatred toward his father in the guise of less objectionable and more justified hatred toward the tyrant. This was also shown in our interpretation of *Hamlet*. If, as a psychologist, one wished to be logically consistent—and considering the immense, still insufficiently appreciated "significance of the father in the fate of the individual" (Jung)—one would have to consider all emperors and princes created by authors (for the time being still ignoring those who existed historically) as substitutes for the father; this has been claimed with solid psychological justification for dreams and neurosis.

As an excellent literary/historical example of the realizability of such a conception, brief reference can be made to Diderot's attempt to reform the dramatic art. In his theoretical discussions of the drama, basing his question on the works of the English naturalists, he asks whether it is only kings and princes who are worthy to be portrayed as protagonists on the stage, or whether the fate of ordinary mortals should not also be portrayed. And what does he do to realize his proposition practically? Instead of a tragedy, whose central figure had always been a king, he writes a bourgeois play *Père de famille* [The father of a family]. That is, he unconsciously participates in our mode of interpretation, replacing the king with the father. Following these proposals for reform, apparently of a literary nature only, but actually deeply personal, arose Lessing's *Bürgerliches Trauerspiel* [Bourgeois tragedy] and Schiller's *Kabale und Liebe* [Intrigue and love]; Diderot's influence can be pursued up to Ibsen's family dramas.

Still, even though we do not wish to go so far as to interpret the dramatic king as a father substitute in all cases, though this is suggested by psychological considerations, we will surely be justified in accepting this interpretation where it is supported by additional evidence. In *Don Carlos*, where the mighty, tyrannical ruler is also the father, the connection is very clear, and we will expect to find it in other dramas by Schiller, though perhaps less clearly. This association is still rather obvious in *Die Räuber* [The robbers], where the old father is, at least, a "reigning" count, and where hatred toward the son, Franz, is motivated by concerns of inheritance. Only deeper analysis reveals that the motivating force in this drama is actually hatred toward the father (cf. chap. 20 concerning Schiller's love for his sister). We should also note here that Schiller initially planned to name this drama *Der verlorene Sohn* [The lost son], which also suggests the dominant role of this complex in the conception of the work. The revolutionary drive for freedom, so heavily emphasized here and so prevalent in all of Schiller's subsequent works, has been identified by literary historians as an expression of hostility toward the duke of Württemberg and his autocratic rule. And from our point of view too, it seems impossible for *Die Räuber* and subsequent works to have arisen without Schiller's strained relations with the duke. Indeed, we must recognize that Schiller intentionally portrayed their relationship in writing certain portions of his works. However, this does not preclude the role of an equally strained infantile relationship with his father in the conception of these works. Indeed, this compels us all the more to adopt this interpretation of the powerful dramatic effect, which would not otherwise be comprehensible, given that the duke's strict measures affected all his students equally.

We need only consider briefly the connection between experience and literary production to come closer to the solution of one of the most interesting mysteries of literary production. In this investigation, we are concerned only with the deepest emotions of the playwright, slumbering in the unconscious; to understand them consciously, we must treat them as though they themselves were conscious thoughts. As the deepest source and driving force of Schiller's dramatic works, we recognize—anticipating our conclusion—hostility and jealous hatred toward the father arising from love for the mother. These feelings arise in earliest childhood, undergo intensive repression, and under the influence of the necessary external events, rise from the unconscious to be expressed. To make this possible, the playwright must occupy himself with a conscious image and work further upon it. He finds this conscious image in the actual experience associated with the unconscious complex. This experience itself is no chance one, but is instead psychically determined. Otherwise how could it correspond to the unconscious complex in all senses? The actual attitude of the adult is, of course, still determined by his infantile psychic configuration and is thus created by the individual himself. The sense in which this is intended is best shown by Schiller's relationship with the duke. It was, insofar as permitted by the environment, a faithful copy of Schiller's relationship with his father. The playwright displaced all his feelings for his father onto the duke (cf. our discussion of the transformation of childhood feelings for the father into revolutionary stirrings against the ruler). The reformulation of all these emotions leads the normal person to subjugate himself to the social authorities; it leads to social organization. In Schiller's case, owing to the persistent effect of powerful childhood impressions, this reformulation of hatred toward his father was unsuccessful, and he became a revolutionary in spirit—an enthusiastic proponent of freedom in every sense. It is only the replacement of the father by the ruler, the duke of Württemberg, that makes comprehensible the strong emotional effect this new relationship had upon Schiller. Just as this interaction influenced the conception of *Die Räuber* in the manner described, its effects are also observed in *Die Verschwörung des Fiesco zu Genua* [The conspiracy of Fiesco in Genoa] and in the characters of President Walter, Philip II, Wallenstein, and Gessler.

It was especially easy for Schiller to transfer his feelings for his father to the duke, since Duke Karl wished to be known as the "father" of his pupils, who were obliged to employ this form of address. This appellation can be frequently observed in various petitions submitted by Schiller. The beginning of one such petition (September 1, 1782) reads: "The inner conviction that my prince and absolute master is also my father now gives me the strength" (Jonas 1892, no. 33). Schiller's last letter after fleeing closes: "With all the feelings of a son toward his angry father" (no. 35). Further, Minor writes (1890, 224): "Schiller complained about the duke but nevertheless loved him. He honored him and hated him simultaneously." Indeed, this sounds like a description of Schiller's relationship with his excessively strict and feared, yet loved and respected, father. In the introduction to the first three acts of *Don Carlos* in *Thalia,* Schiller publicly declares that he does not wish to oppose himself to the one who had until then been his father. He justifies his discussion of his whole relationship with the duke by saying that "there was no more natural way to introduce my reader to the essence of my undertaking than to introduce him to its author." This displacement onto the duke of Schiller's childhood ambivalence toward his father can also be pursued in detail. If one can believe the report of so reliable a contemporary as Andreas Streicher, though he of course took advantage of the opportunity to support his friend Schiller, the duke was by no means the despot Schiller perceived and portrayed. Instead, Schiller's conception of his father as a tyrant, which perhaps more accurately reflected the situation at home, influenced his association with the duke, who according to Streicher's report felt true fatherly feelings for his students and was concerned with their welfare. In this sense Schiller's flight from Stuttgart is to be understood more as an escape from father and family than from the discipline of the ducal school. Schiller himself confirms this in a letter to his favorite sister, Christophine (October 18, 1782), where he writes: "Tell dearest Papa that I wrote to him in the same frame of mind in which he wrote to me, and that I spoke to him in that way with good reason, for I wished to separate his fate from mine." His statement that *Die Räuber* had cost him family and fatherland is to be understood in the same way (Streicher 1965, 94).

Just as Schiller felt bitter toward the duke from the very beginning, his interaction with his father was seldom easy. Very serious differences between father and son are frequently reported (especially in the summer of 1784 and the following year). But even as a child, he feared his father more than he honored him, and Streicher reports (1965, 23) that as a child, when he felt guilty, he voluntarily asked his mother to punish him so that his father would not treat him too severely in his anger. On the other hand, it is easy to understand that the strict and strong-willed father was greatly pleased by the works of his son, in which the absolute power of the father decisively overcomes the son. After reading the first three acts of *Don Carlos* in *Thalia,* he wrote to his son (March 30, 1785): "I find the *Thalia* and especially the portions of *Don Carlos* extremely well conceived and executed—the best of all your works thus far." He expresses similar satisfaction with *Kabale und Liebe,* where the conflict between father and son plays a central role, with special emphasis placed on the superior strength of the father.

If, in supporting our analysis, it appears that we have considered Schiller's life in his parents' home too superficially, this is because the reports are fragmentary and not always reliable and because we do not wish to create the impression that we place too much importance on them, even when they support our position. Indeed, in our investigation we are concerned with the discovery of unconscious emotions and fantasies, which nevertheless express themselves later in the individual's life, still disguised and difficult to recognize, in works of art and in neurotic symptoms. Thus the experiences of the playwright must be considered in an analysis of his works just as the experiences of the neurotic must be considered in the corresponding investigation. From this method, it seems, arise certain perspectives that are very fruitful for understanding the relation between experience and literary production.

Just as the child's relationship with the father serves as a model for the subsequent social orientation of the individual to emperor and fatherland, to temporal and religious authorities, to superiors and rivals, and even to God and religion, the child's relationship with the mother serves as an example for the whole love life of the individual. Literary/historical criticism has determined that the model for Schiller's tyrants, especially for Philip II, which we related to Schiller's childhood orientation toward his father, derives more directly, in fact, from Schiller's strained relations with the duke of Württemberg. Criticism has also sought a model in Schiller's life for the remarkable love of Carlos for Elisabeth and has found it, corresponding fully to our expectations, in the young playwright's love for Charlotte von Wolzogen. On her estate, as a guest of her mother, he found asylum after his flight from Stuttgart and was able to work industriously and in peace on *Don Carlos*. Schiller's mood, his activities, and his experiences during the period in Bauerbach, as well as their effects on the continuously progressing *Don Carlos,* have been described in detail by Gercke (1905). In the second part of his book, one finds in Schiller's relationship with Charlotte an explanation of Carlos's peculiar and contradictory love for the princess of Eboli and for Elisabeth. Detailed parallels can be observed: Schiller's initially hopeful love for Charlotte, the sudden disturbance through the appearance of a competitor (Winkelmann), Schiller's jealousy, his attempt to reiterate his earlier claims, his despair upon recognizing the young woman's affection for the competitor, and finally his resignation.

We can endorse this skillful analysis in all points, but we must also add that this whole experience, as well as its literary manifestations, must be regarded as a reactivation of his relationship with his mother (cf. our discussion of Schiller's relationship with the duke). His attachment to Charlotte certainly had a great, and perhaps decisive, influence on the development of *Don Carlos.* But this recent experience only awakened the same unconscious emotions that had been associated with his mother. In fact, all the real consequences of this experience had already been predetermined by these emotions. Thus the love relationship in *Don Carlos* is not the literary manifestation of Schiller's unhappy love for Charlotte. Instead, both relationships, the literary one and the simultaneous real one, derive from and reproduce Schiller's relationship with his mother. Here, just as with Schiller's relationship with the duke, one has the impression that the literary treatment of unconscious complexes struggling to be expressed is associated with a drive to transform them into actual experience. This resembles the way an actor, through sympathetic understanding, transforms these psychic emotions into action. With the playwright, it is probable that in the various phases of his love life certain infantile erotic configurations are reactivated that then seek a corresponding real experience or assist in creating one. Yet this experience can never be so ideal as to satisfy overwhelming infantile emotions. These therefore turn aside, disappointed by this experience and by reality in general, at last finding their ideal form of expression in great fantasy constructions—works of literature. In his works, the playwright creates for himself the experiences that reality has denied him and that, in a deeper sense, it can in no way provide. For even the experience that he creates for himself and that subsequently brings about the literary manifestation of his emotions is possible only based on childhood fixation, and thus it reproduces, along with the gratification of the wish, all the hindering circumstances.

In the love life of the man, fixation on the mother is expressed, among other ways, by his being interested only in women who already belong in some way to another man—which of course applies to the mother (cf. the theme of the abduction of the betrothed, chap. 4). This condition on love, most clearly expressed in *Don Carlos,* also played a significant role in Schiller's other works and in his life. The first woman to whom he was attracted as a youth, the Laura of his youthful poems, was Luise Vischer, said to have been a captain's widow. His love for the married woman Charlotte von Kalb, with whom Goethe and Hölderlin were also infatuated for similar reasons, is well known. He met her in May 1784 after she had been married barely six months and fell so deeply in love that he was able to bring her to consider divorcing her husband and marrying him. In a letter to Gottfried Körner (July 23, 1787), he speaks of his hopes for a speedy reunion. That his love affair with her was not without its influence on the character of Carlos and his love for Elisabeth and the princess of Eboli is confirmed by Schiller himself in a note to Körner (July 29, 1787). In this context it is especially important to note that his love for Charlotte von Wolzogen was actually a displacement of his older and deeper love for her mother, Henriette von Wolzogen, fourteen years his senior, in whom he saw mother and beloved united.

He writes to Henriette from Mannheim (September 11, 1783): "You were the first person for whom my heart felt pure and unadulterated affection; such a friendship is exalted—not subject to the changes of circumstance. Please continue, my dearest one, to call me your son, and be assured that I can appreciate the heart of such a mother. Our separation, the need for which I cannot reveal to you beforehand, will put my mind at peace—such a peace as I have not enjoyed for a long time."

In other letters, too, he frequently refers to their association in the most tender terms as that of mother and son (Jonas 1892, vol. 1, nos. 67, 86). But the great love of his live, his love for Charlotte von Lengefeld, later his wife, demonstrates in its remarkable evolution and in its similarity to his relationship with both Wolzogens the typical character that reveals to us its infantile origin. When Schiller met both Lengefeld sisters toward the beginning of 1788, he was attracted first to the unhappily married Karoline. The rapturous letters he wrote to her and to both sisters together have led some to believe that he loved both at once and that he hesitated in deciding which he should marry. In any case, it was the general opinion that Schiller had actually loved his married sister-in-law, Karoline von Beulwitz, first, and that he loved her more than he did her sister Lotte; that he married Lotte only because it was the wish of her older sister. It is known that Karoline was initially considering divorce and the possibility of finding as Schiller's wife a sphere of activity corresponding to her talents and wishes. This seems all the more comprehensible since she had already been inwardly divorced from her husband for a long time and had given up living with him. Schiller was by no means disinclined toward this proposal, which fell through because of Karoline's notions of suitability. Here he found his "conditions for love" (Freud) fulfilled: the possibility of winning a woman who belonged to another man, who felt unhappy in her marriage to that man, and who saw in Schiller a "rescuer"—conditions that corresponded fully to his infantile ideal love for his mother.

But "Convenience" [Bequemlichkeit], as Karoline was nicknamed, hesitated to produce such a scandal in the family and brought the situation to a socially acceptable conclusion. At her urging, a conversation took place between Schiller and Charlotte that led to their engagement. By involving herself in this way, however, she reveals her wish not to lose her beloved completely. That Schiller was influenced by a similar wish in marrying Lotte is clearly revealed in that he had always dreamed of living with both women. Thus he actually married his wife as a substitute for her unattainable sister, just as he had loved Charlotte von Wolzogen as a substitute for her mother. This replacement of an unattainable woman belonging to another by her daughter or younger sister—by her attainable image—also belongs to the genre of love for the mother and regularly leads, as we shall demonstrate for Schiller's case, to the replacement of erotic affection for the mother by the less objectionable erotic affection for the sister (cf. below Schiller's love for his sister Christophine). During the first few months Karoline lived with the newlyweds, but this ideal situation, in which Schiller was able to live with both sisters—reminiscent of the situation in his parents' home, where he lived with his mother and his sister—was not to last long. Lotte quickly developed the suspicion that her sister might mean more to Schiller than she did herself. In Jena the two sisters had an open disagreement, after which Karoline withdrew more and more from intellectual and emotional contact with Schiller. In his developing relationship with Goethe, Schiller found a substitute for her. The aftereffects of love for his mother in Schiller's relationship with Lotte also expressed themselves characteristically in that Schiller himself told her frankly (October 29, 1789) that the reason for his long hesitation before deciding to ask for her hand was that he had no longer considered her quite free—clearly revealing his wish for a rival. This wish is also demonstrated in that after their engagement was officially announced in church, he jokingly remarked to his betrothed that it was too bad that Knebel had not appeared to compete for Lotte's hand. Schiller writes (February 14, 1790): "Certain people really ought to play that card so that this story would acquire a tragic twist." Childhood rivalry with the father for the mother's love still had its effects in the marriage of the son.

And it was not enough for the playwright to deal with these emotions in literature only, as he had done most recently in *Don Carlos*. Instead, he sought to realize them in life and to extend them to new experiences. His association with the Lengefeld sisters is an especially apt confirmation of our notion of the relation of experience to literary production. If we consider Schiller's relationship with the two Wolzogens, the mother and her daughter, as an immediate model for Carlos's relationship to Elisabeth (the older, married woman, who actually appears here as a mother) and the princess of Eboli (the free young woman), we shall not be surprised that the two Lengefeld sisters, whom Schiller met only after completing *Don Carlos,* correspond to Elisabeth and the princess of Eboli even more than did the two Wolzogens. Lotte was nicknamed "Propriety" [Dezenz]; her shyness and withdrawing timidity are mentioned especially often (cf. Berger 1905) and contrasted with the rapturous, passionate personality of her older sister. Thus, as a result of his mother complex, the playwright experienced in real life the division of the goals of his affection into enthusiastically reciprocating ones and cool, rejecting ones. In almost all his works the playwright depicted this division, employing Elisabeth and princess of Eboli types. But whereas his connection with the Wolzogens—like his original relationship with his mother and like *Don Carlos*—ended with renunciation, the especially felicitous circumstances of his association with the Lengefelds produced, through displacement to the "sister" (cf. part 2), a nearly perfect realization of Schiller's infantile ideal. Thus we gain insight not only into the complicated and subtle mechanisms of his actual love life but also into its relation to literary production. For the loving association with the Lengefeld sisters, which arose only after the completion of *Don Carlos,* could not possibly have influenced Carlos's attachment to the two women in the drama, and one can only suppose that both the real and the literary relationships sprang from a common psychic source that we believe to be the infantile incest complex and its effects as it is dealt with later in life.

Since it will seldom be possible to present these deeper connections, though they are found in every case, as well as can be done by referring to the wealth of material on Schiller's life, let us briefly consider, before discussing the individual dramas, how his total literary production was dependent on his love life. The great break in Schiller's literary production, which lasted more than ten years—from the completion of *Don Carlos* (1787) to the completion of *Wallenstein* (1799)—becomes comprehensible if one considers that it falls during the time of his great love for the Lengefeld sisters, his marriage, and the first years of married life—events that in the sense of our presentation provided him with sufficient gratification of his unconscious fantasy life. In this connection, Schiller himself writes to the two sisters a month before the wedding (January 10, 1790): "Previously, I was more important to myself, because I had to be everything to myself: my own desires were more moderate and my own heart was able to still them. I embraced the creations of fantasy, literary beings, with a heart full of love—with a spirited joy. Now all that is past, my dearest ones. In thinking of you, my soul consumes all its glowing force, and no other object even suffices to make me warm. I have never been so poor and insignificant to myself as now with the approach of my most joyful happiness."

With *Don Carlos,* Schiller had brought his great internal reaction to subside for the first time through a literary release from his family complex. The same trend was expressed externally in his setting up a permanent residence—after a long period of moving, as if in flight, from place to place—and in his marrying and establishing his own family. Further, when the playwright has Carlos say resignedly at the end of the drama: "Mother, there is a higher, more desirable goal than possessing you," this suggests the dissolution of the infantile Oedipus complex and a turning toward new, higher goals. This was already hinted at in Schiller's sketches concerning Posa. And though the playwright needed intensive dramatic production well into the years of his youth in order to master his strong Oedipus complex until its demise in these resigned words of Carlos, he now needed ten more years to establish the normal orientation to life and humanity made possible and shaped by marriage and the creation of a family. In this first period of inner equilibrium, following upon the period of Sturm und Drang, Schiller enthusiastically dedicated himself to the sciences, philosophy, and history, and it is well known that his study of the last led him back to dramatic production. In his conversations with Dalberg, who was also responsible for the first suggestion to write *Don Carlos,* he seems to have come upon the plan to write *Wallenstein.* But how Schiller has changed in this work! Gone are the powerful words of the impetuous young man and his primal outbursts of hatred for the father. Hostility toward the father appears tempered and clarified in Max's conflict between love and duty, which is still the driving force of the work (cf. especially the Piccolominis); this is still clearly revealed by a few isolated turns of phrase and similes. Thus the father, Octavio, says (2.7): "Then the world will see atrocious things, and with the father's blood the son's blade will drip in ghastly combat."

This attenuation of hatred for the father within the playwright is of course associated with a great change in the technique of production: the need to temper and idealize these primal outbursts, still to be seen in successively evolving versions of *Don Carlos,* no longer exists.

In this connection, Schiller writes to Körner during his unproductive period, providing him with insights into the conditions of his artistic production (May 25, 1792): "A single aspect of an object, and not always the most important one, can often attract me to deal with that object, and it is only during this work that idea develops from idea. What inspired me to write *Die Künstler* [The artists] was obliterated as soon as I finished the work. This was even the case with *Don Carlos*. With *Wallenstein*, though, things seem to be going better." In a letter to Goethe, Schiller also gives special expression to his changed relation to the dramatic material, brought about through a great displacement of affect (November 28, 1796): "It seems that I am very successful now in keeping the dramatic material outside myself and in presenting only the dramatic object. One would almost say that the subject as such does not interest me at all; never have I felt such coolness for the material combined with such warm feelings for my work ⟨displacement of affect⟩. So far I have drawn my main characters as well as most of the minor characters with the pure love of the artist. However, I have a great personal interest in the young Piccolomini, the character second in importance. Here the work will gain as much as it loses."

The great shift in the playwright's inner life cannot be explained by his marriage and its psychological influence on sexuality alone. Rather, this shift must also be explained by the great psychological events in a man's life brought about by marriage: the replacement of the unattainable and forbidden mother ideal by the wife, esteemed in the full compass of sexual life, and a second, perhaps even more meaningful event—becoming a father after having held on so long and so intensely to the role of son. This transformation of emotion, with the associated unconscious fear of retribution discussed above, accounts for the way hatred toward the father is now dampened, gradually giving way to a positive attitude toward him, as can be observed in *Wallenstein*. Once this fatherhood, which is not strictly related to literal fatherhood, has taken place in the psyche, the playwright's earlier productive abilities are reinstated, and beginning with *Wallenstein* Schiller created a new immortal masterpiece each year until his death. But now self-criticism itself had to compensate for the harm it had done him. Schiller writes to Körner (May 25, 1792): "And it has hurt me, actually, for I have already been missing for many years the intensity and the glowing fervor I possessed before I knew of any rules."

Now that we have completed these general discussions, it is appropriate to group summarily the further cases of confirmation for our interpretation without addressing the details; in all cases, readers are referred to the detailed analysis of *Don Carlos*. From the very beginning of *Kabale und Liebe*, the bourgeois tragedy, Ferdinand regards his father, the president, with a coolness behind which outbursts of hatred are all too frequently observed. Here we see the same tense relations between father and son that we observed in *Don Carlos*. Further, many details repeated in *Don Carlos* are already present here. Ferdinand too sees in his father a tyrant and murderer who has come into power through the violent elimination of his predecessor (1.7). On the one hand, Ferdinand too hates and fears his father, and he even threatens him with his dagger (2.6) just as Carlos does (5.4; *King:* "Your sword drawn against your father?"). On the other hand, Ferdinand, like Carlos (2.2) demonstrates readiness for reconciliation (2.7 and 4.5). But whereas in *Don Carlos* the father delivers the son to the executioner, in *Kabale und Liebe* it is the son who brings the father before the court (2.4; *Ferdinand:* "The son will deliver his father into the hands of the executioner"). In *Kabale und Liebe,* that the obvious enmity between father and son arises from the mother complex as described by Freud (1910) is revealed by the personalities of the two female characters and the protagonist's ambiguous relationship with them, similar as it is to the set of relationships in *Don Carlos.* Among the conditions for love evinced by persons whose libido had long been intensely fixed on the mother but was then directed away from her and toward others, Freud observed a peculiar one that is particularly noticeable, since it is strangely opposite to the conception of the mother. This is the preference of such persons for sexually disreputable women. In explaining this strange attraction to the "whore," Freud refers to a situation often observed during the years of puberty—these young men have two separate sexual orientations. They have divorced sensual and spiritual love from one another. On the one hand, they demonstrate a great respect for women, combined with unrestrained [spiritual] love. On the other hand, if the sensual aspect is strong enough to be manifested, then these youths are sexually active only with disreputable women. This is because the noble, pure conception of the (unattainable) mother they have developed prevents them from associating women with sexual pleasure. But given the drives of maturing sexuality, they "open a separate account" for disreputable women, from whom they seek only sexual pleasure.

However, this sharp separation of the objects of love, which arises during puberty, cannot be permanently maintained. With the intensification of sexual needs, a compromise gradually develops as an adaptation to social circumstances that can be designated as the normal solution of this conflict: these men are attracted to someone else's wife—a woman who in a sense is no longer quite pure. This attraction brings about a near reconciliation of the originally divided aspects of the individual's love life. Still, this compromise clearly reveals that these conditions for love arise from the mother complex. During his investigations, in fact, Freud found that the child, on beginning to realize the true nature of the sexual relationship between his parents, considers this a degradation especially of the mother, who is beloved by the child yet unattainable. During puberty he becomes familiar with prostitutes, and reiterating his infantile disdain for sex, he tells himself that his mother, having given herself to the (unloved) father, is actually no better than these women. In his fantasies, he involves the mother in all manner of sexual relationships; in so doing, the desire for revenge upon the father, whom the mother prefers, and the wish for easier access to the mother are expressed. Blinded by jealousy, Hamlet similarly goes so far as to conceive of his mother's marital relations as reprehensible and illicit and even calls his mother a whore.

Those portions of prehistoric infantile fantasies revealed by psychoanalytical research indicate, surprisingly, that the conception of the mother as a whore is by no means as uncommon as one might assume from the consternation with which adults reject such a suggestion. Yet the astonishment with which this suggestion is rejected is easy to understand, given the intense repression this offensive fantasy has undergone. In neurotically inclined persons, this infantile fantasy emerges at the time of puberty in distorted form and expresses itself in their social behavior, which has been precisely described by Freud (1910). In the playwright, however, we observe the fantasy in undistorted form, and though an apparently justified motivation has been provided, this motivation proves on closer inspection to be as untenable as the original infantile justification of the conception. It has been shown that the child in love with his mother, though he apparently places no definite claims on her—and certainly no sexual ones—nevertheless perceives the sexual activity of his parents, upon discovering it, as sexual infidelity by the mother. Hamlet behaves no differently when he calls his mother a whore for going to the bed of his (step)father. At the time of puberty this fantasy—which originally, in a manner of speaking, was purely critical—is reassessed in a positive light: the whore nature of the mother must now enable the son to rid the incest fantasy of its monstrosity and to come closer to the possibility of its realization.

From the same motive arises another equally common fantasy, which has also found precise literary expression in a remark of Hamlet's. He says to his mother: "You are the queen, your husband's brother's wife; and—would it were not so!—you are my mother." Behind the spite expressed in this comment lies the typical wish of every son in love with his mother for the dissolution of the bonds of blood relationship that would make the forbidden sexual relationship possible. If one also considers the like-minded words of Don Carlos—his first in the drama, "O heaven, grant that I might forgive the one who made her my mother," one may suppose that besides the defense mechanisms emphasized, this wish for the dissolution of blood relationship was not without its influence in the assessment and characterization of the step relationship in Schiller's *Don Carlos*. At this point we must emphasize that this parallel between literary works, and almost all the parallels that we will discuss below, are in no sense to be interpreted as derivatives or borrowings, but rather are a demonstration of typical psychic impulses and of the literary means of expression they are associated with. It is in this sense that we should understand Schiller's remark that Carlos "has the soul of Shakespeare's Hamlet" (Jonas 1892, vol. 1, no. 65).

That the conditions for love arise from the mother complex is revealed still more clearly in those men who have been unsuccessful in effecting the compromise required for achieving an approximately normal love life. In these men, accordingly, the split conception of the love object as unapproachable and despised is retained and becomes increasingly intense with sexual maturation. Having observed in the characters of Elisabeth (chaste, pure, and restrained) and the princess of Eboli (passionate, rapturous, and receptive) the first beginnings of this split between eroticism and sexuality in Schiller, and noting that Schiller then encountered these two personality types in the Lengefeld sisters ("Convenience" and "Propriety"), we now find in *Kabale und Liebe* the two extreme examples of this fantasy: the holy, chaste, pure virgin, Luise Miller, and the whore, Lady Milford. That we are dealing with the literary presentation of an originally unified fantasy is demonstrated by the contradictory behavior of the protagonist with respect to the two women; in his mind, the two women exchange their roles and are identified with each other. This contradictory behavior of the protagonist is still externally motivated through the intrigue of the plot, while similar behavior by Don Carlos is apparently motivated by inner forces. Initially Ferdinand conceives of Luise as a pure angel. Give the false suspicions produced by intrigue, however, it is strikingly easy for him to conclude that she is a whore. On the other hand, he initially treats Lady Milford, the prince's mistress, with extreme disdain, only to beg her forgiveness when he is convinced of her inner purity and magnanimity. And when Lady Milford embraces him in a scene (2.3) reminiscent of the princess of Eboli's misleading devotion, he rejects her love just as Carlos rejects that of the princess. In this scene, in which Lady Milford reveals to the president's son her love for him, we observe one further theme Freud has also identified as a typical incest fantasy. The dramatic separation into two love objects, originally united in the mother, can, through the mutual interference of these two opposing tendencies, produce serious psychic conflicts that lead to two distinct outcomes. The individual either sublimates the whore (devotion for Lady Milford) or, through the disappointments associated with the object of devotion, becomes a misogynist (a Hamlet type). One of the most frequent forms of such sublimation is a striving for the moral or social redemption of fallen women, for which a rational motivation can easily be provided in the temptation to which the sexually disreputable woman is continually subject. The redemption fantasy, which is usually realized by marrying such women, has one of its roots in the son's conception, discussed above, that the mother is unhappy at the father's side and wishes to be rescued by her son, who in so doing creates a justification for his claims on the mother. In the scene mentioned above (2.3), which seems like a study for the great scene with the princess of Eboli, the ruler's mistress (the mother) frankly expresses her desire for salvation from sexual decadence:

> *Lady Milford* (very tenderly): Listen, Walter, when an unhappy woman is irresistibly drawn to you by almighty forces; when she presses herself against you with a breast full of glowing, inexhaustible love, Walter, and you still say the cold word "honor"; when this unhappy woman, oppressed by her feelings of shame, weary of vice, heroically uplifted by the call of nobility, throws herself into your arms (she embraces him imploringly and solemnly), having been saved by you, and wishes to be given back to heaven by you; or (she turns away from him with a hollow, trembling voice), when obedient to the horrific call of desperation, fleeing from your image, she falls once again into even more deplorable depths of vice. . . .

But as Freud has demonstrated, this redemption fantasy on the son's part has, in addition to a tender side associated with the mother, an inimical side directed toward the father. When the son begins to think maturely, his gradually increasing and incomprehensible antipathy toward the father manifests itself as a desire for independence from paternal authority. The son wishes to owe the father nothing, but he cannot help feeling that he owes him everything—his very life. This guilt can be relieved only through retribution of like for like—by saving the father's life—as compensation for the son's own birth. We immediately recognize that this fantasy, usually manifested as desire to rescue the emperor, enables the son to express his dislike for the father behind a noble motive. Thus this fantasy represents a stage subsequent to the stage of vengeance for the father's death observed in *Hamlet:* there it is not the rescue of the father that the son strives for, but the punishment of his murderer. The rescue is the prime defense against the son's own feelings of hatred and against his tendencies for self-punishment. Here again we observe the regular development and formation of a motive that proceeds from open hatred toward the father, which can only be gratified by killing him, to a neurotic defense against this impulse, the desire to avenge the father's death, and finally to the fantasy of rescuing the father, the precise opposite of killing him—the ultimate defensive measure. But the deeper motivation of this desire to rescue the father once again shows us only the son's aversion toward the father (cf. the ultimately contemptuous interpretation of the "redemption" of the mother, which equates her with a whore).

As we will discuss in more detail in part 2, this rescue of the father from life-threatening danger in compensation for the son's own life is already encountered in Schiller's first drama, *Die Räuber* [The robbers], or *Der verlorene Sohn* [The lost son], as it was originally titled. Indeed, we already observe in Christian Schubart's story, which served Schiller as source material, the importance of the theme of the rescue of the father from the murderous attacks of his evil son by the rejected good son who has returned unrecognized. Similarly, in the final version of *Die Räuber,* Karl Moor rescues his father from the miserable death by starvation to which he has been abandoned by Karl's brother, Franz. Thus, like Hamlet, whose father lives on as a ghost, Karl Moor avenges the (intended) murder of his father. The only difference is that the playwright's inimical attitude toward his father, personified in Franz, indicates more clearly than the fratricide in *Hamlet* that the son's rescue fantasy arises only to compensate for his earlier fantasy of patricide. That the young Schiller felt strongly his debt to his father for the gift of life is demonstrated in the first version of *Die Räuber,* where Franz philosophizes away every obligation to his family, saying (1.1): "That is your brother! That is to say, he was baked in the same oven as you were, so you should regard him as sacred! . . . But your father is more sacred still! He gave you life; you are his flesh and blood, so you should regard him as sacred! Again, a clever conclusion! I should like to ask why he made me. Certainly not only out of love for me, when I hadn't even yet become an 'I.' " Later (5.2) he characterizes human birth as "the result of a bestial impulse" (cf. Hamlet's revulsion before the marriage bed).

If here, as in Karl's rescue of his father, the oppressive feeling of indebtedness to the father for one's life is especially evident, in *Kabale und Liebe* we find an especially clear and characteristic expression of the revenge fantasy. Whereas in other works the father (emperor) is rescued from life-threatening situations into which he has been brought either through his own fault or by other persons, here it is the son himself who threatens the father's life in order, later, to grant him his life. This configuration, melding patricide and rescue of the father, corresponds closely to our interpretation. Consider act 2, scene 6, in which the president enters the house of the musician:

> *President* (laughs more loudly): An amusing proposition! The father should respect his son's whore.

Luise (casts herself down): O heaven and earth!
Ferdinand (also with Luise; drawing his sword against his father, but then quickly letting it fall): Father! I owed you a life once, but now the debt has been paid. (He sheathes the sword.) There lies the statement of the child's debt, torn to shreds.

In addition to these rescue fantasies involving both parents, a quite special but also typical form of the redemption of the mother plays a role in this drama of Schiller's youth—again in a quite characteristic manner. This is the fantasy of marriage to a fallen woman. It is of no great consequence that the fantasy appears here negatively—that Ferdinand heatedly rejects the offer of his father and the request of Lady Milford herself that he marry the ruler's mistress (1.7):

Ferdinand: Would you wish to be father to the vile son who married a privileged courtesan?

The father's answer is a very clear reference to the "mother character" of Lady Milford:

President: More than that, I would court her myself if she desired a man of my age. . . . Would you not wish to be son to the vile father?
Ferdinand: No! As truly as God lives!

This solution to the son's relationship, too, is a typical incest wish and the complement to the prostitution of the mother. If he is not his father's son, then his mother has of course committed adultery and has in a sense prostituted herself. Thus the son's incest fantasy is stripped of its horror, and hatred of the father is reduced to simple rivalry with an unrelated man.

This perspective provides a deeper understanding of two themes widely represented in literature and widely esteemed by literary historians. Just as the father has taken the bride from the son in *Don Carlos,* and just as they are rivals, to an extent, for the affections of the princess of Eboli, in *Kabale und Liebe* Lady Milford's marriage to the son as well as to the father is considered. But this typical incest fantasy of the abduction of the bride or of competition between father and son also shows that the deepest source for the rivalry of two men over a woman is to be found in the child's rivalry with the father. This theme, which dominates the entire production of numerous writers, will concern us further when we investigate the relationship of siblings in part 2. The opposite configuration, often encountered in the same literary work (cf. both *Don Carlos* and *Kabale und Liebe*), is the protagonist whose affections alternate in double love, between love for one woman and love for another—a pure, noble woman and a sensual, evil one. This theme can be pursued from Lessing's Marwood and Sara Sampson, or from his Orsina and Emilia Galotti, to Wagner (Elisabeth and

Venus) and Ibsen, in whose dramas this theme is dominant. Just as the first theme originates in the child's relationship with the father, we can already recognize it as the expression of fantasies involving the mother and leading to the splitting of the love object into noble and despicable aspects. The sacred, unapproachable aspect is of course the mother in her relationship with her son, but since she gives herself to the father, he perceives her as a whore.

These two themes of rivalry and double love, which we observe in both *Kabale und Liebe* and *Don Carlos,* were also seen in Schiller's own life—in his relationship with the von Wolzogens and with his rival, Winkelmann, and in his association with the Lengefeld sisters, where he felt painfully the absence of a rival. In *Maria Stuart,* both themes are finally expressed clearly and melded with one another. Here too the protagonist stands between two women—the pure, virginal Elizabeth (2.2) and the "courtesan" Maria—both of whom appear as queens (mothers). One can consider both Count Leicester and Mortimer protagonists—two persons who are rivals for the affections of both women. The young Mortimer falls passionately in love with the much older Maria, but Leicester lets it be known that he has established an earlier claim on her hand (theme of rivalry)—that she had been betrothed to him before she was married to Darnley. It is characteristic that Maria's variegated past, far from repelling the inexperienced Mortimer, instead attracts him. And if the degradation of the mother to a prostitute served as a defense against the son's inclinations in *Kabale und Liebe* (he loves Luise, the pure woman), in *Maria Stuart* the original wish for easy access to the woman finds full expression in this theme. In the passionate love scene (3.6), Mortimer reveals to her where his hopes lie:

> You are not without feeling;
> The world does not accuse you of cold severity;
> You can be moved by the passionate request for love.
> You have made the singer Rizzio happy,
> And Bothwell, too, led you away.

Here too the rescue fantasy plays a large role. In fact, the whole drama revolves solely around Mortimer's rescue attempt:

> I wish to save her, I alone!
> Let the danger as well as the fame and praise be mine.

Through individual details, as well as through these typical female characters, the drama reveals its origins in Bauerbach during the time of the composition of *Don Carlos*. Schiller first began to think about *Don Carlos* in May 1783. Like Carlos and Posa, Mortimer and Leicester are, in the final analysis, only personifications of various aspects of the relationship with the mother. Like Carlos, Mortimer falls unhappily in love with the queen (mother), and like Posa, Leicester is able to cloak the whole conflict in a political guise. Mortimer's unexpected and surprising capture by Leicester also reminds one of Carlos's arrest by Posa, which occurs in similar circumstances. In both cases this leads to the death of the stated protagonist. Corresponding to its time of composition following *Wallenstein* (1799–1800), however, the conflict with the father is eliminated and the corresponding emotional content of the drama is dedicated to the presentation of the historically documented animosity between Mary and Elizabeth (who were, by the way, blood relatives). But hatred of the father, too, is revealed in one detail—Mortimer's relationship with his uncle, Paulet; even here, though, this theme is not undisguised. Just as Paulet is Maria's jailer—just as he strictly guards her and makes access to her difficult for Mortimer—Philip, supported by his household, was Elisabeth's jailer, jealously guarding her. Maria has doubts concerning the success of Mortimer's attempt to rescue her:

> And Drury, Paulet, my jailers?
> Their last blood they would sooner—

But Mortimer answers:

> They will be the first to fall by my sword!
> *Maria:* What? Your uncle, your second father?
> *Mortimer:* He shall die by my hand. I shall murder him.

Just as the fantasy of incest with the mother follows upon that of the murder of the father in *Don Carlos* (1.5), here, following these thoughts of patricide, Mortimer experiences the fantasy of union with the beloved:

> Life is
> But a moment. Death, too, is but a moment!
> Let them drag me to Tyburn, let them rend me
> Limb from limb with glowing irons
> For embracing you, O passionately beloved.

In *Die Verschwörung des Fiesco zu Genua* [The conspiracy of Fiesco in Genoa], the second drama of Schiller's youth, which arose between *Die Räuber* and *Kabale und Liebe,* one again finds the two opposing female figures. Here too, under the guise of political intrigue, the protagonist (like Leicester and Posa) is motivated by his affection for two women—his noble spouse Leonore and the "coquettish, bad" Julia, the "Widow Imperiali." The latter character, just like the "ravished," innocent Bertha Verrina, is Schiller's own invention, which he thought it necessary to develop as a counterpart to Leonore. In Fiesco's relationship to her we observe the most tender attempts at approach as well as the coolest rejection when she passionately embraces him (4.12). This sexual aggressiveness by women, elsewhere a male characteristic, is a typical feature in Schiller's works. Not only the Countess Imperiali, but also Lady Milford, the princess of Eboli, and Agrippina offer the protagonist their love with varying degrees of candor and reserve. But all of these are disreputable female characters, and this offering of affection is clearly characteristic of loose women. Originally it derives from the son's wish that the mother would offer him all her love. With the subsequent repression of this wish arises a rejection of sexual activity expressed in the inability to actively win a woman's affection, thus once again creating the need for the originally desired active engagement of the woman. Here the protagonist plays with the affections of the Widow Imperiali but hates her uncle, the prince of Genoa, whose tyranny he wishes to topple. In this "honorable old man of eighty" we see once again the typical disguise of the father as tyrannical prince. Confirmation is provided by the playwright himself: when the rebellious hordes are about to put an end to the old Doria, Schiller has him cry to his defenders: "Save yourselves! Leave me! Instill terror in all nations with the horrific news: the Genoans have killed their father" (5.4).

The complications in the personal relationships, revealed to us principally through historical documents, must remain without discussion here. But we should mention that Fiesco is punished, since, after removing the tyrant, he himself wishes to become tyrant, prince, and "father." That is, he wishes to set himself up in the father's place. Here the political drama stands clearly in the foreground but serves Schiller psychologically as a disguise for his personal opposition to his father, as was also made clear in our analysis of *Don Carlos*. One of his earliest dramatic fragments was entitled *Die Verschwörung der Pazzi* [The conspiracy of the Pazzis], and the dramatis personae of *Die Räuber*, too, are conspirators who wish to "overthrow the laws of the world."

Given this background, we will not hesitate to interpret the conspiracy, indignation, and tyrannicide in *Wilhelm Tell* as further expressions of Schiller's father hatred. But even if *Wilhelm Tell* were the only one of Schiller's works known to us, this interpretation could still be developed and demonstrated with certainty. As much as the expressions of the unconscious are distorted and disguised through powerful cultural inhibitory tendencies, their origin and meaning can still be recognized from certain signs; Freud's term is "the mark" [*die Marke*]. The "mark" that identifies Schiller's *Wilhelm Tell* as an incest drama with special emphasis on hatred toward the father, as characterized above, is Duke Johann's scene (5.2). Just as Tell kills the tyrant Gessler, Duke Johann murders his uncle, Kaiser Albrecht, who denies him his inheritance (cf. Hamlet; Paulet in *Maria*

Stuart). Tell and his deed are central to the plot, however, especially since his deed seems far removed from patricide. Through the justification of self-defense and defense of land, property, and family, it seems not only justified but even laudable as an act of national heroism. Tell's deed is so central to the plot that in many productions up to the present day Duke Johann's scene, the most important scene for understanding the whole drama, has been eliminated. This scene reveals to us that Tell's deed is patricide in disguise. From Melchthal's question regarding Duke Johann, "What drove him to the deed of parricide?" (5.1), we can deduce that Schiller conceived of the relationship between the emperor (father) and his murderer, in a psychological sense, as that of a father and his son. The association of Tell's deed with Duke Johann's, and its designation as a disguised act of patricide, is revealed to us by the powerful emotion with which Tell rejects the association of his deed with the murder of the emperor. It is remarkable that Schiller placed this scene (5.2) precisely where he himself wanted it within the drama, while sticking strictly to the chronological order of historical events in the rest of the work. The always helpful Tell, who retrieves a stray lamb from a chasm, who risks his own life to save Baumgarten, sends Duke Johann away from his home, where he had sought protection; from Tell least of all had Johann expected to hear relentless condemnation of his deed:

> *Tell:* Dripping with the blood
> Of patricide and the emperor's murder,
> You dare to enter my clean home?
> *Duke:* I had hoped to find compassion in your home;
> You too took revenge on your enemy.
> *Tell:* Cursed one!
> How can you compare ambition's bloody sin
> With a father's just defense?
> . . . .
> I raise my clean hands toward heaven.
> I curse you and your deed. I have avenged
> Holy nature; you have violated her.
> I'll share nothing with you. You have murdered;
> I defended what is dearest to me.
> *Duke:* So you cast me away, comfortless, into despair?
> *Tell:* Even speaking with you fills me with dread.

Here, at the height of Tell's defense, when he faces the parricide—the image of his own inner motives—the powerful emotions of rejection begin their transformation into emotions of kindness and sympathy for the parricide, in order finally to identify with him and to be forgiven, along with him, through his atonement:

> *Tell:* Can I help you? Can a man help sin?
> But stand up now. Whatever horrid deeds
> You have done, you are a man, as am I.
> No man shall depart from Tell uncomforted.
> What I can, I will do.

In *Wilhelm Tell,* we see a shift of emphasis similar to that Freud has described as characteristic of the development of dreams. Patricide (the tyrant Gessler's murder), made unrecognizable through repression and even justified (cf. *Hamlet*), is brought into a central position in the plot through the shift of emphasis in Duke Johann's scene. And just as the powerful emotional material of repressed hatred toward the father lends dramatic life to the historical events and characters of *Maria Stuart,* Schiller's enthusiasm for the hero of liberty, Wilhelm Tell, gains strength from deep feelings of father hatred, though there is no room for these to be fully developed within Duke Johann's scene.

After this shift of emphasis, the second most important psychological mechanism in *Wilhelm Tell* is the displacement of emphasis we observe in the famous apple-shooting scene. Here the father aims at the son, but the way Gessler, for whom the second arrow is meant, forces Tell to do so marks him as a "father" with respect to Tell. But in this scene, through powerful defense mechanisms, the emotion of hatred toward the father is associated with the opposite conception of hatred toward the son—of wagering the son's life. Indeed, this hatred is transformed into love: the father does not aim at his child in hate, trying to kill him, but shoots with the highest degree of psychological self-mastery, to save his life. ("Shall I become the murderer of my child?") Thus the whole psychological situation is recast in a moving manner; we recognize this as the essential characteristic of such a displacement of emphasis. But this displacement derives psychologically from Schiller's fatherly feelings (the theme of fear of retribution). As a young man, Schiller would have required neither this displacement nor the whole justification through the parricide Duke Johann.

Confirmation for our interpretation is provided in the numerous parallels to the Tell legend—in tales of the bowman whom a tyrant forces to shoot at a loved one to save his own life. Indeed, variants also exist in which the bowman must shoot at his own father (or brother). The oldest Germanic variant is the tale of the bowman Eigel, brother of the smith Wieland. *Thidrek's Saga* reports how King Nidung forces Eigel to demonstrate his skill by shooting an apple from the head of his three-year-old son.

When the king inquires for what purpose the remaining two arrows were intended, Eigel remarks that they were meant for the king if the first shot had struck the child. Saxo Grammaticus relates the same tale about the bowman Toko; in the corresponding Nordic variant, *Hemnig's Saga,* the target is a hazelnut. In a Hungarian folktale, Tschalo Pischta is forced by a cruel king to shoot an apple from his father's head if he does not wish to be put with him in a place "where neither sun nor moon shines." In Schiller's play, Gessler makes the same threat: "I will have you led away and kept where neither sun nor moon will shine on you so that I will be safe from your arrows." This suggests that Schiller was familiar with the Hungarian version. The same substitution of father for son is also observed in a folktale of the Armenians of Bukovina, in which a "blind prince," blinded by the usurper of his father's throne, wanders in foreign lands accompanied by his faithful dog. From Saint Joseph he receives a golden "wishing arrow" and a salve with which he is to anoint his eyes on the day after next in order to regain his sight. On the following day, however, he is to take part, still blind, in a shooting competition arranged by the king. He shoots his golden arrow, which always returns to him unseen, through a golden ring thirty-three times, whereupon he is forced by the cruel king to shoot thirty-three apples from his father's head. Thereafter he shoots the king and all of his followers with the same arrow. Lessmann (1908), in whose work I encountered these tales, remarks (p. 45) that such tales of the blind bowman are common and suggest that the Nordic Hödr must also be analyzed in this light.

An attempt to explain this strange mythological figure, the blind bowman, leads us to another source of Schiller's *Wilhelm Tell.* Here we must adopt a point of view introduced into the science of biology by the Viennese physician Alfred Adler (1907). He proposes, among other things, that every superior achievement of an organ derives from an original inferiority of that organ, resulting in subsequent superiority through compensation by other organs or by the central nervous system. In addition to the records of various illnesses, he adduces some classic historical examples to support his theory—among others, the eloquence of the stuttering Demosthenes and Beethoven's deafness. Our blind bowman certainly seems no stranger than the deaf musical genius. Since it does not address biological problems but treats relationships in an intuitive manner, the myth can, of course, in no better way represent the original inferiority of the bowman's eye than through his simultaneous blindness. Through this simultaneity, which makes the figure appear so strange, the myth expresses causality—the relation of the inferiority of the eyes to good marksmanship. In addition to his claim that an inferior organ effects its own superior function—for example, the eye of the artist or marksman—Adler claims that an inferior organ effects the characteristic elaboration of certain personality traits associated with the psychomotor superstructure of that organ. The individual will perceive the world and all its phenomena through the modality of such a dominant, inferior organ, will always emphasize perceptions associated with that organ, and will employ comparisons and images from its domain.

In *Wilhelm Tell* we find certain echoes of the bowman's blindness that, without Schiller's necessarily having been familiar with these myths, can be derived from his own psyche. Rudolf der Harras, for example, suggests to Tell's son that he should let himself be blindfolded:

> *Walter Tell:* Why the eyes? Do you imagine that I fear
> The arrow from my father's hand? I'll await it
> Firmly, and will not move an eyelash.

Since we are already familiar with the displacement characterizing the whole shooting scene, it will not surprise us to see the "blindness" displaced here from the bowman to his target. But hints with reference to Tell himself are not lacking; the man who "prides himself on his sure sight" lets his "crossbow sink" at the decisive moment and cries: "My eyes are overcome with dizziness!" Another hint that the shot is actually taken "blind" is perhaps to be found in a remark of Gessler, in which he eggs Tell on:

> You relish the unusual. Therefore I have now
> Selected a feat just for you.
> Another might have second thoughts, but you will close
> Your eyes and undertake the task.

And it sounds like unconscious irony when Berta says immediately thereafter: "Do not joke, my lord, with these poor people." In this connection, another significance of the Melchthal episode—the blinding of the father—becomes clear; its deep association with hatred toward the father and revenge on him also becomes clear. Melchthal, who has revolted against the tyrant, flees. The tyrant gets his revenge by blinding Melchthal's father and robbing him of his possessions. (Gloucester in Shakespeare's *King Lear* meets the same fate.) Thus the son actually puts his own father's life at stake (*Melchthal:* "Because of my crimes, because of my misdeeds!") In this self-accusation by the son, as in all such cases of self-reproach, the wish to harm the father, hidden in the unconscious, reveals itself. And just as the young Melchthal sacrifices his father to save his own life, Tell shoots at his son when coerced by the tyrant. In both cases this coercion serves to motivate and justify the inimical feelings.

It is therefore clear that the Melchthal episode is also a variation on the same theme, revenge on the father, appearing this time with negative features (defense mechanisms). This theme is illustrated most clearly in Duke Johann's scene and in a highly obscure manner in Wilhelm Tell's actions. It is also elaborated in a very dampened form in the Attinghausen episode, in which the rebellion of the nephew, Rudenz, hastens the death of his mortally ill uncle. In this sense one could conceive of Schiller's *Wilhelm Tell* as a powerful symphony of father hatred in which four variations on the basic theme are developed simultaneously, in the manner of a fugue. In some cases these themes appear to have acquired coloring specifically from the eye theme in the psychic superstructure of the work. The source of this superstructure—of this vision complex—can easily be found in defects in Schiller's own vision. Even as a youth he was constantly blinking, as emphasized by his friend Streicher (1965, 63) in his description of the twenty-one-year-old student of Duke Karl: "The reddish hair, the knees inclined toward one another, the quick blinking of the eyes when making an objection." In view of this association, Tell's son's declaration that he will not move an eyelash becomes clearer and acquires a deeper meaning. It sounds almost like a reminiscence of the young Schiller's attempts to break this childhood habit. Later he suffered from inflammations of the eyelids (Jonas 1892, 2:441), and in a letter to his later wife (May 27, 1788) he described himself as nearsighted: "I hope to be at the spa, assuming you mean the one I must travel past, for otherwise, with my nearsightedness, I would probably have to spend a long time looking for you." It is remarkable that Schiller, despite these defects, had a passion for marksmanship. In a letter written in Bauerbach he already expressed satisfaction at having shot a bird of prey (February 1, 1783), and in a letter to Streicher (January 14, 1783) he remarks enthusiastically: "I am planning to spend some time this winter with my friend W. at his estate in Thüringen Forest. I will live only for myself and for friendship, and best of all, I'll learn to shoot, for it's hunting season at the home of my friend." Coincidentally, it seems that Schiller's vision problems were hereditary. The old name "Schiller," given to his ancestors, refers directly to problems of the eye; recent research indicates that the name derives from the verb *schielen* ["to squint, to be cross-eyed"]. We can only silently admire the organic power and psychic transformations that led from a cross-eyed ancestor to the singer of the impassioned hymn to vision (Melchthal's monologue).

Thus it seems clear why Schiller was so attracted by the Wilhelm Tell material. It gave him the opportunity to portray his relationship with his father in a highly exhaustive yet disguised manner, while emphasizing the eye theme. But the objection can still be raised that he could have encountered all these themes in his sources, that he did not invent them himself, and that therefore one can draw no conclusions regarding his psychic life. This objection holds also for the other dramas discussed. Therefore we are now obliged at last to undertake a psychological investigation into the conditions for the author's selection of material.

4 *The Stepmother Theme: The Psychology of the Selection of Material*

Queen: **Do you place your hopes on me, your mother?**
Carlos: **I place them on my father's wife.**

SCHILLER, *Don Carlos*

In the psychological investigation of *Don Carlos,* the figure of the stepmother has been shown to express a compromise between erotic affection for the physical mother and defense mechanisms opposing this rejected passion. Psychic opposition to the incestuous fantasy first effects the dissolution of the physical relationship, but the original erotic affection for the mother is still expressed in that her substitute, the stepmother, is also the father's spouse. Thus the stepmother is simultaneously the nonphysical "mother," whose love for the son is no longer incestuous but nevertheless violates the father's claims and provides a justification for hatred between father and son, rivals for her affection. Not least, love of the stepmother derives from the son's wish to compensate for the age difference between himself and his mother by acquiring a younger mother. The agreement in age usually arises because the (step)mother was originally the son's betrothed but was taken from him by the father. This tendency for the rejuvenation of the mother, however, like the other aspects of the stepmother fantasy, by no means arises from a conscious conclusion that the mother is already too old for sexual love, but only reflects how the fantasy clings to the pleasure-oriented memories of childhood, when the mother appeared to the boy as a young, beautiful woman and the father as an omnipotent man.

According to whether the author places the resistance to incestuous passions in the son or in the mother, as determined by his own psychic constitution, one can distinguish two typical versions of the stepmother theme. The one, which portrays the son's passionate but hopeless love, we shall call the "Carlos schema" after the most significant representative of this group. The other, which portrays the mother's passionate love in the face of rejection by her son, we shall designate the "Phaedra schema." We have chosen these terms recognizing that within these two schemas portraying the passionate love between stepmother and stepson with various shadings of attraction and rejection, it is primarily these two sources, the Carlos and Phaedra legends, that always attract authors to write ever newer versions of the material. An attempt to explain this point brings us to the problem of the selection of material; an approach to its solution now seems to present itself.

The circumstance, apparently in no need of explanation but nevertheless extremely noteworthy, that so many important authors have for centuries occupied themselves with the same material, always creating new possibilities for plot development, has a deep psychological interpretation. From the ambivalence characteristic of all higher psychic operations, which we have also observed in the stepmother theme, it seems comprehensible that not every author will be successful in mustering the significant expenditure of psychic energy and unconscious thought necessary to create such an expression of compromise. The author, whose literary and historical interests are determined by his psychic composition, will gladly adopt such a compromise upon encountering it, since it serves as the perfect means to pacify the inner conflict between his desires and their rejection. But we should not consider this assimilation and reworking of a highly complicated and characteristic creation of the psyche in the superficial manner of the literary historian or even of the author himself. The author assimilates only what corresponds to his innermost feelings. He must, in the true sense of the word, be predisposed to select given material. But even then, whether from a predecessor or from a common source, he does not simply assimilate the theme as it is; he adjusts it psychically, incorporates it into his being, and makes it psychically his own. He does not simply adopt the ready-made schema, but modifies it in various points according to his own personality or the perceptions of the times. He brings the predetermined form and substance to life again with his own means. He fills the traditional forms of presentation with his own affects, thus creating an impressive, living work of art. As we may suppose, he succeeds in this by sexualizing his activity, thus deriving the degree of passion necessary for creation.

The complicated process of assimilating certain material or poetic images to one's own use can be made clear only through its pathological analogue in the hysteric. Here we receive insight into the same mechanism, though it has in this case become much cruder. In the hysteric, the "imitation" of symptoms is well known. It occurs to such an extent that in institutions, all the roommates of a patient acquire one of his symptoms. Freud is responsible for the insight that this is in no way a simple imitation but is, rather, a true "assimilation," arising from the same etiological demand (1909f, 104). The assimilation of literary material by the author is similar. As we have seen, he does not simply come to terms with current conflicts, as Goethe indicated, psychically diffusing them, but must instead, based on his childhood fixations, continually create these conflicts. Of course, in the real world such conflicts can never be fully resolved. Thus the author is led to seek gratification in his unconscious fantasy life. Therefore, as we have suggested extensively above, it is psychologically misguided to look for actual experiences in the author's life as parallels to his literary themes, because the themes are the products of fantasy activity, for which actual experiences are only raw material subject to the most extreme modifications. Since the playwright creates based on inner experiences and not exterior ones (which themselves are often based on inner ones), it is understandable that given the "same etiological demands" in the unconscious he will grasp at such configurations when they present themselves and correspond to his psychic composition. In our case, the common etiological demand would be the incestuous inclination fixated in the author's unconscious, which, affected by defense mechanisms as discussed, adopts the stepmother theme as an appropriate means of expression. The "vague urge to unburden oneself of ⟨quite distinct⟩ conflicting ideas," of which Schiller wrote to Körner (May 25, 1792), brings the author to seek out and cling most strongly to the form that affords these feelings, which are subject to the effects of defense mechanisms, the most perfect means of expression possible.

That he so often seeks out and finds this exemplary form in the creations of earlier authors corresponds perfectly to the suppositions we have had to make concerning the uniformity of the psychic life of artists. We must regard the amazing conservatism of artistic themes and forms as a result of these suppositions. This conservatism is evident not only in our contemporary literature, but perhaps to an even greater degree in the art of the ancient world, where a small number of artistic themes and forms found expression for centuries, undergoing minimal modifications. Only a few great authors are able to express their feelings effectively in forms of their own invention. In this respect, most of the remaining authors can be divided into two groups. The first group are the "adopters," with whom we will primarily be occupied here, who adopt traditional literary materials and forms and whose personal contribution is extremely subordinate to general interest in the material and problems of form. These authors appear to proceed from objective stimuli. In this group are to be found many sublime authors whose use of proven themes has brought them great popularity. The second group comprises authors whose emotions instead strive for original forms of artistic expression but who are incapable of adapting their personal psychic destiny in terms of universal human themes. Whereas the first group illustrates that apparent coincidences of literary history actually result from the psychic needs of authors, the second group illustrates the fate of the "misunderstood" authors who, more or less insistently, always depict themselves and never the problem. They are incapable—not intellectually but psychically—of giving the products of their fantasy the final, universal, but sufficiently idealized form of expression that would make them socially valuable. For psychological investigation, these authors (Otto Ludwig, Christian Grabbe, and others) and their creations are of course just as valuable as recognized great authors. One could even say that they demonstrate more candor than other authors. Their works also aid us in the human understanding of great works of literature and can in this sense be identified with initial outlines, the psychology of which was discussed above—those outlines, specifically, that are incapable of leading to a harmonious final form. As suggested by preliminary versions and fragments, even the great author begins with such personal interests and problems, but he transcends them in the course of his work by transforming them into general human problems—a sublimation of which the subjective author is incapable. We should emphasize here that we must regard this subjectivity as a neurotic personality trait and that psychologically we have no right or reason to claim that these literary achievements have limitations, for such a qualification can be justified only by considering the social value of a work of literature.

Indeed, we must proceed one step further. In the introduction, we demonstrated that the incest theme is found in the works of the most important authors of world literature, thus providing justification for focusing on it in our subsequent research. The works of these authors have entered the emotional life and intellectual culture of society because these authors were able to present shared human themes in a universally accessible and effective form. Of course the author also consciously adopts old, historically documented materials with some frequency. But these materials have been preserved precisely because of their universal effect, which arose exclusively through their perfect literary form, addressing shared human themes. It is this social aspect that determines the value of a literary work and raises the author to the status of a celebrated national hero. In contrast, the works of a subjective author, effective only within a specific small segment of society, are not appreciated. They are ridiculed, quickly forgotten, and removed from the cultural sphere in question, just as happens with the antisocial behavior of the neurotic.

The opinion of Schiller, without a doubt the most popular poet of the German people, regarding both characteristic types of literary creation—free invention and adoption of historical material—is of interest. He writes to Goethe (January 5, 1798): "I would certainly accept the suggestion that I select nothing but historical material; freely invented materials would prove a disaster for me. It is one thing to idealize the realistic and quite another to realize the ideal; the latter is the case with free fictional works. It is within my power to bring a specific, limited body of material to life, to refresh it, and to let it flow forth; the objective determinacy of such material keeps my fantasy within bounds and resists arbitrary decisions on my part." That Schiller also conceived of the employment of historical material as involving personal adaptations is clear from other letters to Goethe. In 1799, in discussing the *Warbeck* material with him, he writes: "I think that one would be well advised always to take the common situation, the time, and the characters from history, but to invent everything else freely. In this way a middle ground would be found, combining the advantages of the historical drama with those of the invented one."

In fact, the most important authors have treated historical material in a similarly free manner. The conditions of this manner of composition perhaps provide a partial explanation for the powerful effect their works have achieved. The sense in which this is meant can best be illustrated by the difference between the treatment of traditional literary material and the treatment of the historical events underlying the literary material. If the author turns to traditional literary material as an appropriate form for expressing his emotions—for example, the Carlos or Phaedra story—he has a relatively smaller task. It is easy for him to relate his own emotional life to the material: not only was it chosen in accordance with his unconscious fantasies, but the form, with which he is already familiar from the works of other authors, lends itself to artistic sensitivity and effect. This is not the case with historical material that has never been used in a literary form. Historical events brought about by upheaval in the real conditions of life do not usually correspond so well to an author's demanding and productive literary fantasy. Here, besides the theme that initially interested him, he finds a large amount of additional material that he cannot relate to. But precisely this impersonal element serves the defense mechanisms striving to disguise personal complexes. This has been observed in

Schiller's dramatic works (*Don Carlos, Maria Stuart,* and *Wilhelm Tell*). With this material, which corresponds less well to the wish complexes of the author but serves his intensified defense mechanisms, there of course arise significant displacements of affect, as we pointed out especially in *Wilhelm Tell* and *Maria Stuart*. But we have learned to recognize even the changes made by the author in historical material as psychically significant expressions. It is just this point of view that justifies us in making no distinction between freely invented material and historical material in our analysis of dramatic works. Both reveal to us in their own way the author's innermost feelings, which, even through the guise of tradition and historical costumes, always succeed in asserting themselves with powerful affective force.

Similarly, Lessing recognizes no basic distinction between a historical work and a freely invented one. "Aristotle long ago decided how much the tragic poet should concern himself with historical truth: only to the extent that the truth resembles a well-constructed fable with which to associate his opinions. He needs a story not because it has occurred, but because he would have had difficulty in finding material more appropriate to his current purposes" (*Hamburgische Dramaturgie* [Hamburg dramaturgy], part 19, July 3, 1767). In a similar vein, concerning the character of Wilhelm Meister, Schiller tells Goethe: "I cannot express to you strongly enough how well you have chosen the character of the protagonist, if such a thing can be chosen." And with keen psychoanalytical insight, Hebbel complains that "even sensible men never cease to quarrel with the author concerning his choice of material, as they call it. Thus they show that they always regard creativity, of which the first stage, the receptive stage, lies far below consciousness and sometimes reaches back into the dimmest reaches of childhood, as a form of 'making,' albeit a refined one, and that they suppose one to have the capacity to make arbitrary decisions in one's creative production to an extent they would surely not expect in real life. . . . One must forgive the author if he does not live up to their expectations. He has no choice. He cannot even choose whether or not to produce a literary work" (introduction to *Maria Magdalena,* 1844).

The modifications the author makes in historical material demonstrate that in addition to the *what*—the actual selection of material—the *how,* essentially giving form to the material, is also important. Thus, given our point of view, which has concentrated on the roughest outlines, it will still be necessary to emphasize significant psychological involvement in the selection of material. Adopting material greatly aids the author in pouring forth his emotions in a traditional form, since through the emphasis on historical interests and aesthetic problems he is brought into a pleasurable situation like that of a spectator at a drama. But as we have seen amply illustrated for the incest theme, adopting historical material also provides him with a far more pleasurable psychic release through the aesthetically justified suspension of unconscious repressions. In the mythical, historical, or literary protagonist, the author finds justification for his own rejected fantasies and feelings, which he would not presume to present, one could almost say, of his own accord. In obtaining release from his unconscious feelings of guilt, he can make the claim that he is, after all, not the only guilty one. Here we are dealing with the powerful psychic mechanism of identification—an important precondition to all artistic creativity and simultaneously the reverse side of the projection mechanism. For the author will naturally be able to identify first with those images he has just projected out from his unconscious in seeking justification for them.

Of course, identification with the historical protagonist is successful only insofar as it favors the tendency for justification. It succeeds completely when the author compensates for what he feels is missing in the historical figure by attributing to the protagonist his own feelings, regardless of whether they fully correspond to historical fact. This explains the free variations upon historical data, so characteristic in the works of great authors. In this sense, generalizing Schiller's own pronouncement on his relation to historical material, we could say with him: "History is only a storehouse for my fantasy, and things must be content to be what they become in my hands" (October 10, 1788). However, if this justification of originally egocentric fantasies through the life of a historically documented protagonist is to be fully successful, the author still requires approval as expressed by the judgment of the people—the success that not only confirms that his justification has been successful, but also shows him that in addition to the protagonist and himself, all the spectators attracted by the literary work have found justification for their own unconscious feelings in the literary work and have rewarded the author for this pleasurable gratification with success, fame, honor, and admiration. Yet the actual reward, given by the author to his public—and vice versa, neither being consciously aware of it—is that the public sanctions the author's justification, thus freeing him from his personal, unconscious feelings of guilt: precisely the service he has just provided his audience. This explains the pride and confidence with which the great author presents his works to society; the timidity with which the dilettante keeps his works secret is also accounted for by their antisocial origin and character.

The Don Carlos Schema

Carlos Dramas

The story of Don Carlos derives, of course, from historical events, though not in the form we know from the literary treatment of this material. Thus, for example, it has not been demonstrated that Carlos loved his father's third wife, Elizabeth. Further, it is not certain that he died at the express wish and command of his father. It is certain only that Don Carlos, probably because he was in sympathy with the revolutionaries, was thrown into prison, where he died in 1568. The historical Philip also had a second son, who succeeded him as Philip III.

Inspired by the still fresh impression of the death of Crown Prince Don Carlos, Lope de Vega (1562–1635), a contemporary of Philip II, wrote a drama, *El castigo sin venganza* [The punishment without revenge]. The place of activity was transferred from Spain to Italy, and the names were changed in deference to members of the royal family still living then. Many literary historians question, by the way, whether Lope even thought of the events in the house of Philip II in composing this drama. I will now present the plot of the drama as given in Wurzbach's book on Lope de Vega (1899).

Duke Luís of Ferrara, a libertine, decides at an advanced age to marry Casandra, the young princess of Mantua, in order to gain an heir to the throne. He sends his illegitimate son Federico to receive the bride. During the journey Federico comes to a river, where he hears cries for help. He rushes forward and saves a young woman whose carriage had plunged into the river. He immediately falls in love with her, but then discovers that she is his future stepmother. After the wedding, Luís neglects his young spouse, with whom he has shared his bed only once. In this, Casandra finds justification for her growing love for Federico, and while the ruler is in Rome she commits adultery with Federico. This is pointed out to Luís in an anonymous letter. He returns, and, by eavesdropping on Casandra's conversation, becomes convinced of her guilt. He has her bound to a chair with her face covered. He orders his son to kill her (the opposite of saving her), claiming that the person under the hood is a dangerous enemy of the state. Suspecting the truth, the son fulfills this command only after great hesitation. After killing Casandra, the prince is also stabbed to death by the guards at his father's command.

In accordance with Lope's freely developed sensuality and lack of sexual inhibition, the incest between stepmother and stepson is really carried out. This differs from all historical accounts and from all other literary treatments. For the same reasons, the typical theme of the bride's abduction by the father is reversed. Here the son attempts to win the bride (the mother) from the father. With this complete gratification is also associated the extreme severity of the punishment (an expression of defense mechanisms). In myth we will also encounter the son's killing of the mother after the act of incest (cf. Nero) as the highest expression of defense mechanisms. But just as the son falls in love with the mother without knowing that she is his father's bride, he also kills her without knowing her identity. From *Oedipus,* we are familiar with this anonymity of a character as a defense mechanism, and we will deal later with its psychological significance. A new wish theme, which is also of great importance, is the union of the lovers in the absence of the father. This absence corresponds precisely to the child's conception of "being dead" and can thus be considered psychologically as the child's expression of patricide. Or more precisely, patricide can be considered the realization of the child's wish for the absence of the disturbing competitor. (This childhood origin of the murder will be discussed in more detail in chap. 5; Lope's incestuous tendencies will be elaborated on in chap. 19.)

Fifty years after the death of Don Carlos, his countryman Don Diego da Euciso wrote a drama in which he figured as protagonist, *Prince Don Carlos*. The English dramatist Thomas Otway (1652–85) also wrote a Don Carlos tragedy at the age of twenty-five, *Don Carlos, Prince of Spain*. Otway, like Schiller, treats the prince's love as incestuous, precisely as though Elizabeth were his physical mother. He portrays Philip as a terrible, jealous tyrant. In 1685 Jean Campistron, a pupil of Racine, wrote a Carlos drama entitled *Andronic*. The plot is transferred from the Spanish to the Byzantine court. Andronic, the son of the emperor of Constantinople, is robbed of his bride by his father. He falls into depression and inactivity. Then the oppressed Bulgarians turn to him for aid. He suggests that his father send him to Bulgaria, but this awakens his father's suspicions, and he forbids Andronic to undertake the journey. He decides to flee. In a last conversation with the empress Irene, when bidding her farewell, he is surprised by his father, arrested, and killed. Irene is poisoned, and the king remains alone.

In his tragedy *Filippo,* the Italian playwright Vittorio Alfieri also deals with the Carlos schema. Alfieri too limits himself to the pure family drama. In the introduction, he remarks that he has adopted those traditions portraying Philip as the suspicious, violent, bloodthirsty Tiberius of Spain. He states that, like most historians, he assumes Carlos's love for his father's third wife, Elizabeth, who was betrothed to Carlos before Philip married her. Further, he states that, differing from all historical accounts, he has "Isabella" die with Carlos, although Elizabeth is generally said to have outlived him by a few months and to have died of natural causes. Alfieri's selection of certain versions, and the expansions and modifications he made in the historical material, reveal his individual inclinations. Since there is an intensification of defense against the son's love for the mother, the father—the main obstacle—comes into the foreground, as already demonstrated in our analysis of Schiller's *Don Carlos*. In Alfieri's drama Philip is actually the protagonist, as indicated by the drama's title. The son projects outward his hatred toward his father; he believes that his father hates him:

> *Carlos:* Yes, far more deeply than he hates those around him,
> Philip hates me.
> . . . .
> For in his bloodthirsty heart he has long been
> Planning my death.

The stepmother, Isabella, tries in vain to make him understand that these fears are unfounded:

> *Isabella:* Anger blinds you, and you imagine in him
> A hatred that can never be found.

But for Carlos, the most important thing is to justify his own hatred:

> *Carlos:* . . . It's true that
> I tremble before him, but I do not hate him.

In this defense against his own hatred and this justification of his hatred by supposing that his father hates him there also lies, in a psychological sense, the punishment for his criminal passions. The final consequence of this tendency for self-punishment (defense) is the demand for the harshest punishment, death:

> *Carlos:* Here, I offer my arms to your chains.
> Here, I bare my breast to your sword.
> Why do you hesitate?

Gomez, Philip's confidant, tells Isabella, who still hopes that Carlos can be saved:

> . . . It is hopeless, alas!
> To chasten his own untamed heart
> Through a sentence of death! No, I see already
> How he pursues his own demise.

This tendency for self-punishment eventually leads to Carlos's suicide. Philip lets Carlos and Isabella, both of whom have been condemned to die, choose between dagger and poison. Carlos stabs himself:

> *Carlos:* . . . I am dying—follow my example!
> Take the goblet—do not hesitate.

Isabella: Yes!
I'll follow you. O death, you are a joy to me.
Philip: Then you shall live against your will.
Isabella: Let me be! Oh, cruel punishment! How?
He dies and I
. . . . . .
Must live at your side?
To bear this, to see you? No, never! I'll die!
If you take the goblet from me, then let your dagger do the deed.
(She quickly grasps the dagger from Philip and stabs herself.)

We must also regard the blinding of Oedipus as an expression of such a tendency for self-punishment, which presumably plays a role in many suicides. But in addition to being a punishment, death here also represents fulfillment of the forbidden wish. Here too, as almost always in the fantasy life of the neurotic and of the artist, dying with the beloved is a symbolic expression of sexual union influenced by defense mechanisms grappling with unconscious guilt.

The drama begins with Isabella's expression of love: "As Don Philip's unfaithful wife, I dare to love his son!" But she is not happy to admit this. Immediately, her powerful defenses against this inclination express themselves: "Alas for me if this passion ever reveals itself to a mortal! Alas for me if he were to suspect it." Then follows the expression of her own attempt to repress this inclination:

Who reads my heart? If only I knew
As little about it as the others.
Then I could deceive myself, flee from myself,
As I am fleeing from him.

In the second act, Carlos and the queen meet. After extensive hesitation, reminiscent of the effects of psychic defense in the neurotic, they confess their love for each other. But Philip's jealousy too is expressed only in awkward hints. He has the idea that his son is stalking him to kill him. For though nothing of the kind has occurred, and lacking any trace of proof, he accuses his son before his councillors:

To avenge himself for forgiven faults
He creeps to my chamber
And beweaponing his hand
With patricidal steel, he approaches me
From behind. He lifts his blade;
He nearly plunges it toward his father's side

When unexpectedly a voice cries out from beyond,
"Beware, Philip! Beware!" It was
Rodrigo, who had come to my assistance. I feel
something like a thrust brush past me.
I look behind. At my feet
Lies only a dagger, and into the shadows
I see my son rush off in wild flight.

Placing the son's murder fantasy in the mouth of the father is an ingenious step, for the father too wishes to kill the son, and it is a familiar occurrence in the psychology of neurosis that the fear of being killed by the son arises in the father as a defense against this wish. The warning voice Philip claims to have heard is characteristic of the paranoid nature of this idea. In addition to providing a defense against his own hatred, this motive also serves to justify the king's hatred for his son: if Carlos wishes to assassinate him, then he is correct in hating him. That this delusion arises from such unconscious argument is clearly expressed in Philip's accusation of his son:

Carlos: What do I hear! Am I a patricide? But no!
You do not believe it yourself. What was
your reason, your suspicion, your proof?
Philip: Suspicion, proof,
and even certainty I derive from your dark animosity.

Yet Carlos remarks quite correctly that it is his father's hatred toward him that has produced this delusion: "You hate me. That is my crime."

At this point it is appropriate to provide a few hints concerning the conditioning factors of the Oedipus complex in childhood from the life of Alfieri (cf. Landau 1899 and Heyse's introduction to his translation of Alfieri). Unfortunately, the playwright's two-volume autobiography was unobtainable. In any case, his interest in the stepmother theme can be easily explained in that his father had married at the age of fifty-five (the old father!) a widow much younger than himself (the young mother!).

The father died after five years of marriage, however, before Vittorio was one year old. Only three years later, his mother married a man of her own age, with whom she lived happily for many years. The son is said never to have had any complaints concerning his stepfather. Alfieri loved his mother very much and was extremely devoted to her his whole life long. With loving words he dedicated to her his tragedy *Merope,* for which Voltaire's and Maffei's tragedies of the same name served as models, as a tragedy of motherly love. Characteristic of incestuous tendencies is that in the tragedy Aegisthus, the son of Merope, kills Polyphontes, who has ambitions for the throne, only after the latter also begins to court Merope. Polyphontes had already killed Aegisthus's father and brothers, but the son takes revenge only when Polyphontes also wishes to marry Aegisthus's mother. Alfieri's preference for "the mother"—for another man's wife—is also expressed in that in 1777, at age twenty-eight, the playwright fell in love with an older woman, Louise the countess of Albany, wife of the pretender to the English throne, Charles Edward Stuart. He lived with her, after a lengthy interruption, until his death in 1803. There will be further discussion of Alfieri's incestuous tendencies and their expression in his works below. At this point it will suffice to mention briefly his works reflecting, to a greater or lesser degree, the incest complex—especially opposition to the father (tyrannicide). Like Schiller, he wrote a *Conspiracy of the Pazzis,* two books concerning tyranny (cf. Schiller's *Geschichte der Rebellionen* [History of rebellions]), and a *Maria Stuart.* Further, among other works, he wrote two Brutus dramas and the tragedy *Agamemnone.*

The German playwright Friedrich Fouqué (1777–1843), inspired by Schiller, also wrote a tragedy *Don Carlos, Infant von Spanien* [Don Carlos, infante of Spain]. In this work the playwright favors the father's point of view, siding with Philip. Unfortunately this rare book (1823) was unavailable, but we can present a few excerpts from Koch's introduction to an edition of some of Fouqué's works in Joseph Kürschner's collection *Deutsche National-Literatur* [German national literature]. Koch writes: "We do not know the extent to which 'the marvelously beautiful and charming mother' (Fouqué's words), the first German in an old French noble family, affected her son's literary sense. The characters Otto von Trautwangen (in *Der Zauberring* [The enchanted ring]), Alwin, and Sintram demonstrate special devotion to their mothers, allowing one to deduce the nature of the playwright's own 'most tender devotion to his lovely little mother' (cf. Fouqué, *Poems,* 3:280, "Das Bild der Mutter" [The mother's image]). A theme observed in the story 'Sintram' and in the novella *Rosaura und ihre Verwandten* [Rosaura and her relatives], 'a terrible dream' whose memory for years fills the dreamer with terror, reflects an experience from the playwright's own childhood." Koch seems to have gained information from Fouqué's autobiography (1840), which unfortunately was also unavailable. His love for his mother is also suggested in that he became seriously ill owing to the pain and anxiety brought about by her death at the end of 1788. His relationship with his second wife, Karoline von Briest, also suggests this. She was much older than he was, and he had already fallen in love with her as a boy (just as he had fallen in love with his mother). Nevertheless, she first married another man (just as the mother had already done, the father having of course claimed her before the boy could). When she finally married Fouqué, she said she had been widowed, but others state that she had been divorced before marrying Fouqué. If that were the case, in marrying her, Fouqué would have experienced a delayed fulfillment of his infantile wish to reclaim his beloved from the man who had taken her from him (the father). This could be considered a real-life fulfillment of the childhood fantasy depicted in his Carlos drama.

In conclusion, we should also mention (cf. Minor) the Carlos dramas of Montalván, Russell, Rose (*Carlos and Elizabeth,* 1802), and Mercier, who handled the plot in fifty-two uninterrupted scenes. G. Döring also wrote the tragedy *Posa* (1821).

Byron's *Parisina*

The material Byron addressed in his narrative poem *Parisina* also belongs to the Carlos schema. The poem was written in 1815 during the short period when Byron lived with his wife.

In his introduction Byron says, "The following poem is grounded on a circumstance mentioned in Gibbon's *Antiquities of the House of Brunswick.* I am aware that in modern times, the delicacy or fastidiousness of the reader may deem such subjects unfit for the purposes of poetry. The Greek dramatists, and some of the best of our old English writers, were of a different opinion: as Alfieri and Schiller have also been, more recently, upon the Continent. The following extract will explain the facts on which the story is founded. The name of *Azo* is substituted for Nicholas, as more metrical. Under the reign of Nicholas III, Ferrara was polluted with a domestic tragedy. By the testimony of a maid, and his own observation, the Marquis of Este discovered the incestuous love of his wife Parisina, and Hugo his bastard son, a beautiful and valiant youth. They were beheaded in the castle by the sentence of a father and husband, who published his shame, and survived their execution. He was unfortunate if they were guilty; if they were innocent, he was still more unfortunate; nor is there any possible situation in which I can sincerely approve the last act of the justice of a parent" (Byron 1966, 6:503).

Byron's fear of offending his contemporaries with this sensitive material and his reference to earlier writers result from a deep psychological confusion of the material with its mode of presentation, for Byron deals with sexual relationships far less openly than did earlier writers. Rather, owing to the advancement of repression, he handles them much more discreetly. He dispenses with the amorous relationship of Hugo and Parisina in a few lines, treating the sexual element so superficially that, just as he intended, one could by no means assume that the relationship was in fact a sexual one. Immediately thereafter, he mentions incestuous dreams (Byron 1966, 6:509):

> And Hugo is gone to his lonely bed,
> To covet there another's bride;
> But she must lay her conscious head
> A husband's trusting heart beside.
> But fevered in her sleep she seems,
> And red her cheek with troubled dreams.

On the other hand, Byron develops the discovery of the attachment and the punishment (defense mechanisms) extensively. The punishment of Hugo and Parisina constitutes almost the total content of the poem. Parisina betrays herself in a dream by whispering Hugo's name. Nor is the theme of the abduction of the bride by the father absent here as a defense mechanism and justification of the son. Hugo says to the father (Byron 1966, 6:516):

> 'Tis true that I have done thee wrong—
> But wrong for wrong:—this,—deemed thy bride,
> The other victim of thy pride,—
> Thou know'st for me was destined long.

Psychological confirmation from Byron's life of the incestuous tendency expressed in the poem happens to present itself in the peculiar relationship of the poet to his mother. But we must first reemphasize our basic discussion of the connection of experience and literature. We certainly will not underestimate the effects of the author's experiences upon his works. But compared with childhood experiences and impressions and their unconscious traces and emotional effects, which no one has previously considered, all subsequent experiences are relevant only insofar as they awaken and revitalize those childhood experiences. Furthermore, the discovery of an actual experience precisely corresponding to an event portrayed in a literary work—for example, the discovery of an actual incestuous liaison—should by no means always be taken as the only proof for the correctness of an interpretation relating the work to the author's life. Indeed, this rare coincidence seems to lead to the false assumption that it must ordinarily be possible to assume an actual event in the life of the author precisely corresponding to the contents of the literary work. Instead, let us reiterate that in literature we are dealing with the expression of repressed and thus unconscious feelings, emotions, and fantasies that in real life can be represented only in a distorted form dependent on societal factors. With Byron, it will in this sense be necessary to bring actual events in the poet's life into the discussion of literary interpretations. This will allow us to gain a psychological understanding of the extended consequences of his relationship with his mother.

Byron was the only child of his father's second marriage, to Catherine Gordon of Gight. He was born in the third year of this marriage (1788). From his first marriage, his father also had a daughter, Augusta. The father, who because of his eccentric tendencies and wanton wastefulness was called "Mad Jack," died three years after Byron's birth (1791). Byron's mother moved with him to Aberdeen, Scotland, while Augusta was raised in the home of her grandmother, the widowed countess of Holdernesse. Since the father had left the family with very little money, the mother was forced to finance her son's education herself. Until the age of ten, he was always with his mother. Then he entered school at Harrow, while his mother moved to Nottingham, where he still visited her frequently, especially during holidays. The following letter, addressed to his beloved half-sister, Augusta, dates from his last year at Harrow (1804):

> You say that you shall write to the Dowager soon: her address is at Southwell, *that* I need hardly inform you. Now, Augusta, I am going to tell you a secret, perhaps I shall appear undutiful to you, but, believe me, my affection for you is founded on a more firm basis. My mother has lately behaved to me in such an eccentric manner, that so far from feeling the affection of a Son, it is with difficulty I can restrain my dislike. . . . She is so hasty, so impatient, that I dread the approach of the holidays, more than most boys do their return from them. In former days she spoilt me; now she is altered to the contrary; for the most trifling thing, she upbraids me in a most outrageous manner. (Byron 1966, 1:43)

The following week he wrote to his sister once again:

> But she has an excellent opinion of her personal attractions, sinks her age a good six years, avers that when I was born she was only eighteen, when you, my dear Sister, know as well as I know that she was of age when she married my father, and that I was not born for three years afterwards. . . . But I am now coming to what must shock you, as much as it does me, when she has occasion to lecture me . . . she does not do it in a manner that commands respect, and in an impressive style. . . . She flies into a fit of phrenzy, upbraids me as if I was the most undutiful wretch in existence, rakes up the ashes of my *father*, abuses him, says I shall be a true Byrrone, which is the worst epithet she can invent. Am I to call this woman mother? (Byron 1966, 1:46)

His aversion toward his mother is also expressed in various other letters, in very insistent terms. This exaggerated emphasis on his disinclination toward his mother is of great psychological significance. To explain it, we must refer to an empirical result of Freud's psychology of neurosis already emphasized earlier. If sexual inclination toward someone is repressed for some reason, it expresses itself as hatred or disinclination toward that person. As we shall see confirmed in our investigation of the Phaedra theme, unrequited love is especially subject to being transformed into hatred. On the other hand, an individual who unconsciously hates someone but who rejects this emotion or is unable to express it will in real life treat that person with tenderness or kindness. This is the case with Byron. He writes that his mother originally spoiled him, and in that period Byron probably felt no animosity toward her. As the son grows older, a mother must of course reduce her need for affection toward him, lest her attachment to her son lose its innocent character. If the coddling of the child reveals a neurotic tendency in the mother, this supposition is further supported in that she was not able to reduce her need for affection in a satisfactory manner but instead, as Byron writes, replaced it with the opposite emotion. Although the son's infantile incest tendencies normally undergo repression with the passage of time, this process was in Byron's case emphasized and accelerated in an unpleasant manner by his mother's growing aversion toward him. Thus the mother's disinclination toward the son can be attributed to her hysteria, while the son's disinclination toward the mother can be attributed to her rejection of his love.

But in other respects, too, Byron's relationship with his mother illustrates several neurotic traits. The fear of being with the person one loves, while simultaneously rejecting this love (hatred), is a defense mechanism familiar from the psychology of neurosis. Byron feared the approach of the holidays and spending time with his mother. This is a reaction to the experiences of early childhood, for while she still coddled him, he was certainly glad to be with her. The mother's understatement of her own age and her pride in her youthful appearance arise from the unconscious wish to be more like the son, while Byron's denunciation of her little lie arises from his own defense mechanisms. We are already familiar with the reduction of the mother's age as an important basic element of the stepmother problem, and this experience from Byron's personal life perhaps explains why he was attracted to Parisina, Hugo's stepmother, who was claimed by the father to the son's detriment. By seducing other men's wives, Byron, like Richard Wagner, avenged himself later in life for the way his mother, the wife of another man (the father), withdrew from him during his childhood. After his unsuccessful marriage to a young woman who had had many suitors, Byron fled to Italy, where he struck up and maintained a number of romantic liaisons, mostly with married women—in accordance with the local custom, according to Byron. There were affairs with Marianna, the young wife of his landlord, with Margarita, the wife of a baker, and with the Countess Guiccioli, whom he met three days after she was married to the sixty-year-old count. He eventually won her from the count after bitter struggles with the old man ("father").

His disguised erotic affection and his jealousy with regard to his mother also reveal themselves in his hatred of her supposed lover (the "father"). In the letter to his sister of November 11, 1804, quoted above, he remarks in this connection: "She is so very strenuous, and so tormenting in her entreaties and commands, with regard to my reconciliation, with that detestable Lord G. that I suppose she has a penchant for his Lordship; but I am confident that he does not return it ⟨Byron's wish!⟩, for he rather dislikes her than otherwise, at least as far as I can judge" (Byron 1966, 1:46).

Typical of the mother's neurotic character is the way, often mentioned by Byron, his mother was wont to upbraid him for the slightest offense—out of proportion to the nature of the infraction. This "displacement of psychic intensity" (Freud) from an affectionate relationship to an indifferent one is a basic principle of the psychology of neurosis. In everyday life it happens only too often that an individual flies into a rage, out of proportion to the immediate stimulus. In every person there are a number of repressed feelings of hatred and anger that may explode simultaneously, given an apparently innocuous stimulus. The conscious distortion and concealment of Byron's aversion toward his mother, which we have previously assumed, and which reveals itself in his exaggerated emphasis on his inimical feelings, is directly conceded in his letters. On November 2, 1808, he wrote to his mother: "If you please, we will forget the things you mention. I have no desire to remember them. When my rooms are finished, I shall be happy to see you; as I tell but the truth, you will not suspect me of evasion" (Byron 1966, 1:194). Toward the end of the same month, however, he writes to Augusta: "I am living here *alone*, which suits my inclinations better than society of any kind. Mrs. Byron I have shaken off for two years, and I shall not resume her yoke in future, I am afraid my disposition will suffer in your estimation; but I never can forgive that woman, or breathe in comfort under the same roof" (Byron 1966, 1:203).

This flight from his mother (from the love for his mother), is of course one of the sources of his wanderlust, which stayed with him his whole life. During the school holidays of 1806, at the age of eighteen, he had already fled from his mother in Southwell to London, "since it had come to threatening scenes between her and her son" (Jessen 1906, 24). Three years later he began the great journey that brought him to Gibraltar, Malta, Constantinople, Athens, and so on, keeping him away from home for two years. He left without bidding his mother farewell and wrote to her, among other things: "The world is all before me, and I leave England without regret, and without a wish to revisit any thing it contains, except *yourself*, and your present residence" (Byron 1966, 1:225). Considering Byron's disinclination to spend time with his mother, we will most likely interpret this statement correctly by assuming that it means the opposite—that Byron wanted to see everything in his fatherland again except his mother. In fact, capricious fate fulfilled this wish. "In the beginning of July 1811, Byron landed in Portsmouth. In London, toward the end of July, he received news of the illness of his mother and left immediately for Newstead. Shortly before his arrival, she suddenly died" (Jessen 1906, 64). One almost has the paradoxical impression that his mother deliberately died just before his arrival to avoid the undesired reunion. For just like the son, the mother also hoped that they would never see one another again. In the mother's case, however, defense against this wish led to self-reproach, which expressed itself in the superstitious fear that she would never again see her son. Jessen (1906, 64) remarks: "During her son's long journey, Byron's mother on several occasions experienced superstitious emotional crises characterized by the belief that she would never again see her son." Of course this superstition was only an expression of her wish not to see her son (her fear of not seeing him), while the psychic counterimpulse, the original and now unconscious (repressed) love for her son reacted with an emotional crisis in the face of this obsession. This transformation of a rejected wish into the superstitious fear of its fulfillment is typical of the mechanisms of obsessional neurosis, and we will also come across it in our explanation of Karl Grillparzer's obsession (chap. 14). It is due to repression through a "reactive complex." The extent to which the poet's aversion toward his mother was reactive, concealing his disappointed love for her, is indicated by the affectionate tones that, despite manifest animosity, appeared upon her death, as reflected in Byron's letter to Pigot (August 2, 1811): "Now I feel the whole truth—that we can have only one mother."

Given this unhappy love for his mother, we are in a position to understand not only the literary fantasy function of *Parisina* but also Byron's unhappy marriage, which was only a repetition of his relationship with his mother. Initially he loved his wife, but he soon felt such animosity toward her that a final break was inevitable. And just as he had fled from his mother, Byron again fled abroad to escape his wife, never again to set foot on his "motherland."

One portion of a letter Byron sent from Verona to his friend Moore (1815) seems especially indicative of the characteristics of psychic processes and of the temporary predominance of certain psychological complexes. This passage is significant in that it was written in the same year *Parisina*, Byron's mother-incest poem, made its appearance. He writes: "The state of morals in these parts is in some sort lax. A mother and son were pointed out at the theatre, as being pronounced by the Milanese world to be of the Theban dynasty—but this was all. The narrator (one of the first men in Milan) seemed to be not sufficiently scandalized by the taste or the tie ⟨Oedipus and Jocasta⟩" (Byron 1966, 3:385).

As suggested by his journals, Byron seems to have himself suspected that the source of his later neurotic sufferings was to be found in his childhood. The early onset of his passions eventually led, as far as we can now surmise, to neurosis. He was already leading a "wild, eccentric life" in Harrow (identification with the father). His marital conflicts have a manifestly neurotic character, and his flights from all painful things at home—his passion for travel—were clearly neurotic in origin. Finally, though, during his last year of life, two months before his death, Byron suffered an apparently hysterical collapse in Missolonghi. He writes in his diary: "Upon February 15 . . . I had a strong shock of a convulsive description, but whether Epileptic, Paralytic, or Apoplectic, is not yet decided by the two medical men, who attend me. . . . It was very painful. . . . I was speechless with the features much distorted, but *not* foaming at the mouth, they say. . . . It lasted about ten minutes, and came on immediately after drinking a tumbler of Cider mixed with cold water. . . . I never heard that any of my family were liable to the same, though my mother was subject to hysterical affections" (Byron 1966, 6:323–24).

The comment that his mother suffered from hysteria fully confirms our interpretation of her relationship with her son and justifies the psychological conclusions we have made, and whose significance was, of course, not clear to the poet at the time he wrote these words.

The Theme of Abduction of the Bride and Relinquishment of the Bride

To the Carlos schema belongs also Jean Racine's *Mithridate* (1673), simultaneously a further demonstration of the playwright's incestuous stirrings and a limiting case, approaching the Phaedra schema. Mithridates' two sons by different mothers, Xiphares and Pharnaces, both love Monime, their father's betrothed. Fearing their father, they conceal their passions until emboldened by the sudden news of his death (the unconscious wish of the sons):

Xiphares: I love her and will no longer conceal it,
Since now my only rival is my brother.

As is evident, hatred of the father is combined here with rivalry with the brother—a complication whose psychological basis will become clear only in part 2 of this work. Even at this point, however, it is clear that after the death of the father the brother replaces him as a competitor for the mother's love. In the same way, in the son's affections, the sister begins to take the place of the rejected and aging mother (cf. Byron). But Xiphares justifies his right to Monime's hand through the familiar theme of abduction of the bride by the father:

> My father was still ignorant even of
> Monime's name when I already glowed
> With pure passion for her.

The son now becomes firm in his desire to take from the father the father's bride (the mother). Monime too loves her future stepson Xiphares. Still, when asked by her slave whether she has revealed her love to him, she answers:

> He still knows nothing; the gods have
> Helped me; boldly struggling with myself,
> I told him nothing, or only half a word.

Soon, though, the false announcement of the father's death is retracted—a detail we will also encounter in the Phaedra schema. Indeed, Monime's whole character approaches that observed in the Phaedra complex. For when Mithridates, believing that he has been betrayed only by Pharnaces, leaves Xiphares to stand guard over Monime, she reveals to Xiphares her love for him but subsequently attempts to avoid him. Upon returning from the land "from whose bourn no traveller returns," Mithridates grows suspicious of his sons, whom he finds, despite his orders to the contrary, with Monime. He is filled with jealous hatred and says to Arbates:

> You see me
> Always burning with one love.
> This heart, nourished by blood, thirsting for battle,
> In defiance of the weight of years and fate,
> Carries everywhere Monime's bonds
> And hates with glowing ire, above all enemies,
> Two thankless sons remaining here.

Mithridates tricks Monime into revealing her love for Xiphares. Realizing she has been fooled, she pushes away Mithridates' hand and openly declares her passion for her future stepson. But she finds offensive the thought of being courted by Pharnaces, the older brother, and expresses her fear of patricide and fratricide:

> Shall I live,
> Shall I wait until Pharnaces, drenched
> With their heartblood, supported by the

> Roman throng, the cruel lust of
> Patricide and fratricide still in his eyes,
> Appears here before me?

Soon, however, Mithridates really does meet his death. Dying, he betroths his betrothed, Monime, to his son Xiphares. Thus the son's wishes are completely fulfilled here; the father, albeit dying, relinquishes the bride (the mother) to the son. But this fulfillment comes only at the cost of displaced incestuous feelings, dampened because Monime is first of all not the physical mother of Xiphares and second, is not even his actual stepmother, since she had never married the father but had only been betrothed to him. This extensive dampening, this "censorship" of incestuous feelings is, however, the necessary precondition for complete fulfillment of the wish, which does not hesitate to buy the mother's love (the love of the father's bride or betrothed) with the father's death. Still, this occurs not through patricide, as in *Oedipus*, but—though the son has wished for it—more innocently, through external causes. Thus the son avoids the need to commit undesirable acts.

Indeed, the rejection of hatred toward the father goes so far that the relinquishment of the wife to the son, motivated by the father's death, seems to result from this rejection. Behind this double distortion (dampening), which features voluntary relinquishment rather than patricide and violent conquest of the "mother," and which involves the father's betrothed in the place of the physical mother, the tendency toward fulfillment of the original incest wishes, in connection with the examples discussed above, is clearly recognizable. The theme of relinquishment of the bride, without the subsequent dampening, is contained in Appianos's tale of the Syrian king Antiochus, the son of Seleucus, who falls in love with Stratonice, his father's wife. He keeps his emotional sufferings to himself, becomes ill, and lies in bed sick and weak, though without pain. However, the doctor, Eristratus, tricks him into revealing his love and convinces the father to relinquish his wife to his son. This tale of Antiochus's love for his young stepmother, Stratonice, related also by Plutarch, was treated more extensively by Matteo Bandello. In 1566 William Painter translated this work into English. Petrarch also related the tale in *Trionfo d'amore* [Triumph of love].

A similar treatment of the same theme is found in Pierre Corneille's *Rodogune,* which Lessing sharply criticizes in his *Hamburgische Dramaturgie* [Hamburg dramaturgy]. After the death of Demetrius, both his sons fall in love with Rodogune, their father's betrothed; this is purely the invention of the playwright. The playwright contrasts their rivalry over Rodogune with their rivalry over the throne, which their mother, Cleopatra, promises to whichever of the two murders her rival, Rodogune. Rodogune, however, learns of the threat and in turn promises her hand to whichever of the two murders Cleopatra.

It can hardly be more clearly stated that in their rivalry over the father's betrothed, the two brothers are really competing for the mother. Lessing's remark concerning Rodogune's age illustrates how this incest fantasy of the relinquishment of the bride to the son influences the historical material:

> Corneille was able to change the historical circumstances just as he saw fit. He could, for example, make Rodogune as young as he wished. And Voltaire is very wrong when he calculates that Rodogune could not have been so young. Voltaire claims that she married Demetrius when the two princes, who were at least twenty at the time of his death, were in their childhood. Of what concern is that to the playwright? Corneille's Rodogune never married Demetrius. She was very young at the time the father wanted to marry her, and not much older when the sons fell in love with her. Voltaire's historical exactitude is insufferable. He should stick to verification of the data in his general history of the world.

This theme of relinquishment of the bride to the son is the exact psychological opposite of the theme of abduction of the bride by the father. This latter theme corresponds to the typical childhood fantasy that although the father has claimed the mother for himself, she was actually meant for the son and is herself dedicated to him. In his ninth book of histories, Herodotus relates one version of the realization of such a fantasy in later life. This is the story of Xerxes, who fell in love with the wife of his brother Masistes. Since she herself was not attracted to him, however, and since he hesitated to take his brother's wife by force, he developed an unusual plan. "He married his son Darius to the daughter of this woman and Masistes in the hope of winning her over sooner . . . and took the wife of Darius (his own son) into his own house; he then lost interest in the wife of Masistes, for his affections changed, and he fell in love with Darius's wife, the daughter of Masistes, and won her over." But his own wife, Amestris, discovered the affair and, assuming that Masistes' wife was responsible for the affair, cruelly maimed her. Before Masistes had time to muster the Baktrian forces and do battle against his brother, he and his sons were murdered at Xerxes' command.

The relinquishment of the bride simultaneously provides fulfillment and revenge for the fantasy of the abduction of the bride. According to Storfer (1911, 17), such themes are frequently to be found in the works of the Russian writer Maksim Gorky: "Here mention should be made of his stories 'Malva,' 'On the Raft,' and especially 'Tartarenchan and his Son.'

In the first story, the son falls in love with his father's beloved. The second story centers on the love of a stepfather and stepdaughter (abduction of the bride: the opposite of the first story). In the last story the son, having returned home victorious, demands from his father the father's beautiful favorite slave."

Der heilige Kuss [The holy kiss], a recently published Renaissance drama by Paul Altholf (1911), involves a similar theme. The son, whose identity has only just been revealed, seduces his father's young wife. Upon the advice of an astrologer, the father renounces the woman and permits her to marry his son, but soon thereafter he has the son killed.

In the works of the Elizabethan playwrights, who as contemporaries and immediate successors of Shakespeare were almost completely under his influence, the themes of abduction of the bride and relinquishment of the bride, arising from the parent complex, are indispensable elements. In *Hamlet* they had already found their highest artistic and highest neurotic expression. We should mention a few works influenced by *Hamlet,* for example, John Marston's *Antonio's Revenge,* based upon a son's revenge on his mother's second husband, the murderer of his father. The central theme of Thomas Kyd's *The Spanish Tragedie* also seems related: a father takes vengeance on his son's murderers (Koeppel 1895, 21). Mention should also be made of Cyril Tourneur's *The Revenger's Tragedy,* where the bastard Spurio hates his father the duke and his legitimate brother and courts the duchess. One is reminded of the fate of Gloucester and his sons in *King Lear* (Koeppel 1895, 39).

The theme of relinquishment of the bride is found in Francis Beaumont and John Fletcher's *Monsieur Thomas*. Valentine, a rich man who is no longer young, returns to London after a long journey accompanied by the young Francisco, whom he has met during his travels and warmly befriended. Valentine is betrothed to his ward, Cellide, who is glad to become his wife despite the difference in their ages. The young foreigner falls in love with her. He carefully conceals his emotions so as not to spoil the happiness of his mentor, but his torment is so great that he becomes gravely ill. An uninvolved friend guesses the nature of his ailment and informs Valentine. The latter relinquishes the young woman to the young man and is rewarded for his sacrifice by discovering that Francisco is his son, long believed dead (Koeppel 1895, 96). Further, in John Marston's *Parisitaster, or The Fawne,* Tiberio, son of the duke of Ferrara, is sent to the court of the duke of Urbino to request for his father the hand of the Princess Dulcimel. She likes the son better than the father, however, and uses her own father as matchmaker, as in Boccaccio (3.3). The duke of Ferrara, who has followed his son to Urbino in disguise, finally gives his consent to the marriage (Koeppel 1895, 27).

This theme of the son who seeks a bride for his father but wins her for himself is a typical product of the incest fantasy. We have encountered it already in Lope de Vega's Carlos drama and will encounter it again in the Ermanaric-Swanhild saga (chap. 5). Further, the story of Combabus gives the impression of complete freedom from the incest complex but nevertheless reveals a connection with it. In Lucian's essay "Peri tes Syries theou" [On the Syrian god], the handsome Combabus is accused of committing adultery with the wife of the king and is condemned to death. In the last hour he is able to prove his innocence, for he had castrated himself upon being named traveling bodyguard of the young queen Stratonice. This unusual caution on the part of the suitor, who anticipates subsequent suspicion, cannot in this form be regarded as a basic theme. Nor can the absence of kinship between Combabus and the king be regarded as such, for we have so often seen the son (and sometimes the stepson or nephew) seek the hand of the bride for his father and then take her from him. I am unfamiliar with the sources of Lucian's tale, but the name of the beloved woman, Stratonice, suggests the story of Antiochus's love for his young stepmother, Stratonice, related by Plutarch, in which the father yields the woman to the son. But the theme of relinquishment of the bride to the son seems to be nothing more than a sentimental transformation of the son's original bride-abduction fantasy, which is usually punished with the castration of the son for the forbidden sexual act. We will deal with this in the section on the castration complex (chap. 9).

The theme of the nephew who seeks the hand of the bride for the uncle but wins her for himself while she is under his protection underlies the Tristan saga. It is observed also in Philip Massinger's drama *The Great Duke of Florence*, based on an older drama, *A Knacke to Knowe a Knave*, whose plot involves a simple dramatization of the Edgar saga. The good king Edgar sends his nephew Ethenwald to request (for the king) the hand of Alfrida. Ethenwald is enchanted by her beauty and spontaneously marries her himself, telling the king that the girl would not have been worthy of him. But Edgar soon discovers the truth and forgives them. As the Ermanaric saga shows (see below), this dampened formulation is also based on the kinship of father and son. In Massinger's drama this is still suggested in the fact that the nephew, Giovanni, is heir to the ducal crown (Koeppel 1895, 117). The Tristan saga, which has come down to us in a late form, still reminds one of "myth of the birth of the hero" genre and incestuous family dramas in that Tristan originally serves incognito at the court of his uncle, who then sends him to ask for the hand of Isolde, and in the theme of the substitution of the bride. The relation of this theme to the incest complex will be discussed below (chap. 11). In the wedding night with Marke, Brengäne, Isolde's trusted companion, substitutes for Isolde, who has already given herself to Tristan.

In George Chapman's *The Gentleman Usher,* this typical fantasy of the son finds a form reminiscent of the theme of abduction of the bride by the father but ends with the sentimental relinquishment of the bride to the son. Duke Alphonso courts Margareta, the daughter of Count Lasso, but without success; the young girl loves his son, Prince Vincentio. This provokes the jealousy of the old duke; his jealousy is also stirred up by his unworthy protégé Medice, who hates the prince. The lovers are taken by surprise, Vincentio is gravely wounded by Medice, and Margareta is so distressed by the false news of the death of her lover that she stabs herself. The doctor heals Vincentio and Margareta, and the repentant duke unites the lovers in marriage (Koeppel 1895, 8). Chapman may have recalled the basic plot of his comedy from an older play, published in 1600 and recently attributed to George Peele, *The Wisdome of Doctor Dodypoll.* Alphonso, duke of Saxony, loves the young Hyanthe, but she loves his son, Prince Alberdune, and is loved by him. In this older work, too, the young lovers ultimately prevail, and the father must yield to the son (Koeppel 1895, 221).

The fantasy of the father's abduction of the bride or beloved (mother or stepmother), also typical of the incest complex, is observed in John Ford's *The Lover's Melancholy.* The beautiful Eroclea must flee her homeland because the old prince, the father of her beloved, seeks her hand in marriage. The young prince Palador becomes despondent, and Eroclea comes to his court dressed as a man. There, after many complications, everything is resolved (Koeppel 1895, 172). In Beaumont and Fletcher's *The Humorous Lieutenant,* Celia, the daughter of King Seleucus, wins the heart of Prince Demetrius. She is a prisoner of war; her true identity has not been revealed. But the father of the prince desires her for himself. At first he desires her only as a lover, but later he even offers her the crown (Koeppel 1895, 83). In *Cupid's Revenge,* by the same authors, one finds a tale from Philip Sidney's *Arcadia.* The son of the king of Iberia has an affair with the frivolous wife of a bourgeois gentleman. The king finds the two together. To protect her, the son pleads her innocence and virtue so eloquently that the old king wishes to win this unusual woman for himself and finally makes her queen. She attempts to continue her punishable liaison with her stepson but is rejected by him. Through her calumny and intrigues, the son is forced to flee for his life (Koeppel 1895, 46).

If in this guise, which differs greatly from the original form of the fantasy, we find the theme of abduction of the bride by the father associated with the forbidden love between stepmother and stepson, here placed back in time before the marriage to the father, further-reaching combinations and complications of theme are found in the play *The Costlie Whore*, by an unknown author. The duke of Saxony notices a woman's glove his son has found in the street. His son, Prince Frederick, discovers that the courtesan Valentia is the owner, and the duke marries her despite his son's protest. The prince takes up arms against his father and succeeds in taking Valentia prisoner. His father falls at his feet and begs him to release her, which he does, but then the prince is taken prisoner himself. The duke signs the death warrant and gives the document to his wife to do with as she pleases. Valentia wishes to grant the prisoner his life in exchange for his love. Frederick rejects her with derision. She has the goblet of poison administered to him and brings his body before the duke. Fatherly love has awakened in him, though too late, and he turns from Valentia in anger and disgust. Then Frederick, who had been given only a sleeping potion, rises, and the duke abdicates the throne in his favor. A novel by Greene, *Saturn's Tragedy* (1605), a novelization of a simple, short account by Aelianus, is cited by Koeppel as the source. Aelianus's account concerns the story of King Psammetichus, to whom the shoe of the courtesan Rhodope is brought by an eagle. He has her sought after throughout the realm and makes her his wife. In Greene's version, Philarces, the son of Psammetichus, is deeply offended to see a whore in the place of his deceased mother. In vain he seeks to dissuade the king from the marriage. Once crowned, Rhodope falls in love with her stepson, and Philarces too yields to temptation. The old king surprises the guilty pair and kills them (Koeppel 1895, 201). This example clearly illustrates the treatment of the incest theme and its dampening by the various adapters of a historical theme. Although with Aelianus, who knew the original meaning of the tale, there is no incest theme whatever, Greene depicts the stepmother's love for the son with a tragic conclusion; in the drama inspired by Greene's novel, the Phaedra schema is adopted and we see a shift toward the sentimental. As we know, the representation of the father's spouse as a whore corresponds to the son's erotic fantasies at puberty when he has become aware of the sexual relations of his parents.

The Phaedra Schema: The Psychology of Literary Adaptation

In contrast to the Carlos schema, which deals with the stepson's passion for the stepmother, we have designated the opposite state of affairs, the stepmother's love for the unreceptive stepson, the Phaedra schema. We derive this designation from the Phaedra fable, which has often been adapted and strongly characterizes this type of plot. Our interest in this material is increased because Schiller, as is well known, translated Racine's *Phèdre* [*Phaedra*] into German. Given the two-sided, ambiguous character of all abnormal and all highly valued expressions of the psyche, it should not surprise us that the writer of *Don Carlos* (the expression of his defense mechanisms in the face of his unrealized incest wishes) should, after the resolution and partial displacement of his primary incest complex, and at the height of his creative power, produce *Phaedra* as a positive complement. The objection that this is not an original work by Schiller, revealing specific aspects of his own inner life, but is only a translation can be laid to rest since, as we have seen, the choice of already existing mythological or historical material does not take place haphazardly but is strictly conditioned by the total psychology of the writer. No one will question that in an original work the author's own psychic life is the only one reflected. But though this is less obvious, selecting works for translation and adaptation provides no less information. Even if Schiller's translation of *Phaedra* were the only symptomatic expression of his incestuous feelings we possessed, though we would have less evidence on which to base our conclusion that they existed, this conclusion would not be completely unreasonable. Since we have already proved the existence of his incestuous passions through a consideration of other works, however, we should not consider the *Phaedra* translation to have arisen by happenstance or for literary reasons alone. Instead, we should consider it too an expression of the incestuous tendencies already familiar to us. Therefore this coincidence will be valuable to us as a meaningful hint concerning the psychic nature of interest in given material per se. This also is relevant for the passive spectator.

Before attempting other proofs, we will certainly not seem too bold in stating that, in a psychological sense, translations and adaptations are in general as valuable as original works. That is, we will assume for them a determinate and multifaceted selection strategy much the same as for original works by the same author. But since the special form and the working procedure in translation, like all specific psychic activities or effects, exhibit unique characteristics, the distinct nature of original works versus translations must reflect a psychologically significant difference. As we can now anticipate, this difference is only a dynamic one; we can best conceive of it by observing its most extreme aspect, the spectator's relation to the creative artist. In the gratified spectator of a work of art, who thus "likes" the work, the same psychic impulses that drove its creator to artistic production are gratified much as in the experience of the creative artist himself. The only difference is that the artist must expend on his own the psychic energy providing these impulses with a means of expression, whereas the spectator, who has stronger (normal) inhibitions opposing these impulses, escapes the need to expend this psychic energy, since this has been done by the creative artist (cf. Rank 1907, 48).

With the creative artist, however, powerful defense mechanisms not infrequently arise in opposition to certain impulses. These mechanisms prevent the resolution and expression of these impulses, as happens in the passive spectator, who must await the independent stimulus of the work of art to experience release from his inhibitions and gratification of his repressed emotions. From the freely creating artist to the passive spectator, we must assume a single chain characterized by the same unconscious impulses and their release in the artistic work. The adapter and the translator constitute intermediate links in the chain. The effects of the artistic work are due to the same unconscious emotions that inspired the creative artist to produce it. (In the spectator these are more deeply repressed.) This provides an independent explanation of the enthusiastic reception and recognition the artistic work receives. This gratification of repressed infantile emotions leads to its favorable reception. But this aesthetic pleasure functions only as a preliminary stage (cf. Rank 1907, 48), making possible the release of more deeply rooted pleasurable emotions. The relation of the translator (or adapter) to his model is in a psychological sense quite similar to the relation of the spectator to the creative artist. If the writer, in attempting to satisfy his need for the release and artistic treatment of certain emotions, experiences powerful inner defense mechanisms that do not even permit him to identify with a historical figure, he will begin to feel that another writer's artistic expression of similar emotions is psychically his own. By identifying with another writer, he will attempt through adaptation to make the other writer's work truly his own. He can do this since, in contrast to the unproductive spectator, he requires only a small stimulus to bring his less repressed emotions into action.

Adaptation thus is an intermediate form—a compromise between inability to write the work on one's own (because of the strong defense mechanisms) and the creative artist's stronger means of reaction—he cannot obtain release simply through being a passive spectator. The writer creates the work in his own language (in the widest sense of the term). He also experiences it psychically, but the psychic energy necessary to conquer his inhibitions has already been expended for him by his predecessor. Now he need only identify with the latter. Here linguistic and formal interest and the enjoyment of the translation process serve as a preliminary pleasure inspiring the writer to further work but simultaneously promoting the attainment of the final pleasure, gained through the resolution of inhibitions.

With Schiller, as we have attempted to demonstrate, love for the mother, anchored in the unconscious, was disguised and repressed by powerful opposite impulses and substitute impulses (hatred of the father). In *Don Carlos,* the only completed drama by Schiller in which erotic affection for the mother is clearly expressed, nevertheless on the one hand defensive mechanisms are projected onto the mother, who is unreceptive, while on the other hand independent inhibiting factors arise (courtly ceremony, etc.). Schiller could not bring himself to portray on his own (cf. the *Agrippina* fragment) the corresponding positive wish fulfillment, as found in Racine's *Phaedra,* where the (step)mother approaches the son lovingly. He was able to do so only in the context of Racine's play and, as it were, take no responsibility for the work himself.

In Racine's drama the stepmother, Phaedra, confesses to her stepson, Hippolytus, her passionate affection for him, which she has attempted to resist (repress):

> *Phaedra:* To flee from you
> Was too little for me. I banished you!
> I wished to appear hatefully cruel to you.
> In order to resist you better, I courted
> Your hatred, but to no avail! You hated
> Me all the more, yet I loved you no less.
>
> (2.5)

Just as Phaedra seeks to stifle her own love through pretended hatred, Hippolytus's defense against his erotic affection for his stepmother is possible only at the cost of the opposite defense mechanism—hatred of her. In his case repressed love for the mother is transformed into hatred (cf. Byron). Similarly, Phaedra's love for her stepson, who rejects it, is later transformed into hatred. In both cases the impossibility of the gratification of these passions (in the one case owing to internal reasons and in the other case owing to external ones) is the reason for the transformation of affect, already familiar to us. Racine himself has Theseus make this point in a fine comment to his son, Hippolytus:

> The hated source
> Of your misogyny is clear.
> Only Phaedra moved your perverse heart—
> Your heart unmoved by licit love.

This remark expresses a correct psychological understanding of the mechanism of sexual rejection (in its stronger form—misogyny), which has its basis in the fixation of the libido on sexual objects from childhood, generally incestuous. That this is also the case with Hippolytus is proved by his relationship with Aricia, whom he loves only as a substitute for the mother, having displaced his incestuous feelings to the younger woman. When his father jealously confronts him with his suspicion [that he loves Phaedra], Hippolytus finally admits (4.2):

Here at your feet
I acknowledge my true sin: I love,
Oh, father, one whom you have forbidden me to love.
I am true to Aricia.

And elsewhere he declares:

I am preyed upon by a passion
That he condemns.

That this love too is opposed by the father and must be concealed from him is the common trait seen also in the erotic affection for one's (step)mother. Thus Aricia is revealed as the substitute for the (step)-mother. Further, he addresses Aricia as "queen," just as he does his (step)-mother. Indeed, the theme of succession to the throne is addressed here once again, though only in passing.

Hippolytus: Has she surpassed all other women
In beauty, or did I hope to gain your throne as well
As a dowry by abducting her? [from Rank's German version]
Let us not permit Phaedra, usurping our claims,
To banish us both from my father's throne
And to promise her own son the spoils. [same, from French text]

That his relationship with Aricia only reflects his relationship with the (step)mother is characteristically expressed in that he conceives of his love for Aricia as secret and forbidden and attempts to resist it, just as Phaedra attempts to resist her love for him.

Hippolytus: I, hate you, O queen? Whatever rumors
Are being spread about my pride, is it thought
That I was born to a tiger mother?
. . . .
You will then perhaps wish to learn of a secret
Which this heart can no longer contain.
. . . .

For six months already, tormented, torn
By shame and anguish, I have carried this arrow in my heart.
In vain, I resist you, resist myself.
I flee you where you are: I find you where you are absent.

By making a secret of his love for Aricia, he lets the suspicion arise that he is guilty of incest; and in a later scene, he says with reference to his love for Aricia [and his silence regarding Phaedra's love for him]:

> Should I mercilessly reveal
> The shame of his bed, and color the forehead
> Of my father with unworthy blush?
> You alone have perceived the terrible secret.
> To you and to the gods I can now confess.
> From you I could not conceal what I wished
> To conceal from myself. Judge whether I love you!

But just as Hippolytus loves his (step)mother in Aricia, in Hippolytus Phaedra loves the more beautiful image of his father. She says to her (step)son:

> Indeed, my lord, I yearn, I burn for Theseus;
> I love Theseus, but not the one
> Black Acheron saw,
> The flattering suitor of all women,
> The abductor who descended
> To desecrate the shadow king's bed.
> I see him true, I see him proud, even
> A bit shy. I see him young and beautiful
> And charming, winning all hearts,
> As one imagines the gods, as I
> See you!

This frank statement, as well as Phaedra's hints of her love for the (step)son (2.5), is possible only because Theseus is believed dead, corresponding to the wish for the absence of the father. But even then it is not possible without Phaedra's involving her nurse Oenone and without the expression of defense (3.1):

> *Phaedra:* Alas, I have revealed myself too openly,
> Daring to disclose my wild wish;
> I have said what none should ever hear!

With the "miraculous" return of Theseus, believed dead (wished dead), from the underworld (cf. the "ghost" of Hamlet's father), this defense is transformed into glowing hatred toward the (step)son. In accordance with the wishes of her mistress, Oenone slanders the son, telling his father that Hippolytus, impassioned by forbidden love, seeks to possess the queen. This fantasy corresponds to the appearance of the son's aggressive feelings toward the mother. Here we encounter a remarkable trait, which will also turn out to be a typical one. Counter to all expectations one might have concerning the relationship of father and son, Theseus, feeling no doubt whatever concerning this slander, is immediately seized by suspicion:

> After your wicked passion
> Has dared approach your father's bed,
> You rashly show your hated head?

Psychologically, this strange twist is very correctly motivated. The father is able to accept this terrible suspicion so easily since he has so long harbored it unconsciously—because the suspicion merely reflects his secret fears. Oenone, therefore, correctly proceeds from the "prior opinion of his father" (3.3). In his suddenly awakened hatred toward his son, Theseus calls down the curse of Neptune upon him. Indeed, this curse is realized with terrible consequences. As in *Don Carlos,* the father kills the son only indirectly, by cursing him, having himself earlier been thought dead. Thus, just as the son wishes for the father's absence, he dies through his father's wish. After Hippolytus's death, Phaedra admits the accusation was false and confesses her criminal affection for her husband's son. Then she takes poison, thus dying together with the son (as in Alfieri's *Philip*), a symbol of sexual union that was already impossible in Schiller's *Don Carlos.*

It will now be of great interest to pursue the advance of repression from Euripides' *Hippolytus* to Racine's *Phaedra.* In Euripides' drama, the actual father (as in *Don Carlos*) always stands between mother and son, who never even express their feelings to each other. The external impediments are thus abundant here, for the internal ones are not yet powerful enough on their own to prevent the repressed impulses from expressing themselves. In Racine's drama, on the other hand, the internal impediments are already so great that in spite of the absence of the father (his death) and the receptiveness of the (step)mother, actual incest does not occur. Further, in Euripides' drama Aricia, freely invented by Racine—the woman onto whom Hippolytus displaces his affections for his stepmother—is absent. Yet Hippolytus is portrayed as a misogynist. This can be attributed to a certain form of defense against his erotic affection for his (step)mother. With the progressive increase in repression observed in the works of the great authors, the internal defense mechanisms become stronger, and the (step)mother becomes more receptive to her (step)son (the son's wish). Accordingly, the external impediments can become weaker without danger that the repressed impulses will express themselves.

That the crux of the Phaedra problem is the (step)mother's freer or more inhibited relations with the son is further substantiated by other adaptations of this material. Most significantly, Euripides himself wrote two tragedies with the title *Hippolytus.* The one that survives, and the one we have just discussed, was titled *The Garlanded Hippolytus* (*stephanephoros*) after the garland Hippolytus consecrates to the virgin goddess Artemis; one could also call this tragedy *The Chaste Hippolytus*. An earlier tragedy, of which only a few fragments survive, is supposed to have been called *The Hooded Hippolytus* (*kalyptomenos*), since Hippolytus is supposed to have covered his head in shame upon Phaedra's open avowal of her love (cf. Christ 1888). In this *Hippolytus,* corresponding to Phaedra's open confession, she was given a more daring character. Wilamowitz-Moellendorff (1875, 210 ff.) even states that in the first *Hippolytus* Phaedra acted seductively toward Hippolytus to a shameless degree. This tragedy, as Christ remarks, is supposed to have proved offensive. Euripides therefore removed the objectionable portions, giving it the form in which it has come down to us. Whereas in the first *Hippolytus* Phaedra openly confesses her love, in the second she even attempts to resist it:

> I began
> By being silent; I hid the torment of my suffering.
> . . . .
> And finally, when despite all my efforts
> I could not master this passion, I chose death as a sure way.

Just as in Racine's *Phaedra,* it is the nurse who brings her to confess her love. Oenone names Hippolytus as the object of Phaedra's passions. Phaedra's defense expresses itself in a characteristic turn of phrase: "You hear the word from yourself and not from me." (Similarly, in Racine's drama she says: "You have said his name, not I" [1.3].) From this and similar details, and from her whole role in the plot, one has the impression that the nurse, like the seer Teiresias in *Oedipus,* is no more than a projection of the unconscious, an embodiment of the impulses Phaedra herself dares not admit feeling.

We might hypothesize about what inspired Euripides to such a revision of the first *Hippolytus,* but given the paucity of biographical information concerning the Athenian tragedians, such suppositions could not be proved. Still, this revision of the original drama can be attributed to very strong defense mechanisms that make the second version look almost like the opposite of the first (serving as a defense against it, just as Schiller's adaptation of *Phaedra* served as a defense against *Don Carlos*). In the first *Hippolytus* the son covers his face in shame, whereas in the second the (step)mother does so (cf. Welcker 1839–41). Welcker also argues that Euripides wrote *Hippolytus* in vexation at the behavior of his wife, Chorilla. Indeed, he was considered a misogynist by his contemporaries and by later classical writers. That too suggests repression of earlier erotic affection for the mother (the theme of the second *Hippolytus*) and would also explain his two unhappy marriages (cf. Byron's marriage). It is not known whether conflicts arose with his son on account of the stepmother (the second wife), but this can be suspected, given that in his works Euripides sides with the father. The incest theme is not rare in the works of Euripides, and one can of course evaluate this circumstance psychologically, even though this material was popular (again, not accidentally) at the time. That this accumulation of incest material and its treatment in the works of Euripides was already noticed in the classical period is demonstrated by the polemics of Aristophanes, who has the tragedian Aeschylus appear in *The Frogs* and accuse Euripides of preferring the incest theme. There we also find hints of a lost tragedy by Euripides, *Stheneboa,* which is supposed to have dealt with material similar to that of *Phaedra*. Further, Euripides handles the story of Phoenix, popular among the tragedians, in a manner reminiscent of his *Hippolytus*. In the *Iliad,* Homer lets Phoenix himself tell his tale (Homer 1974, 9.447 ff.):

> as when for the first time I left the land
> of lovely women, Hellas. I went north
> to avoid a feud with Father, Amyntor
> Ormenides. His anger against me rose
> over a fair-haired slave girl whom he fancied,
> without respect for his own wife, my mother.
> Mother embraced my knees and begged that I
> make love to this girl, so that afterward
> she might be cold to the aging man. I did it.
> My father guessed the truth at once, and cursed me,
> praying the ghostly Furies that no son
> of mine should ever rest upon his knees:
> a curse fulfilled by the immortals—Lord
> Zeus of undergloom and cold Persephone.
> I planned to put a sword in him, and would have,
> had not some god unstrung my rage, reminding me
> of country gossip and the frowns of men;
> I shrank from being called a parricide
> among the Akhaians.

Closely following Homer's account, the Roman tragedian Ennius also adopted the material. Euripides, however, altered the tale in a characteristic manner. In his version, like Hippolytus, Phoenix is innocent. Phthia, his father's mistress, pursues Phoenix with loving entreaties, just as Phaedra pursues Hippolytus, and when he resists her she also slanders him, telling his father that he desires her in illicit passion. Thus Euripides modifies the material, lending it a close resemblance to *Hippolytus*. Nor is the son's punishment absent in *Phoenix:* here the son is blinded by the father.

(In connection with this punishment and with the blinding of Oedipus, see Rank 1911a, 1913.)

The theme of the false accusation of the son by the father's wife (the Potiphar theme) is widely represented in myth and literature and also arises from a certain configuration of the Oedipus complex: it seeks on the one hand to realize the son's incest fantasy without reproach, while on the other hand expressing the fear that the father's suspicions may have been aroused. Of the many literary examples, we shall discuss only two. In Heliodorus's *Ethiopica,* Knemon tells his story. His father takes a second wife and wins her love, but she approaches the son with indecent entreaties: "She called me sometimes her dear child, sometimes her sweet one, then the heir of the house, and then her life. In a word, she mixed the decent names with the seductive, all the while noting which ones made the greatest impression on me; in her dignified expressions, she presented herself as a mother, while in the more indecent ones she presented herself as a woman in love." One night while her husband is away she stealthily approaches the son, "seeking to receive the forbidden pleasure." The son obstinately resists, and the woman tells the father that the son has taken advantage of her, whereupon the father has him whipped. The stepmother continues to spin out her intrigues. She instructs a slave woman to feign love for the son, and he sleeps with her each night. One evening she tells him that his father is away and that the stepmother is with another lover. She encourages him to take vengeance. Armed with a dagger, he enters the (step)mother's bedchamber crying: "Where is the cursed one? Where is the lover of the great, noble heroine?" The startled father springs from the bed and begs on his knees for mercy. The son drops his weapon in fright, whereupon the father has him bound and brought before the judges, who banish him. However, the stepmother, who now loves him all the more passionately, is pursued by the Furies. To resolve the situation, the slave who helped her in the deception offers to assist in slipping her mistress into Knemon's bedchamber by night in the slave's own place. But the slave also brings a jealous admirer and the husband to the bedchamber; everything comes to light, and the stepmother commits suicide.

The same theme is reflected in the tale "The Seven Wise Masters." An Indian king named Kurush has a son whose teacher is the wise Sindibad. Upon completing his education, the son is about to return to his father when Sindibad reads in the stars that misfortune threatens his student; to escape misfortune, the son must not speak for seven days. One of the king's wives attempts to seduce the prince and incite him to murder the king. The prince answers angrily that he will answer her in seven days. Now the queen accuses the prince of attempting to take advantage of her, and the father condemns him to death. By telling a tale about the falsehood of womankind, a vizier persuades the king to postpone the execution, but through a contradictory tale the queen convinces him to reinstate the sentence of death. This is repeated for six days so that the tales of six more viziers alternate with those of the queen until the eighth day arrives, when the prince can once again speak. He now reveals to his father the true state of affairs, and the queen is punished (Griesbach 1886, 54).

The Roman tragedian Seneca also wrote a *Phaedra*. He stuck to the original, more daring version of the plot, as did Ovid in the fourth of his *Epistulae heroidum* [Letters from heroines]. Whereas in Euripides' drama Phaedra's love is expressed by the nurse, in Seneca's drama she confesses her love to the son herself. She is startled to hear the word "mother" from his lips and asks him to call her "sister" or, better yet, "maiden," since she wishes to follow him wherever he goes. In Euripides' drama Phaedra writes a message in which she falsely accuses the stepson. In Seneca's drama she accuses him in person but later also reveals in person the son's innocence. She wishes to be united with the beloved stepson at least in Hades, so she commits suicide beside his body (cf. Schanz 1907). As one can see, Phaedra acts more spontaneously here with the son as well as with her husband. This is also expressed in that the nurse is nearly excluded from the drama, as though the secret impulses no longer require projection to find expression.

The lost *Phaedra* of Sophocles is especially interesting in this connection. Welcker (1839–41) presents some opinions concerning this work. In the Sophoclean drama, presumably, Phaedra takes such decisive steps that defense against her passions can no longer be maintained. We ought rather to suppose for her a completely different personality bearing little resemblance to that of Euripides' Phaedra, who simply suffers. Indeed, in the Sophoclean drama the nurse would have to oppose the acts of her mistress. The depiction of such unbridled passions on the part of the (step)mother for her son by the author of *Oedipus* should not surprise us. Here, though, we also receive confirmation for our interpretation of the stepmother theme as a dampening (displacement) of the love for the physical mother. Indeed, the genealogist Epimenides reports that Laius sired Oedipus with Eurycleia, and in *Scholia in Euripidem: Phoenissae* it is stated that Laius had two wives, Eurycleia and Epicaste [Jocasta]. According to this version Jocasta would only have been Oedipus's stepmother, but in Roscher's *Lexicon* it is stated that this account arose through a later need to dampen the horror of incest.

Just as we were able to study the progression of repression in three separate plots in chapter 2, here we see the same process unfolding within the context of a single plot. We can follow this process from the shamelessly provocative Phaedra of Sophocles to the already less shameless but nevertheless insistent Phaedra of Euripides' first *Hippolytus,* and thence to the Phaedra of his second *Hippolytus,* in which the stepson resists her passions. In that drama, stepmother and stepson never even confront one another. Thence the progression leads to the Phaedra of Seneca, who, corresponding to the licentious times of Nero, again bases the story on the original version. Finally the theme finds its most sublime artistic expression in the stylized tragedy of Racine.

Recently, Gabriele D'Annunzio has produced *Phaedra,* a drama in verse, with which I am familiar only through a short synopsis. In the first act the return to Athens of Theseus, "claimed dead," is awaited. Phaedra's unbridled passions are presented, exemplified by her stabbing to death a slave woman, intended as a gift for Theseus, in a jealous rage. In general, as far as I can gather from the synopsis, the poet attempts to motivate Phaedra's glowing love for her stepson through her sensually passionate nature; in the beginning of the second act, Phaedra is lying voluptuously on her bed, entertaining the loving entreaties of her admirer Aedes. The climax of the drama occurs in the second half of the second act. In this great scene Phaedra pours forth her crazed, fervent love for her stepson, Hippolytus, and attempts to seduce him. He falls asleep, exhausted, on her bed, at which point her passion exceeds all bounds. In her terrible desire and sensuality, she awakens the sleeper with a kiss. Hippolytus rouses with a confused start, declaring: "That was not the kiss of a mother." "I am not your mother," answers Phaedra, and a stream of ardent words of love swells from her lips. She is determined that the stepson shall be hers, no matter what the price. She begs him to kill her rather than go from her: "Tear out my heart, and you will see in it only yourself!" But Hippolytus rejects her coldly and inexorably. Now follows Phaedra's accusation of her stepson. She claims that he has dishonored her, that in sinful passion he has taken advantage of his stepmother. In the last act Phaedra is seen beside the body of Hippolytus, his father having commanded that he be trampled to death by wild horses. She reveals his innocence as well as her own guilt and dies by poisoning herself. In a critique of the drama, De Gubernatis (1909) remarks that D'Annunzio wanted to combine something of the *Hooded Hippolytus,* which failed to please the Athenians, with the famous *Garlanded Hippolytus,* still admired among the works of Euripides. He emphasizes that in a manner characteristically different from the dramas of Euripides and Seneca, and as expressed in the title, D'Annunzio, like Racine, casts Phaedra as the central character. That D'Annunzio wrote the work in only seventeen days speaks for the playwright's passionate involvement in the conception and composition of the work. (Schiller wrote his *Phaedra* in twenty-six days.)

Hans Limbach has also just written a unique *Phaedra* (1911). It closes with the sudden killing of Hippolytus by Theseus and the suicide of the heroine.

Malvida von Meysenbug, Nietzsche's friend, treated the Phaedra schema in a modern context—in a novel set in the time of the Franco-Prussian War. In the novel, the love of a worldly woman for her husband's son, whom she never wished to meet, is connected with the social tragedy of the illegitimate child. Heinrich von Kleist dealt with a noticeably similar theme in his story *Der Findling* [The foundling], which features a strangely psychological treatment of the Oedipus complex (with an inhibited act of incest and the killing of the son as punishment). Here again we observe the theme of sexual pleasure with an unconscious woman, typical of Kleist (cf. *Marquise von O . . .*, etc.), and which was realized in his own *Liebestod*.[1] In George Bernard Shaw's *Misalliance* the theme of the illegitimate son seems to take on almost comedic proportions: the illegitimate son threatens the father with a revolver, accusing him of seducing the mother.

1. [Love-death]—[Kleist shot himself and the terminally ill woman he loved.]

5 The Conflict between Father and Son

And—explain to me, Örindur,
This duplicity of nature!—
At times I wish to see his life, his blood
Flowing away; at times (softly, almost tenderly) I
wish to forgive him.

MÜLLNER, *Die Schuld*

With the repression of erotic inclination toward the mother, when the fantasies based on possessing her become unconscious, the resulting jealous animosity toward the father, as we have seen, tends to intensify to the point of fervent hatred for the preferred competitor. The intensity and permanence of the hatred become comprehensible only if one understands its origin and continuous stimulation by unconscious erotic sources. The child had earlier wished for the temporary or permanent absence of the father in a purely negative sense, in order to possess the mother alone and undisturbed; but with the illustrated tendency for repression the clear wish for the death of the hated competitor now appears, sometimes intensified to the point of murderous impulses. In childhood this typical fantasy of murdering the father—soon repressed—is hardly inhibited by the threat of punishment through the legal system, which, as one knows, does not even discourage adults from committing murder. Instead, the fantasy is inhibited to some degree by external experience, which recognizes and respects the father as the stronger rival, but mostly by the internal sensation of the original affection for the father, which has been largely consumed and concealed by the later sensation of hatred. Nevertheless, its unconscious traces can never be fully destroyed. It is this feeling of affection that, following an act of murder and the associated disappearance of the impulses of hatred, is largely reinstated and intensified to the emotion familiar to us as repentance. One could not conceive of this emotion were it not for the opposing traces of affection remaining. Indeed, in cases of pure hatred the only emotion experienced following the murder is satisfaction.

As illustrated in Greek mythology, the first stage of the repression of the childhood Oedipus complex is reflected in that both of the tabooed acts and the associated fantasies, now repressed, can be experienced only when the parents' true identity is unknown. In the next stage of repression, as we have systematically demonstrated for *Don Carlos* and parallel works, the complex is separated into its two components. In accordance with the tendency for gratification of wishes (rejuvenation, relinquishment of the bride), erotic affection for the mother is dampened to affection for the stepmother or even for the common beloved of father and son. Hatred toward the father increases at the cost of repressing love for the mother and is distinguished from its libidinous counterpart by abnormal exaggeration and fixation. Just as we have become familiar with a series of more and more repressed stepmother fantasies, we can also pursue the historical development of the widely dispersed theme of conflict between father and son, which appears in the legends of nearly all cultures. Psychologically speaking, even though this theme appears in ancient sources, it is already the product of double or multiple repression. Most significantly, the usually bitter and unresolvable conflict is often depicted completely dissociated from its source—sexual rivalry. Thus it is depicted in an unmotivated form. Second, the son does not consciously oppose his rival. Instead, the conflict begins and ends without the father's true identity being revealed. Only after the killing of the rival is his kinship with the victor made clear. In many cases, after the third stage in the process of repression, which we have designated psychologically as "becoming a father," when the legend portrays repentant fatherly feelings, the conflict remains unresolved: the identity of the father is revealed before the conclusion of the conflict, or another character is introduced, destined to be killed in place of the father (splitting of the father). Finally, in a stage of repression leading to repentant self-punishment, the son may be killed by the father. In the following legends, which we shall bring together in a cursory fashion, the conflict usually occurs without the father's identity being known; but in characterizing this form of the theme as the result of repression, we do not mean there must have been older forms of the myths in which the kinship was clear. It is only in a psychological sense that we assume such a preliminary stage. Indeed, since we must assume that the production of myths—that is, gratification in communal fantasies—began only with the repression of individual fantasies, even the first coherent mythological forms must be characterized by repression.

In connection with the Carlos schema, we shall begin with a legend that still shows clearly the sexual origin of the rivalry between father and son but that, like Schiller's *Don Carlos,* ends with the killing of the son. This is the Icelandic/Norwegian saga of Jörmunrek and Svanhild. The mighty king Jörmunrek, upon the advice of his confidant Bikki, courts Svanhild, the daughter of Gudrun and Sigurd. His son, Randver, fetches the bride. Then Bikki, a sower of intrigues, tells the king that they are guilty of illicit relations. Jörmunrek has his son hanged and Svanhild trampled to death by wild horses (cf. Jiriczek 1894).

Here again we find some familiar traits: that the son goes to fetch the father's bride, as in Lope de Vega's Carlos drama, and also the psychologically well-motivated way the father immediately assumes the son's guilt based on the slightest evidence, leading him to have his son killed.

To this group belongs also the German saga of the Harlungs, Emrika and Fritila. Sibich falsely accuses them, telling their uncle, Ermanaric, that they have had their eye on Ermanaric's wife and have threatened to molest her. Ermanaric, driven by anger over their daring and by covetousness for their treasure, deceitfully captures them while their bodyguard, Eckehart, is away and has them hanged (cf. Jiriczek 1894). Here, it is true, the husband's jealous hatred is directed toward his nephews, but in the Nordic version, jealousy is also the reason for killing the son. Jiriczek attempts to explain the subsequent shift from son to nephew as follows:

> That Ermanaric has his son (in the Nordic version) as well as his nephews hanged out of jealousy is certainly not to be accounted for by claiming that the two incidents were incorporated into the saga independently. One of these parallel cases must have been the model for the other. When the saga had made the slain princess the wife of Ermanaric, a poetically unifying move that surely had already occurred in Germany, another motivation for her demise was necessary, and this was most easily to be found in the ancient theme of love between the young woman and her stepson. In the [Nordic] Harlung saga, the golden treasure of the Harlungs is sufficient to explain Ermanaric's violent deed. Avarice and jealousy are motivations that go hand in hand. But the execution of the son in the later German version is completely unmotivated, for it certainly cannot be motivated by the father's avarice. Apparently the theme of jealousy, preserved in the older Nordic version, was lost from the German version, since the Svanhild saga had been forgotten.

That the father's jealousy is unmotivated in the German version should not surprise us. From our psychological research, on the one hand, we know that the motivation for this mortal enmity has become repressed and unconscious. On the other hand, we know that the motivation through avarice, so gratifying to originator and interpreter of the saga alike, is only a substitute motivation inserted to provide a logical explanation—a rationalization—and serves as well in reality as in fantasy. It is necessary in order consciously to justify and make possible the father's killing of the son, which actually occurs because of sexual rivalry (Svanhild saga).

But as soon as we turn to the sagas in which the conflict occurs without the characters' knowing each other's identity, the sexual motivation recedes. In the German saga of Ortnit and Alberich, rivalry over the mother is still suggested. Ortnit, weary of idleness, embarks on a voyage of conquest and receives from his mother a magic ring. On his way he finds a man [Alberich] sleeping on the ground in the forest, dressed in elegant clothing but no bigger than a child. He takes hold of the little man, who gives him such a powerful blow that Ortnit, who has the strength of twelve men, loses his breath. Then Alberich tricks him out of the ring, which had made it possible for Ortnit to see him; he says he will return it to Ortnit only on condition that he be allowed to say whatever he wishes about Ortnit's mother. After refusing for a long while, Ortnit gives in. As soon as he has the ring back on his finger and sees the dwarf standing before him, however, he grasps him by the neck, crying: "Now I have you in my power. Speak, now, but if you value your life, do not dare insult my mother." He has unsheathed his knife and is ready to stab the defenseless dwarf, but the dwarf says calmly: "If you kill me, a son murders his father." Then Ortnit lets the knife fall and says, trembling with anger: "You, my father? Tell me, what riddle is this?" The dwarf continues: "If you will hear me, you shall discover the truth. Your father and mother had been married for a long time and had experienced happiness and tranquillity. But one wish remained unfulfilled: they had no son to inherit their rich kingdom. One day the queen was seated on her bed, lamenting her fate, when I entered her chamber and gave her what she had been longing for." After learning this, Ortnit is overcome with melancholy. He rides back home to the castle dressed in the armor Alberich has given him. He pretends to be a foreign knight and tells the guard he has killed his master (Ortnit). It is only at the sight of his mother that his melancholy abates.

In this saga we easily recognize the elaboration of a typical childhood fantasy. This is the fantasy of the son who takes his father's place with the unfaithful mother and sires a child by her, just as he is himself a child. Here the seduction of the mother is attributed to Alberich, with whom the hero identifies in that he has made himself a mighty father (with the strength of twelve men) and has made his father a little child (his own child). Nevertheless this child can still rob him of his senses with one blow, just as a father could. The ring, which enables the otherwise invisible father to be seen, makes it possible, here and elsewhere, for the son to overhear the sexual relations of the parents, which the now visible Alberich describes (cf. Rank 1913). This argument seems to suggest that it is precisely this situation of overhearing that in general gives the son occasion to identify with the father and to despise the mother ("do not dare insult my mother"). That the son's fantasy can no longer be realized is emphasized by his surrender to the preferred and victorious father, and by his resulting melancholia and contemplation of suicide (he claims he has killed himself).

In an episode of the Old High German *Hildebrandslied,* written about A.D. 800 following an older model, we encounter a completely unmotivated battle between a father and a son who is unaware of the father's identity. The episode portrays a conversation between Hildebrand and his son, Hadubrand, which takes place in front of enemy armies. Thirty years before, Hildebrand had accompanied Dietrich on his flight to the Huns, but he has now returned home. He had left Hadubrand behind, since the child was illegitimate, and now Hadubrand will not believe the old man when he tells him he is his father:

> In that land he [Hildebrand] left behind
> The maiden in her chamber and a child.
> . . . .
> Most likely he no longer lives.

The old man tries to give his son a bracelet, but here too the son suspects treachery and refuses it. Hildebrand can convince no one that Hadubrand is his son, and he does not wish to be accused of cowardice in the face of the two armies. With a heavy heart, he decides to do battle:

> Now the dear child shall strike me with his sword,
> Shall kill me with his blade, or I shall bring him death.

The eighth-century fragment ends in the midst of the battle, and we do not know its outcome. But the whole situation and mood suggest a tragic ending. According to Jiriczek (1894), an Old Icelandic saga that utilizes recollections of German sagas suggests that the death of the son by the father's hand should be assumed. However, later sagas (the Thidrek saga) suggest that the struggle ends with a reconciliation. Thus we see the tendency for repression and dampening at work and must assume that originally the father was killed, though unknown to the son. This is also suggested by the last two lines cited, in which the father twice stresses his probable demise. Later the transformation toward repentant identification with the father brings about the killing of the son. Still later, sentimental tendencies resolve the conflict with a reconciliation. In connection with this progressive repression, it cannot be coincidental that the saga writer, who presumably was personally interested in the story, broke off just before the crucial decision, which was already vacillating in older versions. This enables readers to complete the account according to their own taste. Here we can extend to the creation and retelling of myths a basic principle that we established in our analysis of literary works. We will often find application and confirmation for this principle. The opposing characters in a drama do not represent only contrasts consciously conceived of by the playwright but are instead the necessary expression of psychic conflicts—the unconscious splitting of emotions. In the same way, contradictory and deviating versions of the same theme prove to be the results of a psychic contradiction arising from repression. Therefore, in the process of psychological analysis and synthesis, these versions complement one another.

Before investigating precursors of the battle episode in the *Hildebrandslied* and widespread parallel works, let us discuss a presumably later account that, given the double aspect of the Oedipus complex, reveals its origins in the theme of relationship to the mother through dampening that of father hatred. This is the legend of Milun, poetically rendered by Marie de France (Warnke 1885) and characterized by Hertz (1862) as the Breton *Hildebrandslied.* A young woman becomes pregnant by Milun, a brave knight. Fearing the consequences, she advises him to take the child, when it is born, to her sister, who lives a great distance away and will raise him. The ring the maiden has received from Milun, as well as a letter bearing his name, will be given to the child so he will someday be able to find his father. After the child is born and taken from his mother, Milun sets out on adventures; the maiden, now married, is thrown into prison by her husband as a fallen woman. The story continues twenty years later when the boy is grown. During this time Milun and his fallen lover have been corresponding by means of a swan that functions as a carrier pigeon. When twenty years have passed, the youth arrives in Brittany in search of his father. He shows himself to be a brave knight and defeats all opponents. Milun is worried about his own reputation as a knight, until then unquestioned. After a long period of rest, he decides to set out again to do battle with the strange knight and then search for his son. Not realizing each other's identity, they fight fiercely until the young man finally shoves the old man from his saddle. At this point the old man's helmet is pushed aside, and the young man sees his opponent's white hair. He does not take advantage of his superior position, but brings the old man a horse so the two will once again be on equal footing. Now the old man notices the ring on the young man's hand and inquires about his parents, since he has never fought such a brave hero. The young man relates in detail the whole story of his birth and youth. Through the ring and the letter, the two recognize each other as father and son, and the youth determines to save his mother from the power of her husband, whom she hates, and bring her to his father:

> The son cried: "I'll unite you
> With my mother surely.
> I now depart to slay her husband;
> To bring you peace for all your cares."

On the way to the castle where the mother is held prisoner, however, they are met by a messenger with the news that her husband has just died and that she is free and has been released:

> She thanks God with heart and hand
> When she sees again her handsome son.
> Without asking the relations
> If it be their pleasure,
> He brings his mother peacefully
> To his father as a bride.

In this late legend, so noticeably similar to the *Hildebrandslied,* we easily recognize an Oedipus myth that has been distorted by many transformations and has been sentimentalized. In the original version of this myth the son kills the father, and it is he himself, not the father, who is joined as king with the mother. From our analysis of *Hamlet,* we are already familiar with the mother's second husband as a substitute figure who permits the unhampered flourishing of the son's hatred toward the father (the son wishes to kill the mother's spouse) but also aids the son in gratifying his repressed incest fantasy through identification. Thus the psychic mechanism and tendency in the development of legends becomes comprehensible. It is of no great significance that in this case, just as in *Hamlet,* the stepfather (the second husband) is not killed by the son but instead dies a natural death, again through dampening. That the planned revenge on the father is motivated by his poor treatment of the mother is, as we already know, typical of the rescue fantasy, which entails the son's liberating the mother, who is unhappy as the father's spouse. But since Hildebrand, like Milun, unscrupulously leaves his lover and his illegitimate child, it is probable that he too is punished by the son for his poor treatment of the mother. In the *Hildebrandslied* fragment this is also suggested by the corresponding charge, which Hadubrand pronounces to his father:

> In that land he left behind
> The maiden in her chamber and a child.

This conception of the mother's unhappiness and her desire for release (as well as the corresponding rescue fantasy) is not original but is instead a rationalization, adopted late in childhood, of the individual's own longing for the mother's love, justified by her desire for liberation. The actual origin of this fantasy is found in the earliest years of childhood, when the child, on becoming aware of the parents' sexual relations, assumes, based on his own rough play, that the father is harming the mother (Freud terms this the "sadistic conception of coitus") and that she must be released from his power. From this same source arises the desire, embodied in the stepfather (the second husband), to take the father's place in his relationship with the mother. In the preceding legend all these themes have been transformed in a sentimental manner. Instead of the killing of the father, we observe his rescue, which belongs to a later stage of psychic development. Later (*Hamlet*), this leads to the compensatory avenging of the father. Milun saves the life of his unrecognized father, or grants him his life when, moved by the sight of the white hair, he decides not to take advantage of his own superior situation. Indeed he grants his bitter enemy, fighting for his reputation as a hero, an advantage. In the Oedipus myth too a battle between the son and his unrecognized father occurs at the famous crossroads, but there the fateful error is recognized only long after the murder has occurred. Milun, though, through the ring and the letter, recognizes the error before serious harm can occur.

From our investigations in *The Myth of the Birth of the Hero* (Rank 1909), we already recognize these as typical signs of the son rebellious toward the father and desiring the mother (cf. also the legends in chap. 9). In the Hildebrand fragment too, a ring that the father wishes to give the son, but which the son suspiciously rejects, plays a role that is no longer completely comprehensible. However, we may suppose that it originally revealed the identity of the slain father. For in the Oedipus legend too it is just such a symbol—the pierced feet—that reveals the son's terrible deed. Otherwise Oedipus, like Hadubrand, could have continued to assume that the older man was not his father and that he himself was not the exposed child. Similarly, in *Oedipus* the mother's identity is realized only after incest has been committed. In the *Hildebrandslied,* though, with a strong swing toward the sentimental, the mother's and son's mutual recognition makes incest impossible. According to Freytag (1872), in Greek drama scenes of recognition enjoyed the importance given to love scenes in modern drama. In general the unconscious impact of scenes of recognition, which have such an effect on our emotions and our tear ducts, seems to rest in the distressing possibility—finally eliminated in a gratifying way—that the two could unknowingly do battle against one another (father and son, brothers) or marry one another (mother and son, brother and sister).

Thus the battle between father and son, with the father's identity unrealized, is the opposite of marriage to the unrecognized mother. If, in a large group of legends, only the fateful battle is related, the Oedipus legend, which links both themes in a psychologically logical way, demonstrates that the son kills the father to gain possession of the mother. But that both acts occur without recognition of the parents' identity merely reflects the psychological fact of the repression of these infantile wishes. As this repression progresses, it leads to the isolation of the patricide complex and later to dampening of the complex into the themes of rescue of the father and vengeance for the father.

In his comments regarding the lays of Marie de France, Reinhold Köhler (1899, 259) points out an interesting parallel. Another French lay bears great similarity to the last portion of the *Lay of Milun*. This is the *Lay of Doon,* first published by Gaston Paris (1879, 61–64). Previously it had been available only in the Old Norse prose translation, "Douns ljóð" (*Strengleikar* [Ballads], 9). The lay relates that Doon, a Breton knight, has won the hand of the Lady of Edinburgh by passing certain tests assigned by her to her suitors but leaves her four days after the wedding. Upon departing, he gives her his gold ring and tells her that if she bears him a son, she should give the son the ring when he is grown and send him to the king of France. Indeed she bears a son, and when he is old enough to ride, she gives him Doon's ring and sends him to France. There he becomes an excellent knight. In a tournament at Mont Saint-Michel in Brittany he and his father joust without recognizing one another. The son wounds the father in the arm, causing him to fall from his horse. After the tournament Doon's father asks the victor to show him his hands. On one finger he notices his own ring and reveals that he is the victor's father, whereupon both depart for England, the son bringing the father to the mother. In both poems the son fights with the father in a tournament at Mont Saint-Michel, throwing him from the saddle, and in both poems, the father recognizes the son from the ring he is wearing.

Paris (1879, 60) has already pointed out the many parallels between the two lays, but he did not go so far as to claim definitely that they have a common author. The parallels with the *Lay of Milun* and the resemblance of both versions to derivatives of the Oedipus complex become more probable when we consider also Paris's emphasis (p. 32) on the rescue of the mother from dire straits in the lays *Doon de la Roche* and *Enfances Doon de Maiance* as well.

We will now present without special commentary the widely dispersed and often surprisingly overlapping parallels in the battle between father and son. For their exhaustive compilation we are indebted mainly to the tireless research work of Reinhold Köhler, who unfortunately died too young. In most versions the bitter and grim battle is completely unmotivated or very insufficiently motivated. We now understand this as a consequence of its dissociation from the actual motivation—unconscious sexual rivalry. Earlier, this motivation has been repressed. Corresponding to this repression, which in its later stages leads to sympathy with the father in almost all versions, it is the son who falls (compensatory punishment), while in some versions the battle ends undecided or with recognition and sentimental reconciliation.

Concerning the *Hildebrandslied,* Jiriczek (1894) remarks: "The historical model for Hildebrand is the loyal Gensimund. The change in name probably occurred first in Germany, where the battle between father and son came to be associated with Hildebrand. The legend is widespread. In the eighth century the Irish already sang and told of the tragic death of Conlaoch, who fell by the hand of his father, Cuchullin" (cf. Franz Pfeiffer, *Germania,* 10:338; Campbell 1890–93, 3:184). In *Biterolf,* Dietleib fights his father Diete without recognizing him.

In their edition of the *Hildebrandslied,* the brothers Grimm (1812, 77 ff.) also present the following German parallels. (1) In the novel by Olger Danske, Galder meets his father, Göde, king of Denmark, without recognizing him. They fight with all their might until their kinship is finally revealed. (2) Paltrian and Wigamer discover that they are father and son before doing battle (Hagen 1808). (3) Bogsweiga battles his son, whom he has never seen, but recognizes him from the bracelet he had given the boy's mother as a sign (Uhland 1865, 165).

Köhler (1868) mentions several parallels in his discussion of C. C. Cassat's article on the romance *Richars li biaus,* published in full by W. Förster, in which the hero and his son do battle: (1) Guillaume de la Barre, the hero, and his son, in a Provençal romance by Arnaud Vidal de Castelnaudary (Meyer 1868, 20 and 27); (2) Eglamour and Degrabell in the English poem *Sir Eglamour of Artoys* (Ellis 1805, 537); (3) Renaud de Montauban and Gui in the Italian poem *Anchroia Regina* (Duméril 1839, 123); (4) the father and son d'Ailly in Voltaire's *Henriade* (Köhler 1868). Further, in an editorial note (p. 414) Gaston Paris adds: "One can add to these battles that of Nalabron and Robastre in *Gaufrey,* that of Baudouin and the bastard de Bouillon in *Baudoin de Labaure* (chap. 25), and that of Milun and his son in the *Lay of Milun* by Marie de France; the battle of Renaud and d'Aimon does not have the same character." In his comments on Marie de France, Köhler also cites as examples of battle between father and son that of Gauder with his son Gerant in Berthold von Holle's *Demantin* and that of Sadoc with his son Apollo in the romance *Tristan de Léonois* (Tressan 1788, 7:31). See also Alexander Wesselofsky's comments (1879, 588) and Felix Liebrecht's comments (1879, 406). In the first chapter of his

Russian-language volume *Ilya Muromets and Kievan Heroism* Orest Miller (1869) provides, in addition to Slavic examples, the following distant parallels (after Köhler 1899): (1) Desramés and Rainouard in *Bataille d'Aliscaus;* (2) Malveris and Ysoré in *Prise de Pampélune;* (3) Andronicus and his son in a Greek folk song (Büdinger 1866). Another Russian scholar, Aleksandr Kirpichnikov (1873, 170), adds to Miller's examples the following: (1) In *Gui de Bourgogne,* the children of France go to Spain led by Gui, whom they have elected king. In Spain their fathers, who have been there for many years and do not know them, prepare to do battle against them. (2) In *Gaydon,* Gaydon's battle with Karl is a battle of sons against fathers, in which the sons are victorious. (3) In *Parise la duchesse,* the father besieges his son, whom he does not know, but for whom he nevertheless feels a certain sympathy. Kirpichnikov remarks: "The first two examples are interesting in their collectivity, and the last is interesting in that the battle is transformed into a siege." Concerning the third episode, Kirpichnikov is imprecise. The father, Raymond, duke of Saint-Gilles, besieges not his son, Hugues, but instead his vassal Clarembaut. Nevertheless, Hugues is in Clarembaut's service. In a battle of resistance undertaken by those under siege, however, an actual man-to-man struggle does occur between Raymond and Hugues; the son thrusts the father from his saddle. In this struggle, the duke in *Parise la duchesse* says with reference to Hugues (Guessard and Larchey 1860, 65): "Il ne sai que ce vant ne á que ce puet aler, / Orandroit l'am je plus que nul home charnel" [He does not know that it's nothing to boast about that this should happen, for I love him more than any mortal man].

Ossian's most beautiful poem, *Karthon,* deals with the same legend (cf. *Jahrbuch für Romanische Literatur,* 2:195). Klesamohr has never seen his son, Karthon, since he had to flee before Karthon's birth. Therefore he does not know it is Karthon he is now challenging to battle. Karthon, suspecting that his opponent is his father, seeks to avoid the battle (cf. the old Hildebrand). But the old man (like the son in the *Hildebrandslied*) insists on going on with the battle and stabs his son in the side. Dying, the son names his father. Out of grief, the old man dies four days later. From the psychologically well-motivated circumstance that the opponent who insists on the battle also emerges victorious, we can also infer the original death of the father in the *Hildebrandslied.* The opponent who enters the battle with doubts will not be able to utilize his whole strength and must therefore fall. In the *Hildebrandslied,* a victory for the father would mean the deliberate murder of the recognized son. This explains why the outcome of this battle has undergone so many modifications. Psychologically, the mysterious "voice of the blood," which speaks to Hildebrand and also raises doubts in the mind of Karthon, is only the expression of this indecision, resulting from the ambivalent infantile perspective.

This shifting of perspective is seen very clearly in the Russian legend of Ilya Muromets, where victory belongs sometimes to the father and sometimes to the son; recognition and reconciliation sometimes occur, though elsewhere Ilya Muromets fights and kills his unrecognized son (see "Fürst Wladimir und seine Tafelrunde" [Prince Vladimir and the knights of his round table], in *Altrussische Heldenlieder* [Old Russian heroic legends] [1819], 75).

> Only a few versions have a happy ending, but these are incomplete and defective. It is remarkable that in all of these versions, the battle is divided into two halves. In the first half, the son is always victorious and Ilya is near his end, but then Ilya summons his last strength, overpowers his son, forces him to divulge his name after three inquiries, and releases him on discovering that he is his illegitimate son. The son returns to the mother, Latigorka, discovers the truth of his father's words, and now wishes to take revenge for his mother's shame and his own. He attacks the sleeping Ilya but is smashed against the ground by his father as he awakens. (Bistrom, *Das russische Volksepos* [The Russian folk epic], 6:132 ff.)

In the interesting version at hand, we can grasp not only the progression of the repression of hatred toward the father, but also its origins in the mother complex. The first part of the poem, in which the son is victorious, still clearly reveals the original tendency for the slaying of the father, which was later dampened to the defeat of the son and, in this version, to forgiveness (sparing his life). However, the second portion reveals in a most unambiguous way the original Oedipus complex; the son's illegitimacy serves not so much to dampen the Oedipus complex as to justify it in the sense of the infantile family complex (cf. Rank 1909). If the child in love with his mother imagines that she is being mistreated in sexual relations with the father, this conception is justified (rationalized) here by the illegitimate birth of the son; that the son attempts to kill the father while he sleeps clearly suggests the child's situation in the parents' bedroom, where this complex is decisively reinforced and solidified. Corresponding to the repentant tendency for repression already suggested in the first portion of the poem, the slaying of the son actually occurs in the second portion. Here we repeat the qualification that in our reconstruction of the original theme we claim only psychological, not literary, relevance. It is probable that there was an original version comprising the killing or even the conscious murder of the father, but this is not absolutely necessary. Our conception of the extant versions as secondary transformations refers only to their psychological precursor, regardless of whether this version actually found literary expression. Still, as shown by our psychoanalytical investigation of the psychic life of the individual and by the noticeable characteristics of the legends we have emphasized, the version comprising the killing of the son can be conceived of only as a reactive construction based on the originally successful victory of the son over the father.

The famous episode of the battle between the hero Rustum and his unrecognized son, Sohrab, related in Firdusi's "Shah-namek" (Görres, ed., *Königsbuch* [Book of kings]), is worthy of special mention. Here again the still boyish Sohrab sets out in search of his father in order to take vengeance for the disgrace of his mother, Tahminah, who is considered only Rustum's lover (and who is woman above but snake below) (cf. Rank 1913). Once, during his adventures outside Iran, Rustum had been secretly married to the daughter of a Turanian prince; she had offered to marry him. But like the fathers in the *Hildebrandslied,* the *Lay of Milun,* and other poems, he deserts her immediately thereafter. Finally, father and son come across one another unrecognized. In contrast to the *Hildebrandslied,* where the father hesitates to do battle because of vague suspicions, in the Iranian legend the son is seized by doubts and ominous thoughts while the father (like the son in the *Hildebrandslied*) mistrustfully rejects his opponent's offer of friendship. After several intermediate incidents attributable to an ambivalent point of view, the Iranian legend ends with the son's death. Therefore we are justified in claiming this as confirmation of the original death of the father in the *Hildebrandslied.* Indeed, it was necessary to conclude that the vague suspicions, disturbing sometimes the father and sometimes the son, relate to the imminent doom of that character—the father in the *Hildebrandslied* and the son in the Iranian legend.

Still, that the Rustum legend in its extant form does not demonstrate the psychologically original theme is shown by a detail of the battle, which owing to the alternating advantage of father and of son is reminiscent of the Russian legends discussed above. In Firdusi's version the battle lasts three days. Strangely, on the second day the father, a famous hero, loses the advantage to his still boyish son. Sohrab is already drawing the dagger from its sheath to sever the head of his father, whom he does not know, but the latter has recourse to a trick: he refers to a custom of the land according to which the victor may kill the vanquished only after he has twice thrust him from his horse. Thus the battle continues on the third day. Before this, however, Rustum begs God to restore to him his giant's strength, which had been partially reduced at his own wish. With his giant's strength, he breaks Sohrab in two like a straw. Mortally wounded, Sohrab reveals his identity to his father, proving the kinship with an onyx his mother gave him. The Polynesian and American parallels to the battle between father and son (Ehrenreich 1910) might also be mentioned.

Let us turn now to the most significant, interesting, and valuable works—Greek legends reflecting two variants of the battle between father and son. Both of these strange legends involve Odysseus, and psychologically they complement one another. These legends are known to us mainly through the Greek tragedians, especially through fragments of Sophoclean tragedies. This offers us the desirable possibility of gaining insights into Sophocles' own process of selection, and thus into his psychology. It should not surprise us to find the killing of the unrecognized father dealt with also in other works of the Attic tragedian. Sophocles may have included such an episode of the Odysseus legend in his tragedy *Odysseus akanthopleks e Niptra* [Odysseus killed by acanthus, or The footbath]. In the course of this episode, Odysseus is killed by Telegonus, one of his illegitimate sons, the son of Circe. The tragedy is not extant, but its content may be supposed from the tragedy *Niptra* by the Roman poet Pacuvius. This tragedy is also lost, but more fragments remain. After Odysseus hears the prophecy that he will be killed by his son, he avoids his legitimate son, Telemachus, and does not permit himself to associate with him. However, his son Telegonus, whom Circe has borne him, comes to Ithaca and wishes to penetrate Odysseus's palace, unfamiliar to him, by night. The guards attempt to hinder him, sounds are heard, and Odysseus is awakened. Believing that his son Telemachus wishes to attack him by night, he rushes out, brandishing his sword, and fights Telegonus in the dark. In the course of the fight, Odysseus is mortally wounded.

Here again it is characteristic that Odysseus immediately suspects an attack by his son when he is awakened by the noise, just as do King Philip and Theseus, who are not surprised by their sons' supposedly malicious behavior. With Odysseus, too, such suspicions are assumed always to be present, and the oracle's proclamation predicting his death by his son's hand is only a projection of his own unconscious fears. The inevitable fate pronounced by the oracle is reminiscent of the oracle's pronouncement to Oedipus, also misunderstood. Just as Oedipus assumes that his foster father, Polybus, is the father intended by the oracle, Odysseus, without even thinking of his other son, Telegonus, assumes that his son Telemachus is the murderer the oracle means. In the course of his psychic development, the Attic tragedian, too, must have made the psychological transition from son to father, arising from fear of reprisal. Because we lack biographical and literary material, we cannot pursue this in detail as with Schiller (chap. 3) or Shakespeare (chap. 6). However, this transition is shown in the process of selection, for thereafter Sophocles never dealt with patricide and incest with the mother, but wrote instead of the punishment of the son and dampened (stepmother) or completely hindered incest (*Telephus*). Coincidentally, the little we know of Sophocles' personal life is just sufficient to make very probable our supposition that with the Attic tragedian too the selection process, though it corresponded to the style of the day and was based on earlier traditions, was decisively influenced by personal factors. According to Christ (1888), Sophocles himself is supposed to have had some illegitimate sons. His wife, Nicostrate, bore him a legitimate son, Iophon, who was also a tragedian and who even competed with his father in dramatic competitions. But there are also reports of serious disagreements between father and son. Indeed, the son went to the blood relatives (*phratores*) and accused his father of derangement (*paranaias*). Sophocles is supposed to have demonstrated his sanity by reading the chorus from *Oedipus at Colonus* glorifying Athens, whereupon the judges acquitted him. In this *Oedipus* Sophocles emphasizes the harsh treatment of Oedipus by his sons, Polynices and Eteocles—that is, Oedipus's punishment for murdering his father. This can probably be attributed to Sophocles' own transition from hating son to hated father. This transformation of feelings then found its complete artistic expression in the dramatic presentation of another fable, also taken from the Oedipus legend, which Sophocles treated in his tragedy *Euryalus*. Just as *Oedipus the King* and *Telegonus* embodied the feelings of the son—that is, hatred toward the father (beside erotic affection for the mother)—*Euryalus,* no longer extant, dealt with the father's feelings—that is, hatred toward the son, who thus is also punished in retribution.

According to Welcker (1839–41), the content and background of the tragedy are as follows. After his victory over the suitors, Odysseus travels to Epirus to consult certain oracles. There he sires a son, Euryalus, by Enippe, the daughter of his host, Tyrimmas. When he is grown, the mother sends Euryalus to Ithaca with a token of recognition and a sealed letter, in order to find his father. Odysseus happens to be away from the house, and his wife, Penelope, who has in the meantime heard of Odysseus's infidelity with Enippe, decides to take vengeance. When he returns home, before he can discover the truth, she incites Odysseus to kill Euryalus as an enemy. Thus, without knowing it, Odysseus becomes the murderer of his son.

This episode renders the Odysseus legend even more similar to the Tell legend, discussed in chapter 3, in which the father, though coerced, threatens the life of the son.[1] Interestingly, we already find here the token of

1. At this point, we should mention briefly the similarity, even in the details, between the Odysseus myth and the Tell legend. Odysseus too is a bowman; he vanquishes his wife's suitors with a masterly shot through the twelve ax eyes. He too kills his enemies with his extra arrows. Like Tell, he also makes a journey by water (his wanderings). Indeed, he is even bound to the mast (near the island of the Sirens), just as Tell lies bound in Gessler's ship.

recognition (the ring) and the letter. Elsewhere, as in the case of Uriah [2 Samuel 11], such a letter brings about the death of the rival in love. Here, though, it reveals the son's true identity after he has been killed, and in a series of sentimentally dampened versions it leads to recognition of the son in time to prevent his death. That Odysseus's wife brings about the son's murder out of jealousy not only shows the sexual background of the whole situation but is also clearly reminiscent of the fateful letter King Proetus delivers to Bellerophon in the *Iliad* (6.166 ff.). After an unsuccessful attempt to seduce Bellerophon, the king's wife tells her husband that Bellerophon has been molesting her. Here we glimpse a deep motivation for Penelope's jealous accusation of Euryalus and his death by the hand of Odysseus. Penelope had already been tormented by insistent suitors, and Odysseus had already killed these men, so offensive to Penelope, without scruple.

That such a connection has been lost in Homer's version of the Odysseus legend is demonstrated by Eugammon's *Telegony,* a two-volume epic sequel to the Homeric poem. This epic relates the later fate of Odysseus and his line, presumably based in part on old versions not used in the Homeric epic. Of this work too, which Sophocles utilized as a source for his *Niptra,* only fragments remain. Significantly, it ends with two marriages: Telegonus weds Penelope, his father's widow, while Telemachus, Odysseus's legitimate son, marries Circe, the mother of Telegonus. Whether Sophocles and Pacuvius also adopted this solution is unclear from the few extant fragments of their tragedies. But based on our previous discussion, we can suspect that they did not fail to make use of this marvelous compromise, in which a man has two sons by different mothers and, following his death, each son marries the mother of his brother—a

---

Odysseus too is the only one clever enough to save himself from the storms of the sea while his comrades perish, so that one could just as well say of him what Schiller says of Tell: "He handles the rudder like a bow." The Odysseus myth also emphasizes the hatred between father and son, which becomes all the more interesting for us in that it incorporates and unifies both variants of this complex: Odysseus kills his son Telemachus with a javelin (of acanthus) but is himself killed by Telegonus, his son by Circe, who does not recognize him. Just as Tell attempts to make himself look harmless by affecting simplicity ("If I had my wits, I wouldn't be called Tell"), the clever Odysseus also frequently dissembles. He attempts to avoid involvement in the Trojan War by affecting insanity: he plows with one ox and one horse. But Palamedes, who is even cleverer, is able to outwit him. He places the child Telemachus, Odysseus's little son, in front of the plow to test the authenticity of Odysseus's madness. This incitement to kill his young son is clearly reminiscent of Tell's shot at his own little son, and in the Melchthal episode we once again observe plowing with oxen. Blinding, which is carried out on Melchthal's father, is found also in the Odysseus myth, but in a different context: Odysseus blinds the one-eyed Polyphemus. As a remarkable final parallel, we note Lessmann's remark that Kaiser Albrecht was also one-eyed.

sort of half-mother or stepmother. Thus we find that Sophocles addressed not only the relationship of father and son in its various guises, but also the relationship with the mother—here in its dampened form, the stepmother theme.

According to Welcker, in a second form of psychic defense that went further still, Sophocles may have dealt with the son's desire for the mother in his tragedy *Telephus*. This material, derived from the myth of Atalanta, was taken up by Pacuvius in his tragedy *Atalanta*, whose contents and background Ribbeck (1875) summarizes as follows: Atalanta bears Meleager a son, Parthenopaeus, whom she exposes along with Telephus, born of the secret union of the Arcadian princess Auge and Hercules. The boys are suckled by a doe and then are found by shepherds and brought to King Corythus, who has them raised. In the meantime, Auge has fled to Mysia, where she has been adopted by the childless King Teuthras. Upon the advice of the Oracle at Delphi, Telephus now sets out for Mysia with his friend Parthenopaeus to find his mother. He helps King Teuthras out of a dire situation by conquering his enemies. In return the king's supposed daughter, Auge, Telephus's own mother, is given him in marriage. However, she had sworn to Hercules, when she was his lover, that she would never give herself to another man. She therefore decides to stab Telephus, whom she does not know, in the nuptial chamber. But a snake sent by the gods rises up between them and frightens Auge out of her plan. When she confesses she wished to kill Telephus, he determines to kill her with the same sword. In her fear she calls upon Hercules, to whom she had sacrificed her virginity, and Telephus therefore recognizes her as his own mother.

This fable too includes the two youths (blood brothers or twins); in *Telegony* each one loves (marries) the mother of the other. But the Telephus legend demonstrates that each is actually in love with his own mother. Therefore in other fables they fight with each other, just as they fight with the father in the *Odyssey.* In fact, De Gubernatis (1872, 2:198) relates the same situation, but with full retention of actual incest with the mother [De Gubernatis's English]: "The two youths Aegipios and Nephron are another form of Açvinân, who, hating each other on account of the love which each has for the other's mother, are changed by Zeus into two vultures, after that Aegipios, by a stratagem of Nephron, mixted himself with his own mother."

Concerning the Sophoclean Telephus tragedy, Ribbeck (1875) comments: "It is unambiguously attested that Telephus's danger of falling victim to Oedipus's fate was portrayed on the Greek stage." And Welcker suspects that this scene of recognition between mother and son formed the climax of Sophocles' drama. The dampening of true incest is clear, since mother and son are married, just as in *Oedipus,* but given the scene of recognition, the sexual union does not occur. Erotic affection for the mother is repressed further still in Sophocles' *Phaedra,* where love for the son is openly avowed but is rejected by him; here, owing to the female character's offensive protestations of love, the mother is dampened to stepmother.

Thus, besides the repression through time, reflected in the development of myths and in the dampened transformations of their literary versions (stepmother theme), in each individual case we also see the parallel repression within the individual, which not only is observed in the composition of the individual work (cf. *Don Carlos*) but also expresses itself in the sequence of works by a single writer; these works illustrate the incest complex from its impetuous appearance in puberty, through the stage of fear of retribution, to the clear skies of the father perspective.

In its various degrees and manifestations, the conflict between father and son is one of the most frequently utilized essential themes of the playwrights of all times; as is becoming less and less ambiguous, the aesthetic development of the playwright begins, of course, with the father complex. Below, only a few examples of the rich material can be presented.

In Philip Massinger's tragedy *The Unnatural Combat,* the young Malefort, as avenger of his mother, challenges his father, the admiral of Marseilles. She had been poisoned by her spouse because he wished to marry another woman, more receptive to his sensual nature. The son perishes in the fight, and the father exults over his body (Koeppel 1895, 85). The incestuous origin of the rivalry between father and son is suggested by a shift into the second generation (rejuvenation of the mother—stepmother) in the love of the father for his daughter. The father complex is also the main theme of Massinger's *The Fatal Dowry,* where the young Charolois sacrifices himself for his father, who has died in debtor's prison, by taking up his place there and making possible the father's burial. Moved by this example of filial loyalty, Rochfort releases him and gives him his daughter in marriage. She loves Novall, however, and is surprised by Charolois in Novall's arms. Novall is forced to fight and is killed (shift of the conflict). The father condemns the guilty woman to death, and Charolois carries out the sentence. As his knightly prerogative, Rochfort absolves Charolois of all wrongdoing, but the young man is stabbed to death by a supporter of Novall. In the self-sacrifice of the son for the father, who languished in debtor's prison, Koeppel is very appropriately reminded of Cimon's self-sacrifice for his father, Miltiades, as reported by Cornelius Nepos. In both cases, however, one cannot fail to notice the ambivalent position of the son, who—it is true—sacrifices himself for his father, but only out of an overwhelming sense of guilt toward him. The incestuous origin of this guilt is suggested in Cimon's marriage to his half-sister, while in Massinger's tragedy the original rivalry with the father is represented in the jealous killing of the preferred and envied competitor. In an interesting study, Reik (1912) attempts to show that Richard Beer-Hofmann, in his recent tragedy *Der Graf von Charolais* [The count of Charolais] (1904), was seeking to grasp with greater psychological depth the father complex underlying the story.

Pedro Calderón's *Life Is a Dream,* in which the father cruelly imprisons the son based on an oracular pronouncement, will be discussed below, as will *The Steadfast Prince* by the same playwright, which also deals with the theme of the son's self-sacrifice. In *Cleonnis,* planned by Lessing, Euphaes was to kill his son Cleonnis without knowing his identity. In Friedrich Hebbel's *Agnes Bernauer,* Duke Ernst fights with his son Albrecht because the son refuses to marry the bride his father has selected and instead marries a beautiful young bourgeoise. Agnes worries that the duke may react severely: "And if he draws his sword?" Albrecht responds: "Then he gives me the right to draw my own as well" (2.9). When the old duke hears of his son's marriage (3.13), he indeed lunges at his son with drawn sword, and they find themselves in hand-to-hand combat. But when the son draws close in the fight, the father backs away with the significant justification: "You once saved my life! (With a sweep of his hand) Away! Away!" (5.9). This sparing the son's life as repayment for saving the father's is clearly reminiscent of the son's identical repayment fantasy in *Kabale und Liebe* ("Father, I owed you a life once").

Here only brief mention can be made of how the fight (or in dampened form, the conflict with the father) also appears in countless variations in modern literature as a less offensive expression of the repression of incestuous fixation on the mother. In his great novel *The Brothers Karamazov,* Fyodor Dostoyevsky, whose works almost always concern a murder, has the sons kill their father. Dostoyevsky's political orientation, arising from the father complex, is also interesting from the standpoint of the transformation of feelings. In his youth he belonged to a revolutionary party aiming to overthrow despotism and murder the czar. Upon his return from Siberia, having served his sentence, he became a loyal subject and a defender of despotism. In Dmitry Merezhkovsky's historical novel *Peter the Great and Alexei,* the psychological aspects of which are discussed by Ferenczi (1909, 448), the father's cruel treatment of the submissive son is depicted. And as Freud mentions in *The Interpretation of Dreams* (1909f, 181), Henrik Ibsen, in his freely invented plots, shows a tendency to bring the conflict between father and son to the fore. This is seen most clearly in *The Wild Duck,* where Gregers Werle strongly chastises his father for his ill treatment of and infidelity toward the deceased mother, who lives on in her son's memory as an idealized infantile image. The son, under great psychological stress, now attempts to realize the rescue fantasy, originally associated with the mother, in the happy married life of Hjalmar [his boyhood friend]. In Hjalmar's relationship to his own unhappy father, whom he is ashamed of in polite society but respects and loves within his own four walls, the playwright has portrayed the second component of the childhood orientation, which values the father. In the great argument between father and son [Werle and Gregers], the father utters a line reminiscent of a passage in *Don Carlos,* where Carlos proclaims:

> Why, of a thousand fathers,
> Must I have this father? And he this son before a thousand better sons?
> Two more inhospitable opposites
> Could not be found by nature in all her realm.
> How could she join the polar extremes of humanity—me and him—
> In such a sacred bond?

In Ibsen's play the father says: "Gregers, is there anyone in the world so repulsive to you as am I?" Gregers responds softly: "I have watched you from too close." Werle responds: "You have watched me with your mother's eyes." The son chastises the father even more severely in Ibsen's family drama *Ghosts,* where the hindered sibling incest clearly indicates the incestuous origin of the rivalry (cf. chap. 24):

> *Osvald:* Father—Father—Father! I have never known my father. I have no memory of him, except that he once made me ill!
> *Fru Alving:* It is terrible to think that! Should a child not love his father anyway?
> *Osvald:* If a child has nothing to thank his father for? . . . do you really still cling to the old superstition?

Here, just as in *The Wild Duck,* we observe the theme of the enduring mother, suffering from the father's infidelity, familiar to us from the rescue fantasy. *Ghosts* is also an interesting complement to the theme of repayment for the gift of life, reminding one of Franz Moor's speculations on birth [in Schiller's *Die Räuber*], discussed in chapter 3. Saying that it is she who gave him life, Fru Alving refuses to promise her son that she will administer the poison to him when he has his attack. Osvald responds: "I did not ask you for life. And what kind of a life have you given me? I don't want it! You can have it back." In Ibsen's youthful work *Peer Gynt* as well, which reveals an effusive love for the mother and the identification of the mother with the beloved, Solveig, the relationship with the father is dealt with in a paranoiac treatment of the family complex. Peer Gynt, who has delusions of grandeur and sees himself as an emperor, is declared emperor of the insane asylum. In the "naturalistic" vein, arising from Ibsen's social dramas, the conflict between father and son is commonplace, and here Ibsen, as the originator of the modern family drama, plays a role similar to that we were compelled to assign to Diderot (chap. 3). From the abundance of modern literature, only a few examples of the conflict between father and son can be mentioned here—for example, Georg Hirschfeld's drama *Zu Hause* [At home], Ernst Hardt's *Der Kampf* [The struggle] (2d ed.), Henry Bernstein's *Israël,* Herman Heijermans's *The Ghetto,* and Gustav Wied's story "Aus jungen Tagen" [From youthful days], which depicts the son's fantasy of attacking his father with a knife. Consider also Emile Verhaeren's *Le Cloître* [The monastery], where, with a noticeable exclusion of all female characters, repentance over the killing of the father is portrayed, and Hans Franck's very recent drama *Herzog Heinrichs Heimkehr* [Duke Henry's return] (1911), which depicts the return of Heinrich, believed dead (cf. Theseus), whom his son, the new ruler, refuses to recognize.

In *Die Geige* [The fiddle] (1911), a collection of novellas by Rudolf G. Binding, is found the story "Die Waffenbrüder" [The brothers at arms], which treats the struggle between unrecognized father and son, making reference to figures from the *Nibelungenlied.* In a Prussian mounted regiment, the weaponsmith Thomas Woller, from the Rheinland, and the homeless Daniel Roux, a fencing master, fight side by side against the army of Napoleon III. The two are united by the truest brotherly bonds of fellow fighters, hammered in the hot forge of flaming peril, and when peace is declared Daniel is moved to take up residence in the smith's hometown. It turns out that Daniel is the only one who can plead on his friend's behalf when Thomas falls in love with a strong-willed, obstinate woman. Through her defiance and obstinacy, the beautiful Gertrud, the conceited destroyer of her own brother's business, so irritates Daniel that he acts on her taunts, creeping in at night in his friend's place and taking advantage of her. This secret, well guarded through all the years Thomas and Gertrud live together as man and wife, is tauntingly revealed one day to the widowed Gertrud by Daniel's self-satisfied, gossiping wife. The betrayed Gertrud discloses her sufferings to her adolescent son, who decides to avenge her by attacking his previously respected friend and teacher, and in the struggle with his own unrecognized son, Daniel is killed with his own sword. Gertrud, to whom unclear associations have occurred too late, must bear with her the stream of dark thoughts (cf. M. Wied in *Die Zeit*).

However, we should not conceive of the obvious correspondences in the material—and in the shaping of the basic themes—as literary imitation, influence, or reminiscence, or in the case of the structure of legends, as haphazard thematic ubiquity. Instead, we believe they are explicable in a deeper sense as products of the same psychic developmental process, though we assume that these recurring psychic configurations rely sometimes more and sometimes less on previously existing fantasy constructions, depending on the psychic and intellectual talents of the individual. (In an extremely effective manner, myths provide even completely uncreative individuals with fantasy material.) Often enough, though, this bringing to life of poorly repressed, unconscious complexes through fantasy is impossible, and according to disposition and subsequent fate, a perverse, neurotic, or criminal orientation may result. We need only suppose the case where these impulses—which underlie the incest complex and were originally carried out in real life, later finding expression in distorted dreams and illogical fantasies—break through, on a higher cultural level, into real life, producing the pervert and the murderer. And nothing can better confirm our claim that these repressed impulses live on in all of us unconsciously after childhood, and are active beneath the surface, than that with the elimination of certain inhibitions and with abnormal intensification of the childhood emotions, capable of overpowering the inhibitions, these original impulses blatantly make their appearance.

The Psychology of Parricide

Criminal justice should seek to discover innocence rather than guilt.

HEBBEL, Diaries

The meaning of the infantile incest complex for later acts of murder carried out in highly emotional states cannot be presented here in its full extent, given that the motivation is regularly concealed in the unconscious. But through the association of mother incest with patricide, the Oedipus legend already suggests that even today, at least in the unconscious of the patricide, the same conflict rages, though owing to the process of transformation of affects it now expresses itself only in one-sided, exaggerated, and therefore incomprehensible hatred of the father. Referring to the individual cases of "criminal" incestuous orientation that have been noted in the literature will shed light on the theme of rivalry between son and father, which is of special interest for our investigation and still appears with surprising frequency at our level of culture, leading to attempts on the lives of close relatives. The individual cases will illustrate the psychological relationships presented. First, as purely statistical attestations of the frequency of patricide, let me present the accounts of violent acts I have collected from my daily reading of the newspapers in recent years, which, because of lack of information, cannot be further explained. Most of the cases demonstrate an early, clearly inimical relationship between father and son, which at times seems completely unmotivated and at times is rationalized through material motives, but which proves to be a correlate of sexual rivalry in those cases where the external relationship leads to a revitalization of the infantile incest complex.

Case 1. "They murdered their father. Lemberg. The 14th. In the town of Horozki near Bobrujski, during an argument, the three sons of the farmer Myslowic murdered their father with an ax. They carried their father's body to a field belonging to the next village and let it lie there. The patricides have already been arrested."

Case 2. "Shot by his son. Saint Petersburg. The 22d. Privy Councillor Buschoden was murdered yesterday by his son, who fired six shots at him. The son appears to be deranged. As justification for his terrible deed, he claimed that his father was completely unnecessary in the world. A brother of the murderer is a well-known political refugee living in Switzerland." This case confirms that political insurrection (the brother) arises from the father complex. Further, it clearly shows the motivation for the son's act—a motivation unknown to the son himself. A priori, this certainly should not be viewed as a symptom of derangement, but simply as the psychological expression of repression. If court psychiatrists believe that with a declaration of insanity they have determined the psychological motivation, they are extremely mistaken, even if the diagnosis is correct. It is only in the peculiar logic of insanity—the logic of unconscious thought—that the actual motivation can be found. And though many cruel acts cannot be attributed to normal thoughts and feelings, psychology has taught us that insanity and alcoholism produce no new thoughts and impulses. Instead, through the disappearance of certain inhibitions, these conditions bring about the manifestation of old, repressed thoughts and impulses. Indeed, based on our experience, we must say that these individuals flee into psychosis or alcoholism in order to live out their repressed complexes. Or, more correctly, we should say that repressed drives, demanding realization, have in these individuals become so powerful that they come to the fore, overpowering conscious thought. The truly insane individual, given his deranged unconscious, will perhaps be more likely to reveal the actual motives of his act than the neurotic under the influence of a powerful, repressed affect, who, in a manner extremely confusing to the uninitiated, attempts to rationalize his unknown motives to himself.

Case 3 shows, besides the superficial motivations, the self-punishment suggestive of a deep inner conflict. "A triple murder in England. London. The 19th. The small city of Maldon is in turmoil owing to a triple murder. The landowner Cole had been in disagreement with his son Fredrick for some time. Recently the court declared the father's home off limits to the son, since he had been convicted of theft. Last evening the son lay in wait for the father and hit him with a stick as he was leading a horse into the stable. On hearing his cries for help, his brother-in-law, Major Kitchen, hurried to the stable. The son took a revolver from his pocket and shot his father and Major Kitchen. On being pursued, he shot at his pursuers but finally aimed the weapon at himself, shooting himself in the head."

Case 4 shows rationalization through the money complex (strictness of the father). Here, though, through the intermediate element of prostitution, as in many cases, this represents the sexual. "The murderer of a forester. Berlin. January 25, 1908. The murder at the Mügelsee of the forester Schwarzenstein has been explained in a frightful manner. The father was murdered by his own son. The son, Willi, is twenty years old. He also wished to become a forester and had taken on a job with a master forester. Since he had been declared unfit for military service because of physical weakness, however, he had to give up his career in forestry. He then worked for a short while in a wood yard, but he could never manage to keep a job for long, for he is prone to frivolity. He frequented taverns with female servers and ran up debts everywhere. In desperation, he forged checks in his father's name. Often there were arguments between father and son. The father often complained to acquaintances about his frivolous son. The son had recently inherited assets from his grandfather but did not receive the money, since his father had claimed it, declaring once and for all that he would keep it as long as he lived and would never give it up. After the murder was discovered, it was noticed that the son affected a nonchalant demeanor. . . . Finally the evidence was pieced together and the police arrested the young man today. He was brought to the scene of the crime. There he became deathly white and cried, 'Help! Help!' He will next be brought to his father's body and will be confronted there."

Case 5 demonstrates the murder impulse toward the father, latent in the unconscious, without the assumption of which this unusual deed would hardly be comprehensible. "A patricide incited by the father. Stuttgart. The 27th. The innkeeper Weiss instructed his twenty-three-year-old son, mentally abnormal and lame in both feet, to shoot him with his musket. The son fired the weapon, which had been loaded by the father himself. Since he did not immediately die, though horribly wounded, he begged his son to finish the deed, and the son struck him with an ax. The patricide was incarcerated. The tragedy is said to have arisen from a dispute over money."

Case 6 suggests the Hamlet tragedy converted to a positive view. The father's would-be murderer, the son's representative with respect to the mother, is incited by the son so that he may realize the son's repressed wishes in the son's place. "A child's frightful plan. Marburg. September 22, 1909. A family drama, which has aroused great attention in Untersteiermark, was dealt with today before the local court. When Johann Kasper, director of the Pettau savings bank, entered the garden of his villa outside Pettau at midnight on July 18, a revolver shot, which penetrated his left hand, was fired at him in the dark. Director Kasper, who always went armed with a revolver at night, also fired a shot with his right hand. In the next moment a third shot was fired, piercing his right hand. Disarmed, he fled toward his house calling for help. He called to his wife, who appeared at the window, telling her to give him his second revolver, which he kept in the night chest. Public opinion immediately assumed that the director's wife had herself incited the murder attempt. Kasper's marital life is not happy. Recently Kasper had had to drive a servant away; he whipped his wife and the servant with a dogwhip. After the night attack, the wife was arrested, as well as a seventeen-year-old servant, Josef Gonsa. After a long period of interrogation, he admitted that he had been incited to do the deed—and not by the wife, but by the director's eleven-year-old son, Heribert. Then the young schoolboy was also brought in and after many denials finally confessed that he had incited the servant to shoot the father. As a motive, the boy stated that the father treated him harshly when he brought back poor grades from school. He won the servant over by telling him that after the father's death, Gonsa would be master of the house. It was also pointed out that Gonsa had stated that he would marry the director's widow after the latter's death and would then lead a happy life. Today Gonsa was accused of the crime of attempted incited murder. On account of his youth, Heribert Kasper was accused only of a misdemeanor."

Case 7 reveals even more clearly the role in patricide of repressed feelings of love, transformed into hatred; this occurs through defense of the mistreated mother. Most of these cases are characterized by the youth of the son, near puberty; at this age, intensive struggle with the incest complex is typical. "A fourteen-year-old patricide. Lemberg. In Zawadow, a fourteen-year-old boy has murdered his own father. Johann Kalinczuk, a drunkard known in the area, passed the whole night in a tavern and did not come home until 6:00 A.M. He arrived in a state of great intoxication. His wife severely criticized him for the change in his life. Thus arose an argument that ended in violent acts. Kalinczuk attacked his wife, beat her bloody in his excessive rage, and ripped out pieces of her flesh with his teeth. The fourteen-year-old son defended his mother: he grabbed a hoe and struck his father until the latter fell to the floor, drenched in blood. He gave the dying father a final blow and left the hoe wedged into the father's smashed skull. Then he hurried to the police station, where he reported all that had occurred. He was immediately handed over to the court."

Case 8 features the same scenario: "To free his mother. Attempted murder of the cruel father. Korneuburg. February 17, 1910. In Pernersdorf, on the twelfth of the month, a tragic incident occurred. The innkeeper Richard Ecker had caused his family to suffer incessantly. He had tormented his wife for years and let her suffer want. She had to beg her husband for every cent to buy the most essential articles for the household; he himself never spent anything. More and more ugly scenes occurred in the Ecker home. On the twelfth of the month, at 1:30 P.M., Richard Ecker was found unconscious and seriously wounded in a corner of his cellar. His skull was partially smashed. Beside Ecker lay a so-called mason's hammer with which the frightful blows had been executed. The nineteen-year-old son, Richard, turned himself in to the police as the culprit. He claimed he had carried out the deed out of hatred for his father because he could no longer bear to see the suffering his father caused his mother. It is doubted that Ecker will recover. The young man was delivered to the local court."

With their fantasy of the mother's rescue, which in reality can be carried out only through patricide, these cases remind one of the motivation for the battle between father and son as revenge for the poor treatment of mother (cf. Hildebrand, Milun, Sohrab, etc.), which corresponds to the same childhood perspective.

Case 9 reveals to us—not fully within the framework of the incest complex, but certainly with a related sphere—sexual rivalry for the common beloved (abduction of the bride) as a motive of patricide. "A family tragedy in New York. The millionaire George Sterry was shot yesterday in his office by his own son. The son then committed suicide. In stock exchange circles, the incident has been the subject of much discussion. We are informed that a violent argument preceded the deed. The father wished to hinder the son's marriage to a beautiful but poor young woman and threatened to disinherit his son if he married his beloved against his father's will. It has now become clear that the father had pursued the same young woman with entreaties of love, without intending to marry her. Presumably the son had heard of the father's pursuit of the young woman and had then carried out the murder."

With its substitution of the mother's beloved for the father (cf. *Hamlet*), like the substitution of the beloved for the mother in the preceding case, case 10 demonstrates the uninhibited emergence of emotions based on the repressed incest complex, revitalized by real circumstances. With the punishment of the mother for her infidelity to her son, however, it supersedes the patricide impulse and the associated substitute gratification. "Budapest. The 22d. In Biksoder, the twenty-three-year-old farmer Ugocsan surprised his mother during a rendezvous with her lover. He flew into such a rage that he began to stab the pair in a frenzy. The mother died instantly, and the lover suffered serious wounds. The furious son also stabbed a small child the woman held in her arms, which he supposed to be the result of his mother's relationship."

Case 11 reveals in a completely undisguised fashion the son's jealousy over the mother's affections and his revenge for the mother's infidelity to the son in marrying another—another son, as it were; the man was fifteen years younger than she. "Matricide out of jealousy. The murder of Mme Rachel Waché is being much discussed in Paris, and not without reason, for the criminal deed has an interesting motive. Gaston Waché, the murderer of his mother, seems to be a modern Orestes. Apparently he murdered his mother out of jealousy; she had secretly married a few days before. Mme Waché was already sixty years old. She had four children, three already married. Only Gaston lived with her at home. He is described as a quiet, almost shy young man. It is his mother's marriage plans that upset and transformed him. Mme Waché, the owner of several houses, seeing that her family was well provided for, wished to experience a new happiness in her later years. A stockholder of the firm Bonmarché, named Hajos, had asked for her hand in marriage. He was fifteen years younger than she. Mme Waché's children opposed the marriage, but the mother seemed to fear only the dissatisfaction of the youngest son. She informed him of her marriage when it had already taken place. She also asked that he move out of the house to make room for her husband—who is a widower with three daughters, by the way. This sudden news stunned Gaston. He immediately left the house, dined in a restaurant, and returned in the evening. In the morning he entered the mother's bedroom, and after a short scene in which he heaped reproach upon his mother, he drew out a revolver and fired a shot that immediately killed her. For an hour the son sat in despair before the body of his murdered mother. Then he called a doctor and confessed the crime with crazed agitation. From his statements it seems that he was very attached to the mother. Questions of inheritance are only of secondary concern."

Case 12 illustrates another complication: patricide and multiple sister murder. The patricide is characterized by a superimposed money complex; the first sister was killed in obvious jealous excitement, and the others in clearly sadistic abandon. The especially refined killing of the engaged sister occurred immediately after the well-planned murder of the father, and in connection with the visit to the mother's grave, it suggests obvious jealousy that cannot bear to see the eldest sister, who has now taken the place of the mother, in the possession of another man. "Tragic murder in Mainz. Mainz, December 28, 1908. The quadruple murder by the student Josef Racke of his father and sisters has aroused great interest here. Nikolaus

Racke, representative in the Reichstag and the local legislature, papal chamberlain, and wine wholesaler, had been widowed for the second time in 1904. From his two marriages he had eighteen children, of whom twelve survive. Josef, born in 1887, who has just committed the frightful deed, entered a monastery to take holy orders after completing the gymnasium. However, he later abandoned this intention and has been a university student for the past four years, having studied chemistry and more recently astronomy. For the Christmas holidays, the young student returned from Bonn to his father's home. His own study was in the wing, while the bedrooms of the three daughters, Stephanie, Elisabeth, and Anna, and finally that of the father, were behind the chapel and the dining room. Two other daughters and the second son lived in more distant portions of the great house. On Friday the family had retired after the Christmas celebrations. When Racke and his daughters had not appeared for coffee at 9:00 A.M. on Saturday, a maidservant and the police, who had been fetched in the meantime, discovered the murder of the daughters, who lay in their beds. When the father's bedroom was opened, the same dreadful scene presented itself. The floor of the room was covered with blood, and Racke lay dead in his bed, his head hacked beyond recognition. Father and daughters had been murdered with blows from a heavy, sharp instrument and with revolver shots. Suspicion quickly fell on the young Josef, who was found sleeping in bed. He was arrested and immediately confessed the deed. He related that at about 2:00 A.M. he had crept into the rooms of the members of his family and had murdered them with a bread knife, which he had tied to the barrel of his gun on the first day of Christmas, and with a revolver. He had abandoned his intention to murder his other sisters and his brother, since their rooms were too distant. *The motivation for the deed.* The murderer showed not the slightest trace of contrition and immediately asked for a drink after the first interrogation. On Sunday morning at 8:30 A.M. the murderer was brought before the bodies. Concerning his motive for the grotesque deed he divulged nothing. It seems he committed it in a deranged fit. There are said to have been arguments between father and son recently; the son complained that he was not given enough money to support himself in the university city of Bonn. The eldest of the murdered daughters, Anna, had been engaged to a doctor from Berlin just before Christmas. The student had arrived in Mainz a few days ago to celebrate Christmas in his father's home. On the first day of Christmas he visited the grave of his mother, who died a few years ago. In the morning, the faithful Catholic family had gone to communion together. On the evening of the first day of Christmas, the whole family had sat together in complete harmony. The murderer said that he had deliberately committed the deed after the first day of Christmas because he wanted the family to take communion first. An uncle of the murderer is in an asylum for the insane. The police investigation has concluded that the deed was the work of a deranged person. The individual statements Josef Racke has made are in any case often self-contradictory. During the interrogation, the murderer repeatedly declared that he would be willing to make more detailed statements only to a priest. He exhibited typical traits of religious derangement. In spite of the fact that he suffers from religious derangement, or perhaps precisely due to it, the twenty-one-year-old student had planned the gruesome deed down to the last detail with singularly cold-blooded determination. First Josef Racke killed his father with a sharp bread knife. Then he killed his (engaged) sister Anna with his improvised ax and with the same instrument immediately opened the veins of her left wrist to be completely sure of her death. The two other sisters, Stephanie and Elisabeth, who were sleeping in a third room, were awakened by the events taking place in the neighboring room, and when Racke entered their room Stephanie was sitting up in her bed. Elisabeth had jumped out of bed in fright, and before she knew what had happened, the brother fired two shots at her, of which the first entered just above the heart, killing her immediately, while the second injured her in the right upper arm. Stephanie wanted to flee from the room, but her crazed brother brought her down with the ax. The blow split the girl's face in two. Racke had intended to kill his other siblings as well, in order, as he said, to free them from the cares that life, and he himself, had caused them, but he was already exhausted and thus, fortunately, could not carry his frightful murder plan to its culmination."

With reference to the theme of killing the son, several acts of murder can now be presented in which the father kills his son in a fit of anger. First, as a transitional case, consider the father who claims he used his weapon in self-defense, having been roughly attacked by the son.

Case 13. "Father and son. A frightful family tragedy occurred yesterday evening in the seventh district. A businessman living there shot four times at his son, seriously wounding him; the son, a degenerate individual, was always intoxicated at home and frequently threatened his family. Concerning the deed, we have learned that the sixty-seven-year-old furrier Karl Behr lives with his wife and two sons at Lindengasse 25. Whereas the one son is a comfort to his parents, the second son, the twenty-four-year-old uniform cutter's assistant Josef Behr is a ruffian, a drunkard, and a lout, known to the police. All previous attempts to reform him have failed. The father had become so fearful of the son's wildness that he obtained a revolver for self-protection. Today at 2:00 A.M., Josef Behr came home thoroughly intoxicated. As usual, he began to stir up trouble in the most wild manner. When his family told him to be quiet, he began to swear and make threats. The drunkard answered his old father with such indecent insults and threats that the father, overcome with anger, jumped out of bed and threatened to shoot the degenerate son. Josef Behr is then said to have behaved so brutally that the father feared for his safety. He declares that he grabbed the revolver and shot blindly at the son in self-defense, without really knowing what he was doing. All four shots hit the ill-mannered son. After a vain effort to attack the father, he collapsed, seriously wounded."

Case 14. "Another officer's tragedy. Baden-Baden. The 15th. In nearby Lichtenthal, Major Bauer shot his son three times and then shot himself. The son, twenty-three-years-old, had become engaged against the will of the father, who thereupon refused him all financial support. When the young man made preparations to take his father to court to force him to continue to support him, Major Bauer told him to see him in Lichtenthal. There an animated argument occurred during which the officer committed the terrible deed. Believing that he had killed his son, Major Bauer then shot himself. However, the son is not mortally wounded."

Case 15 shows more clearly the father's jealous feelings toward the son, who is secretly received and financially supported like a lover by the mother. "The family drama of a university professor. Concerning the affair of Artur Joly, a professor of analytical chemistry at the University of Brussels, who shot his only son twice, wounding him rather seriously in both legs, we are informed that inimical feelings have already existed for years between the father and the son, now thirty-seven years old. Professor Joly accused the son of laziness and lack of energy and was very annoyed that the son, who initially was to have become a pharmacist but then learned watchmaking, is not able to support himself. The son states that he has not received from his father sufficient funds to establish a business. The Joly couple live in Brussels, Rue de Robiano 21. Close by, at Rue de Robiano 47, the son had a furnished room. The mother paid the rent and gave the son money from time to time. In the evening, after dining with her spouse, she was in the habit of giving a sign to her son, who would be waiting near the window. He would then enter his parents' home and would be given supper by his mother. Paul was with his mother on the first floor when Professor Joly unexpectedly appeared. He immediately proceeded to his laboratory, on the second floor, and had his supper brought to him there. This behavior on the part of the father angered the son. He hurried upstairs and knocked on the door of the laboratory, which the father had locked, until the latter opened it. When Professor Joly then calmly told his son that he never wanted to hear from him again, the son sprang upon his father and began to choke him. The old man tore himself loose and shot his son twice with his hunting gun. As mentioned, the shots wounded him in the legs. Professor Joly was arrested. He stated that he had fired in self-defense and did not regret shooting his son. Professor Joly is respected by his colleagues as well as his students. He is considered a rather nervous but good-natured man."

Case 16 illustrates similar jealousy toward the young son, and it is characteristic of the family framework of the father complex that the son's murderer is arrested after the deed has been reported by his own father. "The tragedy of a returnee. Zagreb. The 11th. It is reported that Mikulicic, a worker who had returned from America to his home in Pleso, killed his own little son a few days ago. The boy had been born during his father's absence and displayed an obvious dislike for him, so that the father finally murdered his own child out of hate. The murderer was arrested after the matter was reported by his own father."

If this murder of the little son does not seem plausible as an act of jealousy in the sense of our discussion, the reader should be reminded that the sexual aspect of this emotion will not be consciously emphasized, but that the repressed feelings of jealousy work from within the unconscious. To the conscious mind, the motivations of the unconscious seem extremely inadequate and peculiar because they retain their infantile character. Indeed, in the previous case, such a path seems to reveal the murderer's own infantile perspective. After all, it is his own father who hands him over for punishment. Apparently, having hated his own father, the murderer must dimly have feared similar behavior on the part of his son, who hated him. This theme of fear of retribution plays a significant role in literary form (chap. 6) and in the formation of myths (chap. 9).

The importance of the father complex for a psychological understanding of the murder of a man by a man is not specifically limited to the relationship of father and son but is paradigmatic, extending to a far-reaching psychological identity; many acts of murder, especially those committed out of jealousy, are proved from a psychoanalytical point of view to be realizations of the infantile perspective, which originally centered on the father but has, through displacement, acquired another victim. This is especially true of the political murder, with its strong emphasis on opposition to authority. Here we shall not illustrate this fact, proved by psychological insights, through the psychological illumination of such crimes. Instead, we refer readers to the analysis of literary, mythic, and neurotic fantasies, realized on the one hand by the perverse individual and on the other hand by the criminal. Thus the conditions leading to criminality are to be found not so much in any predisposition (cf. Lombroso, who speaks of the "born criminal"), but rather in one's manner of dealing with infantile psychosexuality and especially with the parent complex—all of which is also surely influenced by predisposition. Just as Freud has pointed out the infantile mode of thought of the dreamer and the neurotic, the infantile mode of action could be claimed for the criminal, especially the murderer. However, these individuals should be clearly distinguished from the perverse, for whom Freud has also demonstrated the retention of the infantile mode of action in the sexual realm.

In the perverse individual, the originally polymorphic sexual disposition of the child not only has been fully retained with a certain orientation, but has matured to full sexual activity in the absence of certain inhibitions. In the neurotic, for whom a similar intensification of drives is constitutionally preeminent, there arises, for reasons we shall not further discuss, a sense of guilt intensified by moral, religious, and conventional inhibitions following the attempt to repress these overly powerful drives. This sense of guilt leads to the failure of repression and to the distorted appearance of the repressed emotions as symptoms. The criminal, also an asocial being, stands psychologically between the perverse individual and the neurotic. He has in common with the perverse individual the same potential for action with respect to the environment, in contrast to the neurotic, who turns against his own ego. However, he stands closer to the neurotic in the sense that sexual feelings and affects do not remain in their original realm to seek gratification there. Instead, a unique mode of repression, well known from the development of neuroses and characterized by Freud as displacement, associates them, through deflection and inversion, with other conceptions. Thus the criminal can be characterized as an active neurotic, while the perverse individual is not necessarily neurotic at all. In the original composition of their drives, though, both stand equally close to the neurotic, and in their uninhibited potential for action they have the same relation to the neurotic.

Freud recognized these excessively strong drives, leading to such varied personality types and destinies, in the sadistic component of the sex drive, whose nature and development decisively influence the outcome of the struggle for repression. It should be noted that in the case of the playwright too it is mainly this sadistic emphasis that accounts for most of the acts of murder and cruelty he depicts on the stage and with which he powerfully affects the emotions of the spectators—the same as his own, but more strongly repressed. He is therefore distinguished from the true murderer in the same way he is distinguished, through the literary treatment of his incestuous feelings, from the truly perverse individual, who transforms his incestuous feelings into actual sexual acts. Freud's analysis of obsessional neurosis (1909b) has shown that the artistic or criminal transformation of powerful repressed sexual affects into murderous impulses can occur only through the sadistic component of sexuality. Because of the unsuccessful repression of an overly powerful sadistic component, obsessional neurosis leads to the self-tormenting inhibitions of powerful impulses. The obsessional neurotic often suffers precisely from the belief that he has murdered someone or from the delusion that he is being accused of murder. In other cases he isolates himself within his home so that he will not, in an agitated state, commit the feared murder. But the analysis of these conceptions, which are of course objectively unfounded and therefore apparently illogical, has revealed not only that they correspond to formerly positive, now repressed wishes and impulses, but also that the illogical nature as well as the affective intensity and indestructibility of these impulses is to be attributed to displacement from the originally sexual realm and the corresponding displacement of affects through the sadistic component of sexuality.

In the case of the neurotic, the sadistic component is directed toward the individual himself in the form of self-punishment. In the hysterical individual it is directly expressed in physical ailments, whereas in the obsessional neurotic it is expressed in self-tormenting feelings of guilt and self-reproach. In the criminal, though, it turns to influential persons in the environment who correspond more or less to the sexual goals of the sadistically perverse individual. Paradoxically, the murder fantasies and reproaches of the obsessional neurotic also concentrate on precisely those persons who were valued by him and dear to him. This explains the conflict that the murderer, capable of action, generally feels only after the act—in the form of repentance and a need for punishment. Thus one can in a sense regard the murderer's victim as a sort of pathological substitute for the sexual goal.

Correspondingly, there is a form of neuropsychosis that demonstrates this very clearly and that characteristically is transformed into a murderous impulse (inhibited in the obsessional neurotic). This is paranoia, the psychoanalytical analysis of which has determined that the persecutors feared by the paranoiac, and whose murderer he sometimes becomes, are nothing more than substitutes for formerly beloved persons who, through the outward projection of the transformation of his emotions, are now perceived as enemies. Analysis reveals that the father is the most basic image for the paranoiac; he is beloved in the unconscious and resisted by the conscious mind as an enemy and persecutor. Originally, of course, the child's relationship with the father was similarly contradictory. It is only through this contradiction of emotions that the repentance, aimed at punishment and harm to the self, can be explained. This in turn explains the indifference, so noticeable in these cases, with which the sentence of death is received. This indifference to one's own death corresponds to the similarly weakened conception of death during the murder itself.

In judging the act of murder, far too much use is made of the conscious mind. Psychologically, it is very unlikely that the murderer is able to conceive of death in all its terrible consequences at the moment of the murder, as is assumed by the penal code, based on the old principle of talion. Instead, here too he has instead retained the infantile mode of thinking, permitting him to carry out his infantile impulses in reality. His conception of death corresponds fully to the child's conception of death, discussed by Freud in *The Interpretation of Dreams,* which initially aims only to bring about the absence, temporary or permanent, of the disturbing competitor, who has become intolerable. The child's conception of death lacks any idea of the person's never returning or of bodily decay, terrible when clearly conceived. Similarly, in depicting the killing of the competitor, the playwright, who cold-bloodedly portrays the most frightful acts of murder in his fantasy as well as on stage, aims only for the absence of all disturbing competition or, psychologically expressed, the elimination of the psychic inhibitions. This is of course shown by the typical theme of the father who is thought dead (wished dead) but who nevertheless returns, either alive (Theseus, Mithridates, the old Moor in *Die Räuber*) or as a ghost (*Hamlet*), symbolizing the son's feelings of repentance and reestablishing the psychic inhibitions. The playwright continually strives, with the engagement and sanction of the public, to live out these fantasies. On the other hand, as shown by the facts, the threat and carrying out of punishment have no effect when repentance, a consequence of the associated tendency for harm to the self and self-punishment, does not occur. In these cases, which nevertheless often lead to the murderer's suicide, the death penalty would perhaps be a longed-for conclusion for the psychically lived-out life. Psychologically, though, the death penalty does not even correspond to the principle of talion, which is based on sadism. Psychoanalytical research compels us to conclude that a true psychological understanding of acts of murder can be obtained only through a detailed consideration of the decisive unconscious motives and the special nature and arrangement of the drives that underlie them. One can only regret that in its judgment and treatment of these antisocial elements, society—even if it appreciated the actual driving forces behind their acts—could hardly give due consideration to these psychological facts. However, it may already be possible to conceive of the possibility that prophylaxis will occur as a consequence of the general pedagogical effect of psychoanalytical enlightenment—a by no means utopian hope for the future.

6 *Shakespeare's Father Complex: The Psychology of Dramatic Creation*

The rude son should strike his father dead.
SHAKESPEARE, *Troilus and Cressida*

Shakespeare's hatred of his father, arising from and fed by the unconscious sources of repressed, infantile erotic affection for his mother, is already familiar to us from our analysis of *Hamlet,* where it functions as the driving force of the whole drama. Characteristic and, as we have emphasized, typical of the infantile relationship to the father is the contradictory position of the son, vacillating between affection and revulsion and not permitting him to carry out the wished-for but feared murder of the father, thus leading to the ghostly apparition of the father, killed by someone else. Yet the ghost still provides a means of expression for the repentance of the son, who reproaches himself for having contemplated the father's murder.

One finds precisely the same nuances, the same vacillating, contradictory character, and the same ghostly apparition in Shakespeare's *Julius Caesar;* with Brandes (1895–96, 426), for internal reasons, we must consider this work to have arisen simultaneously with *Hamlet.* The highly similar personalities of Brutus and Hamlet have often been compared. The conflict of emotions played out in Hamlet's unconscious and expressed only through its neurotic effects (the inability to carry out desired acts) is in Brutus partially conscious: "Vexed I am of late with passions of some difference" (*Julius Caesar,* 1.2). On seeing the unsuspecting Caesar, who

Brutus has decided must die, he declares: "The heart of Brutus yearns to think upon it" (*Julius Caesar,* 2.2). Having committed the deed, he justifies it to the people as follows: "If there be any . . . dear friend of Caesar's, to him I say that Brutus' love to Caesar was no less than his" (*Julius Caesar,* 3.2). He claims to have committed the deed out of patriotism: "Not that I loved Caesar less, but that I loved Rome more" (*Julius Caesar,* 3.2). In contrast to the situation in *Hamlet,* this psychic conflict can be expressed here so consciously and openly because it involves not the father, as in *Hamlet,* but rather the tyrant who strives for unlimited power (cf. *Fiesco*). The analogy between *Hamlet* and Brutus's act of murder despite his deep love for Caesar reveals to us the son character of Brutus. Nor are we unfamiliar with the substitution of the tyrannical ruler, the emperor, for the father. In *Julius Caesar* this displacement and substitution make direct wish fulfillment (the murder) possible, just as they allow the conflict to be a conscious one; Hamlet represents the opposite situation—repression and neurosis. Similarly, the ghost scenes in *Hamlet* and *Julius Caesar* (3.4) complement one another. The night before the decisive battle for rulership, unresolved since Caesar's death, the ghost of the murdered Caesar appears to Brutus in his tent and threatens him with reprisal and vengeance: "To tell thee thou shalt see me at Philippi" (*Julius Caesar,* 4.3). In *Julius Caesar* the ghost appears to the actual murderer, whereas in *Hamlet* it appears to the avenger of the murder (defense).

On the other hand, the son relationship, fully present in *Hamlet,* has been eliminated in *Julius Caesar.* The mother, who plays such a significant role in *Hamlet,* is also completely absent in *Julius Caesar; Julius Caesar* appears to be a purely political drama—a drama of men. We have before us a classic example of a drama that, without containing the slightest sexual allusion, nevertheless has its deepest sources and driving forces in unconscious infantile sexuality. This is revealed by the ghostly apparition of the dead Caesar in Brutus's tent. This is the vision of the father, familiar to us from *Hamlet,* which can easily be proved typical and which corresponds to the dream of the father in its artistic guise. Nevertheless, in its affective emphasis the apparition suggests a neurotic attack (vision). Not least of all, the affect of this scene, which achieves full expression through the dramatic portrayal and the effects thereof, leads us to recognize the identity of the ghostly apparitions in *Julius Caesar* and in *Hamlet*—to recognize that they are both apparitions of the father. Hamlet proclaims:

> Be thou a spirit of health or goblin damn'd,
> Bring with thee airs from heaven or blasts from hell,
> . . . .

Thou comest in such a questionable shape
That I will speak to thee.

(*Hamlet*, 1.4)

Almost with the same affectively powerful words, Brutus addresses the ghost:

Art thou any thing?
Art thou some god, some angel, or some devil,
That makest my blood cold and my hair to stare?
Speak to me what thou art.

(*Julius Caesar*, 4.3)

The son character of Brutus is also expressed in that he alone is actually made responsible for the deed. (Cassius, who embodies one side of Brutus's psyche, is also made partially responsible; cf. the splitting in *Don Carlos*.) Brutus alone feels the full weight of this guilt. Indeed, the ghost of the victim appears to him alone. In a peculiar manner, providing evidence for our point of view, the repentance of the "patricide" and his tendency for self-punishment are also expressed in *Julius Caesar*. Brutus and his second self, Cassius, perish not in battle, at the hands of their enemies, but rather by their own hands, in repentance for the murder of Caesar. They perish, made powerless by the memory of Caesar; they perish, as it were, by Caesar's hand. This is also suggested in that they kill themselves with the same sword they used to murder Caesar:

With this good sword
That ran through Caesar's bowels, search this bosom.
. . . .
Caesar, thou art revenged,
Even with the sword that kill'd thee. (Cassius dies.)

(*Julius Caesar*, 5.3)

Brutus directly states that he dies for the dead Caesar and, at the same time, by Caesar's hand:

O Julius Caesar, thou art mighty yet.
Thy spirit walks abroad, and turns our swords
In our own proper entrails.

(*Julius Caesar*, 5.3)

And immediately before his death, Brutus cries:

Caesar now be still.
I killed not thee with half so good a will.

(*Julius Caesar*, 5.5)

At this level of interpretation, the figure of Cassius appears only as the embodiment of the defensive tendencies active in Brutus from the beginning and expressing themselves in self-punishment. From the opening of the drama, Cassius is depicted as a candidate for suicide, and in his first appearance he expresses suicidal thoughts. It is also very significant that Shakespeare has Cassius die on his birthday (5.3), also suggesting his relation to the father.

However, the historical source Shakespeare has been proved to have used, and to have followed almost word for word—specifically Plutarch—states that Caesar considered Brutus his illegitimate son (Plutarch, *Brutus*, chap. 5). This belief gives our conception and interpretation of Brutus's son relationship to Caesar a greater meaning and also leads us to accept it as irrefutable evidence. Indeed, we should interpret in the same manner Caesar's cry, which he is said to have repeated again and again on seeing Brutus approach him with dagger drawn: "You too, my son Brutus" (Suetonius, *Julius Caesar*, chap. 82). In Shakespeare's play the wounded Caesar says only: "Et tu, Brute? Then fall Caesar" (*Julius Caesar*, 3.1). In Suetonius, Caesar actually falls through Brutus's faithlessness—by the hand of his son—and in the same way, as was shown, Brutus actually dies in repentance for the murder of his father—by Caesar's own hand. Thus, although he was doubtless aware of Brutus's son relationship to Caesar, Shakespeare omitted it in his adaptation of the historical sources. We now come to another important realization associated with one observed earlier: it is not only the modifications a playwright makes in the historically documented relationships and characters or in his predecessors' conception of these elements that have deep psychological motivation. The playwright's omissions from the sources have deep psychological motivation as well. These are equivalent to the omissions found in a final draft with respect to earlier versions and arise from a tendency to inhibit the expression of painful, repressed emotions. Shakespeare's strongly affective father complex was undoubtedly of this nature. Indeed, in our conception of the psychology of the selection of material we must now argue for a conclusion that cannot be proved. Given the material recorded by Plutarch, which Shakespeare adopted almost word for word (with the exception of the son relationship), we must actually say that the situation is the reverse of what until now has generally been assumed. One need not first demonstrate that in every case the choice of material has deep psychological motivation for the playwright and that the selection corresponds extensively to his dominant complexes. On the contrary, from the selection and treatment of material, one can infer with great certainty the nature of the playwright's psyche. Not only does he introduce certain contradictory feelings into the historically documented material, which has attracted him because of certain interests—

historical, aesthetic, or otherwise—but also, given such interests, he is always preferentially in search of material that will enable him to express his feelings in their various states of repression and defense (Bleuler's complex: receptivity).

In addition to this highly significant elimination of the son relationship, which is to be equated with the dampening of the mother to stepmother, the few details Shakespeare freely inserted into the story are also of psychological importance. In Plutarch, Brutus's first monologue before the final decision (2.1) is lacking, just as is the dialogue between Brutus and Cassius expressing the same conflict within Brutus's psyche (1.2). Further, the ghostly apparition, which Plutarch does not particularly designate as Caesar's, was specified by Shakespeare as Caesar's. Certain other details also support our analysis (cf. Delius 1882). In addition to all the internal features that characterize *Julius Caesar* as a patricide drama, an apparently insignificant external detail will, after our previous discussion, serve as evidence. This is a figure of speech, which—like all linguistic details, especially similes—the playwright never chooses at random. Rather, figures of speech are strictly determined by the psychology of the playwright; even superficially, they must correspond to the style of the whole work. To assuage Antony, who is disturbed about the murder, Brutus attempts to convince him of the need for the deed:

> Our reasons are so full of good regard
> That were you, Antony, the son of Caesar,
> You should be satisfied.
>
> (*Julius Caesar*, 3.1)

That it is precisely Brutus who says this suggests that Shakespeare was aware of his son relationship to Caesar but eliminated it because of internal inhibitions. For the utterance actually signifies: "The reasons satisfy me, Caesar's son; they should satisfy you all the more." Just as the son's tendency for self-punishment is embodied in Cassius, his feelings of respect for the father are embodied in Antony, who delivers such a pious, yet politically tinged eulogy for the murdered Caesar. The objection, apparently well justified in principle, that Cassius and Antony, like Brutus, are historically documented persons and that they accordingly cannot be personifications of the playwright's feelings as a son, as we claim, can be refuted by pointing out that although these persons are historically documented, their full personalities remain undescribed; only isolated details are reported. To bring them dramatically to life, the playwright in this case, for example, makes use of his various feelings as a son with respect to the father. It is in this manner that these characters acquire dramatically essential continuity, but they also take on a certain one-sidedness corresponding to the psychic point of view in each case and to its opposite impulses.

Here, as in our discussions of Schiller, we have to a seemingly excessive degree claimed psychological significance for individual, apparently insignificant details, figures of speech, and similes. Therefore, before proceeding further with our interpretation of certain details in the works of Shakespeare suggesting the inimical relationship of father and son, we should attempt to justify our interpretation. If we are really to take seriously the parallels between dream and drama, then it is not even sufficient to consider all details, even the apparently most insignificant ones, to be of equal psychological importance. The most important thing is to expect, following our studies of dreams, that the psychologically most important theme of the whole drama may be expressed in an easily overlooked, unobtrusive element. Herein, to an extent, lies of course the aesthetically pleasurable effect. To produce this effect, a "facade" of innocent, inoffensive elements must be presented. Thus, in *Henry VI,* one of the earliest dramas of the young Shakespeare, which might appear to have arisen from historical interests alone, are depicted the horrors of the civil war, which respected no family bonds (part 3, 2.5). In the stage directions we read: "Enter a son who has killed his father, dragging in the corpse." The son, who only now realizes that the slain man is his father, says:

Pardon me, God, I knew not what I did!
And pardon, father, for I knew not thee!

(*3 Henry VI,* 2.5)

This form of defense is already familiar to us from *Oedipus*. But the punishment for the forbidden wish fulfillment immediately follows the act. Immediately after the deed, in the stage directions we read: "Enter a father who has killed his son, with the body in his arms." Similarly, in Shakespeare's first drama, *Titus Andronicus,* which he may have written at the age of twenty, Titus kills his son Mutius in anger but must then, in punishment, chop off his own hand (tendency for self-punishment). This violent murder of the rebellious son was, as Brandes mentions, freely invented by Shakespeare. In *Henry VI* (part 3), the way the two sons react to the news of their father's murder is also characteristic for the expression of feelings of father hatred and of their repression:

Edward: O, speak no more, for I have heard too much.
Richard: Say how he died, for I will hear it all.

(*3 Henry VI,* 2.1)

In *King Lear,* too, the subplot running parallel to the main action contains the theme of father hatred with its typical figures: the loving son, Edgar, and the hating son, Edmund—a splitting of emotions repeated in

Schiller's *Die Räuber* and in *Don Carlos*. (Like Edmund, in speaking to his father, Franz Moor also slanders his innocent and faithful brother by means of a counterfeited letter. Here again—in *Die Räuber* and as regularly observed, in fact—the father is immediately inclined to believe in the son's rebellion.) Through the fault of his evil son, the father, Gloucester, loses both his eyes (cf. Melchthal) and realizes too late his grave error in judging his sons. Here, of course, the playwright's feelings toward his father, contradictory as a consequence of his infantile perspective, are again personified.

Besides these rather undisguised depictions of the split but primarily inimical relationship between father and son, in the ghost scenes of *Hamlet* and *Julius Caesar* we have observed in full clarity the neurotic nature of this relationship; in these ghostly apparitions we have also recognized the markings of repressed father hatred. Similar ghost scenes are also found in other works by Shakespeare written in various periods of his life, however, and based on our findings we have reason to suspect unconscious father hatred as the driving force behind these episodes as well. Three years after *Julius Caesar* and *Hamlet* there arose *Macbeth*, which also contains the typical ghost scene. Driven by ambition, Macbeth murders the venerable King Duncan; it had been predicted that Macbeth would himself become king (the son wishes to put himself in the father's place). But he also has his friend Banquo murdered; he envies him his children. (According to the same prophecy, Banquo's sons will become kings, and thus the successors of Macbeth.) Thus we see the theme of the fear of retribution that seizes the rebellious son when he himself becomes a father. Here the simultaneous killing actually unites Duncan and Banquo as one person. The ghostly apparition of Banquo can therefore be taken as demanding vengeance for the murdered king as well. Banquo's ghost appears at the banquet and sits in Macbeth's place (the father thrusts the son back from the place he wishes to usurp). The first words Macbeth speaks to the ghost are an expression of defense against his feelings of guilt: "Thou canst not say I did it" (*Macbeth*, 3.4).

Banquo's two appearances as a ghost are Shakespeare's free invention (cf. Brandes), and the father character of these appearances as well as of the whole murder is revealed not only in the characteristic ghostly apparition, but also in certain seemingly insignificant details. Like Hamlet, Macbeth is by no means unable to carry out a planned act, but is only incapable of the specific act of regicide. And it is highly significant that the first mention we hear of Macbeth is the report of a soldier attesting to the general's heroic boldness and decisiveness (1.2). Macbeth also fells without a second thought the two servants who guard the king and could reveal his guilt. But facing this one deed, the murder of the king, he hesitates and doubts, just as do Brutus, Hamlet, and Tell. It is his wife who drives him to the final step; she is simultaneously the embodiment of his ambitious wishes. This explains why it is not Macbeth, but rather his wife, who reveals the father nature of Duncan. Referring to Duncan and the planned murder, she [actually MacDuff] says:

> Malcolm and Donalbain, the king's two sons,
> Are stol'n away and fled, which puts upon them
> Suspicion of the deed.
>
> (*Macbeth*, 2.4)

Thus it is fully characteristic of the father complex that after the murders of both Duncan and Banquo, their sons are suspected. Just like the sons of Duncan, Banquo's son, who escaped the attack by fleeing, is suspected of having murdered his father (4.6). Further, that Shakespeare makes Macbeth and Duncan cousins perhaps hints at Macbeth's son relationship to Duncan (cf. Claudius's words: "Our chiefest courtier, cousin, and our son" [*Hamlet*, 1.2]). The connection with Caesar's murder is also demonstrated by a seemingly unimportant detail: Caesar is stabbed twenty-three times, and after the apparition of the murdered Banquo, Macbeth says:

> But now they rise again
> With twenty mortal murders on their crowns,
> And push us from our stools.
>
> (*Macbeth*, 3.4)

Given that there is a similar ghostly apparition in *Richard III*, one of Shakespeare's earliest works, Lady Macbeth's words to the guests explaining her husband's conduct surely apply in all senses to the playwright himself:

> My lord is often thus, and hath been from his youth.
> Pray you, keep seat. The fit is momentary.
> Upon a thought he will again be well.
>
> (*Macbeth*, 3.4)

Just as Caesar appeared to Brutus, the ghosts of all the relatives he murdered so as to succeed to the throne appear to Richard in the night before the decisive battle. Richard, like the Roman conspirators, is felled not by an overwhelming enemy, but rather by the repentance the ghosts have awakened in him:

> By the apostle Paul, shadows to-night
> Have struck more terror to the soul of Richard
> Than can the substance of ten thousand soldiers
> Armed in proof, and led by shallow Richmond.
>
> (*Richard III*, 5.3)

Through the multiplication of the ghostly apparitions and the complication of the murder of relatives, this scene's origins in the father complex are obscured. But its dramatic structure is so similar to that of the scenes of the father's apparition that one must conclude that Richard's dream has the same driving force. Just as Macbeth calls for wine to dull the impression of Banquo's apparition ("Give me some wine. Fill full" [*Macbeth,* 3.4]), Brutus twice demands wine before the apparition of Caesar ("Give me a bowl of wine!" [*Julius Caesar,* 4.3]). In the same manner, in his tent, Richard too twice demands wine before the ghost appears ("Fill me a bowl of wine. . . . Give me a bowl of wine" [*Richard III,* 5.3]). In addition to the internal probability and the superficial similarities, other characteristic details too reveal the incest complex, which also played a significant role in the creation of *Richard III.* Richard's courting of the widow of Edward, whom he has slain, beside Edward's bier is nothing but a dampened form of marriage to the mother:

> What though I kill'd her husband and her father?
> The readiest way to make the wench amends
> Is to become her husband and her father.
>
> (*Richard III,* 1.1)

And speaking of her marriage to Richard, she reports:

> Never yet one hour in his bed
> Have I enjoyed the golden dew of sleep,
> But with his timorous dreams was still awaked.
>
> (*Richard III,* 4.1)

After he is rid of her as well, he decides to marry his own niece, the daughter of the widowed Queen Elizabeth, having murdered her brothers:

> Her father's brother
> Would be her lord? Or shall I say, her uncle?
> Or, he that slew her brothers and her uncles?
>
> (*Richard III,* 4.4)

The ghost seeking atonement, characteristically found in a series of literary works, is in *Hamlet* unambiguously that of the father. Thus this tragedy marks the turning point in Shakespeare's inner life with respect to these feelings. In the works before *Hamlet,* the father complex is only touched upon, expressing itself in minor conflicts. In *Hamlet,* and in the subsequent *Julius Caesar* and *Macbeth,* the conflict is intensified in a neurotic manner. This becomes comprehensible if we consider the fact, pointed out by Freud, that Hamlet was written immediately after the death of Shakespeare's father, with the fresh impression of this "most important event in a man's life"; that is, it "was written in the reactivation of the infantile feelings for the father" (Freud 1909f). It is very probable that, after the death of his father, Shakespeare—like all persons for whom this complex was important in childhood—reproached himself (perhaps unconsciously) for not having been sufficiently loving toward him; for having perhaps even been hard and abrupt; for having been unfair to his father at least in his own thoughts. It is probable that he felt his father did not deserve this hatred and that distress over rejection by his son may have brought about or at least precipitated his death. These doubts concerning the justification of his former hatred are of course reasonable, for the actual source of this hatred, which in its intensity makes this hatred appear comprehensible and justified—that is, the erotic inclination toward the mother—was and is unconscious. To justify this hatred, the conscious mind had developed conventional motivations that to the mature man, under the effect of the feared rival's death, must have seemed insufficient. In short, thoughts of the dead father, connected with self-reproach, gave him no rest. The "ghost" of the dead man always plagued him, demanding vengeance, and the attempt to dispel his memory, to repress it, led to the various artistic products of this complex, which are surprisingly similar to the products of dreams and neuroses.

Among other results this led, through the assimilation of older material, to the composition of *Hamlet*. In this sense, Brandes's comments (1895–96, 401) concerning the first draft of *Hamlet* are significant: "The main interest in this older drama appears to have centered on an invented figure, the ghost of the murdered man, and on his cry: 'Hamlet, revenge!' " In this first draft of *Hamlet,* no longer extant, Hamlet's mother (like Hamlet himself) is supposed to have been much younger. From our point of view this suggests gradual repression. In any case, she was conceived of as young enough to call forth Claudius's passions (and ultimately those of her son); the corresponding derogatory references to her age, found in the final version, were absent in the original one. From the various guises of the stepmother theme, we are already familiar with the rejuvenation of the mother. There is a striking correspondence: in the drama, the father of the prince of Denmark, like the playwright's own father, had just died. Thus Hamlet's reproach, inhibitions, and pangs of conscience are still active. This correspondence suggests Shakespeare's intense identification with his protagonist. For with the later realization of the long-repressed infantile wish for the father's death, arising from jealous love for the mother, a restructuring of the original Oedipus complex occurs (though based on an infantile perspective), owing to the feelings of guilt and the powerful self-reproach that blames the son for the father's death. Through psychic reaction, the father is brought once again into the original position of respected, beloved, honored, noble, and powerful protector of the child, while infantile love and respect for the mother are eliminated and she takes on the despised role characteristic of the later fantasies of puberty, which even blame her for the father's death. Thus Hamlet's reactively exaggerated loving and repentant attitude of atonement toward his father proves to be the literary representation of the same transformations occurring in the psyche of the author himself. The material concerning vengeance for the murdered father attested in the Hamlet legend, with which the playwright was undoubtedly familiar from earlier Hamlet dramas, therefore must have taken on this psychic significance for him at this time.

But just as an affectionate tendency, originally present and never abandoned by the unconscious—that is, a latent homosexual component—is necessary to bring about the reactive loving orientation toward the father, so the condition for the later revitalization of the young son's conception of the mother as a whore is an earlier, deeply felt disappointment in connection with the mother, usually found in the discovery of her sexual relations with the father (and perhaps later, in fantasy or in reality, in her relations with other men). Indeed, in speaking with his mother Hamlet often enough and forcefully enough characterizes his (step)father as reprehensible, and in the sense of his fantasies, incestuous. This disappointment in connection with the mother, the consequences of which we recognize in the eighteen-year-old playwright's unhappy marriage (cf. Byron) to a woman eight years older, also not uncommonly leads, as has been shown by psychoanalytical research, via misogyny, to a complete turning away from women and a simultaneous diversion of the libido to those of one's own sex, based on the originally affectionate father complex. Here we find a source of the playwright's homosexual tendencies. These found their most powerful expression in the sonnets composed in this period, but they also play a significant role in his dramatic works.

That it was actually the death of a parent that brought about such a change in the psychic life of the playwright is also demonstrated in that *Coriolanus*, the only drama besides *Hamlet* to be based on the relationship to the mother, was composed just after the death of Shakespeare's mother (in 1608), just as *Hamlet* was written as a reaction to the death of his father. Like Macbeth, developed three years earlier, Coriolanus is also completely under the influence of a woman, and just as Macbeth's ambition is personified in his spouse, Coriolanus's ambition finds expression in his mother, Volumnia. Every noble deed he has done "he did . . . to please his mother" (*Coriolanus*, 1.1). Here again, behind an apparently insignificant turn of phrase, we find the hint of mother incest. Volumnia says to her daughter-in-law: "If my son were my husband, I should freelier rejoice in that absence wherein he won honour than in the embracements of his bed where he would show most love" (*Coriolanus,* 1.3). We also find here the fantasy, typical of the incest complex, of not being the son of one's own mother. When Coriolanus will not be persuaded, even by his mother, to contemplate reconciliation and mercy for his native city, the mother finally says:

> Come, let us go. This fellow had a Volscian mother.
> His wife is in Corioli, and this child
> Like him by chance.
>
> (*Coriolanus,* 5.3)

These words mollify Coriolanus. In illustration of the psychologically notable relationship of Coriolanus to the opposing general, Tullus Aufidius, which exhibits the most burning hatred combined with direct erotic affection, a characteristic expression of the infantile perspective toward the father, consider the following passage:

> *Coriolanus:* I'll fight with none but thee, for I do hate thee
> Worse than a promise-breaker.
> *Aufidius:* We hate alike.
>
> (*Coriolanus,* 1.8)

Nevertheless, Coriolanus crosses over enemy lines without hesitation, giving himself up to Aufidius:

> O world, thy slippery turns! Friends now fast sworn,
> Whose double bosoms seem to wear one heart,
> Whose hours, whose bed, whose meal and exercise
> Are still together, who twin as 'twere in love
> Unseparable, shall within this hour,
> On a dissension of a doit, break out
> To bitterest enmity. So fellest foes,
> Whose passions and whose plots have broke their sleep
> To take the one the other, by some chance,
> Some trick not worth an egg, shall grow dear friends
> And interjoin their issues. So with me.
> My birthplace hate I, and my love's upon
> This enemy town. I'll enter. If he slay me,
> He does fair justice; if he give me way,
> I'll do his country service.
>
> (*Coriolanus,* 4.4)

His mortal enemy Aufidius receives him with the affectionate love that, given that Coriolanus has turned away from his mother, can only be seen as a revitalization of specifically homosexual drives in the sense of our discussion:

All-noble Martius! Let me twine
Mine arms about that body whereagainst
My grainèd ash an hundred times hath broke,
And scarred the moon with splinters. Here I clip
The anvil of my sword, and do contest
As hotly and as nobly with thy love
As ever in ambitious strength I did
Contend against thy valour. Know thou first,
I loved the maid I married; never man
Sighed truer breath. But that I see thee here,
Thou noble thing, more dances my rapt heart
Than when I first my wedded mistress saw
Bestride my threshold. Why, thou Mars, I tell thee
We have a power on foot, and I had purpose
Once more to hew thy target from thy brawn,
Or lose mine arm for't. Thou hast beat me out
Twelve several times, and I have nightly since
Dreamt of encounters 'twixt thyself and me—
We have been down together in my sleep,
Unbuckling helms, fisting each other's throat—
And waked half dead with nothing.

(*Coriolanus*, 4.5)

The third servant also depicts Coriolanus's reception by Aufidius in a similar manner: "Our general himself makes a mistress of him, sanctifies himself with's hand, and turns up the white o'th'eye to his discourse" (*Coriolanus*, 4.5). In addition, we also find indirect hints of Coriolanus's effeminacy, again usually couched in idiomatic expressions and similes. Thus Cominius says of him, albeit with an emphasis on his youth:

In that day's feats,
When he might act the woman in the scene,
He proved best man i'th'field.

(*Coriolanus*, 2.2)

Further, to his mother's entreaties, he responds:

Away, my disposition; and possess me
Some harlot's spirit! My throat of war be turned,
Which choired with my drum, into a pipe
Small as an eunuch or the virgin voice
That babies lulls asleep!

(*Coriolanus*, 3.2)

We have already claimed that this whole contradictory pattern of behavior, vacillating between the most tender affection and fervent hatred, corresponds fully to the infantile perspective toward the father. And that this regression to an infantile orientation arises not only from the father's death but also from the son's turning away from the beloved mother is very clearly revealed in this drama. Thus Coriolanus, a hater of his father, becomes a hater of his native city, and because of affection for the previously beloved father he becomes the most tender friend of his bitter enemy, by whose hand he nevertheless dies in the end. (Nor is Aufidius, however, unrepentant: "My rage is gone, And I am struck with sorrow" [*Coriolanus*, 5.6].) The father complex is directly suggested in Coriolanus's relationship with his old friend Menenius, whom he respects and characterizes as a father:

> You hear what he hath said
> Which was sometime his general, who loved him
> In a most dear particular. He called me father.
>
> (*Coriolanus*, 5.2)

Further, to the guard who refuses to grant him access to Coriolanus, Menenius says: "You shall perceive that a Jack guardant cannot office me from my son" (*Coriolanus*, 5.2). To Coriolanus himself he says: "The glorious gods sit in hourly synod about thy particular prosperity, and love thee no worse than thy old father Menenius does! O my son, my son! thou art preparing fire for us" (*Coriolanus*, 5.2). After Coriolanus has roughly and inexorably turned away the beseeching old man as well as his mother, Coriolanus himself says:

> This last old man,
> Whom with a crack'd heart I have sent to Rome,
> Loved me above the measure of a father,
> Nay, godded me indeed.
>
> (*Coriolanus*, 5.3)

In this artificially created father relationship we find the opposite situation with respect to Shakespeare's omission of the historically documented father relationship in *Julius Caesar*. Here one receives some insight into the displacement of affect, analogous to dreams, that must occur with the psychic assimilation of historically documented material in order to make possible the uninhibited release of repressed emotions through artistic fantasy. We also gain further insight into the selection of material. We cannot accept the objection that we have chosen random passages in making our determination of the playwright's major complexes. Nor can it reasonably be objected that we are unjustified in introducing these complexes into the discussion of his works. Instead, it appears that the historically documented material chosen by the author, which he need only bring to life with his own affects, could not, as Lessing said, have been invented better by the playwright himself. Here we already begin to suspect the reason for this remarkable correspondence. In this respect, the development of myths is relevant: the creators of the mythic or literary material chosen by the playwright developed the material based on the same eternal human complexes continually experienced by all creative individuals; these complexes present themselves with overwhelming force and demand gratification. They exist not only in the playwright, but also in the founder of religions and in the hero who carries out historically significant acts, and with whom the author can identify just as he can with a mythical hero, even without the half-legendary historical documentation, already adapted to reflect a given complex. It is only under the influence of the same complex that the hero who carries out momentous real-world acts (such as the actual Coriolanus) could have been driven to do so.

In utilizing the source material, in this case a rather extensive, unaltered assimilation of Plutarch, the playwright needed to make only those modifications dictated by his own infantile perspective and repression. These changes should in general be regarded as shifts of affect and outward projections of split emotions. Just as the feelings for the father are multiply split within the psyche of the author, he personifies these feelings in multiple versions of the father, either in recapitulation or in modification of older material. The stage of repression in which the playwright finds himself will determine which one of these figures, all arising from the same underlying complex, he will adopt as the father figure in a given work—again with the justification that he is only adopting preexisting material. In *Julius Caesar* the father figure has been eliminated. In *Coriolanus* it corresponds to the respected, honorable old man, whom the son will offend only reluctantly, while it has been eliminated from the highly ambivalent and mainly inimical relationship with Aufidius. In *Hamlet,* of all possible father figures, Shakespeare chose the revenge-seeking ghost, while the "stepfather" is handled inimically and Polonius is treated with derision.

In *Hamlet,* however, in addition to the reactive need for repentance and atonement that followed the death of Shakespeare's father, a second important psychological event makes the ghost the bearer of the father role and the father the bearer of the ghost's role and characterizes *Hamlet,* as already mentioned, as a turning point in Shakespeare's creative life. This is the previously mentioned conversion of son feelings into father feelings, which clearly appears for the first time in *Hamlet,* stimulated by the father's death and accompanied by fear of retribution. In each case we must conceive of this as a purely psychological event, as a reaction to the now incomprehensible infantile hatred of the father, a reaction that can be coincident with actually becoming a father or can be influenced by that event, but that actually occurs quite independent of it. After all, Shakespeare had already been a father for some years before he began to write literary works. This fatherhood had no deep psychological effects initially and probably could not have, given the playwright's long years of separation from his family. Even the death of his only son Hamnet (1596) seems to have produced no lasting effect on the playwright, working in a completely different sphere of life. It was only with the death of his father that his infantile complexes dealing with his perspective toward his parents awakened, as well as the memory of his own family and of his own dead son. Feeling that he had neglected the boy, he experienced as much guilt in connection with his son as with his father. Thus it was only on the death of his father that the basic transformation in the psychic life of a man that we have characterized as the feeling of fatherhood occurred, just as it ordinarily does, in Shakespeare. This psychic transformation, which makes a father of the son, is of the greatest significance in a man's life and can be compared only to the greatest and most meaningful event in a woman's life, motherhood. Fatherhood is psychically what motherhood is organically. Many utterances and, not least of all, creations of writers are comprehensible only from the psychology of the son. That is, in his thoughts, feelings, and actions, the individual is nothing but a son; he regards everything from this one-sided point of view. With the coming of the father psychology, everything is psychologically reevaluated. Thus in *Hamlet* hatred of the father now appears only in a disguised manner, cloaked in its opposite; and besides the insistent criticism of the (step)father, we also clearly see the wish to justify him. This fatherly point of view of the son, which demands and makes possible the justification of the father, does not result from any better, unbiased insight into actual circumstances but arises because the son now feels himself to be a father and must justify himself psychically toward his own children in order to deal with his feelings of self-reproach. Here again we see the theme of retribution, the fear of a son's similar behavior toward the father who, as a son, has reproached himself for his behavior toward his own father. The writing of *Hamlet* should therefore be regarded as Shakespeare's attempt to eliminate the unconscious split in his psyche, the split between his unconsciously still active infantile feelings as a son (hatred toward the father and erotic affection for the mother), against which powerful defense mechanisms had arisen following the death of his father, and his current feelings as a father—wishing love and obedience from his son and fearing the son's erotic affection for the mother. It is due to this inner conflict that Hamlet, the son who cannot carry out revenge upon his father's murderer, seeing in him the embodiment of his own wishes, is contrasted with Laertes, the son who with all his energies and with full passion demands vengeance for his murdered father Polonius:

> How came he dead? I'll not be juggled with.
> To hell, allegiance! Vows to the blackest devil!
> Conscience and grace to the profoundest pit!
> I dare damnation. To this point I stand,
> That both the worlds I give to negligence,
> Let come what comes. Only I'll be revenged
> Most thoroughly for my father.
>
> (*Hamlet*, 4.5)

While Shakespeare consciously uses Laertes to serve for Hamlet as the image of genuine father vengeance, uninhibited since it is not reactively exaggerated, this complementary figure also serves unconsciously to liberate the playwright's inhibited feelings of revenge and atonement with respect to his father, at least in the splitting of the father-son relationship (Polonius-Laertes). Here again we see, as we did with Schiller, that the character apparently opposite to the protagonist actually lets the playwright gratify those feelings that, owing to strong internal inhibitions, he cannot gratify through the protagonist himself. Thus, as in *Don Carlos*, the characters can be reduced to a series of splittings of the father and the corresponding perspectives of the son. In the old murdered Hamlet (the characteristic identity of name between father and son originates with Shakespeare) is embodied the formerly loved and respected father, now seeking vengeance and atonement. In his murderer, Claudius, in addition to the fulfillment of the son's wishes, is embodied the father hated because of his role as competitor for the mother, toward whom hatred of the father, now sublimated as vengeance for the father, can be more fully expressed, now being only partially inhibited. In Polonius is embodied the disdained and derided elderly father who wishes to keep his daughters for himself, just as the father wishes to keep the mother. In each of these perspectives, the son (Hamlet, as well as his psychological complement, Laertes) has a distinct relation to the father. That the playwright psychically conceived of the murder of the eavesdropping Polonius behind the curtain (already attested in his sources) as a patricide substitute has already been demonstrated by Hamlet's cry after the murder, "Is't the king?" And we have assumed as well that the final murder of Claudius also represents, in its actual psychological significance, the murder of the mother's husband, made possible by the theme of vengeance for the father. This is the basis of the drama.

But the theme of vengeance for the father does not suffice for the playwright as it does for the legendary hero, who purposefully sets out on his mission. Instead, Hamlet is able to kill the king only when the king has poisoned the deeply loved mother. Only then can he carry out the decisive death blow, which he had been saving for "th'incestuous pleasures of his [Claudius's] bed," for life without his mother has no value for him and he, like so many other heroes, wishes to be united with her at least in death. In mythology, we will observe with special frequency this intention of killing the hated competitor during sexual relations ("in th'incestuous pleasures of his bed") as a typical father hatred theme. There we will come to understand its deeper meaning (Cronus's castration wish). It has its origins in the child's overhearing the sexual relations of the parents and his ambivalent reaction to the impression of this event, which in the son usually produces jealous feelings toward the father and sensuous desire for the mother. In connection with this, the son attempts to identify with the father (Hamlet = Claudius, who embodies his incest wishes); thus Hamlet, corresponding to his wishes, gives exaggerated emphasis to his mother's sexual relations, characterizing them as incestuous, just as Schiller initially set *Don Carlos* in the torrid atmosphere of incest. This theme of eavesdropping, present in the sources, is utilized by the playwright three times. Each time, owing to the son's identification with his father, it is the son who is secretly listened to—twice in his mother's bedchamber and once during an encounter with Ophelia: the first time by Polonius, eager to be of service, and the king; the second time by Polonius alone, who loses his life in the process; and the third time, again in the mother's bedchamber, by the ghost of the murdered father, who places himself between mother and son just as Philip does in Schiller's drama. This last circumstance, and the location of the scene in the mother's bedchamber, reminds us of how the jealous son originally listens in secret to the parents and figuratively intrudes between them, placing himself, in his wishful fantasies, in the position of the removed (but reappearing) father (cf. "The Myth of the World Parents" in chap. 9). Another detail that the playwright knew but omits demonstrates that this eavesdropping refers to the sex act. According to Saxo's account (cf. Simrock 1870), the king decides to test the authenticity of Hamlet's dementia through sensual pleasure. In the forest, as if accidentally, Hamlet is left alone with a young woman so that his behavior in love and in the sexual act can be observed. However, Hamlet takes her to a remote place, where he has sexual relations with her far from all eavesdroppers, and he swears the young woman, whom he has known since childhood, to secrecy. Here one easily recognizes the original source of the encounter with Ophelia, where eavesdropping takes place, but one notices again the characteristic omission of eavesdropping in the context of the sex act, repressed by the playwright and therefore painful to him. And in another omission, too, the playwright reveals his defense against adopting those portions of the legend that conflicted with his repressions. In Saxo's account the king decides to send Hamlet, whose presence makes him uncomfortable, to the king of England with a letter instructing the recipient immediately to kill the bearer. During the journey, Hamlet opens the letter and replaces his name with the names of the two men who are accompanying him, and they are in fact executed in his stead. To this extent Shakespeare does adopt the story. In the legend, however, Hamlet also adds to the letter the statement that the king should grant him, the bearer, his daughter's hand in marriage, which also immediately occurs. This detail, a typical element in legend (cf. the letter of Uriah), was also omitted by the playwright, since it constitutes a positive sexual expression.

It would lead us too far afield to attempt to derive this ancient and widely distributed theme—too generally labeled the theme of the letter of Uriah—from the parent complex, as we have done for the myth of exposure of the newborn, with which it is basically identical. We should mention, however, that in such legends the son's claims to inheritance, feared by the father, are not usually associated with jealous affection for the king's wife, that is, the mother (though this is the case with Bellerophon). Instead, they are associated with the theme of the father, jealous on account of his daughter, who wishes to destroy his future son-in-law. As we know, Shakespeare dissociates this relationship from the theme of the letter and extends it to Polonius's relationship with Ophelia. Given the group of legends briefly mentioned here, and the Brutus legend to be discussed below (chap. 8)—which also shows obvious parallels to Hamlet's journey to England—Rosenkrantz and Guildenstern, killed in Hamlet's stead, correspond to the brothers who in related traditions compete with the hero and are eliminated by him. Laertes, to an extent, should also be seen as such a brother figure. This becomes especially clear in the struggle for the love of the sister (Ophelia).

Lastly, in the fencing scene, Laertes takes on a sort of father role toward Hamlet. (It would be difficult to explore exhaustively the multiple aspect and the richness of associations of these creations of psychic compromise.) We are already familiar with such scenes of battle between father and son from mythology. An apparently insignificant shift in the legend indicates that in this murder, as in all the others in the drama, the playwright was gratifying the impulse for the murder of the father. In the legend, Hamlet returns home to wreak vengeance on the same day that memorial rites are scheduled for him. Clothed in dirty rags, he enters the hall, and since he deliberately wreaks havoc with his sword, bystanders secure it in its sheath with a wedge. When all are lying drunk on the floor, he carries out his vengeance; the guests, trapped in the hall by a net, he burns to death. Only then does he seek out his stepfather, Fengo. He exchanges Fengo's sword, hanging on the bedpost, for his own and then awakens him, demanding vengeance for his murdered father. Fengo grabs for the weapon; while he tries in vain to draw Hamlet's sword, now wedged fast, Hamlet kills him with his own sword. That Shakespeare includes this theme again demonstrates the tendency to dampen the patricide complex but reveals, on the other hand, that repressed emotions are gratified through more innocent, psychically less offensive situations. As always in adopting legendary material in conformity with his own deepest complexes, the playwright has, in his own way, substituted an internal motivation for an external one (the stuck sword). With Shakespeare the son is unable to draw his sword against Claudius—not because it is wedged fast, but because of his psychic inhibitions, which do not permit him to kill the king while he is praying (3.3). Hamlet must also be envisioning the actual "crime" of which he himself feels guilty in his fantasies: he wishes to kill Claudius "in th'incestuous pleasures of his bed." In *Macbeth* it is the same conflicting son feelings and father feelings that bring about the murder of Banquo (out of fear of his children) as well as that of Duncan.

In *Hamlet* too it is mainly these feelings that transform hatred toward the father into vengeance for the father. Here we can proceed one step further in our interpretation of *Hamlet*, thus providing another confirmation of our conception of King Claudius as a "father." On the one hand, the psychologically conditioned introduction of the theme of vengeance for the father in place of patricide requires the use of a substitute character, a straw man who to an extent embodies the son's wishes. On the other hand, the revenge on the murderer—the son's killing him—is again nothing but the murder of the rival for the mother, apparently justified by the theme of vengeance. This murder confirms the association of Claudius with the "father." In the often-discussed most important scene of the drama (3.4) Hamlet, in an effort to convince her of the heinousness of her crime, contrasts for his mother the images of the two brothers, her current husband and her former one ("that was, to this, Hyperion to a satyr"). Here it is quite clear that Hamlet sees, in the one image, his father as he admired him in childhood and, in the other, the father he later despised as a competitor for the mother's affections. Indeed, as Riklin (1908) has pointed out in his explanation of the wicked stepmother in folktales, one sees a sexual competitor only from his worst side. In folktales, though, everything is seen from the daughter's perspective. She sees the mother as a rival for the love of the father and therefore, like the son, on the one hand makes her a stepmother, but on the other hand sees her only as the bothersome, irritating, wicked competitor.

The conflict between father feelings and son feelings finds its most perfect, highest artistic expression—and simultaneously its strongest neurotic expression—in the figure of the ghost of the murdered father in *Hamlet*. At first glance it might appear that Shakespeare has provided for us in the character of Hamlet the most reliable material for understanding his own psyche. But this is not the case. The character of Hamlet is already "idealized." That is, several of Shakespeare's psychic tendencies have already been split off from Hamlet and personified as separate characters. Defense against the inimical orientation toward the father, which has become unbearable, leads to projection of the ghost. Here, though, the reaction against this orientation, the fear of being hated in a like manner by one's own son, is also expressed. So in the pronouncements of the "ghost" as well as in many of Hamlet's own utterances, son feelings appear juxtaposed with father feelings. As a son (3.4), Hamlet seeks to separate the mother from the father (Claudius) by disparaging her sexual relations with him:

> Nay but to live
> In the rank sweat of an enseamèd bed,
> Stewed in corruption, honeying and making love
> Over the nasty sty.
>
> (*Hamlet*, 3.4)

But just as he derides his father (stepfather) in this context, Hamlet's own father feelings begin to emerge—the ghost appears, representing the father who fears similar treatment from his son, and the son is admonished to redeem the mother:

> Amazement on thy mother sits:
> O, step between her and her fighting soul.
>
> (*Hamlet*, 3.4)

Similarly, the ghost's utterances are contradictory. The ghost expresses hatred of the father (thus as a son):

> Let not the royal bed of Denmark be
> A couch for luxury and incest.
>
> (*Hamlet*, 1.5)

But as a father and husband, he adds (for his son):

> But howsoever thou pursuest this act,
> Taint not thy mind, nor let thy soul contrive
> Against thy mother aught.
>
> (*Hamlet*, 1.5)

In the ghost's pronouncement, Hamlet's jealous concern for his mother—his feelings as a father who fears and condemns the incestuous tendencies of his son—are expressed more clearly still:

> Ay, that incestuous, that adulterate beast,
> With witchcraft of his wit, with traitorous gifts—
> . . . . won to his shameful lust
> The will of my most seeming-virtuous queen.
> O Hamlet, what a falling off was there
> From me.
>
> (*Hamlet*, 1.5)

In the father's fantasy of the mother's (the queen's) incest with the son lies also the fulfillment of the son's wishes. In the "ghost of Hamlet's father," then, a whole series of powerful unconscious emotions of the playwright coincide and are expressed in compromise: his infantile hatred of his father and his erotic affection for his mother, but also the reactively revalued incest complex that respects the father while despising the mother; and finally also the punishment for these rejected feelings: that is, the fear of similar retribution by his own son. This astounding compromise borders on hysteria, where in every symptom, in addition to various disguised wish fulfillments, we also find a thought process dealing with punishment. In just the same way, in the figure of the ghost, two opposing incest wishes find expression. The playwright was able to express his hatred for his father and his love for his mother, but given the revaluation of his own incestuous feelings—a revaluation emphasizing the viewpoint of the father—he was also able to condemn his son and his wife owing to his fear of similar treatment from them (cf. the identity in name of the old king and the young king in Shakespeare's *Hamlet* and the correspondence with the name of Shakespeare's own son, Hamnet).

This many-faceted internal structure of the figure of the ghost makes it easier to understand why Shakespeare—who as is well known also acted—played the ghost, not Hamlet (as one might expect), in the drama. This suggests that at the time Shakespeare identified more closely with the role of the father. This conception gains in significance given that this role is generally said to have been Shakespeare's best performance. Thus we have an opportunity to investigate the deeper conditioning factors of dramatic ability from our point of view, and I do not wish to pass up this occasion, for Shakespeare's creations lend themselves so well in this respect. In Shakespeare, playwright and actor coincide in the same individual. One sees the development of the actor from the playwright, thus observing the internal relations as well as the differences between them. There is no dramatist whose biography, no matter how accurate, could provide such clear information on the decisive internal events and experiences that dramatic activity springs from as the analysis of Shakespeare's works has provided us. Our attempt to regard acting from the same psychological perspective as the composition of dramatic works is to an extent justified by the results of a deeper investigation of the sources of all artistic creativity, such as the one I attempted to carry out in *The Artist: Preliminaries to a Sexual Psychology* (Rank 1907). Among other results, it was demonstrated (p. 52) that acting is a fully valued psychic act and a more basic release for psychic states than the activity of the playwright. It is actually the actor who must complete the drama, who must do what the playwright wishes to do but, owing to psychic defenses, cannot achieve. The actor "experiences" what the playwright can only "dream." While the dreamer experiences the many-faceted plot internally, however, the actor projects it outward. All characters of the drama are personifications of individual psychic forces in the playwright, who frees himself from his painful inner conflicts through this projection. Thus, to a substantial degree, the creation of dramatic works constitutes a defensive act. The playwright pours forth his innermost feelings, whereas the actor absorbs them within himself—adopts them. To the defensive activity of the playwright, the actor opposes affirmation. Thus the activity of the actor involves mainly assimilation and identification. In a psychological sense, the actor is the positive aspect of the playwright.

Through dramatic creativity, this psychic conflict is only temporarily resolved. (The playwright is continually driven to compose more works based on internally related themes that inspire and grip him and that become uninteresting to him only through the process of composition.) Below we shall apply our insights to Shakespeare's characters, especially the "ghost." The repressed feelings are released only for a time; soon they insistently demand expression and release again. And since Shakespeare, as a child, probably feared his father, the memory of his father is accompanied by anxiety because he has repressed hatred toward him (cf. the similar demonstrated relationships with their fathers of Schiller, Goethe, Hebbel, and other playwrights with affectionate mothers). But acting did not merely permit Shakespeare to deal with his reactions whenever these feelings had developed a certain degree of intensity within him. Indeed, it provided him with much more. While he played the ghost of the father, the ghost of his own father (his painful thoughts of him) could not plague him. As long as he acted, he was protected from it. As a playwright, he had resisted these anxiety-ridden feelings by projecting them outward. As an actor he truly embodied them, portraying them onstage. He thus placed himself in the position of the father and gave expression to his father feelings through identification. Acting also assured him of the successful functioning of his defense mechanisms. As a playwright he had resisted his feelings of hate, but as an actor he once again adopted them by identifying with the ghost of his father, which plagued him, in order in turn to plague as a "ghost" his own son (represented by Hamlet) and to admonish him for his reprehensible thoughts and actions. In the "ghost," however, Shakespeare also identified with the son (compromise) in order to justify his own feelings as a son. Thus he played the role to escape anxiety associated with his hateful and repentant thoughts of his dead father and in connection with the similar feelings he believed he had to fear as a father himself. He played the role to prevent an attack of anxiety, as one might say with reference to certain hysterical phobias, and he played it so well because he needed to act to maintain his psychic equilibrium—one would almost say, to cure himself.

Again this process, as already suggested, can be illustrated only through an example from psychology—the way the symptom of agoraphobia arises (inability to cross a street alone). Freud is responsible for the insight "that the symptom is constructed to prevent the outbreak of anxiety" (1909f, 343). If one forces the neurotic to carry out the act he believes he is incapable of, he will experience an attack of anxiety. "The phobia acts as a fortification against anxiety." In the same way, Shakespeare also constructed his "symptom" (though it was a highly valued achievement, not a disability) to prevent the outbreak of anxiety. We can say this in no other way.

Thus, once again, our investigation has shown how a single chain of early, affectively powerful childhood impressions stretches through reactivation in the "dream of the normal"—and through the fantasy wishes of those especially predisposed—to dramatic production, which obscures these feelings, and from there to achievement as an actor, finally ending, as an ultimate form of defense, in the hysterical attack.

7 Oedipus Dramas of World Literature

The strict law of chastity; aversion to the instinct
To become the father's fellow suitor, the mother's spouse—
All of this I pressed into his young, waxen heart.

LESSING, *Giangir*

Just as the historically documented background material of *Don Carlos* has preferentially been "dramatized" by playwrights of our era—that is, infused with their personal complexes and filled out accordingly—the Oedipus legend, in full correspondence with the principle of repression, was equally popular among classical tragedians. This preference for the Theban cycle of legends over the less violent and more grandiose legends of the Trojan cycle is probably attributable to the themes of patricide, fratricide, and the mother's honor, unconsciously experienced by the playwrights. Such a concentration on these themes is later observed only in the legend of the sons of Atreus (chap. 9), which was actually developed by the tragedians themselves. Aeschylus (525–456 B.C.) had already written an *Oedipus,* which was performed with the tragedies *Laius* and *Seven against Thebes* and the satyr play *Sphinx* (cf. Christ 1888). Aeschylus found the material in the *Odyssey* (11.271 ff.), where Odysseus sees the shades of the dead in the underworld:

> Then came Epicaste, the beautiful, Oedipus's mother,
> Who with a blinded soul committed the foulest deed.

> Her own son, who murdered his father,
> She took as husband! But soon the gods condemned the
> shameful deed.

Aeschylus also borrowed material from another old epic, the *Oedipodeia,* of the post-Homeric epic cycle. He also intensified the horror of the mythological tradition by modifying the legend, making the four children—sired, according to the old epic, by Oedipus with his second wife, Euryganeia—the children of his union with his mother.

In passing, we should note that even Homer, it seems, did not mention Oedipus's fate without internal motivation, for shortly before Epicaste's "apparition as a ghost," Odysseus's own mother appears to her son.

> "Only longing for you, and fear, my noble Odysseus,
> And your sweet image took your mother's life!"
> Thus she spoke. Then my heart swelled with fervent longing
> To embrace her, the soul of my dead mother.
> Thrice I tried to press the loved one to my heart.
> Thrice she glided easily away, like a shadow or a dream,
> From my embracing arms, but all the more did I then long for
> her.
> And I addressed her, said these winged words:
> "Shall we not, in the underworld, embraced by loving hands,
> Ease each other's mournful hearts with tears?"

This depiction corresponds fully to the appearance of the mother in a dream; defense is nicely expressed in the mother's slipping away from the son's embrace.

After Aeschylus and Sophocles, Euripides also wrote an *Oedipus,* which, like that of Aeschylus, is no longer extant. Nauck (1889) also mentions other Greek tragedians who wrote Oedipus dramas: Achaeus, Theodectes, Xenocles, Carcinas, and Diogenes. Nicomachus, Philocles, a nephew of Aeschylus, and Lycophron, the author of two Oedipus dramas, are listed in Roscher's *Lexicon* (1884–1937). Constans (1881, 19) also names as authors of Greek Oedipus tragedies Meletus, Socrates' accuser and "author of an *Oedipodeia,* a tetralogy mentioned by the annotator of Plato; and Aristarchus of Tege, a contemporary of Euripides, according to Suidas, and doubtless earlier than the latter." This impressive succession of Greek Oedipus tragedies (twelve are usually cited) not only demonstrates the creative identification of many playwrights with the hero of the legend, but also reveals the popularity of the material with the Greek people, based on similar psychological motivations.

Of the Roman tragedians (cf. Ribbeck 1875), Seneca wrote an *Oedipus* that distinguishes itself in the special way it depicts Oedipus's guilt. It is not the seer Teiresias who characterizes Oedipus as a patricide, as in the Sophoclean drama. Instead, after a sacrifice and a conjuration of the underworld, the ghost of Laius appears and accuses Oedipus of murder and incest. Creon relates to Oedipus the result of the conjuration, but he is taken prisoner because Oedipus fears a conspiracy. Still, Oedipus continues brooding over the accusation and finally recalls that he once killed a man at a crossroads. As in the Sophoclean drama, the shepherd who reports the death of the foster parents then resolves all mysteries. Oedipus blinds himself, and Jocasta stabs herself at the sight of her blind son. The crime in the presence of the mother complements the mother's self-punishment in the presence of the son: according to Nicholas of Damascus, Oedipus killed Laius before his mother's very eyes. That this circumstance does not hinder their marriage shows clearly that both unconsciously wished for the removal of the father. It is also worthy of comment that in Seneca's play, Oedipus remembers the murder, though he does not yet know it was his own father he killed. Here objections should be raised against a criticism made by Lope de Vega. In his *Poetics*, a poem in which he presents rules for the composition of good *comedias*, he demands especially that the protagonist in no way contradict himself—that he not forget what has occurred. For example, he criticizes Sophocles because Oedipus does not remember having killed Laius (cf. Schaeffer 1890). Of course Lope de Vega did not grasp the deep sense of the legend, which expresses in this way the repression of the patricide fantasy, painful to recall. But Sophocles was also criticized by ancient writers, especially Aristotle, who felt that the late revelation of Oedipus's disastrous fate seemed improbable. In fact Euripides believed Oedipus was intentionally silent about the matter.

In his biography of Julius Caesar (chap. 53), Suetonius claims that Caesar also wrote an *Oedipus:* "One also speaks of writings he is supposed to have composed in his youth, for example, *The Praise of Hercules,* the tragedy *Oedipus,* and collected maxims. In a short and simple letter to Pomponius, whom he had entrusted with the organization of his library, Augustus forbade him to make these works known." Caesar's *Oedipus* is especially interesting, since his incestuous affection for his mother can be psychologically proved. Suetonius remarks (chap. 7): "Even in connection with his worrisome dream the following night—he dreamed that he had slept with his mother—the dream interpreters inspired him with the greatest hopes. They interpreted the dream as an omen of his future dominion over the earth, saying that the mother he had seen lying beneath him was none other than the earth, the all-mother." Plutarch reports the same episode in his biography of Caesar (chap. 34). I also gather from Suetonius's biography that Caesar lost his father at age sixteen and his mother after the subjugation of Gaul. Many accused him of "rejecting his wife, who had already borne him three children, to marry the daughter of the very man whom, sighing, he called his Aegisthus. Above all other women, though, he loved Servilia, the mother of Marcus Brutus" (chap. 50). In his biography of Brutus (chap. 5), Plutarch explains as follows Caesar's special preference and love for Brutus: "They say he did this to please Brutus's mother, Servilia. Indeed it is very likely that as a youth he had already discovered that Servilia was hopelessly in love with him. Since Brutus was born just when she was most enamored of him, he was probably convinced that Brutus was his own son." As we know, Brutus was at the head of the conspiracy against Caesar and is supposed to have inflicted the fatal wound himself: "And thus he was stabbed twenty-three times. At the first stab, he uttered only a wordless sigh, although some report that when Marcus closed in on him, he cried out repeatedly in Greek: 'You too, my son?'" (Suetonius, chap. 82). Here the politically motivated act once again reveals itself as a disguise for an act derived from deep sexual sources; the murder of the political leader, the tyrant, again reveals that it is basically a patricide. Suetonius reports (chap. 88) that it was decided to wall up the curia where Caesar had been murdered and to commemorate the murder on March 15. Brutus's hatred apparently sprang from his jealousy toward Caesar, who had illicitly possessed Brutus's mother, as Brutus knew. Brutus's erotic affection for his mother is expressed in that he married a widow who was in fact a distant relative—the daughter of his uncle Cato (Plutarch, chap. 13). The interesting association of dream, literature, and experience in connection with Caesar is made more complete by Brutus's own dream, in which the murdered Caesar, his father, appears to him. Here the entire incest complex is distributed between two generations—between father and son—so that Caesar experiences love for the mother in the corresponding dream while his son, Brutus, commits tyrannicide, derived from hatred of the father and again associated with the typical dream of the dead father.

From this crux of the incest problem, one line branches in the direction of Caesar: a series of dramas dealing with Caesar's murder. It seems that the undisguised Oedipus material was superseded by the material dealing with Caesar (who himself wrote an *Oedipus*); this material corresponded better to advanced repression. As with the stepmother theme, the attraction of this material for dramatists lies in the dampening of the frightful events effected by the absence of the mother and also by uncertainty concerning the claim that Caesar fathered Brutus. This uncertainty frees the playwright to depict the relationship between Caesar and Brutus according to his own needs—from the closest blood relationship to complete lack of relationship, from direct patricide to tyrannicide with strictly political motivation. In Alfieri's *Bruto secundo* and in Voltaire's tragedy *Mort de César* (1735), the main emphasis is placed on the blood relationship between Caesar and Brutus.

Indeed, Alfieri even has Brutus declare publicly in the Senate that he is Caesar's illegitimate son. Quite to the contrary, in his own *Julius Caesar* Shakespeare speaks not a word about their blood relationship. Instead, Brutus is a conspirator like the others (see the analysis of Shakespeare's *Julius Caesar*). Conti's *Julius Caesar* is also worthy of note, as is the tragedy *Brutus* by the short-lived Joachim Brawe (1738–58), where the son's relationship with the father is handled as a typical defense with respect to the playwright's own unusual death. The son, who on the one hand attempts with the greatest self-mastery to avoid the act of patricide, thereby becomes all the more obsessed with patricidal thoughts, which he can escape only through suicide. "In his works," says Jakob Minor (*Brawes Werke* [Brawe's works], in Joseph Kürschner's collection *Deutsche National-Literatur,* "love for the father is expressed all the more warmly and ardently," since he had already lost his mother at a young age. His premature death, which creates the impression of a suicide brought about by unconscious forces, seems, in connection with the Oedipus complex, like a repentant self-punishment for his repressed father hatred and a return to the beloved, lost mother (cf. also Theodor Körner, chap. 23).

In Voltaire's *Mort de César,* mentioned above, we see again the relation to Oedipus dramas. Voltaire's first play, which he wrote at age nineteen, was *Oedipus* (1718). It is interesting to note how repression is demonstrated by this playwright of our era, though he could not change the basic material. In Voltaire's drama, Jocasta loves neither Laius nor Oedipus, but a third character, Philoctetes. Thus, in her marriage to her son she also feels unhappy, whereas myth emphasizes the unconscious erotic affection between mother and son precisely by emphasizing the happy nature of this union. In Voltaire's drama Jocasta is quite cool toward her son:

Jocasta: Thebes, then ravaged by a cruel monster
Had promised my fidelity to her liberator;
And the sphinx's conqueror was worthy of me.
Egina ⟨Jocasta's confidante⟩: You love him?
Jocasta: I felt for him some tenderness;
But this feeling was no weakness for him.
It was no tumultuous fire, Egina,
No impetuous offspring of enchanted senses.
I did not feel again that burning flame
Which Philoctetes alone has brought forth in my soul.

. . . .

I felt for Oedipus a serene friendship.
Oedipus is virtuous, his virtue was dear to me.

In this attempt at defense against incestuous tendencies, the progress of repression clearly reveals itself. That Philoctetes is at first accused of Laius's murder demonstrates that he, like Claudius, is nothing but an intermediate character, inserted in defense against incestuous tendencies. Supposedly he is the murderer of the father; simultaneously, he is unrelated to the mother (cf. the stepmother figure as a similar expression of compromise).

Before Voltaire, Corneille had already written an *Oedipus* at age fifty-nine [fifty-three] (1659)—shortly after the death of his father. Here again, as with Voltaire, the influence of repression is seen in his weaving in a second love affair. In his *Lettres sur Oedipe,* Voltaire says concerning Corneille's *Oedipus:* "Thus, Theseus's passion constitutes the whole theme of the tragedy, and the misfortunes of Oedipus are only an episode." Constans (1881, 379) also adds: "The denouement is that of Sophocles, but in his treatise on the play, the author tells us that this is announced simply—for fear, as he says, 'of arousing the delicacy of the ladies.' " In Corneille's play, Theseus, prince of Athens, loves Dirce, daughter of Laius and Jocasta and sister of Oedipus, whereas Oedipus hopes that Theseus will marry one of his daughters, Ismene or Antigone, since he has promised Dirce to Creon's son. When the shade of Laius demands a prince or princess of his own blood as an offering of atonement, and Dirce, as his last living relative, is ready to sacrifice herself at her father's grave, Theseus, who wishes to die for her, attempts to convince her that he is her brother and thus must sacrifice himself. Nor, therefore, does he permit her to speak to him of love:

Theseus: My heart hears not at all when my blood speaks.
It cries with love, with love it sighs;
And to taste this sweetness without crime,
It must revolt against the sister's name.
This true cohort in my fond desires
Oppresses the brother and favors the lover,
Apportioning to both a worthy wish
To die as brother and live as lover.
Dirce: Oh, all too salient proofs of Laius's blood!
Heaven, fating you to incestuous flames,
Has uprooted from your heart the fear
That love should feel at the sister's sacred name.
But if the flame has there usurped a place,
Dirce is not at fault for your mistake.

In the end, Theseus marries Dirce. This love affair of Theseus and Dirce, which reduces Oedipus's fate to an episode, was, as we see, not woven into the plot without deeper meaning; the theme of love for the sister, introduced there, played a meaningful role in Corneille's own life, as we will demonstrate below. In addition to these relationships, the daughter's (Dirce's) hatred of her mother, the same-sex parent, is unmistakably suggested and combined with love for the (dead) father (sacrifice at his grave; union in death). In his *Lettres,* Voltaire writes: "Dirce spends all her time deprecating Oedipus and his mother." We will observe a similar situation with Electra, who also hates her mother and her second husband while loving her dead father and her brother (cf. chap. 9).

Twenty years after Corneille's *Oedipus* appeared the *Oedipus* of the English dramatists John Dryden and Nathaniel Lee. In this drama, similar in style to the French tragedy, repression is demonstrated in similar fashion. Constans (1881) remarks: "[In this adaptation] Sophocles' plot is complicated by a mass of details that suffocate the theme." Another of Dryden's dramas, *Aureng-Zebe,* is characteristic of Dryden's incest feelings. According to Herman Hettner's *Literarische Geschichte des achtzehnten Jahrhunderts* [Literary history of the eighteenth century] (1894–1913), the plot is as follows. Aureng-Zebe, the favorite son of the emperor, falls in love with Queen Indamora, a war captive. She returns his love, but the emperor falls in love with her himself. He becomes jealous of his son, rejects him, and since he wishes to withdraw to a quiet life with Indamora, hands over his realm to his second son, Morat. But this son too is seized by the same passion. He mistreats his father and attempts to kill his brother—his most dangerous competitor. Then his own mother, Nurmahal, who loves her stepson Aureng-Zebe with a passion in which Racine's Phaedra is distorted to a caricature, incites a conspiracy to save Aureng-Zebe's life. She is successful, and Aureng-Zebe becomes emperor. Morat dies of grief. The former emperor grants Indamora to Aureng-Zebe (theme of relinquishment of the bride); Nurmahal, who thus feels betrayed, poisons herself. In this drama one finds an accumulation of the most varied but typical incest themes, as discussed above. Dryden's emphasis on love for the sibling is clear in his tragedy *Don Sebastian* (cf. chap. 18).

In our consideration of the Oedipus works of all peoples and times, Constans gives us an idea of the great popularity and incomparable effect of this unique material. Among the independent literary adaptations, Constans (1881, 381) mentions the one by La Motte:

> The improbabilities inherent to the theme of Oedipus itself had made a strong impression on La Motte. In his *Fourth Discourse on Tragedy,* he had at first attempted to correct these improbabilities in the Oedipus plot.

Later, acting on his precepts, he had written successively an *Oedipus* in verse (1726) that, according to Voltaire, was performed four times, and an *Oedipus* in prose that was never performed. "La Motte," says M. Patin, "ingeniously corrects the improbabilities in the fable, but in so doing he removes from the drama all its terror and all its pity." And he adds delicately, "Of his *Oedipus* in verse and his *Oedipus* in prose nothing remains" (Patin 1870–73, 4:157). Father Melchior Folard also wrote an *Oedipus* (Paris, 1722).

Constans mentions four Oedipus tragedies by La Tournelle, from the theatrical library of the duke of la Vallière, which appeared in Paris (1730–31): *Oedipe, ou Les trois fils de Jocaste, Oedipe et Polybe, Oedipe, ou L'ombre de Laïus,* and *Oedipe et toute sa famille.* Following Patin, he mentions also a *Jocaste* by the count of le Lauragnais (1781) and a tragedy in five acts, *Antigone* (1580), by Robert Garnier, which contains the whole intricate family history of Oedipus. The English dramatist William Whitehead (d. 1785) is also supposed to have left us the manuscript of the first act of an *Oedipus.* Constans also mentions an *Oedipus* by Marie-Josef Chénier and remarks: "His *Oedipe-Roi* is hardly more than a free translation." Hans Sachs, who wrote a *Clytemnestra* in 1554, also wrote an Oedipus tragedy titled *Jocasta* (1550). As sources of Hans Sachs's *Jocasta,* Cholevius (1854) names Ovid, Boccaccio, and others, but no ancient tragedies. Events from the birth of Oedipus to the death of his sons Ioristes and Phoristes are dealt with in a few pages. In the same act, Oedipus appears as a babe in arms and as a Corinthian general. In the battle, he slays Laius, leader of the Phoenicians.

Turning from more or less independent Oedipus works, we can now consider the countless translations produced in a wide range of historical periods and societies, attesting to the great interest in the material. Constans remarks: "Abroad, there is a rather great number of tragedies directly imitating ancient works or French tragedies based on the Oedipus theme. We shall limit ourselves to the mention of a few less well known ones. In sixteenth-century Italy, in addition to *Jocasta* by Dolce, and Ruccellaiët d'Alamanni's works mentioned above, we find first a poor imitation of *Oedipus the King* by Anguillara (1565) . . . and finally an *Oedipus* by M. Niccolini, the able translator of Aeschylus." Constans (1881, 376) also mentions an *Oedipus the King* faithfully translated into Italian by a Venetian noble, Orsalto Giustiniano. Salvá (1826) mentions (no. 2021) a Spanish translation of Sophocles' *Oedipus the King:* "Sophocles' *Oedipus the King,* a tragedy translated from the Greek into Castillian verse, with a preliminary discussion of the ancient and modern tragedy, by Don Pedro Estala, Madrid, 1793." Constans also mentions a Dutch translation of *Oedipus the King* by Joost van den Vondel (1587–1679) (cf. Jonckbloet 1870).

This list of original works, adaptations, and translations of the Oedipus drama could easily be expanded upon, either from Constans's book itself, from which only a few of the examples have been presented, or from the literary works that have appeared since Constans's research. Only one very recent work will be cited as an example of how a modern playwright approaches this material, ancient but ever new to the human spirit. I have in mind Hugo Hofmannsthal's tragedy *Oedipus und die Sphinx*, which deals with the prehistory of the Sophoclean tragedy. With Hofmannsthal, much of what was still unconscious for earlier playwrights has become conscious, as one can clearly see from his *Elektra*—a Sophoclean *Electra* brought from the darkness of the unconscious into the light of consciousness. Hofmannsthal's Oedipus drama stands at the end of a long series of Oedipus works, and his treatment of the theme approaches the furthest limits of presentation art can obtain. Beyond these limits, psychoanalysis begins. Thus, in Hofmannsthal's drama, Oedipus learns of his incest and patricide not from the oracle, but in a dream—clearly characterized by Hofmannsthal as a typical one:

Oedipus: Ask me nothing! I dreamed
the dream of life. Like a raging water
my life raced forward within me. . . . suddenly
my hands slew a man:
my heart was drunk with anger's lust.
I wished to see his face, but a veil
hid it, and already the dream raced on.
I found myself in a bed where
I lay beside a woman in whose arms
it seemed I was a god. In such voluptuousness
I raised myself to kiss her face, to awaken
the one embracing me. Phoenix! Phoenix!
There lay a veil on her face; and groaning
with the memory of the man I slew,
which seized me suddenly, my heart convulsed
and wakened me.

In this incest dream, repression is demonstrated in that the faces of the parents are veiled and unrecognized, an expression of defense, whose origins and significance will become clear below. After Oedipus's dream, the oracle is introduced only to interpret it.

"I live and bear it. And now it is revealed."
Thus spoke the god through the twisted mouth
of the ardent woman: "You have atoned for the pleasure
of killing by killing your father; for the pleasure of embrace

by embracing your mother; thus was the dream,
and thus it shall be."

In contrast to Voltaire, who rejects (represses) incestuous love so much that Jocasta is unhappy in her marriage to Oedipus from the very beginning, Hofmannsthal depicts the love between mother and son as the first and only great love of their lives. But a weak sense of the true nature of this love dawns on Jocasta when she first reminds Oedipus of her slain husband and then of her child, believed lost. This occurs in the gripping scene where they first encounter one another [after suspicions arise]:

Jocasta (involuntarily): Laius!
The people: What says the woman?
Jocasta: No, no, a dream. (She grasps at the air; then, with both hands, at her heart, and sinks, crushed): I have never lived!
Oedipus: I know she is not dead. In my arms I hold the world.

. . . .

(More softly, leaning forward): Because of you,
whom I never saw in a dream, I have scorned
the young women in the land of my youth.
Jocasta: (softly, tenderly, with all the power of the most secret passion in her eyes): My son,
was it you I wished to die for,
longing to join my son in death? No dream
would show him to me. Was it because
your living presence was to
pierce me with such a gaze?

Here again we see the effects of the progression of repression in the same material. Using this material, attested in a unified form, each playwright, intensely caught up in the process of repression, expresses artistically his own particular form of repression until at the end of this series of works the unconscious literary content is revealed through investigations by the conscious, thus establishing a goal for artistic production.

The Psychology of Juvenalia

It is comprehensible that such unique material as the Oedipus legend, which exhausts all the relationships of the incest complex in such a comprehensive manner, was so often employed by playwrights—as described—that few ever attempted to create anew a body of similar incest material, and that when this did occur the result was either negative or unintended and distinct (cf. Schiller's *Braut von Messina* [Bride of Messina], chap. 20). Not so much because of the material or because of any interest in its creator, but instead as an illustration of a general and principal point of view, we now turn to a discussion of one playwright's attempt to depict the whole incest complex in another setting and with other characters analogous to those of the Oedipus legend. This is Gotthold Lessing's "draft of a tragedy," undertaken at age nineteen (1748): *Giangir, oder Der verschmähte Thron* [Giangir, or The rejected throne]. The drama, which deals with incest material, is Lessing's first independent draft of a drama of this nature. Lessing's draft arose as the result of a competition with his friend in youth, Christian Weisse. Lessing's source has still not been determined with certainty; his version differs from Weisse's and also from the historically documented material in that Lessing shifts the betrayal from the realm of politics to the sexual realm—a displacement no longer new to us. The stronger emphasis on the incestuous nature of the material is also connected with this. In Weisse's source the sultan's favorite, Roxalana, hates her stepson Mustapha because she wishes to improve the position of her own son. She falsely brings him under suspicion of having engaged in a political plot against his father, the sultan Soliman. Lessing's draft, however, involves Mustapha's love for his father's wife:

Soliman: Already a gray prison holds Mustapha.
The offender—he! Against me? To wield his dagger against me?
The offender—against my wife! The infamy is too great.
Mustapha, if you had strangled me a hundred times,
Mustapha, dying, I would still have forgiven you.
But my wife, you—
Roxalana: Terrible recollection!
With joyful countenance, without red shame,
He spoke such shameful words to me, which, had heaven
Not indulged him, would never have passed
His lips, would never have been uttered.

Before deciding to have his son executed for these crimes, he converses with Temir, his faithful servant and the tutor of Mustapha, who believes he knows Mustapha better:

Temir: Fathers I pictured for him as gods on earth
Through whom the god of gods keeps impetuous youth in check;
Their blessing and their curse are God's;
Who truly honors them has honored God.
The holy bond of marriage, through which the world exists;
The strict law of chastity; aversion to the instinct
To become the father's fellow suitor, the mother's spouse—
All of this I pressed into his young, waxen heart.

Thus Lessing, like Schiller, conceived of erotic affection for the mother, dampened to the stepmother theme, just as though it were actual incest. Here we see one source of Lessing's literary creativity that is still revealed in works of puberty, but that never fully flowered as with Shakespeare or Schiller. The affects of this incest complex spurred the playwright to write works in which the effects of these forces can be revealed only by analysis (cf. *Nathan der Weise* [Nathan the wise], chap. 17). These effects can be more easily seen, as we know, in drafts and fragments. Just as Lessing dealt openly with both aspects of the incest complex in the *Giangir* draft, another fragment, *Das Horoskop,* also contains hatred toward the father in all its intensity, and with the corresponding defense mechanisms. For a long time nothing was known about the sources and development of this interesting draft (Hempel, vol. 2, part 2, p. 746). Schmidt (1899) writes in the second edition of his biography of Lessing: "In search of material analogous to *Oedipus the King* and capable of transplantation, Lessing utilized the fourth *Declamatio major* of the pseudo-Quintilian." In October 1758 he is also supposed to have read the drama *Renegaten* [Renegades] by Breithaupt, winner of the third prize, in which Zapor kills his unrecognized father. In *Das Horoskop,* as suggested by the title, the main theme is inescapable destiny as the ancients conceived it.

Peter Opalinski, the ruler of Podalia, has a son, Lukas. An astrologer consults the son's horoscope and predicts that he will win honor for his fatherland but will then murder his father: "Remember that the one born at this time will be a strong man, but will then become a patricide." In her effort to convince her son to marry Anna Massalska, a prisoner captured and also loved by Peter, Lukas's mother, Arete, reveals to him the entire content of the prophecy. In desperation over his fate, Lukas attempts to shoot himself (3.4), but the shot strikes his father, who has rushed forward to prevent his son's suicide. Before his dying father, Arete now exhorts her son not to marry Anna, for it would otherwise be suspected that he had eliminated his father as a competitor for Anna's love. At this point Lukas again determines to kill himself. In any case, when his father dies and Anna attempts to run from the scene, Lukas, in his attempt to hold her back, falls on his sword and dies.

In the son's triple suicide attempt and in the killing of the father, justified by prophecy and chance, we find an expression of deeply repressed hatred toward the father atoned for by tendencies for self-punishment. That such hatred results in the son's strong wish for self-punishment is also clearly revealed in the short tragedy *Philotas.* Affection for a young woman, simultaneously desired by father and son, substitutes for love for the mother. Just as in *Das Horoskop,* in *Kleonnis,* another unperformed draft, Lessing planned to incorporate the prediction of fratricide and murder of the son (Schmidt 1899, 758): from Lessing's own commentary, it is probable that he intended that Euphaes should kill his unrecognized son Cleonnis (Hempel, vol. 2, part 2, p.668).

Except in these unperformed drafts, though, Lessing's incest feelings are not often openly expressed in his literary works. Still, a typical characteristic of this already familiar means of expression is worth special emphasis: the literary treatment of the incest problem occurs mostly during a playwright's youth, and most of the incest dramas are early works. Besides *Giangir*, one could cite, among other examples, Daniel Lohenstein's *Agrippina*, Voltaire's *Oedipe*, Caesar's *Oedipus*, Thomas Otway's *Don Carlos*, Brawe's *Brutus*, and especially Schiller's *Die Räuber*, Franz Grillparzer's *Die Ahnfrau* [The ancestress], and Ludwig Tieck's *Karl von Berneck*. Some of these will be discussed later.

As an especially instructive example of the powerful role of incest in stimulating the playwright's fantasy, but also in the later dissolution and transformation of these feelings, we can now discuss briefly two works Friedrich Hebbel wrote in puberty that still reveal the incest theme undisguised, though it is otherwise heavily veiled in this writer's works. Hebbel's first literary work, undertaken at age nineteen while he still lived with his parents in Wesselburen, bears the title *Der Vatermord* [The patricide]. Fernando is about to shoot himself because of his gambling debts when Count Arendel falls on his arm and saves him. In his derangement, though, Fernando believes Arendel is the devil and shoots him. Then Fernando's mother, Isabella, worried over his absence, appears and reveals to him that the man he has killed is his father. Fernando replies: "He is not my father; he is my executioner. He branded me in the womb before I was born. He is not my father; he is the seducer of my mother." Here again we find the typical infantile conception of the father as a wicked seducer (cf. Ibsen) and of the mother as a fallen woman (whore fantasy), upon which follows the attempted rescue, with the killing of the father as its goal. Here the repression of hatred toward the father brings about not only the dampening of the patricide to a murder committed without knowledge of the father's identity, as in *Oedipus*, but also the defense, which borders on neurosis, the self-accusations, and the final suicide. As so often, the son's justification lies in the circumstance that he does not murder the count as father and competitor but instead punishes him as the seducer of his mother. The mother's love for the son is also suggested. In the first scene, the mother says in a monologue: "Oh, my son, why are you doing this to me, to me who carried you beneath my heart? Why do you flee from your mother? You are the image of your faithless but still fervently beloved father; you are my only comfort in my sorrow."

Here, it is true, the mother sees the son as a substitute for her husband.

She associates the two of them. Still, in Hebbel's drama, defense against erotic affection for the mother is expressed in that she prefers his hated competitor, the father.

Isabella (throwing herself upon the body, desperately, to Fernando): My son, Fernando, I beg you, I conjure you, give me back the one I loved so tenderly.

Fernando: Mother, you forgive him? Mother, if you forgive him, I shall be a patricide. Mother, Mother, curse him; curse him just once, Mother, only don't let me hear that you forgive him. (He regards Isabella anxiously. She embraces Arendel's body.) Mother, oh, Mother, farewell; you shall see me no more! (He grasps his pistol from his belt and rushes offstage. A shot is heard.)

Isabella (seems to awaken from a dream, then crying out): God! My son! My son! (She collapses.)

Thus the son's suicide occurs not so much in repentance for the patricide as in irritation that his mother rejects his love; he can never forgive her for preferring the father. The mother's suicide, which next ensues, symbolizes the final reunion with the son (and the husband). The short story "Der Brudermord" [The fratricide], written a year earlier, reflects these jealous fantasies and impulses arising from the parent complex. In this tale Eduard shoots his unrecognized brother, who has abducted their common beloved (the mother). Here again we observe the repentant self-punishment of the murderer and the uniting of the lovers in death.

It is remarkable that these incestuous passions no longer appear clearly in Hebbel's later works. He left his father's house and his family at an early age and mastered these youthful impulses. Still, it is clear that his first impulses to write arose out of defense against his incestuous passions and that these infantile affects also stirred the literary fire of his later works. This is proved by Hebbel's diaries, in which he freely exposes his unconscious. Even in later periods of his life, they still provide information on the role of the Oedipus complex in his family relationships. Thus on November 22, 1838, he writes: "How dark and desolate my childhood was! My father hated me, actually, nor could I love him." This unambiguous confirmation of his hatred toward his father is linked with the typical dream of the father's death, described by Hebbel on November 12, 1838: "I cannot rid myself of the thought that I will soon die. In a dream during the night I saw my father, who died long ago, and of whom I have almost never dreamed." That the father was already dead at the time of the dream does not alter the necessary interpretation of this dream as the fulfillment of the infantile wish for his death. We have already determined that the deeply rooted infantile impulses of love and hate remain fully active despite the death of the loved or hated person. Indeed, Hebbel's comment that he almost never dreamed of his father leads one to suspect that the powerful defensive impulses against the wish for the father's death did not permit its realization in dreams while the father was alive. The dreamer's initial thought that he himself will soon die is of course only an expression of defense (self-punishment) against the earlier wish for the father's death. In Hebbel's poem "Geburtsnachttraum" [Dream on the night of birth], we see how this typical dream of the deceased father is expressed through poetic creativity. In this poem, written on March 22, 1835, in Hamburg, Hebbel relates how he saw all his ancestors in a dream:

> My father led the procession silently,
> He smiled over to me,
> But then he turned away
> And his eye became duller.

Nor did the fear of his father he felt as a child ever leave him. At the end of 1834 he wrote: "I dreamed recently that I was back in my anxiety-filled childhood. There was nothing to eat, and I trembled in fear of my father as I used to."

One expression of defense against his hatred toward his father is of interest in that it resembles the reproach of an obsessional neurotic (December 3, 1836): "At 6:00 P.M. on November 11, 1827, as my father lay dying (after I had irked him on Friday, just a day before), I begged convulsively: 'Just eight more days, God!' It was like grasping suddenly at the powers of the Infinite; I can only compare it to grasping convulsively the arm of someone who can bring help or salvation in some terrible circumstance. My father recovered immediately. On the following Saturday, at 6:00 P.M., he died!"

This powerful defensive affect can be explained as follows. The day before, when Hebbel had argued with his father, he presumably wished secretly for his father's death, just as children do almost regularly, and just as Hebbel himself had probably done in the past. Thus he must have perceived the worsening in his father's condition the next day as the fulfillment of his evil wish. We will encounter the same belief concerning the "omnipotence of thoughts" (Freud) in the obsessional neurosis of Grillparzer's brother and Ibsen's *The Master Builder.* Hebbel attempted to reject this hateful thought, to nullify the wish through his prayer. We notice here, incidentally, one of the psychological sources of prayer. The wish that God grant his father eight more days of life served only to pacify his conscience. He wished to feel free of the accusation that he had brought about his father's death by wishing it. However, his emphatic defense against this wish indicates that such a wish did formerly exist.

Many of the thoughts Hebbel entered in his diary for eventual literary use concern hatred toward his father: "A physically weak son who challenges his father to a duel because his father, before his marriage, wasted too much of his son's wealth, that is, because he wasted the good seed, from which his son should have grown, before conceiving him." This accusation, which is not uncommon with neurotics and usually arises from sexual jealousy over possession of the mother, is also clearly observed in Ibsen's *Ghosts*. Similarly, in Hebbel's *Julia*, Count Bertram says to himself (1.6): "You must never make a young woman your wife. Your own son would at some point challenge you to a duel." Then we read again in the diaries: "A son who can prevent his father from committing a terrible crime only by killing him."

However, none of this material was ever performed. Another entry (March 16, 1858) shows how Hebbel resisted the selection of such material. He copied into his diary the passage from the *Iliad* in which Phoenix tells of his love for his father's wife and his hatred toward his father (*Iliad*, 9.448–61). Then he adds: "This would be something for Alexandre Dumas." Hebbel's incestuous tendencies are also expressed in the interest he showed in incestuous crimes. On August 31, 1836, he writes: "Today Professor Mittermaier mentioned a woman who imagines that she should be burned as a witch. . . . A mother seeks to convince her idiot son to murder the stepfather. He answers: 'Eternity is a long time.' She says: 'Your first duty is to me.' She goads him for a full year. Finally, while the father is sleeping, she comes in with two hammers and says: 'Now you must decide whether you wish to leave me or not!' She presses the one hammer upon him and carries out the first blow with the second one." The theme of the mother who incites the son to eliminate the father is reminiscent of the same theme in the Edward ballad (chap. 10).

The rivalry of two brothers for the mother's favor, shifted from the father complex, is shown to be the driving force behind an incest tragedy that, because of powerful inner defenses, remained unperformed. In the diaries we read (December 19, 1836): "Timoleon, who loved like a god, with unspeakable anguish ⟨defense!⟩ and seized by the noblest courage, sacrificed for the fatherland his brother Timophanes, who had become a bloodthirsty, inexorable tyrant. Then he sank into the deepest melancholy ⟨reaction⟩ and wished to starve himself to death ⟨self-punishment⟩ because slander by many of his fellow citizens and his mother's anger had driven him mad and had estranged him from himself. (Jacobi's *Woldemar*, based on Plutarch)." In the margin Hebbel adds: "For a tragedy." One also finds two brothers' struggle over a woman in the "idea for a tragedy" Hebbel sketched at the beginning of 1845: "An extremely beautiful young woman, still unfamiliar with the power of her charms, enters the world from her isolation in a convent. All are attracted to her; brothers fight to the death, friendships are destroyed, and her own female friends, jealous or insulted by the faithlessness of their admirers, desert her. She loves a man whose brother begins to make plots on his life. Terrified by her own power to bring about this situation, she returns to the convent."

A passage from *Agnes Bernauer* demonstrates how this incest theme, in dampened form, still had its effect on Hebbel's literary creations. Here the son is nearly driven to patricide. Agnes says (3.12): "If only things remain peaceful between you and your father. How terrible it was for me before, when friends and brothers fought because of me." Just as Hebbel's infantile hatred toward his father, leading to the literary theme of patricide, is demonstrated by his own words in his diaries, the theme of fratricide also derives from jealous childhood rivalry. Hebbel, who was actually preferred by his mother, imagined that she preferred his brother Johann. We can easily recognize this as a justification of his own hatred toward his brother, which arose through jealousy over the mother. This incestuous jealousy with respect to his brother is expressed not only in the literary works but also in a dream Hebbel notes in his diary (March 29, 1837): "During the night, I dreamed that my mother and Johann had come to Munich." It is clear that the dream should not be interpreted solely based on its obvious content. One of Hebbel's unconscious tendencies seems to have been the desire to disturb, through his own presence, the unhindered time spent together by his mother and his hated competitor. (In the dream, on the other hand, mother and brother come to him to admire his sophisticated urban life-style, of which he was always very proud.)

The strained relations of the brothers, which remained so for their whole lives, are also revealed in friction over money. On January 7, 1842, the playwright writes in his diary: "Another letter from my brother, begging for money. . . . This fellow always wants money. Between him and me there is no relationship except his desire for money!" But Johann's dislike for his brother, favored at first by the mother and later by fate, is suggested in another diary passage (February 14, 1842); this dislike was poorly disguised by an exaggerated friendliness by which the playwright was not fooled: "Today my brother reports to me that Judith has arrived. His letter is rude and impertinent, but it strikes me better than the last one, which was so exaggeratedly sweet. This is the truth, and perhaps I wrote to him a bit too bluntly. It pleases me that he does not seem to have taken it in such a way." This abrupt change in Johann's expression of his feelings toward his brother is comprehensible as a human expression of jealousy, though the playwright may have wished it himself as a justification of his own dislike toward Johann. Finally, a purely reflective diary passage written (September 18, 1838) by the playwright after receiving the news of his mother's death demonstrates that this hateful orientation, displaced from the father to the brother and maintained for the poet's whole life, derives from erotic affection for the mother: "She was a good woman, whose good deeds and less good deeds seem woven together into my own nature. . . . Although she never understood me, and never could have at her level of intellectual development and experience, she must always have had a vague idea of my innermost being, for it was she who always rushed in to protect me from my father, who saw in me (from his viewpoint, correctly) only an ill-mannered, useless, and even malevolent creature. She preferred to take his hardness, which in the truest sense of the word was not lacking, upon herself, rather than give me up to it."

The wish-fulfillment fantasy central to all of Hebbel's repressed incestuous impulses is expressed in his diary entry of September 21, 1846: "Among the first men, there was no blood shame." Here, like Byron in *Cain* (cf. chap. 18), he reveals his longing for this original state.

If young playwrights are attracted by incest material, this not only speaks for the burning intensity of these feelings but also suggests that the energy for literary production derives not least from the affects of this complex even after the playwright's energies have, through human and artistic maturity, mastered other themes. The literary application of incest feelings by youthful playwrights can be easily understood if one relates these feelings to the completely new emotions of puberty, the resulting desire for independence from the parents, and the consequences of this desire, given earlier intense fixation. In the normal individual, incestuous tendencies are dissociated from the parents and displaced to other individuals, but in persons with stronger drives this is not possible. Instead, these feelings remain fixated on the parents but are forced into repression by the onset of puberty. Still, they remain effective from within the unconscious by expressing themselves in unconscious fantasies whose affects provide the energy for conscious artistic achievement (anticipatory aesthetic gratification). Simultaneously, they lead to autoerotic gratification. That is, the playwright does everything within himself, whereas the normal individual adapts his drives and feelings to the environment and attempts to bring them into harmony with that environment. However, this autoerotic nature brings the playwright closer to the neurotic. During puberty, the neurotic usually fails to master the parent complex and regresses further and further into childhood rather than developing a love orientation in the real world. The playwright too probably undergoes this same regression for a time, but then he finds his way back to reality through the social adaptation and shaping of his fantasies (cf. Freud 1912a, 55–56).

In this respect the youthful preference for the incest theme by playwrights, who are later able to extend their infantile affects to artistic interest in other themes as well, resembles the ontogenetic recapitulation of the incest tendencies in phylogenetic development, which also were originally very dominant and relatively undisguised. Owing to the powerful (atavistic) drives of such individuals, these tendencies are found precisely in creative and productive persons. In the process of repression through time, these tendencies have been obscured, displaced, and sublimated, just as occurs in the literarily talented individual in the course of his human and artistic maturation.

8 The Interpretation of the Oedipus Legend

Alas, what is a man!
He who broods over him will die.

SOPHOCLES, *Oedipus*

In his interpretation of the Oedipus legend, Freud assumed its central association with the two typical dreams of the death of the father and of sexual union with the mother. In *The Interpretation of Dreams,* he revealed that these constitute a reactivation of long-repressed infantile wishes. If we pursue further this psychologically well justified parallel between dream and myth, we will notice especially a substantial difference between the mythical and dream representations of the same unconscious infantile wishes. Whereas the two dreams on which Freud based his meaningful insights showed the two corresponding persons in undisguised form, in the myth under investigation the representation of the fulfillment of this wish is possible only because the parents are made unrecognizable. This we recognize as the work of psychic censorship, of a tendency for repression and defense. In their undisguised presentation of unconscious thoughts, however, these two typical dreams constitute a special and highly remarkable exception, distinguishing them from all other dreams. This special characteristic was emphasized by Freud and actually makes unnecessary an interpretation of these dreams in the usual sense. It is obvious that in these dreams the parents are clearly recognized as such, whereas in all other dreams either the repressed wishes or the persons they are associated with must first pass through the distortion and obscuring of psychic censorship. Freud sees this favored position and this exceptional psychic status, enjoyed by both dreams, as significant in two respects. Concerning the dream of the father's death, he says: "First, there is no wish from which we believe ourselves further removed. We believe that the wish for his death 'wouldn't even occur to us in a dream.' Therefore dream censorship is not armed to resist these atrocities, just as Solon's laws included no punishment for patricide. Second, though, this repressed and unsuspected wish is countered especially often by a residue of waking thought in the form of concern for the life of the loved person. This concern cannot enter into the dream other than through association with the same wish. But the wish can be masked by the concern activated in the waking state" (1909f, 188). Only too often, though, this concern—Freud's interpretation of which can be more fully discussed—is nothing more than the reaction to the wish for the death of the corresponding person that has become active in the unconscious. (This is the usual mechanism in neurosis.)

The original nature of this concern is also revealed in the anguish that, according to Freud, ordinarily accompanies these dreams. Thus the dream of the father's death is actually not so undisguised as the other dream, that of sexual intercourse with the mother, which we will soon discuss. Indeed, dreams of the father's death do not particularly emphasize the son's killing of the father, complementary to the act of incest. Instead, most frequently one sees the father dead and feels anguish in association with this. The person of the father is recognized, but this is possible precisely because the death wish has been replaced by concern and mourning for him. In the same manner as this substitution, so occurs, for example, the already discussed transformation of the father-hating son into the avenger of his murdered father (cf. *Hamlet* and Rank 1909). We see the same mechanism at work when a neurotic, who apparently loves his parents very much, suddenly states without cause that his father has died. Instead of an expression of the death wish, we observe a simple report of the fact, just as a dreamer would relate it: "I saw my father lying dead." In the myth, however, the death blow is really carried out on the father, but without the son's recognizing him. Indeed, from the revelation of the oracle, Oedipus knows he must become the murderer of his father. But at the moment of the deed he once again knows nothing about the revelation, and even later he is unaware of having murdered his father. He knows that he will do so, but he does so without knowing it. There is no more instructive example of the effects of unconscious forces and of repression. Thus dream and myth exhibit, each in its own way, corresponding distortions of the original murder impulse. In the dream the father is recognized, but only because the murder impulse is replaced by mourning. In the myth, however, in which the death blow occurs, the father remains unrecognized owing to the repression of this impulse.

The situation is somewhat different for the typical dream of sexual union with the mother and for the relation of the myth to this dream. Often the typical dream of the mother is quite undisguised: it depicts the mother directly in sexual relations with the dreamer. This depends closely on another factor, however, for these clear dreams of mother incest are orgasmic dreams, and in these the tension of the current libido eliminates all defenses without hesitation. In contrast to this dream, the myth in question reveals its repressed nature in the unrecognizability of the mother. Nevertheless, the son knows from the oracle that he will sleep with his mother, a trait recalling the directness of the dream and indicating that the oracle, taken in the legend as an interpreter of events for all to hear, was originally a dream phenomenon, just as Hofmannsthal conceived it in his tragedy.

Just as the son knows of his crimes before he commits them but nevertheless (unknowingly) commits them, the father also knows before the birth and even the conception of the son that the son will commit the crime. Nevertheless the father sires him—intoxicated, as the legend has it, or seduced by the sensuality of his wife (Schneidewin 1852)—after having for years avoided marital relations with her for fear of fulfilling the oracular prediction. In the significant fact that the father already fears his son's incestuous desires before his birth, we recognize an unconscious expression of the father's fear of retribution; mindful of his relationship with his own parents, he fears the same treatment from his son. This theme of fear of retribution, with whose significance we are already familiar, plays a central role in the transformation of son feelings to father feelings (cf. Shakespeare, and cf. the myth of Cronus and Uranus below); and in the Oedipus legend, appropriately, it continues into the next generation, since Oedipus is mistreated and rejected by his own sons, whom he curses (cf. Eteocles and Polynices, chaps. 13 and 21). To prevent the predicted crime of the son, Laius decides to expose the newborn. To be even surer of the child's death, in Sophocles (v. 1032) and Euripides (*The Phoenician Women*, 26.805) the father has his ankles pierced. In the oldest version (cf. Bethe 1891), the boy is supposed to have been put out to sea in a small chest. Periboea, the spouse of King Polybus, pulls him from the water while washing clothes and takes him as her son (Hyginus, fable 66). In *The Myth of the Birth of the Hero* (Rank 1909), in the context of numerous and widely dispersed similar myths, I attempted to provide a psychological explanation for this portion of the Oedipus legend, involving the exposure of the child in a chest, water, and the switching of the parents. All these heroes are born to noble parents and are put in the water in chests on account of an oracle's pronouncement. Later they are rescued by lonely people or by animals. Finally, they regain their noble rights. In Hyginus's legend, exposure in a chest in the water was revealed to be a symbolic representation of the birth process, modeled after the child's tale of the stork, according to which children are pulled from the water by a stork (or another animal) and brought to the parents in a chest. What makes this symbolic representation of the birth process necessary in myths is that myths appear to be constructed from the point of view of the child not yet enlightened about sexual matters. The child's father refuses to answer the question, Where do children come from? or answers it with the tale of the stork, intensifying the child's inimical orientation toward him as well as the child's desire to be introduced by the mother to the secrets of sex. In many myths this question appears rather undisguised. In others it is disguised or concealed to the point of nonrecognition in an obscure riddle (cf. Freud 1909g). As I was able to demonstrate, in the Lohengrin legend this theme appears as a prohibition on asking the question. Lohengrin, who floats on the water in a boat drawn ashore by a swan (stork), forbids anyone, in a reversal of the original situation, to inquire about his origins. In other myths the meaning of this theme appears less clearly and therefore usually in the form of a riddle; that is, as an invitation to investigate—the opposite of a prohibition. Thus it will not be difficult for us to see the same question about the origin of children in the riddle the Sphinx gives Oedipus, which no one before him had been able to solve. Here too, though, a distortion has occurred. The riddle asks: What being is biped, triped, and quadruped, yet has only one voice and changes its form as long as it lives? The answer is man, who as a baby crawls on all fours (like an animal), walks upright on two feet as an adult, and takes on a cane as a third leg in old age. Instead of inquiring, What is man? the question is made into an answer: the being the riddle inquires about is man. Even more frequent than the riddle—the invitation to investigate (for which further examples will be provided)—is the prohibition on investigation, as we observed in the Lohengrin legend. This always reveals itself as a prohibition on inquiry about the secret of sex. Though we shall not go into a detailed interpretation, we should mention the "basic idea of many permitted doors and one forbidden door" (Grimm and Grimm 1816, no. 3, note), which occurs in many folktales and is undoubtedly based on the same thought. In the "Tale of Fitcher's Bird" (Grimm and Grimm 1816, no. 46), the sexual symbolism is easily seen through. Accordingly, the relevant portion is presented here without commentary:

> The evil sorcerer said to the first of the three abducted sisters: "I must travel away and leave you alone for a short while. Here are the keys to the

> house. You may go everywhere and look at everything, but do not go into the little room that is opened by this little key. I forbid you to go there on pain of death." He also gave her an egg and said: "Take care of this egg carefully for me, and carry it always with you, for if it were lost, a great misfortune would occur." She took the keys and the egg and promised to follow his instructions. When he had gone, she explored the whole house from top to bottom. The rooms sparkled with silver and gold, and she thought she had never seen anything so splendid. Finally she came to the forbidden door. She wanted to pass by, but her curiosity left her no peace. She looked at the key. It looked like any other. She stuck it in and turned it a bit, and then the door sprang open. But what did she see when she entered? A great bloody vat stood in the middle, and in it lay dead, mutilated bodies. Next to the vat stood a chopping block upon which there lay a shiny ax. She was so frightened that she dropped the egg she was holding into the vat. She fished it out again and wiped off the blood, but it was no use: the blood simply reappeared immediately. She wiped and scraped, but she could not clean off the blood.

Thus, the evil sorcerer recognizes that she has disobeyed his command and executes her in a cruel manner. The second sister meets the same fate. Only the third sister is able to outwit the sorcerer and is thus successful in rescuing her two sisters.

In the folktale "Marienkind" [Our Lady's child] (Grimm and Grimm 1816, no. 3), many of these traits are weakened and idealized. Here it is the Virgin Mary who hands over to the girl the keys to the thirteen doors of heaven: "Twelve of them you may open; through them you may behold the glory of heaven, but the thirteenth, which is opened by this little key, is forbidden to you. Be sure that you do not open it, lest you be unhappy." Here her finger becomes not bloody, but golden. In spite of this dampening, though, other traits still clearly indicate the sexual theme—for example, the overwhelming curiosity and the anxiety after the deed: "The desire in her heart would not be still; it gnawed and picked and left her no peace. And when all the little angels had finally left, she thought: 'Now I am really quite alone, and I can look through. If I do it, no one will know.' She found the key and inserted it into the keyhole, and when she had done so, it also turned immediately. She felt a terrible fear, slammed the door shut, and ran away. Her fear would not leave her no matter what she did; her heart beat hard and would not be still." From this beating of her heart, that is, from an obvious change in her whole physical state, the Virgin Mary realizes that she has disobeyed her command. The girl's denial that she has disobeyed, asserted with an almost incredible obstinacy, is also characteristic.

In the Greek myth of Ericthonius, the theme of prohibition also occurs as a clear symbolic reference to the sexual riddle. The goddess Athena tries to free herself from the passionate embraces of Hephaestus; his seed falls on the ground, producing the snake-footed Ericthonius. Athena adopts the child and raises it, unknown to the gods, hiding it in a woven basket. (According to Ovid's *Metamorphoses*, 2.532 ff., she appoints two snakes to guard the child.) She then gives the closed basket to the three daughters of Cecrops, telling them to guard it carefully but never to open it. But the three sisters, Aglaurus, Herse, and Pandrosus, even the last, cannot master their curiosity. When they open the basket and see the child with the form of a snake, they go mad and throw themselves off the cliffs of Cecrops's stronghold—even Pandrosus, though according to Apollodorus she escaped the fate of her sisters. The little basket in which the child lies reveals the role of the woman (cf. the exposure in the chest and water), and the snake reveals the man's role (snake feet), but in other respects this Greek myth is obviously connected in several ways with the two folktales above. In the one case the "virgin goddess," Athena, who bears a child without conception, corresponds to the Virgin Mary, while the three sisters, the last of whom escapes the others' fate, correspond precisely to the arrangement in "Fitcher's Bird." The prohibition on opening a lock and the transgression of doing so are common to all three tales.

The outbreak of madness after the revelation of the secret is to be emphasized as a crucial feature of the Greek legend. Freud has pointed out that a number of neurotic symptoms, especially in obsessional neurosis—for example, melancholia—have their origins in the child's unsatisfied sexual curiosity (cf. Freud 1909g). Although in many other legends insanity does not appear as a direct result of sexual fixation or of sudden sexual enlightenment, there is nevertheless a series of heroes characterized, like the classical Oedipus, by aggression against the father; nearly all these heroes appear temporarily stupid, foolish, or mad. Usually, though, these traits are only dissembled. Here, as shown by the folktales of the ever-successful fool, we find an expression of the thought that one can get along best in life by following one's healthy, haphazard instincts without much reflection. However, the specific sign of this stupidity, the child's sexual ignorance, is unmistakable. Thus the dissembling of these traits is most appropriate, for actually the child always feigns stupidity: he knows much more than is generally assumed.

In *The Myth of the Birth of the Hero*, I pointed out the connection between this dissembling of stupidity and the partially guessed secret of sexual origins. This theme occurs in the legends of Moses, David, Cyrus, Hamlet, Kaikhosrav, the younger Brutus, Tell, Parsifal, and others. It plays a role in the Oedipus legend as well, for in Sophocles' drama, while speaking to the seer Teiresias, Oedipus, albeit ironically, calls himself the "unadvised Oedipus," "the ignorant one," though his name signifies precisely the opposite—"the knowing one." It is interesting that the names of many of the heroes cited are not personal names but epithets, usually suggesting the stupidity discussed above. Thus "Tell" signifies "the simple" (recall Schiller's line: "If I had my wits, I wouldn't be called Tell"); the name "Brutus" means "the stupid one, the foolish one"; and according to Detter (1892), "Hamlet" is only "a translation of the name Brutus and signifies a fool, an awkward fellow." Brutus too, who dissembles madness, solves an oracular riddle, as does Oedipus. The riddle concerns the kisses of a mother, whom he interprets as Mother Earth (cf. the same interpretation of Caesar's incest dream). The same Brutus who eliminates tyrants through his trickery then has his own sons executed when he is first consul (fear of retribution). These incest traits occur more or less obscured in the other myths as well. Lessmann (1906) emphasizes that these heroes—Tell, Brutus, and Hamlet—whose names mean the same thing, are tyrannicides, while Moses, David, and Cyrus also revolt against the existing ruler as revolutionaries. We are already familiar with tyrannicide as a substitute for patricide, however, and opposition to the father is significantly intensified through his secretiveness concerning sexual processes, which forces the child to remain stupid or at least to feign stupidity in order to avoid the father's strictness.

That this lack of knowledge is associated mainly with sexual matters is emphasized, corresponding to our analysis, in the saga of Parsifal, who is raised in complete ignorance, in the stillness of the forest, by his mother Herzeleide so that he will escape the unhappy fate of his active, dynamic father. But the boy cannot repress his powerful drive for action; neither his mother's pleading nor the fool's costume in which she clothes him can keep him at home. In his journeys as a knight, he enters the castle of the Holy Grail, where King Anfortas, Parsifal's uncle, is ill with an incurable deep wound in the groin as a punishment for his sensuality. Parsifal would only have had to inquire as to the nature of the king's ailment and the marvels of the castle. Then Anfortas would have escaped his fate and Parsifal himself would have become lord and king of the castle of the Holy Grail. But having been taught in his youth to ask as little as possible (prohibition on inquiry), in his "stupidity" he neglects to ask where he is, and he must leave the castle the next morning, pursued aimlessly by Kundrie, the harbinger of the Grail's curse (theme of misfortune). Only after long sufferings and battles is he able to redeem Anfortas and gain the rank of king. Thus, whereas Parsifal should have inquired (invitation to investigate, riddle) but declines to do so, having been trained to play the fool (theme of prohibition), his son Lohengrin declares a prohibition on inquiry as a condition for the continuation of good fortune. Whereas the Lohengrin legend censures the urgent curiosity concerning the origin of children through a prohibition on inquiry, Parsifal, who since childhood had been forbidden to inquire, remains the "pure fool." He is so dense that the question, Where am I? (in the castle of the Holy Grail), which he should have asked in order to become king (father) himself, does not even occur to him. Similarly, he also reveals himself to be too stupid for love, for he lies beside his wife for two nights without touching her.

Besides this central riddle occupying the thoughts of the child—What is man? Where does he come from?—which always centers on the parents and in many myths is answered with the infantile theory of the basket and the water (cf. Rank 1909), another critical sexual problem appears to play a role, especially in the Oedipus legend. Although this problem cannot be discussed here in full detail, it is appropriate to mention the Sphinx, the remarkable being that asks the difficult and deadly riddle. The Sphinx is a being with a human's upper body and an animal's lower body. We will disregard the as-yet obscure origins of this man-strangling monster, which probably developed in Egypt, and will attempt only to elucidate its nature in close connection with the Oedipus legend and related myths.

I have pointed out (Rank 1909, 88 ff.) that in most of these legends the lowly mother who finds the exposed child and raises it (suckles it) is replaced by a female animal that suckles and protects the abandoned child. In some legends, such as those of Romulus and Cyrus, later rationalistic interpretation has attempted to make the miraculous suckling by an animal seem plausible by giving the women the names of animals, for example, "Cyno" (Persian "Spako") or "Lupa," which in turn are supposed to have given rise to this peculiar detail. But, in both cases, as researchers such as Duncker and Mommsen emphasize, the unadulterated animal fable is the original version and is found as an independent mythological tradition in these two cases as well (cf. Rank 1909). Those aspects dispersed in these cases between two versions of the legend are united in the Oedipus legend by the identity of the suckling wife and suckling animal. Just as the exposure in the basket in the water asexualizes the birth process in an infantile manner, the legend of the suckling animal, to which the stork constitutes a transition, confirms this conception by emphasizing the similarity between human and animal birth: man is a suckling animal. This identification of the mother with a suckling animal seems comprehensible if one considers the everyday fact that the child achieves knowledge of sexual relationships and processes and of their significance not from the unapproachable (noble) parents, but from animals, unashamed and naive, who display their sexual life and their sexual organs in such an open manner.

Therefore the naked Sphinx has a female upper body (down to the hips), including female breasts, characteristic of man's mammal nature. To this extent the nature, form, and significance of the Sphinx can be understood in connection with the riddle as to the origin of children and with the childhood answer to this question. But affixed to the Sphinx's female upper body is the lower body of an animal, bearing the organ characteristic of the male sex—the male member. Disregarding its animal character, the Sphinx is a female being with a male member. As Freud has pointed out, however, this interpretation is typical of the child's conception, which disregards sex differences and is regularly expressed in another "childhood sexual theory" of boys, which "attributes a penis, familiar to the boy from his own body, to all people, including females" (Freud 1909g, 165). The solution of the riddle of sex differences occurs with increased knowledge of sexual matters. Still, "the conception of the woman with a penis returns later in the dreams of adults; in sexual excitation, a man thrusts a woman down, removes her clothing, and prepares for coitus, only to abandon the dream and the sexual excitation on seeing a well-developed member in the place of the female genitals" (Freud 1909g, 165). Before proceeding with our psychoanalytical investigations, we should like to support from a purely mythological perspective the proposal that this dream, related to the incest dream and transformed to include homosexuality and anxiety, is actually one of the unconscious meanings of the Sphinx in the Oedipus legend. In his book *Das Rätsel der Sphinx* [The riddle of the Sphinx], Laistner (1899) argues convincingly that these difficult riddles have their source in anxiety-filled nightmares of interrogation, which we must consider to be repressed sexual dreams (anxiety), given the elucidation of psychoanalysis. Thus, if Laistner has already proved the dream origin of the Sphinx theme, we should consider the woman with the penis, who of course makes the sexual act impossible, to be the cause of the sexual inhibition leading to anxiety. Yet, it will not surprise us that the Oedipus legend—which realizes the dreams of the father's death and of sexual relations with the mother, otherwise associated with intensely painful affects, in a manner so free of inhibition and anxiety—compensates for the corresponding affect of anxiety in the Sphinx dream. This conception of the woman with the penis, significant for the child's psychology, originates with the beloved mother (cf. Freud 1909a), and in the Oedipus legend we were already able to identify the animal Sphinx with the suckling mother. The later incorporation of the Sphinx figure into the myth, assumed by most mythologists, would correspond fully to this interpretation; in our sense, then, the Sphinx would only be a doubling of the mother. According to Schmidt (1877), a modern Greek riddle portrays Jocasta and the Sphinx as one person; Schmidt considers this version to be more original, since in all similar versions it is the wooed queen herself who asks the riddle. The motive for introducing the Sphinx figure, dissociated from the motherly queen, is closely connected with the general obscuring and elaboration of the legend, dictated by the progress of repression. There is solid evidence that the original formulation of the myth may even have exceeded undisguised incest dreams in its unscrupulousness and directness.

But within the framework of this general investigation we cannot go into this mythological reconstruction of the original Oedipus fable in any detail. Isolated reports that have come down to us indicate that it was more violent in every sense. According to Nicholas of Damascus, Jocasta was present at the murder of her spouse. "It is then difficult to imagine how the marriage to the mother was later possible. One would almost suspect that Oedipus also carried out the act of incest immediately after the deed, but this can by no means be reconciled with the excerpt" (Gruppe 1897, 552 ff.). In the pre-Sophoclean epic, the *Oedipodeia,* the slain father is robbed of his weapons. Most significantly, Oedipus takes his belt and his sword, probably as a sign of claiming his father's power. In Greek tradition, loosening the belt is always conceived of as an erotic symbol (cf. Roscher 1884–1937); the god of marriage, Hymen, bears the epithet "the beltless," and Homer (*Iliad,* 14.215 ff.) identifies the belt of Aphrodite, goddess of love, as the source of her magical charms. In the Nordic Thidrek saga, too, a magical belt gives Brunhild the power to successfully defend her virginity against Gunther on her wedding night, and it is only Siegfried, wearing his magic cap Tarnhelm, who is able to overcome her for the king, tearing her belt from her. If the theft of the belt appears here directly as a symbol of rape (of the mother), the sword also appears as a typical symbol of the male member: as a sign of chastity, Siegfried lays his naked sword between himself and Brunhild, claimed for his blood brother. Thus, if we conceive of the similar theme of Oedipus's removing his father's belt and sword as a symbol of his taking possession of the mother (loosening the belt, marriage), perhaps we are justified in interpreting taking the sword as a later dampening of an original castration.

In the next chapter, crucial evidence for this will be provided from a Greek myth of the gods, where the jealously guarded sexual rivalry between father and son is expressed not in the killing, but only in the castration of the father. In the late form of the Oedipus legend that has come down to us, this is perhaps preserved in the piercing of the ankles, turned back on the son as a form of punishment. Just as killing the unrecognized father presumably was originally a willful mutilation, it is likely that the sexual relations with the mother originally appeared undisguised as well. I am thankful to Professor Ernst Oppenheim in Vienna for the comment that it can be proved through comparative mythology that Oedipus, conceived of as a phallic demon, deliberately raped his mother. With the advent of repression, these crass details were first dampened through the unrecognizability of the parents. In a later period of repression, the myth was transformed: in a repentant reversal, the son experiences the cruelty. Thus the myth now expresses the standpoint of the father. Here, of course, the oracle is first introduced. The oracle predicts the death of the father by the son's hand and the son's claiming of the father's wife, thus employing the notoriety originally associated with the two acts themselves as a justification for punishing the son. For based on the oracle's pronouncement, the father punishes the son, carrying out on him what the son, in pleasurable gratification, carried out on the father in the original sense of the legend. The father castrates him (pierces his ankles) and by exposing him in a chest in the water sends him back into the womb, thus transforming the deep association with the mother into the punishment of not coming into the world. (For this reason, too, he abstains from sexual relations.)

The son, who has become guilty of the originally pleasurable deed, actually suffers this punishment through reunion with symbols of the mother. With the exposure of the newborn child, which occurs as a consequence of the disastrous oracular prediction, the foster parents are also introduced. They are identical with the actual parents but, because of repression, are no longer recognized as such. Through their introduction, the old, objectionable contents of the legend can now be portrayed again in disguised form. Oedipus, learning of the disastrous oracular prediction, attempts to escape his fate by fleeing, but in so doing he only establishes it with greater certainty. This is nothing more than the psychological expression of unsuccessful defense against (repression of) these originally pleasurable infantile wishes. Indeed, in *The Interpretation of Dreams* Freud characterizes such defense as the psychic correlate of actual flight. Thus, given the progression of repression, if the original wish fulfillment appears as a tragic fate the hero must face, it is clear that "fate," as well as the oracle, is nothing more than the justifying projection of the son's own wishes (along with their defensive and punishment tendencies) onto an inexorable *fatum*.

Since we are familiar with the legend mainly from the epic poets, though more details are attested in the works of the tragedians as well, the progression of repression can no longer be followed precisely. However, we know that here, as in other popular versions, the poets, struggling with the violent inner conflicts of the Oedipus complex, usually intensify the incestuous aspect. Yet they give stronger emphasis to the opposing impulses for justification and punishment. Thus we know that originally, immediately after the murder, there occurred the rape of the mother, present at the act of patricide. A formal (unwitting) marriage is introduced only later, in the *Oedipodeia*. This marriage was later extended to many years, and Aeschylus even blesses it with children who finally carry out the curse on the father, given the theme of retribution. On the other hand, we know that Sophocles significantly intensified the defense mechanisms: at the crossroads, the father gives the son reason to commit the murder in "self-defense" (an anticipatory punishment and justification of the son):

> From the road the one who led the team
> And the old man himself rashly press me.
> . . . He swings
> His double goad down upon my head,
> But does not live to atone for it; no, in a moment,
> Struck by the staff in my hand, he falls
> Sinking backward, straight from his seat.
>
> (*Oedipus the King*, 804ff.)

The originally conscious incest myth was created purely from the standpoint of the desirous and vengeful son, and the first stage of repression and self-punishment effected a shift to the standpoint of the father and thus the unconscious continuation of the primary wish impulses (oracle, exposure, foster parents). Finally, the third layer of repression and defense is added owing to fear of retribution; it entails the punishment of the father, who has inadvertently become guilty, by his own sons. They mistreat their father just as Oedipus originally mistreated his, and just as Oedipus's father mistreated Oedipus in the second layer of the myth, which deals with punishment. Like the expulsion from Thebes and the aimless wanderings of the blinded Oedipus, the retribution by his son was added to the legend late; through stronger and stronger themes of punishment and defense, the progress of repression brought about an attempt to make the pleasure theme, maintained in all transformations of the legend, at least somewhat more accessible to the finer sensibilities of later generations. To the three-layered structure of repression associated with the father complex corresponds a similar structure associated with the even more objectionable theme of mother incest. First mother incest occurs consciously, following the patricide (castration). Then, in the second phase, it occurs unwittingly through the introduction of the oracle, exposure, and the foster parents. Finally, in the third stage, it leads to a long marriage and the birth of children. In a stage of repression in which the conscious and pleasurable rape of the mother is transformed into the marriage with the mother, undertaken without knowledge of her identity and revealed with horror, the Sphinx is also introduced. As in a dream experience, the feelings of anxiety produced in the process of repression are placed in the figure of the Sphinx.

"The Sphinx was first introduced into the legend when the marriage with the mother had just been established. In connection with an old literary theme, according to which the hand of a princess is won by conquering a monster, this fearful being, localized by legend in Boeotia, presented itself" (Gruppe 1897). From our discussion of the "woman with the penis," we have already concluded that the Sphinx and the mother originally coincided. That is, the introduction of the Sphinx was intended to effect a splitting off of certain objectionable traits in the mother. All of this is confirmed by a modern Greek variant. After the introduction of the Sphinx, its actual mother nature was eliminated by another wave of repression: since the rape of the mother was originally involved, the hero, according to Gruppe, first had to survive a fight with the Sphinx. That the Sphinx falls into the abyss after losing the "intellectual battle" still suggests the hero's original conquering of the Sphinx, which could indeed be considered a heroic deed, while anyone could successfully have solved the clumsy, foolish children's riddle. Now, perhaps, we also understand better why the formerly raped Sphinx/mother asks the youth, struggling to understand sexual matters (exposure, suckling by animals), a riddle concerning the nature of man, and why the hero can marry only after he has solved it—that is, in the original sense, after he has raped his mother (cf. the Lohengrin legend). To an extent, the child's insufficient sexual knowledge (chest, water, suckling by animals, woman with the penis), originally associated with the mother, is tested by the mother herself, and the son demonstrates his superiority by physically conquering her, later dampened to the intellectual sphere. Thus we can perhaps understand also why the land is beset with misfortune before the riddle is solved and why the women are barren, becoming fertile again only after the conquering of the Sphinx. Just as the son rescues the mother from the supposed violence of the father in the typical youthful fantasy, Oedipus also saves the city, symbolized in many versions as a woman, and brings fertility back to the land. Just as patricide becomes tyrannicide, the son's taking possession of the mother is transformed into the liberation of the (home)land.

Thus, if the figure of the sphinx was first introduced as an aspect of the mother in the process of repression and of the construction of mythic levels, it can also be demonstrated that the conception of the woman with the penis, associated with the mother, led—probably in the very latest period—to a remarkable [homosexual] reformulation of the background story, revealed by psychoanalysis to be another product of repression. Freud (1909g) states: "If this conception of the woman with the penis becomes a 'fixation' with the child and survives all influences of later life, making him incapable of renouncing the penis as a sexual object, such an individual must become a homosexual, given an otherwise normal sex life; as his sexual objects he must seek men who, through other physical or psychological characteristics, are reminiscent of women." The Oedipus legend also demonstrates this homosexual fixation of the childhood sexual orientation—precisely, and characteristically, in connection with the Sphinx. The curse of infertility hanging over Oedipus's father is found, according to Bethe (1891), in the *Oedipodeia*. Bethe connects it with the tale of Peisandrus, according to which the goddess of conjugal love sends the Sphinx to Thebes as a punishment because the Thebans have tolerated Laius's criminal love for the beautiful youth Chrysippus. Indeed, the Delphic oracle, which Laius consults concerning this curse, informs him that the wished-for son will kill him, according to Zeus's decision, in punishment for his abduction of Chrysippus, the son of Pelops. And in the *Oedipodeia* we read that Laius sacrifices the newborn boy to the angered goddess Hera as an offering of reconciliation by exposing him in the meadow of Cithaeron consecrated to her. According to the older version of the myth, as Roscher calls it, Chrysippus's abduction and disgrace are the reason for all the later misery in the house of Laius. Specifically, Pelops, the father of the abducted youth, curses Laius, wishing that he have no children, but that if he does, his son kill him. Considering Laius's homosexual inclinations, this curse of childlessness gains a deeper meaning. Indeed, Oedipus himself was considered to have been homosexual in his youth, as shown by the fragments of Praxilla, a woman poet of the fifth century B.C. (cf. Schneidewin 1852). In her story, he was in love with the same youth (Chrysippus) as his unrecognized father; according to Euripides (*Phoenician Women*, 66), Laius is killed out of jealousy over Chrysippus, or in a fight over the youth—the complete opposite of jealousy over the mother. Just as Oedipus is the first and clearest example of incest among the Greeks, his father Laius is considered the original pederast.

We may now disregard the completely impossible demand for a literal psychological translation, as it were, of the legend. Even had we exhausted its unconscious content such an attempt would fail, since we are unaware of the conscious factors leading to its creation. But at this point our psychological experience and insight will easily afford clues. Since Freud began X-raying the psyche, we have known that the child learns to love, in the widest sense of the word, from his father and mother and that this relationship with the parents is exemplary and determinate for the individual's entire life. Erotic attraction to the mother, displaced in puberty from her to other persons, normally determines the selection of the sexual object and the nature of later sexual life. On the other hand, fixation on the mother can lead to perversion (incest) or neurosis, depending on whether and how it is later repressed. The relationship with the father is similar. Normally, sublimated, it leads to a normal orientation toward social authorities, superiors, friends, teachers, and so forth. But its two extreme forms, passionate infatuation and jealous hatred, displaced to other authorities, can lead respectively to homosexuality and criminality. Although stronger affection for the mother is logically associated with jealous hatred toward the father, it nevertheless appears that homosexual attraction to the father is possible only at the price of a general, exaggerated aversion to women, whose primal image is of course the mother.

This is by no means a schematic construction; two students of Freud who make practical use of psychoanalysis for therapeutic purposes have independently made this discovery in working with their patients. Further, I had deduced it from my own material before the publication of their research. Based on a series of analyses, Stekel (1908, 311) comes to the conclusion that "homosexuality is only a special form of neurotic defense"—precisely, "successful defense against the infantile thought of incest." Quite similarly, based on the analysis of one case, Sadger (1909b) concludes that the homosexual suffers from the consequences of the repression of excessively powerful, precocious, libidinous impulses toward women—usually toward his own mother. In the legend of Oedipus, we observe just this same alternation between these two extremes—homosexuality on the one hand and incest on the other. However, in an extremely oversimplified manner, bordering therefore on the neurotic, the legend also demonstrates the psychosexual development that normally occurs in the child, transcending the mutually conflicting feelings for father and mother and thus going beyond incest and homosexuality. This development usually culminates in a normal sexual life. In a characteristic but necessary manner, with greatly distorted extremes, the legend demonstrates that the individual can protect himself from the homosexual fixation of his feelings only through erotic attention to the mother. Conversely, the individual may take refuge in homosexuality from excessively powerful incest impulses. But the legend also demonstrates—and herein lies its unconscious power, which so strongly affects us—how the individual who does not play the two extremes against each other, thus keeping them in equilibrium, must meet with misfortune, precipitating himself and his loved ones into destruction. For what is so horrifically presented in the legend appears even to this day in the unconscious psychological and emotional life of every individual who has become normal. Yet it is only the result of this process—a normal, healthy sex life—that actually appears, revealing nothing of its dark origins. We would know nothing of these processes, despite their mythological depiction and their reappearance in our dream life, if those neurotic persons who are unsuccessful in mastering this Janus-faced complex did not express in crass and exaggerated forms this developmental stage, which has remained on an infantile level, and if they had not learned through psychoanalysis to conquer it.

9 *The Incest Complex in the Development of Classical Myths and Mythological Tradition: Sexual Symbolism*

Brother will deliver up brother to death, and a father his child, and children will rise up against parents and will have them put to death.

Matt. 10:21

For a son is despising a father; a daughter is rising up against her mother; a daughter-in-law against her mother-in-law; a man's enemies are the men of his household.

Micah 7:6

The dreams of normals, the pathological creations of neurotics, and as this research attempts to demonstrate, the creations of playwrights all serve as proof of the universal presence and significance of incestuous impulses in the individual. Further, we have found proof for the originally powerful effects of incest impulses in the mass psyche of whole peoples—in the mythological traditions dear to the people, in part honored religiously, and handed down since earliest times. We have proceeded from the psychological assumption that myths are to be regarded as intermediate between mass dreams and mass literature. In the individual, dreams and literature provide release for the impulses repressed in the course of cultural development—the impulses that have become unconscious. Similarly, in mythical or religious fantasies, a whole people retains its psychic health, freeing itself from these primal drives inimical to culture: it creates a mass symptom for the absorption of all repressed impulses. The gratification of drives, which the individual must renounce as culture dictates, he permits to the mythical gods created in his own image and ultimately, through identification with them, to himself—at least in fantasy. And since one of the first complexes to succumb to repression is the son's aggressive behavior toward his parents—the rape of the mother and the murder of the father—it should not surprise us that the myths of all peoples abound with these fantasies.

Neither, of course, has such an obvious phenomenon escaped the notice of mythologists. Owing to their own repressed orientation toward these psychically offensive themes, however, analogous to that of the myth creators, mythologists have not been able to appreciate their actual significance. Mythologists derive all these myths, certainly with extensive justification, from natural or celestial processes. Accordingly, as one of their chief representatives, Max Müller (1869, 2:143), admits, they have been able to eliminate some of the most offensive details of classical mythology. Of course, it is clear that many mythological traditions, or at least individual elements of them, still clearly reflect, besides their human significance, a sense connected with nature mythology through reference to natural or celestial processes. Undoubtedly this sense was incorporated into the finished myths, just as nature or astral mythologists incorporate it today. In so doing, they are only recapitulating a developmental stage in the creation of myths; this provides them with the justification for their interpretation. For example, if one conceives of Oedipus as a sun-hero who murders his father, darkness, and shares his bed with his mother, the dawn, from whose womb he sprang, this explanation will perhaps suffice if one has modest expectations.

But there is certainly no doubt that these conceptions of incest with the mother and the murder of the father arise from human life and that in this human guise the myth could never have been developed from celestial observation without there being a corresponding psychic conception. This psychic conception could of course already have been unconscious, as it is with contemporary mythologists, at the time the myth was created. Psychologically, though, it is more probable that the myth was originally conceived in purely human terms, as one dreams. In a time when man began to sexualize nature and the universe, the myth was probably cleansed of its offensive nature by introducing a substratum of celestial processes, thus justifying its existence. This is precisely what is done by our mythologists. This is also the case with the numerous mythological traditions held to be agricultural fertility myths, which originally had a purely sexual significance. In a time when man began to cultivate the earth, these myths were extended to the bearer (earth mother) and producer (seed father) of fertility in nature. Therefore when Goldziher (1876, 107) claims that "the murder of the parents and the killing of the child, fratricide and conflict between siblings, and sexual love and relations between children and parents and between brother and sister are the main themes of myth," this is certainly true. But his explanation—that man derives these myths from the observation of nature—is unsatisfactory. Instead, with the same interpretation and tendency as the nature mythologists, man extended them to nature secondarily.

The Myth of the World Parents

One of the best examples of the extension of individual and human incest impulses and fantasies to the universe is provided by the "myth of the world parents," widely distributed among primitive peoples but by no means absent in the cosmogonies of civilized peoples. Frobenius, who has collected a series of such mythological traditions among primitive peoples, characterizes the myth as follows (1904, 268): "In the beginning of things, father sky lay tightly pressed upon the earth," and one must add that in this position they also pair as spouses. "The young son forced the parents apart; the father was forced upward as the sky."

This interpretation is found not only among the great civilized peoples—Babylonians, Egyptians, Greeks, and so on—but also among nearly all primitive peoples. Frobenius writes (1904, 268 ff.):

> In addition, we find this conception of the sky as the father and of the earth as the mother of the universe in all of Oceania, in China, in India, and among the Semites, Greeks, and our Nordic peoples. Nor is it lacking in America; the Zuni have a particularly clear version of the myth. . . . I have encountered this conception in North and East Africa, in Melanesia and Polynesia, in Indonesia, in the American Northwest, and elsewhere. It is an innocent, simple report that nevertheless contains precisely the same elements as the four myths of civilized peoples. In these we always see the father lying upon the mother in more or less obvious sexual union. Then the children revolt. Many children have already been born, and now they wish to come out into the light of day [337].
>
> In Africa, among the Yoruba, the myth is elaborated extremely beautifully. In the beginning Obatala, the sky, and Odudua, the earth, his wife, lie tightly pressed upon one another in a gourd. An argument arises, and the noble husband strikes out Odudua's eye, whereupon the gourd separates and the sky rises upward.
>
> The second portion of the myth concerns the children of Odudua. The boy Aganyu (the firmament) and the girl Yemaya (the water goddess) marry and bear a son, Orungan, another sky god, in whose name Orun, the sun, mightily appears. Orungan falls in love with his mother, and since she refuses to submit to his passions, he pursues and rapes her. Immediately Yemaya springs up and runs away wailing. The son pursues her in order to appease her, and when he has finally almost reached her, she falls astride upon the ground. Her body begins to swell. Two streams spring

> from her breasts, and her body bursts. From the gaps in her body arise fifteen gods, of which the first is Dana, the god of plants, and the second is Shango, the god of lightning. In the listing, always reported in the same order, the sun and the moon are mentioned last. If we reconstruct this case, we will establish a single pair of gods, the sky god and the earth goddess ⟨who are brother and sister⟩. The son is the separating god.

Before we investigate the mythological traditions of civilized peoples, I should point out that we observe in these myths the simple extension of the infantile Oedipus complex to the universe. However, as Ehrenreich (1910) points out, in these myths it is not simply the case that the "creation of the world is conceived to be analogous to animal and human procreation." Instead, these myths arise from a tendency we believe we have identified in the reassertion of the original impulses of the infantile incest complex, now subject to repression. Indeed, with all the clarity one could desire, the myth recreates the original childhood situation, in which sexual jealousy arises when the child overhears the parents' sexual relations. This jealousy strives for the elimination of the father and possession of the mother. Thus all these myths depicting the origin of the universe, or of the gods who created it, as proceeding from one pair of parents are only extensions of the infantile sexual fantasies to the origins of the universe, also mysterious in the childhood of mankind. Since they must necessarily incorporate incestuous unions, specifically between siblings, given the assumption of a single original human pair, they become excellent gratifications and justifications of the originally purely human incest fantasies.

According to Schneider (1907, 435), the Egyptian ninefold deity consists of Ra; his children, the sibling spouses Shu and Tefent; his grandchildren Keb and Nut; and two pairs of sibling spouses, Osiris and Isis, and Set and Nephthys, Ra's great-grandchildren, who were born to Keb and Nut. This uninterrupted succession of generations born of incest proceeds in the guise of the myth of the world parents. "In the beginning, the universe filled a boundless primordial expanse of water (Nun), which held in its womb the male and female seeds, the beginnings of the future world. The first act of creation began with the formation of the egg out of the primordial water, from which the daylight, Ra, the immediate source of life in the realm of the earth, sprang forth" (Brugsch 1888, 101). As a detailed representation of the human act of impregnation, this cosmogony is associated more closely still with the newborn hero, floating, according to the myths, in a little chest (egg) upon the "primeval waters," since Nun means both "young water" and "young child" (Brugsch 1888, 129). Like Gaea in the Greek cosmogony, Ra now produces from himself the first gods, in clear deference to the infantile sexual theories of the unconscious, identified by Freud. Here, though, the myth of the world parents has undergone the typical displacement, brought about by repression, into the second generation. In the Egyptian mythological traditions passed down to us, this is almost always the case (cf. the Osiris myth). Ra's children are Shu and Tefent (air and water), a pair of sibling mates who in turn engender Keb and Nut (earth and sky), again sibling spouses. Originally they lie upon one another until their father, Shu, presses between them, raising up and supporting Nut (Schneider 1907, 430). In the Greek cosmogony Gaea, the earth, arises from the original chaos. From herself, "without friendly love" (Hesiod, *Theogony,* 132), Gaea produces Uranus, the sky. Then, uniting with the sky, her son, she produces six male and six female Titans. This union of the primal mother with her son in order to create the universe plays a great role in ancient Asiatic myths and cosmologies.

In the Babylonian creation myth, the first world arises from the incestuous union of mother and son. "In the beginning there was chaos, called 'ocean' as a man and 'sea' as a woman (Apsu and Tiamat). . . . Their son Mummu . . . presses between them and engenders a new generation, that is, a new universe, with his mother Tiamat" (Winckler 1907, 92). If we similarly consider the Babylonian schema of moon, sun, and Venus as father, son, and daughter or spouse, the female deity appears as the spouse of both the father and the son (cf. Winckler 1907, 79). "In the Egyptian cosmology, Amon appears as Ka-mutef, that is, the spouse of the mother" (Brugsch 1888, 94), and in the Egyptian Osiris myth, to be discussed in detail below, Osiris appears simultaneously as the spouse and son of Isis (Jeremias 1905, 146), although in the later form of the legend, still echoed in the folktales of Bitiu and Anepu, the parent complex has been replaced by the sibling complex. Similarly, in the Japanese sibling cosmology, Izanagi is originally both son and spouse (Stucken, *Mose* [Moses]), just as the Indic Pushan has punishable intercourse with his sister Surga and with his mother (*Rig Veda,* 6). According to Phoenician legend (Jeremias 1905, 141), the spirit burned with love for its own origin and united with it. In Greek legend, the Pleiad Sterope is considered the mother of Oenomaus, but also his spouse (Siecke 1908, 35). Similarly, in one version Orion is considered the son of Oenopion, while in another, he has raped Oenopion's spouse—thus his mother—and for this reason is blinded (cf. Oedipus) by Oenopion (Roscher 1884–1937). In all these double traditions, we see how the original fantasy of mother incest gradually came to seem offensive, therefore being distributed among several apparently contradictory mythological traditions revealing the original sense when brought together again. Thus, in the festival of Ares' (Horus's) return from abroad, described by Herodotus (2:59 ff.), the incest fantasy is only suggested: with his servants, Ares fights for access to his mother because he wishes to have sexual relations with her (Jeremias 1905, 85). Incest with the mother is also seen in the Greek Attis myth, discussed below, and in the myths of Tamuz and Dusares (Jeremias 1905). "As demonstrated by Lenormant (1872, vol. 2, letter 5), the theme of the son in love with his mother appears quite generally in Asiatic mythology; in the ancient Babylonian myth, Dazi, the Hebrew Tammuz, is the lover of his mother, Ishtar. The Egyptians called Amon the spouse of his mother, Neith. Indra . . . unites with his mother, Dahana" (Goldziher 1876, 108 ff.). Similarly, "Azhi Dahaka, a *drudsh,* half man and half monster, is supposed to have committed incest with his mother, Uda, a demon herself" (Geiger and Kuhn 1895–1904, 2:603–4), and Mithra is also supposed to have married his mother (Hüsing 1906). "In the Vedic hymns . . . there are still no genealogies, no permanent marriages between the gods and goddesses. The father is sometimes the son, or the brother the spouse; she who is mother in one hymn is wife in another" (Müller 1869, 2:68).

Similarly, in Rev. 12:1, the queen of heaven is the mother of the victor, while in another verse (21:9) she is celebrated as his bride. "In the myth of the new age, mother and spouse are one" (Jeremias 1905, 409). In the Gnostic doctrines as well, which according to Bachofen (1897) permit sexual relations with the mother, the incest fantasy plays a major role. In an interesting article, as an example of the "numerous incest myths of all peoples dealing with sexual relations between father and daughter, mother and son, brother and sister," Schulz (1911) discusses the doctrine of the Ophites: "In the beginning was Man, the god of gods, who remained as an infinite light in the foundation of the universe. His thought went out from him and became the second man, the son of Man. Between the light and the darkness floated the *pneuma,* the first woman. By shining upon her, in shared love, father and son together sired the Anointed and his sister, Sophia. Thus the first woman committed the sin of adultery, since she was simultaneously at the call of two male beings. She was first a virgin, then a whore, then a mother—the mother of the Anointed, born from her right side, and of Sophia, born from her left side. Whereas the Anointed immediately returned with the mother to the upper light and to the primordial deity, Sophia ⟨wisdom⟩ sank into the darkness in search of her father. From her, as related above, the world was formed." In the mutual attraction between mother and son, and between father and daughter, there is still an echo of the parental incest continued into the second generation. The notion of virgin, mother, and whore in one person is already familiar to us from the typical fantasies of childhood. It is through these fantasies that the early impression of overhearing the parents' sexual relations and the subsequent wish impulses develop into the whore fantasy.

The Castration Complex

In all these mythological traditions, incest with the mother (or in dampened form, with the sister) has been emphasized, while the theme of jealous hatred toward the father recedes through the already described distribution of the incest complex to several mythological traditions or generations. Still, this jealous hatred toward the father finds a special form of expression in another series of mythological traditions. Its clearest expression is in the Greek cosmogony, which derives from Egyptian influences. Modern mythologists (Stucken, Jeremias, and others) characterize this expression of father hatred as the second "primal theme." As with the first theme, we can gain a psychological understanding of this theme by proceeding from the childhood psychology of the individual. Very clearly, this special form of revenge upon the father reveals sexual rivalry as the reason for the son's revolt; hatred of the father is directed only indirectly at the father's life. Instead, it is first directed at his genitals; the son robs the father of his genitals to make him unfit for sexual relations with the mother.

Of the six male Titans of the Greek cosmogony, Oceanus, Iapetus, and Cronus are the most famous. Of the six female Titans, Thetis, Rhea, and Themis are the best known. Hesiod (*Theogony,* 138) remarks of Cronus: "He hated his thriving father." But the father, Uranus, also hates his children (*Theogony,* 155) and banishes them to the deep womb of Gaea, their mother. She urges her children to free themselves and her as well from the wicked father. She justifies inciting her children to revenge, claiming that "he carried out such disgraceful deeds first" (*Theogony,* 166). But only Cronus, the youngest son, who according to Roscher's *Lexicon* (1884–1937) is "especially attached to the mother," proves prepared for the deed: "Mother, I gladly consent and will gladly carry out the deed: for I do not care at all for our ill-reputed father; he carried out such disgraceful deeds first" (*Theogony,* 107 ff.).

Gaea now urges her youngest son to castrate his father with a sickle prepared expressly for this purpose. "At night, when the father again wishes to approach his spouse, his son Cronus severs his private parts and casts them into the sea" (Roscher 1884–1937):

> And the mighty Uranus comes and brings night with him;
> Yearning for love, he embraces Gaea and extends himself

> Toward creation; but then the son seizes him with his left hand
> From behind; with his right hand he wields the giant sickle
> Of long and pointed blade, and quickly severs his own father's
> Privates, throwing them backward again while rushing by.
>
> (*Theogony*, 176 ff.)

After castrating his father, Cronus assumes command and marries his sister Rhea, who bears him three daughters, Hestia, Demeter, and Hera, and two sons, Hades and Poseidon. However, since Cronus fears that his children will treat him the same way he has treated his own father, Uranus (fear of retribution), he devours each child immediately after its birth. Therefore when his spouse, Rhea, is about to bear her third and youngest son, she flees on the advice of her parents to a cave on Mount Ida, where she bears Zeus and keeps him hidden. She deceives Cronus by showing him, instead of the child, a stone wrapped in swaddling clothes, which he also devours. Zeus grows quickly, suckled by the goat (or nymph) Amalthea. Zeus conquers his father, Cronus, with the help of Mother Earth, who gives the father an emetic, causing him to vomit first the swallowed stone and then his children.

According to the Orphic theogony, however, Cronus's fears are realized; lulled to sleep by Night and bound by Zeus, he is castrated just like Uranus (Preller 1854–55). All the other consequences of this deed are also repeated in the second generation, so that the son, with all his experience, appears merely as a replication of his father—a scenario occurring only too frequently in real life. The psychology of neurosis has taught us to recognize the significance of this effect "for the fate of the individual." Zeus too becomes ruler of the world after castrating his father, and he also marries his sister, Hera. But this repetition by the son should be considered not so much a replication as a transformed, new version of the myth. Just as aberrations in the life of the individual necessarily result from individual traits and certain opposite reactions in the younger generation, such new versions offer a people the opportunity to keep abreast of the progress of sexual repression, which can be fully equated with general cultural progress. In the handing down of the myth, castration is perhaps the most important theme. In the standard version, for example, the overpowering of Cronus by his son Zeus no longer appears in the form of castration, as in the earlier generation, but is depicted in a dampened form that does not name the manner of attack. The castration is mentioned only in a special, adjunct version, and the people, now further advanced in sexual repression, no longer see in this castration only the expression of personal unconscious desires to castrate the father. Instead, they have already begun to react against such feelings through their defense mechanisms (exaggerated fear of retribution, anxiety, horror, disgust, etc.). In the third generation, repression progresses further still. In the struggle against Cronus and the Titans, Zeus is weakened by Typhon, a hundred-headed monster born to the angry Gaea and sired by Tartarus: Typhon cuts out the sinews of Zeus's feet with a sickle (as used in the castration of Uranus). Schwartz (1860, 138) considers this to signify castration "modified in a special way." This is easily understood, based on sexual repression, and from our investigation of the Oedipus legend the two objectionable details—that the deed is carried out by the son and that it has purely sexual motives and consequences—are eliminated, while the noncontroversial elements remain to symbolize the incest complex: the sickle (with which the castration was carried out) and the physical form of the deed—cutting off or cutting out certain bodily parts.

The inimical attitude toward the son, as demonstrated by Uranus, appears in another portion of the myth as well—in the relationship of Zeus with Hephaestus, who dares to support his mother, Hera, after she has been severely punished by Zeus. He is cast down from the sky by his angry father; after falling for a day, he plunges half-dead into the earth. Here, then, the father retains the upper hand. This is a condition for his continuing to rule the universe, yet it indicates that fear of retribution plays the main role, given the increased repression of the desire to castrate the father. Indeed, the Zeus myth, in complete contrast to both of its models, is conceived from the father's standpoint. In this sense it is to be considered completely as a reaction to the preference for the son's point of view in the earlier stages, for Zeus was weakened not by one of his children, but by a distant ancestor—an indirect father, so to speak. With a deep understanding of psychological processes and relationships, this victory of Father Zeus (Dyspater, *deus pater,* Jupiter), and thus of authority in every form, is here made the foundation of universal order.

In that Cronus surprises and castrates his father while the latter is engaged in sexual intercourse with the mother, the childhood source of father hatred—which arises from rivalry over the mother—is fully retained. And if under the influence of Egyptian mythology Cronus's mother incest is dampened to sister incest, mother incest does still appear in the preceding generation: Uranus unites with his mother, Gaea. If we reduce this myth, distributed through various stages of repression over three generations, to the original underlying fantasy, we shall be dealing with the unconscious Oedipus complex, which aims for the castration of the father and the rape of the mother. Here one motive for the repression of the Oedipus legend becomes clear. There, both infantile wishes are brought into a causal relation and to actual fulfillment. But the condition for this complete wish fulfillment is that both acts must occur without the individual's knowledge. On the other hand, in the Greek cosmogony, where both acts are carried out consciously, the tendency for repression exerts itself so that the causal relation between the two wishes is eliminated and they are distributed between two generations or, as with the Cronus myth, between two versions, in each of which basic aspects of the repressed complementary wish are still to be found. Thus, whereas in the myths of the gods one of the two wishes is always repressed, the Oedipus legend aims for the complete fulfillment of both wishes. However, this can be achieved only through their removal from the conscious mind.

In addition to the wish complex of the son, Cronus, the myth also reveals that Uranus is castrated because of his sexual relations with his mother. The theme of castration as a punishment for incest plays a great role in the fantasy life of the individual and of entire peoples. At this point we can present a few examples of the rich mythological traditions of all times and peoples, made clear through the development of the incest complex in the individual. Thus the Greek fable of Lycurgus, as told by Hyginus, relates that Lycurgus denied the deity of Dionysus. As punishment, Dionysus makes him drunk. Lycurgus, who feels sexual desire for his mother, is also in the habit of destroying grapevines; he considers wine a dangerous poison. But in his drunken state, brought about by Dionysus, he kills his wife and son (mistaking them for grapevines). He is also supposed to have severed one of his own feet, thinking it was a grapevine ("traditur unum pedem sibi pro vitibus excidisse").

Considering the ancient and generally known phallic significance of the foot, which is also dominant in the symbolism of the Oedipus legend, we can consider this severing of the foot to signify self-castration for desiring the mother. Here, as in many other incest legends (e.g., Laius, Lot; cf. Noah, Mirrha below), the emergence of the repressed impulses is attributed to too much alcohol. This reveals a good understanding of the psychological need for alcohol and of its effects. The conception of severing the foot as castration, which here, as in ancient Germanic tradition, is associated with the self-inflicted injury of a mutilator of trees, receives etymological support as well: *excido* signifies both "cut off" and "castrate." That the drunken man also considers his son to be a grapevine, and thus cuts him down with his knife, seems in this connection to point to a desire to castrate the son. Like the second castration in the Cronus myth, this appears to express the fear of retribution. The father fears that the son will desire his own mother, just as the father desires his. That is, the father fears that the son will desire the father's spouse. Thus he kills both of them together out of jealousy, like a guilty pair of adulterers caught in the act. Proceeding from the child's perspective, many peoples have introduced castration as a punishment for adultery—the Abyssinians, for example (Stoll 1908, 990).

It should also be clear that this infantile form of punishment for forbidden sexual pleasure still appears today in "criminal" deeds, where it is condemned by custom and law. According to Storfer (1911, 29), only incest—intercourse between the physiological or merely legal son and the wife of the patriarch—was looked upon as serious adultery. In the fantasy productions of the individual and of entire peoples, this infantile conception of the punishment is expressed with surprising frequency. Thus, H. E. Meyer (*Indogermanische Mythologie*, 1:16, 27) reports that Indic incubi (*gandharv*) take on the form of the father or the brother when they approach women to sleep with them. In the *Athar Veda* (4:37) there is a passage in which the jealous husband threatens the *gandharv* with vengeance: "I shall rip out the gonads, I shall cut off the rod of the *gandharv* who approaches dancing, the husband of Apsaras, with the bush of hair." Thus, once again, we note castration as punishment for a form of incest reminiscent of incestuous dreams. Castration as a punishment for adultery is found also in the legend of Helen. After taking Troy, Menelaus carries out vengeance on Deiphobus, Helen's last husband, the brother and successor of Paris:

> Atque hic Priamiden laniatum corpore toto
> Deiphobum videt ut lacerum crudeliter ora,
> ora manusque ambas populataque tempora raptis
> auribus et truncas inhonesto volnere naris.

> [And here he saw Deiphobus son of Priam, all his body hacked and his face barbarously torn, face and both hands, and ears lopped from his mangled temples, and nostrils maimed by a shameful wound]. (Virgil 1950, 6:494)

Goethe undoubtedly had this passage in mind in *Faust* (part 2, act 3) when Phorcys addresses Helen:

> Have you forgotten how he who won you,
> Stubborn widow, and happily wed you,
> Grotesquely mutilated your Deiphobus,
> Slain Paris's brother? He severed nose and ears,
> And so maimed further—a horror to behold.

In the legend of the Holy Grail, the sorcerer Klingsor meets a similar fate. Caught in the act of adultery, he is castrated by the betrayed husband and learns sorcery to avenge his shame (Wolfram von Eschenbach, *Parzival*). As is well known, in the original version of the legend King Anfortas too suffers from an incurable wound in the groin, inflicted by the evil

Klingsor as if in revenge, and in which we recognize a dampened form of castration. In Richard Wagner's *Festspiel, Parsifal,* the legend is dampened further still. On the one hand, it is Klingsor who castrates himself ("Powerless to eliminate the sin within, he lays upon himself his own offending hand"). Yet he takes only the "holy spear" from Anfortas, who has been seduced by a beautiful woman. This seems to be a final echo of the myth of the universal parents, in which the sacred phallus is cut from the man during sexual intercourse. (In a single symbol, the spear comprises phallus and deadly weapon.) The Klingsor episode brings us back to the self-castration we found in the Lycurgus legend as punishment for incestuous desires. Castration as self-punishment for the incest wish is also found in the myth of Attis, who appears associated with his goddess-mother sometimes as son and sometimes as lover; at his wedding he is finally driven mad by his jealous mother, who does not wish to relinquish him to any other woman. In his madness, he castrates himself under a spruce (Arnobius, *Adversus nationes,* 5.5).

According to Pausanias, Attis is indirectly the son of the hermaphrodite Agdestis, castrated by the gods. From Agdestis's blood there grows an almond tree. A daughter of the river-god Sangarius places its fruits on her bosom, thereby becoming pregnant; she bears Attis, and when he has grown to be an attractive youth, Agdestis falls in love with him and jealously drives him to self-castration, from which he dies. Agdestis begs Zeus to revive him, but Zeus grants only this favor: Attis's body is to remain free of decay; his hair (symbol of masculine energy) will always grow; his little finger (phallus) will always live and will alone remain in constant motion. Satisfied with this, Agdestis buries the body of Attis. However, she buries his male member separately, and from its blood there grow violets that wreathe [a] spruce tree. (In the same manner, a pomegranate tree had sprung from the blood of Agdestis's penis.) Just as the reestablishment of generative power occurs several times in symbolic guise (in the context of nature mythology), the castration itself occurs multiply. Not only do Agdestis and Attis suffer castration, but as a symbolic substitute a mighty spruce was felled during the spring festival of the goddess-mother Cybele and set up again in her temple. It is known that the priests of Cybele practiced self-castration, though it was later replaced by cuts in the arm. Concerning Attis, Roscher's *Lexicon* states: "He appears as the son of Cybele. However, when he had become an attractive youth, Cybele saw him lying on the bank of the river Gallus and fell in love with him. Her son becomes her lover. This seems to have been the substance of the mysteries of Attis and Cybele. But, the bonds of love with the attractive youth, who places himself fully at her service and swears fidelity to her, are destroyed by a cruel fate: Attis castrates himself as punishment for his unfaithfulness."

Just as castration should be conceived to have originally been a punishment for incest, in the self-castration occurring in connection with incestuous desires we observe the now familiar theme of self-punishment. This ordinarily occurs as a consequence of the repression of a rejected wish and seems to be nothing other than the repressed impulse to commit the forbidden act. Within the context of the later configuration of complexes, this act (in the case of incest, severing the male member) is not carried out on one's own person. This valuation of castration as jealous vengeance on the father and as repentant self-punishment is two-sided (ambivalent)—so fully characteristic of all psychological processes. This duplicity can only be understood, like the whole castration theme in general, in light of the deep insights into the psychic life of the individual, and especially of the child and the neurotic, introduced by Freud's research.

In *The Interpretation of Dreams* (1909f, 181), concerning the representation of the inimical relationship between father and son, Freud already referred to the "castration wish" as an expression of jealous hatred toward the father. In later publications (1909a, 1909g), based on his rich psychoanalytical experience, he has attempted to bring about a greater understanding of this "castration complex." First, the relation of this complex to infantile psychology becomes clear when one recalls the common threat by parents and caretakers that they will cut off the penis of the boy—who "after all is principally governed by stimulation of the penis"—if he does not stop his practice of childhood masturbation. "In its actual relation to the estimation of this member, the effect of this castration threat is an extremely deep and persistent one." When the child, usually upon overhearing his parents' coital activity, begins to masturbate with incestuous fantasies concerning the mother (or sister or other objects with whom sexual activity is forbidden), he associates the threat of castration, usually made by the father, with all forms of genital pleasure, including incest and even adultery. Simultaneously, however, the jealousy and inimical perspective toward the father are usually intensified both through the prohibition on masturbation and through overhearing the parents' coitus. It should not surprise us if the child projects this threatened and feared loss back upon the father, given the "round trip" psychology prevalent in children. This projection back upon the father receives special motivation from the child's already awakened jealousy in connection with the mother's affection for the father. And since the child usually notices or suspects that the father, preferred by the mother, has a bigger penis, it is understandable that the child wishes to deprive the father specifically of this advantage so as to take away the mother's favor. This also explains the occurrence of castration as a punishment for incest, which is regarded only as another form of forbidden genital play. Thence one theme branches off to self-castration:

the same punishment with which the child was threatened because of his forbidden play, and which he had projected back onto the father, is carried out on the son, who wishes to castrate the father out of jealousy over the mother, given that the son himself wishes for incest with the mother or carries it out in his fantasies.

Just as the son's infantile affection for the mother, and the fate of this affection, affect a man's later love life and indeed dominate it, the sexual jealousy of an adult, acquired by the child in his relationship with his parents, is never without its infantile source (Freud 1905), that is, the incestuous affect. It is only logical that the child's first experience of rivalry, his relationship with his father, should in its broadest sense be extended by the adult to all subsequent competitors (cf. the initial displacement to the brother, chap. 13).

From these masturbation fantasies and their forbidden objects, and from intense self-reproach and self-punishment, a broad path leads to artistic fantasy activity. The intensity, richness, and emotional nature of this activity are explained mainly by the infantile sexual impulses that remain ungratified in later life. Here, though, let us mention a minor path that never transcends the castration fantasy. Like the third foot of Lycurgus, Oedipus, and Zeus, the "eleventh" finger also appears in various works as a symbol of the penis, representing it in the context of castration (cf. the story of Hans Carvel and his ring in Rabelais and Goethe). Such a fantasy is also found in Henrik Ibsen's *Peer Gynt*—also in connection with the compensatory mutilation of trees and, as in the story of Cronus, with the use of the sickle. In act 3, scene 2, where Peer Gynt attempts to fell a mighty pine, a young farmhand suddenly appears. Believing himself unnoticed, the young man cuts off his finger with a sickle to avoid being sent to the battlefront.

> *Peer:* But to sever it? To part with a member?
> To think it, wish it, yes! But to do it,
> Truly to commit the deed? What can one say?

And in act 5, Peer Gynt returns to his birthplace for this man's funeral and hears the clergyman's oration:

> You all knew him; his hair was sleek,
> His voice was soft, his carriage unmanly;
> With few talents, he played the shy man's role.
>
> . . . .
>
> But seeing now his mortal ashes, recall
> How he went always with his right hand in his pocket.
> The hand in the pocket: that expressed, you see,
> The man's whole being.

Remember how he bore himself and shyly bowed,
Entering, embarrassed, a neighbor's home.
He lived always alone. He walked still paths.
Though he remained a stranger among us,
And guarded his secret like a thief,
We knew his hand had but four fingers.

Just as the castration fantasy appears here as the punishment of the masturbator, in *Ghosts* Ibsen portrays the masturbator's second typical punishment fantasy. Based on a medically unfounded notion of inheritance, this fantasy is comprehensible only as an expression of the masturbator's guilt. The excessive masturbator believes that he can expect mental deterioration, consumption, and paralysis as consequences of his vice. And though as a consequence of the Oedipus complex these effects are also blamed on the father, the playwright, like the neurotic, still reveals his underlying self-reproach. (*Oswald:* "And then I discovered the truth, the unbelievable truth! I should have kept away from this gay, carefree life with my comrades. It was too much for my feeble energies. Thus, I have myself to blame!")

In the youthful work of another playwright whose psychic state, as can be demonstrated, was affected in no small degree by masturbation, we find the severing of the little finger carried out, for superstitious reasons, on a child. In Heinrich von Kleist's *Familie Schroffenstein,* Barnabe says:

Then the mother, who understands such matters,
Cut off the little finger of the boy,
For after his death, it will do more good
Than the whole hand of a grown man
While he lives.

Nor can it be a coincidence that in Shakespeare's first work, *Titus Andronicus,* chopping off the hand plays such an important role as a form of punishment.

Although these symbolic punishments naturally relate only to the male genitals, literary tradition illustrates the female complement as well, which is also associated with the punishment threatened for masturbation, though it does not directly coincide with this punishment. The threatened punishment for male masturbation is severing the fingers from the hands, as in Grimm folktale 31 (Grimm and Grimm, 1816), where the hands remain intact only as long as they are clean, or in *Titus Andronicus,* where cutting out the tongue also occurs. Correspondingly, the female punishment for forbidden sexual pleasure is sealing the genitals by sewing them shut or by means of a lock. In his *Bijoux indiscrets* [Indiscreet gems], Diderot relates such an episode. According to Diderot, in the Congo adultery was punished by the loss of the male member, which usually proved fatal. He relates the story of an adulterous woman who accuses her former lover of rape. He is about to receive the punishment when a mysterious ring reveals that she has lied, whereupon she herself receives the analogous punishment: her jewel is locked up behind a Florentine padlock. Sewing up as a punishment for incest with the son, displaced in this case to the mouth (as the male punishment may be displaced to the nose), is found in the legend of Saint Andrew (chap. 10). According to a report in *Avenir du Tonkin* [The future of Tonkin], sewing up a woman's lips is also practiced among the Chinese. Numerous references concerning the custom among primitive peoples of sewing up a girl's vagina as a means of preserving her virginity are found in Ploss (1895) and in Stoll (1908, 549 ff.). The idea that the difficulty in entering a young girl is due to sewing up the vagina is expressed in the German slang term for coitus, *trennen* ["separate"]. In German the dragonfly may be called *Teufelsnadel* ["devil's needle"], and the belief that it will sew up the mouths of crying children (Rochholz 1856, 1:347) seems to point to the childhood threat; the *Teufelsnodle* [Aargau dialect] is also called *Wasserjungfer* ["water virgin"].

Like the finger and the foot, the nose is often cut off as a symbolic substitute for castration, as with Deiphobus, whose nose, hands, and feet were severed. This serves as a reduplication and intensification of the desire for revenge, which applies to all competitors. In dreams, neurosis, and folk tradition, the nose typically appears as a symbol of the penis. This is not due either to its histological similarity as erectile tissue or to its biological relation to the penis, discovered by Fliess, but apparently is due to its formal similarity, noted already in the ancient belief: "Robur viri cognoscitur ex nasone" [a man's virility is shown by his nose]. Thus it is understandable that among American Indians adultery is punished by cutting or biting off the nose (Helbing 1908). As a substitute for castration, this also explains the severing of nose or ears, humiliating for the individual involved—a fate so often experienced in time of war by those, supposedly unmanly and cowardly, who are sent back by the enemy as an admonition (cf. Grimm 1899, 468 ff.). Certain ancient mystery ceremonies had the same secret meaning of castration. Cutting into the arm or the forehead can be proved to be a substitute for the castration originally carried out. The famous Auerbach scene in Goethe's *Faust* seems to have the same symbolic meaning. The intoxicated students, bewitched by Mephistopheles, believe they are in a beautiful vineyard. They pull out their knives and grasp each other's noses, which they believe are bunches of grapes, to cut them off (cf. Lycurgus's similar error). With Goethe, who was following more recent literary traditions, the dampening substitution of the nose for the phallus goes one step further, for the noses are not in fact severed at all. Instead, in a sense thoroughly consistent with a child's perceptions, only the threat is made.

The Old Testament Tradition

In the Old Testament as well, the older portions of which are filled with clear as well as disguised incestuous relationships, the castration theme appears in various forms. According to Stucken (1902), Reuben, who slept with his father's concubine Bilha, the mother of his brothers, suffered castration as a punishment for incest. But even in the story of Jacob, who married his mother's brother's daughter (Genesis 28), there are hints of the castration theme. After fleeing from his father-in-law, Laban, on the night before the feared meeting with his brother Esau (whose enemy he had already been in the womb), Jacob dreamed the following dream.

> Then a man began to grapple with him until the dawn ascended. When he got to see that he had not prevailed over him, then he touched the socket of his thigh joint; and the socket of Jacob's thigh joint got out of place during his grappling with him. After that he said: "Let me go, for the dawn has ascended." To this he [Jacob] said: "I am not going to let you go until you first bless me." So he said to him: "What is your name?" to which he said: "Jacob." Then he said: "Your name will no longer be called Jacob, but Israel, for you have contended with God and with men so that you at last prevailed." In turn Jacob inquired and said: "Tell me, please, your name." However, he said: "Why is it that you inquire for my name?" With that he blessed him there. Hence Jacob called the name of the place Peniel, because, to quote him, "I have seen God face to face and yet my soul was delivered." And the sun began to flash upon him as soon as he passed by Peniel, but he was limping upon his thigh. (Gen. 32:24–31)

In addition to its rationalized meaning, which promises Jacob divine blessings as the "bringer of a new age" (Jeremias 1905, 377), this dream has another personal and human meaning. To understand this meaning, we must refer to Jacob's childhood and youth, as Freud has taught us to do in analyzing our own dreams. When Rebekah finally becomes pregnant after twenty years of childless marriage (Gen. 25:20–26), "the sons within her began to struggle with each other" (Gen. 25:22) so that she curses the fact that she is pregnant: "Gradually her days came to the full for giving birth, and look! twins were in her belly. Then the first came out red all over like an official garment of hair; so they called his name Esau. And after that his brother came out and his hand was holding onto the heel of Esau; so he called his name Jacob. And Isaac was sixty years old at her giving them birth. And the boys got bigger, and Esau became a man knowing how to hunt, a man of the field, but Jacob a blameless man, dwelling in tents. And Isaac had love for Esau, because it meant game in his mouth, whereas Rebekah was a lover of Jacob" (Gen. 25:24–28). Then follows the familiar episode in which Esau sells Jacob his tenuous rights as firstborn for a meal of boiled lentils. Thus Jacob, destined to great things, takes one step toward eliminating his brother's slight advantage at the time of their birth. Jacob makes Esau swear to the sale: " 'Swear to me first of all!' And he proceeded to swear to him and to sell his right as first-born to Jacob" (Gen. 25:33). Jacob takes his second step in this direction by diverting his blind father's blessing, intended for his brother Esau, toward himself, encouraged by his mother and through her cunning:

> So he went on in to his father and said: "My father!" to which he said: "Here I am! Who are you, my son?" And Jacob went on to say to his father: "I am Esau your first-born. I have done just as you have spoken to me. Raise yourself up, please. Sit down and eat some of my game, in order that your soul may bless me." At that Isaac said to his son: "How is it that you have been so quick in finding it, my son?" In turn he said: "Because Jehovah your God caused it to meet up with me." Then Isaac said to Jacob: "Come near, please, that I may feel you, my son, to know whether you are really my son Esau or not." So Jacob came near to Isaac his father, and he went feeling him, after which he said: "The voice is the voice of Jacob, but the hands are the hands of Esau his brother." Hence he blessed him. After that he said: "You are really my son Esau?" to which he said: "I am." Then he said: "Bring it near to me that I may eat some of the game of my son, to the end that my soul may bless you." With that he brought it near to him and he began to eat, and he brought him wine and he began to drink. Then Isaac his father said to him: "Come near, please, and kiss me, my son." So he came near and kissed him, and he could smell the scent of his garments. And he proceeded to bless him and to say; "See, the scent of the field which Jehovah has blessed. And may God give you the dews of the heavens and the fertile soils of the earth and an abundance of grain and new wine. Let peoples serve you and let national groups bow low to you. Become master over your brothers, and let the sons of your mother bow low to you. Cursed be each one of those cursing you, and blessed be each one of those blessing you." Now it came about as soon as Isaac had finished blessing Jacob, yes, it indeed came about when Jacob had barely come out from before the face of Isaac his father, that Esau his brother came back from his hunting. (Gen. 27:18–30)

The deception is revealed, and since the blessing can be neither revoked nor repeated, the disadvantaged Esau becomes despondent and angry. He says: "Is that not why his name is called Jacob, in that he should supplant me these two times? My birthright he has already taken, and here at this time he has taken my blessing" (Gen. 27:36). "However, Esau harbored animosity for Jacob on account of the blessing with which his father had blessed him, and Esau kept saying in his heart: 'The days of the period of mourning for my father are getting close. After that I am going to kill Jacob my brother' " (Gen. 27:41). The mother warns her preferred son and advises him to flee to the household of her brother Laban. There, in fourteen years of service, he acquires for himself Laban's two daughters, his own blood relatives, the beautiful Rachel and the plain Leah (Gen. 29:17), but not without an attempt being made to trick him, just as he had tricked his father. After he has served seven years for the hand of Rachel, a great wedding feast is indeed arranged, but the morning after the marriage is consummated, he notices that Laban has married him to the plain Leah. Laban justifies himself by stating that it is not the custom to marry off the younger daughter before the older one. Jacob takes his revenge through the trick of the speckled sheep, having brought about their birth through the use of peeled staves, thus increasing his property so much that he becomes the enemy of Laban and Laban's family (Gen. 30:26–43). With his wives, children, and possessions he flees from his father-in-law, just as he had earlier fled from the anger of his deceived brother, whom he has to fear again upon his return home. Therefore he sends messengers to Esau to inform him of their master's submission and to give him lavish gifts and thus effect a reconciliation (Genesis 32). "And Jacob became very much afraid and grew anxious. So he divided the people who were with him, and the flocks and the cattle and the camels into two camps" (Gen. 32:7). Then he prays devoutly to God, concluding with the words: "Deliver me, I pray you, from my brother's hand, from Esau's hand, because I am afraid of him that he may come and certainly assault me, mother together with children" (Gen. 32:11).

In this worried state, in the night preceding his encounter with Esau, Jacob dreams the dream now fully clear to us, after his previous experiences, as an expression of his desire for forgiveness from his brother and for reconciliation with him. The wrestling match with the strong stranger, who does not reveal his name, anticipates the struggle with his brother, but it also attempts to make Jacob's fears seem illusory by modeling the struggle upon earlier struggles between the brothers. These had already begun in the womb, when they struggled for the birthright of the firstborn; Jacob had grabbed Esau by the ankle so that he emerged limping on one foot. Similarly, he now grasps his opponent by the hip to bring him down. This grasping the hip is also predetermined by earlier events. It suggests, though weakly, that its actual meaning is to be found in the castration complex: in Gen. 25:33 Esau swears his birthright over to Jacob. That among the Jews swearing was effected by placing the hand upon the partner's hip is also demonstrated elsewhere, and it is certain that this swearing upon the hip is only a euphemistic expression of the original swearing while grasping the phallus. There is also etymological evidence for this in German (cf. *zeugen* ["beget"] and *Zeuge* ["witness"]). In this case Jacob is actually grasping his opponent's genitals, just as he had previously grasped his opponent's foot (cf. Oedipus). Thus we sense an echo of the castration wished upon the brother but feared by the individual himself, for the morning after the dream it is Jacob who is limping—who has come away wounded. If we relate it to Esau's oath, grasping the hip, in addition to this symbolic meaning, also represents a reminiscence—a wish underlying the dream, which must be interpreted in historical perspective. Jacob, of course, fears his brother because of the sale of his birthright and, chiefly, because of the deception in connection with their father's blessing. What could be clearer than that he wanted his brother to sanction these two acts, at least after the fact, since they could no longer be revoked? Although in the dream he retains his animosity toward his brother in connection with the oath concerning the birthright (upon the hip), his own repentant feelings effect an inversion upon himself, a self-punishment (limping). Yet the dream is completely successful in calming the conscience of the fearful, repentant deceiver. For he does not let his brother go before his brother has blessed him—before making good his earlier crime through his brother's "voluntary" sanction. That the dream actually does have this liberating effect is demonstrated by Jacob's thanksgiving to God, in which he says that his "soul was delivered" (Gen. 32:30). In this after-the-fact rehabilitation following the unjust appropriation of the father's blessing, brother and father already blend in the dream as a single person. This is clearly shown in that the dream opponent, before blessing him, says: "Tell me, please, your name," using the same words his father had once used. This time, though, Jacob answers truthfully, in humble repentance: "Jacob." This time the change of name, previously effected deceitfully by Jacob, is demanded by the father: "No longer is your name to be called Jacob, but Israel" (Gen. 35:10). Here it is already clear that in the unknown person of the dream, the psychologically simple transformation of father to God has taken place. (Jacob says, "I have seen God face to face" [Gen. 32:30].) And since the dream figure comprises brother, father, and God, all of whom are to forgive Jacob and sanction his deeds, the figure cannot give his name, but instead only blesses Jacob in the name of these three feared opponents. Roscher argues that this dream illustrates all the characteristics of interrogation by the Sphinx, and thus of the nightmare (in Laistner's sense)—namely, a wrestling match until dawn, refusal to reveal names, lameness, and blessing. This is undoubtedly the case.

Based on Freud's research, though, we must consider the nightmare, filled with anxiety, as basically libidinous. Thus the dream again seems to suggest fear of castration. If the sexual content of this dream appears in the repressed form of anxiety, an earlier dream of Jacob, dreamed while fleeing from his home to the household of his father-in-law, Laban, illustrates the positive counterpart of the castration dream discussed above by assuring the dreamer of his great potency. Before Jacob departs, his father, strangely unconcerned about the earlier deception, blesses him: "And God Almighty will bless you and make you fruitful and multiply you, and you will certainly become a congregation of peoples" (Gen. 28:3). As in the preceding dream, the father's blessing is ascribed to God: "And he began to dream, and, look! there was a ladder stationed upon the earth and its top reaching up to the heavens; and, look! there were God's angels ascending and descending on it. And look! there was Jehovah stationed above it, and he proceeded to say: 'I am Jehovah the God of Abraham your father and the God of Isaac. The land upon which you are lying, to you I am going to give it and to your seed. And your seed will certainly become like the dust particles of the earth, and you will certainly spread abroad to the west and to the east and to the north and to the south, and by means of you and by means of your seed all the families of the earth will certainly bless themselves' " (Gen. 28:12–14). Even if we did not know from solid dream analyses and symbolic relationships that in dreams climbing in general, and the climbing of ladders, symbolizes coitus, this dream would still be clear. It clearly deals with ideas of fertility and potency.

We introduced the incestuous elements in the story of Jacob by mentioning the incest of his son Reuben with Jacob's concubine Bilha ("Reuben . . . you have gone up to your father's bed. At that time you profaned my lounge" [Gen. 49:3–4]). And proceeding backward from generation to generation we find an unbroken chain of incestuous relationships. Skipping Jacob's father, Isaac, whose story will be discussed later, we shall go back to Isaac's father, Abraham. Since his wife Sarah is barren, he takes on his brother's son Lot (Gen. 11:30–31); later the two part because of a dispute over the herd, just as did Jacob and Laban. In the destruction of Sodom (fully paralleled in Judges 19 and 20) Lot is saved, and he commits incest with his daughters while intoxicated (Genesis 19). In obvious contrast to Abraham's childlessness we note God's firm promise, in many cases anticipating word for word the blessing of Jacob: "To your seed I am going to give this land" (Gen. 12:7); "And I will constitute your seed like the dust particles of the earth" (Gen. 13:16); "And I shall make a great nation out of you. . . . I will bless those who bless you and him that calls down evil upon you I shall curse" (Gen. 12:2–3). Because of a famine, Abraham now makes his way to Egypt, and since he fears that he will be killed on account of his beautiful wife, Sarah, he tells her to say she is his sister

(Gen. 12:10–13). She attracts great attention at the court and "was taken to the house of Pharaoh" (Gen. 14:15). But for this reason God sends plagues upon Pharaoh, and Pharaoh discusses the deception with Abraham and lets him go on to another country (Gen. 12:15–20). That this episode includes echoes of actual incest is demonstrated by its doublet (Genesis 20). In Gerar too Abraham presents his wife as his sister, and here too "Abimelech King of Gerar sent and took Sarah" (Gen. 20:2). Jeremias remarks (1905, 342): "One should note that Abimelech really wishes to wed Sarah." But God appears to Abimelech in a dream and says to him: " 'Here you are as good as dead because of the woman whom you have taken, since she is owned by another owner as his wife.' However, Abimelech had not gone near her. Hence he said: 'Jehovah, will you kill a nation that is really righteous? Did not he say to me, "She is my sister"? and she—did not she too say, "He is my brother"? In the honesty of my heart and with innocency of my hands I have done this' " (Gen. 20:3–5). In the morning Abimelech calls Abraham and chides him for the deception, as Pharaoh had done before, whereupon Abraham answers: "She is truly my sister, the daughter of my father, only not the daughter of my mother; and she became my wife" (Gen. 20:12).

It is interesting that Sarah's promised pregnancy and the birth of Isaac occur directly after this episode (Genesis 21). According to Bergel (1882–83), the ancient writers of biblical mythology were attempting to provide support for Isaac's "more than doubtful descent from Abraham." They attempt to do this especially by claiming Isaac's birth as a divine promise. This promise immediately meets with the disbelief even of the parties involved: "At this Abraham fell upon his face and began to laugh and to say in his heart: 'Will a man a hundred years old have a child born, and will Sarah, yes, will a woman ninety years old give birth?' " (Gen. 17:17). "Sarah began to laugh inside herself, saying: 'After I am worn out, shall I really have pleasure, my lord being old besides?' " (Gen. 18:12). And after the birth Sarah says: " 'God has prepared laughter for me: everybody hearing of it will laugh at me.' And she added: 'Who would have uttered to Abraham, "Sarah will certainly suckle children," whereas I have given birth to a son in his old age?' " (Gen. 21:6).

Further, later writers of mythology attempted to make Isaac's legitimacy more probable through another version of Abimelech's dream, which leads us to another incest theme in the legend of Abraham: "When Abimelech had Abraham's wife brought to his bedchamber, he was overcome by a deep sleep. In a dream, the angel Michael appeared to him brandishing a sword and threatening to murder him if he touched the abducted wife indecently. Frightened by this dream, he no longer dared to approach Sarah, and her innocence was no longer imperiled" (Bergel 1882–83). If we interpret the threatening guise of Abimelech's dream as a later disguise of adultery, we will recognize the drawn sword, often placed as a symbol of chastity between a man and a woman forbidden to him (cf. Tristan, Siegfried, etc.), as an original fertility symbol, which also explains Sarah's sudden fertility. On the other hand, the sword could be conceived as a threat of castration in punishment for adultery. In this connection one notes that God punished Abimelech and his house with infertility (Gen. 20:18). Even more evidence for this interpretation is that the threat of castration is also suggested in another episode of the Abraham legend, the counterpart of the dream of Abimelech. This is the attempted sacrifice of Isaac by his father, Abraham, which occurs with no motivation whatever and is comprehensible only in light of the myth of exposure; children of adulterous and especially of incestuous relationships (which would be the case with Isaac) are left to die because similar infractions are feared from them. Just as Abraham threatens Isaac with a knife, Laius has Oedipus's ankles pierced. Since we must interpret this, based on a version of the Cronus myth, as a dampened castration, we can also interpret Isaac's unexecuted sacrifice—prevented only at the last moment by the appearance of an angel—in connection with Abimelech's similar dream, as a direct and literal representation of the castration intended for the son.

We can close our arguments with the observation that it is precisely in connection with the birth of Isaac that God establishes with Abraham the covenant of circumcision (Gen. 17:10–27), according to which every male is to be circumcised in the foreskin on the eighth day of life. Of course, with this observation we are far from casting any light on the historical development of the rite of circumcision or its origins. But we cannot avoid pointing out this connection, since we regularly find that circumcision is conceived as a castration substitute in the infantile and unconscious thought of the individual. Still, it is not out of the question that a new understanding of the custom of circumcision may derive from the castration threat. The hygienic motivations have proved invalid (Stoll 1908, 519 ff.), but no others have been proposed in their place. In light of the psychological relationships, and given the evidence of individual traditions and observations, one can perhaps suppose that circumcision, though perhaps not initially, certainly occurred later as a dampened symbol of castration. This supposition is supported especially because among primitive peoples this ceremony marks the beginning of puberty (as with the biblical Ishmael), and because among many peoples it is also practiced on the female clitoris. Stoll informs us (1908, 523) that many primitive tribes believe the purpose of circumcision is to discourage masturbation in boys and that its purpose with girls is to counteract the sex drives experienced in their unmarried state. This suggests that circumcision is a remnant of an originally more severe punishment. However, we believe that especially solid evidence for our position is provided by the fact, also emphasized by Stoll (503), that in 1 Sam. 18:27, David brings King Saul the foreskins of the conquered Philistines as war trophies. Among certain African tribes this mutilation of the defeated enemies extends to the entire male genitalia, a practice carried out while the defeated enemy is still alive. Stoll (994) indicates that according to Schwally, the expression in the Bible refers to a "penis with a foreskin," which suggests that David had the entire uncircumcised penises of the Philistines cut off, "in which case the ancient Hebrew war custom would be fully identical to the northeast African one." Stoll carefully speculates (506): "It seems that the above-mentioned Hebrew custom of robbing the defeated enemies of their foreskins is the northernmost, and clearly dampened manifestation of the custom of employing the genitals of the defeated enemy as war trophies, assuming that the Hebrew custom was the continuation of a tradition, and not an isolated phenomenon."

Just as sibling incest in the Abraham legend appears doubly, which according to Jung (1911, 85) is an expression of its psychological "importance, that is, its libidinous content," sibling incest is introduced in the Isaac legend with the same words (Gen. 26:7). This we consider further evidence that in the Isaac legend we are dealing with nothing more than an elaborated doublet of the Abraham story. Originally, it appears, sibling incest really existed in each of these cases (or mother incest, as Stucken supposes [*Moses*, 555]). With the gradual dampening to incest with the stepsister, or with a woman only claimed to be the sister, each of these variants, all products of repression, becomes an independent version. Thus the original affective interest (libidinous content) is distributed among several dampened doublets. In the Isaac legend we find only a woman claimed to be a sister, not the actual sister, as in the legend of Abraham: "So Isaac went on dwelling at Gerar. Well, the men of the place kept asking with respect to his wife, and he would say: 'She is my sister.' For he was afraid to say 'my wife' for fear that, to quote him, 'the men of the place should kill me because of Rebekah,' because she was attractive in appearance" (Gen. 26:6–7). The wording of this passage corresponds closely to that of Gen. 12:11–12, but if there are still doubts that the Isaac legend is a doublet of the Abraham legend, they should be dispelled by the fact that the whole Abimelech episode, further dampened, and the story of the obstructed spring are also extended to Isaac. From the union of Isaac and Rebekah, incestuous in a sense, arose the inimical brothers Jacob and Esau, whose destinies we have already pursued in our discussion of Jacob's marriage to the daughter of his uncle, Laban, also a blood relative, and of the incest of Jacob's son Reuben with his (step)mother. The parallels between the Isaac and Oedipus legends, pointed out by Stucken, are also worthy of note. Isaac, like Oedipus, was to be sacrificed by his father; like Oedipus (Eteocles and Polynices), he also has inimical sons; and like Oedipus, he is later blind.

In pursuing further the biblical accounts following the reconciliation of Jacob and Esau, we shall be anticipating the theme of inimical brothers, to be discussed in depth in chapter 13. Genesis 34 relates how Jacob's and Leah's daughter, Dinah, was raped by Shechem, the son of Hamor, ruler of the Hivites, and how she was avenged in a bloodbath by her brothers, Simeon and Levi. That the extermination of the seducer and his family functions basically as a castration for the forbidden sexual act is suggested by the pretended reconciliation that precedes the bloodbath. Jacob's sons claim they can accept Shechem's proposal of marriage to their sister Dinah only if he and all his family are circumcised. Shechem agrees, but "on the third day, when they got to be aching" (Gen. 34:25) and are unfit for battle, they are killed by the sons of Jacob. That this terrible revenge by the brothers, who thus reject the rehabilitating offer of marriage, arises from their desire for their own sister is illustrated by the story of Tamar (2 Samuel 13). Amnon, the son of David, falls in love with Tamar, the sister of his half-brother Absalom. He pretends to be ill to gain an opportunity to seduce her. He succeeds in raping her, though she resists, and then he drives her away in shame, insulting her. But "Absalom hated Amnon over the fact that he had humiliated his sister" (2 Sam. 13:22). Therefore, two years later, he has his half-brother murdered by his servants. That he is driven to this act by feelings of jealousy and incestuous desire for his own sister is illustrated by his subsequent acts and fate. He rises up against his royal father, David, who flees from him; Absalom documents his usurpation of his father's power by having "relations with the concubines of his father under the eyes of all Israel" (2 Sam. 16:22). Later he is stabbed to death while hanging from an oak. His father, having regained power, bitterly laments his son (2 Sam. 18:33), who has pursued him with deadly hatred.

Direct murder of the father is exhibited in 2 Kings 19:36 ff., where Sennacherib is killed by his sons, who then flee to the land of Ararat. I have previously discussed other incest accounts from the Old Testament, such as the incest of the other Tamar with her father-in-law, Judah (Genesis 38) (Rank 1912a). In the same article I interpret man's fall into sin as a distorted, rationalized myth of the world parents, transformed from the monotheistic standpoint of the father and ending with the castration of the incestuous son. Stucken, too, proceeding from purely mythological evidence, concludes that the removal of Adam's rib by Jehovah (Gen. 2:21) is a symbolic act of castration. He connects this idea with a similar detail in Greek mythology: from Adam's rib arises the first woman, just as the goddess of love, Aphrodite, arises from the severed phallus of Uranus. Finally, one more illustration from a familiar biblical text will demonstrate the seemingly innocent distortions behind which, according to the commentators themselves, the offensive theme of castration may lie hidden.

The passage concerns Noah, who after the flood became a farmer and planted vineyards: "And he began drinking of the wine and became intoxicated, and so he uncovered himself in the midst of his tent. Later Ham the father of Canaan saw his father's nakedness and went telling it to his two brothers outside. At that Shem and Japheth took a mantle and put it upon both their shoulders and walked in backwards. Thus they covered their father's nakedness, while their faces were turned away, and they did not see their father's nakedness. Finally Noah awoke from his wine and got to know what his youngest son had done to him. At this he said: 'Cursed be Canaan. Let him become the lowest slave to his brothers'" (Gen. 9:21–25). The father's extreme reaction to the son's clearly minor infraction, and the affect behind this whole account, would be incomprehensible were it not for the Haggadic tradition concerning this detail of the Noah myth. According to this version the bad son—Ham, the black one—castrates his father (Sanhedrin, 70).

The Theme of Dismemberment

Our discussion of castration, sometimes carried out upon the father by the jealous son and sometimes upon the son or brother as a punishment for incest, has continually brought us to mythological parallels, and now it leads us to the investigation of another form of the theme. The Egyptian myth of Isis and Osiris, which the Greek myths of Cronus, of his progenitor, and of his successor resemble in many aspects, contains castration by the brother as a punishment for sibling incest in connection with another theme to which we must also devote our attention.

According to the myth, the siblings Isis and Osiris already burned with love for one another in the womb. They paired, and the still unborn Isis bore Arneris. Thus Isis and Osiris came into the world as sibling spouses. They are paralleled by an apparently not original pair of sibling spouses, Set and Nephthys. The latter pair, apparently, were later introduced as a doublet—according to Schneider (1907), as a means to motivate the fighting between Osiris and his brother, Set. Whereas according to the original tradition Set kills his brother Osiris because of Set's desire to be ruler, the later tradition claims that Osiris was murdered because of his incest with his unrecognized second sister, Nephthys, Set's wife; from this union arose the dog-headed Anubis. Set, or Typhon, as he is called in Grecized versions, avenges the adultery of his brother by placing Osiris in a coffin he throws into the Nile, where it is carried out to sea. With the help of Anubis, Isis finds the coffin, brings it back to Egypt, and "opens it while alone, letting her affection and mourning pour forth" (Creuzer 1841, 19). She then buries the coffin with the body in the forest. Typhon finds the body and dismembers it into fourteen pieces (Plutarch, *Isis and Osiris,* chap. 18). Isis now gathers together the scattered pieces in order to reanimate them, but she finds only thirteen. The fourteenth piece, the phallus, has been carried into the sea and swallowed by a fish. In the reassembled body, therefore, she replaces the missing male member with an artificial one made from the wood of the sycamore. "Isis is supposed to have honored them ⟨the genitals⟩ with the same divine honors accorded the other [members]. She had an image of the genitals set up in the temple and caused it to be honored. This member is said to be considered the most important one in dedications and sacrifices to the god Osiris, and it is given the greatest respect. Therefore under the name 'phallus' it is also said to be worshiped by the Greeks, who got their orgies and Bacchic festivals from Egypt, in their secret mysteries and in the sacrifices dedicated to this god" (Diodorus Siculus, *Bibliotheca historica,* chap. 13). With the help of her son, Horus, who according to later traditions was sired by his father after his father's death, Isis avenges the murder of her husband and brother. Between Horus and Set, who originally were brothers themselves, a bitter struggle occurs in which the opponents tear off certain body parts from one another, employing them as powerful amulets. Set knocks out one of Horus's eyes and swallows it. However, he loses his own testicles; according to Schneider, they certainly were originally swallowed by Horus. Finally Set is defeated and is forced to give up Horus's eye. With its help, Horus reanimates Osiris so that he can enter the realm of the dead as its ruler.

In this rich, highly complex, and widely analyzed myth, we can make only brief mention of the layers of repression. As shown by the closely related Greek myth and the related accounts of primitive peoples, the castration of the brother is only an echo carried over from the son's original castration of the father; the most recent layer of repression has dampened this castration to vengeance for the father, carried out upon his brother and murderer (cf. *Hamlet*), and to his reanimation by the son. Thus atonement is made for the original crime. In the Egyptian tale of Satu and Anepu (Set and Anubis), which arose, according to Schneider's sagacious opinion, from the Osiris legend, the whole myth is subsequently diluted to the point of sentimentality; Satu's wife slanders her brother-in-law Anepu by telling her husband that he has approached her indecently (a dampening of incest). To demonstrate his innocence, the brother, falsely accused by the woman, castrates himself (dampening of castration by the brother) and flees. Then, based upon a reactive development similar to the one we are familiar with from the reanimation of Osiris by his son Horus, he is mourned by his brother, who has recognized his innocence. The brother then searches for a sign, previously agreed upon, in order to reanimate his brother, whom—according to the original version of the myth—he has cruelly dismembered. In the Osiris myth, besides the castration of the opponent, there is also a symbolic substitute for castration—the plucking out (and swallowing) of the eye, as observed with Oedipus and with the "Indian Argus."[1] In making this observation, we wish only to address the theme of mutilation, which we must also interpret as a dampening of castration, corresponding strikingly to the tendency for generalization observed in obsessional neurosis. Isis's characteristic construction of the wooden phallus indicates that her mourning relates mainly to the loss of the true phallus. This is also suggested in that in a later version she is still mysteriously impregnated by her castrated spouse. On the other hand, the behavior of the cruel brother demonstrates that in the mutilation he too is concerned mainly with the phallus, since it is the only part that cannot be found, apparently having been disposed of with special care. Indeed, both motivations are unified in a version quoted by Jeremias (1905, 721), according to which Anubis, the son of the adulterous union of Osiris with his sister Nephthys, finds the phallus of Osiris, who had been dismembered by Typhon and his seventy-two helpers; the phallus had been buried by Isis in a box (chest). Thus only the phallus, from which the new age arose, can escape from Typhon. This version clearly demonstrates that Isis originally kept in a box the actual phallus, made immortal, of her spouse and brother, not merely a wooden one. But given the various attempts at dampening and at justification we observe in connection with the theme of dismemberment, it becomes more probable that the original version entailed only castration. According to Plutarch's account, Osiris is divided into fourteen pieces and scattered throughout the land, except for the phallus, which is cast into the sea, as is the chest bearing Osiris's body in the other version. The identity also seems to suggest that the exposure of the "dead" Osiris in the chest is only a symbolic expression of castration and of pious mourning over the honored phallus. For in the respected Attic mysteries at Athens and Eleusis, the phallus, encased in a mystical chest or box, was carried about as a secret treasure, while in the free and uninhibited orgies of Bacchus it is found as an *ithyphallus* (the image of the male

1. A punishment for adultery apparently opposite to castration is found in an Indian legend relating how Indra seduces Ahalya, the beautiful wife of Rishi Gautama. In anger, the betrayed husband condemns the seducer to wear upon his person a thousandfold the member with which he has sinned. Yielding to Indra's desperate pleas, however, he converts this unseemly adornment into the thousand eyes with which Indra's body is now sown.

member set up by the celebrants) or as a model member worn by celebrants clothed as satyrs (Seligmann 1910, 2:196). In Plutarch, Osiris's division into fourteen parts serves to disguise the castration theme; astral mythologists attribute the fourteen parts to the count of days in the lunar cycle. In Diodorus, his brother has twenty-six fellow conspirators. To each of them, in order to reduce his own guilt, he gives one portion of Osiris's body. (None of them wishes to take the phallus, as revealing the chief guilt.) And according to a version cited by Duncker (1855–57, 1:47), there are seventy-two conspirators. In these various versions, corresponding to constantly advancing repression, we observe a tendency to disguise the anger originally associated with the one hated member by distributing it among more and more body parts. The brother, jealous of the sister's love, is concerned more with castrating than with killing his rival. This is revealed not only in that he still feels the need to castrate the body even after the murder, but also in that the recomposition and reanimation of Osiris do indeed occur; Osiris then lacks only his male member, guarded by his jealous competitor. We are dealing with the typical expression of an impulse derived from the infantile affective standpoint, and by no means with a mythic figure. This is demonstrated by the following case, clearly unrelated to Egyptian mythology, cited by Aschaffenburg in *Münchner Medizinishe Wochenschrift* [Munich medical weekly]. This is the case of an "epileptic murderer." In Rügen, on July 1, 1901, a twenty-nine-year-old cabinetmaker's apprentice murdered two small boys; he mutilated them and scattered the pieces, subsequently wandering about for several hours carrying one boy's penis in his pocket.

Here we can discuss only a few examples of the theme of dismemberment, widely attested in myths, folktales, and legends. The meaning of this theme, surely, cannot be resolved in only a single way, but these examples will illustrate the connection of this theme with the theme of castration. As a meaningful hint relating to the incest complex, we must observe that these dismemberment myths concern mainly the relationship between parents and children, though the original configuration sometimes appears shifted owing to secondary influences. The legend of the twin brothers Pelias and Neleus, the story of whose birth is related in the *Odyssey* (11.235 ff.), reminds us of the retention of procreative powers expressed in the Osiris myth. Originally this legend must have been analogous to the biblical tale of Lot and his daughters. Pelias, who has driven his brother away, is dismembered and boiled by his own daughters, who are hoping to make him young again (Apollodorus 1.9.27). Note that the theme of reanimation, intimately connected with the theme of dismemberment, is not intended simply to compensate secondarily for the original murder as in the mythological traditions discussed above. Instead, behind this reanimation,

animation itself—birth—seems to lie. Here we cannot discuss the widely dispersed legends of the water of life (corresponding to the birth waters [cf. Rank 1909]), which effects reanimation (animation). I have also demonstrated (1912a) that this reanimation relates originally to a dismembered snake (and later to other animals, especially birds). In the snake we easily recognize the symbolic substitute for the severed, that is, impotent, phallus in the Osiris legend, reanimated by the "water of life." The idea that in conception or birth man is himself drawn together from various pieces is expressed not only in sexual theories of children, but also in numerous anecdotes (cf. Balzac's *Contes drôlatiques*) and mythological traditions. Of special interest is the archaic German expression cited by Mannhardt (1858, 305), which says of the pregnant woman, "she has a belly full of bones." This clearly reminds us of the detail, emphasized in all traditions, that the bones of the dismembered one are thrown upon a heap or into a kettle (belly) or are tied up in a cloth. Here belongs also the Eddic tale relating how Thor throws upon a heap the bones of the two rams he has dismembered and then animates them through swings of his hammer, recognized as a phallic symbol. Here too a leg is missing, so the rams limp. A typical childhood sexual theory is also suggested in that the dismembered parts are swallowed, like the phallus in the Osiris legend: the child imagines that conception is caused by ingesting food. This usually occurs when fruits symbolizing fertility are eaten. In the Osiris legend, this occurs when Isis swallows the procreative organ itself. To this conceptual framework belongs also a Greek joke relating how a beggarwoman suffering from abdominal pains consults a doctor. He asks her if she has something in her belly (if she is pregnant), and she answers: "How could I? I haven't eaten for three days" (Schultz 1909, 10).

In the folktale of the juniper tree (Grimm and Grimm 1816, no. 47) we find a version of the dismemberment myth completely archaic in some respects, while already strongly distorted in other aspects. A woman who had long been barren finally gives birth to a boy after peeling an apple under a juniper tree and cutting her finger. The boy is as red as blood and as white as snow. He is the joy of his father, but his mother dies in childbirth. The man then sires a daughter by his second wife. Because of her own daughter, the stepmother is jealous of the handsome and beloved boy and decides to do him in. She offers him an apple lying in a chest, and when the boy bends down to get it, she slams the lid shut so that his severed head falls in. Immediately after this deed, though, she is seized by fear. She puts the head back on the body (reanimation), ties it on with a cloth, and places the reanimated boy before the door of the house with an apple in his hand. Then she tells his sister to ask him for the apple, and since he remains silent, she tells her to strike him once on the head. The little sister does just this, and the head goes flying off the shoulders. The girl believes she is guilty of her brother's death and runs crying to her mother. The mother comforts her and proposes that the boy be dismembered and served to his father. This occurs, and when the father, who finds the meal exceedingly tasty, inquires about his son, he is told that the boy has gone to stay with relatives for a long period. The father casts all the bones left over from the ghastly meal under the table, but the little sister, feeling guilty, collects them, ties them up in her most beautiful cloth, and lays them under the juniper tree. From the tree, a bird flies into the air singing:

> My mother butchered me.
> My father ate me.
> My sister Marlenichen
> looked for all my little bones.
> She tied them up in a silken cloth.
> She laid them under the juniper tree.
> Kywitt, kywitt, what a beautiful bird am I!

Through his beautiful song, he assumes power over a golden chain, a pair of shoes, and a millstone, which he lets fall on his father, his sister, and his stepmother; the stepmother is crushed by the millstone, and the bird is transformed into the living boy again. Here we see the apple as a symbol of fertility (and killing), complemented by the "rejuvenating" juniper. We observe also the doubling of the killing and reanimation by mother as well as sister. This corresponds to the splitting of the mother into the noble giver of life and the evil stepmotherly murderer. However, the only characteristic detail we shall emphasize is the father's devouring the son, which seems to suggest an original dismemberment of the boy by the father. In this folktale the originally inimical impulse has been transformed into exaggerated love for the son, whom the jealous stepmother proceeds to dismember.

Grimm and Grimm (1816, 3:85) note the following parallels: "The collecting of bones occurs in the myths of Osiris and Orpheus, and in the legend of Adalbert. Reanimation occurs in many others, for example, in the tale of the 'Merry Brother' (no. 81), in the tale of 'Fitcher's Bird' (no. 46), in the Old Danish lay 'The Spring of Maribø,' and in the German tale of the 'Drowned Child' (1:62). . . . It occurs in the Negro legend of Nanni, whom his mother teaches to put the feathers and bones back together after eating a young cock . . . Thor collects the bones of the rams he has devoured and animates them by shaking them (*Daemisaga*, chap. 83, 1)."

Perusing the rich literary traditions, let us now examine a special form of the theme, already observed in the reanimation in the folktale of the juniper tree. This is decapitation, familiar from the tales of Salome, Judith, and Goliath, associated with the successful reattachment of the head. Consider one version of the folktale of "Faithful Johann" (Grimm and Grimm, 1816, 3:20). Johann is the adopted brother of the king. To save him, the king decapitates his own sons (reanimation by blood). Johann, reanimated by their blood, in turn reanimates them by setting their heads back on their bodies. In the widely dispersed tale of the faithful "Jacob's Brothers," the children are decapitated not by their own father, but by his [pledged] blood brother. Each brother cures the other of leprosy by letting his own children be sacrificed. The children are then miraculously reanimated (Grimm and Grimm 1816, 3:23). However, the versions in which the severed head is initially reaffixed incorrectly or backward (cf. Stucken 1896–1907, 1:136 ff.) remind us of the dismemberments in which a member is lost, leading to defective function.

The dismemberment and reanimation of animals found in many versions constitute a substitute for acts originally carried out on human victims. This is illustrated by a note (Grimm and Grimm 1816, 3:379) indicating that in a legend of the Botswana of South Africa, the rich man tests the friendship of the poor man by requesting that the poor man let his own son be killed; the rich man claims he can be healed only by the son's blood. The poor man agrees, but in the son's place the rich man actually slaughters a ram. Seeing the ram's blood on the ground, the poor man believes his son has really been slain. (Cf. the similar deception of the old Jacob, who believes the animal blood is that of his favorite son, Joseph, cast into a pit by his brothers.) A remnant of the cruel meal of human flesh and subsequent reanimation is still retained when the rich man and his accomplice "eat the flesh of the ram during the night, but throw the bones into a pit (as if to reanimate them), so that there remains not a trace." Grimm and Grimm remark (1816, 3:380): "In this attenuated version, the child is not really killed, as in other versions, and no miracle is required for his reanimation." That originally this legend too not only included the actual killing of the child, but probably portrayed it as carried out by the father, is suggested in that the mother of the child handed over to be slaughtered, the poor man's wife, appears in the first part of the tale as the rich man's wife. The rich man gives her to the poor man, probably owing to a later dampening tendency when the sacrifice of the son by his own father had come to seem too offensive.

These legends in which a sick man wishes to be healed by the blood of the child of his friend or brother actually derive from the father's cruel impulse against his children. This is shown by the versions of "Poor Heinrich" cited by Grimm and Grimm, in which the father murders his sons to prolong his own life. Thus the Norse king Aun (*Ynglingasaga,* chap. 29) sacrifices his nine sons to Odin one after the other. Through each sacrifice, he gains ten years of life, although in the end he cannot rise from bed but suckles like a child. The old Halfdan also extends his life through sacrifices, and in the Indic myth the raja Injad rejuvenates himself by sacrificing his son Kurn (or Purn), who gives his own life for his father. The ambiguity (ambivalence) of all psychic constructs explains why the many other versions mentioned above present the fatal dismemberment as a creative reanimation. This is the case in the myth of Absyrtus (Apollodorus, 1.9.23), who is cut into twelve pieces by the moon-goddess and put together again (procreated) by his father. The German folktale of the drowned child (Grimm and Grimm 1816, 1:79) provides a similar complement to the dismemberment of the son by the mother—observed in the tale of the juniper tree—and a direct parallel to his reanimation (birth) by the sister. The river washes the separate bones of the child onto the bank. The mother collects them in a cloth in order to bury them. When she comes into the church, however, her child in the cloth is alive; he is missing only one bone in his little finger. This is later found and preserved as a relic. With the throwing of the dismembered parts into the river and with the absence of the one member, later revered as a relic, this late version shows the clearest similarity to the castration in the Osiris myth. We are already familiar with the finger as a symbolic substitute for the phallus (cf. Attis, Peer Gynt, etc.). The same holds for the severed and reconnected head, which from our analyses we recognize as a symbol of penile erection.

This conception of the derivation of the legend of dismemberment from the castration complex will of course be doubted and argued against by mythologists, caught up in their own theories. Therefore, while dealing with this theme we would like to demonstrate that our conception is not at all as far from current mythological opinion as one might think. Yet we must emphasize that we regard the crux of the matter from a different point of view. Based on our analytical interpretations, we frequently arrive at the same results as the astral and lunar mythologists (Stucken, Siecke, Winckler, Hüsing, Lessmann, etc.). However, these researchers characteristically attempt to justify the data, as discussed in the beginning of this chapter. Accordingly, though they analyze incest and castration as central themes of mythology to the same extent as we do, or perhaps even more so, they are willing to recognize these themes only as representing celestial events. On the basis of our psychoanalyses, though, we are compelled to see in these elements universal human themes that were later projected into the heavens by primitive peoples, all subject to the same psychological need for justification to which our contemporary mythologists are also subject in their interpretations of these themes. Thus, in the theme of dismemberment (castration) they see an image of the gradual waning of the moon and in the theme of reanimation they see the waxing moon. For us, though, there is no doubt that it was the objectionable castration that later came to be symbolized through these lunar phenomena. It is psychologically unjustified and illogical, and it contradicts our conception of the sexualization of the universe, to claim that man should symbolize a phenomenon as simple as the phases of the moon through something so objectionable as dismemberment or castration of one's closest relatives. The nature mythologists, especially Siecke, have also been of the opinion that primitive man "directly regarded" the inexplicable waning of the moon as a dismemberment. But this would be psychologically inconceivable were it not that this image, taken from earthly life, also has its source in human life and thought (fantasy). On the evidence of the material, however, the same mythologist admits that the moon "was also regarded as the phallus or the testicles of the sky god." Accordingly, he also includes the legends of Osiris's castration and of his wooden phallus in this genre of myths (Siecke 1909, 214). He mentions further (92) that in the *Rig Veda* the moon is depicted as a seed bearer—as a procreative deity, and that it was supposed that he had intercourse with girls while they slept. The supposed influence of the moon on menstruation and pregnancy is of course well known (Siecke 1909, 77). In an earlier work, *Hermes der Mondgott* (1908), Siecke remarks that "in the narrowest phase of the moon" one "saw not only cow's horns, goat's horns, a curved knife, a staff, a snake, a tooth, an arm, a foot ⟨all penis symbols⟩, a pointed shoe, a boat, and God knows what else, but also the erect member of the gods' messenger, who was thought to be hurrying across the sky. And since one saw in the moon the testicles of the sky god, during the new moon he was held to have been castrated" (1908, 81–82). Thus our conclusions are identical to those of mythologists, with the single exception that we do not claim simple projection into the skies but are compelled through psychological analysis of our unconscious to go back to the human sources of these conceptions. We are simply compelled, heavy though the consequences may be, to regard the horrors of mythology as a superseded state in the psychic development of mankind and of the individual. We cannot simply gaze ashamedly into the skies, contenting ourselves with the primitive rationalization of projection.

The Tantalide Legend and Its Dramatic Versions

> **Since the earth had stained itself with sin's corruption,**
> **Since honor and right had fled from hearts gone wild,**
> **Since brothers had bathed their hands in brothers' blood,**
> **Since children had forgotten how to mourn their parents' passing—**

> **To enjoy more securely the stepmother's bloom,**
> **The father wished an early death for his youthful son.**
> **Wickedly entering the son's embrace, the mother**
> **Had brazenly disgraced, unhorrified, the moral guardians of procreation.**
>
> CATULLUS, "Marriage of Peleus and Thetis"

We must also regard from this human point of view the Tantalide legend, which belongs in part to the Greek legends of the gods and, like these, shows Egyptian influences. Only in this way can we understand the fantasies and psychic impulses underlying it, which for centuries provided material for Greek poetry and representational art. The first episode, still dealing with the gods, relates how Tantalus, the ancestor of the Tantalides and a son of Zeus, dismembers and cooks his own son Pelops as a feast for the gods, whom he has invited for a meal. The myth motivates this weakly, claiming he did so to test their omniscience. The gods notice the crime; only Demeter, absorbed in sad thoughts of her lost daughter Persephone, eats a shoulder blade from the grisly dish. As a punishment, Tantalus is sent to the underworld, where he is doomed to suffer awful punishment forever. However, the gods throw the dismembered parts of the boy into a kettle, and the Fate Clotho pulls him out in renewed beauty. But, the shoulder blade Demeter ate is still missing, so the gods replace it with one made of ivory.

Since this dismemberment and reanimation (in which an eaten member, thus lacking, is replaced by an artificial one) strikingly resembles the emasculation of Osiris, the weak motivation that the crime was committed to test the gods seems even less credible. Indeed, in another version, at least a more credible reason is provided for Tantalus's terrible punishment. He is sent to the underworld because of his criminal desire for the mother of the gods, Hera. Tantalus's punishments would also better correspond to this crime. On the one hand, in the form of insatiable hunger and thirst, they suggest the eternal insatiability of desire (libido). On the other hand, in the fear of death brought about by the boulder always looming over his head, they symbolize the repressive effects of this libido, denied gratification. This version, told from the standpoint of Zeus, ruler of the universe, allows us to include the Tantalide legend in the body of incest literature, for after all, according to the story, the son (Tantalus) is punished by the father because he desired the father's spouse (the mother).

Although we shall base our analysis on this reconstruction of the original version, we immediately recognize in the poorly motivated killing of Pelops by his father Tantalus a doublet of the punishment of Tantalus himself—based on the incest complex—by his father Zeus. Therefore we can suppose the punishment of dismemberment—castration—for Tantalus as well. Thus, in the original version Zeus would not have reanimated his son (Pelops-Tantalus) but would have dismembered him. (This can be contrasted with the reanimation of Osiris, already familiar to us, by his son Horus.) This position is supported by the striking detail that the boy, made whole again in the kettle, was initially also cooked (dismembered) in the kettle. However, full confirmation of our hypothesis is found by descending to the next generation, already human. From the identity of names and themes we easily recognize the destiny of this generation as a doublet of the grisly account of the gods.

The sons of Pelops are Atreus and Thyestes. The elder brother has a ram with golden wool, which guarantees him rulership. Thyestes covets this ram. He seduces his brother's wife, Aerope, and receives from her the prized treasure. In revenge for this double crime, Atreus slaughters Thyestes' two small sons, Tantalus and Plisthenes, serves them cooked to his brother, and gives him their blood to drink mixed with wine. Having discovered the crime during the meal, Thyestes flees from his brother to Sicyon. Here it really is Tantalus who is dismembered and served to his father without reanimation, just as we hypothesized for the earlier generation. As in the Osiris myth and the tales of Bitiu and Anepu, the seduction of the brother's wife (dampened incest) is provided as motivation for this revenge. That a second brother is also dismembered with Tantalus corresponds to the reduplication and splitting of the mythological figure, characteristic of a doublet. This is seen also in the brothers Atreus and Thyestes, who apparently were originally one; here too the son is dismembered directly by the father, as in the Tantalus myth, clearly reflected here. That the inimical relationship between father and son actually underlies the legend, however, is demonstrated by an investigation of the further events played out in the third generation.

In Sicyon, Thyestes, having fled from his cruel brother, asks the oracle what revenge he should carry out on his brother. He is told that he will sleep with his own daughter, Pelopia, who will bear an avenger. Like Oedipus, Thyestes attempts to escape the fate revealed in the oracle's pronouncement; but as with Oedipus, this only brings it about more surely still. In *Pelopidae,* based on the tragic traditions, Hyginus relates how this occurs. At night, without recognizing her, Thyestes overhears his daughter Pelopia while she is making a sacrifice to Minerva. In her dance, she has fallen on the altar and has stained her garment with the blood of animals. While she is washing it in the river, Thyestes, seized by desire, springs from the bushes with hooded head and dishonors his unrecognized daughter. During the struggle, Pelopia draws his sword from its sheath and afterward hides it in the temple. From this union is born Aegisthus, who later slays Atreus, his uncle.

While Thyestes is in exile, the land of Atreus is beset by drought and famine (cf. the Oedipus legend), and on consulting the oracle the king is told that these sufferings will end as soon as the expelled brother, Thyestes, is called back. Atreus himself seeks out the brother in his place of hiding, at the court of King Thesprotus of Epirus, and convinces him to return to his homeland by feigning a friendly attitude. Hyginus also relates that Atreus takes from King Thesprotus his brother's daughter, Pelopia, already impregnated by her father, to be his own wife; it had been claimed that she was the daughter of Thesprotus. When he is born, she exposes her child by Thyestes. Shepherds find the child and raise him with goat's milk. This is also the origin of his name, Aegisthus. Later, Atreus discovers the boy and has him raised as his own son. When Aegisthus is grown, Atreus sends out his two grown sons, Agamemnon and Menelaus, to fight their uncle Thyestes, with whom he has argued in the meantime (Hyginus, fable 88). They go to Delphi to ask the god how they can find Thyestes. But Thyestes asks the same oracle how he can avenge himself. He is seized, brought back to Atreus, and thrown into prison. Atreus now calls his foster son, Aegisthus, and tells him to kill Thyestes in the prison. Aegisthus feigns agreement. He bears the sword Pelopia had once seized from her father Thyestes and had later given to Aegisthus. From this sword, Thyestes recognizes Aegisthus as his own son. Thus, unwitting patricide is prevented. Out of shame over her incest with her father, now revealed, Pelopia stabs herself with the sword. But Aegisthus shows the bloody sword to Atreus as proof that he has killed his father, Thyestes. Atreus expresses joy over the supposed murder of his brother, and while he is carrying out a sacrifice of thanksgiving on the seashore, Aegisthus stabs him with the sword. Then Thyestes briefly becomes ruler.

Here we cannot discuss in detail how these incestuous acts of violence, carried out from generation to generation, serve as reduplications of a single family history, later felt to be too objectionable, that we could interpret based on the Tantalus legend. However, this conception is supported in that Homer was still unfamiliar with the enmity between the brothers Atreus and Thyestes. In general, as expressed in a highly relevant comment by Mannhardt (1858), "The curse (in sexual legends), insofar as it extends over several generations, is also a product of more recent periods" (Pelopides, Labdacides). In this connection, this point becomes more interesting for us since several of the episodes are known to us only from works of the Attic tragedians. For a long period, the Tantalide legend was one of their most popular themes. The following information will introduce us to this Tantalide material, reformulated countless times in poetry and drama.

After the murder of their father, Atreus's sons, Agamemnon and Menelaus, flee to King Tyndareus of Sparta, the husband of Leda. There Agamemnon marries Clytemnestra and Menelaus marries Helen, the daughters of King Tyndareus. Before marrying Clytemnestra, following a vision, Agamemnon is supposed to have killed both Tantalus, Clytemnestra's first spouse, son of Thyestes (thus Agamemnon's cousin), and her child from her first marriage. As he lies dying, Tyndareus declares Menelaus heir to the throne, while Agamemnon returns to Mycenae. There he kills his uncle Thyestes and becomes ruler. [Later,] the spared Aegisthus reigns in his father's stead. When Agamemnon has been named leader of the Greek forces attacking Troy and the fleet is ready to set sail from the port of Aulis, the ships cannot proceed for lack of wind. The seer Calchas is consulted and reveals that the goddess Artemis has caused the wind to die down because Agamemnon, while killing his uncle, injured a doe consecrated to her. She can be appeased only if Agamemnon sacrifices to her his daughter Iphigenia. Convinced by his brother Menelaus and pressured by the whole Greek army, Agamemnon finally makes the painful decision to go through with the sacrifice. Telling her that he wishes to engage her to Achilles, he lures her into his camp, accompanied by her mother. After new encounters and arguments between Agamemnon and Clytemnestra, who had discerned the trick, Iphigenia finally volunteers to be sacrificed. But just when the sacred sacrifice is about to occur, she is saved, transported by the goddess to her shrine in Tauris. In her place, Artemis leaves a doe to be sacrificed.

Clytemnestra returns home in a bad humor, and the fleet sets sail. Eleven years after his departure, Agamemnon returns to his homeland. In the meantime, to avenge the death of his father, Aegisthus seduces Clytemnestra, the wife of his foster brother and cousin, Agamemnon. She still bears a grudge against her husband because of the sacrifice of her child; because she wants revenge on her cruel husband, after long hesitation she finally yields to the seducer's entreaties. She shares with him palace and kingdom, just as if he were her second husband. Three children from her first marriage to Agamemnon still live in the house—Electra, Chrysothemis, and the little Orestes. When Agamemnon finally arrives, he is greeted with apparent friendliness and respect, but he is stabbed to death in his bath by Clytemnestra and her lover, who fear that their relationship will be discovered. Cassandra, Priam's daughter, whom Agamemnon had brought back as a prisoner, is also killed, since she arouses Clytemnestra's jealousy. However, Clytemnestra has the populace told that she has taken revenge on her husband only because of his sacrifice of their daughter and because of his adulterous relationship with Cassandra. Then she publicly gives Aegisthus her hand. Electra finds the death of her beloved father extremely painful and immediately has thoughts of revenge. She fears for the life of Orestes, her younger brother, whom she loves even more deeply now that her father is dead, and she sends him to Agamemnon's brother-in-law to be raised so that he can someday return as an avenger. With her mother, though, Electra lives in hateful enmity. Clytemnestra mistreats her daughter in every way and makes her witness her most intimate moments with her lover, Aegisthus. Electra's hatred is increased all the more because Clytemnestra arranges dances of celebration every year on the day of Agamemnon's death.

When Orestes still has not returned after years of fruitless waiting and Electra, owing to false reports of his death, has lost all hope of revenge, she decides to carry out her revenge alone—to kill her mother and Aegisthus. While she is busy with the preparations, Orestes arrives with his friend Pylades. Since Aegisthus is away from the house, the strangers, who claim to be the official bearers of the news of Orestes' death, are received by Clytemnestra. Orestes, encouraged by Electra, now kills his mother; when Aegisthus returns home, he kills him too. But after the deed, Orestes' childhood love for his mother reawakens. Because of his crime, carried out against his mother out of piety, in the Greek worldview, for his father—in a horrible conflict of duty—he falls victim to the Erinyes [the Furies], the avengers of such crimes. As a madman, he is driven incessantly about, accompanied only by Pylades, until he is finally released from the blot of this unjust murder by Pallas Athena and is thus absolved. The Delphic oracle reveals to him that his sufferings will end in Mycenae if he proceeds to the peninsula of Tauris and brings back to Athens the image of Pallas Athena from her shrine. However, Iphigenia, Orestes' sister, had also been transported by the goddess to her shrine in Tauris. In Tauris, the siblings recognize one another; they return with the image to their homeland, where Orestes reigns happily as king of Mycenae for many years. Thus the curse of the house of the Tantalides ends with Orestes.

Of the complex, sometimes more and sometimes less serious incestuous crimes and punishments of this cycle of legends, the final episodes deserve our special attention—not only for their psychological relevance, but also because the murder of Clytemnestra and the subsequent sufferings of Orestes provided the basic material for the extremely numerous transformations seen in Greek literature and art for centuries. At first glance we recognize in this episode a Hamlet tragedy transposed to a feminine point of view. It is Electra who actually nurtures the revenge, serving as *spiritus rector* of the crime—the daughter who hates the mother because of the murder of the beloved father. Her brother Orestes, whom she sent abroad as a twelve-year-old boy and made swear to return as an avenger, though he was not yet aware of his family's bitter destiny, is only a will-less implement in her hands. (Supposedly, she sent him abroad because she feared for his life, but apparently her main goal was to alienate him from his mother.) In Sophocles' *Electra,* this is clear. On hearing the false news of Orestes' death, Electra attempts in vain to win over her sister Chrysothemis as an accomplice, saying that the murdered Agamemnon was her father too. Finally Electra decides to carry out the deed alone:

> Thus I must carry out the deed
> Alone. I shall never give up without attempting it.
>
> (*Electra,* 1219)

> For hatred, long nurtured, is stamped deep within me.
>
> (*Electra,* 1311)

In providing the following special justification, though, she does not realize how old and deeply rooted her hatred will appear to us:

> To see the height of her excesses,
> The bloody murderer in my father's bed
> Lying with my cursed mother, if one
> Can still call her a mother who shares the bed with him!

This expression of sexual jealousy, reminiscent nearly word for word of pronouncements of Hamlet, unambiguously reveals the childhood sources of her hatred. A version of the murder cited by Hyginus (fable 129) is fully consistent with this expression. According to this version, Clytemnestra and Aegisthus are murdered at night in their common bed; Hamlet too wishes to kill his uncle only "in th'incestuous pleasures of his bed." In Aeschylus's *Choephoroi* (the second part of his *Oresteia*) and in Euripides' *Electra,* Orestes first kills the hated stepfather—in the infantile sense the competitor for the mother's love. In Sophocles' tragedy, however, Clytemnestra is killed first, since Orestes is carrying out the deed in the name of his beloved sister and in her stead. When Clytemnestra cries: "Alas for me, I am wounded!" Electra cries out to her brother, as if it is she herself who is murdering her mother: "You can, strike a second time!" In Euripides' tragedy it is more out of fear of the deed that lies ahead than as a precaution for his own safety that Orestes passes himself off as a messenger, and here too Electra must incite her brother to do the deed:

> *Orestes:* To kill our father's murderers, tell me, how could it be done?
> *Electra:* By rashly daring to do what rashly they did to him.
> *Orestes:* And have you the courage? Would you slay with him our mother too?

Electra: With the same ax, the very one that killed our father.
Orestes: Is that your firm resolve? Shall I interpret it so?
Electra: I would gladly die, having spilled my mother's blood!

And of the deed itself, Electra says:

And I stood by you,
I grasped the sword along with you!

Here it is clear that Electra simply uses her brother's masculine strength to carry out the deed, but that she must actually guide the sword stroke in the decisive blow against the mother. And in Euripides' *Orestes*, Tyndareus, father of the murdered Clytemnestra, says unambiguously to the matricides:

Now I could easily incite the citizens against you
And your sister, so that they would stone you to death.
For she herself, more than you, is deserving of death.
She hardened your heart against your mother. She always had
Evil reports whispered into your ears, relating
How Agamemnon's ghost had appeared to her in a dream,
And then of the courtship with Aegisthus.

In this dream appearance of the murdered father's ghost, we find the complete feminine counterpart to the ghostly apparition of Hamlet's father. Hugo von Hofmannsthal, the modern adapter of Sophocles' classical Electra drama, seems, in conscious reference to Shakespeare, to emphasize further still the identical psychic orientations of Hamlet and Electra. With Hofmannsthal, Electra's fervent hatred for her mother, bordering on insanity, is the focal point of the drama. Like Hamlet, Electra seeks to gain advantage by feigning insanity; like the Danish prince, she is visited by the ghost of her beloved and respected father:

Agamemnon! Father!
I wish to see you, leave me not alone today!
As you did yesterday, like a shadow there
In the corner of the wall, reveal yourself to your child!
. . . .
It is the hour, it is our hour,
The hour when they slaughtered you—
Your wife and he who sleeps with her in one bed,
In your royal bed.
. . . .
So you have come again, you place foot before foot,
Suddenly standing there, both eyes wide open.

Just as Hamlet, because of his infantile fixation on his mother, exhibits clear sexual rejection of Ophelia, Electra too seems devoid of all feminine impulses. This is true already in the classical legend, and even more so with Hofmannsthal. (Her name derives from *a-léktron,* "without a marriage bed; unwed.") She appears only as a sexless spirit of revenge whose deadly hatred of her mother, however, can be understood only as an expression of sexual jealousy against her same-sex rival. Already in Euripides' drama, Clytemnestra says to Electra: "It is in your nature, child, always to be dedicated to your father. This is normal; some children favor the husbands, while others favor their mothers." Thus Hofmannsthal's Electra directly expresses the way her libido is fixated on her father: "I had to sacrifice this sweet shuddering to my father. The dead are jealous. And he sent me hatred, hollow-eyed hatred, to be my bridegroom." Thus, Electra's deed can be understood from the infantile point of view, realized in the myth in full detail: the daughter's jealous hatred of her mother on account of her beloved father. But the complex motivation of Orestes' deed requires a special explanation. Of course it should not surprise us that he kills his stepfather, Aegisthus, with a certain conviction and experiences extreme gratification. From the child's jealous point of view, Aegisthus is his father's replacement with respect to his mother—a competitor the mother prefers to Orestes himself. Therefore in Euripides' tragedy Orestes kills his stepfather first. In Aeschylus's tragedy he does so hesitantly and indecisively, but in Euripides' drama he does so rejoicing: "First honor the gods, O sister, as the authors of this joy." Still, when it comes to killing his mother, who is actually the guilty one with respect to his father and sister, he loses his courage and the conviction of his duty to take revenge; he begins to doubt and to vacillate.

> *Orestes* (gazing upon her): What shall we do now? Shall the matricide
> occur?
> *Electra:* What? Are you so moved at the sight of your mother?
> *Orestes:* Alas! How can I murder the one who suckled me and bore me?
> *Electra:* Oh, be not so cowardly! Rise up and be a man!
> *Orestes:* Thus, I should now set for her the same trap—
> *Electra:* —She trapped and killed her husband in!
> *Orestes:* I'll do it, but fearsome is the task that lies ahead.
> I must commit an atrocity, but if heaven wills it,
> So be it! For me the struggle is sweet and bitter!

And after the murder, Orestes relates with horror:

> Oh, did you see how the wretched one drew forth
> Her breast from her robes, showed it to me as I murdered her;
> How she fell so pitifully (the pain, the pain!)
> Upon her poor knees, and I lost my courage?

. . . .
I held my garment before my eyes; the sword
I raised for the sacrifice, letting
It drive through my mother's neck.

In Aeschylus's tragedy, too, Orestes, following the unscrupulous murder of Aegisthus, shies away from carrying out revenge on his mother; he must be incited and encouraged by his friend Pylades.

Orestes: I seek you too. He has already received the full measure.
Clytemnestra: Alas for me! Aegisthus, my strength, dead!
Orestes: You love the man? So lie with him
In one grave. Never again betray the dead one.
Clytemnestra: Stop, my son, respect this breast
From which, my child, so often with soft lips
You sucked the sweet mother's milk, sinking into slumber.
Orestes: What shall I do, Pylades? Shall I spare her?
Pylades: Where does that leave the god with his pronouncements?
Recall your oath and the temple of Pytho;
Never make the gods your enemies!
Orestes: You have won, and well you have admonished me.
(To Clytemnestra) Follow me! For I wish to kill you beside him
Who was dearer to you, even while he lived, than my father.
Sleep also with him in death! You loved him,
Hating the one you should have loved.

Clytemnestra attempts to justify her adultery when her husband was away, saying: "It is painful for a woman to be far from her husband," but in so doing she wounds Orestes' most sensitive spot more surely still, and with that her fate is sealed. For Orestes clearly states that he is punishing his mother not so much because she has murdered his father but because of her love for Aegisthus. Thus for him, as for Hamlet, it is ultimately jealous impulses of erotic affection for the mother that bring him to the murder of his formerly loved mother (cf. the references to the mother's breast). However, the son's hatred toward his mother, arising from jealousy (and thus from love), is no less intense than the relentless hatred on the part of the same-sex child (the daughter), though it is quite distinct in its affective consequences. This is demonstrated by the detail, common to the Hamlet and Orestes legends, that it is her son's displeasure with her second marriage which the newly wedded mother fears most of all. She therefore attempts to remove him [to another physical location], just as she removed his father. Gertrude makes use of Claudius so that her role in the murder of her husband remains unclear, but Clytemnestra is still able to kill her husband with her own hands. Hamlet's mother, too, has eliminated her first spouse and the father of her son so as to give herself to another man. And just as Gertrude uses Claudius to do the deed, Clytemnestra is assisted by Aegisthus. Similarly, Electra makes use of her brother in carrying out her deed. Further, Hamlet hates his beloved mother, having loved her too much, only after she belongs to another man; the same is true of Orestes. Thus, in the fate of Orestes we have a Hamlet tragedy more perfect in some respects than Shakespeare's. Still, we note a characteristic difference: with Orestes, the repression of human emotional life has progressed less far. Orestes is still able to carry out what Hamlet hardly even dares to contemplate, "sicklied o'er with the pale cast of thought." But for Orestes, too, the deed, carried out from the unconscious infantile point of view, in jealousy for his mother and to please his beloved sister, is not without the momentous psychic consequences usually observed with acts carried out in the realization of long-repressed infantile impulses. The repentant matricide is pursued by the Erinyes, the goddesses of vengeance. That is, his conscience gives him no rest. Just as the ghost of the slain father appears to Hamlet, the ghost of the slain mother appears to Orestes and drives on the indolent Furies to take revenge. The ancients considered the appearance of insanity to be an effect of this persecution, the punishment of Erinyes.

> While later writers, corresponding to their external point of view, attributed this effect to the Erinyes' attributes (whip, torch, and *kentron* ["goad"]), Euripides considered insanity to be a direct effect upon the mind itself. In Orestes, insanity appears like a disease (*nosos manias*), with violent attacks convulsing both mind and body, during which he sees the Erinyes in their full horror (*Orestes,* 43, 400, 791, 835; *Iphigenia in Tauris,* 281 ff., 1456). Aeschylus at least hints at this interpretation (*Choephoroi,* 283 ff.). It would be too one-sided simply to claim that this effect was only a "physical ailment, a struggle with epilepsy," as does Hartung (1865–73, 3:68). The local legends of Orestes (Pausanis 8.24.1; 7.25.4) assume that it was a psychic ailment. ("Erinyes," Roscher 1884–1937)

The detailed description of all this suffering, as well as of the Erinyes and their effects, discussed by Roscher, is characteristic of unconscious conflicts, even in the smallest details. Thus, without being tempted to exaggerate and without appearing naive, we can say that the Orestes of the legend shows all the symptoms of psychoneurosis derived from the parent complex, as Freud has also stated for Hamlet. Nonnus, *Dionysiaca* (10:32), states that the Erinyes "bring about insanity by forcefully removing the earlier thoughts." This corresponds fully to the psychology of repression; the Erinyes correspond to outward projections of painful unconscious impulses of defense and repentance. For an understanding of the legend, the following observation is of the utmost importance: the Erinyes were thought to have been active only in the case of incestuous crimes (in the broader sense) and, more specifically, seem to have been involved only when those incestuous crimes were committed in conflict with the original [infantile], now unconscious constellation of wishes—those cases of incest most likely to lead to tumultuous repentance and pangs of guilty conscience. This provides proof for our interpretation.

> Corresponding to the extremely ancient origin of these deities, their effects pertain to the simplest relationships given by nature—to one's duties toward one's parents and closest blood relatives. . . . Judging from the twelve passages in Homer in which the activity of the Erinyes is mentioned, they were originally active in cases of disrespect (eight cases) and when human limitations were exceeded (in the four remaining cases). In Homer the Erinyes appear not so much as avengers, but as defenders of the order underlying family and social life. It was only through the tragic genre that murder and incest came to be emphasized. Of the six Homeric passages depicting the activity of the Erinyes in connection with disrespect for family members, four cases involve the mother, and only one involves the father. Oedipus's sufferings are also attributed to the Erinyes of his mother. ("Erinyes," Roscher 1884–1937)

The one Homeric passage in which an Erinys pursues a son in defense of his father's rights is the story of Phoenix, whom his father curses, calling upon the Erinyes and wishing childlessness upon him since he has slept with his father's concubine at his mother's request (dampened incest). In tragedy, Oedipus also invokes an Erinys; she carries out his curses upon his sons (Aeschylus, *Seven against Thebes,* 722–25, 791, 887).

> The Erinyes also defended the rights of the older brother, demanding obedience from the younger one. Later writers adopt this theme by having murder of the brother or sister avenged by an Erinys. . . . Concerning their role as defenders of the rights of spouses, writers are of differing opinions. In Aeschylus (*Eumenides,* 212, 605), the Erinyes clearly declare that they will not pursue Clytemnestra for the murder of her spouse because he was not a blood relative. This is also the case with Euripides (*Orestes,* 584). On the other hand, Sophocles not only invokes the Erinyes to pursue wives guilty of their husbands' deaths (Deianira in *Thracian Women,* 809, 895; Clytemnestra in *Electra,* 112), but also assumes them to be punishers of adultery (*Electra,* 114, 276). ("Erinyes," Roscher 1884–1937)

There is no doubt, then, that the Erinyes are the projections of unconscious psychic impulses. Sometimes, as protectors of the family order, they prevent incestuous murders or sexual acts, while at other times they appear as the avengers of these same acts. In later literary traditions, they even act as inciters of these crimes. Thus, in their psychic effects, they fully demonstrate the characteristics familiar to us from the repressed impulses that have broken free from the unconscious.

> They are especially fearsome because of the inexorable persistence with which they pitilessly pursue their victims, even in late periods, and are described as *neleopoinoi* ["punishing ruthlessly"] (Theognis, 220), as *hysteropoinoi* ["late-avenging"] (Aeschylus, *Agamemnon,* 58), *hysterophoroi* ["late-bearing"] (Sophocles, *Antigone,* 1074), or *hysteropous* ["late-coming"] (*Orphica Argonautica,* 1167). They are feared for their ruthless execution of their role as punishers, for they punish even those crimes committed without the knowledge of the offender (cf. Oedipus), punishing both gods and men. The one who has committed the infraction is at their mercy and is consecrated to them (Aeschylus, *Eumenides,* 302–4). They establish themselves in his house ⟨within him⟩ and never depart (Aeschylus, *Agamemnon,* 1186–91) until they have thoroughly destroyed it as *holesioikoi* ["destroyers of the house"] and *phthersigeneis* ["destroyers of the race"], but they drive out the victim himself (Aeschylus, *Eumenides,* 210) and follow at his heels (Sophocles, *Electra,* 1387), kicking him so that he falls, until his very death. ("Erinyes," Roscher 1884–1937) [Greek translations: Liddell and Scott, *Greek-English Lexicon*]

In all the details mentioned, if we liberate ourselves from the mythological worldview, we recognize the depiction of a serious psychoneurosis. We do not even require the significant linguistic correspondence noted in the depiction of the Erinyes as *hysteropoinoi* to support our diagnosis of one of the most serious nervous disorders—hysteria. In the unconscious of the matricide, other motives are crucial. These later break forth, producing insanity. This is shown by a version of the myth in which Orestes punishes himself with castration in symbolic form:

> In Arcadia, not far from the later Megalopolis, in the time of Pausanias, there still stood a shrine of the *maniai.* There, after the murder of his mother, Orestes is supposed to have been beset by madness. In his ravings, he is supposed to have bitten off a finger. In commemoration of this event an earthen mound was exhibited upon which a stone finger had been placed. In this stone finger, F. Liebrecht sees the grave of a matricide, for in popular superstition one still encounters the belief that the hand of someone who has killed or struck his mother will grow out of his grave. Belger repeatedly suggests that the stone represents a phallus or a rough, polelike, perhaps even phallic image of Hermes. ("Erinyes," Roscher 1884–1937)

Just as the form and content of Orestes' ailment suggest neurosis, its cure also shows striking similarity to cathartic therapy. Characteristically, the cure rests on the ambivalent nature of the Erinyes or, as we would say today, on the ambivalence of the drives.

> Like many other deities, according to a conception prevalent through all of antiquity, the Erinyes have both destructive and beneficent aspects. Through respectful worship, the terrible goddesses of revenge became benevolent deities: the Erinyes became the Eumenides. Therefore they were prayed to for the prevention of disaster and for the bestowing of blessings. In one temple there existed a double cult of the merciless and merciful goddesses, the Erinyes and the Eumenides. According to the story, they first appeared to Orestes black, but after his cure they appeared white. It is reported also that to the Erinyes he made sacrifices appropriate to gods of the underworld, while to the Eumenides he made sacrifices appropriate to heavenly deities. In Keryneia in Achaia, the ambivalent nature of the goddesses was known, and the transformation of the Erinyes into Eumenides was attributed to Orestes, the mythological founder of the shrine of the Eumenides. They are beneficent when one has become reconciled with them. The myth of the trial of Orestes tends to explain the reconciliation with these goddesses, otherwise so inexorable, and the transformation of the Erinyes into Eumenides. This also constitutes the main content of Aeschylus's *Eumenides*. As benevolent deities they spare the land from the same ill fortune they threatened as punishing deities (Aeschylus, *Eumenides*, 1009). ("Erinyes," Roscher 1884–1937)

At the aforementioned trial, the same result occurs as psychoanalysis, though in a much more complicated way, seeks to effect—that is, the murderer's release from his unreasonable guilt and from his own guilty conscience, which, bearing down heavily upon his psyche, has produced depression. After this release from guilt, the Erinyes also leave him. He is credited with motives justifying his deed, which, like Hamlet, he committed in a conflict of duty, necessarily overstepping his filial duties to one parent. Indeed, the legend relates that he committed his mother's murder out of filial piety for his murdered father; the legend claims that the Erinyes of his father had driven him to matricide, just as the father's ghost incited Hamlet to revenge. However, the analysis of *Hamlet* has revealed that this exaggerated conception of vengeance for the father is only a disguise for the son's infantile wish for his father's death. Thus we can perhaps also understand why the murder of his father may have been subconsciously well received by Orestes as a young boy, now hoping to win his mother for himself, and why a desire for revenge subsequently developed when this hope was so bitterly disappointed. (Claudius too represents Hamlet's wishes.) Thus Orestes has several unconscious motives for matricide that support each other: his jealous hatred of his mother, the Erinyes of his father, and his secret love for his sister. But all of these are complemented by their most powerful counterimpulse, his original infantile erotic affection for his mother, which, disappointed, leads to the outbreak of neurosis. Still, it is only after the deed has been done that neurosis occurs. With Hamlet, it is through neurosis itself that the deed is prevented. Here we see again the progression of repression in the psychic life of mankind. In still earlier stages of psychic development, man was still capable of following his impulses without inhibition or blame. This is shown in that, in the old epics, the Erinyes do not pursue Orestes after the deed. This trait was first brought into the legend by the tragedians because of their own conflicts and feelings of guilt.

10 *Medieval Fables and Christian Legends*

Oh, the unbridled impiety of human desire, O flame devouring reason, producing impiety, consuming justice! . . . What shall we do, good Jesus? One is ashamed to write what follows.

Life of Saint Alban the Martyr

Like antiquity, the Christian Middle Ages are rich in popular stories, legends, and literary works dealing with the incest theme in its many guises. The many adaptations, versions, and translations of this material show great interest in the theme during all historical periods and among various peoples. Although the development of these legends was partially influenced by the traditions of antiquity, the continual assimilation of these themes and their special treatment under the influence of the Christian worldview demonstrate the active unconscious role of narrator and listener in these stories, which differ displeasingly from the naive antique traditions in their voluptuous and torrid fantasies. If we were dealing simply with the assimilation of existing traditions and their extension to the passive Christian heroes—the saints—there would be no explanation for the burning sensuality with which incestuous crimes were aligned one upon the other, approaching the limits of the humanly conceivable. Based on this excess, we must assume that the great repression of drives expressed in Christianity could be maintained only at the cost of a fantasy life pouring forth to the most voluptuous degree; here the repressed drives found a place where they could be played out. In addition to incest fantasies of all types, sadomasochistic impulses especially permeate the stories of the saints and martyrs. It is also clear why much use was made of sexual symbolism, useful in the tendency to disguise such themes.

Even more clearly than the traditions of antiquity, the development of Christian legends reveals that in these productions we are dealing with the wishful impulses of the unconscious, which upon breaking through are simply attributed by a populace to its saints, in whom are found not only gratification for these impulses, but also punishment and forgiveness, often through repentance and penance exaggerated to a senseless degree. Thus the saint suffers for the evil drives of all. Accordingly, he is considered the recipient of the greatest rewards, which are not only heavenly ones; often he receives the highest religious honors from mortal man. Corresponding to the Christian conception of the sinful nature of man, in these legends the main emphasis is on the sinner's remorseful penance and merciful forgiveness. The shameful acts committed in the service of his unconscious drives appear as merely a necessary evil: they produce the deepest possible repentance, allowing the sinner to receive correspondingly greater divine grace.

In their basic scheme, these tales demonstrate so much correspondence with the Oedipus fable that direct borrowing was often thought to have been involved. In Roscher's *Lexicon* (1884–1937), parallels between several of these legends and the Oedipus legend are noted: "In nearly all of these legends the newborn child, like Oedipus in the old legend, is exposed in the sea; like Oedipus, as a youth he goes abroad because of his doubts concerning his true parents. He frees his homeland from an oppressive enemy (analogy with the Sphinx) and marries his own mother without realizing her identity. Here, though, patricide is nearly always absent."

Greith (1838, 154 ff.), Nodilo (1898–1905), and Comparetti (1867) assume a common Indo-European source for these legends and the Oedipus fable rather than direct borrowing. Nevertheless—given our psychoanalytical insights into the development of dreams and neuroses, which demonstrate the striking similarity between the unconscious fantasies of the most diverse individuals without the influence of external models—in investigating the fantasy creations of the individual and of a people, even if they sometimes borrow from older traditions, we can also reduce the striking correspondences in the presentation of the main themes to a psychological identity, thus superseding any original ethnographic relationship.

Here we will not be able to analyze in detail the fantasies underlying these legends. But it will be impossible to misinterpret these fantasies from the false point of view of nature mythology. We need only refer readers to the discussions of the underlying "myth of exposure" and its psychological relation to the "family complex" (Rank 1909). We should also emphasize the psychologically significant fact that the penance following upon the unavoidable crime is usually a repetition (doublet) of the defense against the desired and yet feared fate attempted in the exposure. Just as the punishment found in classical works is replaced in the Christian legends by penance, so the failure to repress these powerful impulses, portrayed in classical works as the inevitable result of "fate," is attributed in the Christian Oedipus tragedies to the devil. By claiming temptation by the devil, the apotheosis of evil, an attempt is made to justify the emergence of these rejected impulses and wishes into reality and fantasy. In a similar way, other religions also conceive of evil spirits and demons as the expression of repressed drives.

In Zoroaster's teachings the demons, whose leader, Ahriman, hastens the development of creation through his inimical strivings, play a great role. Brodbeck (*Zoroaster*) remarks: "From the apocryphal book of *Tobias* and from the *Talmud*, it is clear that the Jews also believed in the demon of evil desires; they called him Asmodei. He was considered the cause of all hysteria in women. On the Persian model, other nervous and mental disorders were also ascribed to evil demons. The role this belief in demons played in the life of Christ and has subsequently played in Christianity is well known."

In their form, their fantastic appearance, and the complications of their incestuous horrors, these legends sometimes remind one of the hallucinations of obsessional neurotics, in whose development the Zurich school has demonstrated the extensive contribution of incest fantasies. But one should not forget that in both cases the wild and offensive fantasies actually belong to the unconscious and only represent a crass projection of the repressed infantile impulses as well as a distortion brought about by conscious contemplation.

Comparetti (1867) remarks that the Oedipus legend itself does not seem to have been very well known in the Middle Ages; a Latin "Lament of Oedipus" (published by Méril Ozanam, Gall Morell, and most recently by Schmidt) and a late medieval "Roman d'Edipus" are based on the legend.

Thus Bernhard Schmidt's remark (1877, 248) has even greater significance: "Many folktales with details from the Oedipus legend are found in Greece. In Zákinthos I was told some folktales describing patricide and marriage with the unrecognized mother or sister." Schmidt then notes also the Albanian folktale, probably hidden somewhere in Greece as well, cited by Hahn (1864, no. 98). This folktale reveals a striking similarity to the Perseus legend and some similarity to the Oedipus legend as well:

> Once there is a king who rules a land. It is prophesied to him that he will be killed by the son of his daughter; this grandson is still unborn. There-

> fore he casts all the boys born to his two daughters into the sea, drowning them ⟨exposure⟩. However, the third boy whom he casts into the sea does not drown, for the waves throw him upon the seashore. There shepherds find him, take him with their flock, and give him to their wives to be raised ⟨rescue⟩. Nights pass, days pass, and the child grows to be twelve years old, handsome and strong. At this time, a *lubia* comes to the king's land. It dries up all the water. It is prophesied that the *lubia* will not again permit the waters to flow until it has devoured the king's daughter. Finally the king decides to sacrifice his daughter. He sends her to the place where the *lubia* waits. There the youth, who happens to be going past, sees her, asks her the reason for her sadness, and promises to save her. He hides, and when the *lubia* comes, he kills the monster ⟨Sphinx⟩. He takes the head of the *lubia* and lets the king's daughter go without telling her about himself. When the young woman returns to the king and tells him how she has been saved from the *lubia,* he announces that whoever has killed it should come to him, for he wishes to make him his son and give him his daughter in marriage. When the youth hears this, he goes to the king and shows him the *lubia*'s head. He takes the young woman whom he has rescued as his wife, and a great wedding is celebrated. During the playing and singing, the youth throws his club, unintentionally striking and killing the king. The prophecy is fulfilled, and the youth himself becomes king.

Comparetti (1867) remarks that the tale is incomplete, having been distorted by the narrator, a woman from Ljabovo. Initially, mention was made of two daughters, both of whom were married. Subsequently mention is made only of an unmarried daughter. Nor is it mentioned whether it is the youth's aunt or his mother who has been widowed. In any case the extra comment, "He did not know that this deed ⟨rescuing the woman from the *lubia*⟩ would be his undoing," leaves no doubt that it was the more offensive incest that occurred—that the hero married his mother. Comparetti also suspects that the conclusion of the tale, in which the hero discovers his origins, is missing. In the failure to mention whether the hero has married his aunt or his mother, we suspect a dampening (displacement) of the original incest theme, just as is demonstrated by his killing his grandfather instead of his father.

Repression progresses further still in the English poem "Sir Degore," in which incest through Degore's marriage to his mother is prevented when he shows her a pair of gloves she laid in his cradle when she exposed him. She had received them from the unknown man who had once taken her by force in the forest. Further, a dagger without a point, left with her earlier, permits Degore to recognize his father, but also prevents his killing him. Here, then, we find neither the killing of the father nor sexual intercourse with the mother: both acts are prevented in time. This is an expression of defense, as found also, for example, in the myth of Auge and Telephus.

A similar prevention of incest between son and mother (preceded, however, by conscious incest between brother and sister) is found in *Patranuelo* by Juan de Timoneda, a Spanish writer of the sixteenth century. Another old English poem shows that the incest was, in fact, originally carried out. This poem is listed by Brunet (1858) under the title "Sir Eglamour of Artois"; he briefly summarizes it as follows: "A child is exposed by his mother in a boat on the open sea. The child is rescued and brought to a king, who raises him and then makes him a knight. The youth later marries his mother without knowing her identity. Finally he atones for his deed through hard penance." In a Scottish ballad, "Brown Robyn's Confession" (Buchan 1875, 1:108), Brown Robyn freely admits that he has sired two children by his mother and five by his sister. While on shipboard, to prevent a threatening storm from bursting forth in full fury, he announces that he wishes to sacrifice himself; he begs to be tied to a beam and cast into the sea. After he has been floating for a few hours, the Holy Virgin appears to him and transports him to heaven in reward for his well-done penance.

Stucken (1896–1907, 54) also remarks that the Norwegian folksong "Agnus Dei" (Warrens, n.d., 4:90 ff.) has a hidden meaning: the child born of incest is exposed in the sea, but his parents must then suffer in hell for their incest.

Numerous other folk ballads deal with the incest theme. We shall mention only the well-known old Scottish ballad "Edward," translated into German by Herder, which portrays a conversation between a mother and her son, who has killed his father at her behest:

> "Why dois your brand sae drap wi bluid,
>   Edward, Edward,
> Why dois your brand sae drap wi bluid,
>   And why sae sad gang yee O?"
> "O I hae killed my hauke sae guid,
>   Mither, Mither,
> O I hae killed my hauke sae guid,
>   And I had nae mair bot hee O."

He makes further attempts to hide the truth, but she continues her questioning and he finally admits:

> "O I hae killed my fadir deir,
>   Mither, Mither,
> O I hae killed my fadir deir,
>   Alas, and wae is mee O!"

"And whatten penance wul ye drie for that,
Edward, Edward?
And whatten penance wul ye drie for that?
My dear son, now tell me O."

He now says that he wishes to wander without rest from place to place (like Cain). Then his mother asks him:

"And what wul ye leive to your ain mither deir,
Edward, Edward?
And what wul ye leive to your ain mither deir?
My dear son, now tell me O."
"The curse of hell frae me sall ye beir,
Mither, mither,
The curse of hell frae me sall ye beir,
Sic counseils ye gave to me O."

In the versions featuring conscious incest between mother and son, seduced by the mother, we recognize the son's wish fantasy, revealed through psychoanalysis: he wishes to be introduced by the mother to actual romantic love. Here belongs the twenty-third novella of Masuccio da Salerno. In the thirteenth chapter of *Gesta Romanorum* as well, an "impure love"—conscious incest between mother and son—is described. The tale is as follows:

> There was an emperor who had a beautiful wife, whom he loved very much. In the very first year of her marriage she bore a son, whom, as his mother, she loved very much, and whom she even slept with each night. When the child was three years old, the king died. . . . And the queen too mourned his death for many days. After he was buried, she lived in a palace and had her son with her. She loved the boy so much that she could not do without his presence, and they always slept together until the boy was eighteen. And when the Evil One noticed such great love between a mother and son, he tempted her into sin, and the son knew the mother carnally. The queen conceived immediately, but while she was pregnant her son, in desolation, left the kingdom and proceeded to distant lands. In the meantime, when her time had come, the mother gave birth to a very beautiful boy, but just after he was born she murdered him by cutting his throat.

The story ends, like most such tales, with confession, penance, absolution, and death.

Here the killing of the father is absent. He died three years after his son's birth. This elimination of the father without the sin of patricide corresponds much better than killing him to the infantile wish for his absence (death). In this incestuous relationship, the emphasis is on the etiology, which corresponds strikingly with the etiology Freud has noted for similar cases of neurosis: the child's sleeping in the parents' bed or room and overhearing their marital intercourse. In his *Violier des histoires romaines* [The flower of Roman stories], Brunet (1858) comments concerning this tale that he has seen similar ones in Vincent de Beauvais's *Speculum historiale*, bk. 7, chap. 93; cf. also Wright's *Latin Stories* (1842, no. 112).

Constans (1881, 121 ff.) also mentions a tale with the title "Fable of the Bull." A widow, tempted by the devil, repeatedly has intercourse with her son. He goes to the pope to confess his sin; the Holy Father keeps him there. In the meantime, the mother brings a daughter into the world, with whom she also goes to Rome a few years later to receive forgiveness from the pope. There she meets her son, and the pope commands them each to wander through the world alone wearing cowhides. Only hands, feet, and face are to show. After seven years they meet again. All three die in one night, amid miraculous phenomena. To this tale, D'Ancona compares a fable published by Méon (1823, 2:394) with the title "The Bourgeoise Who Grew Fat by Her Son" and a fable published by Jubinal (*Nouveau recueil*, 1:79) with the title "Fable of the Bourgeoise of Rome," in which the wife of a rich senator kills her child, sired by her own son. Through a hard penance, she is absolved. D'Ancona also mentions Sánchez (1860, para. 205) and—following Liebrecht—Wright, *Latin Stories* (1842, no. 110). The novella *Gärende Kraft des Geheimnisses* [The seething power of a secret], by Lynkeus [Joseph Popper], deals with the seduction of an inexperienced son by his mother.

The Judas legend shows the greatest similarity to the Oedipus fable. Because of the striking correspondences, most scholars consider it nothing more than a Christian adaptation of the Oedipus fable. According to Diederichs (1880, 119–46), the content of the legend is as follows. Before the birth of Judas, his mother, Cyborea, is warned that she will bring into the world an infamous son who will be the downfall of his people. After the child's birth his parents, to avoid directly killing him, decide to expose him in a chest in the sea. He does not perish, however, but is driven by the waves to the island of Scariot. There he is found by the childless queen and raised as her own child. Later, though, the royal pair have their own child, and the foundling must take his place behind the legitimate child. Judas treats the preferred competitor with meanness and envy and finally murders him. Fleeing the country, he goes to Jerusalem and finds a position at the court of Pilate; Pilate makes him his closest confidant and places him in charge of his whole household. Once, having developed an insatiable craving, Pilate has him fetch some fine apples from a nearby orchard. An argument arises between Judas, anxious to follow orders, and the owner of the garden. In great anger, Judas slays his opponent with a stone, thus becoming, without realizing it, a patricide. Pilate awards Judas the murdered man's wife. She knows nothing of the murder and believes that her husband has died a natural death. Cyborea's sadness over the hard blows of fate that have befallen her lead Judas to inquire about the earlier events of her life. By comparing what she tells him with what he knows of his discovery on the seashore, he realizes that he is to bring the downfall of his people and that he has killed his father and married his mother. Deeply crushed, he takes his mother's advice, goes to the Savior, and confesses his deeds. Jesus receives him with love and makes him an apostle. His betrayal of the Savior is known from the Gospels. It appears that the story of Judas Iscariot, which gradually became a legend, arose from the need to attribute to Judas, the archrogue (as Abraham a Sancta Clara called him) that crime felt, owing to repression, to be especially heinous.

This legend was first recorded (between 1270 and 1298) by Jacobus de Varagine (Grässe 1850), who claims that he took it from an apocryphal tale. It is attested in Latin, English, German, French, Italian, Spanish, Catalan, Swedish, Old Bohemian, and Russian versions. Creizenach (1876, 201) presents two poems in Latin and three in English. As one can see, the Judas legend was widespread and very popular in the Middle Ages. The various adaptations, versions, and editions are listed and exhaustively dealt with by Constans (1881, 98 ff.) and by D'Ancona (1869, preface). Among the works listed, one also finds dramatizations of the Judas legend (cf. Constans 1881): "In an episode in the *Mystère de la passion* of Jehan Michel (fifteenth century), titled 'Vengeance for the Passion of Our Lord,' the scene between Reuben and Judas is treated so as to make Judas more guilty. In the Provençal version the legend has undergone some alterations. Judas, who narrates the story of his own life here, says that his father and mother exposed him in the sea to protect him from the murder of the innocents ordered by King Herod. Through this borrowing from the Gospels, the older and deeper motivation for exposure—the prediction of doom concerning the boy's birth—is made trivial and superficial. The mutual recognition of mother and son, presented beautifully in the *Legenda aurea* version as a coming into consciousness of unconscious suspicions, is in this play presented in a most superficial manner. Before the mother exposes the child, she brands a sign on his back with a hot iron. Thus, after the incestuous marriage, she recognizes him. This theme, the wounding of the child before his exposure, is indeed found already with Oedipus. But there the purpose of the injury was to ensure the child's death. In *Oedipus* the recognition is due entirely to psychic features. Here, though, the mother wounds the child so that she will later recognize him from the scars. In the legends, we shall often find such rationalizations of themes with deep psychological motivation. In this version of the legend, the murder of the foster brother is also absent. Elsewhere this anticipates the elimination of the father, which also occurs out of jealousy. Coincidentally, Judas's father comes to the country where Judas was raised. An argument ensues, and the father is killed. Judas then flees to Judea, falls in love with his mother, marries her, and sires two children by her. The son's incestuous love, already realized by the marriage to the mother, is materialized by the birth of the children. Their birth, as we already know from the Oedipus legend, is a later addition, for the original legend mentions nothing about the children of Jocasta and Oedipus. Judas, after recognizing his wife as his mother, goes to the Savior, who commands them to separate from one another.

Diederichs (1880, 119–46) presents Russian tales related to the Judas legend. A legend from a seventeenth-century collection is as follows: In a city—later it is called Crete—there lives a merchant named Pulivach, who once heard two doves speaking together: "This man will have joy; his wife will bear him a son who will be named Andreas; this boy will kill his father and marry his mother and will dishonor three hundred virgin nuns." Thereupon the man commands that the child be killed immediately after his birth, but the mother considers it a sin to murder him directly. She has the child baptized with the name Andreas; then she cuts open his body with a knife, ties him to a board, and sends him out to sea. In this manner, apparently, she wishes to delay the calamity and avoid direct responsibility for the child's death. The waves carry the boy thirty miles to a convent consecrated to the Mother of God, called the Convent of the Burning Bush. Here the child, now hardly breathing, is found by a nun and brought to the abbess, who determines to save his life. The open wound is sewn shut, and the child is fed goat's milk. The boy is later instructed by a nun and reaches the age of fifteen in the convent. Then the devil, the enemy of Christian people, begins his work and arouses evil thoughts in him. The boy dishonors all three hundred nuns, some by force and some by cunning. "He seduced me," says the abbess, "with many examples of others' transgressions—those of tax collectors, oppressors, and also of all just people of all times. He said: 'They all redeemed themselves with penance and tears and alms.' " Driven from the convent, Andreas then goes to Crete and begins working for his unrecognized father. He is assigned to guard the vineyards and to shoot anyone found there. To test his servant's reliability, the master himself comes out to the vineyard at midnight. Andreas, believing he is a thief, shoots him dead. Thus the second dire prediction is fulfilled. He immediately reports to the mistress what has happened, and soon she chooses him as her husband. The secret, which has been concealed until then, is discovered when the woman becomes aware of the scar on his body and he tells her of his earlier fate. Then Andreas springs from his bed and cries: "Alas for me, wicked man that I am. Before the law, my sin is greater than that of any other man."

His mother then sends him to a father confessor to confess his sins and ask forgiveness. When the father confessor finds his sins too numerous and does not wish to absolve him, Andreas strikes him with a lectern and goes to another confessor. But he also believes it would be sinful to grant him absolution. Andreas strikes this priest too and tries again with a third. Here, though, he has no more success, and the priest receives the same recompense. Finally he turns to the bishop of Crete, whom he knows to be a prudent and God-fearing man. If the bishop too should reject him, Andreas plans to go abroad to the court of a foreign ruler and later to return with an army to take vengeance on Crete and its bishop. However, there is no need for recourse to this extreme plan. The bishop considers this man, full of rebellious energy, to be a chosen implement of God. The bishop, who fears judgment and death, gives Andreas and his mother spiritual counsel and then releases them. As penance, Andreas is lowered into a cellar eighteen feet deep and three feet wide, where he is put in chains. The bishop declares that his sins will be forgiven as soon as the cellar has become filled with earth and Andreas too has been covered with earth. The mother's nose is pierced and a lock is affixed, but the key is thrown into the sea. The bishop declares that her sins will be forgiven when the key again appears. Until then, deprived of her possessions, she is to wander the earth and praise God. The son in his prison is to engage in spiritual exercises. These require pen and paper, both of which he receives.

After thirty years, when the woman again appears before the bishop, the key is found in the body of a fish, and her unusual penance comes to an end, whereupon the bishop has her accepted into a convent. When a visit is made to the cellar Andreas had been lowered into, he is found sitting outside above it, just about to write the last words of the ninth chant of the great canon. Then the bishop and those accompanying him praise God's grace and realize that Andreas too has been forgiven his sins. The canon is read to the people in the church and is still read annually during Lent; on Thursday of the fifth week it is used in the service. Like his mother, the reformed sinner is admitted to a monastery, and after the bishop's death Andreas succeeds him in Crete. The tale closes: "And God granted that Andreas was bishop of Crete for thirty years. He lived reverently and righteously, appealed to God through fasting and prayer, alms and tears, founded many churches, and brought many people to redemption. He was merciful to others and departed for eternal life with Jesus Christ our Lord. Glory be to the Lord, now and evermore, for ever and ever. Amen."

Diederichs remarks that the time of origin of this legend is unknown, but that judging from the name Pulivach it is of south Slavic origin. A Saint Andreas is historically documented, and according to Diederichs this is a case of the use of a saint's name as the bearer of an invented story: Andreas, archbishop of Crete, lived in the time of the Monotheletic controversy. He is supposed to have appeared at the sixth ecumenical council in Constantinople (680) as the representative of the patriarch of Jerusalem. However, there is some doubt about this account. Theophanes states that in 712 he was on the side of the Emperor Philippicus Bardanes and an opponent of the decisions of the council. Diederichs says there is little or no report of his life, and nothing relevant to our story; he says his views are based mainly on the writings of Saint Andreas, especially the great canon of penance, which attempts to bring the soul to realize its sin through a detailed discussion of the sinful soul and through comparisons of the soul with the sinners and the righteous of the old and new covenants.

Here we can discuss only briefly the rich sexual symbolism of the legend and the psychological significance of certain details. We have already mentioned the symbolism of the vineyard and of the locking of the female genitals as a punishment. In his mythological comparisons, Stucken (1896–1907) equates the key swallowed by a fish, which also appears in the legend of Saint Gregory, with the phallus of Osiris, which meets a similar fate. Thus we would be observing here too, as punishment for incest, castration of the man and locking (sewing shut) of the woman. The rape of the three hundred nuns, with characteristic displacement, suggests that, according to the original version, Andreas certainly would not have hesitated to carry out the deliberate rape of his mother too. Also, the murder of the three priests and the "crusade" (against the father), typical of the legends (cf. Saint Gregory) but here only planned, represents patricide—absent, according to literary historians, from the legend.

Also worthy of note is the point, found in other legends as well, that the widow of the murdered man soon takes his murderer as her husband, as the tale naively indicates. This seamless juxtaposition of the two wishes, closely associated in the unconscious, reveals an aspect of the primitive framework, through the disguising and distortion of which the complex legend develops. The same "overhasty marriage" is one of the main motivations for Hamlet's hatred of his mother, and it also intensifies Orestes' inimical stance in the Electra legend.

Diederichs also cites Russian and Ukrainian legends and folktales related to the Judas legend. He further cites versions from the Far North, from Finnish Karelia. But except for the Russian version, there is in his opinion no doubt that these versions derive from the legend of Andreas of Crete. In a Ukrainian tale collected from a tailor in the Yekaterinoslav region, the son kills not only the father but also, when the incest is discovered, the mother. Hereupon follow (as in the tale of Andreas, but with the elimination of the nuns) the injury, the exposure, the discovery and raising of the child, the service under his unrecognized father, his appointment as guardian of the garden, and the killing of the master, who wishes to test him. Then occurs the marriage with the mother, whom he kills as soon as he discovers her relationship to him. There follows the murder of two priests who refuse to assign him a penance, until finally the third one gives him the following task: "Take this coal from a burned apple tree, plant it there on that mountain, bring it water every morning and evening on your knees; water the coal. If the tree thrives and bears ripe apples, shake the tree. If the apples fall, your sins are forgiven." In twenty-five years there are ripe apples. He shakes the tree and all the apples fall except two. Then he returns to the priest, who places him in a well, closes the iron door, piles earth on it, and throws the key into the sea. After thirty years, the key is found in the body of a fish. The place of the penitent one is sought out, but he has already died, and a candle burns over him. Still, he has obtained forgiveness for his sins.

In the double penance, according to Diederichs, one recognizes the incorporation of another version, also attested among the Ukrainians in Podolia, Galicia, and southern Russia. This is the tale of a violent robber who has slain his mother and father and who has sought a means of penance in vain until he is finally given the task of watering the coals of a burned apple tree or a stick of applewood. According to one version, he succeeds in shaking down the last two apples, thrice shaking the tree with the help of the priest. According to other versions, though, he is not successful, which means he has been forgiven his other sins, but not the murder of his father and mother. As the priest's shepherd, he then receives complete forgiveness by striking down a taskmaster who was attempting to draft even the dead into his service. A Finnish folktale also contains this detail—the penitent unexpectedly reaches the goal of his pains and trouble by striking dead someone who is even more guilty than he. Schiefner (n.d., 2:622 ff.) comments on the Finnish tale, based on the version in Rudbeck's collection (1852). A German translation of this tale under the title "Die Weissagungen" [The prophecies] also exists (*Archiv für Wissenschaftliche Kunde von Russland* 17 [1858]:14–20). There the disaster to be brought about by the child is predicted during the night of his birth by two wise men. The child's father happens to overhear their comments. This farmer remains unworried at first, until another prophecy made by the two men is fulfilled, to his horror and that of his wife. Fearing that the child will really end up killing his father and marrying his mother, as has been predicted, the parents decide he must die. They tie him to a board with a wound in his chest and expose him in the sea. The rest of the story, except for the killing of the mother, resembles the Ukrainian legend. Again washed ashore, the child is found by an abbot. When he is grown, he enters the service of a farmer. While guarding the vineyards at night, he has the misfortune to shoot his father, whom he believes is a thief. Later the widow takes him as her husband. The scar on his breast reveals his identity. The strange penance through the killing of a great sinner is found here too (Schreck 1887, no. 25).

Diederichs also cites another version heard by Kostomarov in certain regions. After the birth of his son, a heathen king asks a prophet about the child's future. He is told that the son will be such a sinner as was never before seen on earth; that he will kill his father and marry his mother. The father commands the mother to take the child to the forest where he will be killed by wild animals, but the mother, who is secretly a Christian, does not carry out the order. She makes a little chest and lays the boy in it, with the Gospels on his breast. She then places the chest in the Danube so that the boy will be carried to good people. A monk pulls the chest from the water, baptizes the child, and cares for him in the monastery, where he grows to be eighteen years old. Then the youth departs and comes to a Christian king, whom he supports in battle against the heathens. He conquers the wild and cruel heathen king and decapitates him, though his victim begs for mercy. The assembled heathens beg to be baptized, and this is accomplished in the Danube. They then declare the tyrant's conqueror their ruler, and the widowed queen is requested to marry him. After they have been married seven days, the queen asks about the origins and family of her new husband. Thus she discovers that she is his mother and that in killing the heathen king he has killed his father. She curses herself and him and says that he should make his way to the forests and chasms to be devoured by wild beasts (as at the time of his exposure). As for herself, she declares that she wishes to plunge into the waves that had once carried him away, bringing them both ill fortune. Thereupon he goes to a monk, who assigns him a penance, and in thirty years his sins are forgiven. He dies soon thereafter.

Diederichs finally remarks that in Ukrainian songs as well, fragments of these tales occur. In the songs, though, the exposure always involves two sons (Kostomarov mentions only one son). Thus, in a song of Volhynia, a widow exposes her two newborn sons in the Danube (Jagić 1876, 316). Twenty years later a ship comes up the Danube carrying two valiant young men of the Don. The song continues: " 'Greetings, widow, do you love the young man of the Don? Will you follow the young man of the Don?' 'Oh, I love the young man of the Don and will follow him: I will go with the one myself, and to the other, I will send my daughter.' She took the two into her home and served them wine and meat. 'Oh, you young widow, how foolish you are! You yourself bore us, and put us in the Danube saying: "Oh, you quiet Danube, take my children!" What has the world come to, that a brother does not recognize his sister! What has the world come to, that a son should take his mother! Go now, Mother, and drown yourself, but I will go into the dark forest. May a wild beast devour me!' "

In this Ukrainian song, incest with the mother (and also with the sister) does occur, but the killing of the father is absent—a characteristic variant we will often encounter. In any case, it is remarkable that in almost all of these versions no mention at all is made of the father. Killing the father has been dampened to fatherlessness. This form of the incest theme, too, is represented in numerous songs, tales, and folktales. Novaković (1888, 321–26) reports on the "Oedipus Legend in South Slavic Folk Poetry." He makes reference to Professor Nodilo in Zagreb, who has found great similarity between the Greek Oedipus legend and the Serbian folksongs "The Foundling Simeon" and "Momir and Grozdana." Nodilo even claims that in the Serbian versions there are extremely archaic features and that the ancient Greek tales themselves are only variants on these themes.

The Serbian folk song "The Foundling Simeon" is found in Talvj's translation in *Volkslieder der Serben* [Folk songs of the Serbians] (1853). It is among the oldest Serbian heroic songs, which date from the fifteenth and sixteenth centuries. The song begins with an abbot's discovery of a boy exposed in a lead chest. The boy is brought up, and his great talent soon reveals itself. Still, out of jealousy, his playmates reveal to him one day that he is a foundling. He now departs to find his parents and wanders for nine years. While returning to the monastery, he comes to Buda. The queen sees him, has him called by a servant girl, serves him food and drink, and offers him her love:

> "Stay with me, unknown knight!
> You are worthy of the love of a princess,
> Worthy to kiss a queen!"
> The foundling Simeon, drunk with wine,
> Did as the queen asked;
> Loving her, he kissed her fair cheek.

In the morning, he sees with shame what has transpired, and despite the queen's protests, he departs. On the way, he notices that the Bible placed with him when he was exposed, which he carries always with him, is missing. He hurries back and finds the queen crying pitifully over the book. When Simeon approaches her and asks for the book, she says:

> "Poor Simeon! Ill-fated youth!
> Dark the hour, when you first departed,
> Darker still the hour that brought you to Buda!

When you made love to the queen,
When you kissed her face,
You made love to your own mother!"

Simeon weeps repentant tears, seizes the book, and hurries back to the monastery. When the abbot hears everything, he assigns Simeon a penance. He locks him up in a terrible prison where he is up to his knees in water and where snakes and scorpions abound. He throws the key to the prison into the Danube. He declares that when it is found again, Simeon's sins will have been forgiven. Simeon spends nine years in the prison. Then the key is found in the belly of a fish and the prison is opened. But now both water and snakes are gone. Instead, the area is brilliantly lit and Simeon sits on a golden chair with the Gospels in his hand. Another version, according to which Simeon was born of the incestuous relations of the emperor Stephan and his sister, is related in an excellent translation by Viktor Tausk (*Die Schaubühne,* June 27, 1907). According to this version it is the boy Sava, born of the incestuous relations of Simeon and his mother, not Simeon himself, who is the "enlightener and first great cultural figure of the Serbs."

This displacement of the incest into the preceding generation (doublet) is already familiar to us from numerous instances in Greek literature. It must be interpreted as a later justification of the deeply disturbing incest with the mother. Apparently, incest with the mother was originally committed consciously, though in these complex legends only conscious sister incest, less offensive, still remains. This version of the theme, just like the historical development of continuously more restrictive prohibitions on marriage among blood relatives (cf. chap. 12), reflects the process of repression, which replaces conscious mother incest with unwitting mother incest and therefore introduces conscious sister incest in the preceding generation.

The most familiar of the legends is probably the legend of Saint Gregory of the Rock. A summary, following Cholevius (1854, 167 ff.), is as follows. On his deathbed, a prince admonishes his son and daughter, who are twins, to love one another faithfully. Then the devil leads them to commit incest. The brother sets out with a broken heart for the holy sepulcher and is killed abroad. The sister bears a son, Gregory. She puts him in a little barrel and leaves him at the mercy of the waves. She places with him an ivory tablet inscribed with the secret of his origin. The child is adopted and raised by a fisherman. After six years, he enters a monastery and is prepared for holy orders. When the boy grows up, he happens to learn of his royal descent. He has no fondness for life in the monastery and decides to gain fame by sallying forth as a knight. He climbs aboard a boat and lets the waves carry him (exposure) where they will. They take him to the land of his mother. Here he successfully fights her enemy (father), who wishes to gain her hand through force of arms. In return, he himself receives her hand in marriage. Later, though, the mother discovers from the ivory tablet that she has married her son. Gregory is desperate. Still, he has read in books that God has infinite mercy for the penitent. At his own request, he is brought by a shepherd to a lonely rock in the sea and chained to it, whereupon the shepherd throws the key into the sea. Gregory lives on the rock for seventeen years. Then messengers from Rome find him and report that by God's command he has been elected pope. Simultaneously, the key is found in the belly of a fish. Gregory interprets this as divine confirmation of his absolution. He is taken to Rome and made pope. Attracted by the fame of his holiness, the princess later comes to Rome to confess. Mother and son, wife and husband, recognize one another and remain together to do penance and live a holy life. Indeed, they are even successful in bringing about the redemption of Gregory's father from damnation.

The legend of Saint Gregory is found in the oldest book of folktales and legends of the Christian Middle Ages, the *Gesta Romanorum,* which is supposed to have been compiled in the mid-fourteenth century and was widely circulated after the invention of printing. In Grässe's German edition, the tale of Saint Gregory is chapter 81, titled "Of the Wondrous Grace of God and the Birth of the Holy Pope Gregory." Constans (1881) remarks: "The Latin follows the French poem step by step, summarizing it." Here the king is called Marcus. The sister incest is described as follows: "It happened one night that he was overcome by great temptation; it seemed to him that he would die if he could not carry out his lustful desires upon his sister." She resists a bit, "but he said: 'Whatever happens, I'll have my way,' and he slept with her." She then exposes their son, unbaptized, and asks for a tablet, which she places with him and which asks whoever finds him to baptize and raise him. Concerning the marriage of the mother, the tale continues: "She set the date of the wedding, and when the two of them, the son and the mother, had been married, amid the rejoicing and hearty approval of the whole land, neither of them knowing who the other was, a truly intimate love developed between them." When the mother discovered the incest from the tablet: "She ran and beat her head on the wall and said: 'O my Lord God, my son and my brother's son is my husband.' Then Gregory said: 'I thought I had escaped from danger, and I have fallen into the devil's net. Leave me, my wife, so that I may lament my misery. Woe is me! Here is my mother, my love, my wife. Thus has the devil ensnared me.' " This tale too closes with penance, absolution, and election as pope. The story is also attested in the French version of the *Gesta Romanorum* (*Violier des histoires romaines*) under the title "De l'admirable dispense de Dieu et naiscence de Grégoire Pape de Romme."

Hartmann von Aue (ca. 1170–1220), the author of *Der arme Heinrich* [Poor Henry], adopted the legend under the title "Gregorius, oder Der gute Sünder" [Gregory, or The good sinner], basing his version on an Old French poem. Luzarche discovered the oldest of the three known versions of this French poem in a manuscript in the library of Tours. It was published in 1857 under the title "Vie du Pape Grégoire le grand, légende française." Hartmann's poem was then translated into Latin. An English version exists as well (cf. "Gregorius auf dem Stein" [Saint Gregory on the rock] by Carl Horstmann [1876]). Constans (1881, 116) also indicates that in his edition of *Sir Tristrem* (3d ed., 108), Walter Scott speaks of a poem contained in the same manuscript under the title "The Legend of Pope Gregory." The beginning and the conclusion of the English manuscript are damaged. Constans considers the English version an imitation of the "Vie du Pape Grégoire le grand." There is also a popular German prose version, "Der heilige Gregor auf dem Stein" [Saint Gregory on the rock] (Simrock 1864, 12:83). J. Ruvarac points out that there is an Old Bohemian version of "Carmen de Sancto Gregorio" [Poem of Saint Gregory] in Saxo. The account "Von Sant Gregori uff dem Stein sein Leben" [Life of Saint Gregory of the rock] is also found in *Leben der Heiligen* [Lives of the saints] (Zainer 1471–72).

Constans (1881, 130) mentions Greith's supposition that the successful attempts by Pope Gregory VII to eliminate the abuses that had crept into marriage in the sixteenth century ("the heresies of the incestuous") played a role in his selecting the name Gregorius. Luzel (1881, 2:27 ff.) relates a Breton version of the legend of Saint Gregory. There the hero, born of brother-sister incest and later marrying his mother, is called Cadon.

A Coptic variant of the legend, mentioned by Köhler (1899, 182 ff.), suggests the independent origin of several of these legends. The Coptic version is presented by Amélineau (1888, 165–69) in French translation, under the title "Historie du roi Armenien." Amélineau, unfamiliar with the legend of Saint Gregory, compares it only to the Oedipus legend. In the conclusion of his dissertation on the origins of Hartmann's version, Lippold (1896, 50–64) argues that the legend derives from two late Greek versions of the Oedipus legend in which patricide is absent. This is by no means a proof of borrowing. A psychological analysis of Gregory's killing the man who uses violence in his suit for the hand of the princess easily identifies this as a substitute for patricide. This also lies behind the killing of the heathen king in the legend related by Kostomarov.

As Köhler relates in *Germania* (1870, 284–91), the legend of Saint Gregory was also dramatized by a Spanish playwright of the seventeenth century, Juan de Matos Fragoso. The drama is called *El marido de su madre*

[The husband of his mother]. In this work Gregorio is the son of Prince Carlos of Antioch and his sister Rosaura. Carlos has taken Rosaura by force and has then secretly left the country. Rosaura brings a boy into the world. Soon after his birth, she exposes him in a chest in the river that flows through her park. The chest is carried into the sea. A farmer, Enrique, notices it, has it brought ashore, and raises the boy as his own son. Once, in anger, Enrique reveals that Gregorio is only a foundling. As proof, he gives him the tablet found with him, stating that he is the son of an unhappy mother and a traitorous father. In the meantime, the duke of Tyre has attacked Rosaura's country, for she has rejected his suit. Gregorio, who has left his foster father, takes up service under Rosaura, becomes a general in the army, and conquers the duke. The people wish for the marriage of Rosaura and Gregorio. Shortly before, Carlos, still passionately in love with his sister, arrives at Rosaura's court disguised as a certain Gerardo. Noting the resemblance, however, Rosaura suspects that he is her brother. Therefore, on their wedding day, she tells Gregorio that she has promised not to marry before she receives news of her brother. Until then they will be married in the eyes of the world only, but not in reality. Gregorio is satisfied with this. During the night the captured duke of Tyre, released by a lady of Rosaura's court, attempts to murder "Gerardo," but Carlos calls for help in time. Half dressed, Gregorio emerges from his bedchamber. Rosaura notices the tablet hanging from his neck and thus realizes his identity. Still she does not reveal who she is, saying only that she cannot marry a foundling. Gregorio then leaves Antioch secretly to become a hermit in the wild mountains of Syria. In the last act, Enrique meets Gregorio without recognizing him and reveals to him an important defense secret. Rosaura also goes to the mountains to see the holy man, and finally a priest arrives, telling him that a voice from heaven has declared him patriarch of Antioch. Enrique discovers that Carlos is not the blood brother of Rosaura but had been secretly adopted by her parents, who wanted a male heir. After this revelation, Gerardo/Carlos, in Rosaura's retinue, reveals his identity, and Rosaura offers him her hand in marriage. The hermit says that she is already married to Gregorio, however. Then Rosaura realizes that Gregorio is her son by Carlos: Gregorio reveals his identity after an angel hands him the patriarch's staff.

In this drama, defense against incestuous tendencies is revealed especially clearly. The son does indeed marry the mother, but sexual relations do not occur (cf. the myth of Auge and Telephus). Instead, the wedding is completed only in a ceremonial sense. However, sibling marriage is made possible by the opposite mechanism; incest has already occurred, and defense is effected through the revelation that the two are not siblings. This carrying out the deed with simultaneous defense against it is typical of dramatic portrayals of the incest fantasy (cf. Goethe's *Die Geschwister* [The siblings]).

To the legend of Saint Gregory are related several Italian works. There is a short folk poem published in 1806 ("Tre pellegrini" [Three pilgrims]), whose plot begins in Turin. There is a folktale from Sicily, recorded in our day and presumably derived from the legend of Saint Gregory, as suggested by the name of the hero, Crivolio (Gonzenbach 1870, 159). Here the plot is shifted to a bourgeois sphere; knightly service has no place. The monastery, the abbot, and other details are also absent. In both tales, though, the father remains alive, participating in both penance and forgiveness. Hermann Knust (1866) also relates a Tuscan version. To avoid dividing their inheritance, brother and sister decide to remain unmarried. They take up an incestuous relationship with one another. The father throws the son born of this union into the river. The little box with the child drifts ashore and is found by a rich man who has the boy raised along with his own son. At one point this actual son reveals that the boy is a foundling. Thereupon the boy decides to go out into the world to search for his parents. "During this trip he is taken in as a beggar boy by his true parents, who do not realize his identity, and when he has grown, the father himself, who wishes to abandon his sinful relationship with his sister, brings about the young man's marriage to his mother. Only too late, from a lock of red hair, does the mother recognize her son." After everything has been revealed to him, he withdraws to the desert to do penance. He stays there two years, is then elected pope, and announces that he will absolve all who come to him. The parents come to him; he hears their confession and then reveals that he is their son. They finally die united.

In this interesting version, patricide is replaced by the son's naive fantasy wish that his father relinquish the mother to him of his own free will. We have already recognized this as the dampened form of the theme of relinquishment of the bride.

The Bulgarian legend of Paul of Caesarea, reported by Köhler in *Germania* (1870, 284 ff.) and originally appearing in a seventeenth-century manuscript, is related to the Gregorius legend. Here brother and sister decide to live as man and wife, just as in the previous legend. The reason is clear: it would be undesirable for another man to acquire the sister and, with her, half the kingdom. "The brother took the sister and they had a son, saying: 'It is not proper to keep the child, since it is born to brother and sister.'" They expose the child; he is found and brought to King Herod, who adopts him. "And the mother discovered that there was a young king in that country, and she did not know that it was her son. She sent him a letter asking him to marry her. And he celebrated his engagement to his mother and took her to be his queen, and became king in the city of Caesarea." However, he then discovers the circumstances of his birth from a letter his parents had once written, which he receives from his foster father. He also discovers the secret of his marriage and becomes despondent. "And from then on he no longer approached his mother, and the queen wondered why he no longer visited her bed." Paul then goes to see John Chrysostom and tells him everything. John assigns him a penance. He is bound hand and foot to a column standing in the water. John throws the key that opens the lock into the sea, saying: "He will be forgiven when the key reappears." In the end, the key is found by a fisherman; Paul's sins are forgiven.

The form of double incest we have observed thus far—conscious incest between brother and sister and the marriage of their son and his mother, ignorant of each other's identity—did not suffice for the elaborate fantasy life of the Christian Middle Ages. The desire for intensification of sinful atrocities led to the first incest between father and daughter. The son's mother is also the sister, and double incest occurs with the same person: doubling, as observed in the other variants, is no longer required. This original relationship is dealt with in "Historia Albani martyris" [Story of Saint Alban the martyr], related by Haupt (1860). The story is found in a Roman manuscript. Alban, born of a union between father and daughter, is exposed by his parents and raised by the king of Hungary. As a youth, he is married by his own father, unaware of his identity, to his own mother—also his sister. For some years he lives with her happily married, until the incestuous abominations are discovered. In penance, all three go separately into the desert, where they remain for seven years. After this period they reunite. They must spend the night in the forest, and the son prepares a bed of leaves on the ground for his father and his mother (who is also his wife and his sister). He himself keeps watch from a tree. Then, says the legend, the devil rekindles the flame of criminal passion in the old father, and when the night has almost passed, the father again sleeps with his daughter. The son sees this from the tree, hurries up to them, and kills his shameless parents with his staff. He covers their bodies with leaves.

Concerning the unusual conclusion of the Alban legend, for which there is no parallel in any of the other legends, a few comments are appropriate. In the second portion of the legend, all the crimes are consciously committed. The son consciously kills his father when he catches him once again engaged in conscious incest with the daughter, Alban's wife. That the son kills the father during sexual relations with his mother (or immediately thereafter) is already familiar to us (cf. the myth of Cronus), and we will observe it again in several cases (with Saint Julian, in a special form). Here the infantile origins of jealousy are clearly emphasized. The child, who loves the mother, hates his father, who possesses the mother and stands between her and the son. In his unconscious fantasies, the boy puts himself in the father's place. He wishes to play the father in order to possess the mother. This infantile wish is actually realized, for father and son really possess the same woman, the son's mother. The child's overhearing the marital relations of his parents is also expressed here in a very naive form. Since the son is no child here, but a grown man, the infantile wish for sexual relations with the mother and the elimination of the father becomes fact. That the son also kills the mother here is related to his also possessing her earlier. Indeed, in the Ukrainian tale too he kills the mother after the incest is discovered. In addition, killing the mother is justified by jealousy, as with Orestes: the son kills his mother because she gives herself to his competitor (his father) and not to him. This wish must be gratified in his unconscious.

There are also many versions and adaptations of the Alban legend. In *Germania,* Reinhold Köhler (1870) provides some information on these legends. He notes, inter alia, that two fragments of a twelfth-century poem from the lower Rhine dealing with this legend were published by Lachmann in *Abhandlungen der Berliner Akademie.* In *Serapeum* (1868, 99), Johann Kelle also published the introductory words of some tales from the Fürstenberg manuscript of the Latin *Gesta Romanorum;* these tales are absent in the published Latin version. The eleventh of these tales concerns the legend of Saint Alban. Constans (1881, 118) remarks that in *Gesta Romanorum* he came across a tale (no. 244) that for the most part contained the details related in "Vie de Saint Albin." The only discrepancy is that in the *Gesta* the second portion of the legend, concerning the conscious crimes, is appended (cf. the discussion above). Thus, in the other versions the conclusion of the legend is absent. Karl Greith (1838, 159) has also published a version from a fourteenth-century manuscript in the Vatican library. Here mother and son separate after the incest is discovered and end their days in penance. Further information concerning the various versions is provided by Constans (1881, 114–15) and D'Ancona (1869, 25–26).

The legend was translated into German by Albrecht von Eyb and appears at the end of his *Ob einem manne sei zu nemen ein elich weibe oder nit* [Whether a man should take a wife or not] (1472, 108b–115). Andreas Kurzmann has also translated the legend into German (1897). There are two French translations. In his *Bibliothèque* [Library], Antoine du Verdier (1585, 103) published "La vie de Monsieur Sainct Albain Roy de Hongrie et Martyre," an undated tale of Parisian origin. In *Manuel du libraire* [Bookseller's handbook] Jacques-Charles Brunet (1860–65, vol. 5) published "Vie de Monseigneur Saint Albain Roy de Hongrie," which originated in Lyons in 1483. Raimon Ferraut's Provençal version (before 1300), "Cell que volc romanzar la vida Sant Alban," has been lost. Köhler is also of the opinion that there must have been an old Spanish version too, but he is unaware of publication data. Durán did publish a popular romance in *Romancero general* (1851, nos. 1302, 1303) concerning the life of Saint Alban, but there are discrepancies with respect to the Latin original. In this romance, Alban's father is Hisano, one of the eight princes of the kingdom of Hungary. During the night he takes advantage of his beautiful daughter, threatening her with death if she does not submit (conscious incest). King Albano of Hungary finds the exposed child and raises him as his own son. When the young Alban is twenty, the king tells the eight princes to send him pictures of their daughters, which he shows to his son. The son falls in love with the picture of Hisano's daughter, his own mother, and marries her. In his choosing the unrecognized mother, the power of incestuous affection is illustrated very well. Subsequent events are identical to those of the Latin version, related above, and the conclusion is retained. Finally, Köhler cites a modern Spanish book of folk material containing a prose version of the romance. Durán mentions that the legend is still very popular in Spain. A contemporary folk song of Lower Brittany also deals with material related to the Alban and Andreas legends in an edifying manner, and not without poetic charm (Quélen 1868, 88 ff.).

Following our discussion of Saint Alban, it is appropriate to discuss the legend of Saint Julian the Hospitaler. Surprisingly, he is called the "Catholic Oedipus," though in this tale the incest fantasy is concealed beneath a layer of repression that can be penetrated only by comparing this legend with that of Saint Alban. The story is found under the title "Von der Sünden Vergebung" [On the forgiveness of sins] (*Gesta Romanorum*, chap. 18 in Grässe's German edition, 1905, 3rd ed., Leipzig):

> Once there was a warrior named Julian who was destined unwittingly to kill his parents. One day, while this noble young man was stalking a buck, it suddenly turned to him and said: "You, who are pursuing me, will be the murderer of your father and mother." When Julian heard this, he was very much afraid that the buck's prediction would come true. Therefore he left his family, traveled far away, and came to a distant region where he entered the service of a prince. Here he conducted himself so well, both in battle and in the palace, that the prince made him his military commander. He gave him the widow of a castellan in marriage, and as a dowry Julian received her castle. However, Julian's parents, saddened by the loss of their son, had been wandering everywhere searching for him. Finally they arrived at the castle. Julian's wife noticed them, and since he was not at home, she asked them who they were. They told her the story of their son,

and since she had often heard these things from her husband, she realized that they were his parents. Thus she received them both cordially, and out of love for her husband, she let them use her own bed, having a bed made elsewhere for herself. In the morning, Julian's wife went to church; Julian entered her bedchamber to awaken her. But when he saw two people lying together in her bed, he assumed that they were his wife and a lover. Silently, he drew his sword and slew them both together. But when he went outside, he was surprised to see his wife coming toward him. He asked her who the people sleeping in her bed were. She said: "They are your parents, who have sought after you for so long. I let them sleep in our bedchamber." When he heard this, he fell to the ground and nearly died of fright. He began to weep bitterly, saying: "Woe is me. What shall I do? I have killed my dear parents. For the buck's words have come true. I wanted to go away from them, and in so doing, I have brought about their death. Now farewell, sweet sister, for I shall rest no more until I know whether God has accepted my repentance." But she said to him: "Dear brother, may it never happen that you leave me and depart without me. Since I have shared your joys, I also wish to share your sorrows." Then they built a hospice. On one occasion, they took in a man who revealed himself to be a divine messenger. He told them that the Lord had forgiven Julian and that shortly they would both die blessedly.

In the legend "Sanctus Julianus Hospitator" we have an excellent example of how the sexual origin of the theme of a legend can become gradually obscured while other themes, such as that of the sinner and of divine grace, are emphasized, annihilating the deeper meaning of the original theme except for some faint traces. The whole presentation of the legend, typical for the incest complex, leads us to suspect that incestuous impulses underlie the killing of Julian's parents, though he is unaware of their identity. Though neither desire for the mother nor hatred of the father is mentioned in the legend of Julian, one detail—apparently unimportant and coincidental, but actually very significant and strictly determinate—clearly reveals the connection with the sexual. This is the peculiar way the parents are killed. The tale states that Julian kills them both together with his sword. In the legend of Saint Alban, however, we have already come across a similar situation emphasizing the sexual relations of the parents. The only difference here is that the son, Julian, has never had the mother. Here this wish is repressed. Still, the more complete motivation for Alban's similar killing of his parents reveals the theme of mother incest, repressed in the legend of Saint Julian. Further, another hint leads to the same conclusion. In the legend of Alban, where incest with the mother actually occurs, the woman whom father and son have both had is, of course, the same person. In the legend of Julian, in defense against incestuous impulses, the father's love and the son's love are distributed to two women; a doublet is introduced. But the unity of the two women, wished for by the son, is still revealed in that in his unconscious, his mother takes his wife's place (in the marriage bed). Sexual relations with the mother have been dampened to a simple association of mother and wife. This unconscious fantasy, however, calls for the corresponding physical reactions, expressed as a tendency for punishment: since his unconscious wish is to possess his father's wife (his mother), the love affair of his wife with another man now arises as a punishment fantasy. Indeed, that the other man is his father is clearly indicated in the story itself, although this is known to Julian only unconsciously. Thus he does not recognize his father. This nonrecognition of the father, though, is a typical expression of repression in connection with the death blow (cf. Oedipus). It is a defense mechanism against incestuous feelings of jealous hatred. Still, the deeper motivation for Julian's punishment fantasy concerning his wife's sexual relations with his father is actually found in an infantile impulse: the father, who is now taking Julian's wife from him, has already taken from him the beloved woman, his mother, once before, when Julian's incestuous affection was awakening (abduction of the bride). Here, as with a neurotic symptom, the unconscious impulses are distorted, appearing only in a repressed form as defense mechanisms. The actual drives remain unconscious. This is most clearly demonstrated by comparing the legends of Julian and Alban: things that remain unconscious fantasies in the former appear as conscious deeds in the latter. Alban consciously kills his father, whereas Julian kills him in the belief that he is killing his competitor for the love of his wife (mother). Alban has really had his mother, whereas Julian only associates her unconsciously with his wife. In the end, Alban consciously kills his mother out of jealousy, because of her relations with his father. Julian kills her in the belief that he is killing his "wife" for her infidelity. Thus, based on his infantile perspective, Julian identifies his parents' marriage with his own. In Julian incest is incompletely repressed, expressing itself (unconsciously) in jealous fantasies associated with his own wife. Still, the son's observation of the parents' sexual relations is common to both legends. The only difference is that with Alban the whole impression, as well as the murder, is conscious, whereas with Julian it is unconscious (displaced). Here we see the typical distinction between the murderer who consciously murders the person for whom he feels sexual hatred and the murderer who resists and represses his hatred, displacing it to another person.

The legend of Saint Julian has also been dramatized. Lope de Vega treated it in his legendary *comedia El animal profeta y dichoso parricida San Julian* [The prophetic animal and the blessed patricide Saint Julian].

Wurzbach (1899) considers this one of Lope's best dramas. He summarizes the plot as follows: A buck prophesies to the future saint, who has brought it down in the hunt, that he will kill his parents. Thinking that he has caught his wife with a lover, he fulfills the frightful prophecy and kills his father and mother. He does penance for his sin by devoting his life to the care of the sick, and finally he sees his parents freed from purgatory and received into heaven. Lope's incestuous tendencies are also noted elsewhere. His famous contemporary, Doctor Antonio Mira de Amescua (1578–1635 [1644]) is also supposed to have written a drama *El animal profeta y San Julian* (Schaeffer 1890). Note that the legend of Saint Julian is further dealt with in two Spanish romances (Durán 1851, 2:332 ff.). Much of the incest material adopted by Spanish dramatists originates in old popular ballads.

Finally, in his masterly novella *Saint Julien l'hospitalier,* Gustave Flaubert intensifies the material psychologically—one would almost say psychoanalytically. He treats the material artistically and in a technically consummate manner. Here the buck's prophecy becomes Julian's own tormenting delusion: "The prophecy tormented him; he resisted it: 'No, no, no, I cannot kill them.' But then he thought: '*But if it were my wish . . . ?*' and he feared that the devil would plant in him this desire." As a consequence of this psychic conflict, he becomes ill. "For three months, his mother prayed with fear and anxiety at the head of his bed, and his father walked incessantly about the house, sighing. He employed the most famous doctors, who prescribed numerous medications. . . . When Julian had fully recovered, he obstinately refused to hunt." (Rejection of the use of arms.) His fear intensifies to a delusion expressing itself symptomatically. "One day a saber given to him by his father slipped from his fingers, coming so close to the old man that it cut his overcoat. Believing he had killed his father, Julian fainted. He paled at the sight of drawn swords." "On another occasion he cast his spear in the direction of two white, flapping wings, thinking he had seen a stork. He heard a piercing cry. It was his mother, whose long-brimmed head covering was now pinned to the wall. Julian fled from the castle, never to return."

The author motivates Julian's thirst for murder with the sadistic impulses of the child, who had originally been pampered, "whose little bed was stuffed with the finest down." After the deed, in repentant humiliation, he "prepared a penance shirt with iron spikes." He wishes to punish himself, for he still dreams of killing his parents. "Every evening the sun poured blood into the clouds, and every night, in his dreams, the murder of his parents was repeated." This is comprehensible if one reads the author's description of Julian's sadistic pleasure in killing. He depicts Julian strangling a dove while feeling deep pleasure, and he pictures the murder of the parents, arising from infantile jealousy, in a similar manner: "A man sleeping beside his wife ⟨mother⟩. Overcome by unbounded anger, he fell on them with stabs of his dagger, stamping and frothing and bellowing like a buck."

The intensification of the incestuous abuses through the double relationship of mother and son is also found in the Italian legend "Vergogna from the Kingdom of Faragona," extant in poetic and prose versions of the fourteenth and fifteenth centuries (cf. D'Ancona, Constans, Diederichs). Here too the first incest occurs between father and daughter; the second occurrence is between the fruit of this union and the mother. After their life of repentance and holiness, the pope commands that mother and son be buried together in one grave. He has an inscription made for them that the editor says can still be seen in the monastery of Santa Presidia. It reads: "Here lie two bodies, mother and son, brother and sister, wife and husband, nobly born of the realm of Faragona, and they are in paradise." Constans (1881, 120) comments:

> Here is a very precise detail that seems to indicate that we are dealing not with a purely imaginary legend, but with an actual fact. But this epitaph is found in many other places, always in the context of an appropriate tradition; this eliminates all possibility of authenticity. Julian Medrano, a Spanish writer of the sixteenth century, also claims to have seen near Bourbon the home where this is supposed to have occurred and to have read the following inscription on the two spouses' tomb:
>
> Here lies the daughter, here lies the father,
> Here lies the sister, here lies the brother,
> Here lie the wife and the husband;
> Still, only two lie buried here.
>
> [Cf. Dunlop 1814, 209]

Millin (1790–99, vol. 3, chap. 28, p. 6) claims to have read a very similar inscription in the college church of Ecouis, where tradition held that one of the lords of Ecouis lay buried with his daughter Cécile, born to him of his own wife without his knowledge, and whom he later married in Lorraine, unaware that she was his daughter. The legend does not state how her identity came to light. A similar story, according to Millin and many others, was told at Arlincourt, near Amiens, where the same epitaph was seen. In the seventeenth century Gaspard Meturas (*Hortus epitaphorum selectorum* [Collection of selected epitaphs]) reproduced the epitaph and claimed it could be found in a church of Clermont, in Auvergne [cf. Margaret of Navarre, *Heptameron,* 2:449, and D'Ancona 1869, 45]). These are not the only testimonies we could cite. With Mone (1833) and D'Ancona, we are inclined to see here nothing but a product of fancy and to count this epitaph among the enigmas of genealogy.

Such an inscription is found also in a story (*Anthropophyteia,* 3:65) in which the son has relations with his unrecognized mother and then marries the daughter born of this union, also unaware of her identity. Her epitaph reads:

> Here lie buried:
> The brother with his sister,
> The wife with her husband,
> The father with his child.

An interesting form of double incest (father-daughter, son-mother) is found in a Cypriot folktale first published by Sakellarios (1868, 147 ff.) and also related by Schmidt (1877, 249). A man has three daughters, whom he cannot marry off. Since he lives on the seashore, in a place where ships moor, he affixes the pictures of his three daughters to the door of his house to attract suitors. A captain appears who wishes to marry the youngest of the three daughters, Rosa, and indeed he receives her hand in marriage. But on the night of the wedding, when he is about to go to bed, a ghost appears to him telling him to keep away from his wife, for she is destined to bear a son to her father and later to marry the son. Then the captain asks for the eldest daughter and receives her hand in marriage. The same thing happens to another man, who also relinquishes Rosa and marries her second sister. A short while later, Rosa asks the eldest sister to let her take her place in bed with her husband for one night. The sister refuses, and Rosa discovers the reason for this rejection. Then she goes to her second sister and asks the same favor, also without success. Finally she decides to eliminate her father in order to prevent the fulfillment of the prophecy. She has him killed by peasants. That this killing is only a representation of unsuccessful defense against incestuous affection between father and daughter is revealed in two details. First, Rosa remains unmarried (fixation on the father). Second, in the continuation of the story, she does become pregnant by her father, albeit through a miraculous conception, and brings into the world a son who then marries her. On the grave of the father, buried in a distant land, there grows an apple tree. The daughter eats the fruit of this tree without knowing its origin and thus becomes pregnant. The same *conceptio oralis* is found in the Attis myth and is typical as a defense against incest with the father. When Rosa hears that an apple tree stands on her father's grave, she guesses how she became pregnant and decides to kill the child as soon as it is born. Upon his birth, she stabs him several times in the chest and places him in a little box, which she throws into the sea. The boy is found and raised by a sea captain. During his journeys the boy, who is carrying on his foster father's business, comes to his mother's country. He hears the story of the three sisters, marries one, his mother, and sires children by her. The scars on his breast reveal his identity. Rosa, seeing that the prophecy has been fulfilled, jumps from the roof and is killed.

Besides this form of double incest, a second variant also occurs. Just as the son born of the incest of father and daughter marries his mother in the earlier versions, here mother and son are first united, and the daughter born of this incest marries her father (who is also her brother). Constans (1881, 125) considers this version of the tale to be the more popular one.

Margaret of Navarre's story (in *Heptameron,* vol. 2) in which a young man unknowingly marries the daughter he has sired by his mother is well known. "A young gentleman, fourteen or fifteen years old, desiring to sleep with one of his mother's ladies, slept with his mother herself. In nine months she bore a daughter sired by her son. Twelve or thirteen years later, unaware that she was his daughter and sister, and she unaware that he was her father and brother, he married her." The Italian Bandello, unfamiliar with this account, relates the same story. Constans (1881, 124) also mentions Brevio (1545). All the authors relate the account as though it were fact. The first two place it during the reign of Louis XII, at the court of Jean d'Albert and Catherine of Navarre. Brevio places the story in Venice, shortly before he recorded it. Horace Walpole—who, as he claimed, knew neither the account of Margaret of Navarre nor that of Bandello—dealt with the same material in his drama *The Mysterious Mother.* He maintained that in childhood he had heard it said that a lady had asked Archbishop Tillotson for advice, for she had borne a daughter by her own son, and her son was now about to marry this daughter without knowing her identity, thus becoming her father, brother, and husband. The archbishop advised her to leave the two in their ignorance.

Constans (1881, 125), following D'Ancona, mentions the novella *La mayor confusión* [The greatest confusion], found in *Sucesos y prodigios de amor* [Events and wonders of love] by Juan Pérez de Montalván, which is probably also independent of the works by Margaret and Bandello. In this version the first incest is not between brother and sister (as with Saint Gregory), but between son and mother, in accordance with the original version. However, in the second occurrence of incest, as a form of defense, the spouses are unaware of their crime. This is true also of the version found in *Bibliographie des ouvrages relatifs à l'amour* in the appendix of a volume entitled *Usage des romans.* Here the great "Barrière," the "Terror of the Turks," unknowingly becomes the father and spouse of his sister. The two spouses are left in ignorance concerning their relationship, which is revealed only after their death. The last examples cited lead directly to the relationship between father and daughter. Owing not only to the wealth of information, but also to its psychological peculiarities, this theme will require a separate discussion.

11 *The Relationship between Father and Daughter in Myth, Folktales, Legends, Literature, Life, and Neurosis*

He's father, son, and husband mild;
I mother, wife, and yet his child.
How they may be, and yet in two,
As you will live, resolve it you.

SHAKESPEARE, *Pericles*

Like the erotic attraction of the son to the mother, the loving interactions of father and daughter are among the typical human impulses that, in the process of cultural development, have been subjected to the same process of repression, leading to the development of similar substitutes in mythological, literary, and neurotic fantasies. Here too, though, the woman appears to be less favored by nature and life than the man. Just as the fantasy creations of the mother complex are presented from the son's perspective, only later being inhibited or dampened by the father, who is uneasy or disturbed in his possession of the mother, the fantasy substitutes created by the father-daughter complex are not presented from the perspective of the young child, the daughter, as one would expect from analogy, but are instead dealt with mainly from the standpoint of the father. Just as the man is the active partner in wooing and in procreation, so too the development of myths and religions, as well as artistic activity, is intended to gratify and justify male sexual fantasies. Even in the few mythological passages in which the loving passion seems to be presented from the viewpoint of the daughter, one has the impression that this is only a justification of the father's shocking desires; an attempt is made to shift the blame for the seduction onto her. In admitting the daughter's purely passive role—used in the service of masculine tendencies—in the incest fantasies of the father, it should be noted that this attraction is by no means one-sided. On the contrary, psychoanalysts first became aware of these matters when in the treatment of neurotic women they recognized repressed childhood attraction to the father, with corresponding jealousy toward the mother, as an etiologically significant factor. In this fact, though, we find valuable evidence for our framework. Whereas the man (father) is able to live out his repressed incestuous impulses toward his daughter in violent and satisfying fantasies, in the woman (daughter), for whom such a solution is not available, the repression of attraction to the father, objectionable in our culture, frequently leads to neurosis.

A second difference with respect to the mother complex is based on the physiological, sociological, and psychological peculiarities of the father-daughter complex. The incest between son and mother, as well as the fantasies that replace it, are considered by consciousness—probably owing first to physiological sensations—as a more serious infraction than a union between father and daughter. The internal, physical blood relationship that unites the son with the mother is of course not present to the same degree in the kinship between father and daughter. In addition, with the mother, the significant age difference usually impedes the realization of the fantasy, whereas the man, sexually potent for a longer time, draws new sexual powers from his blossoming daughter. Third, the father has an authoritative influence over his daughter, a *patriae potestas*, lending more force to whatever impulses and wishes he may have than is possible in the son's subordinate relationship with the mother. Thus it should not surprise us that incest between fathers and daughters (often stepdaughters), especially rape of the daughter, is among the most frequent of sexual crimes. Frequently this relationship, felt to be much less objectionable than that between the son and the mother, appears in the productions of fantasy as conscious incest; this is less frequently true for mother and son. The tendency for repression then asserts itself, just as in real life, in that only one partner (usually the father) appears to be seized by the forbidden passion, while the other partner (usually the daughter) rejects the approach with revulsion or attempts to escape it by fleeing.

In mythology, where conscious incest between father and daughter occurs often enough, repression still occurs, but in an interesting form—that of symbolic disguise. In the Cypriot folktale (Sakellarios 1868, 365), we have already seen the prophesied (wished for) sexual relations of the daughter with the father replaced by the daughter's eating an apple from the tree growing on her father's grave (cf. the phallus growing from the son's grave in the story of Orestes). Especially often, though, in various myths, and with noticeable correspondence to neurotic fantasies, the father unites with the daughter in the form of a snake. Considering the universal phallic significance of the snake, this would appear to be a sexual tautology if it did not represent the remains of an unsuccessful attempt to disguise the act. Thus, according to an Orphic tradition, Zeus is supposed to have united with his daughter in the form of a snake (Roscher 1884–1937). We find the same symbolism in Nordic mythology, where Odin, said to have sired Thor by his own daughter, Jord, proceeds to Gunlod, locked up in the rocks, in the guise of a snake and rests for three days in her arms. The same snake symbolism proved effective in the development of symptoms in the first case of hysteria treated using Josef Breuer's cathartic approach (Miss Anna O.) (Breuer and Freud 1909, 15 ff.). Alfred Adler has also reported occasionally about a patient who said she had been united with her father in the guise of a snake (sometimes a bird). When she drew this act at the request of the doctor, the snake was unambiguously revealed to be a penis symbol. Preuner (1864, 410) cites a similar myth concerning the chastity of the *bona dea:* "In vain, her father sought to overcome her by beating her with myrtle rods, for even when he had made her drunk, she had not yielded to him. Only when he approached her as a snake was he able to rob her of her chastity." Schwartz (1874) also discusses this myth.

One of the most famous classical fables, the tale of Myrrha, also involves the daughter's love for her father. According to Apollodorus, the major details of the myth are as follows. Smyrna or Myrrha is supposed to have been inflamed by Aphrodite with criminal love for her father. With the help of her nursemaid, for twelve nights in succession she was able to trick her father into believing she was another woman. (Lot's daughters also deceived their father.) When he finally recognized his daughter, he pursued her with drawn sword, but Myrrha begged the gods to spare her and was transformed into a tree. Ten months later the tree burst, and Adonis came into the world. Aphrodite was so charmed by his beauty that she hid the child in a box (exposure theme) and secretly gave him to Persephone, who did not wish to give him up until Zeus resolved the conflict between the two goddesses by decreeing that Adonis was to spend one portion of the year with Persephone in the underworld and the other with Aphrodite in the world above. According to Ovid (*Metamorphoses,* 10.435 ff.), after sleeping with her father Myrrha is supposed to have hidden in the forest in shame and to have been transformed there by Aphrodite into the tree from which flows the sweet balsam myrrh. When the father split this tree with his sword, Adonis is supposed to have been born.

Behind this symbolic representation of the tree split by a sword, we easily recognize a disguised representation of coitus, which, apparently inexplicably, occurs in addition to the daughter's seduction of the father. On closer inspection, though, we notice that the symbolic representation concerns only the father's sexual wish and act, clearly referring to the repression of the passion originally attributed to the father. This passion is clearly revealed by the symbolic representation and also by his inimical pursuit of the daughter, in which a rationalized remnant of the original rape of the fleeing and resisting daughter is retained. The same tendency for repression and justification is served by the theme of the father's intoxication (he is possessed by his passion). In a later version (cf. Hyginus, fable 164), it is the daughter herself who makes her father drunk and not, as elsewhere, the servingwomen who empathize with the daughter's desire for love. However, a fable related by Herodotus (2.131) reveals that the daughter was originally made willing and available by the servingwomen, in the service of the father's passions. This fable concerns the golden cow that King Mycerinus of Egypt had made as a grave monument for his beloved daughter, who had died young: "Some tell of this cow and of the colossus; how Mycerinus loved his own daughter and later raped her; thereupon the girl is supposed to have hanged herself in shame, and he buried her inside that cow. But the mother cut off the hands of the servingwomen who had given the daughter over to her father."

Cutting off the hands is typical for this group of myths. Now we can return to the justification of the father's passions in his intoxication and in his seduction by his daughter. This theme, of course, appears again in the biblical account of Lot and his daughters (Gen. 19:30 ff.), who make their father drunk and lie with him for two nights in succession in order to be impregnated by him:

> Later Lot went up from Zoar and began dwelling in the mountainous region, and his two daughters along with him, because he got afraid of dwelling in Zoar. So he began dwelling in a cave, he and his two daughters. And the first-born proceeded to say to the younger woman: "Our father is old and there is not a man in the land to have relations with us according to the way of the whole earth. Come, let us give our father wine to drink and let us lie down with him and preserve offspring from our father." So they kept giving their father wine to drink during that night; then the first-born went in and lay down with her father, but he did not know when she lay down and when she got up. And it came about on the next day that the first-born then said to the younger: "Here I lay down with my father last night. Let us give him wine to drink tonight also. Then you go in, lie down with him, and let us preserve offspring from our father." So they repeatedly gave their father wine to drink during that night also; then the younger got up and lay down with him, but he did not know when she lay down and when she got up. And both the daughters of Lot became pregnant from their father. (Cf. Nyctimene's treatment of her father in Ovid [*Metamorphoses*, 2:589 ff.].)

A continued incest fantasy is found in the Iranian myth in which the father, who has no son, sires a granddaughter by his daughter, a great-granddaughter by his granddaughter, and so forth, for nine or ten generations, until finally the last daughter bears him a son (Lessmann 1908). In the Indic myth, Prajapati takes his daughter Ushas by force (Goldziher 1876, 223). Given these undisguised expressions of the father's passions, repression recalling the Myrrha fable is also observed. According to a Polynesian creation myth (Stucken 1896–1907, 244), Tane sires a daughter whom the people make his wife. When she discovers that she is living with her father as his wife, she flees in shame and kills herself (cf. White 1887–90, 1:131 ff.). Another form of defense is also found in a primitive people. The city of Dsiampa (Cambodia) was destroyed because the king married his own daughter (Bab 1906, 281). The story of Jezdegerd II has the same unhappy ending. He is supposed to have married his own daughter and then to have killed her (Nöldeke 1887, 106).

In "Harpalyce," though, a tale of Parthenius (no. 13), the father is punished. By his wife Epicaste, Clymenus has two sons and a daughter, Harpalyce. She is extremely beautiful, and he falls in love with her. Initially he attempts to master his passion, but later, with the help of her nursemaid, he makes love to her. Soon after, when she has married Alastor, Clymenus pursues them and abducts his daughter to Argos, where he takes her by force in public view. In revenge, she kills her younger brother and serves him to her father as a meal. Upon her request, she is transformed into a bird. Clymenus kills himself on becoming aware of her terrible revenge. Parthenius also tells of Larissa, with whom her father, Piasus, slept before her marriage to Cyricus. Strabo (12.621) adds that Larissa threw him into a wine vat. Thus he atoned for his crime. Of Roman authors, Virgil should still be mentioned. In the *Aeneid* (6.623), he portrays the punishment in Hades of Phlegyas, who raped his daughter before her marriage. We should also mention two poems of Catullus. In one the father sleeps with his married daughter, and in the other he sleeps with his son's wife.

In legends and folktales the father's attraction to the daughter plays a much greater role than in myths, where the son's relationship to father and mother is dominant. The familiar and widespread legend of King Apollonius of Tyre is of ancient origin and underlies Shakespeare's *Pericles*. Presumably the material derives originally from a Greek work of the fifth century, of which a Latin translation is extant. In the Middle Ages the tale was translated into almost all European languages and is attested in numerous manuscripts, editions, and adaptations. In one of these forms it found a place in the *Gesta Romanorum* (no. 153). In 1461 Heinrich Steinhöwel composed a version of this variant in verse, and then it was taken up in books of folk material. In the twelfth century Godfrey of Viterbo included the story in his great chronicle, from which John Gower took it in the fourteenth century, including it in the eighth book of his *Confessio amantis* [Lover's confession] (Brandes 1895–96, 833).

In the following highly abbreviated summary, I follow the *Gesta* and Simrock (1870, vol. 3). King Antiochus Seleucus rules in the city of Antioch. When his beautiful daughter is of marriageable age, his wife dies, leaving her dear child in the father's care. While several suitors seek the hand of the beautiful and virtuous maiden in marriage, the father himself falls so much in love with her that one day he takes her by force. "While he secretly acted as her spouse within his own four bedposts, he thought of a new means to drive away his daughter's suitors in order to enjoy the possession of her undisturbed. Therefore he announced that whoever desired his daughter's hand would have to solve a riddle as proof that he possessed enough wisdom and insight to succeed Antiochus upon his death. Whoever attempted but failed to find the solution was to be beheaded by the sword. He had this written in large letters on the gate." In the *Gesta*, the riddle is as follows: "I am engaged in crimes; I devour my mother's flesh; I sought after my brother and my mother's husband, but I cannot find him." In Simrock, the riddle is this:

> I feed on the flesh of my mother
> And surely, I am my own mother;
> My father is also my son
> And seeks to win my love.
> I am his mother, daughter, and wife;
> But no matter how he caresses me
> The brother still does not appear
> Who would be my son and my grandson.

Many brave princes fall victim to the king's cruelty; to scare off the other suitors, he even has those beheaded who find the solution. Then Apollonius, a mighty king, arrives in Tyre. He discerns the solution of the riddle, suggesting the father's incest with the daughter, but he must then flee from the king, who is all the more embittered. First he lands in Tarsus, where he prevents famine by distributing his provisions. Then, proceeding further, he is shipwrecked and loses all his possessions.

Here an apparent episode from the Oedipus legend is inserted. Apollonius, thrown ashore naked, is fed and clothed by a fisherman, who also shows him the way to the royal palace. At the foot of this road he assists the king while he bathes. The king invites him to the palace, gives him gifts, and serves him food and drink. He tells the king's daughter, Lucina, his story, and she comforts him. Then he marries her; when she is already pregnant, a ship arrives from Tyre with the news that the sinful King Antiochus and his daughter have been struck by lightning and that the city of Antioch has selected him as its king. Apollonius sets sail for Tyre with his wife. On the way, a violent storm arises at sea. The queen gives birth prematurely and lies as though dead. According to the old custom, the captain urges Apollonius to throw her body overboard immediately. A watertight coffin is made and sealed well with pitch so that she will not sink but will be carried ashore by the waves to be buried with royal honors. On the third day the waves bear the coffin to the coast of Ephesus, not far from the home of the doctor Cerimon, who revives the apparently dead woman and consecrates her to the service of Diana.

Apollonius brings the newborn child, who would not have been able to survive a longer voyage, to the city of Tarsus, which he had once saved from famine. He names his daughter Tharsia, after the city, and has her cared for by Stranguilio and his wife, who raise her with their own daughter, Philomancia. The child's nursemaid, Licordis, remains with her. When Tharsia is twelve years old, she learns from her dying nursemaid that she is actually living with foster parents. Since Tharsia is becoming more and more beautiful, while her foster sister recedes into the background, the foster mother decides to kill Tharsia, but the foster father objects. Still, she assigns her servant, Theophilus, to kill the girl. Just as he is about to carry out the deed, she is abducted by pirates so that he is able to claim she is dead. Tharsia is taken to Mytilene, where the mighty king Athanagoras rules. She is put up for sale at the market; the king wishes to buy her, but a procurer, who pays a higher price, obtains her for his brothel. Her first client is the king, but she implores him to spare her and tells him her story. Then the king says: "Your misfortune touches my heart. The same thing could some day happen to my own daughter!" He gives her money and leaves her untouched. The same thing occurs with all her subsequent clients. The procurer is so angry about this, despite his profit, that he orders his servant to deprive her of her virginity by force. But she arouses his pity too and proposes to bring in more money through her talents than through the sale of her body. She sings at the market, asks riddles, and wins great popularity and acceptance.

In the meantime, Apollonius has come to Tarsus to fetch his now grown daughter. When he does not find her, he falls into despair and commands his men to throw him into the sea. With difficulty, his men convince him to change his mind, but he swears never to cut his beard or change his clothes until he has found his daughter. He goes into the lowest hold of the ship, falls to the floor, and forbids anyone to disturb him on pain of death. During the homeward journey, the ship is driven into the harbor of Mytilene. King Athanagoras hears the foreign king's unusual story, and after attempting in vain to comfort the unhappy father, it occurs to him to send the talented Tharsia on board to cheer him up. There, she sings:

> I must live in the house of shame
> But I am chaste and pure.
> . . . .
> The water is my fatherland.
> My father I have never known,
> But his name is known far and wide.
> God grant that I see him!

Apollonius tells her to leave him, and she promises to go if he can solve the three riddles she asks. The first riddle deals with a house, and the solution is water; the second riddle concerns a giant—the ship's mast. The third riddle, surely the principal and most significant one, is associated through its unambiguous sexual symbolism with the riddle of Antiochus. (The solution is a ball.)

> Smooth outside, rough inside,
> They pound coarse hair into my maw
> Until I'm full as full can be.
> They give me many a hard blow
> So I go soaring up and down.

"Then she sat down on his lap and kissed his lips tenderly, attempting to comfort him. She embraced him, and did not wish to leave him." He pushes her away so that she is wounded in the forehead. Then she laments her fate, which has brought her ill fortune since childhood; but while she is telling her story, Apollonius recognizes her as his daughter. King Athanagoras asks for her hand in marriage, since he had spared her virginity before and has reunited her with her father. Apollonius consents and is then instructed in a dream to look for his wife Lucina in the temple of Diana in Ephesus. "She was still as beautiful as eighteen years before; the pure service of Diana had preserved her freshness so that she was the most radiant of the virgins." Then the spouses recognize one another and are reunited, and various persons involved in their fate are rewarded or punished.

In this highly complicated and multiply elaborated legend we recognize the late product of the repression of an earlier thematic core. This is still fully preserved in the introductory episode concerning the incest of King Antiochus with his daughter. But in the discovery of Apollonius's daughter and her liberation from the brothel, the theme has already been transformed to the sentimental. A psychological understanding of other tales constructed according to the same schema makes it clear that the romantic and improbable themes of the exposure of mother and child and the abduction by pirates, and so on, were introduced because of a single tendency—the tendency to bring the unrecognized father and daughter together, leading to their mutual recognition. And we can quickly conclude, as suggested by the multiple doublets in the legend, that the nonrecognition of the daughter was originally intended to make incest possible between the unrecognized parties; in the underlying story of Antiochus, this still occurs consciously. If this were not the case, there would be no explanation for why Apollonius waits eighteen years, until his daughter is of marriageable age, before seeking her out. In the same way, the original Antiochus story states that his wife died just when the daughter had reached the age of marriage. Here, we notice, as in the Griselda legend, the persistent tendency for the father to wait until his daughter is of marriageable age and then to take her up in the place of the old and now unattractive mother. In the Griselda legend this occurs directly through the father's marriage with his own daughter, which in attested versions has already been reduced to a pseudomarriage with the rationalized purpose of testing the fidelity of the first wife, whom he then, as though in the daughter's place, also marries a second time.

In the Apollonius legend, however, it is very clear that we are basically dealing with the replacement of the aged mother by her youthful image, her daughter. This is shown in that Apollonius, who now must renounce marriage with his daughter, at least gets back his wife as young as she was eighteen years before, at the time of their daughter's birth. He then marries her again (in the daughter's place). (Consider the opposite situation, the aging statue in Shakespeare's *The Winter's Tale,* behind which the father's love for his daughter also lies.) Based on our assumption that in the second part of the story, the Apollonius legend, undisguised incest with the daughter is preserved just as in the earlier story, only in a more distorted and dampened form, we recognize in this desire for daughter incest—desperately maintained despite the tendency for repression—the reason for the disjoining and doubling of the original, simple core legend. As I have demonstrated in a similar manner for the Cyrus story, all the king and daughter characters prove to be doublets of the pair originally living in an incestuous union. Apollonius is identified with the king of Antioch in that after the latter is eliminated, he becomes his successor. Just as King Antiochus gives the suitors a riddle, at the end of the story Apollonius, like a suitor (unknowingly) of his daughter, must also solve a riddle. In the same way King Athanagoras, who in the brothel treats Tharsia like his own daughter and thus spares her, proves to be a doublet of

Apollonius, who can no longer possess his daughter either, yet does marry her in the guise of Athanagoras. That the Apollonius story derives from the tendency for marriage with the unrecognized daughter is also revealed, finally, in the third doublet of the father-daughter pair—in King Archistrates and his daughter Lucina, who marries Apollonius without his having told her his name or origin (cf. Lohengrin). Thus she marries him unknown, just as he would wish to marry his daughter. As soon as he tells her his name and becomes the successor of Antiochus—that is, as soon as he recognizes that he is living incestuously, as did his predecessor—there occurs the exposure of his wife, thought dead. Indeed, in the conclusion, at the time of the second marriage, she is once again identified with the daughter. Just as with the wife's exposure, there are also multiple doublets of the daughter's rescue from danger, all for the sole purpose of making marriage with the unrecognized daughter possible. She escapes from the servant who has been ordered by the "stepmother" to kill her, as well as from the servant in the brothel who has been ordered to deprive her of her virginity. Here we recognize that her foster parents (as in a typical family romance) are actually no more than a doublet of her own parents. It is the father who opposes the killing (exposure) planned by the mother; this seems like a distant echo of the original tendencies.

Here we should point out that the mother's death when her daughter reaches marriageable age not only is an expression of the father's wish to exchange his spouse for his daughter but, as Riklin points out (1908), also corresponds to the jealous wish of the daughter, who wishes to take her mother's place with the father (identification). Then the father's second marriage, which brings a stepmother into the home, also represents for the daughter a substitute gratification for the unrealizable incest wish; similarly for the father, the second marriage substitutes a young spouse for the daughter. This is clearly shown by the folktales, to be discussed below, in which the father, after a long search, still finds no substitute for his dead wife but instead decides to marry his daughter. Finally, the brothel fantasy should be emphasized as a psychologically meaningful and interesting element of the Apollonius legend. This element is found in the unconscious fantasy life of many individuals, and in female neurosis almost always. It expresses, on the one hand, the father's wish for easy and guiltless access to his daughter (cf. her attempt to seduce him in the Apollonius story) and corresponds to the son's fantasy of the mother as a whore. On the other hand, given certain psychoanalytical discoveries, one must derive this fantasy from the daughter's psychic relationship to the father. Based on my experience, I would say this is the crux of an understanding of the psychology of prostitution.

Here, though, we must continue without demonstrating this interesting connection through appropriate material. Rather, in a purely schematic fashion, and in connection with the son's fixation on his mother, a type of love precisely described by Freud, we shall sketch the corresponding female type—the fixation of the daughter on her father. In their love life, such young women show the following patterns, sometimes complemented by opposing characteristics, given the corresponding outcome of repression:

1. They are attracted to older, established men from whom they gladly accept financial support, as if from the father. This usually leads to a mild form of prostitution.

2. They prefer strong, energetic, robust men who are their intellectual and social superiors and who patronize, protect, and defend them.

3. Like the son in the corresponding fixation, they are faithful, loving one man only, or else they represent the pure prostitute type who, in going from man to man, continually realizes in disappointment the irreplaceability of the beloved father. Even when they wish to be faithful, their unconscious perspective, which in the loved one sees only the father, often brings them to dissolve the relationship, intolerable in the long run. That is, they usually love "unhappily," following the example of their first attraction.

4. They like to deprive other women of their husbands or lovers. This can be attributed to jealous rivalry with the mother and appears to be a specific condition for love.

5. Either they want to have no children, since they themselves, through identification, represent both mother and child, or they wish for a child without coitus. Sadger (1909a, 24) has analyzed this as an extension of the actually forbidden sexual relations with the father.

6. The woman directly becomes a prostitute. The incipient tendency for this is already found in many of these traits. Thus she avenges herself because she cannot have a certain lover by taking all lovers. She seeks to realize her incest fantasy in another form of "censured" intercourse. That in doing so she can also play the "mother" with respect to the man has its solid psychological basis, since she truly does identify with her mother, in whom, like the son, she originally saw a whore seducing the adored father.

That the father in the story of Apollonius saves the daughter from the brothel with her virginity intact corresponds fully to the son's rescue fantasy, which again honors as a saint the mother, who had been degraded to a whore (cf. Freud's characterization). Here the ideal image of the virginal mother establishes itself. This image is common to the son, who loves his mother, and to the daughter, who wishes to have a child by her father without the rejected sexual union.

The fable underlying *The Winter's Tale,* one of Shakespeare's last dramas, fully corresponds to the schema found in the Apollonius fable. As one might suspect, we observe the same tendencies and the same repressions opposing them. Leontes, the king of Sicily, suspects his beautiful and chaste wife Hermione of adultery with his friend in youth, King Polyxenes of Bohemia. He therefore commands that her newborn daughter be exposed. The child is saved and returns to her father's palace as the bride of Polyxenes' son, Florizel. She is joyously received by her father, who has been enlightened as to the unfounded nature of his suspicions.

As in the Griselda fable, this second marriage with the wife, believed (wished) dead, is only a substitute for marriage with the daughter. This is directly seen in the work Shakespeare employed as his source. This is the much-read novel of Robert Greene (1588) titled *Pandosto: The Triumph of Time*. Here we can easily grasp the work of repression, which dampens the fantasy of marriage with the unrecognized daughter to a second marriage with one's own spouse. The wife, believed dead, does not retain her youthful appearance, as in the story of Apollonius. On the contrary, when her husband catches sight of her true-to-life statue, he is amazed at her aged appearance. This is another result of repression that opposes the unconscious tendency for a second marriage. It is instructive to observe in various examples how echoes of the original motivation are still preserved in Shakespeare's drama. This is especially true of the resemblance of mother and daughter, which is typical for the whole father-daughter complex, and which reveals that the second marriage indeed constitutes the replacement of the aging wife by the blossoming daughter. Leontes promises not to marry "Unless another, / As like Hermione as is her picture, / Affront his eye." After he recognizes Perdita as his own daughter, he cries out: "Oh, thy mother, thy mother!" And just as he sees in Perdita the rejuvenated image of his wife, he sees in her husband, Florizel, his own rejuvenated image (or that of his brother-double Polyxenes). He says to him:

> Your mother was most true to wedlock, Prince,
> For she did print your royal father off,
> Conceiving you. Were I but twenty-one,
> Your father's image is so hit in you,
> His very air, that I should call you brother,
> As I did him.

And when Polyxenes does not wish to permit Florizel to marry the shepherdess Perdita, Florizel asks Leontes to exert his influence, for his friend, King Polyxenes, can refuse him nothing. Then Leontes says jokingly, but revealing the deepest theme of the material: "Would he do so, I'd beg your precious mistress."

John Webster's tragedy *The Thracian Wonder* involves the same requisite elements—exposure and the interval of time. Pheander, the king of

Thrace, has his daughter, who has just given birth, exposed along with her child and her lover. Without recognizing each other, the lovers live in the same area, dressed as shepherds. When fourteen years have passed, King Pheander visits the region. He falls in love with the shepherdess and leads her away to sire a prince by her. But before the incest occurs, he discovers that she is his daughter, and everything is happily resolved (cf. Bodenstedt 1858–60, vol. 1).

Before further analyzing the father-daughter theme in the richly developed world of medieval legends and folktales, let us consider programmatically a derivative of the theme, so widespread in the myths and adaptations of all times and peoples that we must include here a brief description of its basic elements. In the Apollonius legend, to keep the suitors from his daughter the father poses a riddle. For the suitors, solving it proves just as fatal as not solving it. In other cases, though, this has been replaced by a difficult, fatal task—often a direct struggle with the father. The father, who does not want to relinquish his daughter to any of the suitors and therefore sets up nearly impossible conditions, does this, as the Apollonius legend reveals, because he wishes no one else to have her; ultimately, he wants to possess her himself.

The riddle is encountered again in the famous Persian fable of Turandot (i.e., Turan's daughter), which Schiller dramatized based on Carlo Gozzi. Here, as in the Griselda fable, a distorting shift of the psychic accent from the significant to the subordinate has occurred. Originally it was the father, enamored of his daughter, who asked the suitors the riddle. In the Persian fable it is pronounced by the daughter herself, uncomprehending in her cruelty, and against the will of her father. The riddle asked by the father appears again in *The Merchant of Venice,* where Portia's suitors must demonstrate their wisdom by correctly choosing between three chests (as is supposedly also the case in the legend of Apollonius). This is an element Shakespeare borrowed from the *Gesta Romanorum* and from a novel of Masuccio da Salerno. With an insight into her unconscious destiny reminiscent of the analyses of Jung (1909), Portia says: "Oh me, the word, 'choose'! I may neither choose who I would nor refuse who I dislike; so is the will of a living daughter curbed by the will of a dead father." Here, we should also recall that in the Apollonius legend the riddle dealing with incest, to which the riddle of the sphinx is related, corresponds to the epitaphs suggesting incest that we discussed in connection with the legend of Vergogna, which deals with father-daughter incest. Liebrecht (1869) notes this connection with the comment that in both cases the unborn child of the father and the daughter is thought of as speaking. We should also mention the epitaph of Lucretia Borgia, who was supposed to have had incestuous relations with her father and with her brother, Cesare. Thus she was the daughter of her father, Alexander VI, as well as his lover, and as her brother's lover, she was her father's daughter-in-law. Reference to these relationships is made in her epitaph:

> Hic jacet in tumulo Lucretia nomine, sed re
> Thais, Alexandri filia, sponsa, nursus.
>
> [Here lies entombed one named Lucretia—in truth
> Thais, Alexander's daughter, wife, and daughter-in-law.]

We encountered another form of keeping the suitors from the beloved daughter in the "letter of Uriah." The father attempts to eliminate his undesirable son-in-law (for every son-in-law is undesirable to him) through the most varied means, but finally the position of the suitor is victoriously asserted over the father's resistance. Here, as in the unconscious fantasy, the father, who previously kept the mother from the son, is melded with the father (stepfather), who now is reluctant to relinquish his daughter at the time when the adult selection of the love object occurs. Now the struggle is directed against this (step)father, just as it was previously directed against the physical father (cf. the Telramund figure in my interpretation of the Lohengrin legend). The suitor's struggle with the father of the beloved corresponds to the son's struggle with his father. In the epic "Kudrun," Hagen of Ireland will give his daughter only to the man who is stronger than he is; those he beats are hanged. The Greek fable of Hippodamia has the same meaning. Hippodamia's father, Oenomaus, has declared that suitors must beat him at chariot racing to win her hand in marriage. Thirteen youths have already died in this way. Out of love for her fourteenth suitor, Pelops, Hippodamia cunningly brings about her father's death by loosening the spokes of his chariot wheels. In distorted versions the young woman, held to be of a militant personality, is portrayed as participating in this competition with the father herself, as in the myth of Atalanta, in which other details also correspond to the father-daughter schema: her exposure by the father, who hopes for male heirs, and her decision to remain a virgin and to flee the society of men, which corresponds on the one hand to fixation on the father but also seems, on the other hand, to be an echo of his precautions for her safety. Finally, though, Atalanta agrees to fulfill her father's wish that she marry, but on condition that her suitors do battle with her using their weapons. The victor will receive her hand in marriage, but the vanquished will die.

Here we notice that the battle with the Nordic Brunhild must also originally have been fought against the father; this is still clearly suggested by the theme of her seclusion by her father, Wotan, who engulfs her in a sea of flames impenetrable to even the hardiest hero (cf. Rank 1911b, 138). In other versions this seclusion supposedly occurs in the interest of retaining her virginity, as in the myths of Perseus, Gilgamesh, Telephus, and Romulus (cf. Rank 1909), in which the father secludes the daughter in an isolated place. In those cases in which his strict command of chastity is disobeyed, the daughter and her child are persecuted with an implacable hatred comprehensible only as coming from the rejected love of the competitor (cf. the evil father-in-law type in the Lohengrin legend; Rank 1911b, 113–17). In German sagas and folktales, too, this isolation of the daughter by her envious or jealous father is often encountered. This is the case in the story of the "Great Wolfdietrich" (*Hugdietrich*, ed. Holtzmann, 1865), in which the king of Salonica keeps his daughter locked in a tower. Hugdietrich, disguised as a young woman, is able to penetrate the tower and fathers a son (Wolfdietrich) by the princess. He keeps his son hidden in a wolf's lair (exposure, cf. Rank 1909). Similar details are found in the tale of Frederick of Normandy. In Ulrich Futerer's tale, similar details are related concerning the daughter of King Salabrei of Babylon: Lorandin, who escapes his pursuing father by means of a mighty jump, lauded in legend, wins the hand of the incarcerated daughter for King Bermund of India. Hagen (1850, 1:143) speaks of a princess (Hildburg) defiantly locked away by her father, "for whom even the father probably has his desires" (like Sidrat). The parallels with another tale (Grimm and Grimm 1816, vol. 3, no. 6) show what unusual rationalizations this jealous Argus nature of the father undergoes as the story is passed down without being understood. In one version the princess is pursued by mice, so that her father knows no other way to save her than to build a tower in the middle of a great river and bring her there. However, she becomes pregnant when a stream of water enters her window; she exposes her child; and so forth. Here it is clear from the whole context of these adaptations and from the details of later versions that the tale is a symbolic depiction of persecution by the father.

A Hessian tale of this genre shows the motivation for the father's acts more clearly still. In this tale the king decides that his daughter shall not marry. He has a house built for her in the forest, in the most profound isolation. She is forced to live there and never sees any strangers. However, she too becomes pregnant by drinking from an enchanted spring; she exposes the child; and so forth. Koeppel notes a tale published in the sixteenth century in many languages in which Isabella, the beautiful daughter of the king of Scotland, is locked up in a tower by her father, who does not wish to marry her off. The young Aurelio makes his way to her, but they are apprehended and perish. Finally, an Armenian tale drastically illustrates how the father attempts to protect his daughter from the advances of other men. This is the tale of Assly, the daughter of a priest, and the Tatar prince Kyaram. Assly is covered from head to toe in an impenetrable, unremovable, indestructible enchanted gown. It is studded from top to bottom with a long row of buttons; each one fastens by itself as soon as the next one is undone. Assly's father wove and prepared this gown himself to protect her from advances of every kind.

Legends of the daughter's persecution by her father, structured on the model of the Apollonius legend, were highly popular and widely distributed in the Middle Ages. In his exhaustive collection (*Gesamtabenteuer* [Collected tales], 2:59, 3:154), Friedrich von der Hagen (1850) has brought together most of the legends of this genre. As an example for this whole group, let us consider briefly the story "The Russian King's Daughter." In Russia there reigns a mighty king. He has a beautiful wife and an even more beautiful daughter who wishes to marry no man who does not please her. The father likes the sight of his daughter above all else, and when the mother dies and the gentry encourage him to remarry in order to produce an heir, he wishes to marry only a woman as beautiful as his daughter. But such a beautiful young woman is nowhere to be found, so the king swears to remain unmarried. However, the gentry consult together, and with gold and silver they purchase from the pope a decree stating that the king may marry his daughter. He rejoices greatly and makes splendid preparations for the wedding. When the daughter learns that she is to marry her father, however, she cuts off her hair, throws off her bridal gown, puts on a gray shirt, and scratches her face so that it is bloody. All are appalled. The father faints, but on regaining consciousness he orders his daughter exposed in a barrel in the sea. She is borne to Greece, where the king marries her. At this point follows persecution by the wicked mother-in-law. This thematic doubling shows that the Greek king is to be identified with the first king and that in the original version the exposure occurred when it was discovered that incest had unknowingly occurred or when the children of conscious incest were to be eliminated. Indeed, when the Greek king is away from home, his wife brings a son into the world and writes this news to her husband. But the evil mother-in-law replaces this letter with a false one (cf. the letter of Uriah) reporting the birth of a devil. Just like the first king (doublet), this king also commands his marshal to expose mother and child in a barrel that is to be thrown into the sea. The barrel is carried to Rome, and when the Greek king discovers that he has been tricked, he also proceeds to Rome. The king of Russia is also in Rome to do penance. When the pope hears the two kings' story, he realizes that the woman rescued in Rome is the lost wife and daughter they mourn.

"The Story of the Patient Helena" (Simrock 1864, 10:501 ff.) is constructed according to the same schema. King Antonius of Constantinople falls in love with his daughter. Like Apollonius's daughter, she escapes being raped by her father through abduction by pirates and is wed by King Henry of England. Betrayed by her evil mother-in-law, she is forced to flee. First, though, one of her hands is severed, and from this defect she is later recognized. In addition, the tale has been greatly elaborated and interwoven with other themes. The novel appeared in France in 1586 and has become common Germanic folk material. Von der Hagen cites Dutch (1621), Danish, and Swedish versions, and an Icelandic version in verse. He has already identified the marriage of Constance, daughter of King Tiberius of Constantinople, to the sultan, possible only with the permission of the pope, as disguised father incest. He supports his argument by noting that a Middle English song in stanzas, which runs precisely like the story of Constance, relates the following: the king's daughter, Emare, resists her father, and having been exposed, arrives in Wales, becoming the king's wife. A Norman-English chronicle of the mid-fourteenth century tells the same story, as do John Gower (*Confessio Amantis,* 2.38) and Geoffrey Chaucer ("The Mannes Tale of Lawe").

In the thirteenth century there appeared in German a similar romance, "Vom Grafen Mai und Beaflur" [Count Mai and Beaflur]; the major events of its plot follow those of the Swedish poem. Beaflur decides to flee to escape her father's advances. She boards a small, tightly caulked ship in which she sets sail on the high seas. She is carried to the land of Count Mai, who marries her against the wishes of his mother. A war calls him to Spain. During his absence, Beaflur bears a beautiful boy. The mother-in-law (like the father in the legend of Offa) falsifies the letter the messenger is to deliver to the king. She accuses Beaflur of infidelity and claims she has given birth to a wolf. Another forged letter commands that she be killed with her child. But since the king's men take pity on her, innocent as she is, she and her child are secretly brought to the ship she came in. She is carried to Rome, where she is reunited with her spouse after eight years and reconciled with her father.

The oldest Italian version, in *Pecorone* (10.1) by Giovanni Fiorentino (about 1738), relates that Dionigia, the daughter of the king of France, flees not from an insistent father, but from marriage with an old prince. She becomes queen of England, is persecuted by the mother-in-law, and so forth. The first of the French versions, which are the most widely distributed, is the thirteenth-century "Roman de la manequine" [Romance of the mannequin] by the northern French Philippe de Reims, in which three effigies are burned in the place of the condemned persons. The king of Hungary must promise his wife that his daughter will succeed to the throne. Thus he wishes to marry her himself, with the approval of the pope and his vassals. However, the daughter refuses and cuts off her left hand (cf. Helena). She throws it into the sea, where it is devoured by a sturgeon.

The father decides that his daughter must burn, but the knights merely burn her in effigy, setting her in a boat in which she is borne to Scotland. The king (father) marries her. Later, based on forged letters, she is to be burned again. Once more two effigies appear (for herself and the child), and once more she is placed in the boat. Finally, in Rome, everything is resolved. A religious drama, one of the *Miracles de Nostre-Dame,* written in the fourteenth or fifteenth century, is based on this romance. Another such drama of the same period seems to diverge from the romance. In the Helena romance, the emperor wears Helena's hand, which never decays, in a little box around his neck. Here we see significant relations to the phallus of Osiris (also swallowed by a fish) and to the threat of punishment and the punishment fantasy involving the father's severing of the hands upon discovering the daughter's masturbation.

Even more clearly than in this group, in which the persecution of the daughter, arising from rejected love, is continued by the mother-in-law in an apparently loosely appended addendum (cf. Rank 1911b, 117 ff.), the father-daughter theme is preserved in a series of legends in which the father first pursues his daughter with entreaties of love and then appears again as an evil father-in-law who continues to persecute and torment her in her marriage. To this group belongs the English legend of King Offa, related by Matthew of Paris in his Latin life of the two kings of the West Angles, Offa I and Offa II.

After Offa becomes king, having lost his way while hunting one day, he comes across the daughter of the king of York. She has rejected the unnatural entreaties and advances of her father and has for this reason been led into the forest, where she has been left without food. They spend the night together in the hut of a hermit who shows them the path out of the forest. Then Offa takes the woman as his wife, and she bears him many beautiful children, sons and daughters. Later Offa goes to war. After his victory in the war, he sends a messenger to announce the good news at home. The messenger happens to meet the queen's father, who falsifies the letter. The forged letter claims that Offa has been vanquished, that he sees this as God's punishment for his marriage to a heathen woman, and that she is to be taken into the wilderness with her children; their hands and feet are to be severed, and they are to be killed. The cruel command is not carried out in its entirety; the children are mutilated and killed, but the mother is spared. A devout hermit finds the bodies, and through his prayers they are brought back to life. He keeps them and their mother in his hut in the forest. When Offa returns, he hears of their execution and falls into such deep melancholy that he nearly goes mad. After a long while, though, while hunting, he happens to come to the hermit's hut, where he finds his wife and children. Concerning this legend, Müller (1869) remarks very astutely that one may suppose the battle Offa must win before his marriage [*sic*] suggests that the hero can marry only when he has freed his future wife from the suitor who is oppressing her. Here this suitor appears as her father (battle). "We can also suppose that as Offa's inimical complement, he actually constitutes, with him, a single person. Therefore the killing of the children, for which the legend places the blame on him, should actually be attributed to the father" (Müller 1869, 432).

In Italian, Gianfrancesco Straparola relates the story "The Girl in the Chest" in the manner of a folktale. Thebaldo, prince of Salerno, promises his dying wife that he will marry only that woman whom his wife's wedding ring fits; the only such woman is his daughter Doralice, whom he desires. With the help of her nursemaid, she hides in an exquisite chest (exposure) that is sold to the king of England. Her father comes disguised as a merchant, kills his grandchildren with the queen's knife, and brings about her punishment as a child murderer. Naked, she is buried up to her waist in the earth. Finally, the nursemaid discovers the truth, and Thebaldo is drawn and quartered.

From Rittershaus (1902), Riklin (1908) has compiled several folktales that in more or less elaborated form deal with the same schema of the daughter's sexual persecution by her father. One of these is the tale "The Father Who Persecutes His Daugher" (Rittershaus 1902, 133, no. 31). A prince kills his parents and his sister to become ruler himself. Some years later he marries a beautiful princess, and in a few years they have a daughter, Ingibjörg. By the time Ingibjörg has grown up, her mother is on her deathbed. She summons her child and tells her that after his wife's death, the evil father will desire to sleep with his daughter and will tie her up with a cord to prevent her escape. Therefore Ingibjörg should tie her bitch to the cord as she herself flees. All of this occurs, and in a ship (exposure) Ingibjörg arrives in a foreign kingdom where the young unmarried king meets her in her hiding place, a farm, and takes her as his wife. She makes him promise never to accept a guest for the winter without her knowledge. This does occur, however, and the persecution by the winter guest (father) begins. He kills her child and ruins her life, but through a magic spell she is saved and the father is punished.

The tale of Björn Bragstakkur follows the same schema. Björn lives deep in an isolated forest and forces a princess whom he has abducted to marry him. When his wife dies, he also wishes to marry his daughter, Helga, but she escapes in the usual way. In a slightly different guise, the tale "Helga, the Farmer's Daughter" (Rittershaus 1902, no. 40) deals with persecution by the (step)mother. From her dying mother, Helga has received an awl that can say "yes" when told to do so. One evening the father is about to take her by force, but she claims that she must still tend the fire. When she has gotten outside, she sticks the awl into the wall and tells it to say "yes." There follow flight, marriage with the father-doublet, persecution by the mother, and the happy ending. Finally, following Riklin (1908), I shall cite "The Tale of the Fair Sesselja" (Rittershaus 1902, 217, no. 51). For a long time, a king grieves over the death of his wife. He declares that he will marry only a young woman who is as beautiful as the dead woman was, and who resembles her. One day, when he sees his young daughter Sesselja in her mother's festive gown (substitution wish), even more beautiful than his wife was, he is overcome by the wish to marry her. In the continuation of the tale, the doubling becomes very clear. Like the exposure and the interval of time (cf. the tale of Apollonius), it has the purpose of allowing incest to be carried out, at least unknowingly, since it could not be consciously carried out in the first portion of the tale. (Here the incest is symbolically disguised through a bird.) In the second portion, the royal father is replaced by a prince. Sesselja flees from her father's kingdom and is taken in by poor people in a foreign land, who pass her off as their own daughter (family romance). Once, while she is tending sheep and believes no one is watching, she puts on her mother's festive gown (doubling) and is brought to the king's daughter as a servant (reintroduction into the original milieu). This princess is also called Sesselja—"Sesselja the Haughty"—and is thus identical with the heroine (doublet). This is also suggested in that she rejects all suitors (fixation on the father). In a dream, the princess is miraculously impregnated by a bird that has been rescued by the servant Sesselja. She realizes this when she touches the gold given her by her father, which retains its luster only when touched by a virgin: the gold turns black. To conceal the pregnancy from the father, when the child is born the servant Sesselja places her own hand on that of the princess and declares that she herself is the mother. Her identity with "Sesselja the Haughty" is clear, just as is the identity of the first king with the prince who springs forth from the bird, and who also marries the original Sesselja.

In an especially refined manner, this tale attempts to make possible the conscious incest foiled in the first part of the story. It does this by contrasting the royal father and his daughter Sesselja with a second pair, the prince and the second Sesselja. In addition, the tabooed sexual act with the father is depicted in symbolic guise. In my discussion of the Lohengrin legend (Rank 1911b, 113–17), I attempted to explain in this light a group of folktales in which the persecuting father also finally marries his daughter in the guise of another king, his noticeably ill-defined, shadowlike double, as in the legend of Apollonius and all its parallels presented here. One of these is the familiar tale of "Allerleirauh" [Fur all over] (Grimm and Grimm 1816, no. 65). A king promises his wife, on her deathbed, that he will marry no one who is not as beautiful as she herself and who does not have the same golden hair. However, there is no such woman to be found until the king sees in his maturing daughter the image of her beautiful mother. The daughter attempts to dissuade the father from his decision: as a condition for marrying her, she assigns him various difficult tasks, just as the jealous father assigns them to the suitors in other tales. She demands three fine dresses and a coat made of all sorts of furs and animal skins. When the king fulfills these superhuman demands, the daughter flees, taking these treasures with her: she puts on the coat of fur and blackens her face and hands with soot to escape recognition. In the forest, she is found by a king who at first takes her for an animal. She is forced to perform menial tasks in his kitchen (Cinderella). During a festive celebration she mingles with the guests for a short time, having washed her face and put on her fine gown (cf. the festive gown of Sesselja's mother). She now attracts the king's attention. The king asks for her hand several times: the third time, when she has already put her coat back on and blackened her face, he recognizes her from her ring as the beautiful guest at the ball and marries her.

In this tale too the initially desired conscious incest becomes possible as incest committed without the knowledge of the parties involved: the daughter blackens her face so she is not recognized by her father. Similarly, the daughter of the Russian king scratches her face. In chapter 13 especially, we shall become familiar with applying soot to the face, which makes possible unwitting incest with the sister. We recall that in incestuous dreams the unrecognizability (disguise) of the face plays the same role, making possible the incest of Pelops with his daughter in the Tantalide legend.

As in "Allerleirauh" and "The Russian King's Daughter," in a German tale (Grimm and Grimm 1816, 182), "The Little Dog Quedl," Mathild, the beautiful daughter of Henry III, wishes to become ugly so that her father, who has fallen in love with her, will no longer desire her. God does not grant her this wish, but the devil appears and promises to transform her father's love into hate if she will be his [the devil's]. She sets the condition that he must find her sleeping three nights in a row, but her handiwork and her little dog always keep her awake. The devil becomes angry and disfigures her face so much that her father loses his passion for her. Without going into a deeper analysis of this tale, in which the devil, who wishes to possess her, once again only represents the father, we should refer to another parallel to this disfiguration, noted by Stucken (1896–

1907). In a tribal legend of the Ainu (Brauns 1885, 167–70), a princess becomes hairy all over because she resists her father's embraces. Then she gives birth to dogs that are later transformed into humans. As with "The Little Dog Quedl" and the dog that the daughter leaves the father in her stead (ties to him) in the Icelandic folktale, we notice that this dog too was originally a transformed image of the father in which his sensual, sexual aspect is symbolized (cf. the prince transformed into a bird in "The Tale of Sesselja").

Another German tale, "The Tale of Hülfenberg" (Grimm and Grimm 1816, no. 181), tells of a saint who was a beautiful princess whom her father fell in love with. In her need, she implores heaven for help. Suddenly she grows a beard (animal-hair theme), bringing an end to her beauty.

The Lithuanian tale "The Rat Who Wed the King's Son" corresponds to the Icelandic tales in which the dying mother warns the daughter about her father's advances. In the Lithuanian tale, a king has a beautiful wife and a beautiful daughter. His wife dies, and he wanders from country to country in search of a wife, but nowhere does he find a woman as beautiful as his wife or his daughter. Then he says to his daughter: "We shall become man and wife!" The princess answers: "How can we become man and wife? I am your daughter and you are my father!" With the help of her dead mother's ghost, she is able to escape the advances of her father, who then shoots himself. In Campbell's collection of Gaelic tales (1890–93, no. 14), we find the tale "The Princess Who Wished to Marry Her Father." The king wishes to marry only the woman whom his dead wife's clothes fit. The daughter, the only woman they do fit, flees across the sea in a tightly sealed chest and becomes a kitchen maid at a king's court. Finally the prince marries her, recognizing her from her lost shoe, which fits only her (Cinderella). The relation of this tale to the Cinderella genre becomes even closer when we recall that there the heels of the two evil competitors, the sisters, are cut off, just as hands are severed in several of the tales of daughters who oppose their fathers (cf. "Helena," "Roman de la manequine"). In Giambattista Basile's *Neapolitan Pentamerone* (3.2) (no. 22 in Liebrecht's translation), a king loves his sister, Penta, especially because of her beautiful hands. Then she has her hands cut off and sends them to him. He has his sister put into a sealed chest and thrown into the sea. A chieftain rescues her, but his jealous wife throws her into the sea again. Then a king brings her to his wife. Dying, she gives them her blessing as man and wife. In all other versions, though, the young woman who is wed to the father or warned of the father by the dying mother is their own daughter. Here then begins the common schema associated with sibling love. Falsification of a letter, persecution, and final reconciliation follow. Chopping off the hands occurs in "The Ballad of Duke Herpin of Bourges" (Simrock 1864, 2:408–11). Herpin desires his daughter. Deeply disturbed, she chops off her hand and throws it into the sea. She is then expelled, and so forth.

In our discussion of "Roman de la manequine" we have already noted the similarity of the hand—cut off, swallowed by a fish, and preserved in a little box—to the phallus of Osiris. We have also indicated that this detail is probably conceived as a punishment for masturbation, which serves the daughter as a substitute for intercourse with the father (cf. "Allerleirauh," in which one finger remains white). Finally, the tale "Das Mädchen ohne Hände" [The girl without hands] (Grimm and Grimm 1816) shows the distortions undergone by the theme of father-daughter incest and the related masturbation complex. Without realizing that his daughter is there, a poor miller promises the devil, who has offered his assistance, whatever is standing behind his mill. When the evil one comes to fetch her in three years, she washes herself so that she is completely clean (cf. washing off the soot in "Allerleirauh"). Thus the devil cannot touch her. At his command all water is kept from her, but with her tears she washes her hands clean. Then, at the devil's command, the miller must cut off his daughter's hands (cf. the dismemberment in "Fitcher's Bird"). She weeps upon her stumps until they are clean, however, and the devil must leave her. She goes into the world; in a garden, she plucks fruits from the trees (also a typical masturbation symbol) with her mouth. The king marries her and has silver hands made for her (cf. the golden finger in "Marienkind" [Our Lady's child]). During his absence she bears a child, but the devil exchanges the letters, condemning her to be exposed with her tongue cut out and her eyes put out (doublet of exposure by the father). (In another version [Grimm and Grimm 1816], it is the stepmother who, more naturally, exchanges the letters.) But the punishment is carried out only on an animal, while she herself goes to live with her child in a forest. After searching for seven years, the king finds her and marries her again.

That this folktale with its doublets is originally based on conscious father incest, carried out unknowingly in the second portion, is demonstrated by a variant from Zwehrn, cited by the Grimms. The introduction reads: "A father desires his own daughter as a wife. When she refuses, he has her hands ⟨and breasts⟩ cut off and has a white shirt put on her. Then he expels her into the world" (Grimm and Grimm 1816).

In contrast to naive folktales and legends, which represent the father's erotic affection for the daughter as a natural phenomenon, occurring almost universally, in literature this theme appears relatively seldom. This can be explained in that the author or playwright, as we have seen, usually portrays the perspective of the son (with respect to father, mother, and siblings), gaining a father perspective only in the course of development from the psychology of the son to that of the father. Therefore it is no coincidence that dramatic adaptations almost exclusively involve mythological or historically documented cases of father-daughter incest. The playwright, as is especially clear in Shelley's *The Cenci,* is able to portray these cases in such a way that opposition to the lustful father, who takes the sister from the son just as he takes the mother, again dominates. In his tragedy *Thyestes in Sicyon,* Sophocles probably dealt with the incest of Thyestes and his daughter Pelopia, as portrayed in the Tantalide myth. Concerning the few fragments that remain of this tragedy, Welcker (1839–41) writes: "*Thyestes* surely involved the incest, committed unknowingly, of Thyestes and his daughter Pelopia, dwelling in Sicyon, from which Aegisthus was born." Lessing, too (1790), assumes that *Thyestes* involved the incest of father and daughter. Just as Sophocles portrayed unconscious sexual attraction to the mother in *Oedipus,* so that *Oedipus* expresses his feelings as a son, *Thyestes*—presented from the man's point of view, as already suggested by the title—deals with his feelings as a father. He had already expressed these in *Oedipus at Colonus,* in which the father's curse falls upon the ungrateful sons, while the loving daughters remain his true companions and caretakers until his death.

Here we should also mention the legend of Herod's stepdaughter (Mark 6:17–24). This legend has been dramatized by modern playwrights, who emphasize Herod's lustful desire for his stepdaughter. Herod, who has married the wife of his brother Philip and is therefore criticized by John, has John taken prisoner; he has him beheaded at the request of his stepdaughter, Salome, who asks this at her mother's instigation, for he has agreed to grant her any wish in compensation for her dancing. In his story "Herodias," the widely read Flaubert calls the stepdaughter, unnamed in the Gospels, Salome; in Josephus Flavius, Herod's sister appears by the name of Salome. Flaubert's designation can be seen as a subtle reference to Herod's incestuous passions (cf. also his marriage to his brother's wife). Recently Oscar Wilde's *Salome,* which places the theme in the steamy sensuality of the Orient and also addresses the incest theme more clearly, has become especially well known.

Salome: No, I'll not stay, cannot stay.
Why does the quadrumvir always stare at me
With his mole-eyes under
their trembling lids? Strange, that my mother's
husband should look at me so. I know very
well what this means; yes, I know.

(act 2)

In Hermann Sudermann's tragedy *Johannes,* the dance of Salome before her stepfather becomes a voluptuous striptease.

In his tragedy *Mirra,* Vittorio Alfieri deals with the story of Myrrha. The powerful repression that incestuous impulses have undergone in the course of cultural development is clearly revealed in this tragedy. In Alfieri's drama, there is no mention of the sexual relations of father and daughter found in the Greek myth. Indeed, the forbidden attraction is not even articulated; but subtle hints of this attraction lead to Mirra's doom. Thus in this drama, as in *Hamlet,* the way the material is treated already approaches the highest form of defense; this is the only way the incestuous impulses can now be expressed.

Mirra, the daughter of King Ciniro, is to be married to a noble prince. The closer the day of her marriage to Pereo approaches, the more melancholy she becomes. No one can understand this, and she herself is silent about it; but when her nursemaid makes an incidental comment, she believes that her secret has been discovered—the secret she wishes to keep even from herself. After postponing the wedding as long as possible, she must finally set a firm date. She declares that she will leave her parents directly after the ceremony and will travel to her husband's country. During the wedding, Mirra is tormented by the Furies, and the ceremony must be interrupted. Here again the Furies appear as an expression of defense against incestuous feelings of hatred, for Mirra hates her mother, Cecri, her competitor for her father's love.

Cecri: But, what do I see? Child,
Are you angry with me? You reject me?
You withdraw from my arms? You glance, my child, with dour intensity,
Upon your mother, too.
Mirra: Ha, seeing you is only too painful. You
Rend my heart all the more with your
Embrace. But what am I saying?
. . . .
If you truly pity my sufferings,
Once again I beg you, kill me. ⟨Defense; punishment⟩
Cecri: Cruel one! How can you incessantly
Repeat such bitter words? No, from now on,
I shall guard your life.
Mirra: You'd guard me? And I
Would always have to see you? Before my eyes
You'd always stand? I'd sooner bury these eyes
In deep, surrounding darkness;
With my own hands I'd sooner

Tear them from my very face.
Cecri: Oh, heaven!
What do I hear? Are you mad? My blood freezes.
Do you hate me, then?
Mirra: You are the first,
The only, the eternal, unfortunate cause
Of all my misery.
Cecri: Such a word! Oh, daughter?
I the reason? But even in streams of tears. . . .
Mirra: Mother, woe is me, forgive! It is not I who speaks;
Through me there speaks an unknown power.
Mother, you love me much too much. And I . . .

In an afterword to the drama, Alfieri comments: "At this point in the drama, I hope that everyone will see and feel that something stronger than herself is speaking through Mirra's mouth and that here it is not the daughter speaking to the mother, but the unhappy, desperately loving woman speaking to her beloved and preferred rival." The unconscious has awakened, has taken control over the conscious, and now speaks through her. The father, Ciniro, also feels great attraction to his daughter, but he attempts to repel it.

Ciniro: My heart is breaking.
And yet, as a final test, I must,
Though I love her without measure, at least
Conceal from her a portion of my feeling.

He then tells her to reveal the object of her secret love.

Oh, speak as to a brother. For I know
love too. But the name—

Mirra does not wish to name the object of her affections, but accidentally she lets out one word that reveals all.

Mirra: Yes, I love, since you force me to speak.
I love hopelessly, desperately.
But neither you nor anyone shall ever know
Whom I love. He himself does not suspect it,
And I almost deny it to myself.
. . . .
In the name of heaven, let me
Flee forever from your eyes.
Ciniro: My daughter,
My only beloved, oh, what are you saying? Come
To your father's arms. . . . What? You repel me

As if mad? Thus you
Despise your father. You harbor such a lowly passion
That you hesitate. . . .
Mirra: No, lowly it is not,
Sinful, indeed, but never—
Ciniro: What are you saying? Sinful!
If your father himself does not condemn this love
Then it cannot be so. Therefore let me know.
Mirra: You would see the father himself shudder,
If only he knew. Ciniro!
Ciniro: Ha, what do I hear?
Mirra: What am I saying? Oh, I know not what I am saying.
I do not love. No, don't believe it!

One continually sees her attraction in conflict with her defenses. These defenses finally culminate in the death wish. She says to her father:

Shall I die
Far from you? Oh, happy my mother—she
Shall be allowed to die at your side.
Ciniro: What are you saying? What fearful light bursts forth
From this word? Godless, you—
Mirra: Oh, heaven,
What have I said? Woe is me! Where am I?
Where shall I hide? Where shall I die? Ha, your sword
Shall serve me—
(She grasps the sword from her father in the greatest haste and stabs herself.)

In the introduction to his translation of this drama, Heyse comments that Alfieri himself considered *Mirra* his most absorbing work. Byron, who saw it in 1817 in Bologna, admits that it brought him to a deathly struggle with tears, held back with difficulty, and to paralyzing shudders such as had seldom been produced in him by a literary work.

With Alfieri, the repression of incestuous affection goes so far that a spectator unfamiliar with the fable does not directly learn that Mirra is in love with her father. Alfieri was very much aware of this, for he writes in the afterword mentioned above: "Given this supposition [that the spectators are unfamiliar with the fable], they should consider very carefully and without bias whether this young woman, if she were not called Mirra, would appear in the course of the drama to be more in love with her father than with any absent brother, close relative, or nonrelative, whom she would be forbidden to love for any reason." Alfieri makes this comment to show that he understood how to deal delicately with the controversial material, but in attempting to justify himself he only reveals his repressed emotions.

In one of his masterly novels, Stendhal relates with historical accuracy the story of the Cencis. It deals with Beatrice Cenci, who was executed on September 11, 1599, for the murder of her father, who had inhumanely tormented her and had repeatedly taken her by force. Stendhal portrays Francesco Cenci as having a cruel, sadistic nature, as having "an unbounded and unnatural hatred for his children, which began in their earliest childhood when they could not possibly have offended him. . . . Every day, beyond reason, he beat with a stick his young daughters, who lived with him in the palace. . . . He cried out that he would be happy only when all of his children were under the ground. . . . He now attempted with threats and violence to rape his own daughter Beatrice, who had already grown to be a beautiful young woman, and made all sorts of advances toward her. He told the poor girl the most frightful things, which I hardly dare repeat; he told her that the children of the love between father and daughter would surely be saints and that all the great saints honored by the church had been born in such circumstances—that their maternal grandfathers had been their fathers." Beatrice then had recourse, along with her similarly tormented mother, to the most extreme form of defense; she hired assassins to murder her father and was then executed herself.

Of the dramatic adaptations of this material, we should mention Shelley's tragedy *The Cenci*. The poet obtained the material from a historical source that also mentions the incest; in a preface to the drama, Shelley describes his work with the historical sources. It is of great psychological interest to pursue the way the poet—based, demonstrably, on his own complexes—formulated the material so that the cruel and lascivious father appears primarily as the oppressor of his sons, whose opposition to their father is aroused by the fate of their sister Beatrice. It is known that the playwright, who was expelled from Oxford University at age nineteen for his atheism, made an early break with his father. His father provided him only minimal financial support; his whole life long, Shelley nurtured an intense hatred for all the commands of authority. From a number of letters of his youth (June 1811 to June 1812), recently acquired by the British Museum from a private collection, it is clear that Shelley, despite his difficult financial position and his young age, abducted the young Harriet Westbrook, a sixteen-year-old schoolgirl, to rescue her from her father, who wished to force her to continue in school. From this juvenile perspective, in which his own strict father and the strict father of his beloved were melded into a single object of hatred, his interest in the material and the manner of treating it evinced in the drama are comprehensible.

The old Cenci hates his sons, two of whom he indirectly kills through his curse (wish). His son Giacomo also hates him but dares not transform his unconscious impulses for murder into thoughts, let alone deeds (2.2). However, Orsino, the cunning prelate, brings Giacomo's hateful fantasies into consciousness, so that he finally cries out:

We
Are now no more, as once, parent and child.
But man to man; the oppressor to the oppressed;
The slanderer to the slandered; foe to foe.

Finally, in his colloquy with Orsino, he even utters the word "parricide":

That word "parricide"
Although I am resolved, haunts me like fear.

But through hints of the incest that has occurred, Orsino is able to awaken Giacomo's jealousy:

Fair sister, thou in whom
Men wondered how such loveliness and wisdom
Did not destroy each other! Is there made
Ravage of thee? O, heart, I ask no more
Justification! Shall I wait, Orsino,
Till he return, and stab him at the door?

But powerful inhibitions hinder him in the execution of the deed; finally he agrees to have his father assassinated. In Giacomo, defense against father hatred is expressed in a form already familiar to us, and typical in its deep psychological motivation: the fear of retribution, the fear that his own son will treat him the same way (cf. Cronus). With anticipation, Giacomo awaits the messenger who will bring him the news that his father no longer lives:

The hours crawl on; and when my hairs are white,
My son will then perhaps be waiting thus,
Tortured between just hate and vain remorse;
Chiding the tardy messenger of news
Like those which I expect. I almost wish
He be not dead, although my wrongs are great.

As he did earlier by alluding to the rape of Giacomo's sister by her father, Orsino is now able to rouse Giacomo's jealous hatred again through the memory of his dead mother. The incestuous origin of this hatred is clear: it is jealous affection for the mother and the sister. Sexual love for the sister, which is hardly suggested in the drama, will be revealed in part 2 as a displaced form of love for the mother. Here this displacement is very well motivated through the early death of the mother, for which the son, based on his infantile perspective, holds the father responsible. But the old Cenci, too, justifies his hatred of his son with suspicions of Giacomo's jealousy concerning his stepmother, Lucretia. Upon Beatrice's avowal that she had meant her father no harm, Cenci answers:

> Nor you perhaps?
> Nor that young imp, whom you have taught by rote
> Parricide with his alphabet? Nor Giacomo?

Here, then, we observe the stepmother theme in its characteristic form, for which we can derive a new motivation from the standpoint of the father. Just as for the son the death ("absence") of the father is the necessary condition for incest with the mother, for the father (and also for the daughter) the "absence" of the mother is the necessary condition for father-daughter incest: competitors must first be eliminated.

In a drama of our time, Ibsen's *Rosmersholm*, repression in the depiction of the incestuous affection between father and daughter goes even further than in Alfieri's *Mirra.* After the death of her mother, Mrs. Gamvik, Rebekka is taken into the home of Dr. West. She has sexual relations with him, is finally adopted by him, and cares for him until his death. However, Dr. West, though not legitimately, is also her true, physical father. This fact is hardly suggested in the drama. It is obscurely suggested that West is Rebekka's father, but the existence of their sexual relationship is suggested more obscurely still. The entire incest complex, placed in the time before the action of the drama, is so obscured (repressed) that the uninformed spectator can hardly guess the actual state of affairs. The dialogue (act 3) in which Rebekka discovers that Dr. West is actually her father and in which Rector Kroll begins to suspect that she has had sexual relations with him is so characteristic of the effects of repression that I shall present it here in abridged form.

Kroll: I really believe you knew the whole story. Otherwise, it would seem very strange that you would permit Dr. West to adopt you.

Rebekka (standing up): I see! Now I understand.

Kroll: And that you took on his name. Your mother's name was Gamvik.

Rebekka (going to and fro): My father's name was Gamvik, sir.

Kroll: But your mother's profession ⟨midwife⟩ must surely have brought her into constant contact with the district doctor.

Rebekka: Yes, you are correct.

Kroll: And as soon as your mother died, he took you in. He treated you roughly, and yet you remained with him. You know that he won't leave you a red farthing. You've received only a chest of books. And yet you still hold with him. You indulge him, caring for him until his last breath.

Rebekka (standing by the table, regarding him scornfully): And you explain my doing all of this by claiming that there was something improper, something criminal about my birth!

Kroll: What you have done for him I attribute to a natural, childish instinct. Otherwise I consider your behavior to be a consequence of your origins.

Rebekka (vehemently): But there is not a word of truth in what you say! I can prove it! At the time of my birth, Dr. West had not yet even come to Finnmark.

Kroll: Excuse me, Miss, he arrived there a year before your birth. I am quite certain of that.

Rebekka: You're mistaken, I say! You're thoroughly mistaken.

. . . .

Rebekka (walks to and fro wringing her hands): That's impossible. You're only trying to deceive me. It's not true at all! It can't be true! Never!

Kroll (rising): But my dear, why in God's name do you take this so to heart? You really shock me! What must I think and believe!

Rebekka: Nothing. You should neither think nor believe a thing.

Kroll: Then you must explain to me why this matter—this possibility—upsets you so.

Rebekka (composing herself): But that is quite clear, Rector Kroll. I do not wish to be considered an illegitimate child.

Kroll: Well, as you wish. Very well, for the time being, we'll be satisfied with this explanation.

With the modern playwright, the incestuous relationship is hardly suggested. As with the sexual attraction between mother and son (Oedipus, Hamlet, Carlos), we observe continually increasing repression of the attraction between father and daughter, expressed in the increasing obscurity and delicacy with which this incestuous relationship is depicted. This process of repression extends directly from Myrrha's conscious incest with her father, from which a son also arises, to the incest of Thyestes with his daughter, committed unknowingly but followed by death as a self-punishment; to the subtle treatment of the Myrrha fable in Alfieri's drama, where the mere thought and its expression prove fatal; and finally to Ibsen's *Rosmersholm,* where powerful inner inhibitions render a clear expression of unconscious emotions impossible.

Of modern works dealing with erotic attraction between father and daughter, Gustav Geijerstam's psychologically masterly novel *Kvinnomakt* [The power of woman] is worthy of special attention. In this novel a young girl's love for her father is depicted, along with her aversion to her "unfaithful" mother. The father says: "I believe she hated her mother—not because she would have hated her otherwise; instead, she hated her for me" (p. 183). After the divorce, she wishes to take up the role of the mother and all other women with respect to the father, "more like a loving wife than a child" (p. 150); she is jealous when he speaks with other women (e.g., Elise). Further, the author makes the sensitive general comment: "A father left alone with his daughter easily takes on in his behavior toward the child a certain something that shows how little he can forget the difference in their sex" (p. 277).

The stepfather's sexual desire for the stepdaughter is depicted in Ferdinand von Saar's story "Die Steinklopfer" [The stonebreakers], where Tertschka tells the young laborer Georg about her stepfather: "Believe me, he won't let me go, and certainly not with you! I haven't mentioned this before, but now I must tell you. Even while my mother was alive, he often wanted to be tender with me, but I avoided him and threatened to tell my mother. Last summer, though, he came back alone from the tavern and started again, and said he would marry me. And since I wouldn't hear of it, he wanted to use force. But I defended myself and told him what I think of him. Since then he hates me to the core and takes his revenge where he can" (p. 145).

Dr. Reik informs me that conscious incest between father and daughter occurs also in a novella Guy de Maupassant published in *Gil Blas* (January 23, 1883) under the pseudonym Manfrigneuse, *Monsieur Jocaste*. A young woman marries an aging man. In her unhappy marriage, she carries on an affair with a young man. While pregnant, she feels that death is near and makes her lover swear to care for her child. After many years, he hears of the death of the old man and remembers his promise. He seeks out the young woman, who has now grown up, and is so overwhelmed by her resemblance to her mother that he falls in love with her, although his suspicion that he is her physical father conflicts with this attraction. Finally he does marry her, though, and in the story within the story, the author defends this incestuous union. Oskar Pfister mentions the artistic depiction of the father complex in the novella *Die Tochter von Oberbühl* [Oberbühl's daughter], by the Swiss author Jakob Frei. Further, we note Korfiz Holm's novel *Die Tochter* [The daughter], and especially his more recent works. In a recent novel, *Die Toten des ewigen Krieges* [The dead of the eternal war] by Waldemar Bonsels (1912), it gradually becomes apparent that Afra was both lover and natural daughter of the deceased landowner.

Of modern dramatic presentations of the father-daughter complex, we should briefly mention Gerhart Hauptmann's early drama *Vor Sonnenaufgang* [Before sunrise] (1889), in which one scene depicts the father's crude lust for his daughter. In the dream play *Hanneles Himmelfahrt* [The ascension of Hannele] by the same playwright, the crude, lustful father is contrasted with the idealized god/father presented in the form of the respected teacher. In Arthur Schnitzler's tragicomedy *Der Ruf des Lebens* [The call of life], the sickly old father keeps his blossoming young daughter under his thumb. She must eliminate the inhibiting old man in order truly to live.

Further examples of the modern treatment of this material under the pressure of increasing tendencies for repression include Herbert Eulenberg's drama *Anna Walewska* (1889). The plot centers on the theme of incest. Count Wladimir and his blossoming daughter live alone in their castle. When a suitor appears, the father's jealousy is awakened, and he shoots the man dead. His passions for his daughter now seethe unhindered, leading to the death of both father and daughter. In his tragedy *Sonnenfinsternis* [Eclipse] (1908), with extensive reference to the story of the Cencis, Arno Holz has depicted the consequences of incest between father and daughter amid extensive literary disguises. Ferdinand Ritter von Feldegg's rustic drama *Urvolk* [Aborigines] (1911) seeks to fulfill the original wish by transforming it into a popular mode of defense: the supposed father eloquently defends his right to any sort of relationship with his supposed daughter, but it is finally revealed that she and the farmer are not blood relatives.

In concluding this chapter, it is appropriate to demonstrate through a few case histories how often such relationships between father and daughter must occur, given that they become known with such comparative frequency. Storfer (1911, 17) emphasizes that among the Orang Sakai of Malacca, the fathers themselves have *jus primae noctis* with their daughters. In the area of culture history, this fact is of interest. Beginning with this original custom, Storfer attempts to explain several of its peculiarities. In his *Mystères de Paris* [Secrets of Paris], Eugène Sue expressly mentions that in the lowest strata of society fathers often have sexual relations with their daughters. Marcuse (1908, 130) writes: "The father who has been widowed early sometimes seduces or rapes his daughter even in her youngest years, later having a permanent 'relationship' with her, lasting years or even decades, and ending only with the death of one of the parties, or with the daughter's marriage, or through their arrest. Often the last two cases bring only a temporary interruption. Initially the arrest usually occurs not in connection with the discovery of the incestuous relationship, but owing only to abortion or infanticide, which the young woman has carried out or is suspected of having carried out. Of eighty welfare dossiers State Councillor Schmidt has received, forty mention father-daughter incest, flagrant procurement, or professional prostitution" (1908, 133). Bloch (1909) notes a case reported by Public Prosecutor Dr. Kersten (1904). The case involved a sixty-five-year-old mason who sired a daughter by his eighteen-year-old stepdaughter and then had sexual relations with this daughter when she was thirteen. From my reading of the newspapers in recent years, I have collected a number of characteristic cases, most of which again cast an interesting light on the psychology of the murders and attempted suicides. With the exception of the acquittal, the following case is reminiscent of the story of the Cencis.

Case 1. "Zagreb. December 23, 1910. Today, the thirty-four-year-old Elisabeth Magenheim was brought before the local court. On the night of November 6, she slew her spouse, a well-known businessman, with an ax. She received the sympathy of the entire city when it was revealed that her marriage had become a true martyrdom for her. The businessman had not only mistreated his wife severely, but had also maintained a relationship with his stepdaughter, a fourteen-year-old girl, for an extended period. During the night in question, a struggle arose between the spouses owing to the savage father's attempt to misuse his own daughter also, a ten-year-old child. In the face of his threats to kill her and the daughter with his knife, the mother could defend herself in no other way than to grab an ax and split his skull. When she was arrested, public sympathy was so great that within a short time one thousand crowns had already been collected for the woman and her children. In yesterday's trial, the court acquitted the woman by reason of self-defense."

The following four cases became known because of the murder of the children.

Case 2. "A grim family picture. Korneuburg. On June 30, 1909, Karl Krisch, a miller's helper residing in Stetteldorf, reported to the police in Oberhollabrunn that on June 8, 1906, his sister-in-law Karoline Assmann, a minor, had borne a child and had killed it. The child was found in a basket in the woodshed. The girl's father, the master miller Franz Assmann of Stetteldorf, was informed and fetched his daughter and the child's body a few days later. Karoline Assmann had buried the body in a woodshed in Stetteldorf, and upon investigation the remains were in fact found there. Karoline Assmann declared that she had strangled the child out of shame, for it had been sired by her own father. She claimed she did not know whether it had been alive when she strangled it. Karoline Assmann, who had taken a position in Vienna, was arrested. On Saturday, Franz Assmann and his daughter appeared in court and were accused of the crime of incest. The father was also accused of seducing his daughter to commit indecent acts. Both pleaded guilty. Franz Assmann was sentenced to three months in prison with strict regimen and Karoline Assmann was sentenced to one month in prison."

Case 3. "Incest. Graz. February 20, 1907. Yesterday afternoon the twenty-year-old Anna Marche of Eisbach, a carpenter's daughter, was arrested for the murder on January 27 of her newborn child. The girl stated that she had committed the deed out of shame, since the child had been sired by her own father. Marche is the father of several children, of whom Anna is the eldest. He was arrested and handed over to the court."

Case 4. "An abuser of his daughters. Arad. January 8, 1908. In the parish of Simonfalva, the landowner Alexander Keresztessy was arrested based on information from an anonymous party. He had had sexual relations with his twenty-year-old daughter. Twice this relationship had led to consequences that had been eliminated through the intervention and assistance of her mother. In the investigation, it was revealed that the man had also had sexual relations with his fourteen-year-old daughter. Keresztessy and his wife, who was also arrested, have submitted an exhaustive confession."

Case 5. "Quintuple child murder in Munich. A frightful quintuple child murder was discovered here today. For years, the smith Johann Höfling had sexual relations with his two stepdaughters, aged twenty-three and twenty-four. Six children arose from these unions; at the command of the father, five of these were killed by the daughters, who held them under water until they drowned. The smith's wife, who had knowledge of her husband's relations with her daughters, raised no objection to these murders. Höfling buried the bodies in the cellar. The brother of the two sisters has now informed the authorities that one of them is once again looking forward to the joys of motherhood. Thus it will still be possible to save one doomed child from the hands of the depraved."

Case 6 leads to attempted suicide by the victim. "Raped by her father. The thirteen-and-a-half-year-old Emma Nowak sprang from a second floor window into the courtyard of her home at Steinergasse 3. Fortunately, she was not injured. Police Commissar Hernals investigated the motive for the act and concluded that it was fear of punishment that had led the child to seek death. Emma had been to the cinema and had remained away from home for some time. Since she had been roughly treated by her father for some time, she attempted suicide out of fear of punishment. However, she has also accused her father, the thirty-seven-year-old baker's assistant Karl Nowak, of a much more serious crime. She declared that the monster had raped her repeatedly. Since it was determined that the child's accusations are based on the truth, Karl Nowak was arrested on the 22d and handed over to the court."

The following cases, 7 through 11, demonstrate how the libidinous impulse, when direct expression is inhibited, can be transformed into a criminal act—often the murder of the sexual object.

Case 7. "Attacked by her stepfather. Budapest. A few days ago the shoemaker Viktor Rytko reported that his stepdaughter, the eighteen-year-old shop assistant Hedwig Geyer, had stolen a large sum of money from his wallet and had then fled with a young man. Today the police were able to apprehend the young woman. She, however, denied having stolen any money from her stepfather and declared that he had pursued her with indecent entreaties; she stated that it was for this reason that she had left her parents' home. When confronted with his stepdaughter, Rytko declared that he would be willing to withdraw the accusation if she would go home with him. She rejected this suggestion with indignation, whereupon Rytko drew a small bottle of vitriol from his pocket and threw the contents in her face. She was seriously injured and was taken to the hospital."

Case 8. "Child murder and suicide. Kraków. This afternoon the railroad engineer Andreas Czedyk fired three revolver shots at his eldest daughter, mortally wounding her. She was fifteen years old. Then Czedyk turned the weapon toward his own head and killed himself with a shot through the temple. Czedyk had pursued his own daughter for some time with entreaties of love. His wife had recently discovered this and had wanted to send the girl to relatives, but the father carried out the awful deed before this could be arranged."

Case 9. "Father and daughter. Trieste. June 15, 1908. Yesterday morning, the forty-two-year-old Alexander Colussi, watchman at the poorhouse morgue, attempted to rape his own twenty-one-year-old daughter there. A violent struggle ensued. Finally the father murdered his daughter by stabbing her in the neck with a knife. He then went home, took poison, and shot himself in the head. He was soon dead."

Case 10. "Murder by a madman. Trento. In Trento, the master stone carver Negriolli, confined to the hospital as a dangerous alcoholic, shot his own daughter with a revolver after making a successful escape. He had designs on his daughter and did not wish to give her up to anyone else. After the deed he fled to the roof, where he was pursued by police and guards. When apprehended, he declared that he was very pleased with his deed."

Case 11 is perhaps comprehensible in connection with incest. "The frightful act of a father. Trier. Early in the morning, in a nearby town, the vineyard owner Herges shot his two daughters, ages twenty-one and eighteen, while they slept. The murderer has suffered an emotional collapse, but he refuses to provide any information as to the motive for his deed, which no one can explain in any way."

Case 12, like the case after it, illustrates father-daughter incest committed without the knowledge of the parties. This is especially interesting because of the instinctive object selection between father and daughter. "Married to his own daughter. Bromberg. Thomas Molland was arrested and accused of marrying his own daughter. Molland has recently returned from America. More than thirty years ago, he had emigrated to America and had left his wife and children in Bromberg. For twenty years he sent no word, so he was declared dead. The widow entered a new marriage. Molland's daughter, twenty-one, decided to search for her father in America. There she met a man who courted her and whom she also liked, although he was already rather advanced in age. Now Molland has returned with his wife and three children to Bromberg. There it was discovered that his wife is his daughter. The investigation seeks especially to determine whether the man knew that his chosen bride was his daughter at the time of the wedding. In any case, in America he had taken on a new name."

Case 13. "How one becomes one's own father. The *Graz Montagszeitung* (November 1907) reports that the Graz city tribunal is dealing with an interesting decision, based on the following story. Many years ago, a worker had a relationship with a loose woman. The relationship was not without its consequences, but it lasted for such a short time that the man even forgot the woman's name. Years passed, and then he met a young woman whom he liked and who was also attracted to him. They entered an intimate relationship, and when consequences resulted, he married her; there were no apparent impediments. They lived together without event until it was discovered one day that the man had married his own daughter, born of his earlier relationship. The affair came to the attention of the authorities, and the pair was brought before the judge and accused of incest. However, the court acquitted them, since there had been no intent to do wrong, or even negligence. Still, the fate of the child born of this marriage entered in good faith is now in question. It must be determined whether it will be considered legitimate or illegitimate and thus whether it will receive its father's name. This is the legal side of the question that the city tribunal must decide. Indeed, an unusual scheme of relationships exists between the three persons. The said worker is the father of his wife, and thus his own father-in-law. However, as the father of his wife, he is also the grandfather of his child. And since he is the grandfather of his child, he must be his own father."

In the complications of relationship, this last case is reminiscent of the Christian legends. Through its preconditions it also reminds one of the case of Molière. In 1622 the playwright married Armande Béjart. He was forty and she was nineteen. She was held to be the younger sister of Madelaine Béjart, Molière's former lover. In the marriage certificate, she was also listed as the sister of Madelaine. This information was later revealed to be false, though not during Molière's lifetime: it was later established that Armande was Madelaine's daughter. Immediately after the wedding the rumor spread in Paris that not only was Armande Madelaine's daughter, but Molière was her father—that he had married his own daughter.

These rumors became so persistent that Montfleury presented an indictment against Molière to the king. The king, however, dismissed all rumors and became godfather to the couple's first child. Thus the affair was put aside. After Molière's death, it was established that Armande was indeed a daughter of Madelaine, not her sister, but the identity of her father is unknown. Still, it is clear that Madelaine maintained an intimate relationship with Molière for some time. Incidentally, his marriage with Armande was a very unhappy one. Molière did love her passionately, but she is said to have been flighty and unfaithful. Later she also had an affair with Molière's pupil and adopted son Michel. The couple soon parted permanently.

We also know that Lope de Vega, though there was no incest, harbored a conscious passionate affection for his daughter. When his daughter, Marcela, born in 1605 to his lover Doña María de Luján, entered a convent, Lope wrote: "She whom I loved so tenderly, more like a lover than a father, whom I clothed in the fairest garments of gold and silk—she has withered. Her fine garments have become plain; she has slept on chaff, barefoot and naked. She is without the pleasures of life" (Wurzbach 1899). The opposite situation, the daughter's passionate veneration of her famous or important father, nourished by erotic impulses, can easily be related to infantile fixation. This is demonstrated by the family history of Byron, who, as we have mentioned, had a special liking for *The Cenci* and *Mirra*. From his marriage he had a daughter, Ada Lovelace, who was raised far from her father and in complete ignorance of his importance. Later she parted with her mother and, unlike her mother, "upheld the memory of Lord Byron with passionate veneration" (Engel 1904).

12 Incest in Historical Times: Tradition, Custom, and Law

> **It is the custom among the Persians to marry one's mother; in Egypt and Athens to enter legitimate marriages with one's sister. Your memorials and tragedies glory in incest, about which you gladly read and hear. In the same way, you worship incestuous gods who cohabit with their mothers, daughters, or sisters.**
>
> ARNOBIUS, *Adversus Nationes*

Having recognized the power of incestuous desires in the fantasies of the individual and of a people, we can expect that they were also fulfilled in the real life of ancient peoples far more often than in later periods; this is also suggested by the especially strict customs, taboos, and punishments that attempted to counteract these desires. Indeed, the historical works of the ancients are filled with incest. Considering the numerous cases of which we have no knowledge, the documented examples, considered noteworthy in some sense, suggest the great intensity and frequency of incest. One can say that the sexual life of the ancients was permeated with incestuous tendencies. We will be able to understand this psychologically comprehensible circumstance even better when we note the words of reliable observers and statisticians, who state that in our time and on our cultural level incestuous relationships still occur with shocking frequency. On the other hand, psychoanalysis demonstrates that in raising children, one crucial requirement is that these impulses be repressed. Unsuccessful repression leads to the emergence of neurosis, perversion, and criminality; yet in some cases, given the appropriate predisposition, these impulses are lived out in a desirable manner in artistic fantasy.

Among many ancient peoples, as well as primitive peoples of today, sexual relations among blood relatives not only were not forbidden but were gladly undertaken and even directly encouraged, reference being made to divine example. This is especially significant for our conception of repression through time, still relived today by the individual in the development of his psychic life.

Schiller-Tietz has compiled a series of relevant examples: "Thus it is sufficiently well known that the ancient Peruvians married their mothers, sisters, or daughters without regard to blood relationship. The children of the first Inca married each other, and after that time, it was the custom in the princely house that the Inca could marry only his sister in order that the blood of the royal family remain pure. According to the chronicles, this was carried on for fourteen generations. Following this example ⟨which itself makes reference to divine example⟩, the warriors are also supposed to have married their own sisters. . . . There is no doubt that among the ancient Persians there were no restrictions at all as to marriage with blood relatives. It was not only brothers and sisters who married among the Persians, but even fathers and daughters or mothers and sons. Indeed, for certain religious offices, persons born of such unions were required" (Schiller-Tietz 1892, 7 ff.). That the son could marry his mother after the death of his father, and that this occurred especially often among the magi, is mentioned not only by Arnobius but also by Herodotus (3.31), Diogenes Laertius (*History of the Philosophers,* 1), Plutarch (*Artaxerxes,* chap. 26), Ctesias (*Persicha,* chap. 47), Agathias (2.23), and Heracleitus (*Fragments,* chap. 7, ed. Müller). Constans cites further examples (1881, 35), stating: "For the rest, one will do well to note that to a certain degree Oriental customs authorized the union of son and mother, if one is to believe Catullus and Sextus Pyrrhonicus (*Hypotypos,* 3.24), according to whom the magi were born of such incest, and Lucan, who claims that the situation was the same among the kings of the Parthians."

In Herodotus we find a fully characteristic extension of this Persian custom. He emphasizes especially (1.137) that among the Persians "no one had ever killed his father or mother. Instead, when it appeared that something of the sort had occurred, it always turned out that such deeds had been committed by adopted children or bastards. Indeed, they opined that it would be quite unnatural for a child to kill his own father." Since we do not consider the emphasis on this situation to be a reaction to successful repression, we will note a significant connection with the fact that marriage with the mother was permitted. To an extent, marriage with the mother eliminates the erotic, affective sources of hatred toward the father. That in the education of boys the Persians systematically attempted to dampen the father complex further still can be deduced from another comment of Herodotus, appearing just before the previous one (1.136): "Before the age of five, a boy does not come before the eyes of his father, but remains with the women." Thus, precisely in the years that are crucial in the development of the later psychosexual orientation, the child is, on the one hand, fully isolated from his father, and on the other hand is brought into such proximity with his mother and the other female members of the household that condoning incestuous marriages becomes almost essential.

Further, Schiller-Tietz (1892) continues: "Nor did the ancient Egyptians observe any restrictions on marriage. Among their kings, marriages with sisters occurred frequently, especially in the house of Ptolemy. Cleopatra, for example, was born of a brother-sister marriage and was the granddaughter of another brother-sister pair. Her grandmother, Berenice, was simultaneously the niece and sister of her husband."

Thus comment must already be made concerning the incest complex of siblings, to be treated in detail in part 2: we must state that the sexual attraction of siblings (with its negative consequences—hatred toward the brother and jealousy), which we have come to recognize in the psychic life of the individual as a second, less shocking level of parental incest, is etiologically nothing but the necessary consequence of the original but soon forbidden marriage between parents and children. We will not be surprised to see marriage with the sister occurring all the more frequently in the traditions and customs of peoples, though our evidence is limited to historical times. Behind these customs originating in relatively late periods and the commentaries concerning them, we can suppose—based on our experience with the psychic life of the individual—a more shocking period in which parental incest was not yet forbidden. Sibling marriages, permitted so universally and without restriction, were intended to prevent and obscure this parental incest.

Erman (1885, 221) reports that "in Ptolemaic and Roman Egypt, marriage with the sister was actually the rule. Of the rulers of the Ptolemaic dynasty, most had married their sisters, and under the emperor Commodus, two-thirds of all the citizens of the city had also done so. Apparently marriage with the sister, which seems highly criminal in the light of our moral customs, was considered the most obvious and natural thing, just as among contemporary Egyptians the cousin is considered the most natural and sensible marriage partner. Further, the gods had already set an example, for the brothers Osiris and Set had married their sisters Isis and Nephthys."

Of the historically attested incestuous relationships among civilized peoples, a few are worthy of special mention. Curtius reports that Sysimithres, satrap of Soediana, was married to his own mother, but this marriage is not presented as any sort of exceptional case (cf. Kossmann 1905). Antiochus X also married his mother, Cleopatra (Winckler 1907, 121).

Plutarch reports that Artaxerxes was married to his daughter (Marcuse 1908, 144). Schrader also mentions isolated cases of marriage between children and parents among Indo-European peoples (1901, 910), and further cases are found in Bachofen (1897). It is not only the ancients themselves who in justifying their incestuous unions referred to the deities representing their own repressed complexes. For example, Winckler is also of the opinion that these special rights, later reserved for the king alone, obligated him to a life reflecting mythological tradition, but that this tradition was itself of astral origin. However, this again implies a perpetuation of the cult of the deity or of celestial observation. Thus special reference must be made here to the psychological conception of this development discussed by Freud (1909h, 131): "From the development of the ancient religions, it seems that many things that mankind had renounced as 'criminal' were attributed to a god and still permitted in the name of the god. Recourse to the deity was the way man freed himself from domination by evil, socially harmful drives. It is therefore no coincidence that all human characteristics and the misdeeds associated with them were attributed to the old gods without restriction. Still, it is no contradiction that it was not permitted to justify one's own misdeeds through divine example." Universally permitted incest, not yet rejected in human life, was thus the original state. Repression began with "displacement" of incest to the deity, and later to the king, considered divine, so that to him everything was permitted, just as was originally the case with the pater familias. When these royal privileges met with repression as it continued its advance, however, the kings, interested in keeping these privileges, referred to divine example. Indirectly, though, they were only indicating the universally human character of these impulses and suggesting to the people that such marriages had once been condoned by all. With this more recent appearance of impulses previously repressed with difficulty, the role of religion, culminating in the justifying projections of the gods, was actually completed, and it was now necessary for laws to keep these impulses in check through prohibitions and punishments. Thus, as Winckler believes, the king subsequently led his life in accordance with mythological tradition, but only because he required this tradition to justify his own regression to an earlier stage of repression. In mankind real events, as well as the development of religion and myths, flow from the same powerful drive sources; just as religion originally arose through the repression of drives, in accordance with appropriate psychological motives it is also used to justify these impulses when they appear.

So, for example, Diodore writes (chap. 27): "That which is counter to the customs of all other peoples, it is said, was legalized in Egypt; it was permitted to marry one's sister because Isis had been so happy in such a union." Among the Persians, in addition to marriage between parents and children, such unions between siblings were also permitted. In many portions of the *Zend Avesta,* the scripture of the Parsis, marriage between first cousins (*khatuda*) is praised as a union especially pleasing to the deity. Further, a woman could marry two brothers in succession (Brodbeck, *Zoroaster*). The history of the Achaemenids, the oldest Persian dynasty, also mentions many marriages between siblings. As the first example of sibling marriage, Herodotus (3.31) cites the marriage of Cambyses, who was seized by love for one of his sisters (they shared both father and mother) and wished to take her as his wife. Since he realized that this was unusual—for until then the Persians had entered no unions with their sisters—he inquired of the royal judges whether there existed a law permitting what he desired: marriage with the sister. The judges immediately responded with a just answer ensuring the safety of their own position: they had found no law compelling brother to marry sister, but they had found one permitting the king of the Persians to do whatever he pleased. Thus Cambyses married his beloved sister, and soon thereafter also a younger sister, whom, however, he soon killed (Duncker 1855–57, 4:429 ff.). This report illustrates fully the tendency for justification discussed above and reflects in part its historical development.

Among the Greeks, too, according to the oldest traditions, marriage with the sister was permitted. This is suggested not only by the divine "example" of Zeus and Hera (actually the divine reflection of humanity), but also by many naive accounts. In the *Odyssey* (Homer 1961, 10.7), Homer mentions without the slightest shock that Aeolus, son of Hippotes and a friend of the immortal gods, married his sons to his daughters:

> Twelve children had old Aiolos at home—
> six daughters and six lusty sons—and he gave
> girls to boys to be their gentle brides;
> now those lords, in their parents' company
> sup every day in hall—a royal feast
> with fumes of sacrifice and winds that pipe
> 'round hollow courts; and all the night they sleep
> on beds of filigree beside their ladies.

Later, in the Athens of Solon, marriage with the paternal half-sister (*homopatrios*) was the only form of sibling marriage still permitted. Among the Romans, even this form of half-sister marriage was no longer permitted, though marriage between first cousins did occur. Concerning sibling marriages among the Greeks, in his foreword to his *Biographies,* Cornelius Nepos makes the following comment: "Thus, for Cimon, the famous Athenian, it was no scandal that he was married to his sister, for his fellow citizens had precisely the same custom. According to our moral laws, this would be criminal." And concerning the marriage of Cimon himself, imprisoned after the death of his father (Miltiades) because he could not pay his father's fines, Nepos relates: "Feelings of attraction and local custom had led him to marry his half-sister, Elpinice. Still, a certain Callias desired the hand of Elpinice in marriage. He was not of noble birth but had attained great wealth through mining. He encouraged Cimon to relinquish Elpinice to him and promised to pay Cimon's debts for him if he would agree. Cimon rejected this offer, but Elpinice declared that she would never permit a son of Miltiades to die in prison, especially since it lay in her power to prevent this. She said that she was determined to marry Callias if he would keep his promise."

With the restrictions placed on incest by custom and law, however, the act was only removed from public view; it did not cease to exist. This is indicated by the innumerable accounts of incestuous crimes, which became interesting only after the restrictions had come into effect. Thus, in chapter 7 of his biography of Caesar, Plutarch gives an account of Publius Clodius's incest with his married sister. Incestuous relationships, originally permitted, were simply reported with surprise as matters of fact in later societies on a higher cultural plane. In still later periods they were noted only as exceptional cases intended to deter readers from incest, or only in a disguised form resulting from the progress of repression.

As the second account in his book *Love's Woes* (20 B.C.), Parthenius of Nicaea relates the story of Polymele, loved by her brother Diores, who finally did persuade his father to permit their marriage. Further, in the story of Leucippus (no. 5), he relates the entire account of an incest tragedy. After Leucippus has long attempted without success to master his passion for his sister, he confesses his passion to their mother and threatens to commit suicide if she does not assist him. She arranges for the sister to sleep with him. However, the sister's betrothed discovers this and informs their father, Xanthius, of his daughter's infidelity—but without naming her lover. The father apprehends the siblings flagrante delicto, and the daughter rushes in shame from the room. Believing the young man to be the lover mentioned by his daughter's betrothed, the father wounds him. In his efforts to escape, the son also gravely wounds his father. In the eleventh tale, Parthenius discusses resistance to sexual passion between siblings as exemplified in the love of Caunus for his sister Byblis, on account of whom he fled the country, since she, to his horror, had also confessed her love for him.

The seventeenth tale, "Periander's Mother" is of special interest. There, in summary, it is related that Periander, a Corinthian, was originally mild and calm in nature. Later, though, for the following reasons, he acquires murderous traits. While he is still very young, his mother develops a strong passion for him. For a time she gratifies her desires by embracing the boy. Subsequently, though, her passions grow and grow, and she is no longer able to master her illness. Finally she tells her son that a very beautiful woman is in love with him and that he should not leave her alone any longer. Initially he refuses to enter a punishable union with a legally married woman, but since his mother does not cease to admonish him, he finally agrees. And on the night agreed upon by her son, she directs him not to light any lamp in his bedchamber and not to force the woman to speak. These things too she requests out of shame. Periander promises to obey his mother in all of this. Thus, arrayed in her finest jewels, she goes to him in the night and leaves before morning. The next day she asks him whether he is satisfied and whether he wishes the woman to return. Periander answers that he would very much like this, for he himself experienced no little pleasure. She continues to visit him every evening, and Periander, beginning to feel love for her, wishes to know her identity. Having failed to convince her to speak, one night he finally lights the lamp in his bedchamber. Recognizing his mother, he wants to kill her, and is prevented from doing so only by a demonic apparition. From this time on he is mentally deranged and begins to act in the cruel manner that leads to the suffering of so many of his fellow citizens. The mother kills herself in despair.

This criminal love of a mother for her son, also mentioned by Diogenes Laertius of Aristipus (1.96), becomes even more interesting in light of the story of Periander's ancestors and of his own subsequent life (cf. Herodotus, 5.92). The story of Periander's father, Cypselus, has all the characteristics of the "myth of the birth of the hero." Corinth was ruled by the Bacchiads, "who married only within their own family. However, Amphion, a member of this family, had a lame daughter called Labda. She was wooed by Eetion, son of Echecrates, for none of the Bacchiads wished to marry her. . . . Eetion had had no children, either by this woman or by any other." The oracle at Delphi prophesied that he would have a tyrannical son (warning), and since this prediction corresponded to one attested earlier in the family of the Bacchiads, they decided to kill Labda's child upon its birth (sentence of death). When Labda had given birth to her child, they sent ten men to kill the child. "Labda, who knew nothing of these affairs and therefore believed that these men had come in love and friendship, fetched the boy and handed him over to one of them. They had agreed that the first one who should hold the boy in his hands should cast him to the floor but when Labda brought the boy and had handed him over to the man, the boy smiled at him as if divinely inspired, and when he saw this, the man felt pity for the boy and did not wish to kill him. He handed him over to the next man, but he in turn handed him to the third, and so on. Thus each of the ten men gave him to the next one, and none of them was willing to kill him. They therefore handed the child back to his mother. Then they stood before the door and argued among themselves, one always blaming the other, but all of them especially blaming the one who had first received the child, accusing him of breaking his word. Finally, after some time, they decided to go in together and attack the child simultaneously. Nevertheless, Corinth was to experience unhappiness from the house of Eetion. For Labda had been standing at the door and had heard all this. Since she feared they might reconsider and would indeed take the child and kill him, she went and hid the child where she thought he was least likely to be found—in the flour box (exposure in a little chest)—for she knew they would search everywhere when they returned to look for the child. Now they came and searched the house, but when they could not find the boy, they decided to go home and tell those who had sent them that they had done everything they had been commanded. . . . But now Eetion's son grew up, and since he had escaped from this danger, he was given the name Cypselus ⟨chest maker⟩." Based on the ambiguous pronouncement of an oracle, Cypselus then gained control over Corinth, which he ruled as a cruel tyrant. After thirty years he was succeeded by his son Periander. "Initially he was much gentler than his father. However, after coming into contact, through messengers, with Trasybulus, the tyrant of Miletus, he became even more bloodthirsty than his father." We are already familiar with the way his transformation to a cruel tyrant is motivated in Parthenius's story, and Periander's subsequent behavior also suggests this interpretation. He had married Lyside, the daughter of the tyrant Proclus of Epidaurus. This spouse, whom he tenderly called Melissa, he later murdered secretly and for unknown reasons, but the murder appears to be a consequence of his unvented rage against his mother, pouring forth after the fact. He sent [cf. Herodotus (book 2)]

> messengers to Acheron of Thesprota concerning communications from the dead in connection with the missing pledge money of a guest. Then Melissa appeared and said that she would under no condition reveal the whereabouts of the pledge money, for she was freezing and naked: the clothes she had been buried in did her no good, since none had been burned with her. As a sign that she spoke the truth, she declared that Periander had placed a loaf of bread in a cold oven. When this was told to Periander (and he took this to be a true sign, for he had had relations with the dead body of Melissa), he had a herald announce that all the women of Corinth should congregate in the temple of Hera. They then proceeded to the temple as though to a festival, adorned in their finest jewels. However, he had assigned his lancers to assist him in the temple and stripped all the women

naked, free women and servingwomen together. He brought all their raiment together in a pit and burned everything, with prayers to Melissa.

Just as the myth of exposure is extended to Cypselus and sexual relations with the mother are extended to his son Periander, the enmity between father and son over the mother is delayed until the third generation. Herodotus reports (2.50–51):

For after Periander had killed his wife Melissa, he also met with the following misfortune. He had had two sons by Melissa, seventeen and eighteen years old. Proclus, lord of Epidaurus, their maternal grandfather, invited them to visit him. He treated them with great friendliness, as was fitting, for they were the sons of his daughter. And as he was bidding them farewell, he walked along with them and said: "But my children, do you know who murdered your mother?" The elder brother did not take these words to heart, but the younger one, Lycophron, became very sad on hearing this, and when he arrived in Corinth he did not speak to his father, feeling that he was his mother's murderer. When his father addressed him he did not speak, and when asked questions he did not respond. Finally Periander became angry and drove him from the house. And when he had driven him away, he inquired of the eldest son what the grandfather had said to them. The son, however, answered that they had been received with great kindness. But Periander said that there could be no other possibility—that the grandfather must have given the boy food for thought. He never ceased asking about this. Finally the son remembered and told his father. Periander also took these words to heart, but not wishing to appear soft, he sent a message to the people who were harboring his banished son, forbidding them to give him lodgings. . . . After this pronouncement, no one wished to speak to the son or give him shelter; indeed, he himself believed that he should not violate the prohibition, but instead wandered among the pillared halls. On the fourth day, though, Periander caught sight of him and noticed his unkempt state, for he had neither washed nor eaten. He felt pity for him. His anger left him, and he approached the boy saying: "Dear son, which would you prefer, your current state or everything that I now possess, if you will do your father's will? For you are my son, you are king of rich Corinth, yet you lead a beggar's life, for you are recalcitrant and angry with the one whom you should least of all treat in this manner. If such a misfortune has occurred as the one you suspect I am guilty of, then that is my own misfortune, and I carry the greatest burden, having brought it upon myself. Now, though, you have seen how much better it is to be envied than to be pitied, and also what it means to be angry with parents and those more powerful than you. And now come home with me." Thus he sought to win him over. But the boy still refused to answer his father, saying only that before God he was deserving of holy punishment for even

> entering a conversation with his father. Then Periander realized that his son's disturbance was incurable and could not be eliminated. He had him taken from his sight and sent to Corcyra [Corfu], for Corcyra was also subject to him. And when he had sent him away, Periander did battle with his father-in-law Proclus, since the latter was mainly responsible for this whole misfortune. He captured Epidaurus and took Proclus captive.

When Periander was old and no longer had the energy to govern, he sent for Lycophron, for his elder son was dull and slow. But Lycophron did not even honor the messengers with an answer. Nor did he yield to the entreaties of his sister, whom their father sent to trick him. And when he finally agreed to return to Corinth on condition that his father exchange residences with him, the citizens of Corcyra murdered him to prevent the appearance of Periander in their country. Then Periander took revenge on them by having three hundred boys, sons of the noblest men of Corcyra, sent to Alyttes in Sardes to be castrated.

In returning from these half-legendary citations to actual history, we should mention one case that Tacitus mentions in his *Annales* (6.49):

> In those days Sextus Papinius, of a consular family, chose for himself a sudden and terrible end, plunging straight to his death. His mother was blamed for this. Long rejected, she had been attempting through flattery and even luxury to seduce the young man to commit that deed ⟨incest⟩ from which he was able to escape only in death. She was therefore accused in the Senate, and though she threw herself at the senators' feet and spoke of common grief, of the weakness of a woman's heart in such unhappiness, and of other sad and lamentable things relating to the same sorrow, she was banished from the city for ten years, until such time as her younger son should have the dangerous years of adolescence behind him.

The numerous poems of Catullus (nos. 88–91 and others), for example, in which he accuses Gellius and others of incest with mother and sister and also mentions that marriage with the mother was practiced among the Persian magi (no. 90), suggest how frequently incestuous relationships occurred, or can at least be presumed to have occurred, in later Rome as well—and not only among royalty, despite express prohibitions and strict punishments.

Among the ancient Hebrews, too, as is demonstrated by passages from the Old Testament, marriage to the paternal half-sister was permitted (e.g., Abraham and Sarah). In confirmation of the frequency of such marriages, Nöldeke (1887) mentions the expression "my sister, my bride," which occurs so frequently in the Song of Solomon (cf. Schiller-Tietz 1892). That among the ancient Egyptians lovers, or man and wife, addressed each other as "brother" and "sister" demonstrates that he is correct. This is observed, for example, in love songs (cf. Schneider 1907, 211 ff.) and is apparently a last echo of formerly permitted sibling marriages. Among the Jews such unions must still have occurred in later times, as is demonstrated in Ezek. 22:11: "His own daughter-in-law a man has defiled with loose conduct; and his sister, the daughter of his own father, a man has humiliated." Only after the exile were such marriages forbidden in the priestly laws (see below).

Having so often noted incest among civilized peoples, we should not be surprised to encounter it in primitive societies. According to Schiller-Tietz, "the Alfur of Minahassa trace their descent from Lumimunt, who united with her son Toar, while the Kalang of Java and the Nias also claim descent from mother-son unions, and the Savun trace their descent from a brother and sister. Although these and other tales can be explained with reference to nature myths, they are nonetheless reliable reflections of customs and modes of thought in ancient times." Schiller-Tietz also mentions the "custom among high-caste Balinese of wedding to one another twins of the opposite sex upon the achievement of marriageable age. Although this is no longer practiced today, such twins are still referred to as *kembarbuntjing* ('betrothed twins'). . . . Among the Batak of Sumatra, it is still considered most desirable to marry a cousin—the daughter of the maternal uncle. This was the rule in ancient times, and the custom is still so common that a man still addresses his betrothed or his wife as *born ni datulang* ('daughter of the maternal uncle'), even if she does not actually stand in this relationship to him. Conversely, a woman calls her lover or her husband *ibebere ni danang* ('son of the paternal aunt')" (Schiller-Tietz 1892, 15).

According to Winckler (1907, 93), "we have determined that in South Arabia, where a certain form of polyandry is practiced, a father and his eldest son shared a wife, while each younger pair of brothers also had a common wife." Strabo (16.783) reports on sexual relations between mother and son among the Arabs; he also mentions the same custom among the magi (15.735) and the Hibernians (4.201). As a monument to this earlier period, a complete Arab Oedipus legend has been preserved that, based on several independent traits, Goldziher (1876, 216) believes was composed free of Greek influence. One of the many Nimrods appearing in Arab legend, the son of Kena'an and Salcha, was exposed by his parents because of a frightening prophecy. They hoped he would die and thus bring his father no harm, but he was miraculously saved and suckled by a female tiger. (Arabic *nimr*, "tiger," is said to be the origin of his name.) Later he was raised by the inhabitants of a nearby village. When he had grown up, he gathered together a great army and fought against his unrecognized father, Kena'an, whom he killed in the decisive battle. In triumph he entered the capital city and married his mother, Salcha. Characteristic of this "Oedipus legend" is the absence of those defenses or themes of repression that are so characteristic of the Greek legend.

Finally, the aborigines of Cooper's Creek in South Australia relate in a sort of world parent myth that after the creation brothers and sisters and other close relatives married one another. In Indonesia (West Java), the Baduvi have propagated for centuries exclusively through incest. Sibling marriages are also observed among the Kamchadals and the Wangoro. Arrago writes that frequent sibling marriages are found in Guam; indeed, such marriages are considered the most natural and appropriate unions. Further, sibling marriages are not uncommon in the royal houses of Baguirmi, Siam, Burma, and Polynesia. Morgan describes the Malay group marriage of brothers and male cousins with their sisters as the most archaic of all kinship systems encountered thus far, attesting to a stage far back in prehistoric times (cf. Marcuse 1908, 145).

Similarly, Winckler (1901) derives sibling marriage from the simplest types of kinship systems, for within the gens all are brothers and sisters. However, he states that the words "brother" and "sister" themselves fully obscure the original situation, for the terms originally signified something quite different than they do now. That kinship terminology plays an important role has been demonstrated in the stepmother complex and in that unrelated marriage partners are often still designated by terms referring to the original relationships. Whatever meanings the terms "brother" and "sister" may have acquired, the terms originally referred to the blood relatives who were the offspring of the group marriage. Among the peoples who still demonstrate the more primitive stages, we therefore find the first regulations, restrictions, and punishments aimed at continually narrower avoidance of incest. Indeed, "the peoples who have not yet been touched by modern civilization generally extend the restrictions on marriage much further than is the case among more advanced societies; these restrictions often comprise all members of the tribe or clan, and their violation is considered a serious crime" (Westermarck 1908, 7).

"Among many savage groups, fear of sexual relations with relatives is so great that it has led to the prohibition of marriage with members of the same tribe and has brought about the establishment of exogamous marriage. It cannot be doubted that the prohibition of the marriage of relatives and the extreme fear of endogamous, and especially incestuous, unions, already represent a reaction to bad experiences" (Marcuse 1908, 141). According to Westermarck's convincing argument (1908, 11), "the abduction of women from other groups arose mainly from an aversion to strong endogamy," and in the custom among many Australian aboriginal tribes of exchanging the bride for a female relative of the husband we can see not only a very characteristic echo of the original marriage of these relatives themselves, but also a highly refined manner of ensuring that such a union does not take place. Recently Freud was able to provide a psychoanalytical explanation for the extremely extensive totemic marriage restrictions of the Australian aborigines, which reveal, among other things, a special fear of incest with the mother-in-law. He described these restrictions as a form of infantilism recurrent in neurosis.

That these restrictions were originally intended to prevent repudiated incest with the mother while still permitting sibling and father-daughter incest as substitutes is demonstrated in a comment by Winckler, which confirms our conception of repression (1901, 16): "According to whether the society is patriarchal or matriarchal, all the children become members of a gens differing from that of one of the parents. Indeed, they originally became members of the father's gens, since matriarchy was the original form: only the mother of an individual can be determined. In this manner sexual intercourse with the mother is avoided and all males become brothers of the father. On the other hand, sexual relations between brothers and sisters and between fathers and daughters not only are not avoided, but are intentionally brought about, for paternal relationship, since it cannot be proved, is not recognized." Later, then, the restrictions are defined more and more narrowly through modifications of the system until they include all members of the tribe or clan. Among certain peoples with whom repression has progressed especially far—for example, the Chinese—marriage with a person bearing the same family name is considered criminal, even if there is no relationship (Westermarck 1908, 7). In this restriction, extending even to those bearing the same name, we find an interesting complement to the custom of addressing the marriage partner with the term designating the originally permitted, related sexual object (sister, cousin, etc.). This custom is observed in many cultures (cf. the Egyptians, Bataks, and Arabs; the Song of Solomon). We see here that through these restrictions an attempt was made to counteract even the smallest possibility of incestuous relationships or those that might appear to be incestuous. The prohibition of marriage with persons bearing the same family name is also found in the statutes of Manu, which strictly forbid such unions (Schiller-Tietz 1892, 21). "In connection with the totems (family names) of the Indians of North America or with the castes of the Australians, we observe the same precept, and apparently this custom existed also among the Highlanders of Scotland. . . . Precisely the same dictum is also observed among many primitive peoples of the Indian archipelago; on Sumatra, it is observed among the Malays and the Bataks. . . . Among the Khond of India, such a marriage within the tribe or within the extended family is considered incestuous and is punished by death" (Schiller-Tietz 1892, 21–22).

Among the cultured peoples of antiquity, and among contemporary ones, we find that the punishments receive greater emphasis than the restrictions. "In the canons of Vishnu, it is stated that sexual relations with one's own mother, daughter, or daughter-in-law are among the most serious crimes, and can be expiated only through death by fire" (Westermarck 1908, 7). That we are confronted in the later priestly laws of the Old Testament with the strictest possible restrictions and punishments for every form of incest should not surprise us, given the incestuous unions with which the older portions of the Bible are filled. Thus Marcuse remarks (1908, 44): "That incest must have existed in ancient Israel is demonstrated by Moses' strict law, 'whosoever approaches his mother to lie with her, let him be killed.'" Further, in 1 Cor. 5:1 we read: "Fornication is reported among you, and such fornication as is not even among the nations, that a man has [a wife] of his father." The strict restrictions of Lev. 18:6 ff. on the degree of blood relationship permitted in marriage are well known: "You . . . must not come near, any man of you, to any close . . . relative . . . to lay bare nakedness. I am Jehovah. The nakedness of your father and the nakedness of your mother you must not lay bare. She is your mother. You must not lay bare her nakedness. The nakedness of your father's wife you must not lay bare. It is your father's nakedness. As for the nakedness of your sister, the daughter of your father or the daughter of your mother, whether born in the same household or born outside it, you must not lay bare their nakedness. As for the nakedness of the daughter of your son or the daughter of your daughter, you must not lay bare their nakedness, because they are your nakedness." And so the restrictions proceed through the whole gamut of relationships. The more serious infractions are punished with the death of both parties, while the less serious ones are punished with childlessness and infertility. Similarly, we read in Deut. 27:20–22: "Cursed is the one who lies down with his father's wife, because he has uncovered the skirt of his father. . . . Cursed is the one who lies down with his sister, the daughter of his father or the daughter of his mother."

The Chinese, who extend the restriction to those bearing the same name, punish "marriage with the sister or the mother with death, and consider incest to be the worst crime of all; they consider even unions with distant relatives to be incestuous" (Marcuse 1908, 140). "According to Medhurst, among the Chinese the punishment for incestuous relations with the great uncle, the father's cousin, the brother, or the nephew is death. Whoever marries his mother's sister is strangled to death" (Westermarck 1908).

Based on our psychoanalytical experience, we can also regard the well-known, exaggerated love of children exhibited by the Chinese as a remnant and consequence of intense repression and sublimation in dealing with the incest complex. P. J. Hoogers (1910) provides some interesting details concerning the relationship of children and parents among the Chinese.

> Love for the parents is the highest commandment of the Chinese moralists. But this commandment is so all-encompassing that it comprises everything that is considered good and just. Every conceivable virtue is demanded in the name of love for the parents. Tseng, a pupil of Confucius, states that every fault is simply a lack of love for the parents. Indeed, if one is a poor employee, an unfaithful friend, or a cowardly soldier, this is seen as an offense against the parents, thus conflicting with the highest commandment of Chinese ethics. In China, it is the highest honor to be known as "a good son," and for many generations the emperors themselves appended to their names the word *xiào,* "good son." However, this reverence for the parents is exaggerated to a peculiar degree. Filial love demands that while the parents live, the child never go too far from them; above all, he should never go to a place unfamiliar to them. Thus the missionaries have the greatest difficulty explaining to them Christ's first visit to the temple, for the Chinese consider it contrary to good conduct that a twelve-year-old boy should visit the temple without his parents' knowledge. They are still more offended by the Scripture, "A man shall leave his father and mother and shall cling to his wife," for according to the Chinese hierarchy, the parents and even the brothers are more worthy of love than the wife. The sacred writings of the Chinese complain that this dictum has often been violated. It is written: "If you lose your wife, you can marry another." The wife is not a blood relative, and it is blood relationship—that is, descent from the same parents—that is all-important to the Chinese. It is explained that one must care for one's body and one's health because the substance of the body is from the parents; whoever neglects or harms his own body is injuring his parents. This explains the incredible caution, and cowardice, of the Chinese. Never would a Chinese climb a mountain, never would he approach a cliff. If one were to have to undergo an operation or an amputation as a result, this would be perceived as profane and contemptible behavior toward one's parents. Most of the faults of the Chinese are nothing but exaggerations of this one virtue. Respect for the parents justifies everything: cowardice, fleeing from the enemy, avoidance of work. The good consequences are less relevant. One of these, surely, is the major role the parents play in marrying off their children. Having no children is one of the three

greatest sins against one's parents. This explains the rapid propagation of the Chinese and their hatred of any form of celibacy. "Person without heirs" is a Chinese insult. When the parents die, mourning lasts three years. This period lasts so long because the first three years of a child's life are the most difficult for the parents. This long mourning brings with it significant disturbances in social life. Not only does the mourner often leave his home and move into a hut, but he also gives up his profession for three years. One can imagine the disarray caused by such a custom, especially among high officials. Indeed, the emperor can release his officials from these strict dicta, but the chronicles have often severely criticized emperors who have too frequently placed matters of state before respect for the ancestors.

The special role of the mother-in-law in Chinese marriages is also significant in a psychoanalytical explanation of fear of incest with the mother-in-law. Concerning this, I shall cite the personal observations of Katharina Zitelmann (1912):

> The Chinese wishes to have very many sons . . . for the purpose of marriage among the Chinese is the birth of a son, who will be able to make offerings to the dead father. This explains why the Chinese wishes to have many sons. Since these are married off very young, but remain in the father's household, the mother often has many daughters-in-law to supervise. Everything she has suffered in life she now takes out on the daughters-in-law. The tyranny of the mother-in-law is one of the sad aspects of the customs of the land. It must be admitted that it is difficult for her to train the completely unskilled children who come into her home as daughters-in-law to perform the duties of the household. Still, they are treated as servants or as slaves and punished in the cruelest manner. The suicide of daughters-in-law is not uncommon. In effect this punishes the mother-in-law, for it gives the family of the unhappy daughter-in-law the right to intervene. The young husband never defends his spouse against his mother's cruelty, since respect for the parents is the first commandment for the children. He hardly knows his wife and usually never becomes well acquainted with her, for private conversation between the spouses is impossible. The wife lives in the women's quarters and the husband lives with the men. If this is the situation in the wealthiest households, one can imagine the situation in poor families, who must live cramped together in little huts. It is said that a young woman has only one means of defending herself against her tormenter: she may emit a fearful scream that will cause the neighbors to come running. The missionaries tell the most delightful tales about this.

Here, behind the negative mass of powerful repressions and sublimations, we still see a bulwark against formerly positive desires and affects.

Further, Japanese mythology again reveals the original existence of sibling marriages, later strictly prohibited. According to Japanese mythology, the first human beings were the brother and sister Izanagi and Izanami, who paired according to the example of the birds. Krauss states that the oldest law codes mention marriages with siblings, as well as with aunts, nieces, and stepmothers. In the same law codes, incest between parents and children is mentioned as a crime. In Japan today, sexual relations with the concubine of the father or grandfather or with the spouse of the son or nephew receive the same punishment as relations with a paternal aunt or sister (Krauss 1911, 114). "It is clear that the Japanese has an aversion to sexual relations with a sister or maternal half-sister but does not avoid the paternal half-sister" (94). That according to Krauss *imo* means both "wife" and "younger sister" suggests how frequent sibling marriages must have been in earlier times (114).

According to Schiller-Tietz (1892, 22), as the punishment for incest, which is often the same as that for adultery, "in most societies the guilty parties are drowned. They are placed together in a sack or basket weighted with stones and thrown into the water. Among the Buginese, if the guilty parties are of noble family, they are placed on a raft of banana fronds and driven out to sea. Burying alive and burning alive also occur in certain tribes as punishments for incest."

In our modern, civilized states the concept of incest, as Marcuse argues (1908),

> is not uniformly defined in the legal codes and is not punished everywhere in the same way. There is no punishment for incest in France, Belgium, Portugal, Spain, Vaud, or Holland. In Italy and Neuchâtel it is punished, but only when a public scandal has been produced. In England incest is punishable only in the ecclesiastical courts. However, this is not the case in Scotland, the colonies, or America. Only in the remaining legal systems, and thus by no means in most systems, is incest mentioned. Still, as noted, in comparing these legal codes, there is no uniformity. While all classify sexual relations between ancestors and descendants, or between siblings, as incest, some also include more distant relatives such as in-laws in the definition. (Marcuse 1908, 138)

Thus in some states marriages between uncles and nieces, and less frequently between aunts and nephews, are permitted, whereas in others they are prohibited. In Spain and Russia, first cousins may not marry. In England, as in Germany, marriage with the spouse of a deceased sibling is prohibited. In Russia, even seventh cousins may not marry. Westermarck (1908) notes further variations in marriage restrictions based on tribal, racial, national, and religious distinctions. Marcuse makes the interesting comment (1908, 145) that the conception that royal families should not pollute their blood with that of less noble families has led to the notion among members of the current dynasties and the "high nobility" that the marriage partner must be of equal birth: "Indeed, in our royal families, incestuous marriages, or at least those closely bordering on incest, between multiply and closely related persons have been raised to the status of governing principle of the royal house."

Despite all these taboos, restrictions, and threats of punishment, the tendency for sexual intercourse with one's closest relatives, deep-seated in human nature and barely kept in check by education and culture, not only appears in our dreams, in the creations of literary fantasy, and in neurosis, but also expresses itself in forbidden acts still frequent to this day. This is demonstrated by an examination of the history of the customs of modern civilizations. In dealing with this immense theme, which is of such importance for our research, we will require more than a brief summary.

With reference to the aforementioned criminal cases of our own day, which demonstrate especially well the jealous rivalry between father and son and the tender affection of father and daughter, consider the following observations chosen at random. Bloch (1909, 701) emphasizes that in certain historical periods a shocking increase in incestuous unions can be noted; for example, during the French rococo period. Many historical examples of this type are also found in his volume *Neue Forschungen über den Marquis de Sade* [New research on the marquis de Sade] (1904, 165–68). There he argues that

> the peculiar tendency for incestuous relationships that made its appearance during the rococo period, as if through mass suggestion and with such shocking frequency, can be considered a characteristic psychosexual phenomenon of the times. Everything that the marquis de Sade relates about incest in *Justine and Juliette* and *One Hundred and Twenty Days of Sodom*, every combination and every refinement, had already been carried out by him in reality! Nicolardot says that incest should be called "la péché philosophique," for the philosophers of the period sought to justify it. In the supplement to *Journey of Bougainville*, Diderot declares that incest is an inconsequential matter. Even the notorious regent Philippe d'Orléans had sexual relations with his two daughters, the duchess of Berry and Mademoiselle de Valois, as well as with Madame de Ségur, one of his illegitimate daughters. De Terray enjoyed the favors of a young woman who was his daughter by his former mistress. How often de Sade praises just this fantasy as the culmination of physical pleasure! The notorious Marshal Richelieu also had such a relationship with his own daughter, Madame Rousse, his illegitimate daughter by Madame Capon. Cardinal de Tencin, archbishop of Lyons, also had his own daughter as mistress for a long period.

It was de Fleury, however, who realized de Sade's ideal: he was the lover of a grandmother, mother, and daughter. In his youth, he had an affair with a woman much older than he. Later, he had an affair with their own daughter, who married Monsieur de Mondorge, his uncle. The third affair was with the daughter of the latter two, whom he finally married. In 1764 a couplet describing the relationship of the duke of Choiseul, who lived in more than fraternal intimacy with his sister, the duchess of Gramont, became popular. The degree to which intellectuals were fascinated by incest at the time is illustrated by the peculiar plan, "le plan plus secret et plus chéri," that Mirabeau related to Madame de Monnier in his secret letters to her; they also include frightful blasphemies that the publisher, Cottin, has omitted from the text. Mirabeau wanted not only his children by Sophie, but also their children and grandchildren to live in perpetual incest in order to avoid every "mélange de sang," and so that there would always be a Sophie for him and a Gabriel for her. In this respect too we observe the resemblance of Mirabeau's fantasy to that of the marquis de Sade.

Rétif de la Bretonne also poured forth his incestuous ideas (cf. Bloch 1906, 381 ff.). Regarding Rétif's peculiar conceptions of incest, Bloch remarks:

> I regard his frequent comments concerning the pregnancies of his illegitimate daughters, which have more than anything led the critics to doubt his veracity, as nothing but the products of a degraded imagination. He seems to have found unusual sexual pleasure in the fantasy of sexual relations with his own children. In many cases he claimed paternity only for the purpose of wallowing in this fantasy. Of the countless sexual relationships Rétif claims to have had with his own children, a few may actually have occurred. In his dissertation, Hassler does consider Zéphire to have been his illegitimate daughter and later his lover. Usually, though, Rétif only reflected the "thermometer of his heart," fancying that so many of the beautiful women with whom he had relations were his daughters. It does seem unlikely that nearly all of his children could have been girls. This demonstrates that we are merely dealing with the fantasies of the peculiar personality described above.

Theodor Mundt (1857, 141 ff.) reports that many years ago in Paris it was rumored that in the faubourg of Saint-Antoine over six hundred workers lived with their own daughters in incestuous relationships, and he adds: "Actual instances were probably not lacking, and many sexual relationships of this type, though not in the number supposed, were doubtless maintained in Paris, especially during the Republic of 1848. The French nature does not seem so filled with innate revulsion at the thought of incest as is, most noticeably, the German nature" (Bloch 1906, 182). Wherever the orgiastic element of sexuality receives special emphasis, the primordial infantile incest impulses reappear. A comment by Löwenfeld (1908) is of special interest. He states that sexual aberrations, with special emphasis on incest, figured in the rites of a witches' sabbath. In confirming this, he quotes a passage from an old description of a witches' sabbath: "Their dances finished, the witches and warlocks proceed to couple. The son does not spare the mother, nor the brother the sister, nor the father the daughter. Incest is common; even the Persians were of the opinion that to be a good sorcerer and magician one had to be born of a mother and son."

We have already mentioned the love of Ninon de Lenclos's son for his unrecognized mother. In Holland's edition of the letters of the princess of Orléans, we find (December 23, 1701) the story of a woman who had married, unaware of her error, her own son, whom she had left at a foundling home; she had turned to a confessor for advice. Also of interest is a report of Napoleon's forbidden passion for his sister Pauline, which recent biographers have sought to confirm (cf. D'Alméras 1908). It is certain that Pauline Bonaparte, the "tinsel queen," one of the most unrestrained *amoureuses* who ever lived, was passionately in love with her brother and was extremely jealous of his spouses. After his abdication (1814), Napoleon called his mother and sister to him in exile on Elba, and it is in this period that rumors place the forbidden relationship of the siblings.

Completely unique is the relationship of "der alte Fritz" [Frederick the Great] and his sister, revealed by a curious exchange of letters that until recently was available only in the original French edition (*Oeuvres de Frédéric le Grand*), but which Wilhelm Langewische-Brandt now includes in German in the appendix of the volume *Eine preussische Königstochter* [A Prussian princess] (see Wilhelmine 1910). In this correspondence, which the siblings have their dogs address to one another, they reveal their physical desire for each other. The sister's lapdog expresses himself in a femininely reserved manner, but the brother's bitch expresses herself quite openly: "But my most charming Folichon ⟨the margravine's whippet⟩, are we to enjoy these pleasures only in our imagination? Shall we not carry out in reality what is the passion of our hearts and the height of our wishes? Shall we be as foolish as humans? They feed on wishes and are satiated with fantasies, and while they waste their time with useless projects, death secretly approaches and whisks them away with all their plans. Let us be wiser. Let us not merely run after the shadow, but grasp the thing itself." The sister's love letter begins with the following words: "I am not accustomed to accepting compliments. I have always obeyed the laws of strictest chastity observed by the ladies of my country, and I have always atoned for romantic heroism in a little adventure in which my waistline has suffered a bit. But I can forgive Folichon for things that I could never tolerate in a bourgeois dog." She had already been married for fifteen years when she wrote this, and there is no evidence in the subsequent correspondence that any actual intimacies occurred. However, these letters reveal the tendency for such intimacies most unambiguously.

Concerning the frequency of incestuous crimes in our time, Marcuse (1908, 130) comments: "Knowledge of such sexual aberrations reaches the public only very seldom. It is generally supposed that these occur with extreme infrequency, but the specialist knows that this is completely incorrect." It must also be emphasized that according to Marcuse, most of the rural portion of the populace shows a tendency for incest.

Finally, let us discuss two very recent cases of sibling incest. The first concerns seduction by the stepsister.

> An unparalleled case of immorality between stepsiblings was dealt with yesterday before the district judge in Währing. The locksmith Wilhelm H. appeared before the police in Währing and accused his stepsister, Anna Z., who resided with him, of continuous attempts to seduce him, all of which he claimed to have rejected. However, he stated that on the previous evening she had taken advantage of his total inebriation and had seduced him. The police made inquiries, and although H. wished to withdraw his accusation after the fact, both he and his stepsister were accused. The pair sorrowfully confessed the crime. H. maintained his claim that he had been seduced while he was no longer in control of his faculties, and his sister confirmed this completely, adding that she was in love with her stepbrother but that he had rejected her. She claimed she had not known that her seduction of her stepbrother was a criminal offense. A doctor called as an expert witness testified that the act could not have been committed in a state of complete inebriation and that the protestations of the accused could not be believed. However, it should be noted that since the incident Anna Z. is looking forward to the joys of motherhood. The judge pronounced both parties innocent, since he does not dispute H.'s claim of inebriation and since the statute of limitations had expired in the stepsister's case.

The second case was reported by the Rome newspapers during the work on this book (summer 1906) as a "Lovers' tragedy between siblings."

> In Rome a few days ago, a handsome young man stood before the jurors—Corporal Roberto Tommasini of the military band. He was accused of having maintained an incestuous relationship with his sister and of having shot her. He had been possessed by intense passion for his sister, Amabilia, for some time. She responded with the same feelings for him. To escape from her own feelings, the young woman became engaged to another man, while Tommasini sought comfort with a lover. But all his efforts were for naught. Since their passion was greater than their reason, they decided to die together. The first, sure shot put an end to the sister's life; the second shot penetrated the brother's breast without killing him. A note found with the

wounded man indicated that both parties had gladly looked forward to death: "Who can keep two hearts from loving one another? Whoever has a heart will forgive us and weep for us. Death is our life. We are young, but what future awaits us?"

In this case too we find all the typical characteristics of incest: the infantile sources, the attempts to resist the mutual attraction, the flight to other lovers and failure with them, and finally the shared death, which appears here quite clearly as a symbol (and substitute) for sexual union. Of course Tommasini denied having had anything more than a deep, chaste attraction to his sister. He claimed it was slander by the sister's fiancé and other cruel parties that had led them to seek death. Experts declared that Tommasini had been so much under the influence of pathological passion and excitation that his responsibility for the crime appeared to be greatly diminished. The jurors agreed with this conclusion and declared the young man innocent owing to his inability to comprehend the consequences of his actions at the time of the crime.

This historical sketch has illustrated in tradition, custom, and law the powerful means by which societies attempt to repress primitive incestuous desires. As we have already pointed out, based on psychoanalytical insights, the widespread opinion that avoidance of incestuous relations is a phylogenetically inherited human instinct can no longer be maintained. What is more, such an assertion loses all credibility in the face of the strict prohibitions, threats, and punishments we see adopted to maintain this supposedly inborn instinct. As Marcuse has demonstrated, these are adopted not because experience has shown that incest regularly produces harmful consequences for the offspring, but because they are psychologically required at a certain level of culture (stage of repression). Sociologically, too, it was with the establishment of restrictions on incest that our own culture began. These primitive tendencies and all the emotional complexes associated with them then became subject to repression. Then arose the passionate fantasies of the realization of these infantile wishes continually reflected in myth, religion, and literature. At times these infantile wishes are so resistant to repression that they lead to neurosis, criminality, or perversion, while in some cases special talents permit their sublimation through artistic creation.

PART II

The Relationship between Siblings

13 *The Significance of the Sibling Complex*

Indeed, it is said that we all descend from such relationships.

IBSEN, *Ghosts*

It is only through the primary parent complex that the significance of the sibling complex can correctly be appreciated and understood. This is because one's relationship with siblings is revealed by psychoanalytical research to be a "second edition," less intense but unchanged in content, of the etiologically earlier relationship with one's parents. Therefore everything that has been said concerning the child's relationship with the parents applies, with corresponding modifications, to the relationship with siblings. Since the original Oedipus complex quickly falls victim to repression, the impulses associated with the parents but rejected by the individual are then easily associated with the siblings, automatically present as substitutes. In the context of the siblings, these impulses are able to develop in a less impeded and more lasting manner.

This displacement of the Oedipal perspective to the siblings is further promoted by the family structure created by the very birth of siblings. The first child—let us imagine the case of a boy—regularly and inevitably becomes part of this new structure. Experience has shown that he first receives the newcomer, who has taken from him his preferred status, with intense animosity. Thus a deviation is already found for a portion of the inimical affects derived from the parent complex. If the newcomer is a little brother, this brother gradually takes over the father's position as competitor for the mother's affections. Being of equal status or, more frequently, in an even weaker position, the younger brother makes a better enemy than the immensely powerful and feared father: the older brother will have more success against the younger brother than against the father. But even if the newcomer is a little sister, it is only with time that tender impulses begin to break through the originally inimical ones (ambivalence). This also occurs in the case of a younger brother, but less intensely and with slightly different overtones. Just as the younger brother becomes a competitor in place of the father, but reduced to childlike proportions, the sister is later seen as the ideal substitute for the mother. In the fantasies of the brother, she generally takes on the image of the pure female ideal. The mother, because of her relationship with the father, is usually unworthy of this status in the eyes of her son. This displacement is encouraged because the siblings, through their similarity in age, thought, and emotion, stand much closer to one another than to adults, widely separated from them by the great chasm of culture.

Between siblings of the opposite sex growing up together, a close bond develops; they feel that they belong together. The bond is strengthened by sharing little secrets kept from the parents. Much more frequently than is generally supposed, brother and sister, encouraged by sleeping together, already engage during childhood in the mutual removal of clothes and in erotic touching and play. Often these activities are an attempt to imitate the overheard or suspected sexual relations of the parents ("playing father and mother"). Such childhood sexual traumas are commonplace in psychoanalysis. They not only are found in the childhood of subsequent neurotics, but also exercise their inhibiting effects from the unconscious later, their affect having been kept alive only through intensified fantasy activity. In the normal individual these impulses and experiences sink into the unconscious, whereas in the playwright they continue to fill and dominate his fantasy life, even in his later years.

The persistence with which these creations of fantasy dominate the works of the playwright is partially explained in that these creations are substitutes, more capable of entering the conscious and standing in the place of the more repressed and rejected parent complex. In reviewing the grouping of our material, this circumstance is seen to reflect the developmental process. Phylogenetically too, according to this process, the work of repression begins with mother incest. In its place sister incest may appear, until it too falls victim to repression (cf. chap. 12). Accordingly, we found the development of myths and legends, the first products of the poetic "collective spirit of the people," filled with productions brought about by the repression of the parent complex. In the literary works of the individual, these productions still retain a very significant role, but one reduced through advancing repression and partially unconscious. Yet the sibling complex, which belongs to a later developmental stage and falls victim to a later layer of repression, has a relatively small role in myth and can easily be classified as a subcategory of the parent complex. In the works of the individual, though, the sibling complex lives out a much fuller, more varied, and richer life than the parent complex. In the context of the parent complex the dominant tendency is to emphasize excessively the inimical relationship with the father at the tender mother's expense. With the sibling complex, besides isolated cases of hatred of the brother, the incest fantasy is often associated with the sister. If the sexual union of the siblings does not figure directly in the fantasies of the individual, it at least appears in a distorted and disguised form (see chap. 17 for the relevant mechanisms).

Thus, whereas in part 1 the broadly mythical creations of the incest complex were most significant and required detailed analysis, the creations of literary fantasy will have the greatest significance in part 2. The sibling complex does also play a lesser role in dreams, mythology, legends, folktales, history, neurosis, and criminality, and in this introductory chapter we shall deal with these aspects in summary fashion before discussing literary works.

That in mythology, too, sister incest usually represents mother incest directly, or is derived from it, seems to have become clear to certain researchers unfamiliar with psychoanalysis. Thus Stucken regards Abraham's union with Sarah as representing original mother incest. Jeremias (1904, 82) also comments: "The relationship of sibling spouses and the relationship of the son-husband with his mother-wife (which is equivalent) are illustrated most clearly by the myths of Tammuz, Attis, and Dusares." It was already necessary to discuss certain myths dealing with siblings in part 1. We mentioned the Egyptian legend of Osiris, the Greek myth of Cronus and Zeus, who married their sisters, the Japanese legend of Izanami and Izanagi, who procreated in imitation of the birds, and several other legends. In creation myths, especially, in which we recognized cosmologically depicted incest fantasies, sibling incest is found in primitive cultures in a typical form interpreted by astral mythologists as a representation of the relationship of sun and moon. Indeed, this is the form in which the tales themselves are presented; but as can be demonstrated, this occurs in accordance with a rationalizing tendency lacking true insight.

Frobenius (1904, 347) presents some of these myths.

> North American tribes say that the moon is a young woman and that the sun is her brother. She visits her brother secretly during the night but is

> finally discovered, since he has left a mark on her face with his black hands ⟨handprint⟩. The same myth not only occurs in Panama, but must also have existed in Oceania, for Bastian remarks that the moon is sometimes darkened by the hand of Mani ⟨the sun god⟩, and in these areas the moon is considered feminine. Tina is said to be Mani's sister. Thus everything corresponds. . . . Among the Cherokees, on the other hand, the sun, a young woman, lived in the east, while the moon, her brother, lived in the west. The young woman had a lover who always visited her in the dark. He came by night and departed before daybreak. She wondered who it could be. To find out, one night she rubbed his face with ashes ⟨handprint⟩. When the moon rose the next evening, its face was smeared. Then the sister knew it was her brother who had visited her. She was so ashamed that in the future she kept as far away from her brother as possible.

Among the Chiglit Eskimos, who live near Indians, the same tale is again encountered in the form of a creation myth (Petitot 1886, 7). The first two humans were brother and sister. By night the sister is seduced by her unrecognized brother. Finally, to determine who her nightly lover could be, she blackens her hands with soot and leaves marks on his face. The next morning she recognizes her brother and flees from him, but he pursues her passionately.

Up to this point the tale is related in purely human terms, and it should be interpreted in those terms. Undoubtedly the tale reflects the effects of the first prohibitions on sibling marriage among these peoples. The conclusion of the story, which relates that the pursued sister rose to the sky as the sun, while the brother continues to pursue her as the moon, is also undoubtedly the product of a still later stage of repression. At that stage of repression, even the mythological representation of sibling incest was found objectionable and was therefore projected from the earth to the sky. The tendency for this projection is a justification in a double sense. It is at once an expression of defense placing these rejected impulses of human psychic life into the farthest possible external realm and an expression of comparison (identification) through reference to divine (celestial) right, held to be an example for mankind. We are already familiar with this mechanism from chapter 12. Before continuing with the discussion of the human (psychological) content of these legends, we should mention a Greenland legend very similar to the creation myth from northwestern Canada (Rink 1875, 236 ff.): "Here, too, the moon is feminine, and is pursued every night in the dark by a young man. The man is her brother. Upon his white jacket she has left some sooty spots ⟨handprint⟩, and is thus able to recognize him. The woman cuts off her own breast and flees. The woman becomes the sun and the brother the moon" (cf. Frobenius).

One notices the obvious relation of these tales to the tales of pursuit of the daughter by the father (chap. 11), which also include the theme of disfiguring the face, severing the breasts, and so on. Thus one immediately recognizes the full significance of the incest complex in these cosmologically presented productions of fantasy. In both types of legends, the man consciously desires his daughter or sister. In both types of legends, applying soot to the face originally served to make incest possible through nonrecognition. Later versions that interpret the use of soot as a strategy to permit recognition are a secondary product of advancing repression.

The close relation of these tales of siblings to the father-daughter tales is demonstrated by the Italian folktale "The Girl without Hands" mentioned above. It is constructed precisely according to the father-daughter schema, but instead it involves the sister. After the death of his wife, the king takes it into his head to marry his own sister, Penta, and tells her so. In her desperation, she severs both her hands and sends them to her brother with the comment that he should "gladly enjoy that which he seemed to wish for more than anything in the world." The king orders her exposed at sea in a chest sealed with pitch. After many adventures, she is fished up in a foreign city. After the death of his wife, the foreign king marries her. Now follows the birth of a son during the king's absence; the mother informs him by letter. The letter is falsified so that mother and child will be sentenced to death; however they are only exposed in the wilderness, where a sorcerer finally resolves everything happily and she regains her hands.

As in the related father myths, the incest fantasy asserts itself through doubling. The king who marries Penta, who has been fished from the water, after his wife dies is of course the doublet of the king who wishes to marry his sister Penta after the death of his wife. The exposure (the two doublets are to be combined) could originally have occurred when the king recognized his disfigured sister as his spouse (perhaps from her hands).

However, the father's severing the hands or breasts of the daughter who refuses to submit is also reported as a punishment. In contrast, in the sibling myths listed the hands are covered with soot and the handprint serves as a sign leading to recognition. In a legend of the Indians of the lower Fraser River (American Pacific Coast) reported by Stucken (1896–1907), the same tale appears in a purely human form and concept. One night the sister smears her lover with soot; then she recognizes him the next morning as her brother, who has led her to commit incest. On finding that she is pregnant, she is filled with intense shame and begs the brother to go far away with her. But when their son grows up, he notices their great resemblance to one another and discovers the whole truth. Brother and sister willingly die by fire (Boas 1895, 37 ff.).

Ernst Siecke, one of the founders of lunar mythology, has also pointed out repeatedly that these incest fantasies portrayed in celestial form are also numerous in the myths of civilized Indo-European peoples. He cites a number of gods and goddesses, emphasizing the parallelism of their names. In each case, they are "children of the sky" and siblings: "Since they approach one another, these siblings are also bride and groom, man and wife" (Siecke 1897). Of such related pairs, Siecke lists Dianus and Diana, Phoebus and Phoebe, Iolaus and Ioleia, Pyrrhus and Pyrrha, Liber and Libera, Niödr and Nerthus, Fjorgym and Fjorgyn, and many others. In one hymn of the *Rig Veda* (10.10), Yama and Yami wed. Here too Siecke sees clues indicating that the siblings Freyr and Freya were also spouses (1897, 23 ff.): "Later, of course, Gerdha ⟨the same goddess by another name⟩ took the place of Freya." The parallelism in name that Siecke points out very nicely shows the sibling relationship where it has not been preserved genealogically but has been eliminated because it was felt to be offensive. Two of Siecke's examples utilizing this method of interpretation will demonstrate that in myths, too, names are highly significant.

The first example deals with the Trojan cycle and the other with folktales.

> Paris was also called Alexander, and Cassandra was also called Alexandra. The parallelism in name leads one to conclude that these two siblings were originally closer to one another and that Helenus, the twin brother of Cassandra, is only a derivative or doublet of Paris. Through his spouse, the moon-goddess Helena, Paris is unambiguously placed among the gods of light. ⟨If Helenus is Paris, then we also have the pair Helenus and Helena.⟩ Apparently he is a sun hero. Therefore the female Alexandra, associated with Alexandrus, can be nothing but a moon-goddess, and thus of the same nature as Helena. Her other name, Cassandra, is apparently derived from *kasi-andra* "she who has brother as husband." This is of course supported by the ancient myths relating that sun and moon are brother and sister, but also husband and wife. (Siecke 1901, 69)

Siecke's second example (1892, 7 ff.) concerns the Grimms' folktale of the white bride and the black bride: "Sun and moon are like man and wife, and also like brother and sister. In the most ancient times, it was possible for them to be both simultaneously. In later times such relationships came to be considered offensive. Therefore many old tales had to be altered to a degree. Originally, of course, the king fetched his sister and bride himself." Recently Siecke (1909, 92) has discussed the peculiar legend "that Faunus impregnated his feminine counterpart Fauna ⟨wife, sister, and daughter⟩ in the form of a snake."

The Nordic saga of Sigmund's union with his twin sister Signy also demonstrates the parallelism in name as well as the twin relationship. According to the *Völsunga-Saga*, the brother commits the incest unknowingly; only the sister is aware of it. Signy, who has two sons by Siggeir, realizes that only a true Völsung can serve as avenger. Unrecognized, in a disguise, she approaches her brother, and from this union is born Sinfjötli. Here again we see the theme of disfigurement applied to bring about the act of incest.

In noting another myth from the Nordic tradition, we shall approach the greatest and most significant group of myths—those involving enmity with the brother, so characteristic of the sibling complex. This enmity is portrayed in a manner analogous to the treatment of enmity with the father, derived from the parent complex. This competition usually arises because of jealous rivalry over a woman, often the brothers' sister, and even where this original relationship has already been weakened or fully eliminated, it is still clear that the woman is a surrogate for the mother. In passing, mention should be made of the inimical pairs of brothers already mentioned: Eteocles and Polynices, Atreus and Thyestes, Jacob and Esau, Perez and Serah, Osiris and Typhon (Set), Romulus and Remus, and so forth. At this point we can turn to our discussion of the Nordic myth of Baldr and Hödr, which, though it is generally interpreted as a nature myth, stands close to the myth of the blind bowman. The blind Hödr shoots his brother Baldr with the young twig of mistletoe (blind = unknowingly) supplied to him by Loki, disguised as a woman. From the two versions of the myth, Snorri's *Edda* account in Icelandic and the version of Saxo Grammaticus, which Müllenhoff claims is much older, it is clear that the two brothers oppose each other on account of their love for the same young woman, Nanna, who according to Saxo Grammaticus is their sister. Baldr is presented as the one Nanna favors, but he is shot by Hödr, who in Saxo's version is not blind. Then Baldr's brother Vali appears as his avenger and slays Hödr (Böklen 1907, 136).

Just as the sisterhood of the two brothers' common beloved is muted in later versions of this saga, this may also hold true for the famous biblical brothers Cain and Abel. Cain, like the Roman Romulus, is presented as a founder of cities. After the murder of his brother, he founds the first city and names it after his son Enoch (Gen. 4:17). According to the biblical account, Cain becomes jealous of his brother because Abel's offerings are pleasing to God. Literary treatments of this story show that their authors felt this was not sufficient motivation. Rather than portraying the conflict as arising over the brothers' love of God, writers have often portrayed it as centering on the brothers' love for their parents, especially their mother. In Gabriel Legouvé's version, *La mort d'Abel* [The death of Abel] (1792), Cain hates his brother because Abel is preferred by their parents. Similarly, in his "erotic mystery" *Die ersten Menschen* [The first men], Otto

Borngräber attempts to portray the conflict as arising out of sexual rivalry over the mother. Even Böklen, who stands firmly in the camp of the nature mythologists, notices the absence in the biblical account of all explanation for why Abel's offerings found favor in the eyes of Jehovah while Cain's did not (1907, 115). Just as playwrights have intuitively substituted the parents (the mother) for the "jealous" God and have portrayed the brothers as vying for the love of their parents, Werner Moser (1903) concludes that in Jehovah's place there was originally the common sister of Cain and Abel. Each wished to take her as his wife and attempted to gain her love through gifts. Indeed, as Böklen mentions, a later Judeo-Christian tradition takes this theme of sexual rivalry in the context of the incest complex as the basis of the biblical account, apparently highly distorted and ethically tendentious. According to this tradition, Cain was jealous of Abel because Adam and Eve wished to give his twin sister to his brother in marriage (Böklen, n.d., 67). But in the talmudic story of Cain, incestuous jealousy also appears as the driving motive for the fratricide. In the Midrash it is written: "Rabbi Huna teaches that they fought over the twin sister who had been born together with Abel. Abel made claim to her because she had come into the world with him, but Cain believed he had the right to her as firstborn" (Weil 1845, 38). From psychoanalyses of neurotics we realize that this rivalry over the (incestuous) love object is only a renewal of early childhood rivalry, ultimately dealing with possession of the mother. This is confirmed in the works of creative artists.

According to a personal communication from Dr. Federn, there exists a painting, probably by Anselm Feuerbach, that portrays the awakening of Cain's enmity toward his brother; Cain watches with jealousy and hate in his eyes as the young Abel is suckled by Eve. In his novel *Pastor Klinghammer,* Wilhelm Hegeler portrays the same source of later competition and enmity between brothers. In the novel, rivalry over a woman, ending in the murder of one of the brothers, forms the central core of the plot: "The pastor no longer knew when the enmity between him and his brother had begun. It was probably as old as the brother himself. It seemed to him that in childhood, when he had seen the beautiful little boy in his happy mother's arms, the tormenting thought had already awakened in him: 'He will achieve everything which you strive for with the whole force of your passion, and which remains forever forbidden to you' " (p. 7).

In the Bible, the theme of the inimical brothers is noted frequently. In addition to the story of Esau and Jacob, the brothers' hatred of Joseph should be mentioned, as well as the fratricide committed by Jehoram (2 Chronicles 21) and the murder by Absalom of his brother Amnon, who had raped their sister Tamar. Minor skillfully relates the frequency and powerful effect of this theme to the first impressions of childhood: "The theme of the inimical brothers is the oldest tragic conflict legend and literature have dealt with. It dates back to the Bible. A significant portion of its elemental power, so often felt, derives from the fact that this impression of enmity is among the earliest of our childhood. Our first love and our first hate involve the brother; our first rival is our brother" (Minor 1890, 302). Significantly enough, in the Bible, which projects events in the life of the individual back into human history, the first murder is a fratricide. In Lithuanian mythology, too, the first murder occurs when Ugniedokas kills his brother Ugniegawas (Friedrichs 1909, 317).

Concerning the enmity of Amnon and Absalom, Winckler remarks (1895–1900, 2:228): "When we have two brothers with sun (Tammuz) nature, one of whom is the spouse of the common sister, of Ishtar nature, we have the basic characteristics of the Ishtar/Tammuz myth. Ishtar appears in her two roles as virgin and as spouse, while Tammuz appears in the corresponding roles—as sibling spouse and celibate brother. One of the brothers kills the other—the theme of hatred of the brother." Winckler, who also subscribes to a purely astral interpretation of the myth of the Dioscuri, remarks (1905–6, 2, pt. 1:49 ff.): "In ancient accounts of man's beginnings one finds everywhere the tale of the two brothers (half-brothers), one of whom is killed or must yield to the other in some way. The two brothers are bound by love yet separated by hatred. . . . Brother and sister are simultaneously spouses. Often the theme of the inimical brothers is motivated by their love for the common sister and spouse, whom one brother steals from the other. In myth, though, doppelgängers often appear in the place of the brother. Nevertheless, they show the same characteristics as he does." Even in the Greek legend of the Dioscuri, we find both the theme of inimical brothers and the incest theme in distorted, dampened form. Castor, the mortal son of Leda, and Pollux, her immortal son, take vengeance on Theseus for abducting their sister Helen. In the same way, Simeon and Levi avenge their ravished sister Dinah (Gen. 34:25–31), and Absalom takes vengeance on his brother Amnon for raping their sister Tamar. In that story it is clear that the rape of the sister originally relates to incest, with the disfavored brother taking vengeance on the preferred one. In the myth of the Dioscuri, in which the brothers are bound by love, they avenge the sister together; enmity and abduction of the bride are displaced to another pair of twins (doublet). Castor and Pollux at first appear bound by deep love to their distant relatives, the brothers Lynceus and Idas. Later, though, they have a falling out with them and abduct their brides, the daughters of Leucippus (complement to the abduction of Helen). Then Lynceus, Idas, and Castor fall in battle; only the immortal Pollux remains unharmed. In later versions, though, he sometimes shares the fate of mortality with his brother Castor.

Before we attempt to discuss in brief our interpretation of this theme of the twin brothers, recurring so often in typical form and guise, we should emphasize that this original theme of the pair of twin brothers lives on in the numerous folktales of brothers in which rivalry over a woman (sister) is significant. Wundt, who discusses these tales in detail (1909, pt. 3) and stresses their origins in human life and their human content (282), remarks strikingly (277): "In all mythology, there is a constant trait: pairs of friends are preferentially placed in contrast to the inimical brothers. The friend selects his friend by free choice. The brother, however, especially in Oriental legends, is the born enemy of his brother. . . . Therefore this contrast is also intensified when an originally allied pair of brothers is transformed into an inimical pair (cf. Eteocles and Polynices, Romulus and Remus)." In contrast, wherever the enmity between the brothers is portrayed as congenital, the myth may relate that this enmity originated in the womb. This is the case with Esau and Jacob, and in the Argive legend of Acrisius and his brother Proetus (Apollodorus 2.2.1).

In a German folktale (Grimm and Grimm 1816, no. 60) the theme of the rival brothers is strongly distorted, though it does retain some of its original traits. By slaying a vile dragon, one of the twin brothers wins the hand of the king's daughter. However, he is beheaded by the marshal, who presents himself as the dragon's killer. The brother is reanimated by his loyal animals, and just a year later he arrives at the wedding of the princess and the marshal. There he presents the seven tongues he had cut from the dragon and receives his bride. The impostor is executed. Once, in the forest, a witch turns him and his animals to stone, and his twin brother, who in the meantime has come to the court, is taken for the missing husband of the queen—indeed, himself takes on this role. At night, though, he lays a two-edged sword between himself and his brother's spouse as a *symbolum castitatis*. Here we see the original rivalry of the brothers, though in sentimentally dampened form. In the evil marshal, who robs the victor of life and bride, we also recognize the split-off doublet of the brother, who wishes to take his brother's place in the marriage bed. Even though a strong dampening and a shift toward the sentimental have occurred in the folktale, it is clear, given the manner of development of legends, that he did take his brother's place in the marriage bed in the original version. Here, as in many other places, in the analysis of the creations of mythology in the light of the advancement of repression, Wilhelm Müller's striking comment is relevant (1856, 422): "Often, to understand the significance of an entire myth, one must assume that what seems about to occur, but is prevented, really does occur." Through sentimental dampening, the loyal brother, who has not touched the bride, releases the brother and his animals from the spell. Nevertheless, the bitter payment the loyal brother receives for this clearly shows that originally the relationship of the brothers was thoroughly inimical: when the brother tells his reanimated brother that he has been taken for the missing spouse and has slept in the young queen's bed, "he becomes so jealous and angry that he draws his sword and cuts off his brother's head." That the second brother's reanimation now occurs through the same animals and the same herb as that of the first brother, beheaded by the marshal, confirms once again that these scenes are to be interpreted as doublets. Finally, through sentimental dampening, the main theme of sexual rivalry is again addressed. Both brothers approach the young queen, who becomes confused about which of them she should consider her husband. Seeing the collar of one of the animals, though, she recognizes her true spouse. Nevertheless, as they are going to bed, she asks her husband why he has always laid a two-edged sword between them in their bed, and he recognizes that his brother has been truly loyal.

In their comments on this tale, the brothers Grimm note a great many interesting variations of this genre, some involving the father's locking up the daughter. In the folktale "Wasserpeter and Wasserpaul," the theme of sexual rivalry is clearer still. The one brother, released from a spell, returns and finds the other in his place; he kills him out of jealousy. Hearing of his loyalty, however, and that he has laid a sharp sword between himself and the queen, the true husband reanimates his brother with the water of life. In particular, the Grimms emphasize the similarity of this formulation to the saga of Sigurd. They support this observation with several noticeably parallel details. In this connection, we are interested only in the theme of sexual rivalry. Like the married brother in these folktales, in the German saga Sigurd frees the bride, Brunhild, from the dragon and also separates himself from her. "The brother with the same form is Gunnar, the blood brother, with whom Sigurd exchanges form. Indeed laying the sword between does occur, but in the opposite context" (Grimm and Grimm 1816).

If, in comparison with the German folktale and its significant parallels, we bring up the similarly structured Egyptian tale of the brothers Bitiu and Anepu and the Osiris legend underlying it, we find the originally inimical rivalry of the brothers over the love of their sister. This rivalry ends with the castration of the brother guilty of incest by his competitor, who presents himself as the sister's avenger. As with the parent complex, incest and castration are found to be the primal themes of the sibling complex, based as it is on the former complex. Thus we can appreciate Schwartz's observation (1860, 138 ff.) that the name "Castor" may originally have signified "the castrated one" and may have become associated with Castor without there being a corresponding legend.

In this connection Schwartz convincingly emphasizes that one of the brothers is usually considered to be of divine origin, of heroic character, and immortal, while the other is assumed to be of human origin, weak, and mortal. Fated to perish young, he leads a shadowy existence beside his heroic brother. "This contrast of the weaker brother as opposed to the strong hero is observed also in the relationships of Heracles and Iphicles, of Agamemnon and Menelaus, and of Hector and Paris, while all of these are reminiscent of Siegfried and Gunther. Here the weaker one is the spouse (of Brunhild or Helen), while it is the stronger one who must fight to gain her hand." From the perspective of castration, it would also be clear why Gunther is unable to deprive Brunhild of her virginity on the wedding night. Similarly, the immortality of the one twin brother (Pollux or Heracles, etc.) could be derived from the children he is destined to sire.

Given the two primal themes, in this pale, shadowy, weak, and mortal twin brother we not only recognize the brother eliminated, through castration, from competition for the sister, but are also in a position, given our understanding of the "myth of the birth of the hero," to comprehend the apparently most important source of the theme of the twin brothers. For the same tales of the Dioscuri are found widely among primitive peoples and include all the obvious details. Ehrenreich, especially, has noted this. In one aspect of the legend, he finds the key to understanding the theme of the twin brothers (1910, 239):

> A peculiar and still unexplained trait, frequently found in America, is that only one of the brothers has divine qualities, while the other is considered purely human. His father is a mortal who impregnates the mother only once, her elder son having been sired by a god (cf. the legend of Heracles). Accordingly, this second son is weaker and has human imperfections. In another variation on the theme, the second brother arises from the discarded afterbirth of the elder brother. This "child of the afterbirth" is one of the most frequent figures of legend among the Plains Indians. In this respect it is interesting to note the African belief that the afterbirth is a brother, an alter ego of the child. Therefore the child must preserve the remains of his umbilical cord, with which his soul or life energy stands in a mythic relationship, for the rest of his life.

Here belongs also the concept, widespread among the Australian aborigines, of a protector spirit born simultaneously with the child. The significance attributed to the afterbirth is also demonstrated in that in Japan it is ceremonially buried.

At this point, in random order, we can note several mythological and historical manifestations of the sibling complex. This will cast light on the wide distribution and typical guise of these themes. We have already mentioned the institution of sibling marriage in many cultures. In his first book of histories (chap. 13), Diodore derives this custom of the Egyptians from their mythology (the Osiris myth). Wiedmann reports that in an Egyptian tale, Ahure marries her brother Nenefar-Kaptah in accordance with the old custom observed in royal houses. We have already mentioned that the royal families of Peru procreated through incest. Multatuli (1901, vol. 1, chap. 20) relates the story of the two Peruvian royal twins, Telazco and Cuzco, both of whom loved their sister and were also loved by her. In Multatuli's work one also finds other hints of childhood love for the sister. Thus, Walter also relates the story (p. 127) of a boy who wishes to follow his little sister to heaven: "He said he was engaged to her, . . . that he loved her so dearly that he would gladly marry her." Bab (1906) reports similar accounts of primitive peoples. The queen of Inthapataburi (Cambodia) married her brother; this marriage was without issue. Yami begged her brother to become her spouse, though without success. In Indic accounts, Pusan has relations with his sister Surga (*Rig Veda* 6). Herodotus (3.31) names Cambyses as the first Persian king to marry his sister: "He won the love of one of his sisters and wished to take her as his wife." The royal judges found that this marriage, previously considered a crime among the Persians, was actually legal. Shortly thereafter, though, Cambyses also married his second sister, whom he then murdered. Indeed, Cambyses committed this deed out of jealousy, for the sister mourned the murder of her brother Smerdis, whom Cambyses had had killed based on a dream. Herodotus (1.35) also mentions the story of Croesus, who permitted his son to go hunting despite an ominous dream, leading to an unknowing fratricide. In Xenophon's *Anabasis* (1.8.26), Cyrus fights against his brother and wounds him. In Wolfram von Eschenbach's *Parzival,* the hero fights against his unrecognized brother Feirefiss.

In the *Epistulae heroidum* [Letters from heroines], Ovid relates the story of the famous lovers, the siblings Macareus and Canace, also dealt with by Euripides in his tragedy *Aeolus.* In Virgil's *Aeneid* the story of Dido, who married her uncle Sichaeus, illustrates the theme of the brother who appears as the jealous avenger of the sister and the competitor for her hand: her brother Pygmalion kills his sister's spouse while she is fleeing from him [Sichaeus]. (A similar love affair has occurred in Italy in our time; cf. the Bonmartini case below.) In Heliodorus's *Ethiopica,* to ensure their safety, the beloved, called Chariclea because of the whiteness of her hands (cf. Penta, soot), claims that her lover, Theagenes, is her brother. This theme, already familiar to us from the legends of Abraham and Isaac as a dampened form of incest, is found also in other portions of the work, as well as in many later Greek works and in the tale "Ismenias and Ismene" by Eustathius. Among the loving relationships discussed by Parthenius, several involve siblings. These include the story of Polymele, beloved by her brother Diores, who wished to marry her, the story of Leucippus, who was in love with his sister (chap. 12), and the story of Caunus, who loved his sister Byblis. Greek legend claims the descent of Byblis from Minos, in whose family sinful relationships were prevalent. When Minos made clear his desire for his grandson Miletus, whose looks attracted the grandfather, Miletus fled to Caria in a small boat on the advice of Sarpedon. There he founded Miletus and sired the twins Caunus and Byblis by Eidothea, a daughter of the local Carian king, Eurytus. According to the usual version, it was Byblis who felt the sinful attraction. When she confessed it to her brother, he fled the country in horror (doublet of the father) and founded the city of Caunus in southern Caria. However, Byblis, still consumed by passion and tormented by the thought that she had driven her brother from his homeland, hanged herself from an oak. From her tears sprang the spring of Byblis (Ovid, *Metamorphoses,* 9.450 ff.). In contrast to this version, there is another claiming that it was Caunus who felt passion for his sister; since he could not master it, he fled from his father's house. In this version, too, Byblis hangs herself. In his novella *Die Richterin* [*The judicatrix*] (chap. 17), Conrad Ferdinand Meyer refers to Byblis's sinful love. Pierre Louÿs has related her story in "Byblis," and in his *Chansons de Bilitis,* which he claimed to have translated from classical Greek, he says of a young man: "He is so beautiful that his mother cannot embrace him without blushing."

In Arthurian legend, Mordred is sometimes Arthur's nephew and sometimes his illegitimate son. Giglan explains why: "Mordred was his illegitimate son whom he had sired by his sister before his marriage, not recognizing her." In *The Thousand and One Nights* we encounter the theme of sibling love again and again, for example, in the "Tale of the First Calender" and in the "Miraculous Tale of Omar Alnuman and His Sons Sharkan and Dhul Makan." In one of the tales the caliph's son retreats with his beloved sister into a subterranean cavern, where they are later found, burned to ashes. In Boccaccio's *Decameron* (day 5, story 5), a young man falls in love with his sister, whom he does not know. When he is about to carry her off, he finds himself in hand-to-hand combat with another suitor. In German folktales (Grimm and Grimm 1816) the theme of sibling love is often encountered. It is found, in a very interesting guise, in the tale "Seeburger See" [Seeburg Lake], which describes the formation of this lake near Göttingen. "In olden times, where the lake is now, there was a proud castle. In the castle lived a count named Isang who led a godless and wild life. Once he broke through the holy walls of the convent of Lindau, seized a nun, and took her by force. No sooner had he committed the deed than he realized that the woman upon whom he had just brought shame was his own sister, who had been secluded from him until then. Indeed, he was horrified; he sent her back to the convent and did a great penance, but still his heart did not turn to God. Once again he began to live by following his lusts." Soon, though, reaction is observed. The depiction of his psychic state resembles the confession of a neurotic suffering from pangs of guilt and deluded self-accusations. In the story, with its symbolic manner of presentation, the outbreak of neurosis is associated with a white snake enabling humans to understand the language of the animals. "Afterward, all the sins and crimes he had previously committed weighed down upon his heart and stood so clearly before him that he could not ignore them. He was beside himself with anxiety. 'I feel so hot,' said he. 'It seems like the fires of hell.' In his fear he went back to the courtyard, but all the animals there—the chickens, ducks, and geese—were running about telling one another about his decadent life and his horrid crimes." The cock warns him of the impending destruction of the castle. He flees and watches from afar as it sinks out of sight. Then the count turns to God and does penance for his sins.

In "Sündliche Liebe" [Sinful love], also among the German folktales related by the Grimms, the incest theme appears in still another psychologically interesting guise. "On the Petersberg near Erfurt, a brother and sister are buried together; they are pictured on the rather impressive gravestone. The sister was so beautiful that the brother, after spending some time abroad, fell deeply in love with her and sinned with her upon his return. Immediately, the devil ripped off their heads. Their images were carved on the gravestone, but the heads soon disappeared from the carving too. New heads of brass were affixed to the carving, but these too disappeared. Indeed, if one simply drew new heads in chalk, they were gone by the next day." This disappearance of the heads is strongly reminiscent of the defense mechanism of incest dreams in which the forbidden partner's face is not seen and of the other techniques aimed at the enactment of incest (disguise, soot, etc.) appearing here and elsewhere as punishments (severing of the hands).

In the tale "Die Heidenjungfrau zu Glatz" [The heathen maiden of Glatz], who "had shot her brother with bow and arrow," the illicit love of the heathen maiden and her brother is described. Because of their love, they are despised and their lives are imperiled. Through her magical charms and her strength she repeatedly escapes, until finally she is apprehended and incarcerated.

Pauli relates a legend (published before 1597) widespread in the sixteenth century. The son of a wealthy man of Groningen becomes a hermit and lives for a long time in quiet contemplation and meditation. In a dream, a voice tells him it is the Lord's will that he commit one of three sins. He must either become totally inebriated, break his vow of chastity, or commit murder. As the apparently least harmful sin, he chooses inebriation; he writes to his sister and asks her to visit him and bring wine. She arrives, and at first they converse in a quite decent manner. "But gradually the brother becomes aroused and takes his sister by force. After the deed he thinks, 'She will have a child by me, so I shall first let her go home.' Then he goes to her home and murders her. Thus he commits all three sins, having supposed that he had chosen the least of them." The legend then relates that this sinner, who sinned against his will, does penance and is elected pope.

At times sibling incest occurs in folktales as well. In a Hungarian folktale (Erdélyi 1850, no. 11), a king wishes to marry his seven daughters to his seven sons. Laistner mentions a similar Serbian folktale in which a youth accomplishes the difficult tasks required to win the hand of the princess but is cast into the dungeon by the king, who breaks his word. Finally, though, he appears in all his wondrous glory. Still, he is not able to free the princess from the mountain of glass, for the king is his father and the princess is his sister. Laistner comments: "Through this relationship, a major portion of the old folktale of the glass mountain is eliminated. One variant attempts to find a substitute: it is related that in the forbidden chamber there resides a young woman who finally becomes the prince's spouse." To this folktale can be compared two Serbian folk songs from volume 2 of Vuk's edition: number 27, "Dušan Wants to Marry His Sister," and number 28, "The Marriage of Dušan's Sister." In another variant, the same is related of the emperor Constantine and his sister Jelena. Serbian heroic legends also relate the story of the robber leader Predag, who shoots his brother Nenad on seeing him for the first time but then stabs himself when he learns from his dying brother that he has committed fratricide. The story of Francesca da Rimini is historically documented. In 1275 she was married to Gianciotto Malatesta, the lord of Rimini. Because of her attraction to his brother Paolo, Malatesta murdered them both in 1288. In *The Divine Comedy,* Dante recalls Francesca's demise. This theme has been adopted by Silvio Pellico, Johann Uhland (unfinished), Paul Heyse, Martin Greif, and recently Gabriele D'Annunzio. In his drama *Pelléas et Mélisande,* Maurice Maeterlinck deals with similar material. The aging, jealous Golo murders his brother Pelleas because his wife, Melisande, now loves him.

In concluding this chapter dealing with the rich domain of the sibling complex, having seen its significance in the structure of myths, folktales, and legends, we should also note the neurotic and "criminal" expressions that, as with other complexes, are also observed. Interestingly, in criminal cases conflicts with the brother occur far less frequently than the innumerable conflicts with the father. Still, cases of bitter enmity between brothers do exist, not seldom leading to murder and death.

Crimes arising from sexual love between siblings are far less numerous than those arising from the father's passionate love for his daughter. To the examples of love between recognized siblings noted at the end of chapter 12 should be added an example of sibling love without the knowledge of the partner's identity, reminiscent of mythological cases. Consider the following newspaper account (December 25, 1910): "His sister's bridegroom. According to Russian press reports, a young lieutenant from Yalta has shot himself after learning that the young woman to whom he had become engaged was his own sister. The officer had met the young woman through her foster parents. A few days before the wedding was to be celebrated, it came to his attention that his betrothed was the daughter of his own mother. The young woman, who has no knowledge of the reasons that led to his suicide, is torn with grief. Out of deference to the families struck by this bad fortune, the names of the parties involved have been withheld by the Russian press."

The affair of the Countess Bonmartini was much discussed a few years ago. She is supposed to have arranged the murder of her husband by her brother, who was also her lover. The jealousy of the brother-in-law is one of the typical reactions encountered in the psychology of hatred of the brother; it too can be clearly traced in the life and works of authors (cf. Schiller, Goethe, Wagner, and others below). Recently there occurred in Paris an unusual murder noted by Josef Friedjung (1912, 293). He states that based on our psychological insights the supposed motive for the murder can be understood as "an unusual rationalization of incestuous jealousy."

"On May 22, 1911, the talented painter Amélie Lhermite was murdered in Angers by her brother. The murder, which at first seemed mysterious and incomprehensible, was shockingly clarified in court yesterday. . . . Eugène Lhermite claimed that he had loved his only sister passionately. The only meaning in his life had been to ensure her future happiness. However, their grandmother, father, and mother had all died insane, and the two of them were also under the threat of insanity. When the sister reported to him one day that she was planning to marry, he begged her to give up this idea in order to avoid bringing new candidates for insanity into the world. The sister would not listen to these arguments. She rejected with horror his proposal that they commit suicide together. In court, he claimed that he had had no other choice; killing her was the only way to end the family's bitter curse. He also stated that a sentence of death would be the best thing for him as well."

Friedjung remarks: "Whoever has come to understand Freud's teachings will hardly be satisfied with the interpretation of the deed presented by the murderer before his judges and, apparently, generally accepted. Surely the French are familiar with less drastic measures than murder and suicide in order to avoid passing down the trait of insanity. We do accept Lhermite's claim that he loved his sister and that he wished to dedicate his life to her happiness. When she wished to give herself to another, the brother, whose libido was fixed on the sister, acted in the same way as many another pathologically uninhibited lover."

Finally, reference should be made to two cases of neurosis derived from the sibling complex. These cases illustrate the typical emergence of repression at the time of puberty and should prove instructive. We should note that incestuous attraction to siblings is a regularly occurring feature in the psychoanalysis of neurotics and that every practicing analyst is familiar with many such cases. In his capacity as spiritual adviser, Pastor Pfister of Zurich had occasion to notice and come to an understanding of two cases involving young persons not seriously ill. The first report concerns two brothers who harbored thoughts of death and felt murderous impulses toward one another. Cain and Abel fantasies played a great role in this connection. The younger brother suffered from violent, unconscious murderous impulses. Without realizing it, he associated all daily experience—everything read and thought—with the murder of the brother. Characteristically, he hated no other boys—only his brother. The second case concerns an intelligent, ethically sensitive youth who had been in despair for six months following a dream of incest with his sister. Immediately upon awakening, he had the impression that the dream was true; he could not rid himself of this thought. After suffering for half a year, he asked his sister directly: "Did I commit incest with you?" He was finally consoled by her assurances that nothing had occurred between them in the slightest, "though at first, doubts as to my innocence did return a few times." During analysis, it was revealed that "the siblings had slept in the same room until they were fifteen, that is, until after the dream. The girl had often spoken in discreet terms of a topic (birth) that seemed to arouse the boy's curiosity and always produced pleasurable feelings in him. It is understandable that the brother's sexual desire was unavoidably directed to the sister. The ugly thought was always rejected with horror. . . . The interpretation of the dream was now clear: the image of incest provided fulfillment of the repressed wish."

Having established in this introductory chapter the psychic-infantile nature of the sibling complex, subject to repression and struggling from the unconscious for expression, we shall turn to the wildly exuberant sibling incest fantasies of the most important authors of all times and places, and to their many guises and variations.

14 *Grillparzer: A Contribution to the Problem of the Relationship of Literature and Neurosis*

In my pain she left me melody and speech
To lament my sorrow's deepest need:
And when in my torment my human voice failed me,
A god enabled me to speak of what I suffer.

GOETHE, *Tasso*

Franz Grillparzer's first work, *Die Ahnfrau* [The ancestress], demonstrates very clearly the close connection of the parent and sibling complexes. Here we find only slight deviation from the typical form of parental incest drama: the son kills the father but loves the sister instead of the mother. The drama can be summarized as follows. The ancestress of the Borotins, who was murdered by her husband because of her infidelity, is condemned by a curse to wander without rest through the rooms of the palace until her descendants have died out. The last three members of the family are the old Count Borotin, his son Jaromir, and his daughter Berta. As a child, Jaromir is abducted by the gypsy Boleslav, who raises him as his own son and makes a robber of him. Jaromir happens to meet Berta and falls in love with her. The old count has no objection to their relationship. While Jaromir is staying at the count's palace, soldiers come to capture the robber band led by Jaromir. While the robbers are being pursued fighting breaks out, and Jaromir kills the old count without realizing he has killed his own father. Gradually it becomes clear to Jaromir that he too is a Borotin—that he is his father's murderer and his sister's lover. Beside Berta's body, he dies in the arms of the ancestress, who closely resembles her.

One notices the typical wish for elimination of the father, and one sees that defense against this impulse—repression—is expressed through killing the father without knowing his identity. We know that Grillparzer never had a loving relationship with his father. In his autobiography he wrote: "Actually, I never loved my father tenderly. He was too harsh." Even more important than his inimical relationship with his father is the expression of love for the sister, observed in *Die Ahnfrau:* Grillparzer himself had no sister. If we disregard the vacuous objection that any playwright could deal with the incest theme without personal involvement, we are presented with a psychological riddle. If Grillparzer had had a sister, it would be clear how his love for his mother had been displaced to that sister—a process discussed in chapter 13. However, from his relationship with his father we can conclude that he did have an affectionate attachment to his mother in early childhood. Indeed, based on the intensity of the defense mechanisms, one must suppose that this affection was powerful enough to be displaced to a fantasy image—the sister. This would correspond fully to Grillparzer's neurotic character. To a high degree he shunned sexual activity, preferring the woman created by his fantasy to any real one.

But the question remains why the figure in this fantasy was specifically a sister. One can suppose that the playwright, given his immense need for love, developed the fantasy that he had a sister, for powerful inhibitions prohibited him from finding gratification in the real world. His rejection of sex also acted to determine the form and orientation of these fantasies, which caused him to desire a woman whom he could love but not possess sexually. This sister fantasy is confirmed for us in the poem "Abschied" [Farewell], written by Grillparzer on departing from Gastein on August 1, 1820, and addressed to Frau Josephine von Verhovitz. There we read:

Madame, you were a mother to me;
   My mother is now at rest.
Your admonitions were like hers.
   Your call was like her call.
Madame, you were my sister,
   Though sisters I never had,
But emotion and fantasy
   Have pictured to me how dear and fine
It would be to be glad of oneself in another,
   Of another in oneself;
To be two, and yet one,
   Intimately united.
Madame, you have taught me well
   What a wife should be.

. . . .
But Madame, I have no home,
No ties plaited by love.
My mother they have carried away
And sisters I never knew.

In addition to passionate longing for a sister, the poem reveals that his incestuous tendency has been displaced from the mother to the sister: the married woman is lauded as mother, sister, and wife. Here an unconscious motivation for the development of the sister complex may become clear to us. Since he creates mainly unconsciously, the playwright never pictures his emotional and love life in a manner precisely corresponding to reality. Still, he makes modifications only to the extent determined by inner objections (Freud's "psychic censorship"). Each one of his works is "truth and poetry." With Grillparzer, of the actual incestuous affection for the mother, only "the incestuous," the forbidden love, has found its way into his work; owing to the repression of this affection, "the mother" does not appear. As a substitute for her, based on the infantile perspective, affection must be displaced to the sister.

As Abraham (1909, 113) and Stekel (1909, 32) have discovered, this displacement from the forbidden sexual object, the mother, to the sister is often expressed in marriage to a cousin, permitted in our society. Stekel points out that Grillparzer actually was in love with his cousin Marie Rizzi and was also infatuated with Charlotte Paumgarten, the youthful spouse of another cousin. In this connection we should perhaps mention that in Grillparzer's portrayal, King Ottokar is related to his spouse "in an impermissible degree" and that she is much older than he. Another unconscious factor favoring the sister fantasy is Grillparzer's hatred toward his brother, which played a major role in his psychic life. Love for the mother with hatred toward the father and love for the sister with hatred toward the brother are so closely associated in the psyche that one of these impulses seems to require the other as its complement, even if the essential persons do not exist in reality (cf. Schiller's brother hatred, chap. 20). Thus Grillparzer may have developed the fantasy of competition over a sister to justify his hatred of his brother.

In real life, however, the reason for the development of this fantasy was competition for the mother's affections. We continually return from the sister to the mother and must suppose that behind the "sister," Berta, stands the mother. This also makes sense, given that the old count's wife is absent and Berta takes her place. A passage from act 3 confirms this interpretation. Berta discovers that Jaromir is a robber and rejects him. He embraces her knees and says:

Take me! Take me!
Mild as a mother, lead
Me, your child, as you please.

Here this unconscious displacement is revealed in that Jaromir addresses his lover, who is actually his sister, as if she were his mother. Here is the same identification of wife and mother found earlier in the poem "Abschied"; here the mother is represented by the imaginary sister. But the figure of the ancestress herself reveals more clearly still the underlying theme of love for the mother. Grillparzer indicates that the ancestress bears such a resemblance to Berta that both Jaromir and the old count confuse them. In the final scene, in which Jaromir once again confuses the ancestress with Berta, she says to him:

I am not your Berta!
I am the ancestress of your house,
I am your mother, sinful son!

These words provide the key to understanding the entire drama. When the old count and Jaromir confuse Berta with the ancestress, the mother of the family, they are doing precisely what Grillparzer did himself, for in his unconscious he also confused his mother with the imaginary sister, putting one in the place of the other. Here, though, the situation is reversed. From the real mother and imaginary sister, the configuration in real life, derive the real sister and imaginary mother (the specter) of the drama. Defense against erotic affection for the mother effects this displacement in psychic emphasis. The specter (the ancestress) is reminiscent of the ghost in *Hamlet,* and this correspondence is not just superficial but is a result of the same psychic mechanisms. In *Hamlet* we determined that the ghost of the father represents unsuccessful defense mechanisms and that the work of repression transforming the father into an uncle has remained stalled in an intermediate stage. Here, similarly, the process of repression transforming the mother into a sister remains incomplete. Behind the sister, who has come into the foreground, and who resembles the mother in body and countenance to the extent that they are confused, stands the specter of the original mother. Through the activity of psychic defenses, however, she becomes the ancestress, the mother of the whole family. If one adopts this interpretation of the drama, several scenes, especially the two in which Jaromir confuses her with Berta, acquire a deeper meaning. In act 2 the ancestress approaches him from Berta's room and gestures to him "with both hands, from the distance":

Jaromir: I should depart? I cannot, cannot!
When I see you, so beautiful, so charming

Before my drunken eyes,
I am drawn to you!
Ha, I feel the dawn of the day
In the most secret depths of my heart,
And emotions that still slept
Rouse themselves and wake.
Can you let me suffer so?
Shall I perish here before you?
Have compassion for my sorrow,
Let me enter your chamber!
Has love ever hindered
Its strongest desires?
(Hurrying toward her)
Berta! My Berta!

(As he approaches her, the specter extends her right index finger and arm toward him.)

Jaromir (starts back with a cry): Ha!

This powerful affect of defense against the love impulse can be understood only in the context of incestuous attraction to the mother. The dark final scene also becomes psychologically comprehensible, given this interpretation. Instead of the sister, with whom he has arranged to flee, the ancestress—the mother, enters the tomb.

Jaromir: For they say—how absurd!—
That you are my sister!
My sister! Laugh, girl,
Laugh, laugh, I tell you!
Ancestress (with a hollow voice): I am not your sister.
Jaromir: Yet you say it so mournfully.
My sister! Laugh, I say
With my father, laugh about something else!
Come! All is prepared for our flight.
Ancestress: Where is your father?
Jaromir: Silence!

Three times, with growing intensity, she inquires about his father. This question about the whereabouts of the murdered father is reminiscent of the question the mother asks Edward in the Scottish ballad discussed above (chap. 10). Jaromir suggests that the killing of the father derives from jealous affection for the mother when he says that he would seize the young woman even from the arms of her mortally wounded father:

If I go, woman, you will follow me,
And even if your father came

And took you in his arms,
With his great mortal wound
Which cries out "Murderer! Murderer!" to me,
My hand you'd not escape.

Here we recognize the infantile origins of this incestuous tendency. Like Cronus and Hamlet, Jaromir wishes to kill the father while he is in the mother's arms—to take the mother from him. Here too, union with the mother is symbolized by death. Jaromir attacks the mother, but she defends herself:

Ancestress: See the bridal jewels I bring!

(She grasps the cloth from the covered bier. Berta lies dead in the coffin.)

Jaromir (falling back): Alas for me! Deception, child of hell!
All for naught! I will not leave you!
There is Berta's face,
My proper place! (hurrying toward her)
Ancestress: Then come, doomed one!

(She extends her arms; he falls into her embrace.)

Jaromir (crying out): Ha!

(He falls back, takes a few faltering steps, and finally collapses on Berta's coffin.)

The ancestress "bends down to him and kisses his forehead, raises the lid of the coffin, and closes it sorrowfully over both corpses."

Characteristic of the incest wish is that Jaromir, though he already suspects that Berta is his sister, does not abandon his hopes of taking her as his wife.

And if she, she whom I love,
Love, nay, long for—
If she were my sister,
What could explain this hot passion
Which drives me, flaming, toward her?
Sister! Sister! Deranged delusion!
Is the brother so attracted?
When Hymen's torches glow for us
And we fall into each other's arms
In the glowing union of the marriage bed,
Then only shall I say she's of my blood.

The conscious thought of incest with the sister was not shocking to Grillparzer because he unconsciously knew he was free of such a desire: his love was for the "ancestress"—the mother. That this youthful work was shaped by his own powerful complexes was clear to the playwright himself—so clear that it is embarrassing for literary critics who espouse the "purity" of his fantasy life. A year after writing *Die Ahnfrau,* he wrote: "Go out into life, let sorrow and suffering besiege the defenseless breast, and it will be hair-raisingly clear to you what lies behind *Die Ahnfrau.* You will see that this 'something,' at least subjectively, is no empty 'nothing.' " In these words we find expressed the playwright's unconscious suspicions concerning the deepest sources of the drama. In a comment from his autobiography this is clearer still: "The performance of *Die Ahnfrau,* though excellent, made the most terrible impression on me. It was like a bad dream made manifest before me." And in a letter to Adolf Müllner, the author of *Schuld* [Guilt], he admitted (1818): "I cannot deny that it was rough, purely subjective outbursts that gave *Die Ahnfrau* most of its power. As the drama progressed, it was more the feelings of the playwright than those of the characters that were significant." And though he claims to have written *Sappho* under precisely opposite conditions—as a purely intellectual exercise—he admits (in the same document) that this material too "truly lived within him." Nor did Grillparzer fail to generalize—quite correctly—these personal experiences of the subjective determinacy of literary production. In *Studien zur englischen Literatur* [Studies in English literature], commenting on Shakespeare, he writes: "I believe that a literary genius can give us nothing he has not found within himself; that he can never depict a passion or emotion he has not felt as a human being in his own breast. . . . In my opinion, only a person with intense passions can be a playwright, though these emotions may be held in check by the rein of reason and therefore may not appear in daily life."

At this point we should refer to the psychological source of the changes Grillparzer made in the text of *Die Ahnfrau.* It might appear that these changes were based on purely external considerations; supposedly they were suggested by Grillparzer's friend Schreyvogel. The changes concern the depiction and deeper motivation of the ancestress theme. In the first version the deeper motivation was only dimly suggested; Grillparzer was called a "tragedian of fate," an appellation he strongly objected to. We will demonstrate that the construct of the incest drama does overlie the "tragedy of fate" as a genre (cf. chap. 22). The hesitating and vacillating nature of the characterization of the ancestress becomes comprehensible when we recall that behind it are hidden Grillparzer's most secret unconscious wishes, while extremely powerful defenses operate in opposition to the conscious presentation of this "symptom." From our analysis of drafts and fragments, we are already familiar with a playwright's uncertainty and vacillation when his deepest and most personal emotions are involved. As a consequence of powerful psychic inhibitions, these impulses either undergo characteristic modifications or simply are not dealt with (cf. Schiller's drafts of *Carlos* and the *Agrippina* fragment).

That *Die Ahnfrau* arose from two psychic "centers," which at first appear to bear little relation to one another in the conscious mind of the playwright, is characteristic of the nature of literary fantasy. Behagel writes (1907, 11): "For a long period, in Grillparzer's psyche there lay two distinct images, side by side yet separate. The first was the story of a robber who flees to a palace, pursued by the authorities. There he has a love affair with a chambermaid and is captured in her room. The second concerned the legend of the last female descendant of an old house; because she resembles the old grandmother of the family, who haunts the house as a specter, she brings about the most frightful confusions of identity." "One morning," writes Grillparzer in his autobiography, "as I lay in bed, both ideas met, complementing one another. Before I arose and dressed, the outline of *Die Ahnfrau* was complete." Behagel adds: "Thus, that the image rests in the unconscious does not always indicate an unchanging perseveration. The transformation can, of course, be so slight that the playwright does not consciously notice it. In this case fantasy separates disturbingly conflicting thoughts, creating two wholes in the place of the single original image." Grillparzer's description (cf. his autobiography) of the origins of *Die Ahnfrau* sheds much light on the process of literary creation and its relation to neurotic outbursts of the unconscious. After the playwright had written eight or ten verses, he went to bed: "Then I suddenly found myself in a strange sort of turmoil and was overcome with a feverish heat. I tossed and turned the whole night. The next morning I arose with the feeling of a grave illness approaching. Then I noticed the paper on which I had written the verses the previous evening. I sat down and wrote more and more; thoughts and verses came of their own accord."

Here, though, we are by no means dealing with some sort of exceptional emotional state. Instead, almost all playwrights have admitted experiencing such states, attesting to the impulsive and uncontrollable nature of literary affective life. Thus, while conversing with Johann Eckermann, Goethe remarked: "Every product of the highest quality is beyond human control—sublime, beyond all earthly power. Such things . . . are related to the demonic, which does with the writer as it will, though he believes that he is acting on his own impulse." And shortly after the composition of *Werther*, Goethe confessed in a conversation with Soret: "In other times, it was different with my works. Before their composition, I had no conception or impression of them whatever. Instead they came over me suddenly, demanding creation. I felt myself instinctively driven, as if in a dream, to write them down on the spot." In *Dichtung und Wahrheit* [Poetry and truth] this process is described in greater detail: "Short poems had so often come to me spontaneously, without my being able to reproduce them later, that I sometimes ran to my desk without taking the time to straighten out the paper if it lay at an angle. Instead, I wrote down the whole poem diagonally, from beginning to end, without moving from the spot. At such times I preferred to grasp the pencil, which more willingly followed my hand. For it had occurred a few times that the scraping and splashing of the quill awakened me from my somnambulent composition and distracted me, strangling the little product in its very birth." And it is not only short poems that arose in this way. Indeed, Goethe once remarked that he had written *Werther* "rather unconsciously, like a somnambulist." Dilthey (1906, 176) describes the young Goethe engaged in the composition of the first *Faust:* "To Jacobi, at that time, he seemed possessed—almost never permitting himself to act arbitrarily. Again and again fantasy, through poetry, freed him temporarily from the turmoil of his life by raising life into the world of illusion. He unburdened his soul by giving expression to his cares."

The situation was similar with Schiller. In Gohlis, the engraver Endner is supposed to have found him lying on the floor, trembling convulsively, while occupied with the outline of the scene between the princess of Eboli and the prince (Minor 1890, 526). Mention is also made of his panting and stamping during the conception of *Die Räuber.* Schiller himself said that he could compose only in a sort of "pathological" affect: "I will work on *Wallenstein* as much as I can, but nature's pathological interest in such literary work is extremely exhausting for me" (December 8, 1797, in a letter to Goethe). In Goethe's answer to this letter, he reveals his own mode of composition: "I can very well imagine how you work. Without a vivid pathological interest I have never been able to portray a tragic situation either. Therefore I have more often avoided such situations than sought them out. Was it among the merits of the ancients to be able to approach the most tragic material as a mere aesthetic game, whereas with us nature's truth must be involved if such a work is to be produced? Indeed, I do not know myself well enough to know whether I could write an actual tragedy. Still, I'm frightened even at the thought and am almost convinced that I could destroy myself through the very attempt" (December 9, 1797).

Hebbel expressed similar feelings when he wrote to Uchtritz upon the completion of *Gyges:* "When I have finally rid my soul of such a work, for a time I feel as though I am without head and viscera. Composition is for me a sort of somnambulism and takes hold of me as bloodletting does in the physical domain. I would be exhausted were there not always great pauses between my individual works. I do not give myself over to these pauses without protest, but in the end they are as essential to me as sleep." Further, Christoph Wieland reports similar states for Heinrich von Kleist:

"Another trait of his, and one more fatal than the others, since it often seemed to border on insanity, was his habit of muttering to himself while at table. At such times he had the air of someone who believes he is alone, who is preoccupied with other places and other concerns. He finally confessed to me that in these moments of distraction he was working on a tragedy of which he had such a high and perfect conception that he had not yet been able to get it down on paper."

"When Turgenev wrote, he was in the power of an inexplicable force that dominated and drove him. He saw a certain image, an individual form or group of forms in a certain light and with certain nuances of color. This image would come to him incessantly—would torment him for weeks or months, demanding artistic production. In their behavior, language, and experiences, his characters gradually became clear images. Will and fate brought with them catastrophe and solution. He suffered and groaned under the internal compulsion to write; he strove to escape it, but finally acquiesced to its ineluctable power, proceeding to his desk with exclamations of comic desperation" (Reibmayr 1908).

Alfred de Musset's feverish, painful inspiration is described in similar terms: "Creativity confuses me and makes me shudder. The process of writing, always proceeding more slowly than I would wish, makes my heart pound furiously. Weeping, repressing loud cries only with difficulty, I give birth to an idea. At first I am intoxicated with it, but the next morning I find it repulsive. If I try to revise it, it only becomes worse. I am no match for it; I decide it is best to forget it, to await another inspiration. Still, the next idea comes over me so confusedly and with such force that my poor being cannot grasp it. It oppresses and torments me until it achieves realizable form, but then my other sufferings begin—the pangs of birth; true physical pains I cannot define. Such is my life when I fall into the power of this immense artist within me. Thus it is better for me to live as I intend to; it is better for me to indulge in excesses of every sort so as to slay this gnawing worm others timidly call 'inspiration,' but which I frankly call 'illness' " (George Sand, *Elle et lui,* 1; cited by Ribot 1902).

In the spontaneity of creative inspiration, on which conscious intent and will have no effect, we can see the immense power of unconscious fantasies. Thus we should regard the exceptional physical and psychic states that occur with such frequency during creative inspiration as the effects of infantile affects, powerfully breaking forth from the unconscious. In many cases one has the impression that these physical manifestations, reminiscent of fevers, do not stimulate or promote literary production but rather are consequences of the creative process and explicable in the light of the infantile affects awakened by fantasy. If we suppose that a playwright deals, for example, with the inimical relationship between father and son in some historical, political, or general human guise, and in terms of his own strongest complex, we cannot doubt that through occupying himself with this theme his infantile perspective is unconsciously reanimated. Since he has long ago repressed the associated conceptual framework, this perspective is no longer appropriate for the adult, who then rejects it. Thus it is old, repressed infantile affects that place the playwright in this special state of productive excitation. To an extent these affects provide the driving force for literary production. To an extent, though, they are rendered harmless in that they are diverted to the production of the exceptional physical and psychic state. These phenomena, experienced by the playwright as disturbing and irritating by-products of literary production, are not merely associated with the actual nature of literary production. Rather, they are its very purpose; they function to divert powerful accumulated infantile affects that have remained with the playwright more vividly and energetically.

Grillparzer's boundless jealousy, whose sources we have identified for the most part as incestuous infantile affects, speaks for his infantile perspective toward his parents. In the candid pages of his diary, he writes: "I am vengeful. Indeed, I transcend myself when I am able fully to gratify this passion. I believe it would kill me to be unable to take vengeance on someone who has insulted me. This passion expresses itself with special vigor when jealousy is involved. This emotion, despite all others, is the strongest one in my heart; neither love nor sensual pleasure, though they are extraordinarily strong in me, can compete with it. And never did this passion manifest itself in a more frightful and repugnant way than when K. wished to kiss Antoinette. I cannot describe my emotions. I shook and shivered like one consumed by fever. My teeth were on edge, my fists were clenched. If only I could rid myself of the memory of that day."

Further comments concerning his emotional sufferings are found in his diary (1827): "If I were ever to put the history of the development of my emotional life on paper—but it will never come to that—one would think it was the case history of one deranged. The disconnected, contradictory, spontaneous, and spasmodic nature of my emotions is beyond description. Today ice, tomorrow fire and flames. At one moment intellectually and physically impotent, but in the next instant overflowing, unlimited." One year later he writes: "I could well refer to my current state, although it expresses itself mainly in my emotions, as a sickness, and since it is also associated with a physical discomfort known only to myself, there is all the more reason to call it that."

The playwright himself realized better than many literary historians how closely such outbursts resemble neurotic states. As long as they believe the genius is especially favored by God and completely different from normal and pathological individuals, literary historians will attempt to wash playwrights clean. Yet we should not allow ourselves to be misled by Grillparzer's depiction of psychic torment, bordering almost on the pathological; we cannot agree with Stekel's confusing declaration that the playwright is generally a neurotic. Instead, we should at least attempt to bear in mind the only thing that is actually clear in this connection—that the creative artist's achievement, which has a liberating effect for him while being highly valued by society, will always distinguish him from the uncreative neurotic so clearly that the distinction can never be blurred, despite the extreme similarity of the preconditions for creativity and neurosis. One cannot simply identify the work of art with dreams. Nor is one justified in identifying the work of art as a neurotic symptom or in branding its creator, so long as he remains capable of production, a pathological neurotic. Instead, a deeper understanding of the psychic relationship of the playwright and the neurotic will lead us to conclude that although the playwright stands close to the border of neurosis, and may sometimes cross it, he is generally able to avoid neurosis through his artistic production. Today more than ever, I still subscribe to this assertion of many years ago (cf. Rank 1907).

Confirmation for this position is provided by several statements of prominent playwrights themselves. [Rank cites a passage in Byron's letter to Miss Milbanke, October 10, 1813, in which the poet claims his literary activity has saved him from insanity.] Byron also writes: "To withdraw myself from myself (oh that cursed selfishness!) has ever been my sole, my entire, my sincere motive in scribbling at all; and publishing is also the continuance of the same object, by the action it affords to the mind, which else recoils upon itself." And concerning *The Giaour* and *The Bride of Abydos*, he writes: "It was written in four nights to distract my dreams from X. Were it not thus, it had never been composed; and had I not done something at that time I must have gone mad, by eating my own heart." Enclosing the conclusion of *The Bride of Abydos*, he also writes to Thomas Moore: "All convulsions end with me in rhyme."

Otto Ludwig appears to have dealt with new material like a disease: "If I were unable to get it down on paper, I think it would cost me my life" (*Studien*, 2:243).

With reference to an essay that had predicted he would one day go mad, Hebbel (*Diary*, 3:254) uses almost the same words as Byron to describe the liberating power of creative activity: "Such an opinion is, by the way, not completely unfounded, in that it is based upon a certain degree of insight into the creative process in the soul of the author, and overlooks only the liberating power of creativity." Elsewhere we read the clinching conclusion to this thought: "A repressed or otherwise impossible mental 'birth' may, like an impossible physical birth, bring destruction, whether it be through death or insanity. One is reminded of Lenz, Goethe's friend in youth, of Hölderlin, and of Grabbe" (preface to *Maria Magdalena*). On New Year's Day his diary reads: "I need a receptacle for so many of the things I think and feel lest all these things, having torn themselves loose from my inner being, come back to destroy me." In a similar vein, Goethe writes to Auguste von Stolberg (March 6, 1775) concerning his first conception of *Faust:* "Today was wonderful. I sketched, wrote a scene. If I were not writing dramas now, I would perish." And with deep insight into the psychotherapeutic effects of artistic production, he says in *Dichtung und Wahrheit:* "And so began that inclination from which I have never been able to diverge—the inclination to transform whatever gladdened or tormented or otherwise occupied me into an image, a poem, and to come to terms with myself about it in order to improve my understanding of the externals and to give myself inner peace. This talent was probably more useful to me than it ever was to anyone else, for my nature continually cast me from one extreme to the other. Therefore all the things that have become known about me are simply fragments of a great confession, which this small book is a daring attempt to complete."

After the impulsive and somnambulistic composition of *Werther,* the author felt that this catharsis had saved him from suicide. In a letter to Carl Zelter, he says regarding suicide: "Surely *Werther* leaves no one in doubt that all the symptoms of this mysterious disease, as natural as it is unnatural, have swept through my inner being. I know very well how many decisions and struggles I had to go through to escape the waves of death, just as I have also saved myself with great effort from many a subsequent shipwreck." Not insignificantly, Goethe refers to the causes: "This aversion to life has both physical and moral causes. These we can leave to the physician and the moralist, respectively." The special nature of these causes is unambiguously pointed out in another passage from his autobiography: "But it was too late! I had really lost Ännchen, and the madness with which I avenged my mistake upon myself—raging in upon my physical nature in many demented ways in order to do harm to my moral nature—greatly contributed to my physical maladies, because of which I lost some of the best years of my life. Indeed, I would perhaps have perished entirely from this loss if literary talent with its healing powers had not proved so especially helpful."

Nor have authors ever considered their own lives and works to be of high quality; they have instead, with deep psychological insight, regarded them as a last resort undertaken to preserve their psychic equilibrium. Thus Schiller writes to Henriette von Wolzogen (May 30, 1783): "How insignificant is the utmost greatness of an author compared with the thought of living happily." Byron writes in his diary (November 24, 1813): "But I do think . . . the mighty stir made about scribbling and scribes . . . a sign of effeminacy, degeneracy, and weakness. Who would write, who had anything better to do? 'Action—action—action'—said Demosthenes. 'Actions—actions,' I say, and not writing,—least of all rhyme. Look at the querulous and monotonous lives of the 'genus.' " [Rank cites a passage in Byron's letter to Miss Milbanke, October 10, 1813, in which the poet expresses his conviction that an active life is more desirable than the life of a sedentary dreamer.]

Upon the death of Jean Paul (October 17, 1825), August Platen writes in his diary: "If the literary art did not hold mankind as if by force, who would submit to it?" This conception of art as a weak surrogate for life is expressed especially strikingly by Richard Wagner. In the beginning of 1852, he writes from Zurich to his friend Uhlig: "My dear friend! My own thoughts about 'art' often come to me, and usually I cannot help thinking that if we had life, we would need no art. Art begins precisely where life ends. When we have nothing, we cry out through art, 'I wish.' I cannot imagine how it could occur to a truly happy man to produce 'art' [*Kunst*]: it is only in life that one 'can' [*kann*]. Is our art thus nothing more than an admission of our impotence? Surely! Our art is, at least, and so is all the art we can imagine, given the perspective of our current dissatisfaction with life! All art is a wish expressed as clearly as possible." He repeatedly expresses similar views. Thus he writes to Mathilde from Paris (May 2, 1860): "Yes, always to be in conflict, never to find total inner peace, always to be agitated, attracted and repulsed—such, truly, is the eternally seething process of life, from which the artist's enthusiasm bursts forth like a flower of desperation."

Characteristically, though, great authors have always represented this conflict between art and life, which ends with the renunciation of life, as the choice between woman and art, thus unambiguously revealing the meaning of "life." Not only have they stated this directly, as above, but they have also, and far more frequently, revealed it in generalized statements, to a degree unconscious and to a degree deliberately obscured. Ibsen's "last word," his dramatic epilogue *When We Dead Awaken*, portrays nothing but the artist's painful realization that he has wasted his life by engaging in fantasies rather than living.

> *Rubek* (seriously): This artist's life—all artistic activity and everything related to it—now seems so completely empty, hollow, and futile.
> *Maja:* What would you have in its place?
> *Rubek:* Life, Maja.
> . . . .

Rubek (repeatedly, as though dreaming): A summer night in the mountains. With you. With you. (His eyes meet hers.) Oh, Irene, that's what our life could have been. But we've both let this all pass us by.
Irene: We will only see what we have irrevocably lost when . . .
Rubek (regarding her inquisitively): When . . . ?
Irene: When we dead awaken.
Rubek (shakes his head mournfully): Yes, but what will we see then?
Irene: We will see that we have never lived.

Recently, in his strongly autobiographical drama *Gabriel Schillings Flucht* [Gabriel Schilling's Flight] (1912), clearly based on his personal experiences, Gerhart Hauptmann has dealt with this same theme of the artist's need to choose between woman and artistic creation.

With the exception of *Die Ahnfrau* and two works of puberty to be discussed below, both of which derive from his hatred of his brother, Grillparzer's works reflect his incest complex only in a highly obscured form (cf. *Traum ein Leben* [Dream as life]) and through extensive displacement of affect (cf. *Medea*). Once again we see that as with Hebbel, Schiller, Kleist, and many other playwrights, a few fragments written during puberty and one or two youthful works appear to be violent and impulsive reactions to the infantile incest perspective whereas later works seek, with varying degrees of success, to withdraw from this theme, though the dramatic formative power of the playwright continues to be fed by the still active infantile affects. In seeking to understand literary creativity, this observation is significant. One could, of course, make the alternative claim that the playwright's personal involvement with the incest complex is relevant only in that the expression of his artistic abilities enables him to master it in early life (puberty), given that it is dominant after the separation from the parents. In the same manner, it would be claimed, artistic expression enables him to resolve in a gratifying way other psychic conflicts that may subsequently arise.

Based on our experience with the psychology of neurosis and with comparative ethnopsychology, however, the incest complex, which Freud recognized as a determinate, etiological factor in neurosis, can be said to play a rather significant role in the emergence of artistic production and in the nature of its content and form. With the repression of the real possibility of incest there begins mythic fantasy activity based on the Oedipus complex. In the same way, within the individual, given insufficient repression of these impulses and the appropriate personality and intellectual ability, literary fantasy is produced when the displacement of the libido from the parents, required during puberty, fails owing to excessively strong fixation. In his work the author is saying, as it were, that he has not mastered the parent complex. In turn, this determines his personality traits. It causes him to remain on a certain primitive level of emotional development approximately corresponding to the stage of myth development in the history of culture.

But we can describe the role of the incest complex in the emergence of the literary creative drive more precisely still. Earlier we mentioned that the individual must possess the appropriate intellectual ability. This can be considered a necessary precondition for his experiencing the incest complex through literary fantasy. But we also know from psychoanalysis that such precocious special talent, already evinced by most authors in early childhood, is paralleled by precocious sexual development. In turn this sexual development is only the expression of sexual drives originally stronger in these individuals than in others. Through their precocious tendency to activation, though, these drives effect, on the one hand, the intense fixation on parents and siblings characteristic of the incest complex and, on the other hand, a corresponding excess of fantasy activity, necessary for the author in his production. Thus, in the final analysis, what the author has in common with the neurotic is an abnormally strong sex drive, precociously demanding activation and fantasy activity, as well as the powerful inhibitions necessary to keep the sex drive in check, which constitute the feeling of guilt. In terms of the emergence of these conflicts, psychic development in the author and the neurotic proceeds in quite parallel fashion. Then, however, the creative artist finds a way to relieve himself of the harmful excess of indomitable drives and oppressive feelings of guilt in a justifying, liberating manner sanctioned by society, whereas the neurotic, alternating between his drives and his feelings of guilt, is never able to master the conflict at all.

This relation between artistic creation and neurosis becomes quite clear when we compare Grillparzer with his brothers. The playwright was the eldest son (born 1791). A year later his brother Karl was born, and the next year Kamillo was born (died 1865). The last brother was Adolf (born 1800). At the age of seventeen (1817), having attempted unsuccessfully to find liberation through writing a literary work, Adolf fell victim to his own neurosis and drowned himself. The life of Grillparzer's mother, too, ended in suicide during an episode of derangement. (Grillparzer himself stated that she suffered from *mania menstrualis periodica*.) The mutual relations of the brothers were by no means loving. In his autobiography, Grillparzer writes that it would be impossible to conceive of more disparate characters than he and his brothers. In two dramas of his youth written at age seventeen, nine years before *Die Ahnfrau*, brother hatred is the dominant theme. In *Blanka von Kastilien* [Blanca of Castille], Fedriko hates his illegitimate brother Don Pedro, king of Castille, and loves his brother's wife, Blanka, who returns his love. This typical theme of rivalry between two brothers over a woman (usually the sister) corresponds to the rivalry of father and son over the mother. With Grillparzer this common love object of the two brothers represents, of course, not the sister but the mother. This is already revealed in that the object here is a married woman (cf. Freud's "rescue type") rather than an unmarried girl, as it usually is with sister incest. Thus Don Pedro, the king, represents both the hated father and the likewise hated brother, here portrayed as an illegitimate brother. In this figure of compromise, too, we again find hatred of the father displaced to the brother (cf. the king in *Hamlet*). In addition, all the characteristic traits of incest drama are to be found here. Fedriko prays to the Holy Virgin "that she protect me from bad dreams!" The sexual union of the lovers is symbolically replaced by their shared death. When Fedriko sees that all is lost, he cries out: "Now, though death come to us, / It cannot part us; it can only unite us."

In another work of Grillparzer's youth, *Robert, Herzog von der Normandie* [Robert, duke of Normandy], Heinrich hates his brother Robert—a situation analogous to that of Franz and Karl Moor. Except for its appearance in these two dramas of youth, hatred of the brother almost never appears undisguised or as the dominant theme in Grillparzer's other works. It does, however, appear in the tragedy *Ein Bruderzwist in Habsburg* [A conflict of brothers in Habsburg], where it is significantly associated with unconscious homosexual tendencies. Since it does not in general find expression in his works, however, hatred of the brother appears more clearly still in his family relationships, especially in the fate of Karl Grillparzer. Though the playwright was later able to repress his infantile hatred rather successfully after gratifying it in the works of his youth, and to sublimate it for the most part into the realm of ethics, unsuccessful defense against this hatred drove his brother Karl to neurosis. The valuable psychological insights to be gained from this case justify its detailed explication. On March 30, 1836, Grillparzer began a voyage to France and England. In June of the same year he received word from his friend Karajan in Vienna that his brother Karl (born March 1, 1792, died January 30, 1861), then a tax official in Salzburg, had on May 13, 1836, declared before the court in Vienna, while in a state of derangement, that he was guilty of the murder of a journeyman. He had made this declaration secretly and on his own, having left his employment and his wife and children. On June 30, 1836, in a letter to Karajan, Grillparzer remarked that he himself would attempt to avoid succumbing fully to the family illness that plagued the sons of his father. In the same letter he writes: "My brother has already done such crazed things without being deranged, but for his own good derangement is the better interpretation; I hope that his case will continue to be seen in this light." In July 1836 Grillparzer, having returned to Vienna, composed a "Report for the Vienna Criminal Court on His Brother Karl." This extremely important document may be found in the edition of letters and journals of Grillparzer published by Sauer and Glossy. In this report Grillparzer attempts to explain his brother's actions. By attempting to explain his own unconscious impulses, he is able to interpret his brother's obsessional neurotic symptom with astounding success. He was not, of course, in a position to grasp the complete solution, partially because of his own unconscious desire to avoid its discovery. Here I shall present excerpts from Grillparzer's report; several portions will be important for understanding the symptom.

The report begins: "Karl Grillparzer, the second son of Wenzel Grillparzer, still remembered here as a renowned lawyer, already exhibited traces of his character in his earliest youth. He is of a reserved, shy nature. Initially he is very much enraged by misfortunes, but then he gives way to anxiety and despair. He means well, by the way, and has a harmless nature capable of heartfelt affection." Grillparzer then relates a good deal of information from his brother's childhood. Although interesting, it is not of great significance for analysis. Then Karl became a soldier: "Partially in fear of its being discovered by the French that he had ransomed himself, and partially in fear of bringing about the death of our gravely ill father by causing him to worry about his son, he once again departed immediately after visiting me and speaking with me; he subsequently sent no word for eight years." After the fall of Napoleon, Karl again returned to Vienna. "Our father was dead, and I was unable to do anything for Karl. He therefore remained what he was—a common soldier. However, I did earn enough to ensure that he was admitted to the military hospital, sent to the clinic, and handled there with care, for he suffered from headaches that had developed into a terrible migraine." When Karl left military service, the playwright secured him a position as a tax collector.

> During his entire service, he was guilty of one single infraction of discipline. This incident bears such a resemblance to the current case and, in illustrating his specific emotional state, does so much to explain the case that it cannot be overlooked. After a stormy argument with his superior, a tax collector known to be of a repulsive nature, he left his position and his family, leaving a written note and not waiting for permission. He came to me in Vienna and declared that he no longer wished to live. Immediately, though, he broke into tears, admitted his mistake, and, crying like a child, allowed me to take him home and appeared ready to return. . . . These outbreaks of half physical, half moral inner distress—never accompanied, incidentally, by actual derangement—were frequent earlier but have not been repeated for twelve to fifteen years. They characteristically begin with

> utter despair, pass to a stage of wild obduracy, and finally end in the most complete remorse and repentance. At such times my brother always sees himself as isolated from human society—doomed to unhappiness. He is overcome especially by an almost superstitious fear of losing me, his brother, whom he, not without some justification, regards as his only support. Last year, when I wished to undertake a trip to England and France, he wrote me the most pitiful letters, imploring me to consider the dangers of such a trip and what would befall him and his family were I to meet with misfortune. He could be reassured by no arguments. When I actually did begin my trip this March, therefore, I took pains to inform him and especially to assure him that the monthly sums I had been sending him, partially to cover his bail and partially to lighten his household expenses, would continue to arrive. I am convinced that this alone led to his subsequent state of derangement. It has been emphasized that about six weeks before his disappearance he had been unusually depressed. He spoke with no one, greeted no one, and paced back and forth silently, absorbed in himself. This period coincides precisely with my departure. His old fear had returned; he believed that I was in danger and that he himself and the fate of his family were in jeopardy. Given his isolated locale, without a friend to comfort him, with a wife who, kind as she is, cannot at her level of education provide him stability, it was inevitable that this anxiety should quickly become an idée fixe. Unfortunately, the letter from my attorney with the monthly sum, which had been mailed on May 3 and had arrived in Salzburg on May 5, did not arrive in Grossgemein until May 15, when he had already left (May 13). He assumed that I must have met with some misfortune leading to the suspension of the payments. Even that he went as far as Vienna in his subsequent derangement demonstrates how firmly his fear had expressed itself; he had the vague impression that only in Vienna could he receive definite information about my fate. I do not know whether he still recalls this train of thought. With my knowledge of his character and emotional state, however, I am convinced that this was his reasoning at the time.

Grillparzer also remarks that an impairment in his brother's logical faculties was involved. "Thus, with problems on all sides, his mental constitution was no longer up to such a blow. He left family and position and was seen for three full days in Salzburg, where he wandered about the streets, absorbed in reading a paper he held in front of him. Finally he arrived in Vienna, where he surrendered to the authorities, declaring himself guilty of the horrid crime equally foreign to his gentle nature and his state of mind." One more passage from Grillparzer's letter to Karajan should be cited: "Self-reproach during his journey, his helpless position in Vienna, where he had gone mechanically, having always gone there in such cases when he needed help from me, and worry about providing for his family brought about the temporary derangement of his mind."

Based upon this characterization by Grillparzer and the declarations of doctors, and since his implication in the murder was shown to be groundless, Karl was released. It was declared that he suffered from "melancholic derangement"; he was retired by the tax authorities and given a pension at half his salary.

This case is instructive in several ways. Grillparzer's success in analyzing the symptoms is astounding. The main point, Karl's superstitious fear that his brother would meet with an accident, was correctly emphasized by Grillparzer as the driving theme of the neurosis. But he did not understand the deeper source of this fear and its association with the charge of murdering the journeyman. Psychoanalysis reveals that such unconscious, apparently absurd, obsessional neurotic delusions and accusations should be interpreted as repressed wishes for the death of a previously loved person. Hatred toward his brother, derived from childhood rivalry, which the playwright was able to deal with in literature and thus master, led in the brother's case to unsuccessful repression and neurosis. Grillparzer's understanding of his brother's obsessional neurotic state speaks for his own similar perspective toward Karl, later successfully mastered; in his interpretation, he progressed so far that only the last point remains to be supplied by psychoanalysis. Still this point does, of course, cast the entire situation in another light. That Karl had already once left their father's home after an argument with his brother and had sent no word for eight years suggests powerful repression of his hateful thoughts toward his brother and his fear of their expression. In the same way he later left "his job after a stormy argument with his superior, a tax collector known to be of a repulsive nature" and set out to see his brother in Vienna and tell him he no longer wished to live. In his superior, owing to a displacement, he once again saw only his older brother, with whom he had previously also had an unpleasant argument.

However, the unconscious feelings of hatred and the murderous impulses directed toward his brother now turned against Karl himself as an expression of defense (self-punishment). This also explains his prevailing tendency "to see himself as isolated from human society—doomed to unhappiness." It also explains his continual self-reproach, finally culminating in his self-accusation in connection with the murder. This self-reproach, justified in a sense, was derived from his repressed feelings of hatred and his murderous impulses and expressed itself consciously in the defensive form of exaggerated fear concerning the health and life of his brother. This expression of repressed death wishes in the defensive form of exaggerated fear concerning the person toward whom there is unconscious deathly hatred is typical in neurosis. The same was true of Byron's mother. We should also refer to Freud's excellent analysis of a hysterical young woman (1909f) who in a state of frenzied delirium expressed extreme animosity toward her mother, though in her subsequent phobic stage she suffered from the agonizing, obsessional neurotic delusion that some misfortune had befallen her. "Wherever she was, she had to hurry home to reassure herself that her mother was still alive."

Here it is quite clear why a trip undertaken by the unconsciously hated person can so easily lead to the outbreak of neurosis: the trip realizes former infantile conceptions of "being away," of the final absence of the disturbing competitor. At this point the most likely conscious thought is probably that misfortune is more apt to strike during a trip than at home. Such a worry is not at all neurotic. It becomes neurotic only when it becomes overpowering: the "dominant" idea brings about the repression of all other ideas. This neurotic trait corresponds to a neurotic reaction against unconscious death wishes and to the resulting self-reproach. When this self-reproach became unbearable, Karl always needed to be reassured that all was well with his brother. This explains why he so often visited him unexpectedly in Vienna: he needed to assure himself of his brother's existence. But the possibility of doing this was taken from him as long as his brother was traveling. Further, that he returned to Vienna under the compulsion of his unconscious impulses reveals once again his attempt to assure himself of his brother's well-being, though he hated him unconsciously. ("He had the vague impression that only in Vienna could he receive definite information about my fate.") That he finally turned himself in for murder precisely in Vienna, where he found his brother absent, leads us to the solid conclusion that behind the journeyman he had supposedly murdered he saw his brother Franz.

Nor was this "journeyman" chosen haphazardly. The wandering journeyman, the typical traveler, is after all a familiar figure (Brother Straubinger). Thus, by means of this bridge supported also by other, unknown motivations, the tendency for repression may have displaced the murderous impulse directed at the brother to the typical traveler, the wandering journeyman. That Karl himself had traveled extensively as a young man also determined the selection of the journeyman in connection with his tendency for self-punishment. Based on his unconscious hatred and his defense against it, Karl's compulsive neurotic act, translated into conscious terms, could be summarized as follows. Karl, always worried about the life and health of his brother (reaction against the unconscious death wish), knows that his brother is traveling, but he has received no word from him. If his brother had really met with disaster while traveling, Karl would have been firmly convinced, given his unconscious wish for just that result, that he himself was at fault. He would believe that his brother had perished because he, Karl, had wished it. This accounts for the way he is plagued by his conscience. Since he is unable to assure himself of his brother's well-being and has heard nothing from him, he concludes (since he unconsciously wishes it) that Franz must have met with disaster—that he must be dead. Thus his wish has been realized. Accordingly, Karl must have murdered him. This accounts for the self-accusation in connection with the murder. Its displacement to the journeyman is the condition for its admittance to consciousness.

In this distorted form, the unconscious impulses could easily have effected their physical realization. If Karl had really murdered a journeyman, his brother Franz would not have been able to explain Karl's derangement, nor would his judges. He would have been convicted as a murderer. But it is clear that in that case the unconscious mechanisms would still have been functioning in precisely the same way. The only difference would have been the final result—there would have been a physical, outward realization rather than the internal release conditioned by intense repression and leading to neurosis. Seen in this light, this case provides insight into the psychology of the criminal and of the murderer. In a murder, the psychological motivations and processes are not as clear and obvious as one might think. Most strikingly, the murder impulse is frequently directed toward a person whom it originally did not concern at all, but toward whom it has been directed owing to repressions and displacements. I certainly do not wish to claim that the murderer is always a neurotic. But like the playwright, the murderer can often be a neurotic. He suffers, however, from an "active" form of neurosis manifesting itself in actions rather than in the fantasies of the passive psychoneurotic. From this neurotic component derives the significant conclusion that with the actual murderer as well, the source of the immense, abnormally powerful affects providing the driving energy for the act of murder cannot be discovered without recognizing the unconscious motivations.

Indeed, it is this affect, appropriately employed, that reveals the nature of the actual motivations. In this case the affect from earliest childhood of hatred toward the firstborn brother combined with rivalry over the mother would be the deepest motivation for the murder. An attempt is made to realize the infantile wish for the absence of the competitor. Here we have proof of the generalization that the criminal brings about the realization of the infantile thought. As Freud discovered, the neurotic has retained the infantile manner of thinking. In the same way, one must suppose that the criminal carries out this infantile thought in reality. Even the playwright retains the infantile manner of thinking, though in a perfected, sublimated way. This is shown by the shared enjoyment of the child and the playwright in rhymes and in playing with words. Whereas the playwright Grillparzer, highly valued culturally, dramatically kills his hated brother in his works, in the illusory world of the theater, in Karl the same murderous impulses are extended to real life and stamp him as culturally inferior. Whereas in *Die Ahnfrau* Franz airs his impulses of hatred as a robber and murderer (Jaromir), Karl nearly becomes a robber and murderer in reality. Finally, a citation from Hebbel's diary demonstrates that this comparison is more than a play on words: "Shakespeare's creation of murderers was his salvation. Thus he was not compelled to become a murderer in real life. And if this is saying too much, given Shakespeare's vast literary power, one can certainly conceive of a broken literary talent in whom elemental life—restrained in others, having previously been brought into balance, but unchecked in the creative artist, necessitating a struggle for balance—could break forth into deeds because his artistic productions are stifled or stillborn."

15 The Ancestress Schema: The Psychology of Aesthetic Effect

Be gone, frightful woman!
Murderer of children, brother, and father!
What have I to do with you?

GRILLPARZER, *Die Tragische Muse*

As in part 1, where we discussed the literary expression of incestuous attraction between parents and children, typical forms of drama are found here too. We shall refer to one type, hatred toward the father and love for the sister, as the "ancestress schema" after this important representative of the type. I shall discuss two dramas of this type, Calderón's *Devotion to the Cross* and Voltaire's *Mahomet*. Both works have special interest for us. Calderón's drama was Grillparzer's model during the composition of *Die Ahnfrau*, and Goethe translated Voltaire's tragedy into German. In his autobiography, Grillparzer describes the awakening of his compulsion to write: "I came across Schlegel's translation of several dramas of Calderón, of which I was attracted especially by *Devotion to the Cross*." We know that such attraction arises from the reader's unconscious impulses, which overlap with the impulses unconsciously expressed by the playwright in his work. From the special case in which simple aesthetic enjoyment is not sufficient, leading the reader to create an independent adaptation or translation, we derive valuable information concerning the conditions for aesthetic enjoyment and for the effect of art. The effect of art is influenced by unconscious themes in a highly determinate manner, though these may not be revealed in the creative output of the individual himself.

An outline of Calderón de la Barca's drama is as follows. Curcio has a son, Lisardo, and a daughter, Julia. Eusebio, who has fallen in love with Julia and wishes to draw near her, is challenged to a duel by her brother, Lisardo. Lisardo is killed by Eusebio, and Curcio places his daughter in a convent. Eusebio, who has become a robber in the meantime, penetrates the convent. At this point, earlier details become relevant. Curcio had once been separated from his wife for eight months. When he returned, he found her eight months pregnant, and he believed she had been unfaithful to him. Under the pretext of a hunt, he lured her into an isolated wooded area to kill her for her crime. She swore by a cross that stood in a lonely clearing that she was innocent. He was about to cast himself at her feet in penitence and beg forgiveness, but his suspicions and his self-assurance got the better of him. He lunged at her several times with his dagger, then left her for dead at the foot of the cross. On returning home, he found her there with a baby girl (Julia) in her arms. In attempting to stab her, he had actually missed. She had succumbed at the foot of the cross because she was about to bear twins, both of whom were born with the mark of a red cross on their breasts. She had left one of the children, Eusebio, in the clearing. Thus we learn that Eusebio is in love with his twin sister Julia without realizing her identity, and that he has killed his brother Lisardo, likewise without knowing his identity. He loves Julia so passionately that even the walls of the convent pose no barrier for him. He says, like Jaromir in *Die Ahnfrau:*

> I shall go on,
> Though the lightning blind me.
> Through the flames I'll venture in.
> No, not even all the flames of hell
> Shall turn me from my course.

Julia responds with the same love. When Eusebio enters her cell and calls her name, she says, awakening:

> Who calls my name?
> God, what do I see approaching?
> Delusion of my heart,
> Dream image of my delusion, be gone!

But Eusebio is not daunted:

> The passion storming within me
> Breaks all bonds.

He continues until she gives in:

> *Julia:* Close the door
> Of my cell, and may the moment

Grant you brief happiness.
Fear is dispelled by fear.
Eusebio: How powerful is my love!
Julia: How tyrannical is my fate!

But before he can experience her love, he notices the cross on her bosom, identical to the mark on his own breast. Horrified, he flees from her arms. Now, though, her curiosity has been aroused:

What? Now, finally,
When your pleas have won my heart,
When your wishes have conquered me,
When your sighs have moved me,
When your tears have softened me,
. . . .
So that I offend God twice,
As God and as my sacred spouse—
Now you flee from my arms,
You turn away from your prize,
You reject me before you have possessed me?

In this prevention of actual incest—though the incest would have occurred without the knowledge of the siblings' identity—we see the expression of psychic defense against incestuous attraction. We are already familiar with this from the love of mother and son (e.g., Auge and Telephus). The desire for the actual fulfillment of love with the desired person and the inability to enact this desire at the crucial moment are traits found also in neurotic sexual abstinence. As long as Julia resists, Eusebio desires her passionately; when she is ready to yield, he flees her. Julia, in contrast, who has refused for so long to submit to her suitor's entreaties, longs for him when he is gone. She therefore leaves the convent to seek him out. With a mob of peasants, Curcio pursues the robber band led by Eusebio. Then, without knowledge of each other's identity, father and son fall upon one another. Each thanks God for the opportunity for revenge. But soon this mutual hatred between father and son is transformed to mutual sympathy (ambivalence). In this manner Calderón expresses his defense against hatred between father and son. Indeed, this defense goes so far that both experience the strongest reaction to their former hateful thoughts—the desire for self-punishment. Eusebio says:

And thus, quite crazed,
I should like to kill myself, and in so doing avenge you.
Take vengeance on me! My life
Lies offered at your feet.

And when the peasants are closing in on Eusebio, Curcio says:

They are closing in. Oh, if only someone
Could save your life now, Eusebio,
Even if he should lose his own life doing so!

Finally the determined peasants mortally wound Eusebio, the hated robber, though Curcio attempts in vain to protect him. In examining Eusebio's wound, Curcio notices the cross and thus recognizes him as his son. Julia, who had fought on Eusebio's side against Curcio and his retinue, now learns that Eusebio is her brother. When Curcio learns that she was in love with her own brother, he wishes to kill her by his own hand. She begs for help in the name of the cross and promises to atone for her sins in the convent. "When Curcio is about to stab her, she embraces the cross on Eusebio's grave and ascends with it into heaven."

With the exception of hatred toward the brother, none of the unconscious wishes is fully realized in an undisguised manner. Hatred toward the father is expressed only in the form of defense against this impulse, and union with the sister is not even realized in its ideal form—through shared death. Julia ascends into heaven whereas Eusebio dies an earthly death. Instead of the fulfillment of the wish, actual incest, we see here the repression of the wish and the "killing" of Calderón's love for his brother, personified in Lisardo.

In Calderón's drama *The Triple Revenge,* one finds almost the same schema as in *Devotion to the Cross.* The robber Lope loves his sister Violante without knowing her identity, but incest does not occur. Hatred of the (supposed) father is also greatly dampened.

Very little is known of Calderón's life, especially his relationship with his family. We know only that he had a sister (Dorotea) who had lived since her youth in the isolation of the convent (as did Julia in *Devotion to the Cross*). She died one year after he did. He also had two brothers—an older one, Diego, and a younger one, José. Thus his love for his sister and his hatred toward his brothers, passions often depicted in his dramas, become comprehensible (cf. also chap. 19). If one now compares *Die Ahnfrau* with *Devotion to the Cross,* one sees the same schema in both, provided one ignores hatred toward the brother—a hatred personified in Calderón's drama by Lisardo. Indeed, given his complex of jealousy toward the brother, the playwright himself eliminated Lisardo at the beginning of the plot. The correspondence is striking. In both the father, a widower of many years, lives with his daughter. The son has been lost in childhood and has become a robber. The two siblings happen to meet and fall in love. Further, both dramas include the pursuit of the robber band by the father, the wounding of the son, and the final death of both siblings. With Grillparzer, however, the son kills his own father, though unaware of his identity. In this respect, and in that there is no fratricide, Grillparzer deviates from the schema he found in Calderón's drama.

But such deviations do not occur by chance, or because of aesthetic considerations. Instead, they are strictly determined by Grillparzer's psychology. We have seen that with Grillparzer the most powerful impulse of the incest complex was hatred toward the brother. What especially attracted him to Calderón's drama was hatred toward the brother, expressed in its crassest form—murder. This also corresponded well to the dampened form of hatred toward the father. These two factors, as unconscious driving forces, led Grillparzer to imitate (adopt) the incestuous relationships depicted in *Devotion to the Cross*. Here we see that Grillparzer by no means made any basic changes in these relationships, as it might appear. Instead, corresponding to his own psychology, he only shifted the emphasis within the schema. He removed the emphasis on hatred toward the brother, so powerfully stressed by Calderón, by eliminating it altogether. However, he added emphasis to the theme of hatred toward the father, dampened in Calderón. Indeed, he simply shifted the emphasis from fratricide to patricide. This displacement, albeit in the opposite direction, is typical, as discussed in chapter 13. The inversion in Grillparzer's work occurs because his hatred toward his brother was more intense than his aversion toward his father. Thus he experienced fewer inner inhibitions to the expression of his father hatred than to the expression of his brother hatred. Now it is likewise clear why he was no longer able to portray fratricide in *Die Ahnfrau*—why he avoided all the painful emotions associated with brother hatred, the sore spot of his psyche. This avoidance is an expression of psychic defense against his brother hatred. Here too we are now in a position to understand another factor made clear by the presentation of love for the sister in *Die Ahnfrau*. Grillparzer simply adopted the theme of love for the sister; but from its position in the schema as a powerful remnant, it reveals its original relation to hatred toward the brother. The painless emotion of love for the sister is substituted for the painful theme of brother hatred. Freud has emphasized that such replacement of a thought by its opposite is a typical form of neurotic repression. The repression of a painful thought occurs in that the opposite of the thought to be repressed is excessively emphasized. Here, though, we are dealing not with true opposites, but rather with impulses that, like opposites, have deep mutual associations. In addition, it is frequently love and hate that undergo such mutual replacement. In our analysis of Schiller's love for his sister (chap. 20) we shall have occasion to demonstrate another such theme of reaction.

Voltaire's *Mahomet* is also conceived according to the same schema as *Die Ahnfrau.* Palmire, Mahomet's slave girl, and Séide, his slave, are in love, though they do not realize they are siblings. Their father is Zopire, the sheriff of Mecca, in whose home Mahomet has left them as hostages. Father and children fail to recognize one another. The prophet loves Palmire; in the name of Allah, he commands his follower and slave Séide to kill Zopire—Séide's own father. In return he promises him Palmire, though he knows that Séide is her brother. He has no intention of keeping his promise. Instead, after the deed, he intends personally to eliminate Séide in order to secure possession of Palmire. Séide's first attempt to kill his unrecognized father is unsuccessful:

> How changed I feel suddenly
> (Drawn away by this terrible god)
> Toward you, you whom I cannot hate.

In Séide's words, defense against father hatred is clearly expressed. In the end, though, he does kill Zopire. The dying man learns that Séide and Palmire are his children. Indeed, he has dimly suspected as much. The children also learn that Zopire is their father. Séide dies, poisoned by Mahomet, who wishes to secure his position with Palmire. But Palmire stabs herself when she discerns Mahomet's modus operandi.

> *Palmire:* My blood? With joy it would flow for Séide.
> *Mahomet:* You love him so?
> *Palmire:* Since that day when Hammon
> Entrusted us to your holy hands
> This feeling has grown, quietly overpowering.
> We loved; our love sprang forth from nature.
> Years passed. At least we learned
> The sweet name of our happiness:
> What we felt, we now called love.

Here too it is only the murderous impulses toward the father that find expression, while sexual union with the sister does not occur. Here the will of Allah, representing the individual unconscious, takes the place assigned in ancient times to fate or the oracle and in the Christian Middle Ages to God and the devil. After the patricide, Séide says to Palmire:

> The deed is done.
> I have broken no law; I obeyed.
> I grasped him with fury; the weak one fell.
> I stabbed, prepared to strike again.

When Mahomet commands him to commit the patricide, he answers:

I hear the voice of God. You command,
And I obey.

Indeed, from his youthful drama *Oedipe* (chap. 7), we are already familiar with Voltaire's incest complex.

16 Goethe's Love for His Sister

Say, what has fate in store for us?
Say, how did it bind us two so well?
Oh, in lives lived out before
You were my sister or my wife.

GOETHE, "To Frau von Stein"

Goethe's translation of Voltaire's drama *Le fanatisme du Mahomet le Prophète* [The fanaticism of Mahomet the prophet], which he produced in 1799 at the request of Duke Carl Augustus, already reveals to us the most significant complexes of his psychic life and literary production: opposition to his father and love for his sister. Goethe's strained relationship with his strict, stubborn father is sufficiently well known from his detailed biography, and we know how often his kind mother, filled with love for her son, had to intercede between him and his father. Here we are interested only in the unconscious continuation and consolidation in the incest complex of this opposition to the father. It is also well known that Goethe felt the deepest affection for his mother his whole life long. From his obviously libidinous fixation on his sister, we can conclude that with Goethe, the parent complex originally played a strong role. As in Grillparzer's *Die Ahnfrau,* an early displacement from the mother to the sister occurred. In his artistic production, rivalry with the father emerged explicitly only in a few literary fantasies and fragments. But the few instances in which it broke forth reveal powerful unconscious sources of affect that account for a major portion of his productive energy. Even in his youthful drama *Götz von Berlichingen,* in which Götz's wife, Elisabeth, is modeled after the playwright's mother, while the psychological opposite of the mother is personified in the sensual, seductive Adelheid, Goethe's hatred of his father and its motivation in sexual rivalry find expression in an apparently insignificant detail. Franz, who poisons his master in order to rescue the woman he loves and win her for himself, says in her arms: "Heaven holds no bliss for me. I would murder my father if he fought with me for your embrace" (first draft of *Götz*).

It is of great interest that Freud reports a similar comment by an obsessional neurotic (1909b, 390). In this individual, the main source of the illness was the infantile perspective of hatred toward the father. "Several years after the death of his father, on experiencing the pleasurable sensations of coitus for the first time, he was struck with the idea, 'This is marvelous; for this, one could kill one's father!' " As a child, the same patient had had the obsessive fear, "If I feel the desire to see a woman naked, my father will die." In this connection, that the young Goethe was already planning a drama about Julius Caesar while in Strasbourg (1770–71) becomes even more significant. Initially he planned to deal with Caesar's entire life; later he wished to deal only with his murder. Eventually he dropped the plan entirely. It is characteristic of the powerful defenses that inhibited his father complex that one further plan also remained unexecuted, never progressing beyond the writing of a few fragments. This is the tragedy *Elpenor,* which was to deal with an accomplished fratricide and an attempted patricide. Like Hamlet, Elpenor becomes the avenger of his pretended father, murdered by the latter's brother: Elpenor is to avenge the murder by killing his own, unrecognized, father. *Elpenor* was begun on August 11, 1781. In 1783 Goethe once again took up the material after a long interval. Then he again abandoned the project, never to return to it. The fragment first appeared in 1807. On May 7, 1807, Goethe wrote to Zelter concerning *Elpenor:* "When a project ceases to flow smoothly, one is never sure whether it is one's own fault or the fault of the material. Usually, though, one develops a distaste for what one cannot complete."

In the episode of Ferdinand and Ottilie in *Unterhaltungen deutscher Ausgewanderten* [Conversations of German émigrés] (1795), rivalry with the father is also suggested. Of Ferdinand we read: "Although he had taken his father as his model in other respects, he now envied him as his competitor. The father was in possession of everything the son desired. . . . The son then believed that the father should sometimes 'do without' so that the son might also enjoy. . . . He became depressed, and one could say that at these moments he had no respect for his mother, who could not help him, and hated his father, who, as he saw it, was always standing in his way."

In the novella *Der Mann von fünfzig Jahren* [The man of fifty years], begun at an advanced age (1807–8), rivalry between father and son arising from love for the sister is depicted in an unusual guise—from the perspective of an aging man. Goethe portrays the baroness as seeing her brother's attraction to her daughter from a humane point of view: "She recognized the impression that the only respectable man who had become so well acquainted with a young woman must necessarily make upon a free heart, and how from this situation there might develop not childish respect and trust, but instead an attraction that could reveal itself as love, as passion." Goethe clearly stated that this attraction on the part of the old major toward his niece actually represents a displacement from the major's own sister to her younger image: "Since her youth, the baroness had loved her brother so much that she preferred him to all other men, and perhaps even Hilarie's [her daughter's] attraction was, if not derived from this preference of her mother, at least fed by it. All three were now united in one love, one comfortable unity, and so they passed their happiest hours. Finally, though, they again became aware of the world around them, and the world seldom tolerates such emotions. One also thought of the [major's] son, to whom, as he very well knew, Hilarie had been promised." Thus the novella is based on the father's passion for the young woman who has been promised to his son and who, furthermore, is also his blood relative. In the story this relationship is doubled and, characteristically, corresponding to the fatherly feelings of the old Goethe, it is the father who is preferred in the second relationship as well. For the son loves a widow whom he finds so attractive that when his father is about to meet her, the son says: "By God! I feel it. I see you as the rival of your son." Indeed, upon their first encounter, the widow already praises the father to the son's detriment, "thereby producing in the young man a very mixed sensation of satisfaction and jealousy."

Goethe's erotic attraction to his sister Cornelia is expressed in a much more powerful and undisguised manner. She affected him not only in the selection and form of his material, but also in his real love life. Concerning the relationship of the siblings, Witkowski writes (1903): "He already loved her tenderly when she lay in the cradle. He brought her everything and wanted to be the only one to feed and care for her. If the child cried, he gave her bread, and if anyone wished to take the child away, his ire was boundless. Since all his other siblings died so young, these two remaining children formed an even closer bond. In their free hours they hid together behind the stove, strolled together through their native city, or wandered through the gardens or to Bockenheim. Whenever Wolfgang was made to stay at home, he found in Cornelia 'a companion who grew always more agreeable.' " He concealed from her his first "love" for Gretchen. But after Gretchen's death, he poured out the great pain of his heart to his sister. She was the first to comfort him and even felt a secret satisfaction at being rid of a competitor. In 1765 Goethe went to Leipzig. From there he wrote to his sister (May 11, 1767): "By God, my sister, Leipzig will never provide me with one young woman like you." In his letters from Leipzig, he uses the tenderest terms of affection with reference to his sister. He calls her "little angel" and generally expresses himself like one in love. The later alienation between the siblings, for which Cornelia's marriage was mainly to blame, only shows once again Goethe's intense erotic affection for his sister. He was never able to come to terms with her marriage, and his affection for her was easily disturbed by genuine feelings of jealousy. In *Dichtung und Wahrheit* Goethe directly describes his relationship with his sister as an erotic one: "That interest of youth; that astonishment at the awakening of sensual drives that form mental images and of psychological needs that adopt sensual form; all the considerations of these events that keep us in the dark rather than enlighten us, like a fog that, not wishing to lift, envelops and does not illuminate a valley; many false paths and confusions that therefore arose—all these things the two siblings shared hand in hand. They were even less able to become enlightened about their unusual state because the more they wished to approach each other, to step into the light, the more they were kept apart by the sacred timidity of close relationship."

Johann Eckermann (1827) cites another remark of Goethe's that we can interpret in the same manner. The conversation concerned Hinrichs's book *Das Wesen der antiken Tragödie* [The nature of classical tragedy] (1827). Eckermann states that in his discussion of *Antigone,* Hinrichs had only her character and manner of action in mind when he remarked that family piety appears purest in womankind and purest of all in the sister—that it is only the sister who can love the brother in a completely pure and asexual manner. "I should think," answered Goethe, "that the love of sister for sister would be even purer and more asexual. For after all, we know that countless cases have occurred in which the most sensuous affection has existed between sister and brother, either known to each other or unknown." At one point in his *Italienische Reise* [Italian journey], he also discusses the relationship between siblings; quite unintentionally, he reveals his incestuous interest in anecdotal form. At another point (October 25) he discusses an unpleasant travel companion: "After some hesitation, he asked me quite seriously to enlighten him concerning another point, for he had heard from his priest that we ⟨Protestants⟩ are permitted to marry our sisters, which would certainly be quite shocking. When I denied this and tried to instruct him concerning certain worldly teachings of our doctrine, he was not especially inclined to pay attention, for he found the topic too mundane."

Here a wishful fantasy appears to be expressing itself or at least finding gratification. Indeed, Goethe's entire love life, so peculiar and enigmatic, can be understood only from his childhood fixation on his sister and mother, which he never entirely mastered. Generally reminiscent of the proverbial "poet's unhappy love," Goethe's peculiar love affairs are characterized by his infantile relationship with his sister and can be understood only from that perspective. His preference for women already spoken for (Charlotte Buff, Kestner's fiancée and the muse of *Werther;* "Max" La Roche, wife of the Frankfurt merchant Brentano; Frau von Stein, wife of the equerry) is derived from the "mother type" described by Freud. Both mother and sister were unified for him in Charlotte von Stein, whom he loved with a passion mysterious even to himself. "Your relationship to me is so sacred, so unique, that for the first time I truly feel, 'This cannot be expressed in words, this cannot be seen' " (August 8, 1776). In one of his letters written from Braunschweig in French, he writes: "My love for you is no mere passion. It is a disease, a disease dearer to me than the most perfect health, and from which I cannot recover." If one wishes to understand how this unattractive, sickly, aging, and by no means understanding, tasteful, or intellectual woman was able to infatuate the playwright for many long years, one must recall that she was for Goethe a substitute for his aging mother and his sickly, unattractive sister. Although the playwright himself repeatedly expresses this thought, one can by no means conclude that he was fully conscious of this connection. This powerful unconscious connection occasionally finds expression in similes, hints, and poetic images. Indeed, those very biographers who speak of "his motherly and sisterly friend" would object strenuously if, given our psychological insights, we were to take them at their word. On May 24, 1776, Goethe wrote to Charlotte: "Thus this relationship too, the purest, most beautiful, and truest I have ever had with any woman except my sister, has now been disturbed!" On February 23, 1776, he writes: "If only my sister had a brother somewhat as I have a sister in you." There are many similar quotations. In the mystical aspect the poet feels in his relationship to the adored woman, we also recognize an unconscious stylization of his childhood fixation on mother and sister. This is true of the references to mysterious relationships predating current earthly life (and going back to the mother) as well as of those to be experienced in a future life. "It seems to me almost unpleasant that there was a time when you did not know and love me. If I come again to this earth, I will request of the gods that I love only once; if they were not so ill disposed toward this earth, I would beg for you as my partner in life." However, from another quotation one senses that it is through his beloved that he would wish to be reborn: "I should like to give you my life, my entire being, in order to receive myself again from your hands. This is already true to an extent, and that is what I hold most dear" (March 13, 1781). Thus, in his unconscious fantasy, mother and beloved are truly one, and even his conscious pronouncements must necessarily bear witness to this deep alliance. Words generally uttered only to the mother are addressed to the beloved: "You know that my only wish is to be able to be completely thankful to you, for I owe you everything." "Your approval is the best fame to me, and if I place a high value on my reputation, it is because I do not want you to be ashamed because of me." His infantile perspective toward his beloved is most clearly expressed in the poem Goethe wrote to Frau von Stein on April 14, 1776.

It is only to us two poor lovers
That mutual happiness is denied.
To love one another without understanding one another,
To see in the other what the other never was,
Always searching for the happiness of dreams,
Hovering in the peril dreamed in dreams.
. . . .
Happy the one occupied by a mere dream,
Happy he whose premonitions were in vain!
For us, alas, every presence and every glance
Confirm dream and premonition all the more.
Say, what has fate in store for us?
Say, how did it bind us two so well?
Oh, in lives lived out before
You were my sister or my wife.
. . . .
You tamed my hot blood,
You gave direction to my wild, wandering course
And in your angelic arms
My suffering heart found peace.

It is only on the basis of this infantile fixation of the libido on the sister (and mother) that we can fully understand the psychological significance of the fact that Charlotte can be considered the muse of the most mature and deepest creations of Goethe's genius. In a complete psychological sense, she represented for Goethe mother and sister. Not only through her "mother" and "sister" aspects, but also through her restraint, reminiscent of his childhood relationship to his sister, she brought to life the old, repressed conflicts that now demanded presentation and expression in artistic creation.

In this respect, we should refer to the detailed description of this mechanism presented in the discussion of Schiller's dramatic works. Further, we should also consider one pronouncement by Goethe himself that shows how his supposed muse could only have played a subordinate role as opposed to his infantile ideals: "My conception of women is not abstracted from reality. Instead I was born with it or it somehow developed in me, God knows how. My women are all better than women found in real life." Below, then, in our search for the deepest psychological understanding of the dramatic creations *Tasso, Iphigenie, Egmont, Elpenor, Die Geschwister,* and others, we can disregard the influence of Charlotte, though we in no way underestimate it. Instead, we shall look back to the deeper influence of the beloved childhood companion. It was this influence that itself shaped Goethe's alliance with his beloved as one problematical for real love but conducive to literary fantasy production.

There are two typical themes, especially, that occur throughout Goethe's works and that can be understood only from the perspective of the parent complex displaced to siblings. One of these is a specific manifestation of the love conflict between two men over one woman; the brother appears as the sister's protector and rescuer—as opposed to her suitor, lover, or spouse (Dioscuri theme). We already recognize the second, complementary theme of a man's vacillation between two women. In the typical form of the rivalry between two brothers over the same young woman (sister), the first theme is found in the musical comedy *Claudine von Villa Bella,* in which the bandit Crugantino wounds his brother Pedro, whom he does not recognize at night, in order to deprive him of a young woman. In *Clavigo*—written in a short time to win a bet but representing, according to Goethe himself, a poetic penance for his abandoning Friederike Brion—Beaumarchais passionately hates his sister's seducer, Clavigo. Clavigo has taken Marie not only from her brother, but also from her betrothed, Buenco (sexual splitting of the brother). Unconsciously, the playwright actually conceives of this inimical relationship of the brother to the sister's seducer as that of two brothers who are rivals for the sister's love. This is revealed by the final scene, in which the dying Clavigo, having been wounded by Beaumarchais, says beside Marie's coffin: "I thank you, brother! You have married us!" (He sinks down upon the coffin.) Beaumarchais thrusts him away, crying: "Away from this saint, you cursed one!" Further, Clavigo continually implores his friend Carlos to spare his murderer, saying: "Spare my brother!"

This identification of the jealous rival with the brother, who is unconsciously associated with such rivalry, is comparable, psychologically, to the identification of the beloved with the sister, also revealed by the name given her. Just as Goethe repeatedly called Frau von Stein "sister," he also wrote to Countess Auguste zu Stolberg (January 26, 1775) referring to her as "the dear unnamed one": "My dear one, I wish to call you by no name, for what are the names 'friend,' 'sister,' 'beloved,' 'bride,' 'spouse,' or a word constituting a complex of all these?" Further, this type of psychic betrayal is not uncommon in daily life, for it sometimes occurs that a lover is presented as "sister" or "cousin." In general, though there is conscious motivation for this, additional unconscious motivation is almost never lacking. Just as Beaumarchais takes vengeance on the seducer of his beloved sister, Götz avenges Weislingen's betrayal of Götz's sister Marie (identity of name with Beaumarchais's sister), and Valentin attempts to take vengeance on Faust for the seduction of his sister. *Egmont* is based on a conflict similar to the one that underlies *Clavigo*. Brakenburg loves Klara just as Buenco loves Marie, and he hates the preferred competitor, Egmont, just as Buenco hates Clavigo. Behind the almost asexual Brakenburg lies the "brother" who is to protect his sister from the seducer. The playwright suggests this when he has Klara say to Brakenburg: "My brother died young; I have chosen you to take his place." A similar conflict underlies *Tasso*. Here again we see the same displacement of the main accent to a small, apparently incidental detail. Here again the playwright longs for the lofty, unapproachable "saint" against the will and behind the back of her brother, the duke of Ferrara. Here too the names play a significant role. They make it easier for the playwright to identify with his characters and to rid himself of old, repressed affects. The poet, disappointed with life at the princely court, wants to head for Rome and speaks of his visit with his sister, who bears the same name as Goethe's own sister, Cornelia. He says (*Tasso*, 5.4):

> For I must hurry to Sorrento.
> There lives my sister, who with me
> Was my parents' joy in sorrow.
> On the ship I'll be silent; I'll walk
> silent ashore; softly
> I'll ascend the path, and at the door I'll ask:
> "Where lives Cornelia? Show me the way!"

With Goethe, this typical theme of the brother's revenge on the sister's seducer can be understood as a compromise between two impulses. One of these is unconsciously concerned with the sexual possession of the sister and finds expression in the seduction fantasy, which views the sister as a fallen woman (Gretchen, Marie, Klara). The other expresses itself as a tendency toward self-punishment and effects the repression of the first impulse. It always brings about the demise of the seducer (Clavigo, Egmont) or of the brother (Valentin). Indeed, these two figures represent only projections of the playwright's psychological conflict. Here we also find a path to understanding Goethe's actual love life, which appears to be characterized by constant, unconscious reproach for his "infidelity" toward his sister. This allowed him to break loose again from every new love object following a brief involvement. Only when the beloved provided a complete substitute for the sister, as with Frau von Stein, did Goethe feel free of this reproach, which increased the tendency for self-punishment in the playwright and his protagonists in the same manner as defense against the incest wish. But Goethe himself played the same role of "protector" with respect to the sister, though in the conventional form of the protective brother who advises his beloved sister not to marry, since he does not wish to lose her tender affection to any other man. In his conversations with Eckermann, Goethe comments concerning his already deceased sister (March 28, 1831): "She was a remarkable being. Morally, she stood very high and had not a trace of anything sensual. The thought of giving herself to a man was repulsive to her, and one can well suppose that this led to many an unpleasant moment in her marriage. Women who feel the same aversion or who do not love their husbands will understand what this means. Therefore I could never conceive of my sister as married. Rather, as the abbess of a convent she would have been in her proper place. And since she was not happy in her marriage, though her husband was among the finest of men, she was passionately opposed to my planned marriage with Lili."

As is revealed by the last words, the powerful infantile perspective is active in the sister just as in the brother. She too advises her brother not to marry, since she does not wish to give him up to any other woman. But this does not occur in the way Goethe imagined. Justifying his own emotions, he presumed that his sister was completely without sensuality. Actually, she was without sensuality only in her relations with others. Witkowski too remarks that she was hungry for love but feared all physical contact. We recognize such behavior as typical sexual reticence. We know that this is a reaction to sensuality precociously awakened and activated in childhood. Under the pressure of high moral demands, such sensuality is soon deeply repressed. Thus we can understand why her marriage to Schlosser, whom she wed in 1773 against the will of her brother, must have been an unhappy one. (She died three and a half years later after giving birth to her second child.) In a parable composed in 1776, her husband confessed that she was repulsed by his love.

From his fixation on mother and sister, the second typical theme of Goethe's work also becomes comprehensible. This is the typical incest theme of a man's vacillation between two women. With Freud, we were able to derive this theme in Schiller's work from the child's ambivalent feelings toward the mother. Here, on the one hand, the child sees in the mother the noble, unapproachable saint, whereas on the other hand he sees her as the woman who serves the lusts of his father without a will of her own. Thus we understand how it becomes easier for the boy to displace his affection from the mother to the sister, who is closer to him in age, maturity, and outlook. Most significantly, since the sister has no sexual relations, the brother can hold nothing against her on this count. When there is a brother, competition for the sister cannot be as intense and serious as competition in the context of the parent complex. The sister falls into one of the two mother roles—usually into that of the pure, chaste, adored one. However, that she is basically a substitute for the mother is often revealed in individual traits. Of these, the "whore fantasy" seems to have been especially emphasized with Goethe. Many of his female protagonists are fallen women, or at least women exposed to temptation. Weislingen stands between two women—the delicate, chaste Marie and the wild, sensual widow Adelheid. This theme is observed in Tasso's two Leonores, who call each other "sister." In *Stella* we see in the double marriage an attempt to realize the fantasy of the unification of mother and sister in a single love object (Count von Gleichen). Even in the playwright's own late marriage, this condition for love makes its appearance, though not in such a transparent manner as in Schiller's double love. With his sensual passions newly awakened in Italy, Goethe turned to Christiane, the "treasure of his bed," raised up from the lower classes (rescue fantasy); the reverse side of his mother/sister ideal he found embodied in the restrained Charlotte.

The clearest proof of Goethe's unconscious incestuous attraction to his sister is provided not by a description of his life or by observations passed down to us—for these are necessarily silent concerning unconscious impulses—but by his literary works, decisively influenced by unconscious perspectives and all too clearly permeated by this complex. In *Wilhelm Meister,* which Goethe began in the year of his sister's death (1777), in the story of Augustin and Sperata (book 8), he presented his childhood wish fantasies relating to the sister, but in the repressed form of unconscious sibling incest. At this time the memory of his painful loss was still fresh, and his childhood emotions with respect to his sister had been reactivated. In the story the Marquis X, a rather eccentric man, has four children. The third son, Augustin, is brought to a monastery because of his weak constitution and his tendency to see visions. Finally, though, he returns home completely broken. His father also has a daughter; he is ashamed of her and has had her raised in secret. This daughter Sperata, meets Augustin, who is slowly recovering in their parents' house. The two fall in love and have a child who later appears as Mignon. Though it is discovered that the relationship is incestuous, Augustin does not wish to leave Sperata. He cannot believe that she is his sister and that nature could so far counter morality. Finally, though, he is convinced. In desperation he flees, but he is apprehended and brought back to the monastery. He then becomes neurotic and is plagued by hallucinations. When word reaches the monastery of the death of Sperata, who dies insane—and word of the miracles associated with the corpse—he again flees, searches for the corpse, and wanders into the wide world. Finally a hallucination drives him to suicide.

The opposite of this wish gratification—possible, owing to repression, only in an unwitting manner (nonrecognition)—is found in the one-act play *Die Geschwister* [The siblings]. Goethe composed this work during a few days in October 1776 as a "general confession" of his love for Charlotte von Stein. Nevertheless, his infantile erotic affection for his sister found unconscious, naive fulfillment in this work, for the blood relationship of the lovers turns out to be erroneous. Thus nothing stands in the way of a loving bond with the "sister." Nor is jealousy lacking toward the rival, Fabrice. It is this jealousy that drives Wilhelm to the decisive confession of his love for Marianne. Like the tale of Augustin and Sperata, this material was freely invented by Goethe. Here follow a discussion of the plot and a few characteristic excerpts.

After the death of his friend in youth, Wilhelm takes on her daughter, Marianne, whom he raises claiming that she is his sister. Wilhelm loves Marianne. At the beginning of the work he says in a soliloquy: "Marianne! If you only knew that the one you consider your brother is working for you with quite different emotions and hopes! Perhaps! . . . Oh! It is so bitter. She does love me, as a brother. No, alas! This is disbelief again, and disbelief never produced anything good." Then Fabrice, Wilhelm's friend, presses his suit for Marianne. The fear of losing her drives Wilhelm to reveal his secret; jealousy toward Fabrice brings Wilhelm to confess his love. In general, Wilhelm's jealousy is clearly emphasized. He is also jealous of the little boy whom Marianne likes very much, and whom she sometimes takes into her bed.

> *Marianne:* I would gladly have let him stay. I only know that my brother does not approve, so I abstain. Sometimes the little thief himself asks permission of Wilhelm to sleep with me.
>
> *Fabrice:* But doesn't the boy disturb you?
>
> *Marianne:* Oh, not at all. He is so active the whole day, and when I come to him in bed, he is as good as a lamb. He is a dear. He embraces me as he is able. Sometimes I cannot bring him to sleep.

Anyone who knows from the study of neurosis how frequently a child's sleeping with an adult (usually the mother) assists in the fixation of the libido in the incest complex, and anyone who is familiar, from observation, with the sleeping together of siblings of approximately the same age and with its later consequences for infantile fixation, will easily see in this dramatic depiction a reflection of similar sensually stimulating experiences and impressions from Goethe's own childhood.

Marianne does not reject Fabrice's suit, but she tells him that he should speak with her brother and that she does privately love her brother and would not gladly leave him. In the conversation concerning Fabrice's suit, she says to Wilhelm, whom she still considers her brother:

> Let us always live together as we do now. For only with you can I live. The feeling has always lain in my soul, and all of this has brought it out so strongly. I love only you!
>
> *Wilhelm:* Marianne!
>
> *Marianne:* Dear brother! . . . You could long have known it. Indeed, you've known it since our mother's death, when I came to you in childhood; I have been with you ever since.

Wilhelm reveals the whole secret to her as follows:

> *Wilhelm* (embracing her): You are mine, Marianne!
>
> *Marianne:* God! What is this? Can I return this kiss? What sort of a kiss was that, brother!
>
> *Wilhelm:* It was not the kiss of a restrained, seemingly cold brother, but the kiss of an eternally, uniquely happy lover. (At her feet): Marianne, you are not my sister!
>
> . . . .
>
> *Marianne* (regarding him): No, it's impossible.
>
> *Wilhelm:* My beloved, my spouse!
>
> *Marianne* (embracing him): Wilhelm, it is not possible.

Goethe's work with the Iphigenia myth and his special manner of treating it show how such a dominant sister complex can affect the realization even of material associated with solid tradition. Orestes commits matricide in deference to his sister [Electra], although this conflicts with his infantile emotions; erotic affection between Orestes and his sister [Iphigenia], merely suggested in classical tradition, is expressed by Goethe not only in Iphigenia's direct loving affection for her brother, but also in that with deep human and psychological insight, and at variance from all other versions, he portrays her as curing the matricide, who is tormented by the Furies. Countless articles and essays have attempted to explain this cure through the sister, but the deepest, ultimate explanation lies in the playwright's own unconscious incest complex. Like Orestes, after turning from his "unfaithful" mother, he found comfort and a substitute in the pure, sacred love of his sister. In this light we can understand Iphigenia's words to Orestes and his response.

Iphigenia: Oh, if the voice of mother's blood calls down
To hell with muted tones,
Shall the pure sister's words of blessing not
Call from Olympus helpful gods?
Orestes: In your arms, with a free heart, let me
For the first time find pure joy!
. . . By your touch,
I was healed. In your arms,
The sickness grasped me with all its claws
For the last time; horribly it
Shook my very marrow. Then it fled away
Like a snake to its hole.

And elsewhere Orestes directly expresses the beneficial influence of his sister upon his repressed infantile affections:

Since my youngest years, I have
Loved nothing as I have loved you, Sister.

And in his exhortation to his beloved sister—"Come down with me, childless and guiltless"—we recognize once again the jealous rivalry of the brother who does not wish to relinquish his sister to any other man and who claims her as his own. But this liberating breakthrough of the unconscious wish, manifest in the cure, is preceded by defense against this tendency, expressed, in agreement with the classical tradition, in Orestes' disguising himself from his sister. In the initial nonrecognizability of the brother, we easily discern the typical theme of recognition of siblings, which underlies both the "Harfner" episode and *Die Geschwister,* and which Aristotle already designated as the most effective element in tragedy. But even in this defensive form, the sister's passionate affection for her brother finds expression.

Iphigenia: Oh, hear me! Behold me, see
How after so long my heart opens to the joy
Of kissing the head of the one who is
The dearest the world still can give me!
Orestes: Beautiful nymph,
I do not trust you and your compliments.
Diana demands strict servants,
And will avenge her desecrated shrine.
Take your arm from my breast!
And if you wish to love a youth and save him,
And if you wish to offer him tender joy,
Then turn your thoughts to my friend,
A worthier man than I.

In connection with love for the sister, brother hatred is also expressed. Pylades claims that he and Orestes are brothers who have quarreled with a third brother over their father's inheritance.

> We are of Crete, the sons of Adrast:
> I am the youngest, Cephalus is my name,
> And he is Laodamas, the eldest of the house.
> Between us, rough and wild, our middle brother stood;
> Already in our boyhood games
> He spoiled the unity and joy of earliest days.

Differing from every other version, in Goethe's drama Orestes has himself presented as a fratricide.

> *Pylades:* . . . Soon the fight
> For kingdom and inheritance split the brothers.
> I was inclined toward the eldest. He slew
> Our brother; because of his blood guilt,
> The Furies drive him mercilessly about.

Hatred of the brother and father are united in Iphigenia's tale of the prehistory of the Pelopides.

> Soon, Thyestes dishonored
> His brother's bed. Avenging, Atreus drove
> Him from the realm. Deceitfully, planning grave deeds,
> Thyestes had already taken a son from his brother,
> Had in secret raised him, calling him his own.
> This son's heart he filled with anger and vengeance,
> Sent him to the royal city
> To kill his own father in his home.
> The youth's plan was found out. Cruelly,
> The king punished the sent murderer, thinking
> The youth to be his brother's son. Too late
> He learned who died before his drunken eyes,
> Tortured.

The playwright's identification with his protagonist, Orestes, allowing him to create the work, is revealed not only in that at the first performance of *Iphigenie auf Tauris* on April 6, 1779, Goethe himself played Orestes, but also in that he had already compared himself previously to this neurotic of antiquity. In 1775, after his voyage to Switzerland, he wrote to Karschin: "Perhaps I am again being driven by the invisible scourge of the Eumenides from my homeland." His intense interest in the material and especially in scenes of recognition, of which he often made use, is attested by his draft of an *Iphigenie von Delphi,* about which he commented on

October 18, 1786, saying that between sleep and waking he had come across the plot outline, in which a scene of recognition would be of central importance: "I myself cried about it like a child." Here the rivalry of sisters over the brother is expressed.

In his *Italienische Reise* [Italian journey], Goethe writes (October 19):

> On the journey here from Centro, I wanted to continue my work on *Iphigenie* [*auf Tauris*], but instead, my muse showed me the plot for *Iphigenie von Delphi;* I had to develop it. Here, as briefly as possible, is an outline. Electra, with some hope that Orestes will bring the image of Diana from Tauris to Delphi, appears in the temple of Apollo and dedicates to the god, as a final offering of penance, the ax that has brought so much sadness to the house of Pelops. Unfortunately, one of the Greeks approaches her and tells her that he has accompanied Orestes and Pylades to Tauris and has seen both led to their deaths, having himself been able to escape. The passionate Electra is beside herself and does not know whether to direct her ire toward men or gods. Meanwhile Iphigenia, Orestes, and Pylades have also arrived in Delphi. When the two sisters meet, mutually unrecognized, Iphigenia's sacred composure contrasts strangely with Electra's earthly passion. The Greek who had escaped notices Iphigenia; he recognizes the priestess who was to sacrifice the friends and reveals this to Electra. She is about to murder Iphigenia with the same ax, which she again seizes from the altar, but a fortunate turn of events averts this last disaster from the siblings. If this scene succeeds, it will be one of the greatest and most moving things ever to be seen in the theater. But where are hands and time to be found, though the spirit is willing?

17 Defense against and Enactment of Sibling Incest

Of all things, I found it worst of all for two people in love to discover finally that they are related or are siblings.

GOETHE, *Die Geschwister*

Under the pressure of moral defense, the undisguised enactment of the sibling incest fantasy, rejected by progressing repression, has brought forth a number of configurations. These can be divided into two large groups. The one theme of sibling recognition attempts, following the classical Oedipus schema, to realize the incest through lack of knowledge of the relationship; the kinship is discovered only after the sin has been committed, though in secondary derivations this may occur just in time to prevent the act. In Goethe's *Die Geschwister,* however, a new form of defense against and enactment of sibling incest appears. This we shall refer to as the theme of the suspension of sibling relationship. Whereas in the first form the forbidden act of incest naively occurs without knowledge of the partner's identity and the impulses of repentance and defense appear only after the relationship is discovered, this second form of the theme demonstrates a more complete wish fulfillment, less oppressed by guilt, in that the inhibitions are present from the beginning, since the relationship is known. Nevertheless, the kinship proves false, allowing the supposed siblings to seal the forbidden bond. Here then, in a refined way, the mechanism of the discovery of kinship, which originally served for defense, is used for the purpose of enacting incest in a disguised manner. Thus, if the first form of the theme, reduced to a logical formula, claims that the man who is unconsciously fixated on his sister loves his (unrecognized) sister in every woman, the second form of the theme asserts the same, but with a slightly different emphasis. It reveals the wish that the actual kinship not stand in the way of love toward the sister.

The Theme of Sibling Recognition

In his *Poetics,* Aristotle already claimed that it is particularly effective for relatives, ignorant of their kinship and about to bring upon themselves the guilt of serious sin, to experience an emotional scene of recognition. And in his *Technik des Dramas* [Dramatic technique], Freytag (1872) mentions that in Greek drama, scenes of recognition occupied the same position as love scenes in modern drama.

In Adolf Müllner's *Der neunundzwanzigste Februar* [The twenty-ninth of February], two spouses realize they are siblings after many years of marriage (cf. chap. 22). Similarly, in Ludwig Tieck's *Eckbert* it is only after incest has occurred that the kinship is discovered (cf. chap. 23).

In François Chateaubriand's novel *Les martyrs,* René enters a monastery after discovering that he has embraced his sister in incestuous love. Recently, in his one-act cycle *Geschwister* [Siblings] (1902), Christian Kraus has dealt with incest committed by siblings without knowledge of their kinship, which is discovered only later (cf. chap. 24).

Finally, we should mention the very recent tragedy *Der Feind und der Bruder* [The foe and the brother] (1911), by Moritz Heimann. In this drama the young wife of a Venetian count flees her husband with a young man of her retinue toward whom she feels deep affection. When the betrayed husband sends word to her that she has fallen in love with the son of her father, she kills her half-brother to spare him knowledge of their incest. She then stabs herself beside his body:

> I loved you! Thus the siblings in paradise
> loved one another! My brother!

The love of another (full) brother for this same sister is also suggested:

> She loves her brother, she loves him sisterly;
> And is a sister not a woman,
> Though she be a sister?

That the half-brother, with whom she has unknowingly committed incest, is only a doublet of the full brother, produced by dampening, is suggested in that he is confused with the full brother. He also has the same name as the father. Defense against unknowing incestuous inclination is revealed in the youth's resistance to adultery with the wife of a man who has acted as his father.

More frequently though, the lovers recognize each other as siblings before the longed-for but rejected union can occur. This is the case in Christoph Wieland's novel *Geschichte des Agathon* (1766), in which the poet artistically depicts his own psychic development. Agathon, who has been raised to serve in the temple in Delphi, falls in love with the virgin Psyche, also dedicated to the service of Apollo. Later it is revealed that she is his sister. After many adventures and revelations presented in the typical form of the family romance, Psyche meets the son of the ruler of Tarentum. She falls in love with him and marries him, "in many respects the second Agathon." In the conclusion of Wieland's story of Danae, the relationships between the characters are discovered. The presentation of the sibling recognition theme found in Lessing's *Nathan der Weise* [Nathan the wise] is probably the most familiar. The temple functionary rescues the Jewish girl Recha from the fire and falls deeply in love with her in spite of himself until it is discovered that she is his sister. In the tender attachment of Saladin to his sister Sittah, we find a doublet of the theme of sibling love. Some of Lessing's other formulations of the incest complex have already been mentioned (cf. chap. 7). In Voltaire's tragedy *Zaïre,* the depiction of the incest complex resembles that in *Nathan der Weise:* Zaïre and Kerestan are in love without realizing that they are siblings.

In August Kotzebue's comedy *Der Rehbock, oder Die schuldlosen Schuldbewussten* [The roebuck, or The guilt-ridden innocents], a situation is depicted in which the sister (the countess of Eberfeld) falls in love with her brother (Baron Wolkenstein, acting as an equerry). A second pair is also presented: the brother (the count) and the unrecognized sister (Baroness Freiling) are in love. After these innocent transgressions have been revealed, a near realization of the incest fantasy is effected. Now becoming his brother-in-law, the baron, repeatedly referred to by the count as "brother," marries the sister of the count, who himself is married to the baron's sister. Before the solution of these masquerades, the incest situations are brought to the brink of consummation, especially in scenes in which the count attempts to win the sexual favors of his sister, disguised as the wife of a land tenant. A similar scene is found in the four-act comedy *Die beiden Klingsberg* [The two Klingsbergs]. In this play, in a number of romantic involvements, father and son are portrayed as rivals—from the chambermaid to the Italian dancer, who receives father and son one after the other; from Amalie, temporarily separated from her husband, to Henriette, the son's betrothed and his later wife, whom the father tries in vain to lure away from him. In one scene (3.13), in a rendezvous with the old count, the woman he expects and loves has been replaced by his own sister.

He is about to make her a proposal when his son appears as a competitor. The deep source of the rivalry between father and son for the mother's love is suggested in that the object of the most serious competition is identified with the deceased mother through name and external circumstances (3.6).

Adolph: She bears the name of my mother.
Count: Your mother was a very fine woman.
Adolph: And yet only a poor, unknown girl.
Count: You won't find a girl like your mother in half of Europe.
Adolph: . . . I have found her.

In Kotzebue's numerous works, several themes from the incest complex are employed in sentimentally dampened form.

In Ludwig Anzengruber's novel *Der Fleck auf der Ehr* [A stain on honor], a farmer's wife has an illegitimate daughter by a neighbor, whose son later falls in love with the girl. The father feels compelled to inform his son that he is in love with his sister, and the son renounces his love. Similar material and presentation of the theme are found in Ernst Zahn's novel of country life, *Herrgottsfäden*. Russi, the servingman, has seduced Rosi, Furrer's daughter, but Furrer refuses to grant her to him. Russi leaves, but he returns years later as a powerful entrepreneur and attempts to avenge the insult done him earlier by bringing about his enemy's social ruin. Tobias, the illegitimate son of Russi and Rosi, joins in the discussion with Furrer. Tobias is secretly engaged to Josepha, Russi's legitimate daughter. Rosi reveals that Josepha is his sister. Tobias tells his sister, and they separate forever. Shortly before they part, we read: "Then Tobias remained standing and listened. He placed his arm around her and his gaze met hers. 'Can you fathom it? We are brother and sister,' said Tobias. He could hardly breathe. 'Don't speak of it,' begged Josepha, trying to go on. He held her fast. 'What I feel for you is not brotherly love,' he stammered. She felt his hot breath on her cheek." In his novella *Die Geschwister* [The siblings], Zahn also deals with the unconscious libidinous fixation of brother and sister on one another. Here the rescue fantasy underlies the whole theme. Indeed, in nearly all of Zahn's works, we find the theme of sexual attraction between close relatives, sometimes more and sometimes less clearly. In *Lukas Hochstrassers Haus* [The house of Lukas Hochstrasser] we see the father's affection for the son's lover. In *Erni Beheim* we see the attraction of mother and son, and in *Vinzenz Püntiner* we find the attraction of brother-in-law and sister-in-law.

The Theme of Suspension of Sibling Relationship

We have observed this theme not only in the classically noble portrayal found in Goethe's *Die Geschwister,* but also (cf. chap. 10) in Juan de Matos Fragoso's legendary drama *El marido de su madre* [His mother's spouse], in which two lovers discover that they are not siblings after all. In *Der neue Menoza* [The new Menoza] (1774), by Michael Reinhold Lenz, the author attempts to justify the marriage of siblings under certain conditions. Finally, though, it is revealed that the spouses are not siblings at all. In his love life Lenz, who acted like a child and wished others to treat him as one, showed a tendency always to approach other men's lovers. Psychologically, this tendency is comprehensible from the incest complex. In his drama *Die Freunde machen den Philosophen* [Friends make the philosopher], he treats the theme of double marriage.

The theme of suspension of sibling relationship is depicted with artistic perfection in Konrad Ferdinand Meyer's novella *Die Richterin* [*The judicatrix*]. Wulfrin and Palma are considered half-siblings, the children of Comes Wulf, who was poisoned before Palma's birth by his third wife, Stemma the judge; indeed, Palma was another man's child. Although at the beginning of the tale attempts are already made to establish that the siblings have different mothers, that they also have different fathers is at first concealed from these two characters, passionately in love. They do not realize that they share "not a drop of blood in common." Palma, born later, loves with wild passion her [presumed] brother—who had always lived far from her—and thinks only of him. With him, though, the incestuous passion, which first appears when he sees his sister, expresses itself initially only as inhibition—in the form of sexual abstinence. But after they have been together for a short time, tender affection toward the sister is also awakened in the rough brother, and it is an accurate reflection of childhood jealousy that his uninhibited passion for his sister appears precisely at the moment of her betrothal to the soft Graciosus. "If one of the violent men hiding in the Rhaetian cliffs had covetously attacked Palma, Wulfrin might have defied him to his face and drawn his sword from its sheath, but Graciosus was so passive that Wulfrin would not have been able to resist. And he himself felt that he was being driven by the dark and frightening thought of marrying his sister."

But since she has accepted Graciosus's offer of marriage only in deference to her beloved brother, she immediately breaks off the engagement—simply out of spite, as she thinks. In vain he sends his sister away. He must admit: "I desire my sister!" Now raving, he has his stepmother told to "prepare the hall and prepare the feast. Light a thousand torches! . . . I shall marry my sister!" In vain the mother attempts to comfort and strengthen him: "I embraced her in every woman, for I am wed to her eternally. No, I cannot live." After Palma has finally discovered the secret of her origins, Stemma admits before the emperor, who acts as father to her child, that she murdered her spouse and that Palma was born out of wedlock. Thus the tie of blood is no longer an impediment to the loving bond.

Knowing from Meyer's life how intensely he was fixated on mother and sister, and how his sister Betsy, especially, stood by him his whole life long, lovingly prepared to sacrifice herself for him, one will easily recognize behind the historical guise of this tale the original fantasy of the boy who ascribes marital infidelity to his mother to justify his being in love with his sister and eliminate the objectionable nature of this affection. The psychological significance of this fantasy in the mental life of the author is already revealed in that the unfaithful wife who eliminates her husband has a doublet in Faustina, whose daughter rescues Wulfrin from enemies just as his own sister Palma does. Here we gain insight into the author's powerful parent complex, which underlay his love for his sister. To this complex corresponds the typical fantasy of puberty, artistically presented, which also underlies *Hamlet*—the fantasy that the unfaithful mother eliminates the father and through this fulfillment of the repressed, jealous infantile wish makes it impossible for the son to seize her from the father or to take vengeance on the father, these acts being resisted by the son's defense mechanisms.

Wulfrin declares: "As a seven-year-old, I fled from home and ran to King Karl, for my father had taken my dear sick mother from me and placed her in a convent." He rejects the suggestion that he take vengeance on his father, saying: "I knew what one owes one's father. He had committed crimes against my mother, and his memory, except for his deeds in war, is bitter to me." Nevertheless, he sometimes suffers pangs of conscience owing to the unexplained sudden death of his father, and in his desperate attempts to free himself from the bonds of sinful love for his sister, he addresses the dead man in the hope of learning from him whether Palma is his child. "When he won back his inheritance, the image of his father and his childhood mood were reawakened. . . . 'In the end he is my father, and he will stand by me if he can. If he is there at all, he will not let me perish miserably.' "

Childish respect for the father is revealed more clearly still in the doublet figure of the emperor who, significantly, attends a mass for the soul of his own father at the beginning of the tale and finally acts "as father" for Palma, now wedding her to her "brother." And concerning the complaint that Wulfrin has been slow to avenge his father's death, the emperor Karl says: "I have just prayed for the soul of my father. Childhood ties reach beyond the grave. I think you should not be absent before the judge: you owe it to your father."

The split perspective toward the father, a mixture of childish respect and jealous rivalry, is expressed in Wulfrin's indecision concerning his revenge and in the split between murdered competitor and powerful, superior emperor. Similarly, the double perspective toward the mother is expressed in the split between the dear, gentle mother, mistreated by the father, and the beautiful young stepmother.

" 'It is true, my lady,' the courtier [Wulfrin] continued frankly, 'that I could never abide you, and I shall tell you why. That old man, my father, was a rough and violent man. I am sad to say it, but he mistreated my dear mother; I believe he beat her. I do not wish to think about it. He locked her in a convent as soon as she became ill. So it is not surprising, given human nature, that I wanted nothing to do with you, the one who drove her from her place.' "

But in the depiction of the elderly father, whom Wulfrin describes as "drunken and ardent, but with gray hair!" and of the very young stepmother, we easily recognize the psychological identity of these father and mother derivatives and the son's wish to take possession of the mother after the elimination of the father. Here, though, the mother is replaced by her rejuvenated image, available for sexual relations—the sister. This displacement is modeled after processes in the infantile psychology of the playwright.

In connection with this, owing to the strong correspondence in the presentation of themes, we should mention the novella *Von zwei Geschwistern* [Of two siblings] by Otto Sachs, who died young. As with Meyer, the plot involves conscious perpetuation of a criminal sibling love affair. Here, though, the kinship is suspended, freeing the couple to engage in sexual relations, on the basis of a document so dubious that the two lovers can never be sure of their destiny; the brother is destroyed by his pangs of conscience. The influence of Meyer's novella is observed even in small details. As in Meyer's work, the story begins after the father's death. As in Meyer's work, the son has been away from home for many years and has never seen his sister. In both works it is clear from the beginning that the two siblings have different mothers, and in both works they are later claimed to have different fathers as well. Indeed, reference to historical or legendary example is not lacking. Just as Meyer refers to Byblis, so Ippolito, the sinful brother in Sachs's novella, makes reference to historical example: "What law restrained the duke of Valentinois, Cesare, who in his inebriated exhilaration openly boasted that he had enjoyed the favors of his sister? He was the son of the pope, who himself . . ." Indeed, even the torrential storm that parallels the storm of passions is not lacking here, and like Wulfrin, Ippolito also pushes his sister violently away when his passions first burst into flame. Finally, like Meyer, Sachs motivates the mutual attraction of the siblings through the absence of opportunity to become acquainted in early childhood, so that they first meet as mature adults.

Despite these correspondences, perhaps not fully conscious, reflecting the same psychic perspective, it cannot be denied that this writer demonstrates originality. Here the theme is presented more freely and spontaneously than in Meyer's artistically perfected tale; therefore in several respects it is perhaps more human and psychologically more accurate. Here the beloved brother's love for the mother, that is, the mother of the "sister"—a love only assumed in Meyer's novella—is clearly portrayed. Here too the brother does claim that he "had to leave his homeland because of disagreements with his stepmother, who dominated her aging spouse. But there were also those who said that his hatred for this woman sprang from excessive love for her, forcing him to avoid her in order to escape a conflict with his most sacred obligations." It is only after her death that he returns to protect the sister. Later in the story it is indeed revealed that the son had loved his stepmother passionately, and in this connection it seems no coincidence that he bears the name Hippolytus. Here too, behind the heavily emphasized sister complex, we can still see his love for the mother; the displacement of erotic affection from the mother to the sister is suggested not only in that Ippolito makes his sister his bride in the chamber of her mother, longed for in vain, but also, and more clearly still, through her repeatedly emphasized similarity to the mother. "Each day Ippolito saw more and more clearly the resemblance of her features to those of her mother." The most significant departure from Meyer's novella is that the siblings refer to an admission of infidelity found in a poem by the father's deceased second wife without inquiring whether this admission is grounded and whether there is actually any doubt about the identity of the sister's father. In this unresolved doubt we have a fine literary example suggesting the omnipresence of guilt consciousness and the great power of incestuous passion, which eliminates all inhibitions. "Thus the blinding intoxication of love turned the lovers' suspicions to certainty, turned appearance to reality." "No! It is not this piece of paper that convinced you! Your unrestrained, powerful, sinful desire for forbidden pleasure has blinded you and presented illusion as truth." Thus the mechanism of suspension of kinship fails here owing to certain infantile perspectives found in the psychic life of the author; this failure, noted by Sachs himself, reveals that in this presentation of the theme we are dealing with nothing more or less than unreproached enactment of the incest fantasy. Whereas the brother is continually tormented by doubts, pangs of conscience, and feelings of penitence, the sister directly confesses: "Even had I never doubted that Ippolito was my brother, I would have acted no differently." And before her judges, who wish to spare her the most severe punishment, she does not hide her true feelings: "I would have done the same even had I been sure he was my brother, for I loved him."

In the novel *Die Epigonen: Familien-Memoiren in neun Büchern* [The epigons: Family memoirs in nine books], by Karl Immermann (1796–1840), the theme of suspension of sibling relationship finds unusual expression. Hermann adores the beautiful Johanna, who has left her husband, Medon. They take leave of one another in the house of Flämmchen, another young woman who had fallen in love with Hermann. "He held her hand tightly and asked softly, 'Do you love me, Johanna?' 'With all my heart,' she answered. 'Must it always be blood alone that makes brothers and sisters? Can the purest bond never be created by feelings, choosing freely and beautifully? No, I shall not give up the belief that such attractions are possible. From the first moment I saw you, you seemed like a brother to me. Let me be as a sister to you! And as a souvenir of this hour and of my confession, you shall receive the best that a woman can offer.' She threw her arm around his neck, and her beautiful, virginal lips met his. Slowly raising herself, she said, 'Seeing this, who would not cry out that this is passion, a crime? So little do we understand the secrets of the heart.' " During the night he is secretly called to Johanna's chamber, where he makes love to a woman he believes is his beloved. However, he soon learns from a letter left for him by his father that Johanna is indeed his sister—that they have the same mother but different fathers. He now falls into a severe neurosis from which he recovers only on hearing, after the death of Flämmchen, that it was she and not his sister with whom he had made love that night. Finally, though, a near incest fantasy is realized: after the death of his uncle, Hermann marries Cornelia, though it is supposed that he is her nephew.

The theme of suspension of kinship is found in a psychologically interesting form in Paul Heyse's 1862 novella *Der Weinhüter* [The winekeeper]. Andree, who has fled from home because of cruel treatment by his mother, works as a winekeeper. Andree loves his half-sister, Moidi, more than he wishes to admit to himself. At first this affection is expressed only in defensive symptoms: "While he spoke these words, she had approached him trustingly and had placed her arm lightly around his neck. But as if a specter had touched him, he withdrew forcefully, thrusting her and her affections away. He was breathing hard. 'Leave me,' he gasped, 'do not touch me. Ask me nothing; go away, as far as you can, and never come back.' " "Since his childhood, he had not dared to kiss her red, easily laughing mouth. But the timidity with which he regarded her was mixed with a dull, passionate torment, and her soft breath, caressing his face, made his heart pound stronger."

The sexual abstinence typical in connection with incestuous attraction is also expressed in characteristic fashion: "He himself found the company of all young women uncomfortable, and he was always disgusted by lovers' small talk. . . . But with a peculiar expression of fear, he looked into his sister's face whenever she expressed her simple thoughts of the future; it seemed to him that a separation from her was somehow to be avoided."

He becomes directly jealous of her once she has openly declared her affection for her brother: "It also happened on more than one occasion, for example on holidays, that she did not come to the place agreed upon. Feverish with jealousy, he would keep watch over the road to her house to see whether she was being detained by visitors. He lay waiting in ambush. . . . He was unhappy. He felt dimly that his behavior was not correct and honorable. Why did he not grant his sister what all young women deserved—freedom of choice in wishes and affections? With hot fear he rejected these thoughts, but they only returned more insistently. Indeed, they did not share the same father. But were they siblings any less for that?"

Out of jealousy over his sister, he nearly kills a soldier. He flees from his homeland not so much to escape punishment as to escape, in a way, his passion for her. While he is residing in a monastery abroad, the woman he has considered his mother dies. On her deathbed, between moments of delirium, she has admitted that Andree is not truly her son, but only a foster child. After the death of the "mother," the "sister" visits him in the company of her betrothed and informs him of her mother's admission. The suspension of the blood relationship has a liberating effect on him: "When Moidi first told me that her mother had found me abandoned or had brought me down from the pastures, from God knows where, it was like being suddenly freed from the glowing chains and bonds I had always dragged about with me, which had not fallen from me even in the monastery. For not even in holy confession was I able to admit what I have endured the past few years on account of Moidi. I was not able to admit that I would have perished if another man had married her. And I knew very well that it would be a mortal sin had I really been her mother's son. Still, I could not rid myself of these thoughts, for they were stronger than my small understanding of such feelings, my religion, and all else."

His painfully repressed passion bursts into flame. He takes Moidi from her betrothed and makes her his wife. Again, though, as in most treatments of the theme of suspension of sibling relationship, we observe the underlying incest fantasy: the suspension of kinship is based on highly doubtful grounds with which defense and penitence can be associated. For on finding that she is pregnant, the sister feels new doubts about whether her mother's delirious utterances should be believed; she wonders if she and her husband are in fact siblings. (This return of the old incest fantasy is expressed more clearly still in that during their journey, the two present themselves as brother and sister.) She suffers terribly from these thoughts and has the "brother" return home to ascertain the full truth. She cannot even be convinced by the priest, the only one who knows the secret, that Andree is not her brother. She still suspects that her mother lied on her deathbed in denying that she was the mother of Andree. Only after the priest has named Andree's true mother, and after this woman has acknowledged her maternity, do Moidi's suspicions leave her; the two become a happy couple. As in most literary works of this type, in addition to affection for the sister, a remarkable attraction between mother and son is also suggested. She is unknown to him until his wedding, but he feels greater attraction to her than is usual with a godmother: " 'I have always felt great love and respect for you. . . . For in the whole world, it is only with you that I have found peace and tranquility.' Then she lifted him up; in tears, she looked into his pale face. Nor did she restrain herself, but held him tightly in her arms and kissed him long and warmly on mouth and eyes."

The theme of suspension of sibling relationship is found also in the last novel of the recently deceased Wilhelm Jensen, *Fremdlinge unter den Menschen* [Strangers among men]. Gerhart, the illegitimate son of a French officer, falls in love with Egge Tribelius, the foster daughter of the pastor and his wife in Ratekau. It is ultimately revealed that she is Gerhart's sister, while the protagonist discovers that his father is the noble marquis de Boissy. After these revelations, the lovers share a not unwelcome death on the high seas. The underlying mother complex is suggested in the unusual attraction of Cordula, Egge's mother, to her daughter's bridegroom and brother, the hero of the tale.

The typical close connection between the theme of suspension of sibling relationship and the parent complex, and the way that in the years of puberty the identical fantasies of the family complex lead to the same manifestations, we find demonstrated in the tragedy *Die Hochzeit zu Barcelona* [The wedding in Barcelona], the first work of an unnamed twenty-year-old playwright published in Vienna in 1891. Here too the siblings, burning with sinful passion for one another, know from the beginning that they have different mothers, and here again (with the help of a ring) it is later revealed that they have different fathers as well. Whereas in Meyer's novel this revelation allows the lovers to engage in sexual relations without guilt, and whereas in Sachs's novella inner doubts and self-reproach disturb and destroy their loving happiness, in this tragedy, after the suspension of kinship the lovers do indeed marry; but their sexual union occurs only symbolically, in their shared love death. Here too Don Carlos, count of Bucar, meets his stepsister, Donna Alma, when he is already fifteen years old. Immediately he falls passionately in love with her.

Don Carlos: I loved in you more than a sister;
I trembled and fled. But you too,
Pure as you are, loved me even more. (Alma nods painfully.)

He is disinherited and banished by his father, against whom he has drawn his dagger; but after a life of wild adventure he returns to his homeland just when his father has died and his sister is about to marry Don Garcias, according to the wish of the deceased father. He now loves his sister more passionately than ever and does not wish to relinquish her to any other man. At this point the king, on his deathbed, reveals that Don Carlos is actually his own son; at the last minute, Don Carlos is able to thwart the consummation of the marriage. He is too late to stop the ceremony, but on the wedding night he murders the husband before sexual relations can occur. Nevertheless, he meets the same fate himself before he can enter the longed-for union with his pseudosister, liberated in this manner. He is pursued by Don Raphael, who wishes to possess the virginal widow of his murdered brother, Don Garcias, for himself. Don Carlos poisons himself and his beloved, whom he has just married. In the relationship of Don Garcias and Don Raphael, who had courted Donna Alma even earlier than his brother, jealous brother hatred derived from rivalry over the same woman is depicted.

The violent elimination of the preferred older brother, in realization of Don Raphael's secret wish, was a fantasy so emotionally charged for the playwright, himself the eldest sibling, that he expressed it in two doublets as well. Don Raphael tells his brother's bride the story of his life, while claiming that he is describing a friend:

Guido, whose bride was taken
By his brother, after he had already
Robbed him of his father's inheritance.

After his brother's murder, Don Raphael asks the new king for the widow's hand in marriage, but the king hesitates, citing ecclesiastical laws limiting marriage. Still, Don Raphael justifies his suit with an example:

Hear me, señor, they were not wed.
In this way, Pedro of Castille
Took Don Juan's widow as his wife,
Slaying his own brother at the altar—
A thing I have not done, my lord.

In addition, we find doublets of the theme of brother hatred in the enmity felt by the newly crowned king, Don Pedro, toward Don Carlos, whom he must recognize as a son of the old king and thus as a brother and a pretender to the throne. Here the extensive psychological identity of various dramatic forms becomes apparent. This is true not only of the relations of the inimical brothers, but especially of the doubling of the father figure. Immediately upon the death of his father, who has disinherited him, Don Carlos returns home, only to be recognized by the dying king as his own son; he is elevated to the rank of prince. As is usual in the family romance, the substitution of king for father improves the pedigree of the protagonist; both father doublets leave the son free to do as he pleases. But in a third form the father, as a competitor, is directly killed by the son. This third father doublet is Don Garcias, whom Carlos murders on the wedding night before the eyes of his "sister." Here the identification of the spouse of the "sister" with the royal father, in the sense of the infantile Oedipus complex, is transparently indicated in that at the moment Carlos murders his "brother-in-law," his actual father, the old king, dies. Another indication of Garcias's "father character" is provided by the rescue fantasy associated with him, for Carlos boasts that he has twice saved his life. Still, given the ambiguous infantile orientation, this does not prevent him from drawing his dagger against him, just as he had done once before when facing his supposed father. Just as Carlos, in murdering Don Garcias, actually murders his father, he also identifies his beloved "sister" with his mother; this is especially clear in light of the typical fantasy that supposes the mother is unhappy as the father's spouse. Indeed, Carlos rescues the sister from the arms of a spouse she does not love. (After the reduction of the doublets, it is also clear that when Carlos finally kills Raphael, he is actually killing his brother.) And just as it is suggested that the "father" once poisoned the "mother," a supposition probably to be interpreted in multiple ways, Carlos also poisons the pseudosister when he has finally married her. Here again, behind the excessively emphasized sibling complex we find the underlying parent complex; we see clearly how the youthful playwright attempts to realize these repressed, libidinous family impulses through fantasy and to become free of them. Here again the theme of suspension of sibling relationship reveals itself as a disguising wish mechanism functioning to make the incestuous union possible under the guise of permitted affection. In all these cases, this is revealed not only in that the two love each other despite their supposed kinship and admit this after its suspension, but also, and especially clearly, in that the powerful guilt consciousness accompanying the forbidden passion still prevents the playwright from permitting the sexual union of the lovers after their kinship is suspended. Just as the mechanism of suspension of sibling relationship fails in Sachs's novella, here too, owing to the same psychic inhibitions caused by the powerful feelings of guilt, the effect of its suspension is thwarted. For this group of literarily depicted fantasies, the following passage from the tragedy just discussed certainly holds true:

> Indeed, the prince
> Don Carlos of Navarre desired her.
>
> . . . .
>
> *Don Pedro* (as if trembling): The brother? The woman he believed to be his sister?!
> Is there proof? Seems it not like incest,
> Committed, at least, in thought?

Recently Hermann Bahr, who has often attempted to include in his works the problem of incest, has treated the theme of the suspension of sibling relationship in a comedy *Die Kinder* [The children] (1910). Professor Scharitzer forbids his daughter to marry the son of Count Gandolf, with whom she has fallen deeply in love. His very understandable reason is that he is himself actually the father of the young count. The two lovers do not wish to be separated, however, and the comedy ends with their marriage, made possible when it is revealed that the supposed daughter of Professor Scharitzer is actually the daughter of the old Count Gandolf. Thus the fathers had been reversed.

The same theme of recognition of the sibling in connection with the theme of suspension of kinship was previously dealt with by Bahr in his novella *Die Stimme des Bluts* [The voice of the blood] (1909). The young husband reveals to his wife, whom he has known since childhood, that the man whose death she is mourning was not her true father. Indeed, he tells her they both share the same father. "If we are brother and sister, I can love you no differently. No, I cannot." Defense against incest now follows in the revelation that he is actually the son of her supposed father. "It is very simple. We had simply reversed our fathers." Later, though, when the wife seeks to justify actual sibling incest, the incest theme, providing the emotional basis of the work despite strong opposing tendencies, is revealed. "If you had proved to me that we were brother and sister, perhaps I would have been confused, perhaps for a week, but I would have survived it. Finally, I would have. Am I your sister if I feel that I am your wife? I am what I feel. Shall I let others dictate what I am? I am not like that; I'm not! I cannot change my feelings, come what may." In addition, in the daughter's instinctive affection for her actual father, the father-daughter complex is touched upon, while in the father's response to the daughter's affection, rivalry with the father for the love of a woman is suggested.

The Elizabethan Dramatists

Among Shakespeare's successors on the English stage, the theme of actual, supposed, or prevented sibling incest was one of the most popular basic elements of dramatic technique. Emil Koeppel (1895), who has distinguished himself through his study of the sources of these dramas, remarks that "the forbidden territory of incest had a strong attraction for many dramatists of the period, just as it did for many highly talented writers of the beginning of our century. Mental illness also occurred in epidemic proportions." This theme returns with tiring monotony—especially in the works of Francis Beaumont and John Fletcher.

In the drama *A King and No King,* presented in 1611, Beaumont and Fletcher depict the passion of King Arbaces for his sister. Arbaces reveals his feelings to his loyal general, Mardonius, who attempts in vain to dissuade him from this sin. In one great scene (4.4) the two lovers acknowledge their passion for one another. Still, they are separated by the fear of sin, and they vow never to commit incest. In the fifth act the solution is presented: they are not really related, and their love is thus no sin (cf. Koeppel 1895, 178 ff.).

In *Woman Pleased,* by the same authors, Isabella, the voluptuous wife of the greedy jeweler Lopez, is repeatedly tempted to the brink of ruin by a young man who is finally revealed to be her brother and who claims that he only wished to test her (cf. Koeppel 1895, 89). In *The Fair Maid of the Sun,* Fletcher gives Cesario's relationship to his sister Clarissa an incestuous coloring. Clarissa says (5.3):

> We lov'd together, you preferring me
> Before yourself, and I so fond of you
> That it begot suspicion in ill minds
> That our affection was incestuous.

In the same work, hints of mother incest are also found. Mariana, who fears for the life of her son, Cesario, declares that he is only her foster child. Based on this revelation, the duke declares that she, the mother, must either marry Cesario in compensation for the false hopes awakened in him or hand over to him the greater part of her fortune. This conflict, which is eliminated by an explanation to the opposite effect that Mariana whispers to the duke (5.3), is found also in Nicolas Caussin's *Cour sainte* [The holy court] (1632) and in Nathaniel Wanley's *Wonders of the Little World, or A General History of Man* (1678).

In John Ford's drama *'Tis Pity She's a Whore,* after confessing his criminal desire to Frater Bonaventura, Giovanni reveals his passions to his sister Annabella (1.3), leading to incest. In contrast to Beaumont and Fletcher's drama, Annabella then marries Soranzo, and the crime is discovered. Giovanni stabs his sister to death. He and Soranzo also meet violent deaths. Koeppel maintains that Ford derived the plot from an account, then related in various versions, of an incestuous relationship that actually existed in Normandy in 1603, during the reign of Henry IV. The French chronicler Pierre Matthieu (1606) provides an account in his *Histoire de France*. The crime occurred only after the marriage of the sister; thus she also became an adulteress. The sinners left the house of the betrayed husband, but he discovered them in Paris and brought them to trial. Good words were said on their behalf, but the king could permit no mercy, given their heinous crimes. Brother and sister were executed.

In its main details, the version of a contemporary French novelist, François de Rosset, agrees with Matthieu's account. In his *Histoires tragiques de nostre temps* [Tragic tales of our time] (1619), the seventh account is entitled "Des amours incestueuses d'un frère et d'une soeur, et de leur fin malheureuse, et tragique" [The incestuous affections of a brother and a sister, and their unfortunate and tragic end]. In the ninth account, "De la cruant d'un frère exercée contre une sienne soeur, pour une folle passion d'amour" [A brother's violence against a sister because of a mad passion of love], the brother stabs his sister to death. For a discussion of a modern presentation of the drama *'Tis Pity She's a Whore* in the French translation of Maurice Maeterlinck, see the review by Jacques du Tillet (1894). In *The Fancies, Chast and Noble*, Koeppel (1895, 185) also sees "a true product of Ford's diseased fantasy." Octavio, the marquis of Sienna, already rather advanced in years, has three women raised in the secrecy of his palace. He calls them his "fancies." Their duenna tells them the most frightfully obscene tales. A fourth young woman, the beautiful and chaste Castamela, is forced to associate with these young women by her brother, whom Octavio had rescued from need and given a lucrative position. In this case, too, it seems that Castamela will have to pay with her honor for the favor shown her brother. Finally the playwright reveals that Octavio's "pseudoharem" comprised the daughters of his deceased sister and that Castamela was the woman betrothed to his nephew.

This apparent incest is reflected in similar, dampened variations on this theme produced by the Elizabethan dramatists with seemingly inexhaustible energy. Especially often, we note the theme of the brother who takes bloody vengeance for his sister's honor, seizing her from her spouse or lover. This is the case in John Ford's *The Broken Heart*. Before the drama begins, the young Spartan Ithocles has taken his sister Penthea from her betrothed, Orgilius, and has forced her to marry Bassanes, whom she does not love. Orgilius takes vengeance for his beloved and for his lost happiness by murdering Ithocles (Koeppel 1895, 172 ff.). That this vengeance for the dishonored sister (Dioscuri theme) derives from the sexual jealousy of the brother is demonstrated by a theme clearly developed in Philip Massinger's *The Duke of Milan*. Here the brother takes vengeance on the duke, who has seduced his sister, by attempting to seduce the duke's chaste spouse. The "temptation over the cross," found in Miguel de Cervantes' 1615 *comedia Los Baños de Argel,* can also be explained within the framework of the incest complex.

Concerning Massinger, Koeppel remarks (1895, 98): "As in the last two dramas discussed, the main theme in *The Renegado* is sibling love. The wish to avenge a dishonored sister provides the main motivation for the brother's actions. In *The Duke of Milan,* Francisco destroys Duke Sforza's happiness because Sforza has seduced his sister Eugenia. In *The Bondman,* the Theban Pisander hurries to Syracuse to punish Leosthenes, who has seduced and deserted his sister Statilia. Similarly, in *The Renegado,* the Venetian Vitelli, disguised as a merchant, proceeds to Tunis to find and avenge his sister Paulina, who has been abducted by the Venetian renegade Grimaldi. It is only in this third treatment that the theme is effectively expressed from the very beginning." In Massinger's *The Guardian,* the subplot includes the theme of sibling love. "Jolante's husband, Severino, has fled the country because he is supposed to have killed her brother in a duel. The voluptuous Jolante falls in love with another man, whom she has her parasite Calipso bring to her. During the night when she is awaiting her lover, her husband returns and cuts off the nose of Calipso, who has taken the place of her mistress" (Koeppel 1895, 142). The man Jolante desires is finally revealed to be her own brother.

In George Chapman's *Revenge for Honour,* a whole gamut of incest themes can be seen. Abrahen, the son of the Arab caliph Almanzor, hates his older half-brother, Abilqualit, the heir to the throne, because he stands in the way of his ambitions. This hatred is increased through the discovery that Caropia, the beautiful and sensual wife of General Mura, adored by both brothers, has chosen the older brother. Through Abrahen's clever game of intrigue, his brother loses favor with their father and is accused of raping Caropia, a crime for which the laws of the land stipulate the punishment of blinding. However, Abrahen wishes for Abilqualit's death. He organizes a revolt of the soldiers on behalf of the condemned prince. When the revolt breaks out the caliph orders his older son strangled, since, given the son's popularity, he fears him as a competitor. Abrahen's next victim is the despot himself. In eliminating his father, he uses a handkerchief. Immediately the murderer seizes the crown. He is also successful in seducing the unscrupulous Caropia, hungry for power, and believes that he has now acquired all the honors and happiness of his dead brother. But Abilqualit is not dead. His faithful eunuchs have not carried out the sentence. Having learned of Abrahen's crimes from Abrahen's monologue beside his supposedly dead body, Abilqualit arrives to expose his brother and to demand the crown for himself. Abrahen stabs Caropia and himself to death. Before she dies, though, Caropia still has enough energy to stab Abilqualit, whom she does not wish to relinquish to any other woman (cf. Koeppel 1895, 71 ff.).

Shelley

Percy Bysshe Shelley (1792–1822), who so much enjoyed dwelling on his ethereal conceptions and who shared country, time, and to an extent destiny with the more realistic Byron, also demonstrates that his love life was anchored in the incest complex, which provided the inspiration for a significant portion of his literary creations. In our analysis of *The Cenci,* and in connection with his early atheism, we have already derived his burning hatred of tyranny—evinced throughout his life and works—from his powerful early opposition to his father, toward whom he felt antipathy his whole life long. As a child, Shelley is already supposed to have learned a curse against king and father and to have entertained the fantasy that his father wanted to commit him to an insane asylum (Richter 1898, 15). When at age nineteen he was expelled for his atheistic opinions, a confrontation with his father was inevitable. "In a poetic epistle to Graham, Shelley speaks of his father with derogatory remarks" (Richter 1898, 62). At age seventeen he wrote his "thriller" *Zastrozzi,* so different from the works of the later sensitive poet. (On her deathbed, Olivia Zastrozzi, seduced and abandoned by Duke Verezzi at age fifteen, makes her son Pietro promise to avenge her. He stabs his father to death and also wishes to kill his half-brother [Richter 1898, 25].) The first political verses Shelley wrote as a student at Oxford were "glowing with hatred of tyranny" (Richter 1898, 38), and the "fathers" he depicted in his works were, like the old Cenci, "a complex of all cruel and evil human drives" (Richter 1898, 397). This is true of Rosalind's father in the poem *Rosalind and Helen* (1819), "in whom Shelley simply personified paternal tyranny as such" (Richter 1898, 343). And in the poem *The Fugitives,* "amid thunder and lightning, the poet sees his past before him. Like a specter, a dark image from his life rises from the dark background of the storm. Suddenly his father and his youth stand before his eyes. On the tower, his father stands like a specter boding death. The wild winds are calm compared with his voice. With a wild curse, he sends the storm upon his son—the last, the last and dearest one to bear his name" (Richter 1898, 554).

Behind this insistent father complex, dominant in the psyche of the poet, his relationship with his mother, with a few exceptions, is almost completely obscured. However, Shelley's love life and his poetic ideal of love seem to have been influenced unusually clearly by the sibling complex, and in our opinion this "led [him] repeatedly to make the marriage of siblings the subject of his works" (Richter 1887, 4). Concerning the circumstantial reasons for his infantile fixation on his sister ideal, Richter remarks (1887, 3): "For the joy of a close relationship with the mother, which transfigures the youth of so many poets, was not granted Shelley. With his unceasing need for love, he had only his younger sisters, who sat fascinated around him while he told them fantastic tales: of the giant turtle and of the large snake that had lived earlier at Field Place. These were the first expressions of his poetic fantasy." His favorite sister was Helen, seven years his junior, whose name he also gave to the heroine of a poem (*Rosalind and Helen,* 1818) in which he deals with sibling love. One year earlier (1817), almost at the same time as Byron in *Manfred* and *Cain,* he had dealt with the theme of sibling love in the poem *Laon and Cythna,* which, after the deletions and changes demanded by the editor, received the title *The Revolt of Islam.*

The siblings Laon and Cythna, who grow up together as children, are separated. Cythna takes the name Laone (cf. Siecke's parallelism of names), and later she meets Laon but does not recognize him as her brother. Together they flee from their enemy and rest in a ruin. "Now silent, driven by a dark feeling, they recognize one another. Silently, one awakens common memories in the other, and their old love overtakes and overpowers them with omnipotent power so that they exchange kisses that fill their melting hearts and consumed limbs with a warm glow; they spend two days and nights in the stormy joys of love. This is one of the most powerful, but also one of the most tender, of all erotic poems. Still, Laon and Cythna are siblings" (Richter 1898, 296).

After Laon and Cythna have sealed their bond of love, they tell each other of their experiences. Cythna has fallen victim to "the cold tyrant's cruel lust" just as Beatrice Cenci succumbed to the lusts of her father. Laon attempts to save his unrecognized sister from persecution by the tyrant, just as Shelley abducted his youthful love Harriet from the power of her father and even entertained the fantastic idea of "abducting his sisters, winning them for a higher destiny than that of two heiresses" (Richter 1898, 195). Finally Laon and Cythna are to be burned at the stake at the command of the tyrant, but through an ethereal vision, they emerge purified from their death by flames. In his first draft, "Shelley glorified the loving bond of brother and sister as superior to others in the intensity of attraction" (Richter 1898, 298), but during the printing of the work, upon the insistence of the publisher, Shelley was forced to transform Cythna from Laon's sister into his childhood playmate—an orphan raised in the house of his parents (Richter 1898, 200). In the idyll *Rosalind and Helen,* begun at the same time, the fate of the poet and his loved ones served as a model, as so often before, and it is characteristic that in this mainly autobiographical poem depicting the fate of his loved ones through that of two families, he once again took up the theme of sibling love.

"Rosalind . . . was deeply in love with a youth. For three years they loved one another, and finally the day of their wedding approached. But as they stood at the steps of the altar, Rosalind's father, who had been away for many years, appeared among the assembled guests and interrupted the ceremony with the words: 'Hold, hold! . . . I tell thee 'tis her brother!' The young man fell dead" (Richter 1898, 335). After the death of her father, Rosalind marries a hard, cruel man—a typical personification of paternal tyranny. From the perspective of the poet, it is clear that this man derives from the father image, for "Rosalind was scarcely able to bear the torment of his deeply hated embrace" (Richter 1898, 343), and even from the grave his cruelty and tyranny still pursued her (Richter 1898, 336).

In addition to the sibling incest prevented by the appearance of the father, the same poem includes a reference to a legendary example of sibling love, a device so well liked by writers (cf. Meyer's reference to Byblis in *Die Richterin,* etc.). With Helen's favorite spot in the forest is associated a terrible legend based on actual events.

> For here a sister and a brother
> Had solemnised a monstrous curse,
> Meeting in this fair solitude:
> For beneath yon very sky,
> Had they resigned to one another
> Body and soul. The multitude,
> Tracking them to the secret wood,
> Tore limb from limb their innocent child,
> And stabbed and trampled on its mother;
> But the youth, for God's most holy grace,
> A priest saved to burn in the market-place.

In the prologue to *Laon and Cythna,* Shelley states that he had simply sought to treat sibling love as an ethical problem with the didactic secondary goal of teaching the virtue of tolerance. This statement can be regarded as an expression of defense brought about by his powerful unconscious resistance to this repressed complex. That all the critics accept Shelley's statement shows that they lack the essential sensitivity required for understanding poetic abilities. The true poet is no sophist, no matter-of-fact fellow who takes on ethical or purely intellectual problems as his themes. The true poet does not consider the pros and cons in deciding to support one side of an argument or another. Instead, he is more a man of affect. Indeed, he is a primitive, presenting nothing that does not proceed from his inner being, demanding expression. Since we know that these motives for production had long been repressed, however, now carrying out their functions from the unconscious, we will not take the poet's own attempt to explain the products of his own unconscious as the final word on the subject. Instead, we shall concentrate on the naive form of expression found in the work itself. The most common error made in the interpretation of literary works, dependent as they are on the inner life of their creators, is that such secondary rationalizations by the creators themselves are taken at face value. Thus critics have been inclined to derive Shelley's undeniable opposition to paternal authority from a striving for freedom and a need for independence found in his character (apparently ab ovo). They claim that this striving for freedom could not tolerate paternal authority. Etiologically, though, these traits developed in precisely the opposite sequence. Opposition to the father, which emerged in childhood, was later extended to opposition to all authority.

Critics have made the same error in analyzing sibling love in Shelley's works. His preference for free, yielding behavior on the part of a woman in love—behavior conflicting with all the limitations of convention—was as undeniable as his hatred of his father. Thus it has been claimed that he also glorified sibling love, condemned by convention, because of this attitude—as if in obstinacy or, as Adler would say, in "male protest." The same has been claimed for Byron. Here again, the psychological situation is actually the opposite. His sibling love, derived from his infantile perspective, was an impulse that, for its gratification, would have demanded breaking down all social conventions. Therefore he illustrated his passion specifically through the theme of sibling love, also maintaining it as a real condition for love throughout his life. As with Schiller and others before, we are now in a position to prove our conception of the underlying, significant status of the incest complex in Shelley's works from the total picture of his personality. If the theme of sibling love had been for Shelley a purely intellectual exercise, it would be unclear why subtler references to this theme penetrate his whole literary production and why it was necessary for him to play out his love life in the typical forms of the incest complex. In our conception, though, life and creative works serve equally as gratifying expressions of the repressed impulses striving for realization.

When Shelley was seventeen, he fell in love with his beautiful cousin Harriet Grove—his own age and very similar to him. We have learned to interpret such affection for distant relatives as derived from repressed incestuous tendencies. Approximately one year later, the break with Harriet occurred. She herself brought it about, and Shelley was deeply hurt. But one year later he fell in love with the sixteen-year-old Harriet Westbrook. It can be no coincidence that she bore the same first name as his first love. Another circumstance that essentially predestined her to be Shelley's chosen love object was that she was the classmate of his sister. When Harriet called upon him to free her from the tyranny of her strict father, indicating that she was ready to make her escape, for the poet—anchored in the Oedipus complex—all the conditions for love were now in place. Here he had everything required by his fantasy: the struggle against a tyrannical father, and a woman with an open, yielding manner defying all social convention. Indeed, Shelley fled with her under the most arduous conditions, and a month later they were married. The initially happy marriage, which later ended in divorce, is interesting because in this marriage Shelley was able to realize another fantasy, the fantasy of "double love." From Schiller's double love, we are already familiar with this fantasy in its relation to the sibling complex. Shelley too felt a double love, and he was always able to satisfy his need for an ideal, intellectual, "sisterly" friend in women other than his wife. For a long period it was actually Harriet's sister who lived with the young couple, until they tired of her. The situation was similar with Lady Hitchener, the "sister of his soul," who also lived for a long time in the couple's home until the poet tired of her too, seeking a substitute in Harriet de Boinville. Precisely the same schema in the choice of love objects is observed in his second marriage. After the suicide of his first wife, he also married Mary, who gave herself to the divorced poet freely, defying all social conventions, over the strong objections of her father, who never forgave Shelley. Here again, Mary's sister accompanied the two lovers on their flight. Despite frequent conflicts, she lived in their home for many years. Their communal life was so intimate that the poet was considered the father of his sister-in-law's child, actually sired by Byron. It cannot be denied, however, that he wrote her rapturous love letters (Richter 1898, 478). In this second marriage, too, the poet sought to gratify his need for "sisterly" love, especially in his friendship with Countess Emilia Viviani, who had to await her marriage behind the walls of a convent and longed for wordly love. She called Shelley "her dear brother" and his wife "her dear, beautiful sister" (Richter 1898, 483). Shortly after he met Emilia, Shelley composed the beautiful fragment *Fiordespina,* from which he is supposed to have adapted several passages in *Epipsychidion.* "Fiordespina and Cosmo are siblings and grew up together as Shelley wished that he and Emilia had done: hearts dedicated to each other in true love should be close from birth and share all things" (Richter 1898, 485). Indeed, his female ideal, glorified in many poems, seen longingly in his dreams in youth, but never attained in life, can be derived from the unattainable, idealized love object. This is also true of *Epipsychidion,* a poem in which Shelley immortalizes his love for Emilia, addressing her as "Spouse, sister! Angel!" (cf. Goethe's poem to Frau von Stein).

> Would we two had been twins of the same mother!
> Or, that the name my heart lent to another
> Could be a sister's bond for her and thee,
> Blending two beams of one eternity!
> . . . .
> Say, my heart's sister, wilt thou sail with me?

Strongly suggesting the forbidden, censured nature of this love, the poem also includes the words:

> Emily,
> I love thee; though the world by no thin name
> Will hide that love from its unvalued shame.

The love ideal, which appeared to him "in the golden spring of his dawning youth," unattainable in life, is expressed in the youthful work *Alastor* (1814), in which the youth seeks in vain the beloved of his dreams. The same theme appears again in the fragment of a fable (Richter 1898, 485). As in *Epipsychidion,* the sibling lovers appear once again in the extant fragment of the drama *The Sensitive Plant.* The beloved can respond to the youth's passion "only with sisterly affection," while he addresses her as "friend, sister, beloved" (Richter 1898, 564).

Given a poet with a powerful, repressed complex pouring forth even in far-removed allusions, we can assign increased psychological significance to the amassed expression of these allusions in images, similes, and characters. In the most unrelated situations, the image of the siblings imposes itself ineluctably upon the poet. Thus, in the poem *An Exhortation* (1819), he speaks of "chameleons" and their "brother lizards." In *Ode to the West Wind* (1819), he calls the spring air the West Wind's "azure sister." In the poem *A Vision of the Sea* (1820), he writes:

> Like a sister and a brother
> The child and the ocean still smile on each other.

Countless such excerpts from Shelley's works could be cited. One allegorical guise should also be mentioned, strongly reminiscent of similar productions of the Gnostics. The plot of the poem *The Witch of Atlas* (1820), which Mary considered an agglomeration of ideas, is as follows (Richter

1898, 457): "In the Golden Age, before Time and Change bore their twin children Truth and Error . . . Time and Change were daughter and father, and the children arising from their incestuous relationship were Truth and Error." Finally, in *Lines Written among the Euganean Hills,* the poet adopts a similar image from *Paradise Lost* (book 5): he refers to Sin and Death as "the incestuous pair"—mother and son (Richter 1898, 347).

18 Byron: His Life and Dramatic Works

Love is not the principle passion for tragedy . . . unless it is Love, furious, criminal, and hapless.

BYRON to MURRAY, January 4, 1821

George Gordon Byron's case is especially valuable as a test of our model because it shows the essential and strictly determinate connection between experience and literary production in the deeper sense to which we have repeatedly referred, distinguishing it from the superficial concept of this connection. It is not Byron's living illicitly with his half-sister Augusta that brought about his interest in the theme of sibling love. Instead, the childhood experience of premature and intense fixation on the mother brought about by an early sexual maturity (cf. chap. 4) determines later experience and artistic production in like manner. Since Byron was unable to resolve this early fixation on his mother straightforwardly and could do so only through intense repression tending sometimes to hatred and sometimes to homosexuality, he spent his whole life seeking a substitute for this first, lost affection. Therefore, based on the model of his initial love for his mother, all his passions were intense and powerful, but they were of short duration and thus necessarily numerous (cf. Freud's "sequentiality" [*Reihenbildung*]). Thus, after a brief period he separated from his wife (cf. chap. 4); similarly, his intimate union with his sister soon gave way to aversion, following the example of his childhood perspective toward his mother. His childhood and boyhood affections, concentrating mainly on relatives or on older or married women, are comprehensible given early repression of his sexual attraction to his mother and the search for this lost ideal. One passage in his diary reveals the relation between his literary production and this premature, incestuously fixated eroticism. He writes that his first literary attempts date from 1800, when he first fell passionately in love with his cousin Margaret Parket. At age fourteen, he fell in love with his relative Marianne Chaworth, two years older than he, whom he had met while visiting his mother in Nottingham. Among these substitutes for his previously beloved mother, his half-sister Augusta was an object corresponding especially well to the infantile ideal. First, she was a blood relative. Second, she was already married when Byron became more familiar with her. Thus infantile feelings of guilt did not hinder this relationship; indeed, they furthered it. Augusta Leigh was born in 1784, the daughter of Byron's father by his first marriage. The following year her father married Catherine Gordon of Gight, Byron's mother. Augusta was raised in the home of her grandmother, the widowed countess of Holdernesse, and Byron came into frequent contact with her only after she had already been married for some years and was a mother.

Still, at age sixteen he already wrote to his half-sister Augusta (March 22, 1804): "Although, My ever Dear Augusta, I have hitherto appeared remiss in replying to your kind and affectionate letters; yet I hope you will not attribute my neglect to a want of affection, but rather to a shyness naturally inherent in my Disposition. I will now endeavour as amply as lies in my power to repay your kindness, and for the Future I hope you will consider me not only as a Brother but as your warmest and most affectionate Friend." In 1811 he wrote to her: "My dear Augusta, I wrote to you yesterday, and as you will not be very sorry to hear from me again, considering our long separation, I shall fill up this sheet before I go to bed. I have heard something of a quarrel between your spouse and the Prince. I don't wish to pry into family secrets or to hear anything more of the matter, but I can't help regretting on your account that so long an intimacy should be dissolved at the very moment when your husband might have derived some advantage from his R.H.'s friendship. However, at all events, and in all Situations, you have a brother in me, and a home here."

Indeed, in June 1813 Mrs. Leigh left her home, "Six Mile Bottom," and moved in for an indefinite period of time with her half-brother Lord Byron in London. He had already broken off his liaison with Lady Carolyn Lamb and had intimate connections with two other married ladies of the aristocracy. Already in the beginning of 1814, in Holland House, Byron expressed unusual views concerning the relationship of brother and sister. These comments were considered scandalous; he later openly admitted to his affair with his sister. When Byron was married, he was wont to speak of his sister as a fool. Nevertheless, he complained continually about her absence and declared that no one had ever loved or understood him as well as she.

The discovery by Byron's wife of this affair led to their divorce; based on the "Astarte documents," Meyerfeld (1908, 709) demonstrates in detail how this occurred. "Already on the second or third day of their honeymoon in Halnaby, the specter of suspicion appeared between them. The young woman, who had read Dryden's tragedy *Don Sebastian, King of Portugal,* made a completely innocent reference to the drama, which involves the criminal union of a brother and sister. Byron suspected that she wanted him to divulge his past. He erupted in a strange and violent manner that awakened the first indefinite but highly painful suspicion in his wife. Her first thought was that he had perhaps had a love affair with a girl who had later turned out to be his illegitimate sister—a suspicion that seemed possible, given his father's life-style. . . . The seed of suspicion germinated when in April 1815 Mrs. Leigh came to London and spent ten weeks with the newlyweds at 13 Piccadilly Terrace. The suspicion, once aroused, was only increased by Byron's bitter allusions, concerning which Augusta successfully dissembled indifference. However, his young wife, now suspicious, could not help noticing Byron's passion for the other woman, which expressed itself with special force precisely then. At such moments she was convinced of his earlier guilt and even thought that the affair might be resumed." Byron's spouse now made every effort to keep Augusta from her brother. When he noticed that Augusta had thus been removed from his power, he felt unbounded ire against his wife and his sister, who had turned against him. He attempted to rid himself of his wife and drank so much brandy that he was near insanity. To take vengeance on both women, he took a *maîtresse en titre;* he seemed to look on this as a greater insult to Augusta than to Lady Byron. Disagreements became more and more frequent, and Byron and his wife finally separated in 1816, when Augusta admitted everything to Lady Byron, repeatedly expressing to her, not only orally but also in letters, her sincere penitence.

The love letters Byron wrote to his sister while he was still married, attempting from abroad to convince her to resume the alliance, show very clearly not only the sensual nature of his attraction, but also that it was firmly rooted in powerful childhood emotions. On May 17, 1819, he wrote to Augusta Leigh from Venice:

> My dearest Love, I have been negligent in not writing, but what can I say? Three years absence and the total change of scene and habit make such a

> difference that we have now nothing in common but our affections and our relationship. But I have never ceased nor can cease to feel for a moment that perfect and boundless attachment which bound and binds me to you, which renders me utterly incapable of real love for any other human being—what could they be to me after you? We may have been very wrong, but I repent of nothing except that cursed marriage and your refusing to continue to love me as you had loved me. I can neither forget nor quite forgive you for the precious piece of reformation. But I can never be other than I have been, and whenever I love anything it is because it reminds me in some way or other of yourself. For instance I not long ago attached myself to a Venetian for no earthly reason (although a pretty woman) but because she was called ⟨short word crossed out⟩ and she often remarked (without knowing the reason) how fond I was of the name. It is heartbreaking to think of our long separation, and I am sure more than punishment enough for all our sins. Dante is more humane in his "Hell" for he places his unfortunate lovers (Francesca of Rimini and Paolo, whose case fell a good deal short of ours, though sufficiently naughty) in company, and though they suffer it is at least together. If ever I return to England, it will be to see you and recollect that in all time and place, and feelings, I have never ceased to be the same to you in heart. Circumstances may have ruffled my manner and hardened my spirit. You may have seen me harsh and exasperated with all things around me; grieved and tortured with your new resolution and the soon after persecution of that infamous fiend who drove me from my country and conspired against my life by endeavouring to deprive me of all that could render it precious. But remember that even then you were the sole object that cost me a tear. And what tears! Do you remember our parting? I have not spirits now to write to you upon other subjects. I am well in health and have no cause of grief but the reflection that we are not together. When you write to me speak to me of yourself and say that you love me. Never mind common-place people and topics which can be in no degree interesting to me who see nothing in England but the country which holds you, or around it but the sea which divides us. They say absence destroys weak passions and confirms strong ones. Alas! mine for you is the union of all passions and of all affections, has strengthened itself but will destroy me. I do not speak of physical destruction, for I have endured and can endure much, but of the annihilation of all thoughts, feelings, or hopes which have not more or less a reference to you and to our recollections.

Byron's passion for his sister becomes even more interesting because it can be followed from early childhood displacement from the mother and over a series of "forbidden" youthful relationships with married women as a gratification of creative fantasy, finally reaching a level of maximum defense and culminating in neurosis. As Byron himself wrote in a letter to his friend Thomas Moore (January 5, 1816): "I could not write upon any thing, without some personal experience and foundation." Thus our conception of repression and of the substitute gratification of rejected affections through fantasy in literary production gains support in that in his mystery *Cain,* a few years after the dissolution of his liaison with his sister, when he had already had to give up all hope of winning her back, Byron took refuge in the infantile fantasy of mankind—in the "original state" assumed in justification of incestuous affections. In that state incest with the sister is no sin; indeed, it is an act required for the maintenance and propagation of the human race. Cain has taken as wife his sister Adah, who is even presented as a twin sister ("born on the same day of the same womb"). This original naive justification of incestuous affections and its later revaluation as a sin are portrayed by the playwright in characteristic manner.

> *Adah:* . . . Love me—I love thee!
> *Cain:* More than thy mother, and thy sire?
> *Adah:* I do. Is that a sin, too?
> *Lucifer:* No, not yet;
> It one day will be in your children.
> *Adah:* What!
> Must not my daughter love her brother Enoch?
> *Lucifer:* Not as thou lovest Cain.
> *Adah:* Oh my God!
> Shall they not love and bring forth things that love
> Out of their love? have they not drawn their milk
> Out of this bosom? was not he, their father,
> Born of the same sole womb, in the same hour
> With me? did we not love each other? and
> In multiplying our being multiply
> Things which will love each other as we love
> Them?—And as I love thee, my Cain! go not
> Forth with this spirit; he is not of ours.
> *Lucifer:* The sin I speak of is not of my making,
> And cannot be a sin in you—whate'er
> It seem in those who will replace ye in
> Mortality.

However, Cain not only has taken his sister as his wife, but has also slain his brother Abel—a theme Byron adopts from the older traditions but motivates through childhood rivalry brought about by jealousy toward the competitor, preferred by mother and father (God). Lucifer, who eggs Cain on to commit fratricide, personifies, as the playwright himself saw it, the unconscious wishes and impulses, just as does the devil in Christian legends and the oracle (fate) in classical works.

Lucifer: And thy brother—
Sits he not near thy heart?
Cain: Why should he not?
Lucifer: Thy father loves him well—so does thy god.
Cain: And so do I.
Lucifer: 'Tis well and meekly done.
Cain: Meekly!
Lucifer: He is the second born of flesh,
And is his mother's favorite.
Cain: Let him keep
Her favor, since the Serpent was the first
To win it.
Lucifer: And his father's?
. . . .

Lucifer: And the Jehovah—the indulgent Lord,
And bounteous planter of barred Paradise—
He, too, looks smilingly on Abel.
Cain: I
Ne'er saw him, and I know not if he smiles.
Lucifer: But you have seen his angels.
Cain: Rarely.
Lucifer: But
Sufficiently to see they love your brother:
His sacrifices are acceptable.

After the frightful deed, the mother curses the murderer of her favorite son with a typical expression of fear of retribution:

May all the curses
Of life be on him! and his agonies
Drive him forth o'er the wilderness, like us
From Eden, till his children do by him
As he did by his brother!

In the context of the sibling complex, this fable presents the precise counterpart of the Greek Oedipus legend. Even references to the dream through which Cain attempts to justify his deed to himself and to his highest judge are not lacking.

I am awake at last—a dreary dream
Had maddened me.

However, a significant difference is found in that with Cain, both the incestuous union and the murder of the competitor are carried out consciously. Still, this uninhibited and undisguised realization of the infantile fantasy is possible only based on the myth of the first human parents and their offspring, which justifies incest. After abandoning hope of real gratification, the playwright's incestuous tendencies find justification, comfort, and at least ideal gratification in the literary recreation of the perfect wish fantasy. Given the same impulses, however, *Manfred* shows the reaction of repression intensified almost to neurotic defense. Manfred attempts to rid his conscious mind of all thoughts and memories of his sister; he attempts to resist his rejected passion and therefore demands "oblivion" from the seven spirits: "oblivion—self-oblivion." Corresponding to the high degree of defense, the memory of the repressed thoughts brings about an "attack":

Seventh Spirit (appearing in the shape of a beautiful female figure):
Behold!
Manfred: Oh God! if it be thus, and *thou*
Art not a madness and a mockery,
I yet might be most happy. I will clasp thee,
And we again will be—
(The figure vanishes.) My heart is crushed!
(Manfred falls senseless.)

In the same manner, the actual apparition of the beloved Astarte produces an attack:

Manfred: One word for mercy! Say thou lovest me.
Astarte: Manfred! (The spirit of Astarte disappears.)
A spirit: He is convulsed.

Defense against the incestuous passion is expressed in that Astarte, his sister, is no longer alive. Indeed, it is not even directly stated that Astarte is his sister. Manfred himself is especially unable to utter this statement. He says only:

Thou lovedst me
Too much, as I loved thee: we were not made
To torture thus each other—though it were
The deadliest sin to love as we have loved.

The old servant Manuel goes furthest in suggesting the incestuous relationship of Manfred and Astarte:

Count Manfred was, as now, within his tower—
How occupied, we knew not, but with him

The sole companion of his wanderings
And watchings—her, whom of all earthly things
That lived, the only thing he seemed to love,—
As he, indeed, by blood was bound to do,
The Lady Astarte, his—

Hush! who comes here?

The breaking off at this point is characteristic for defense against the rejected idea.

Manfred also makes allusion to dreams:

I can bear—
However wretchedly, 'tis still to bear—
In life what others could not brook to dream,
But perish in their slumber.

On October 12, 1817, Byron wrote to his publisher, John Murray: "And as to the germs of *Manfred,* they may be found in the Journal which I sent to Mrs. Leigh." This journal later ended up in Murray's hands, and he destroyed it. Lovelace censures him for this and has established that its destruction did not occur at Lady Byron's request or through her influence. Instead, it was the firm wish of Mrs. Leigh that the journal be destroyed, as she claimed, "for Mrs. Byron's sake." Concerning the deeper sources of *Manfred,* in which some saw only a glorification of the Swiss Alps and an imitation of *Faust,* a portion of a letter to Murray (1820) is revealing: "But it was the Staubach and the Jungfrau and something else, much more than *Faustus,* that made me write *Manfred.*"

Finally, from Byron's poem to his stepsister, two stanzas particularly indicative of the passionate nature of his love can be cited.

Though human, thou didst not deceive me,
Though woman, thou didst not forsake,
Though loved, thou forborest to grieve me,
Though slandered, thou never couldst shake;
Though trusted, thou didst not disclaim me,
Though parted, it was not to fly,
Though watchful, 'twas not to defame me,
Nor, mute, that the world might belie.

From the wreck of the past, which hath perished,
This much I at least may recall,
It hath taught me that what I most cherished
Deserved to be dearest of all:

In the Desert a fountain is springing,
   In the wide waste there still is a tree,
And a bird in the solitude singing,
   Which speaks to my spirit of Thee.

19 ~ *Biblical Incest Material in Dramatic Works*

Among the first humans there was no blood guilt.

HEBBEL, Diaries

Cain's Fratricide

Byron's *Cain* mystery has shown us how adopting Old Testament material provided the playwright uninhibited realization of his childhood complexes, which reflected the complexes of the childhood of humanity. Corresponding to the displacement of affect, which is furthered by the biblical account already distorted and reformulated in a religious context, Cain's fratricide, in connection with his revolt against God/father, is especially emphasized by playwrights too. In the religious plays of the Middle Ages, Cain's fratricide was a popular theme. A religious drama of the seventeenth century by M. Johannsen is entitled *Von Kain dem Brudermörder* [Cain the fratricide]. Friedrich Klopstock also developed the Cain character with great power in his *Tod Adams* [Death of Adam]. In biblical dramas after Klopstock, the tragic theme of Cain and Abel has often been treated. Later, Maler Müller wrote *Der erschlagene Abel* [Abel slain], adapted from Salomon Gessner's idyll. He has Cain curse his parents because they have caused him to murder his brother by their preference for Abel. The idyllist Gessner wrote *Der Tod Abels* [The death of Abel]. Cain hates his brother, who is preferred by God and his parents and is therefore always happy and glad. After a reconciliation brought about by the parents, his dislike for his brother once again awakens. In a dream, an angel of the underworld shows Cain his own descendants enslaved and oppressed by Abel's, and Cain commits the murder. The parents bury the body of their dead son and forgive the murderer, but he is tormented by pangs of conscience and finds no peace. With his wife and child, he leaves for barren lands, never before trodden by men. Gessner wrote *Der Tod Abels* at age twenty-six, when he was devoted to his sister with the first deep affection of those youthful years.

Landau (1899) claims that the similar dream of fratricide in Alfieri's *Abele* was influenced by Cain's dream in Gessner's drama. In both dreams, powers from hell are employed to tempt Cain. Alfieri began the drama in 1786 but did not complete it until several years later. Finally, we should mention a modern treatment of this theme, Otto Borngräber's philosophizing sexual tragedy *Die ersten Menschen* [The first men] (1908). With sharp psychological insight, the poet presents the fratricide as a result of sexual rivalry for the mother's love. Cain desires her, but she is repulsed by his animal lust. Instead, she feels erotic attraction to the more tender Abel. Sensual desire for his mother torments Cain even in his dreams, where he sees his mother's naked body, and is expressed in violent outbursts toward his father, Adam, and toward his preferred brother, whom he finally kills, believing that Abel has had sexual relations with Eve. In act 2, scene 2, the consequences of object selection by the mother are very nicely depicted. Abel and Eve see each other one night from a distance and marvel—until they recognize one another as mother and son—that they had never seen each other in this way before.

> *Chabel:* Never, Chawa, did I see you like this, Chawa.
> *Chawa:* Never did I love you so much.

Cain has the same experience. During the night, he finally believes that he has found a woman. Lustfully he rushes forward, but he recognizes her as his mother.

> *Kajin:* I have rushed impetuously through the whole world, finding no woman. But now I have found a woman, and it is she!

In another passage, fixation on the maternal ideal is expressed:

> *Kajin* (absently): I shall rush impetuously through the wide world. I shall find a sweet, wild woman. Sweeter than you! Wilder than you! More beautiful, more beautiful than you!! (He wishes to depart.) I . . . love you . . . Chawa! I cannot leave.

Amnon's Incest with Tamar: The Spaniards (Lope de Vega, Calderón, Cervantes)

In the works of Spanish dramatists, along with the homosexually tinged theme of disguise, the theme of sibling love plays the most important role. This is especially true with Lope de Vega, whose parents died in his earliest childhood. Since he grew up with his sister Isabel and a brother, it is understandable that in Lope the parent complex was replaced to such a great extent by the sibling complex. We should mention that Lope's first wife was also named Isabel. Given the determinacy of names, it seems that this is no coincidence. It should also be mentioned that in 1588 Lope's brother died in his arms after a sea battle—clearly an important event in the psychic life of the playwright.

In Lope's drama *La fianza satisfecha* [The satisfied pledge], a young Sicilian, Leonido, who commits every crime simply out of a strong lust for sin, attempts to dishonor his sister. When she resists, he wounds her. He also wounds her husband, Dioniso, whom she has called to her aid. He also slaps his father in the face after his father has criticized this behavior. Later, while sleeping on the beach, he is captured by Moors; their king gives him to his spouse, Lidora. Lidora falls in love with Leonido and gives him his father and his sister, Marcela, who have also been captured as slaves. He kicks his father, puts out his eyes, and makes further attempts to dishonor his sister: he threatens to kill their father if she does not submit to him. Lidora disapproves. She calls for help and prevents him from committing further evil deeds. Leonido walks to the coast, where he meets Christ, by whom he is moved to repentance and penance. He lets himself be captured by the king, whose enemy he has become in the meantime, and is crucified. During the execution Gerardo, the father, regains his sight. Finally it is revealed that Lidora is also a sister of Leonido. Thus Leonido has barely escaped incest with both sisters.

Just as hatred for the father is frequently replaced by the less objectionable competition with the brother and even leads, as with Schiller, to the fantasy image of the brother, for Lope, who essentially knew only his brother, vengeance against the father is less associated with guilt and can thus be more freely expressed. The sadistic note in Leonido's vengeance, as well as the subsequent penance and tendency for self-punishment (Leonido allows himself to be captured and crucified) is patterned after drives in Lope's own psyche. Initially Lope led an extravagant, wild life, denying himself no sexual pleasure. In the last years of his life, however, he became devout and lived in the seclusion of a monastery. Every Friday, in remembrance of Christ's passion, he would flagellate himself until bloody (Wurzbach 1899). In most of his *comedias* of the saints, the saints flagellate themselves. In many of Lope's dramas, sensual attraction between brother and sister forms the core of the plot.

In *El vaquero de Moraña,* King Bermudo discovers the loving attachment of his sister, the infanta of León, to Count Manrique of Saldaña. He has him taken to prison and has her locked in a convent. Both escape and are engaged as the servants of a noble. Doña Elvira tends the cows. King Bermudo sees her while hunting, falls in love with her, and asks her to let him visit her the next night. Before this occurs, however, they recognize one another as brother and sister. In *Las almenas de Toro* [The battlements of Toro], Don Sancho, who has never before seen his sister Elvira, falls in love with her at first sight. He wants to win her at any price. When he learns that she is his sister, he is seized by hatred. He does not want any other man ever to possess her. He conquers her town, Toro, but she escapes and, disguised as a peasant, wins the love of the prince of Burgundy, who finally marries her. In *La carbonera* [The charcoal vendor], the king Don Pedro the Cruel falls in love with his sister Leonora, who is disguised as a charcoal vendor. Simultaneously, though, he hates and vilifies his young sister, whose whereabouts his mother has always kept secret from him. Thus he simultaneously hates and loves his sister. Through an unusual compromise of wish and counterwish, desire and defense meet in one expression.

Besides love for his sister, Lope also felt hatred toward his brother. In his *comedia* titled *La niña de plata* [The girl of silver], mortal enmity is depicted. Don Pedro the Cruel lives with his half-brother, the duke Don Enrique of Trastamara, and their enmity leads to Pedro's murder. A Moorish doctor prophesies that Pedro will kill Enrique's mother and that Enrique will murder him in revenge. Thus, incestuous impulses toward the mother or stepmother are mixed with fraternal enmity. Brother hatred is also the theme of *El triumfo de la humildad y soberbia abatida* [The triumph of humility and downcast pride]. King Trebacio abducts his brother's beloved and humiliates his brother in every conceivable way. He finally has him imprisoned without reason. Later Trebacio is overthrown, and the rejected brother is named ruler. Finally he can extend his hand to his beloved. When Felipe cannot climb the steep steps to the throne, Trebacio is forced to lie on the ground while Felipe walks over him. Here we see defense against masochistically derived brother hatred: what Trebacio has done to his brother he must now suffer in return. Finally, we should mention the tragedy depicting the battle of the Horatii and the Curatii as related by Livy (1.26). Lope deals with this plot in *El honrado hermano* [The honored brother]. In the battle, the eldest of the Horatii is the victor. As he is about to march into the city, celebrated by all, his sister Julia chides him for having killed her betrothed, one of the young Curatii. Angry because she does not celebrate him as the victor along with the others, he plunges his sword into her breast. Once again the unconscious motivation is the brother's jealousy toward his sister, who gives more importance to the death of her betrothed than to her brother's victory. In *Horace,* Corneille deals with the same material.

In his drama *Los cabellos de Absalón* [Absalom's hair], Calderón de la Barca deals with the incest of Tamar and Amnon. The first act depicts the incestuous love of Amnon for his half-sister Tamar. The second act presents Absalom's vengeance for Tamar, and the third depicts Absalom's anger toward his father, David, and his death (Schaeffer 1890). Here we find a case of plagiarism unparalleled in world literature. The entire second act of Calderón's drama is copied nearly word for word from *La venganza de Tamar* [The vengeance of Tamar] by Tirso de Molina, a predecessor of Lope. Tirso's work includes the rape of Tamar by her half-brother Amnon and her revenge at Absalom's feast. Further, the first act of Calderón's drama contains a scene from the second act of Tirso's work: at the request of Amnon, Tamar acts as his supposed lover. One should take note of Calderón's powerful repression of his incestuous passions, evinced in other works and distinguishing his psychic life from that of his sensual forerunner Lope de Vega. Given his carefulness as a writer, Calderón had no need to increase his rate of production through intentional or unintentional borrowings. Again this contrasts with the fabulously productive Lope, who claimed, certainly in exaggeration, to have written 1,500 works, of which 450 are extant. Thus one can perhaps consider this plagiarism by the sensitive Calderón, involving specifically the uncomfortable problem of the incest complex, in a light favorable to the playwright. In this plagiarism we see a disinclination to deal with complexes that Calderón, writing under the pressure of powerful repressions, was unable to portray himself.

In his tragedy *Tiridate* (1691), Jean Galbert de Campistron portrays a similar relationship, effected by intense repression and related to the love of Amnon for his sister Tamar. (His *Andronic* deals with the Carlos theme.) The action occurs at the court of the king of Parthia. The king's son, Tiridate, is passionately in love with his sister, Erinice. He is depressed, weeps constantly, and—like Phaedra and Alfieri's Mirra—carefully keeps his love secret. When he accidentally reveals his intentions, he punishes himself, committing suicide by poison. Here the progress of repression conditions the guilt consciousness and the tendency for self-punishment at the mere thought of gratifying the rejected impulse.

Of the dramas of sibling love in Spanish literature, one *comedia* by the famous Miguel de Cervantes should also be mentioned. In *La entretenida* [The kept woman], the student Cardenio is able to gain entry to the home of Marcela by pretending to be her cousin Don Silvestre de Almendárez, supposedly arriving from Lima. As her cousin, he asks for her hand in marriage. But Marcela feels no attraction to her supposed relative. Rome refuses to grant a dispensation for the forbidden union, and the student's ruse is uncovered by the arrival of the real Silvestre. Still, Marcela does not marry this Silvestre either. Marcela's brother, Don Antonio, loves another Marcela who resembles his sister. He treats his sister in such a way that she suspects he has impure thoughts about her. When he is about to ask for the second Marcela's hand in marriage, his competitor, Ambrosio, shows him a letter in which she has agreed to marry Ambrosio. Thus Antonio must give up his suit (Schaeffer 1890).

Finally, we should mention a few works by the famous Guillén de Castro y Bellvís (b. 1569), known as the leader of the Valencians. In *El desengaño dichoso* [The happy disappointment], a queen desires her daughter's suitor and even attempts to slay her husband, who also demonstrates a love for his daughter exceeding the limits of paternal affection. In *El amor constante* [The constant love], the king of Hungary wants to reject his wife and gain a woman secretly married to his brother. When this woman resists, he has her poisoned and her husband—his brother—killed. However, he himself is stabbed by the son of the slain couple. In *El caballero bobo* [The foolish gentleman] a young man wishes to kill his sister's betrothed, dress in his clothes, and play the role of her betrothed, to whom he bears a great resemblance. In *El nieto de su padre* [The grandson of his father], the plot deals with complex blood relationships, as suggested by the title.

It is also worthy of note that Grillparzer, who greatly admired the Spanish dramatists and dealt with the love of brother for sister in his first work (after reading Calderón's *Devotion to the Cross*), makes this comment concerning the drama *Lo que puede una sospecha* [What a suspicion can do] by Antonio Mira de Amescua in his *Studies on the Spanish Theater:* "I confess that I do not understand this work. Doña Inés is the sister of Don Carlos, but then she speaks of him as her lover."

20 Schiller's Sibling Complex: The Mechanism of Displacement of Affect

And if she, she whom I love,
Love, nay, long for—
If she were my sister,
What could explain this hot passion
That drives me, flaming, toward her?

GRILLPARZER, *Die Ahnfrau*

Just as Schiller depicts rivalry with the father over possession of the mother in *Don Carlos*, in *Die Braut von Messina* [The bride of Messina] he depicts the jealous affection of brother for sister. In literature as in life, erotic affection for the sister can be expressed in a much freer and less disguised form than erotic affection for the mother. For the same reason—reduced inner inhibitions—rivalry with the father can be replaced by jealous hatred toward the brother, particularly in those cases where family relations permit the displacement of affect from a real, guilt-producing perspective to a mere fantasy perspective corresponding to the wishes of the individual. Thus, before providing a psychological explanation of this displacement of affect, we will need to concentrate on the strictly individual conditioning factors in the selection and development of material. In looking at this tragedy of fate from a psychological perspective, we should not be led astray by the observation that Schiller had no brother; we should not hesitate to derive the theme of brother hatred in *Braut von Messina* from Schiller's own life. Previously we solved the riddle of love for the sister in Grillparzer's works by claiming that love for the mother was displaced to the imaginary sister, a person existing only in fantasy and therefore serving as a less objectionable substitute in the context of incest. Similarly, Schiller's brother hatred can be derived from his guilty father complex through a displacement permitted by fantasy.

Schiller commented that in this work he intended to deal with "a freely invented, not historical, but simply passionate and human plot." His note to Goethe (October 2, 1797) shows the extent to which the plot for this drama, published at the end of 1802, ultimately derives from the Oedipus complex: "These days I have been very much occupied with seeking the material for a tragedy that will resemble *Oedipus Rex* and will provide the playwright with the corresponding advantages." He places the Oedipus complex in the background of the plot, before the beginning of the drama, in which he portrays only its consequences, corresponding to the fate of Oedipus's sons Eteocles and Polynices. This seems almost like a projection of his own psychological displacements. In Schiller's drama the curse, which he employs like the ancient oracle as an expression of inevitable doom brought about by personal, inner causes, applies to the father of the inimical brothers. The father has taken his spouse, Isabella, from his own father. His own father therefore curses him, wishing that the children of this (nearly) incestuous marriage may bring ruin upon themselves and the whole family.

Chorus: It was also abduction, as we all know,
That brought the wedded wife of the old prince
Into a criminal marriage bed,
For she was the father's choice.
And the progenitor sowed in anger
The terrible seed of frightful curse
Upon the sinful marriage bed.

In contrast to *Don Carlos,* in which the father takes the betrothed from the son, here it is the son who takes the father's betrothed. The curse is to be fulfilled in the current generation. The prince dreams of two laurel trees between which there grows a lily. But the lily becomes a flame, destroying everything around it. His wife, however, dreams of a lion and an eagle playing tame and free at a child's feet. A wise Arab interprets the prince's dream to mean that he will become the father of a daughter who will be the ruin of his two sons, but a monk interprets his spouse's dream to mean that this daughter will be able to reconcile the conflicting personalities of the two brothers. Based on the interpretation of his dream, the prince commands that his daughter be killed, but based on her own dream, the mother strives to spare the child. She is successful in concealing her daughter in a convent, where she grows up. Then the father, who had been able to keep the hostile energies of the brothers in check, dies. The mother cannot keep peace between the brothers, but finally she arranges for them to meet in reconciliation. She chides them, saying that they do not even know why they hate each other:

> But the origin of your quarrel
> Lies in the early days of naive childhood.
> It is your quarrel's age that should disarm it.
> Ask yourselves what first divided you.
> You do not even know, and if you should discover it
> You would be ashamed of your childish quarrel.

Thus Schiller clearly indicates the infantile origin of this impulse. Also, the lack of rational arguments, emphasized by the mother, is characteristic of incestuous hatred, whose actual causes are of course repressed. In her joy, the mother reveals to her newly reconciled sons that their sister lives; each of the sons responds that he has found a comrade for life whom he wishes to present to the mother. But both share the same beloved—their own sister Beatrice. Psychologically, then, their reconciliation is neatly motivated, for each of the brothers must unconsciously believe he possesses the sister, the cause of their hatred. Therefore each is willing to be reconciled with the other. Don Manuel, the elder brother, had met Beatrice while hunting, having pursued his prey as far as the garden of the convent. He describes the meeting:

> Her glance forged deep into my soul,
> And quickly my heart was transformed.
> What I said then, and what the blessed one
> Responded, do not ask:
> It all lies like a dream behind me,
> A dream from childhood's dawning days;
> On my own breast I felt hers beating
> When I again came to my senses.

Beatrice returns Don Manuel's love:

> There he stood, suddenly, at the convent gate,
> Beautiful as a god and manly as a hero.
> No words can name my feelings.
> A stranger, he came to me from another world,
> And quickly, as if it had always existed,
> The bond was sealed that no mortal can dissolve.

However, she is also attracted to Don Cesar [the younger brother], who has fallen in love with her at his father's funeral.

> There, at those solemnities,
> When the prince was laid to rest,

I paid dearly for my daring;
Only heaven saved me when
The youth approached,
A stranger, eyes ablaze,
Penetrating my whole being
With his terrifying gaze,
Peering into my very heart.
My breast still shudders with cold horror
When I think of it.
Never, never, can I gaze
Into my beloved's eyes,
Conscious of my quiet guilt.

The night before the reconciliation of the brothers, Don Manuel had abducted Beatrice from the convent and had hidden her so as to bring her to the palace after the meeting with his brother. Don Cesar learns of Beatrice's abduction. He hurries to the place where she is hiding, now finding her in his brother's arms. His old hatred flames up again, sparked by jealousy; he stabs his brother. Beatrice is brought to her mother, who explains to her that she is the sister of the inimical brothers.

Beatrice (sinking upon Isabella's breast):
Can this really be your heart?
And everything I lived a dream?
A difficult, terrible dream? Oh, Mother!
I saw him fall dead at my feet.

Finally Don Cesar kills himself in repentance over what has occurred. Various lines in which Isabella calls Don Manuel her "better son" (4.5) or says of him, "Oh, he was always a blessed child to me" suggest that the murder of the brother preferred by the beloved was also brought about by the mother's preference for him.

The extent to which the presentation of this tale, drawn together from literary sources of the most varied sort, was influenced by personal complexes is best demonstrated in that in his youth Schiller had already become familiar with the theme of inimical brothers and had employed it literarily, though it did not arise directly from his life. Most of his models, however, especially those that most affected him, dealt only with the rivalry of two brothers in love with the same young woman; given his individual perspective, Schiller transformed this woman into the sister of the two competing brothers. In *Die Räuber*, Schiller portrayed the competition of two brothers over the same woman in the usual way. Going back to the infantile sources of his literary development, we find that his strong attraction to his sister was already linked with guilt at an early age and could thus be so easily associated with the theme of the competing brothers. In *Schillers Leben bis 1787* [Schiller's life until 1787], Charlotte von Schiller mentions that the child's earliest dramatic attempt was "a dramatic poem, *Absalon,* of which Schiller now remembered only the ideas." Given his religious upbringing, it is not surprising that Schiller took his material from the Bible; we can assume that the youth's intense interest was sparked by Absalom's inimical insurrection against his father, David, and by the incest of Absalom's sister Tamar with her brother Amnon. It was probably here that Schiller first found love for the sister associated with hatred toward the brother and the father (displacement from father to brother). Thus, in this dramatic study written in childhood, the later playwright—the youthful author of *Die Räuber* and the mature creator of *Die Braut von Messina*—reveals himself completely. The progression from *Absalon* to *Die Räuber,* which also deals with insurrection against the father and sexual rivalry with the brother, is easily seen. Another youthful work, also lost, was entitled *Kosmos von Medicis.* The drama concerned the conspiracy of the Pazzis against the Medicis and was based largely on *Julius von Tarent* by Johann Leisewitz, which portrays the same historical background and deals with the struggle of two brothers over the same woman (cf. chap. 21). In *Morgenblatt* (July 30, 1807), Petersen, Schiller's friend in youth, writes (cf. Goedecke): "*Kosmos von Medicis* was the first tragedy Schiller undertook and worked on for a long period with highly concentrated energies. The drama shared much in common with *Julius von Tarent,* but it was by no means identical to Leisewitz's work, on which, to an extent, it was based. Schiller also rejected and destroyed the entire work. However, he later adopted individual images, plot details, thoughts, and original ideas from this work in *Die Räuber.*" Still, in the intentionally archaic *Braut von Messina,* the theme of brother hatred was also influenced by classical models, specifically the Oedipus legend as it developed in the works of the tragedians. Soon after completing *Don Carlos,* Schiller turned to classical literature. He was especially fascinated at the time by the Oedipus plays of Sophocles and of the Greek tragedians, and he began to translate Euripides, attempting to translate into German isolated scenes from *The Phoenician Women.* In Euripides' drama Jocasta, "Oedipus's spouse and mother," as she is listed in the dramatis personae, appears onstage. She has not committed suicide after the discovery of the incest. She relates her fate in a monologue [translated from Schiller's German rendition]:

> Unknowingly, the unfortunate one
> Courted his mother. Nor did she know
> That she embraced her son. Thus I gave
> children to my own child.

The main theme of *The Phoenician Women,* however, is the mutual hatred of Oedipus's two sons, Polynices and Eteocles. Jocasta says [translated from Hartung's German rendition, cited by Rank]:

> When brown beards had covered my sons' chins
> They locked their father behind bars,
> Hoping fate would be forgotten.
> He lives still in this house. Struck by fate,
> He poured out upon their heads this crazed curse:
> That they should vie for inheritance of the house
> with naked steel.

Among the excerpts Schiller translated we also find some dealing with brother hatred.

> *Polynices:* Warned by a secret fear, lest brother hatred slyly strangle me . . .
> *Eteocles:* And I too hope to rob you of your life.

Schiller's adoption of the theme of brother hatred was certainly influenced also by Jean Racine's *La Thébaïde, ou Les frères ennemis,* with which Schiller was also familiar. Act 4, scene 3 of Racine's drama is very similar to the opening scene of *Die Braut von Messina.*

Schiller's first significant dramatic work, *Die Räuber,* which he completed at age twenty-one, shows very clearly the playwright's father hatred, which lived on in the brother hatred theme. Schiller's father hatred made use of the adopted figures of the inimical brothers to express the playwright's ambivalent childhood perspective toward his father. Here the theme of brother hatred, apparently in the foreground of the drama, is revealed as an artistically perfected representation of the playwright's conflicting feelings toward his father. The feeling of enmity, later intensified through rivalry over the mother, is powerfully opposed by the originally affectionate and admiring perspective. Therefore the son forced into the role of robber is portrayed as the good, loving son with respect to the father, and the inimical and hateful feelings toward the father can be expressed in the other son without inhibition.

Franz hates his brother Karl not only because Karl is physically and intellectually superior, but also because he is preferred by the father and mother. While Karl is studying at the university, Franz discredits his brother in the eyes of his father and forges a letter in the father's name eliminating all Karl's hopes of forgiveness by the father. In unbounded anger and hatred of mankind, Karl becomes the leader of a robber band and hopes to take vengeance on the world. While in the forests of Bohemia, Franz attempts to win his brother's betrothed, Amalia, for himself.

In order to assume power, he has locked his father in a distant cell, leaving him to starve to death. Karl, who happens to come to this region with his robber band, frees him and reveals his identity, whereupon the old man dies. Karl kills Amalia at her own request; Franz strangles himself with a hatband.

The underlying theme of *Die Räuber*—the theme of the son who attempts to express his split (ambivalent) perspective toward his father through murder and rescue fantasies carried out by two opposing figures—becomes even clearer if one refers to Schiller's source. This was Christian Schubart's tale "Zur Geschichte des menschlichen Herzens" [The tale of the human heart], which appeared in *Haugs Schwäbisches Magazin* in 1775. The plot of Schubart's tale is as follows. Karl is expelled by his father, and since his brother has intercepted his explanatory and conciliatory letter to his father, he takes on work incognito as a servant near his father's home. Through a coincidence, he is able to rescue his father from the hands of disguised murderers, three of whom he kills. The fourth declares penitently that Wilhelm, the attacked man's own son, has hired them to commit the murder. Karl reveals himself to his father as the "lost son." The father laments the injustice done to Karl and even forgives the evil Wilhelm at Karl's request. As Minor (1890, 295) emphasizes, Schubart himself had more than literary interest in this material, for in his own family his quick genius contrasted with the sober diligence of his brother. As revealed by Schubart's own life, however, these relationships are undoubtedly much deeper. His powerful defenses against his hatred of father and brother are revealed not only in the sentimental conclusion of the tale, but also in that Schubart repeatedly attempted to deal with the theme of inimical brothers in various unfinished works. The tendency for self-punishment, which inhibited his unconscious murderous impulses and was realized, though in a manner contrary to his conscious wishes, in his long incarceration for his political activities, can be most clearly seen in the *bänkelsänger* [minstrel] romance "The Patricide's Curse." The father, who has been chained in prison for fifteen years, rises up during the wedding of his criminal son. In the end the son must pay with his life for his crimes against his father, though the father had treated his own father in the same way (theme of retribution).

In Schubart's tale—which, as Minor says, provides the background rather than the content of *Die Räuber*—brother hatred has no place at all. It is only the split perspective toward the father that is expressed in the fantasies of rescue and murder. Schiller, too, derived his treatment of the material and the affects employed in his drama from this complex. This is clear in that the title originally chosen by the playwright himself was "Der verlorene Sohn" [The lost son]. In the original draft, the theme of insurrection against the father must have been dominant not only in the title but also in the plot. This can be demonstrated by a characteristic excerpt from the first edition, eliminated in later ones. In act 4, to the accompaniment of the lute, the robber Moor sings a dialogue on the subject of patricide in the historical guise of a discussion between Caesar and Brutus. According to Minor (1890, 347), this song provided the germ for the last scene of *Fiesco* and for the Posa scene in *Don Carlos*. In the song, given his youthful opposition to his father and to Duke Karl, Schiller supports Brutus, the champion of freedom, while opposing the tyrant. For example, consider the following verse from this song:

> Oh, a deathblow from Brutus's sword!
> You too, Brutus, you!
> My son, you've killed your father; my son, the earth
> Would have bowed to you as your inheritance.
> Go! You became the greatest of Romans
> When into your father's breast your dagger pressed.
> Go, and cry it to yon gates:
> Brutus became the greatest of Romans
> When into his father's breast his dagger pressed.

The later elimination of this "patricide dialogue" speaks clearly for the conflicts that opposed themselves to these impulses soon after their expression. This provides another example of our statement that in first drafts repressed emotions express themselves more impulsively and in a much less disguised manner than in the final draft, much more strongly controlled by consciousness. From all of this, and in light of this playwright's transference of affect, discussed in chapter 3, we can suppose that his original interest in the material was based on the well-elaborated father complex in Schubart's tale and that in the process of conceptualizing and composing the work, which lasted for several years (age seventeen to age twenty-one), the psychic emphasis gradually shifted to brother hatred, which for Schiller was not associated with self-reproach. This resembles Grillparzer's displacement to the love of a fictive sister, demonstrated above. This displacement of emphasis to the "brother" (cf. Absalom, the Medicis), which occurred early in the young poet's life, becomes comprehensible when we recall the ambivalent perspective of the son in revolt against the father. In *Die Räuber,* too, despite the portrayal involving two opposite characters, this leads to a significant compromise with respect to patricide. This same compromise establishes itself in Shakespeare's ghosts, in the specter of the ancestress, and in the appearance of the old Moor. The father has been eliminated—removed in the infantile sense. Yet he lives on, finally appearing to take vengeance on the treacherous murderer—precisely as did the father's ghost in *Hamlet*. In *Die Räuber*, Karl's behavior toward his brother Franz demonstrates the same ambivalence. Here the playwright reveals not only the displacement of affect, but also the psychological identity of the two brothers, whose being can be understood only as the embodiment of Schiller's own split perspective toward his father. In Franz's discussion with Pastor Moser in the final act, patricide and fratricide are directly associated with one another.

> *Franz:* Tell me, what is the greatest sin . . . ?
> *Moser:* I know of only two. But they are not committed by men, and it is not men who exact punishment for them.
> *Franz:* Tell me these two!
> *Moser* (very meaningfully): The one is called "patricide," the other "fratricide."

The son's indecisive, almost neurotic perspective is expressed by Schiller in that having killed his father in the guise of the evil Franz, he now not only rescues his father but even takes vengeance on the disloyal son [first ed.] as the robber Moor (cf. *Hamlet*). If a strong tendency for self-punishment is revealed here and in Karl's surrender [to the legal authorities], the psychic association of the two brother figures is seen in that Karl, reminiscent of Hamlet, feels incapable of carrying out vengeance on his brother. Whereas in the final version self-punishment is carried out not only by Karl, but also by Franz, who strangles himself, the initial one is also clearer on this point. Karl forgives his brother for everything he has done to him personally and wishes to punish Franz only for killing their father. Still, he is unable to do so. Amalia, too, says of the great robber: "He couldn't even bear to see a fly suffer!" The robbers, with great difficulty, rescue Franz from the burning palace into which he has run in desperation. He is brought to Karl alive, but Karl feels incapable of putting him to death himself, saying: "His mother was also my mother!" He has him executed by the robber band: Schweizer announces that the band condemns him to death by starvation in the same tower in which he had kept his father imprisoned.

> *The robber Moor* (walks toward him nobly and painfully): Son of my father! You have taken my heaven from me. May you be forgiven this sin. Descend to hell, son of ravens! I forgive you, brother! (He embraces him and hurries away. Franz is thrust down. The band laughs at him derisively.)

Thus with Schiller the theme of brother hatred now expresses the son's ambiguous perspective, derived from the father complex. This displacement of affect found powerful impulses and powerful support in Schiller's love for his sister, which had already attracted the young playwright to the Absalom material; which led the young playwright to meld the theme of the rivalry between two brothers over a young woman, taken from *Julius von Tarent,* with the plot of *Die Räuber;* and which finally led the mature writer of *Die Braut von Messina* to portray this woman, loved in common by the two brothers, as their sister. From the attachment of the two siblings, it is clear that Schiller loved his sister Christophine. Still, this was only a displacement of his erotic affection for his mother, just as his fictive rivalry with his brother was derived from opposition to the father. Thus, although the boy actually loved mother and sister together, in Schiller's dramatic works we have found the common love of two rivals (father and son) for the same love object (the mother). Father hatred becomes powerful and fixated through childhood rivalry over the mother, but its rejection, brought about by erotic affection for the sister, leads to the almost paranoiac fiction of the rival brother, through whom all repressed impulses derived in real life from forbidden feelings toward father, mother, and sister can be released in an uninhibited manner.

We now understand that the dominance of brother hatred in a playwright with no brother and the dominance of love for the sister in a playwright lacking a sister derive only from defense against the complementary wish. If we now fill out these psychic mechanisms with their content—their affects—we will be able to say that Grillparzer, as a consequence of defense against these impulses, released his erotic affection for his mother and the affect of brother hatred through his "love for the sister," harmless and unobjectionable to consciousness, while Schiller released his affects of love for the sister and father hatred, displaced through repression, through the brother. However, with these peculiar displacements of affect the playwright does not escape the general laws of psychic life. He behaves exactly like the normal person who, in an apparently insignificant and indifferent context, releases powerful, repressed affects. He behaves like the dreamer, whose affects do not appear to be sufficiently motivated in his manifest dream situations because their actual sources are hidden behind the dream situation. Finally, he acts precisely like the obsessional neurotic, for whom a similar false association of affect and imagination is of course characteristic. But whereas the normal person, the dreamer, and the playwright are able to free themselves from their oppressive affects through these psychic mechanisms, the neurotic is unsuccessful in this endeavor.

Schiller's relationship with his sister Christophine and his brother-in-law Reinwald deserves special discussion because of its influence on his literary production. Schiller had three sisters. The eldest of the three was Christophine Friederike, the playwright's beloved sister. The marriage of Schiller's parents had produced no issue for eight years until Christophine's birth. Note that Friedrich, the second child (born two years after Christophine), was the only son, and four daughters were subsequently born, two of whom died young. The two surviving daughters were Luise (born 1765) and Nanette (born 1777), who died unmarried at age nineteen. Friedrich and Christophine (like Goethe and Cornelia) formed an extremely close bond in their earliest childhood, since initially they were the only offspring. All the biographers emphasize this heartfelt affection: "The bond that already united sister and brother was only made firmer by such shared, heartfelt feelings. None of his younger sisters was as dear to Schiller as this eldest sister, and none was so similar to him in appearance, intelligence, or personality. These similarities extended even to their handwriting, which was nearly identical" (Hoffmeister 1838, 1:8).

At the time of Schiller's flight from Stuttgart, Christophine was his only confidant. Two years later Schiller asked his father to let her come to Mannheim and keep house for him. This wish that his sister keep house for him, typical of affection for the sister, seeks to unite spouse, in charge of the household, and mother, concerned with the son's good fortune, in a figure of compromise. In the lives of Ludwig Tieck and Richard Wagner, we shall find the same wish as an expression of the same unconscious impulses. We can also demonstrate its presence with Kleist, and we are already familiar with it in the life of Byron. Schiller's father opposed this plan, however. Apparently under his influence, Christophine herself rejected this offer when in the same year she wrote to her brother (November 25, 1784): "Since you know how familiar I am with your circumstances, you should share all of your worries with me. Of course I would actually be able to help you very little, but is it not a comfort to be able to open one's heart completely to another person? At least this would certainly be true for me. Is your sister, who has already suffered so much, not worthy to be your friend, to take upon herself the whole pain of your soul? Believe me, my dear one, my soul has already suffered much on your account. Forgive me my weakness in admitting this to you; in writing you this, I am too overcome by emotion to conceal it."

Unconscious loving affection for the brother permeates the letter, but this affection strives not to exceed the limits of sibling love. And in a similar emotional state, Schiller wrote to her on New Year's Day 1784: "In my lonely hours I have often considered your future fate, and how often you have been the heroine in my fondest dreams!" Only too soon, though, these fond dreams of his beloved sister's future were harshly interrupted. In May 1783 Schiller's friend Reinwald had seen a letter from Christophine in Schiller's home that pleased him so much that he expressed the desire to establish a correspondence with the young woman. Later he asked permission from Schiller's family to visit her at their home, "Solitude"

[French]. Finally, in 1784, he asked for Christophine's hand in marriage. It is characteristic of Schiller's passionate love for his sister that his wish that she move in with him arose in the same year Reinwald began to court her. The wish almost resembles a struggle over the sister, and subsequently such a struggle was indeed carried out quite vehemently.

Here it is also clear that the draft of *Die Braut in Trauer* [The bride in mourning], which arose in the same year, represents Schiller's wish for victory in this struggle—his wish to gain his sister for himself. Here again we see that the rough draft reveals the playwright's personal feelings with much greater clarity than the final version. In *Die Braut in Trauer,* the son hates the father and the beloved sister's husband in a manner fully corresponding to the unconscious perspective of the playwright himself. In *Die Räuber,* the original drafts of which have unfortunately been lost, we observe the displacement of the psychic accents. The fantasy making the sister's husband a rival brother comes to the fore, and with it the inimical brothers; hatred of the father is dampened and love for the sister is completely disguised, though it can easily be discerned behind the pale figure of Amalia. She lives in Moor's home; the old man considers her his daughter and addresses her as "my daughter," while Franz treats her as a sister:

> *Franz:* Our souls harmonized so well . . .
> *Amalia:* Oh, no, that they never did!
> *Franz:* Oh, they harmonized so well that I always thought we were twins!

And in the third act he says to Amalia: "You know what you were to our family. You were considered Moor's daughter. His love for you survived even death."

Unconsciously, then, Schiller treated Amalia as the sister of Franz and Karl. However, that he does not present her as their sister is an effect of the powerful defenses we find emphasized in the draft of the second part of *Die Räuber* (*Die Braut in Trauer*).

Neither Christophine nor her parents opposed Reinwald's suit. Reinwald then accompanied Christophine when she visited her brother in Mannheim. "Schiller was unfavorably impressed when he saw that his joyful, cheerful sister was determined to share her destiny with a man twenty years her senior, whose small income and hypochondriacal tendencies promised little happiness. He shared his impressions with the family, and his depiction of Reinwald's character brought a temporary halt to the suitor's dealings with the family. From the study of psychic life, we are also familiar with the expression of affection in this resistant guise. It is observed in fathers who oppose the marriage of their beloved daughters and in mothers who oppose the marriage of their beloved sons. Still, Schiller's protest was later ignored. After her engagement, Schiller wrote to Christophine (September 28, 1785, from Dresden): "But no reproaches, good sister. Perhaps my earlier doubts and my apparent disapproval have caused you to lose my trust, and perhaps your suspicions that my advice was not unbiased have harmed your devotion to me." Schiller's unconscious erotic affection for his sister is expressed nowhere more clearly than in this apology for his unsuccessful effort to thwart her engagement. In 1786 Christophine and Reinwald were married. The marriage was a very unhappy one, and a few years later the mother already regretted that Fene (Christophine) was married to Reinwald—influenced, of course, by her own unhappy experiences in marriage. In May 1796 Schiller's mother was very ill, and Christophine was asked to come to the family home to help with the housekeeping. Reinwald, who is supposed to have been very stingy, consented to allow her to make the trip only when Schiller himself asked the favor of him and offered to pay all expenses. After a very short time, however, Reinwald demanded that his wife return. The mother wrote to Schiller (September 28, 1796) that Christophine "unfortunately expressed a painful compulsion to return to her husband, though she can expect no comfort or encouragement from him."

But Christophine herself wrote to her brother (July 21, 1796): "I have seen here so many things Mama has had to be satisfied with; I have seen so much that I would not gladly trade places with her. You see, dear brother, I cannot leave him forever. He is growing old and weak and needs my care, and I would have no more peace if I were to have to blame myself for failing in my marital obligations." On May 21, 1802, she wrote to her brother: "Through all the changes in my life, you remain just as dear to me, though I have not been able to prove this to you in deeds. But I have often been saddened that I could not do this for you. You must often have mistaken my true sentiments, because I could not act as my heart dictated and often had to repress my love for you. . . . For a long time I have not been able to speak so freely with you because I was really foolish enough to believe it unjust to write to you without his knowledge. Forgive this weakness—sometimes I myself cannot understand it—and love your Christophine no less."

After their mother's death (June 9, 1802) she wrote Schiller: "Cotta visited us for a moment and told me that I should send you an address." This was a means of making possible a private correspondence between the siblings, completely unknown to her sullen husband, which was often to provide the sorely oppressed Christophine a means of revealing her heart to her sympathetic brother. An interesting example parallel to this secret correspondence is found in the study of the psychology of neurosis. For this example I am grateful to Dr. Freud. It concerns a pair of siblings who later became neurotic. Psychoanalysis revealed mutual sexual attraction between them, and this attraction had expressed itself in their removing their clothing in each other's presence. When these sessions came to an end and the brother took up his studies far from the sister, they corresponded like two secret lovers, *poste restante,* addressed each other formally, and called each other "monsieur" and "madame." This tendency for alienation from one another can be compared to the offers of friendship (replacing the sibling relationship) expressed by Byron and Schiller. The sensation of guilt that Christophine admits to feeling owing to this secret correspondence indicates the unconscious erotic nature of this liaison, in which the brother was treated like a secret lover. Christophine's inner conflict, brought about by her erotic affection for her brother and her disenchantment with her marital duties, is most clearly expressed in a portion of a letter written in December 1802: "My conception of love was probably too idealistic to be realized. Now I can see that, and I must be content to find the shared feeling of what I would hope to find in another heart and would hope to be able to return." In a letter to Schiller's widow shortly after his death, Christophine attempts to eliminate the painful distinction between sibling love and sexual love by identifying with her brother's wife, thus becoming his lover, wife, and sister in one person: "Oh, my dearest, I press you to my heart as the only dear thing the beloved one has left me in this world. . . . May his memory be holy to me. May it inspire me to do good, to fulfill my duties so that I may someday be worthy to join him again. . . . Oh! His sisters were unable to be much for him. Such was the will of fate; I should not complain. But you have been for him everything we could not be. May God reward you for this!"

This splitting (and attempted reunification), through compromise, of the components of incestuous love—a splitting revealed so clearly in Schiller's works and reminiscent of the split consciousness of the neurotic brought about by unconscious repression—was not without consequences for his sister's emotional life. We must attempt to understand it in the context of the disappointments of her love life, for she later suffered from hysterical attacks. Long after her brother's death, she wrote to his widow, Lotte: "Further, I am sensitive to everything that upsets my heart and I believe it would be best for me to be as calm as possible, for this inner feeling also has its physical effects on my body and produces a sort of tension I have never before experienced. This is probably the consequence of so many sufferings my heart has endured over the long years."

However, Christophine's unhappy love life is to be explained not only by her erotic affection for her brother and her aversion toward her older, sickly husband. On the contrary, owing to repressed infantile impulses, her willing marriage to this man was doomed to unhappiness. Here again we gain psychoanalytic insight into the devastating effects of the parent complex. His sister's infantile perspective is a complete feminine counterpart to Schiller's Oedipus complex. Just as the boy displaced to his sister his original affection for his mother, the sister herself had never fully overcome her first infantile fixation on the father. Instead, she found in her brother a rejuvenated substitute for her aging and sullen father. In the same way, in her old, sullen, and sickly husband she also sought a substitute for her father. From psychoanalysis, we know that such an unusual choice of object as made by Schiller's sister regularly derives from infantile fixation of the libido on the father. In a letter to her brother, she also defends the deceased father against her brother's criticisms (May 21, 1802): "But he was so gentle, if one just knew how to handle him. Oh, I often think of him—of his good side, too. This provides me an excellent account of myself, for I have many of his faults. I must treat my husband more like a father, weak and in need of my help."

Here she directly identifies her husband with her father, perceiving their shared traits to be age, infirmity, and the need for physical care—in short, her asexual relationship to both of them. Her naive wishes, so inclined to entertain the fantasy of replacement of the mother, were already so repressed in the neurotically disposed girl that when they finally found partial realization in later life they produced only a defensive reaction. While already married and managing the household during her mother's illness, she wrote to her brother (July 21, 1796): "I have seen here so many things Mama has had to be satisfied with; I have seen so much that I would not gladly trade places with her." Unconsciously, though, in returning to her unloved husband, for her a father substitute, she did trade places with her mother. And when she later did fulfill her brother's wish that she keep house for him, this too occurred only as a result of her old, long-repressed infantile wish to play the role of her mother with respect to her father. This wish was displaced from the sexual realm to the harmless function of housekeeping. Thus on January 25, 1803, she wrote to her brother concerning her husband: "I already told him long ago that if he ever mistreated me I would take refuge with you." The father not only was the superior competitor for the mother's affection with respect to the playwright but had also won the heart of the playwright's beloved sister. Thus it is no surprise that this side of the incest complex, accessible to the son only through his emotions, also found expression in his literary fantasies. In *Luisa Miller* [*Kabale und Liebe*], the old, sullen father, lovingly provident toward his daughter, is a nearly perfect reflection of Schiller's father. Here the father attempts to rescue his fallen daughter and win her for himself. Similarly, the old Verrina is beside himself when his daughter is deprived of her innocence; in the same way [sic] Thibaut curses his daughter in *Die Jungfrau von Orleans* [The maid of Orleans]. In *Turandot*, Schiller, following Gozzi, addressed the fable of the daughter who is infatuated with her father and kills all her suitors. Finally, in *Menschenfeind* [The enemy of man], the father directly attempts to avoid marrying off his daughter. Indeed, he makes her promise to remain unmarried (scene 8).

In two drafts left us by Schiller, the many-faceted, multiply branching incest complex, with all its complicated emotional relationships, is expressed in a much less disguised, more complete manner than in his artistically perfected fantasy creations. In these drafts his fantasy productions still pour out uninhibited. Indeed, in a letter to Körner (December 1, 1788), the playwright himself identifies this as the precondition for literary production (cf. Freud 1909f, 72 ff.). Here we gain highly instructive insights concerning the development of the obscured, dampened, polished work of art—insights into the working of unconscious fantasy creation. Thus, when the playwright sees himself as incapable of presenting in their original form the unconscious fantasies of his psyche, struggling for liberation and representation, we have convincing evidence that he does feel that they are objectionable. In the draft "Narbonne, oder Die Kinder des Hauses" [Narbonne, or The children of the house], Louis Narbonne has his brother Pierre murdered because the latter is about to remarry. Schiller summarizes the plot as follows: "Louis Narbonne had Pierre poisoned and was able to place the blame on Pierre's own son, whose conduct also assisted him in this effort. He arranged things so that the son fled on the day of the murder, perhaps in despair in connection with another crime. Thus it was assumed that the son was the murderer, while the actual murderer came into possession of all the son's rights. After six or eight years, Narbonne courted the woman originally destined for the unfortunate one." And in the margin, Schiller writes: "Everything must come together to suggest patricide, and also to explain the flight of the supposed murderer."

In this fratricide, displacement from the father is suggested in that the blame for the murder is shifted to the murdered man's own son. In the drama, the murderous impulse toward the father, repressed into the unconscious and displaced by the playwright's defense mechanisms to the fictive brother, becomes a fratricide, while the patricide appears to be fictive. Here we clearly see the displacement of affect brought about by repression. But if we recall Schiller's jealousy toward his brother-in-law Reinwald, to whom he did not wish to relinquish his beloved sister, new light will be shed not only on this fratricide, but also on the figure of the fantasy brother in Schiller's later works. From this hatred of his sister's husband, it is only a small step to the transformation of this hated competitor into the "brother." And in fact, Schiller always addressed his sister's husband as "brother." Immediately before Christophine's marriage, he wrote to Reinwald: "Why should we continue to address each other formally? I am surprised that neither of us has yet come upon the idea of putting an end to this: Are we not brothers? Certainly! And are we not brothers-in-law or becoming brothers-in-law?" This supports our conception of the creation of a fantasy brother—a competitor for the sister. Just as the father was Schiller's competitor for the mother's love, in analogy to this relationship he created a fantasy rival—a brother competing for the love of the sister (a brother whom the father nevertheless underlies). Thus Pierre's murder is actually nothing more than the elimination of the father figure—the rival from childhood brought to life once again by the present marriage of the sister. The continuation of the story shows that this must be assumed. It was to include both the son's unconscious attraction to the mother and the love between brother and sister.

It was supposed that the murdered Pierre had no heirs and that two children born to Madame Narbonne had perished in an accident. "About a year before the disappearance of the children, Louis had been visiting. At that time he had had forbidden relations with Madelon, who then was a young woman. Together they had plotted the elimination of their children."

"After Louis had come into possession of the house, he gave Madelon great authority there. He also promised to marry her. But when other marriage plans arose, it became necessary for him to come to an agreement with her and to find her a husband. She herself wished for a change in plans and had turned her thoughts to Saintfoix. Louis was by no means opposed. Saintfoix was twelve years younger than she, although his actual age was unknown. At the time of the action, she was thirty-four years old but claimed to be twenty-seven. Saintfoix was twenty but was considered twenty-three." Six years earlier (at the age of fourteen), Saintfoix, now a young man, had been taken into Louis Narbonne's home as an orphan. "But a woman of Narbonne's household, Madelon, was attracted to him and had plans to marry him."

Louis was attracted to a beautiful, noble, and rich young woman, Victoire de Pontis. "Victoire had often had the opportunity to see Saintfoix. She soon felt attracted to him, but this feeling seemed hopeless. . . . Saintfoix adored Victoire from the moment he first laid eyes on her, but he did not presume to approach her. He had met another young woman, Adelaide; she, like him, was an orphan. He had once done her a great service and had a tender friendship with her, but for Victoire he felt passion and adoration." "Adelaide feels a strong sympathy with Charbot (Saintfoix), but this feeling is certainly not love."

At one point Adelaide sends an old woman claiming to be her mother to the goldsmith bearing a precious piece of jewelry, for she is in need. In the meantime, Saintfoix visits her. One sees an innocent attraction on the part of the young woman and appreciation and sympathy on the part of the young man. They tell one another about their lives, and Saintfoix suggests that she go with him. Just when Saintfoix is present, however, Adelaide is apprehended by the police, since it is suspected that the jewelry in question is not her own. "She is taken into custody and brought before Victoire's father, Bailli. Saintfoix approaches Bailli, who does not leave him; he approaches Victoire and asks her to put in a good word for Adelaide. Victoire is surprised: jealousy and affection bring her to a clearer expression of her passion. She declares that she is in love with him, and he also declares his love for her. At the moment of their greatest passion, Louis Narbonne enters with Bailli. They have witnessed what has occurred. To both of them, Saintfoix must seem unappreciative and impious toward those who have done him favors."

Through the jewelry, all is revealed. Louis Narbonne has already suspected who Saintfoix and Adelaide are. "Finally the revelation is unavoidable, and he must recognize them as his own children. However, they do not wish to dispossess him. . . . As soon as Narbonne realizes the identity of Saintfoix and Adelaide, he wishes to assist them in their flight. . . . Narbonne requests a chance to speak with Adelaide and Saintfoix. As a consequence, he offers them his assistance in fleeing secretly. Of course, they reject the offer. . . . After Louis had discovered Saintfoix's true identity, he could no longer entertain the thought of the latter's marriage to Madelon. . . . Madelon had sold the two children to a gypsy woman when the elder was only four years old. As fate would have it, this gypsy woman is in the city. She is recognized by Madelon and apprehended by the police. Adelaide also recognizes her with horror. Thus it becomes clear that Adelaide is the daughter of Pierre Narbonne."

Although the relationships in this complicated and hastily sketched story are not always clear, it is nevertheless evident that it deals with several typical themes from the incest complex. Madelon loves her own son Saintfoix without realizing his identity. She would marry him were it not that he adores Victoire. In turn, his father also loves Victoire. In addition, Saintfoix appears to feel a strong attraction to Adelaide, who is either his sister or his cousin. The complications and the unclear details of the story are apparently the result of psychic censorship. Here this censorship already has a strong influence on the draft and prohibits the playwright from completing the work.

There is another draft by Schiller that is much clearer and was therefore even more inappropriate for completion. It is, however, of great interest because it provides a link between *Die Räuber* and *Die Braut von Messina* while simultaneously encompassing all of Schiller's works and focusing on his unconscious manner of presenting themes. The fragment, which occupied the playwright for nearly twenty years, arose in 1784, two years after the completion of *Die Räuber,* and bears the title *Die Braut in Trauer, oder Zweiter Teil der Räuber* [The bride in mourning, or The robbers, part 2]. On August 24, 1784, Schiller wrote to Dalberg: "After *Carlos,* I shall undertake part 2 of *Die Räuber.* It will be a complete playwright's apology to part 1; in it, all immorality must be dissolved in the most elevated morality."

In this second portion of *Die Räuber,* which one can also consider an "interpretation" of part 1, Schiller's incestuous passions are expressed in a much less disguised manner than in part 1. Thus we gain new psychological confirmation of our conception of drafts and fragments. In these we have been able to observe the emergence of the unconscious much more clearly than in completed works, for the expression of unconscious impulses in works intended for the public seems to be associated with a higher degree of disguise (repression). Given our previous findings, this fragment casts an interesting light on the nature of dramatic production and on its deepest driving forces in the psychic life of the playwright. In this draft we recognize the same incestuous impulses we observed in *Die Räuber,* in *Carlos,* and in *Kabale und Liebe.* We can see how hatred toward the Piccolominis and toward Duke Johann in *Wilhelm Tell* derive from these emotions. But the actual circumstances of Schiller's life are also clearly reflected here, and besides his love for his sister Christophine, which found clear expression in the siblings' correspondence, we also notice aversion toward the father and hatred toward the sister's spouse, the competitor for her love.

The portions of the fragment relating to incestuous passion can now be presented in full: "Karl Moor (Count Julian) is the father of a son (Xaver) and a daughter (Mathilde). The daughter is to be married, but the brother loves her passionately and cannot bear the thought of losing her to another man. He has thus far been able to conceal his passion, and no one but the sister knows of it. The father is strict, and is feared. . . . As the wedding day approaches, the brother's passions burst forth. He confesses his passion to his sister; his mind drives him on; he fears his father and feels a certain antipathy toward him. The father is strict with him. . . . A parricide must be committed, but what kind? Father kills the son or the daughter. Brother loves and kills the sister ⟨cf. Karl Moor⟩; father kills him. Father loves the son's betrothed ⟨cf. Don Carlos⟩. Brother kills the sister's betrothed. Son betrays or kills the father." In this draft, all Schiller's incestuous passions are united: his hatred for his father and the defensive tendencies (punishment) opposed to it (the father kills the son); love for the sister and defense against it (the brother kills her); hatred of the competitor for the sister's love ("bridegroom"; brother). Love for the mother (cf.

Don Carlos) is revealed only in defense, in the father's revenge: the father loves the son's betrothed. However, the son's betrothed is simultaneously his sister. Concerning Xaver's hatred toward his father, Schiller writes further: "Xaver goes his way alone, lacking all childish attraction. He feels nothing but fear toward his father."

Realizing that this draft arose in the year of Christophine's engagement to the unappealing Reinwald and represents the playwright's reaction to this event, one will understand the theme ("The daughter is to be married, but the brother loves her passionately and cannot bear the thought of losing her to another") as a direct and undisguised expression of Schiller's feelings. However, Schiller himself was by no means fully conscious of these feelings. Instead, from the unconscious, they strove for expression. This rivalry with the "brother" Reinwald over the sister reawakened childhood rivalry with the father over the mother and the sister. Therefore this rivalry found expression in the draft as well. Like the theme of the sister's marriage, the protagonist's dislike of his strict father is also a direct reflection of the childhood perspective of the playwright himself. Like the various versions of a myth, the various possibilities for parricide express as many impulses and counterimpulses in the psychic life of the playwright. But only one of these, the rivalry with the competitor over the sister, was able to persist for two decades (when circumstances were completely different and it had receded into the unconscious), ultimately finding expression in *Die Braut von Messina*. As far as the playwright's conscious is concerned, however, this occurred not for the sake of the playwright himself, but in the service of a higher task, an artistic problem that the mature Schiller, inspired by the course of Goethe's development, had set for himself in reviving classical tragedy in the manner of *Oedipus Rex*. The fragment of *Die Braut in Trauer* is so valuable to us—indeed, the bride of Messina is a "bride in mourning"—because it shows that even the most sublime work of the playwright, apparently inspired only by the highest aesthetic interests, is nurtured by his infantile affective sources. In the literary work, a continuing attempt is made to realize, though in a highly distorted form, the old repressed wishes of childhood.

21 *The Theme of Brother Hatred, from Sophocles to Schiller*

But the origin of your quarrel
Lies in the early days of naive childhood.
It is your quarrel's age that should disarm it.
Ask yourselves what first divided you.
You do not even know, and if you should discover it
You would be ashamed of your childish quarrel.

SCHILLER, *Die Braut von Messina*

We found that in the development of *Die Braut von Messina* Euripides' *The Phoenician Women* and Racine's *Frères ennemis* played a not insignificant role. The theme of brother hatred, central to the plots of both dramas, proved fruitful for Schiller, since the playwright, as we have seen, had been interested in this theme since childhood. Indeed, directly influenced by Leisewitz's *Julius von Tarent,* this theme is observed in his very earliest literary efforts. However, Leisewitz's drama itself stands near the end of a long series of dramas extending from Sophocles to Schiller, all addressing the theme of brother hatred—usually arising from the brothers' love for the same young woman (the "sister"). This line of development does contain several interruptions and deviations, but all the deviations and detours finally converge. A historical overview of the various portions of this line of development can easily be provided.

The Greek Tragedians and Their Imitators

The Greek tragedians drew the material for their tragedies of brother hatred, like most of their material, from mythology or from epic developments of the mythological tradition. In Greek mythology, two pairs of brothers are especially important. Both pairs were famous for their fanatical hatred and were always highly attractive to the tragedians. From the Oedipus legend, Polynices and Eteocles, the sons of Oedipus, form one pair, while from the Tantalide legend, Pelops's sons Atreus and Thyestes form the other. Dramatic works can be classified based on their derivation from one legend or the other.

Eteocles and Polynices

It is no coincidence, but instead is psychologically quite comprehensible, that we also come across the second level of the incest complex, the relationship of siblings, in the Oedipus legend. It is the intense psychological association of the various incestuous impulses that in this manner finds expression in mythology. With playwrights, too, we have been able to demonstrate the same association of impulses.

The mutual hatred of the brothers Eteocles and Polynices as well as their struggle for rulership is portrayed, in conformity with epic and tragic tradition, as the result of a curse uttered by their father. However, various motivations for the curse are encountered. In the epic Theban cycle, concerning the war of the seven against Thebes, two curses pronounced by the old Oedipus are presented as deeper motivations for the brothers' hatred. When Polynices sets before himself the table of his ancestor Cadmus and the goblet of his grandfather Laius, having been expressly forbidden to do so, and when Eteocles fails to prevent him from doing this, Oedipus curses them, condemning them to conflict and war over their father's inheritance. On another occasion, when they have failed to send him the customary portion of their sacrifice, their old, embittered father's anger again flares up over this seemingly minor infraction and he curses them, condemning each to die by the other's hand. The sorely tested Oedipus, who himself had risen up against his own father, feels deliberate insult in the slightest infraction of filial piety. In the tragic tradition, this aspect is emphasized even more strongly. In *Oedipus at Colonus* (1354 ff.), Oedipus curses his sons because they have driven him from his homeland. Here, then, the hatred between father and sons is primary. He prophesies that they will die by each other's hand. In this reciprocal murder, we once again observe an ambiguous figure of compromise in which, besides fulfillment of the wish for the brother's murder, defense against this wish is also expressed through the receipt of the same punishment. In his tragedy *Seven against Thebes,* Aeschylus directly associates the curse called down upon the sons with the crimes of their ancestors. The "first Theban woman" says of Oedipus:

When he discerned with whom he had begotten them,
The last, pitiful offspring of the house,
He took upon himself a doubly heavy burden:
Criminally, the father evaded the criminal children,
Who grasped the ruler's staff.
Blinded by his own murderous hand,
The suffering man fled, calling down upon his house,
His bloody house, nothing but the curse of blood again:
In mutual murder the dynasty would end.

However, this curse expresses only the unconscious emotions of the sons and is an expression of their deep mutual hatred. Eteocles responds to his brother's challenge to a duel with the words:

Where could a better fighter be found?
Prince against prince; brother against brother;
Enemy to enemy. Thus shall we stand.

Eteocles also mentions his dreams:

Yes, when our father's curse upon us is fulfilled
And all those dreams
Which terror brings to me again each night.

Finally a messenger reports that the brothers have died in a duel, each having killed the other. In Aeschylus's drama, Jocasta is no longer living. Nor does Polynices appear onstage. In contrast, in Euripides' *The Phoenician Women,* which Schiller studied intensively, Jocasta and Polynices both appear. The inimical brothers come together in their mother's presence. Just like Isabella in Schiller's *Braut von Messina,* she attempts to reconcile her children. But in Euripides' drama the two brothers are unrelenting in their hatred:

Polynices: I would gladly know your position before the towers.
Eteocles: But tell me, why?
Polynices: To meet you and to kill you there.
Eteocles: That is also my desire.

A messenger then describes the brothers' fierce battle.

They swiftly fell upon each other
Like wild boars, gnashing their cruel teeth,
With lightning shooting from their eyes, their glance twisted with envy:
Frothing at the mouth, they attacked one another.

They kill one another, and Jocasta kills herself beside their bodies. Euripides motivates the curse with the supposition that the grown sons have imprisoned their father so that his fate will be forgotten. It cannot be supposed that this invention of Euripides influenced the similar scene in Schiller's *Die Räuber* in which the father is imprisoned by the son. This is even less likely, given that Heinrich Gerstenberg's *Ugolino* was probably Schiller's model. However, the independent treatment of this theme by two playwrights belonging to widely disparate cultural periods is of greater psychological interest. Therefore we cannot go astray in seeking in this theme too the expression of a typical impulse in the psychic life of the son. Here again we recognize one of those peculiar formations of compromise whose ingenuity is exhausted in a few stereotypical forms. We see how this expression of compromise, the imprisonment of the father, satisfies the childhood wish for his absence while simultaneously giving expression to defense against the later form of the wish—the wish to kill the father—in that the murder is avoided: the disturbing father is eliminated without resort to patricide. He may, like Theseus, be sent alive to the underworld; like the old Hamlet, he may wander as a ghost from the nether regions. He may, like the old Moor, be imprisoned in subterranean cell. He may, like the son in Gerstenberg's drama, be buried alive. In all cases, he is eliminated without patricide.

In Euripides' *The Phoenician Women,* besides hatred toward the father, love for the mother and the sister is also suggested. This probably explains Schiller's interest in this work specifically. When Jocasta once again sees her son Polynices, she says:

> My child, oh, my child!
> Now, after so many thousand days, I at last see
> Your face again. Oh, let your mother's arm embrace you. Let
> Me rest with you, cheek to cheek. May the richly luxuriant
> Curling forest of your shining black hair shade my neck.
> Oh, joy, oh, joy! Finally now,
> So unexpected, unforeseen, in your mother's arms!
> How can hand and eye, word and glance, or foot
> Dancing circles around you
> In such ecstasy
> Ever have their fill, intoxicated
> With the joy of former happiness?

It should also be remarked that in *Scholia in Homeri Iliadem,* which relates the plot of the *Oedipodeia* (4.375), Astymedusa's slander of her stepsons is provided as a motivation for the curse Oedipus pronounces over his sons. She claims they have attempted to dishonor her (cf. Roscher 1884–1937). This is probably a late construction parallel to the incestuous crime of the father. From the Phaedra fable, we are familiar with slander by the stepmother as a form of defense against the son's incestuous passion.

In *The Phoenician Women,* one also finds a tender suggestion of sibling love. Upon seeing her brother from the walls of the city, Antigone says:

> Oh, if only my foot could rush with the clouds in the wind
> Through the skies, swiftly flying
> To my brother's breast. If only my arms could embrace
> His neck—beloved, unhappy fugitive—
> After so long!

Antigone's love for her brother Polynices is the central theme in Sophocles' *Antigone*. Antigone buries the body of her beloved brother Polynices against Creon's express command, though she knows she must atone for this deed with her death. Yet she is glad to die for her brother. Here again we observe the theme of shared death. In addition to this devoted attraction of siblings, other incestuous impulses are addressed in the drama. On Creon's command, Antigone is imprisoned in an underground cell to die of starvation (the typical death by starvation during imprisonment). However, Creon's son, her cousin Haemon, who is in love with her, penetrates her cell to save her. He threatens his father, who wishes to stop him, with his sword:

> With wild eyes the son now stares at him.
> Scorn in his face, he draws in response
> His two-edged sword. Though swiftly drawn,
> His father evades it. Then the miserable one turns
> Its savage blade upon himself; where he stands, raising his arm,
> Deeply he pierces his breast with the blade. Still conscious
> He falls into the limp embrace of his beloved,
> And gasping he pours out his life in a swift stream,
> On her white cheeks now blood red.

Here again the shared death represents the sexual union, prohibited in reality. In addition, the suicide occurs as an expression of defense against the murderous impulses directed toward the father. When Haemon's mother learns of the death of her son, she kills herself in order to follow him.

In his first tragedy, *La Thébaïde, ou Les frères ennemis* [The Thébaïde, or The inimical brothers] (1664), the young Racine dealt with the hatred of Polynices and Eteocles. Its subtitle, *The Inimical Brothers,* was also adopted by Schiller for his tragedy *Die Braut von Messina*. Other correspondences are also to be found that leave no doubt as to Schiller's literary dependence on Racine. It should be noted that the introductory scene of *Die Braut von Messina* is quite similar to act 4, scene 3 of Racine's drama.

As Schiller did later, Racine derives the hatred of the brothers from infantile sources so that it actually lacks logical justification:

Creon: But if he yields rulership to you,
You must, it seems to me, temper your hatred.
Eteocles: But it is not his avarice I hate.
No, it's he himself I hate!
Unyielding enmity burns within me.
This enmity is not the fruit of one year;
It was born with us, Creon. With life,
Its dark anger surged into our hearts.
From earliest childhood . . . no, what am I saying?
We were already enemies at our birth.
Such were the unwholesome consequences
Of our parent's unholy marriage bond.
. . . .
Indeed, it would displease me if he
Were to render rulership to me: he should rather
Flee from here—not go peacefully from me.
I wish to render him no half-enmity.
I fear his friendship, Creon, more than his anger.
May his anger justify my own,
Opening the floodgates of my burning hatred.

Here Racine clearly expresses that the struggle for rulership is only a theme superimposed on the unconscious infantile rivalry. Here we also find a clear expression of the mechanism of justification. The one brother wishes for the other's hatred and even provokes him to justify his own hatred. In Racine's drama, too, Haemon loves his cousin Antigone, but he is killed when he attempts to separate the two fighting brothers. After Haemon's death his father, Creon, hopes for the hand of Antigone, his niece, in marriage. Thus father and son are suitors competing for the same woman. This appears to be a completion and an explanation of their enmity, unmotivated in Sophocles' work.

Further dramatic versions of the conflict of the Theban brothers are listed by Constans (1881, 385 ff.). Brief mention should be made of the *Thébaïde* by Jean Robelin (1684) and of an imitation of Racine's drama by Luisa Bergalli, *La Teba* (1728). Alfieri also addressed this theme in *Polinice:* Aeschylus's *Seven against Thebes, The Phoenician Woman* by Euripides, and *The Phoenician Women* by Seneca served as his models. In Alfieri's drama, too, Oedipus has already been imprisoned for three years. Alfieri's drama was imitated by Gabriel Legouvé in his *Etéocle et Polynice* (1799). In his *Timoleone* as well, Alfieri addressed the tragedy of the mother standing between the two inimical brothers (cf. his Carlos drama, chap. 4).

Atreus and Thyestes

Like the hatred of Polynices and Eteocles, the hatred of the brothers Atreus and Thyestes cannot be documented as a purely mythological tradition. Homer, who relates in detail the family drama of the house of Agamemnon, son of Atreus (*Odyssey* 3.262–314 and 11.405–39), reports nothing of the fearful deeds of his ancestors (Tantalus and Atreus). He considers the crimes to have begun with the descendants of Atreus (*Odyssey* 11.437). As commented in Roscher's *Lexicon,* Hyginus's version of the legend of the Pelopides, Atreus and Thyestes (legends 87, 88, 252), seems to be based on later epic and tragic poets. Just as the brother hatred of Eteocles and Polynices is depicted as the consequence of their parents' crimes, the legends of Atreus and Thyestes could have arisen, as suggested in Roscher's *Lexicon,* from the need to derive the crimes in the house of Agamemnon from an earlier generation, thus justifying them to an extent. The details of the legend important for us were presented in the discussion of the Tantalide legend (chap. 9). The brother's hatred flares up in their conflict over a woman. Thyestes seduces the spouse of his older brother, and the terrible revenge contrived by Atreus then leads to the further acts of cruelty. Here the justification of the brother hatred in sexual rivalry is clearly pronounced, and once again we see only the childhood rivalry for the love of mother or sister perpetuated in mature sexual life. That in this case the plot deals not only with the brothers' love for the same woman but with the seduction of the wife only confirms our belief that the conflict ultimately arises from competition over the mother and that in his older brother Thyestes sees only a substitute for the father. In depictions by many playwrights, the presentation of the theme is strengthened in that Thyestes is portrayed as being in love with Aerope even before her marriage to Atreus. Thus the older brother takes the beloved woman from the younger brother just as the father takes the (step)mother from the son. Thus, in Voltaire's *Pélopides,* Thyestes says:

> But I shall tell you that before the fatal marriage
> My rival celebrated in this sacred place,
> I loved, I idolized the daughter of Eurystheus.
> . . . .
> Indeed, it was from me one dared abduct her.
> If despair was ever warranted . . .

Similarly, in Christian Weisse's *Atreus and Thyestes* (2.4), Thyestes says to his brother:

She was already mine before you forced her
Into the fetters I have sprung.

In its various forms and versions, the legend of Atreus and Thyestes was already very popular among the tragedians of antiquity. Jakob (1907) names nine Greek playwrights, among them Sophocles and Euripides, and nine Roman playwrights who produced dramatic versions of the legend under various titles. Of these dramas, though, only one has come down to us complete—Seneca's *Thyestes*. This tragedy was very popular among later dramatists. It has been translated into many languages and has also been imitated more or less closely by modern playwrights. Jakob (1907, 19) lists twenty-five translations in Germanic and Romance languages: ten in French, four in Italian, four in English, six in German, and one in Spanish. He also lists (p. 25) eleven imitations or more or less independent modern adaptations of the material: six in French, two in Italian, one in English, and two in German. The main sources for these Thyestes dramas were Seneca's *Thyestes* and Hyginus (legend 88). The plot of Seneca's drama is as follows. Angered by his wife's adulterous relations with Thyestes, Atreus decides to take frightful vengeance upon his brother: he will serve Thyestes his own sons, conceived in adultery, as a meal. Atreus tricks his brother into approaching him by pretending to want a reconciliation. With his three sons, Olisthenes, Tantalus, and a young boy, Thyestes comes to the palace of Atreus. He is received by his brother in a friendly manner and offers him his own sons as a guarantee of good faith. Atreus proposes to his brother that the two share rulership. Then a messenger tells the chorus that Atreus has killed his brother's sons, cooked them, and served them to their own father; he has served him their blood to drink. This final vengeance is enacted before the spectators. Thyestes places to his lips the goblet filled with the blood of his sons. Then the lights are extinguished, the sun is eclipsed, the thunder rolls, and the table falls in pieces to the quaking earth. When Thyestes asks in terror for his sons, Atreus spitefully asks him whether he can still recognize them in the bloody remains. Then Thyestes cries out the now famous words: "Agnosco fratrem" [I recognize my brother]. When Atreus finally discloses to him that he has eaten the flesh of his own sons, Thyestes flees his frightful brother, cursing him.

Hyginus (legend 88) relates the subsequent course of events. (A more detailed account is found in the discussion of the Tantalide legend, chap. 9.) In Sicyon, Thyestes rapes his unrecognized daughter, Pelopia. He then visits King Thesprotus, leaving soon thereafter. Since an oracular pronouncement demands that Thyestes be brought back, Atreus appeals to Thesprotus. There he falls in love with his niece, Pelopia, whom he believes is the daughter of Thesprotus. He takes her back to Argos as his wife. There Pelopia bears Aegisthus, actually sired by her father, but believed by Atreus to be his own son. When Aegisthus is a youth, Thyestes falls into Atreus's hands. Atreus commands Aegisthus to kill Thyestes (the youth's own father). Before the deed can occur, though, all is revealed. Pelopia kills herself. Aegisthus murders Atreus on the bank of the river and becomes heir to the throne with his father.

From these traditions, modern playwrights have generally selected isolated episodes, while modifying the others or inventing new ones. Some of these invented themes again exhibit the typical character of literary presentations of the material arising from the underlying incestuous tendencies. Thyestes' incest with his daughter is the only example of incest in the myth. Indeed, the myth concerns mainly the murder of relatives and the hatred of father and brother. Still, these apparently asexual passions reveal the incestuous emotions of love underlying them. This is demonstrated, for example, by the seduction of the brother's wife. The playwrights now confirm for us the correctness of these associations: based on their own unconscious emotions, they provide the love impulses complementing the impulses of hatred attested in the myth. Thus, in his *Thyestes* (1681), the English playwright John Crowne introduces love of the sister as a complement to hatred toward the brother. Thyestes has raped his brother's wife Aerope. The fruit of this union is Philisthenes. Antigone, the daughter of Atreus and Aerope, and thus Philisthenes' half-sister, loves this youth passionately. She attempts unsuccessfully to flee, but Atreus feigns reconciliation. He promises Philisthenes Antigone's hand in marriage and has Thyestes summoned back. The half-siblings are wed with great ceremony. But immediately after the wedding, Atreus murders Philisthenes and serves his flesh and blood to Thyestes. Finally Aerope kills the hated Thyestes, and Antigone ends her own life. Jakob (1907, 57) expressly notes that the half-siblings' love episode is clearly an invention.

In his tragedy *Atrée et Thyeste,* Crébillon adapts the material in a similar fashion. Atreus raises Philisthenes, the son of his wife Aerope and Thyestes, as his own son. He hopes some day to use Philisthenes, who believes himself to be a son of Atreus, in the murder of Thyestes. This detail is an imitation of Aegisthus's supposed patricide. But the playwright also modifies the incest between father and daughter, which does not mesh well with hatred of the brother. Instead he introduces love for the sister: Philisthenes loves Theodamia, a daughter of Atreus born to him by another wife. When Philisthenes, warned by the voice of nature, refuses to murder Thyestes, Atreus reveals to him that he is Thyestes' son. Thus both patricide and incest with the sister are prevented. Jakob correctly compares and contrasts this portrayal and that of Crowne (1907, 28):

> The theme of criminal love between brother and sister is common to the English and French dramatists. But the English tragedy differs from the French one in that the lovers have the same mother and different fathers, whereas in the French one they share a father but have different mothers. Another difference is that in Crébillon's drama, Theodamia and Philisthenes do not at first know of their close relationship. Only later is it revealed to them, at which time they renounce their passions. With Crowne, on the other hand, Antigone and Philisthenes are fully aware of their relationship but nevertheless marry without hesitation. Given French sensibilities, Philisthenes had to renounce his love as soon as he recognized his beloved as his sister. During the Restoration, though, English spectators were not yet offended by incest.

Crowne's psychological motivation for presenting the conscious incestuous passion is probably to be found in the fictive nature of the relationship—in the certainty that this passion will not be realized; the playwright and the public knew that the wedding was only a ruse of Atreus. Jakob also concludes that in Crébillon's drama the [step]sibling love episode could be the playwright's own invention.

In his *Pelopée* (1733), Abbé Pellegrin complicates the material in a more interesting way. As a complement to the supposed patricide, he introduces attempted incest with the mother. Aegisthus falls in love with his mother, Pelopia. He abducts her from Thyestes (his father), who is secretly married to her (his own daughter), and brings her to Atreus. Here we find the typical incestuous impulses of the son. Without recognizing her, he falls in love with his own mother and takes her from his father, of whose identity he is also unaware. Concerning this portion of the plot, I quote Jakob (1907, 101):

> Through a coincidence, Atreus discovers that Aegisthus is the son of Thyestes. The king, plotting revenge, immediately decides to convince the son to murder his father. He promises the youth Pelopia's hand in marriage if he will kill Thyestes. Atreus does not suspect that she is Aegisthus's mother. At first the youth objects to the murder plan, but when he discovers that Pelopia loves Thyestes, whom he now considers his rival, he agrees to carry out the deed. In the meantime, Atreus has persuaded Pelopia to reveal her secret marriage to Thyestes. Now he also knows that Aegisthus is her child. He conceives the diabolical plan of actually solemnizing the marriage of Aegisthus and Pelopia, Aegisthus's own mother. But first the youth must kill his father. Thyestes and Aegisthus are about to approach each other at the site of combat when Sostrate rushes up to them and reveals their close relationship. Thus patricide is still avoided. At the same time, the youth laments that Pelopia is his mother.

Here we gain insight into the psychologically interesting fact that playwrights derive the typical impulses of hatred between father and son or between brothers from incestuous sources by supplementing the corresponding impulses of love with material from the unconscious. Of course this does not always occur in the same context, as was the case with the playwrights above. Instead, this may occur in distinct works.

Thus Lessing's friend in youth, Christian Felix Weisse, whose *Atreus and Thyestes* (1766) we discussed above, dealt with sibling love in another tragedy. In his tragedy of the Pelopides, the inimical brothers recede into the background. Instead he places the supposed patricide in the foreground. In *Sophie, oder Die Brüder* [Sophie, or The brothers], Weisse deals with love for the sister. According to Minor (1890), the plot of this drama is as follows: Sophie is in love with her stepfather's younger son, Ferdinand. To save the family fortune, though, her stepfather has decided that she must marry his elder son, Karl. The lovers decide to flee, but Karl intercepts them, bringing Sophie to the altar by force. He then takes her to the marriage bed sedated with opium. When Ferdinand attempts to abduct her again, Karl attacks him with a sword. Sophie thrusts herself between the hostile brothers and is pierced by the sword. Karl then claims that Ferdinand is her murderer, but Ferdinand demonstrates his innocence by stabbing himself to death. The father, who had suspected nothing of his younger son's love for Sophie, now punishes Karl.

Here, besides love for the sister and hatred toward the brother, hatred toward the father also plays a role. In an original drama, *Pleisthenes,* Euripides also dealt with the hatred between father and son in the legend of Atreus and Thyestes (cf. Hyginus, legend 86). Having been banished, Thyestes raises Pleisthenes, a son of Atreus, as his own son. When Pleisthenes has grown, he sends him to murder Atreus, whom the youth does not know is his father. He is apprehended, however, and Atreus, falsely believing that he is punishing his brother's son, kills his own son (cf. Roscher 1884–1937).

The love affairs of Aerope were often dealt with by the tragedians as well. It had once been prophesied to her father that he would die by the hand of one of his children. Therefore he handed her and her sister over to Nauplius with instructions to sell them abroad. Nauplius brought them to Argos, where Aerope married Pleisthenes. From this marriage, according to one tradition, sprang Agamemnon and Menelaus. According to other traditions, though, she bore these children not to Pleisthenes but to Atreus. Therefore it has been supposed that she married first Pleisthenes and then his son or father, Atreus. After her separation from Thyestes, Atreus had her cast into the sea and served Thyestes his three sons as a meal. This myth was adapted by Sophocles in his tragedy *Atreus and the*

Mycenaean Women and by Euripides in *Kressai* [The Cretan women] (cf. Nauck 1889; Welcker 1839–41).

Nero and Britannicus

Seneca, in whose tragedy *Thyestes* love for the sister is barely suggested, dealt, like Weisse, with this complement to the brother hatred of Atreus and Thyestes in the tragedy *Octavia* (attributed to Seneca). Octavia, the daughter of Claudius, was wedded to her stepbrother, Nero, through the efforts of Agrippina, Nero's mother and the second wife of Claudius. This occurred after the murder of Silanus, Octavia's betrothed. Tacitus (12.4) reports how this was brought about: "Thus, in order to gain favor with Agrippina, Vitellius joined in her plans. In secret he prepared accusations against Silanus, who did indeed have a beautiful and frivolous sister, Junia Calonia, who had also been Vitellius's own daughter-in-law quite recently. The basis of the accusations was linked to her: Vitellius portrayed the relationship of the siblings, not incestuous but less than cautious, in a scandalous light. The emperor gave credence to these accusations; owing to his love for his own daughter, he was more inclined to believe ill of his son-in-law." After the murder of Silanus, Octavia's father, Claudius, was also killed by his wife, Agrippina, who is then supposed to have seduced her own son Nero to commit incest (cf. chap. 3). In addition to Nero's marriage to his stepsister, we note also his hatred for the stepsister's brother, Britannicus. Nero had Britannicus poisoned during a meal; he collapsed before his sister's eyes. Later Nero wished to rid himself of his stepsister and spouse, Octavia, in order to wed Poppaea Sabina. In Seneca's drama the people support Octavia, and in his anger Nero orders her death. Seneca's drama is introduced by a dialogue between Octavia and her nurse, accompanied by the chorus. In the dialogue, the crimes that have occurred in Nero's house are presented to the spectators. After Nero has divorced her and married Sabina, Octavia remarks characteristically that she is glad she is now only the sister of the emperor.

Contrastingly, in his own drama Alfieri portrays Octavia's passionate love for her stepbrother Nero. This drama deserves notice as a complement to his numerous tragedies of brother hatred. In his *Britannicus* (1669), Racine portrays the murder of Nero's stepbrother. Portions of Schiller's translations from this work have been preserved. In Racine's drama, too, the sexual source of this brother hatred is clear. Nero has Britannicus's beloved, Junia, abducted and falls in love with her himself. In Racine's *Bajazet* (1672) as well, hatred between the two brothers, Sultan Amurat and Prince Bajazet, is central to the plot. In *Bajazet*, though, rivalry over the same woman, Amurat's favorite Roxane, is suggested only in its defensive form.

Schiller's Predecessors: Sturm und Drang

Whereas the fratricide dramas discussed thus far seem closely related and dependent on one another through their common plot, the works we shall discuss below can claim greater psychological importance insofar as they are more or less independent of one another. Indeed, they arose almost simultaneously, and it is only through their shared theme that they form a single group. It is characteristic of Schiller's epoch that in the Schröder-Ackermann competition for the best original tragedy in German in 1775, three dramas dealing with fratricide were submitted: Leisewitz's *Julius von Tarent, Die unglücklichen Brüder* [The unhappy brothers] by an unnamed playwright (Sauer suspects that the drama is a first draft of Berg's *Galora von Venedig* [Galora of Venice]), and finally Friedrich Klinger's *Die Zwillinge* [The twins], which won first prize. In brief, the plot of *Julius von Tarent* is as follows. The sons of the prince of Trento, Julius and Guido, both love Blanca, who has become a nun. The father wishes to wed his heir, Julius, to Cecilia, the daughter of his sister, but Julius abducts Blanca in order to flee with her. However, Guido waits in ambush for them and murders his brother. Here again we find the typical struggle of two brothers over the same woman. The father's hatred, developed beside the brother's jealousy, suggests that behind this woman lies the primal image of the mother. Leisewitz was inspired to write the drama after reading the fictitious account of Cosimo I, grand duke of Florence. On December 21, 1799, he wrote to the librarian Reinwald, Schiller's brother-in-law: "I first got the idea for this drama from the tale of Cosimo I, grand duke of Florence, and his sons Giovanni and Garsias. However, since I found neither the characters nor the historical details especially pleasing, I chose this middle ground between history and invention." According to the historical accounts, the younger son, Garsias, a prince with wild, untamed passions, killed his elder brother during a hunt. He is also supposed to have been stabbed to death by his avenging father when brought to confess before his brother's bier. Strangely, a similar event occurred in the Medici family less than one hundred years before the reign of Cosimo I (cf. Minor 1890, 138).

Giuliano, the grandson of an earlier Cosimo di Medici, and Francesco Pazzi both loved a certain Camilla. Giuliano married her. In revenge, Francesco, with Bernardo Bandini, attacked the Medicis in church, and Giuliano was killed. Leisewitz uses the names "Julian," "Franz," and "Blanka" (Cosimo's granddaughter). That Julian is portrayed as an intimate friend of Franz only increases their similarity to the inimical brothers of the later period (cf. Minor 1890, 138). As may be supposed from the titles of lost works written in youth (*Kosmos von Medicis; Die Verschwörung der Pazzi gegen die Mediceer* [The Pazzi conspiracy against the Medicis]), Schiller was also familiar with this background material. At approximately the same time, it was adopted in Germany by Brandes (1775) and soon thereafter in Italy by Alfieri in his tragedy *La congiura dei Pazzi* [The Pazzi conspiracy]. In his published discussion of his tragedy *Don Garzia,* which deals with the same material, Alfieri declares: "A brother who kills a brother and a father who avenges his dead son by killing another; surely, if ever there was a violent and terrible catastrophe—one occurring at a time of supreme piety—it was this one" (1803, 6:160). Alfieri became familiar with the material from Niccolò Machiavelli's account of Florentine history, in which the conspiracy of the Pazzis is discussed (book 8).

The name of the woman loved by both brothers in the story of the Pazzis, Camilla (family name: Cafarelli), made its way not only into the plot of Schiller's *Die Räuber,* but also into Klinger's *Die Zwillinge.* In that work Guelfo hates his twin brother, Fernando, and is in love with his brother's bride, Camilla. Although they are referred to as twins, Fernando enjoys the rights of primogeniture and has been declared heir by the father. Guelfo, however, is not satisfied with this arrangement. He turns to Dr. Galbo and his mother to ask which of the twins first saw the light of day. Since the mother names Fernando, he feels that she loves him [Guelfo] less. The mother's preference for Fernando corresponds to Camilla's preference for him, for she is only a substitute for the original relationship to the mother. Here it is clear that jealousy toward the same-sex firstborn derives from incestuous passions, for the firstborn can claim the love of the parent of the opposite sex at the expense of a younger sibling. Thus the younger sibling feels he has been unfairly disadvantaged. Hatred toward elder siblings is also based in part on their more advanced sexual development. Klinger, who was probably a "younger son" himself (he had a brother and a sister, Agnes) seeks to circumvent the disadvantaged position of the second-born by making the brothers twins. But since Fernando, despite this circumstance, still enjoys the rights of the firstborn, the ambiguous character of this unsuccessful attempt at compromise is clearly revealed.

In the very first scene, Grimaldi mentions that in a dream, Guelfo has cried out: " 'Fernando'—as one calls one's deadly foe." Finally Guelfo indeed kills his brother Fernando in the forest. By the time he comes home following the murder, he has repressed the memory of the event: "*Guelfo*: I've slain no one, I know no—age! I had no brother!" We are already familiar with this form of defense. Beside the body of the slain brother, however, the memory of the murder comes back to him and he freely confesses it, whereupon his father, the old Guelfo, slays him. This death scene is better motivated than in Leisewitz's drama, for the young Guelfo hates his father; for him, death by his father's hand is welcome not only as a punishment for his brother's murder, but also as an expression of defense (punishment) against his own murderous impulses toward the father. But his hatred of his father is also motivated. The mother does love her son Guelfo. She says to him: "You shall have this kiss! You shall have it, pressed from your mother's lips, my wild son Guelfo! Do not resist, Guelfo, this kiss with all your mother's love!"

However, Guelfo is convinced that she prefers his brother—a motivation for his own hatred now familiar to us as justification; since the mother actually prefers Guelfo, despite his conviction that she prefers his brother, it is clear that we are dealing here with justification. "Is it not so, my Guelfo? You love your mother, who loves you so, who sighs and prays day and night that you will be kind and return her love. My strong Guelfo, let me rest beside you. You have been so kind to me this hour and your whole life through."

But for his own justification, Guelfo requires the conviction of his mother's preference for his brother. This is reminiscent of Hebbel, who in his youthful poetry introduced the mother's preference for the brother as a justification for his own hatred, though he himself was apparently the preferred son. Thus Guelfo says to his mother: "Weep! Weep! Lament! Go running to your Fernando, Mother!"

Here the incestuous source of the jealousy toward the firstborn brother and the deepest motivation for the murder are clearly pronounced. This is the supposed or actual preference by the mother for the elder brother. Further, in the context of the mother's incestuous affection, we also observe the identity in name of father and son. Psychologically, this identity in name is only an expression of this affection and demonstrates the identification of father and son from the mother's perspective. In act 3, when Guelfo is taking leave of his mother, his own affection is also expressed:

> *Guelfo:* Farewell, Mother! Mother, farewell!
> *Amalia:* Oh, Guelfo, not so! In the morning I'll softly creep to you. In only a few hours the night will be spent. I shall see you. . . .
> *Guelfo:* Good night, glorious mother!
> *Amalia* (turning at the door): Good night! Good night, dearest Guelfo!

Thus the relationship of Amalia to her son is depicted just like that of two lovers. From her words beside the body of her son, it is clear that she also conceives of her relationship to her sons in this manner: "No! No! My only one did not do this! Does he not love his mother? Would he slay her beloved?" Like Leisewitz's tragedy, this drama also had a strong influence on Schiller's first production. Given the importance of names in literary works, it is entirely possible that in his use of the name "Amalia" in *Die Räuber* Schiller was influenced by the Amalia of *Die Zwillinge*, for Amalia von Edelreich takes the place of the spouse with respect to the old Moor and the place of a sister with respect to the brothers. (Originally, the Amalia of *Die Räuber* had been called Camilla, the name of the young woman loved by both brothers in *Die Zwillinge.*) This association of the young woman loved by both brothers with the mother and sister also accounts for the fact that in most dramas of brother hatred the mother is absent: she is implicitly present in their common beloved. Thus Klinger's Amalia may have had an influence on Schiller's *Die Räuber.*

Similarly, Klinger's drama *Die falschen Spieler* [The false players] seems to reflect elements of Schiller's work. In *Die falschen Spieler,* just as in *Die Räuber,* the two sons' mother is lacking, and Juliette, like Amalia in *Die Räuber,* is "a distant relative" of the old Stahl, whose son Franz is slandered by his stepbrother Karl in a falsified letter and therefore falls victim to the stepbrother's plots. Here too, as in *Die Räuber,* the two sons are named Franz and Karl. Klinger, though, makes them stepbrothers, a dampening that seems like an expression of defense against the intensification of the conflict of the twin brothers. In Klinger's works these extreme treatments of the theme of brother hatred reveal his intense psychological involvement in these creations, for he does not depict his actual relationship with his elder brother. Instead, in *Die Zwillinge* he attempts to conceal his hatred toward the firstborn through the twin theme, while in *Die falschen Spieler* he attempts to reduce its force through the stepbrother theme. Only in the first drama of his youth, *Otto,* does the theme of fratricide by the younger brother present itself (cf. Sauer 1901). In this drama the father has a falling-out with his son because the son has married the daughter of the father's enemy. The son strives for the throne, although his father and elder brother both lay claim to it. Inimical brothers appear also in Klinger's *Stilpo.*

In considering other playwrights who have dealt with the theme of inimical brothers, one should note especially Voltaire's *L'enfant prodigue* [the prodigal son], which was not without its influence on Schiller's *Die Räuber.* Indeed, this is revealed by the first title of Schiller's youthful drama, originally called *Der verlorene Sohn* [The lost son]. In Voltaire's work the father is a weak man who can easily be manipulated. The elder son, Euphémon, is a lascivious person who wanders about abroad, having been rejected and disinherited by his father. His betrothed has now been promised to his younger brother. Euphémon returns unrecognized to his homeland and takes on employment under his brother, reminiscent not only of Schubart's tale but also of Karl Moor's visit to his father's castle. In Voltaire's work, though, all ends happily: after being recognized and forgiven, Euphémon marries his bride.

Further, after writing a *Don Carlos,* Thomas Otway wrote a tragedy titled *The Orphan* (1680). Two brothers, Castalio and Polydor, love the same young woman, Monimia, who has been raised with them ("sister"). Castalio secretly marries her, and they agree upon a sign by which she will permit him to enter her chamber by night. The chamber is to be completely dark, and neither of the lovers is to say a word, lest suspicions be aroused. Polydor, however, has overheard the discussion of the secret sign but knows nothing of their marriage. Therefore he believes that in making use of the secret sign and going to Monimia in his brother's stead, he is doing no wrong. The next day, though, all is resolved. Castalio stabs his brother to death, whereupon Monimia takes poison and Castalio commits suicide.

In Beaumont and Fletcher's drama *The Bloody Brother, or Rollo, Duke of Normandy,* Koeppel (1895, 122) finds noticeable parallels to *Die Braut von Messina:* the inimical brothers, their comrades who intensify the conflict, the significant figure of the unhappy mother, the reconciliation of the brothers brought about by the mother's entreaties, and the murder of one brother by the other are all reminiscent of *Die Braut von Messina*. After murdering his younger brother, Otto, Rollo also has his elderly tutor executed for daring to report the deed. A sudden passion for Edith, his tutor's daughter, is his undoing: he is murdered in her house. In *The Elder Brother,* by the same authors, two brothers are also in conflict over a woman.

Of playwrights who have dealt with brother hatred or fratricide, Henry Fielding is also worthy of note. In *Tom Jones* he portrays two contrasting brothers. Mention should also be made of Richard Cumberland (*The Brothers*) and Jean-François Regnard (*Les Ménechmes, ou Les Jumeaux* [The Menaechmi, or The twins]). In *Das Mündel* [The ward] by August Iffland, two brothers again conflict bitterly over the love of a woman. In Stäudlin's ballad "Die Brüder," Karl is murdered at the door of the bridal chamber by his jealous brother (cf. Minor 1890).

22 The Tragedians of Fate

Do? Man himself does nothing.
He is ruled by hidden counsel,
And must do as it commands.

MÜLLNER

From our perspective it seems significant that the concept of the tragedy of fate, which to some extent materializes the inevitable destiny of the classical Oedipus legend, fully overlaps incest drama in content. This is true not only of the playwrights designated by literary historians as "tragedians of fate" but of all dramatic creations that, influenced by romanticism, make use of the dramatic technique expressed most clearly in the Oedipus tragedy: for example, Schiller's *Braut von Messina,* Grillparzer's *Die Ahnfrau,* Friedrich Fouqué's *Pilgerfahrt* [Pilgrimage], Achim von Arnim's *Auerhahn* [The capercaillie], and Ludwig Tieck's *Karl von Berneck,* among many others. The disastrous signs, omens, fateful pronouncements, and curses—the whole mystical apparatus of the tragedians of fate—are, like the classical conception of fate and the belief in oracles, the belief in demons, or the blaming of the devil, nothing but the tangible expression of the individual's unconscious impulses, whose effects are perceived as the influence of exterior evil forces and are projected outward in defense and justification. This fate, toward which man is driven against his conscious will by his repressed drives, regularly proves to be a reaffirmation of infantile incest impulses rejected by the adult and operating in the realm of literary fantasy. This fact is very valuable to us as proof of the playwright's powerful preoccupation with this complex, for we have recognized more and more clearly that the fantasies and affects corresponding to infantile incest impulses form the basis of the playwright's productive force.

Zacharias Werner

The plot of Zacharias Werner's tragedy *Der vierundzwanzigste Februar* [The twenty-fourth of February], well known as a paradigm of the tragedy of fate, is as follows. Kunz Kuruth has married Trude against his father's will. After his father has once again made disparaging remarks about his wife, Kunz flings a knife at him but misses. Still, anger and shock bring about the father's death. Dying, he curses his son and his descendants. That the father is not killed directly by his son's knife, but only indirectly, can easily be understood as the expression of defense against the impulse to murder the father. This is all the more true since the fate of Kunz's father seems well deserved. Kunz justifies his deed to himself with the thought that his father had once grasped by the hair his own father, who had often tormented him, and brought him to the ground; Kunz's father had revealed this once while intoxicated. Trude then bears a son, and five years later a daughter. On the anniversary of his grandfather's death, the seven-year-old boy sees his mother slaughtering a cock. He then plays cook and cock with his own sister, slitting her throat—naturally using the same knife that Kunz had used against his father. Kunz curses his son and in his anger wishes to murder him, but the mother saves him and sends him to relatives. The parents are on the brink of financial ruin. After some years, the now wealthy son returns to his place of origin and takes lodgings with them for the night; they fail to recognize him. After a conversation among the three, somewhat reminiscent, in its hints of relationship, of the revelation in Sophocles' *Oedipus,* the son retires to his room and decides to delay until the next day the revelation that he is their son. While he sleeps, Kunz and Trude, influenced by mystical signs, attempt to rob him of his money. Half asleep, he cries out "Thieves! Murderers!" Then Kunz stabs him twice in the chest. Only too late does he learn that he has killed his own son. However, the curse upon the family has now been fulfilled.

Just as Kunz in effect kills his father, who had mistreated his own father, in the end he kills his own son as well, even though the son had initially been rescued by his mother. The theme of abduction, placed in the foreground (but seldom, as in real life, the actual driving force behind a murder), obscures the more deeply rooted complex of jealousy, barely hinted at in the drama. Yet we recognize rivalry over the mother as the deepest source of enmity between father and son, and if this is not apparent in the drama, the recapitulation in three successive generations of the enmity between father and son, a significant affective remnant, suggests an underlying repressed complex associated with the mother's love. This complex was expressed in Werner's peculiar love life, his Don Juanism, his three unhappy marriages, and his deep sense of personal guilt. It is well known that Werner was deeply devoted to his mother. He even traveled with his third wife to Königsberg to care for his mother, who was suffering from a mental disorder. The date of her death, February 24, 1804, then became the title of his tragedy. Through this significant "mark" [*Marke*] alone, the work is characterized as a typical incest drama with exaggerated emphasis on father hatred, increased through the repression of erotic love for the mother.

Adolf Müllner

In 1810 Müllner founded an amateur theater in Weissenfels. Comedies were performed, and Müllner himself sometimes appeared as an actor. On February 24, 1812, Zacharias Werner's tragedy *Der vierundzwanzigste Februar* was performed on this stage; Müllner played the leading male role. Three months later he completed his own "February drama," *Der neunundzwanzigste Februar* [The twenty-ninth of February], and in October of the same year he completed the drama *Die Schuld* [Guilt]. We are familiar with this "personalization" of another playwright's material—filling an adopted form with the contents of one's own psyche—as a typical means of liberation from complexes and of justification. Further, it is only in a superficial sense that Müllner actually referred to his predecessor's "February drama." He made use of the mystical mood of the drama of fate and of Werner's technique of revelation, but he used these formal techniques to portray his own powerful complexes.

Therefore, when Müllner took up this material and shaped it further in the sense of the incest complex, he not only revealed his own unconscious impulses but also reinstated the actual meaning and psychological relation of the themes, isolated and disguised in Werner's drama. The content of Müllner's drama is as follows: Walter Hort is married to Sophie. They have a son, Emil, who is eleven years old. Ludwig Hort, Walter's uncle, returns from abroad—unrecognized—to Walter's home and reveals that Sophie is Walter's sister.

> *Stranger* (Ludwig): Walter, I am your uncle.
> Your wife is your sister.
> . . . .

> . . . God is angered,
> For the union mocks their father.
> And they mourn, having learned today
> That only separation can atone for him.
>
> *Walter* (starts up and grasps the deer hunter): Separation?
> *Sophie* (painfully): Separation?
> *Walter* (embracing Sophie): Never!
> Even if our father has died because of us.
> You are still mine, just as before.
> I have won you at a high price.
>
> *Sophie* (lamenting): After all, did we know who we were?

Thus, though they now know they are blood relatives, they do not wish to leave one another. This detail clearly reveals that ignorance of their kinship is only an expression of defense against incestuous impulses.

After this accidental sibling incest has been exposed, the incest, now conscious, calls forth powerful defense mechanisms demanding self-punishment. When Walter is about to kill himself, the young Emil cries out:

> Father, stop! Kill me first!
> . . . .
> . . . Have mercy, wed me
> With Klärchen, my bride!

Klärchen is his deceased sister. Thus Müllner introduces the sibling incest impulse in Walter's children as well. The young Emil's death wish can be clearly recognized as a symbolic expression of erotic affection:

> *Emil:* Do you still remember? In this very room
> We always played man and wife.
> You yourself married us!

Finally Walter plunges a knife into his little son's breast. Through this displacement, Walter escapes self-punishment, but in his son he punishes the forbidden sibling incest, for Emil also loves his own sister. Walter's impulses of paternal jealousy also lend intensity to his feelings against Emil, whom the mother loves with complete devotion.

The killing of the boy at his own wish and the sibling marriage later offended the Vienna censors; Müllner followed the advice of a friend and dampened the incest to a merely suspected sibling marriage, while portraying the killing of the child as unintentional. The drama was then performed in Vienna with the new title *Der Wahn* [The delusion].

Thus, whereas Werner avoids every incestuous affection, instead portraying the jealous emotions of hate in triplicate, Müllner reiterates the dominant complex of his psyche—sibling love—and suggests the rivalry complex in the dampened form of the unintentional killing of the son.

The sibling complex is central to Adolf Müllner's literary creativity; it seems to constitute the content and driving force of his entire literary production. In *Die Schuld,* Müllner's most effective drama, often performed and very popular in its day, the main theme is jealous rivalry with the brother for a woman's affections. The appearance of sibling love in connection with this theme indicates the underlying incest complex, in all probability originally parental. Corresponding to the unique technique of such dramas, the various emotions of the incest complex that are present in the background to the plot are gradually revealed or, as is often the case, merely suggested. This reflects the resistance of consciousness to recognizing these repressed wish fantasies.

The spouse of Edwin, the count of Örindur, is now expecting a child after many years of childless marriage. The fragile health of the countess requires a journey to a spa. There she brings a boy, Hugo, into the world, but the child dies soon after birth. Laura, a friend whom the countess has met at the spa, gives the desperate mother her own child of the same age so the count may be spared the bitter disappointment of his hopes. But Laura has her own reasons for this apparently noble gesture. She "loved her firstborn son beyond reason." While expecting her second child, her firstborn in her arms, she had come across a gypsy woman while taking a walk. She had refused the woman a small gift, and the woman had uttered the curse:

> For many days you'll be tormented
> Before you're delivered of your burden!
> If you bear a boy
> He'll strangle your firstborn;
> If a girl, he'll be her death,
> And you shall perish in sin!

Indeed, after days of suffering, she bore a boy whom she named Otto. Since the first part of the curse has now been fulfilled, she fears the fulfillment of the second part and thus relinquishes her child in order to avert fate. The countess of Örindur renames the boy after her deceased son Hugo and presents him as her son. Laura tells her husband, Valeros, that Otto has died. Only when she has borne a daughter, Jerta, does the countess reveal to the count the secret of Hugo's birth. However, the feudal lord makes Hugo his legal heir all the same. After Count Edwin's death Hugo ventures to Spain, where he was born and where he now hopes to find his true parents. There he meets Carlos, and soon the two become fast friends. Hugo and Elvire, Carlos's wife, fall passionately in love, and in a fit of jealousy Hugo shoots his friend Carlos in the forest. However, Carlos is the son of Valeros. Thus, without realizing it, Hugo has killed his own brother, as the fateful curse had predicted. After Carlos's identity has been revealed to him, Hugo justifies his deed with their mutual hatred and with his jealousy:

> I imagined I was killing my friend;
> That is all I can say.
> Carlos, eager to avenge a crime
> I did not commit,
> Was plotting my death. (Indicates Elvire)
> She sent me
> A word of warning.
>
> *Elvire:* Oh, God! It was
> Only my fear of the danger;
> Only the first anger!
>
> *Hugo:* No, indeed!
> I set out to make amends.
> . . . .
> Do you know what jealousy is? Its fire
> Drove me out into the forest!
> . . . .
> I was permitted to move a finger
> In order to lead Elvire back home.

Hugo and Elvire later marry and venture to Örindur's castle in the north. It is at this point that the drama begins. Just like Sophocles' *Oedipus*, the drama deals with the revelation of unknowingly committed acts. In the castle lives the unmarried Jerta, the countess of Örindur, considered Hugo's sister. Nevertheless, she loves him in a more than sisterly manner and says to his spouse, Elvire:

> We are competitors.
>
> *Elvire* (wounded): Sister!
>
> *Jerta:* Hugo, I fear, is
> Only the idol of your passions.
> (With intensity)
> I—I love him, soul for soul,
> As one loves above in the light.

The first revelation occurs when Hugo reveals to his supposed sister, Jerta, that he is not her brother. This revelation causes her to shrink back from her affection for him:

> The dream image has dissolved,
> Nature is unbound.

Never more may I embrace you
For you are no Örindur.
Between love and desire
The partition has fallen!

When Elvire discovers that Hugo and Jerta are not siblings, she believes that she has been deceived from the beginning:

That is why this sister
Impudently called herself
My competitor today.
. . . .
Why did she conceal
For months
From me, her friend,
That the bond of blood was lacking?
Hugo: You are unjust! It is because
I first told her today.

The revelation of the fratricide, central to the plot, is accomplished through Valeros's arrival at Örindur's castle. Although Carlos had supposedly committed suicide, Valeros is convinced that he was murdered and has undertaken a quest to find the murderer.

Wondering whether I'm fleeing him
Or approaching nearer to him
His ne'er-seen image stands before me
Ever shifting, mild and wild. (Approaches Hugo)
And—explain to me, Örindur,
This duplicity of nature!—
At times I wish to see his life, his blood
Flowing away; at times (softly, almost tenderly) I wish to forgive him.

Since the sought-after murderer is his own son (and also the brother of the murdered man), these words unconsciously reveal the split relationship of the father with his son. This reluctance to punish his son's murderer has a simple psychological explanation. It has been noted that Laura, Valeros's wife, had passionately loved her firstborn son, the murdered Carlos. To this affection on the part of the mother toward her son corresponds the father's hatred and jealousy towards this preferred competitor. Unconsciously, Valeros wished for his son's death. Therefore he cannot punish the one who has realized this wish, the murderer of his son, especially since the murderer himself is identical to the beloved yet hated son. His suspicion that his son did not die a natural death is also comprehensible in light of his unconscious reproach (conscience). Valeros's self-reproach expresses itself in the wish for self-punishment. He challenges Hugo to a duel and eggs him on in the hope of falling by his son's hand. Besides the tendency for self-punishment, hatred toward the son is also expressed in this challenge:

Valeros: Fratricide in my house!
This shame, by heaven, can be washed clean
By blood alone. Today is the day
He fell, and today Carlos's murderer,
Or I, shall fall as well.

Initially Hugo opposes the duel, but when Valeros calls him a coward, he becomes enraged:

Hugo (beside himself, raising his dagger): Death and hell!
Valeros (taking position and drawing his dagger):
At last! Come out, raging tiger,
And fall upon my breast.
Hugo (after a brief respite): No! Cursed be my hand
If it reveals this blade.
May rust devour it in its sheath.
Valeros (fighting with rising fury):
Ha! Let us fight on! If you dare not,
Boy, then die!
. . . . . .
We cannot both live!

He hurries toward Hugo to run him through, but Hugo stands quietly. Elvire, who has entered, runs up to them. She separates them, and soon, recognizing that they are father and son, they lie reconciled in one another's embrace.

Hugo (sinking, deeply moved): My father!
My God! In your arms?
Valeros: Otto! Dear one—only one!
All, may all be forgiven.

Hugo, however, sees only one means of atoning for his crime; he kills himself. From the words of the mortally wounded Hugo, it is clear that this suicide, as a self-punishment, arises from defense mechanisms against brother hatred and against the father hatred underlying it.

Jerta (approaching hastily and falling into his left arm):
Count! What are you doing?
Hugo (permitting the bloody dagger to fall at her feet):
'Tis already done, but poorly. I struck better at him.

Before his death, he wishes to save Elvire and advises her to flee. He hopes they will once again see one another

> There, where sister, friend, and wife
> Are loved with the same love.

Here again we see the identification of wife and sister in connection with the suspension of relationship. We observe also the symbolism of the shared death, for Elvire kills herself before Hugo's eyes.

Although the drama emphasizes less-than-subtle effects, at times it reveals, despite its crude form, such a correct perception of deep unconscious associations that we can regard it as a symptomatic expression of the playwright's own psychic conflict. This determination is fully supported by Müllner's biography and his unusual literary development. He was born in 1774 and raised in the home of his grandmother. Beginning in 1793, he studied law for some years. Only a few literary attempts date from his youth. The most significant of these is the two-volume novel *Der Incest, oder Der Schutzgeist von Avignon* [Incest, or The protective spirit of Avignon] dealing with the marriage of a brother and sister. When Müllner later became a lawyer, settled in Weissenfels, and entered society, the springs of his literary inspiration ran dry. Later, though, inspiration returned with renewed vigor. Nevertheless, in this period we still find the same psychic conflicts. In Goedecke's summary it is stated that "the theme of the rivalry of brothers over the same beloved formed the narrow frame of his literary inspiration. This can perhaps be partially attributed to the fact that he loved the young Amalie von Logau, promised to his older stepbrother, as much as he hated the stepbrother, who had tormented him since childhood." After his stepbrother's early death, he married Amalie at age twenty-eight. The marriage was not happy for long. His spouse soon became alienated from him, and this state lasted until Müllner's death. The sudden drying up and subsequent reanimation of his creative energies can be considered in parallel with the gratification of his infantile wishes arising from the parent complex. The reawakening of his creative energies can be attributed to this alienation, this "ungratification" of his childhood impulses. External circumstances served only as the immediate stimulus.

Actual circumstances in Müllner's life, as well as his neurotic perspective, are reflected most clearly in the story "Der Kaliber" [The caliber]. The entire tale, which reads almost like the account of a psychoanalysis, is formulated with the same revelatory technique employed in *Die Schuld*. Here follows a brief synopsis of the denouement alone. Ferdinand (behind whom lies Müllner's persona) is passionately in love with Mariane, the young woman originally promised to his older brother Heinrich, and she returns his love. While in the forest, the brothers begin to fight. Ferdinand attempts to strike his brother's hand with a pistol. The weapon fires, and Heinrich sinks down dead. Ferdinand reports to the magistrate that his brother has been shot by a murderer. He depicts events quite differently from the way he believes they occurred. He claims that he had gotten behind his brother and had suddenly heard cries for help. He claims further that it was his sudden approach that caused the murderer to fire the fatal shot. Before the magistrate, he expresses the most extreme self-reproach for having brought about his brother's death, claiming that various incidental circumstances, which he could have altered, led directly to Heinrich's death. He becomes depressed and finally insane. Two days before his wedding to Mariane, he declares that he is Heinrich's murderer. In the end, though, through the caliber of the weapon, the actual murderer is found. In the same moment as Ferdinand's pistol had discharged, a robber had shot Heinrich from the thicket. Thus his belief that he had killed his brother turns out to be unfounded, and his apparently false declaration to the authorities is revealed to be correct.

In its psychic mechanisms, this erroneous self-accusation of fratricide precisely parallels Karl Grillparzer's self-accusations; even the neurotic displacements coincide. With Ferdinand, too, resistance to the powerful wish to kill the brother becomes an obsessive idea leading him to perceive every misfortune that befalls his brother as the effect of this wish. With Müllner, this obsessive idea is only suggested, and in the scene portraying the supposed murder of the brother the psychic mechanisms of the obsessive idea are materially portrayed. Here again we encounter the association with money and suicide plans as a reaction to the murderous impulses felt toward the brother.

From his own life, as we have seen, Müllner carried over the theme of the rivalry of two brothers unaltered into his literary creations, which strongly resemble a confession. But only seldom do psychic inhibitions permit the direct revelation of repressed impulses. Thus in *Die Schuld,* besides Müllner's favorite theme, we also encountered the theme of supposed sibling love (Jerta), and in *Der neunundzwanzigste Februar* the theme of brother hatred is completely absent, whereas love for the sister is strongly emphasized. In other dramatic works by Müllner, as in *Die Schuld,* however, the rivalry of the inimical brothers over a woman does occur—compare *König Yngurd* [King Yngurd] and Müllner's last work, *Die Albaneserin* [The Albanian woman] (1820). Since Müllner appears to have had no sister, it seems that once again we have an example of the replacement of a resisted idea by the reaction against it, as observed with Grillparzer and Schiller. Just as Schiller regarded his sister's husband, his rival for her affections, as his brother, addressing him accordingly, Müllner regarded the woman for whom he competed with his brother as his sister.

This is also suggested in that in *Die Schuld* Hugo calls Elvire, his brother Carlos's wife, "sister." In act 3, scene 2, he says to Valeros: "Elvire was as dear to me as a sister." And in act 4, scene 8, he says to Elvire herself: "Carlos was my brother again, / And you were my beloved sister!"

From our knowledge of these mechanisms, we can conclude that displacements and replacements of the parental love object (the mother) by other persons, like those observed behind the fantasy figures of Schiller and Grillparzer, also played a role in Müllner's love for the sister. From this incestuous fixation on the mother, we can understand the rejection of sex by Müllner and many other playwrights, usually expressed later in life in passionate affection for an unattainable person or one with whom sex is forbidden. For Müllner, then, the woman he cannot possess because she has been promised to his brother becomes the woman he is not permitted to desire: the sister. Therefore, in life and in literature, wherever one encounters an obvious rejection of sex, though it may appear to be sufficiently motivated by a failure to pass beyond autoeroticism or by a displacement to homosexuality, one may conclude with certainty that it is ultimately derived from an original, underlying fixation on the incest complex. For incestuous tendencies are one of the sources of the rejection of sex in the adult—an aversion to fulfilling the real demands of love associated with exaggerated passion and the need for such passion. The individual incapable of dissociating these infantile impulses from the originally beloved objects of the immediate environment will, in the worst cases (psychoneurosis), be incapable of normal love for a new object. In less extreme cases, such an individual will always retain a certain aversion toward the new object. In this group belongs the creative artist. In incest dramas, his symptoms reveal that he has been unable to deal successfully, once and for all, with his incestuous impulses. In life, therefore, he nearly always loves "unhappily."

23 The Romantics

Bride and sister
You are to your brother.

WAGNER, *Die Walküre*

Even more than the tragedians of fate, from our psychological point of view every single representative of the romantic school, the effects of which are still seen in our modern art, would be worthy of investigation in a detailed and thorough monograph if one wished to illustrate exhaustively the immense significance of the incest complex for the love ideal and artistic creation of the romantics. According to Ostwald, classification as a romantic indicates only that an artist exhibits a certain psychological type. The discussion offered here can do no more than begin to demonstrate that emphasis on the incest complex was the special trait of the romantics. Given the extensive and varied material, our discussion must be restricted to a sketch of major points in the lives and works of the most important representatives of romanticism.

Ludwig Tieck

Ludwig Tieck not only provides a classic example of the initial breaking forth of the dramatic creative urge in the context of the incest complex but also serves as the clearest illustration of fixation on the incest complex and of failure to move beyond the affective level of puberty and its conflicts—a failure so characteristic of the romantic personality type. Tieck's first great tragedy, *Karl von Berneck,* written at the age of twenty (1793), shows all the characteristics of the incestuous tragedy of fate.

The Berneck family and its castle are plagued by an old curse. Every Saint John's eve, an icy gray specter walks about the castle. It is the ghost of the first owner, who murdered his brother. Whoever is greeted by the specter must die within the year. The ghost will continue to haunt the castle until one man of the family kills his own brother, without their being enemies. The drama begins with the return of the old and melancholy Walter, lord of the castle, after sixteen years spent on a crusade. Just as Agamemnon is killed by Aegisthus, Walter is killed by his wife's lover. Oppressed by the curse that has befallen the house, his younger son, Karl, also leads a melancholy existence. In revenge for his father's death, Karl kills his mother and her lover with the cursed old sword of his ancestor, used in murder before. Karl's older brother, Reinhard, has a more placid personality but becomes Karl's bitter enemy when he discovers that Karl loves and is loved by the gentle Adelheit von Orla, whose love Reinhard seeks to win for himself. Out of jealousy, he determines to murder his brother. He finds him sleeping but is suddenly moved to compassion. His thirst for murder is transformed into tender affection, and he voluntarily yields his beloved to his brother. Still, he cannot escape the curse. When the lovers are about to take each other's hands and seal their engagement, the murdered mother's ghost appears between them. Tormented by Furies, Karl demands that his brother kill him; he does not desist until Reinhard, tenderly embracing him, plunges a dagger into Karl's breast. Reinhard enters a monastery.

We already recognize the frequently intertwining themes of the plot as derived from the incest complex. In the foreground stands brother hatred due to love for the same woman and motivated by the curse. The impulses of repentance and defense are especially emphasized: the transformation of thirst for murder into tender affection; Karl's longing to die by his brother's hand; Reinhard's murder of his brother while tenderly embracing him. In this context the voluntary relinquishment of the common beloved to the competitor should also be viewed as a sentimental wish fantasy. From our discussion of the theme of relinquishment of the bride to the son, we are already familiar with the deeper sources of this fantasy in the parent complex. In Tieck's drama, too, beneath the superimposed sibling complex, the underlying parent complex still shines through clearly. Like Hamlet and Orestes, Karl von Berneck appears as the avenger of his father, who has been killed by the mother's lover upon returning home. Like Orestes, he not only murders the lover but, owing to unconscious, jealous impulses, murders his mother as well. These impulses are able to become conscious in the brothers' love for the same woman (the mother). Like Orestes, though, Karl is driven mad by the Furies of the murdered woman. The appearance of the mother's ghost between the betrothed lovers clearly suggests the son's incestuous affection for his mother: he can neither marry nor love any woman, because in every woman he sees his mother—because his "mother's ghost" stands between him and his beloved. In infantile fashion, he has fixated his love on his mother.

Based on this example, it will be of interest to observe in the individual psychic development of this playwright a mechanism completely characteristic of the drama of fate, which already found its classical expression in *Oedipus*. The sibling complex, strongly emphasized in Tieck's works, represents a displacement of the repressed parent complex of childhood and in the psyche lies constantly superimposed upon it, strengthened by the continuing presence of love for the sister. In dramatic works as well, the sibling complex comes to the fore; the deeper and more powerfully repressed parent complex, corresponding to its infantile origins, is projected back into the distant past and placed among the events before the plot of the drama in question. In *Karl von Berneck* the protagonist appears as the avenger of his murdered father, whom he, like Hamlet, can eliminate only in the guise of stepfather in love with his mother. However, one of the first stories written by the especially precocious Tieck at the age of eighteen still portrays the father complex directly. In the story "Abdallah" (1791), the protagonist, seduced by an infernal spirit, delivers his father to his deadly enemy the sultan, in order to win his own beloved, a daughter of the sultan. At the wedding feast he is overcome with the guilty emotions of a patricide. In their depiction, the youthful Tieck must have been acting in reaction to his hateful infantile perspective toward his strict father. This ambivalent perspective leads to splitting the father figure into the hated sire and the hating sultan. Thus the sultan's daughter is simultaneously characterized as a "sister." Like its complement in *Karl von Berneck*—the appearance of the slain mother between the wedded lovers—the awakening on the wedding day of pangs of conscience concerning the patricide indicates the sexual-incestuous roots of the hate and murder impulses.

In the same year he wrote *Karl von Berneck*, the productive twenty-year-old also produced a shorter drama, *Der Abschied* [The farewell] (1792), also involving the theme of the husband's return, a favorite theme retained in later works as well, whose incestuous significance we are familiar with from *Karl von Berneck*. The returning spouse is killed by the husband his beloved has married in his absence; this new husband kills her as well. In *Karl von Berneck*, this theme of killing the returning spouse appears as the realization of the typical infantile fantasy of the absence of the father (through travel or death). Here, though, the theme is employed in the context of the sibling complex. Luise, who has married a man she does not love, tells him that the picture of her absent beloved, which she keeps in her room, is that of her dead brother. This theme of the returning spouse is encountered in all of world literature, especially in folk songs, though it usually appears completely dissociated from its roots in the incestuous family complex. Still, it derives originally from the infantile incest complex and is comprehensible only from that perspective. This theme of the returning spouse, which also underlies the Agamemnon and Oedipus legends, is depicted from the son's point of view and represents his wishful fantasy: the impeding father is eliminated, and the son takes possession of the mother unhindered. This is clear not only in that the father is murdered—or in a later, sentimentally dampened version, voluntarily relinquishes the beloved to his competitor—but also from the typical infantile fantasy of the absence or departure of the father, who, like the father in the Phaedra schema, is believed (i.e., wished) dead. Yet the theme of the husband's return proves conducive to a later version depicted from the father's perspective, since in the guise of the stranger who arrives to disturb the marital relationship and finds his wife unfaithful, the fantasy of the young son who finds the mother already in the father's possession also finds expression (cf. my interpretation of the Lohengrin legend).

In Tieck's story "Die Versöhnung" [The reconciliation] (1795), the theme of the husband's return is employed in the following manner. Accompanied by a female friend dressed as a man, the wife ventures forth to meet her returning husband; the husband believes his wife is in the company of a lover and murders them both. The son of the returning husband and the murdered wife, wishing to seek adventure, now leaves the monastery where he has been living. In a cave, he meets his uncle, who was betrothed to his mother's murdered confidante. From him he learns that his father, having committed the hasty murder, can find no peace in death; the son releases his father through prayer.

This sentimental dampening of the son's revenge on his father for the ill treatment of his mother corresponds fully to Tieck's powerful defenses; Tieck's protagonists are thoroughly obsessed with pangs of conscience and psychological torment. The same experiences that underlie "Abdallah" and *Karl von Berneck* also form the basis of Tieck's first novel, *William Lovell* (1795–96), and even in 1815 Tieck commented that these themes would always continue to occupy him. In the novel, the father forbids his son's marriage, thus giving rise to all subsequent conflicts.

Besides the theme of the husband's return, derived from the parent complex, Tieck's passionate love for his sister played a major role in his literary works—usually involving the rivalry of two friends (brothers) over a woman—and also to an extent in his private life. The theme of incestuous sibling love is portrayed most clearly in the original tale "Der blonde Eckbert" [The fair-haired Eckbert] (1796). Eckbert lives with his wife, Berta, in a childless marriage; the couple live in nearly total seclusion. Only Eckbert's friend Walter visits them from time to time. At one point Berta tells Walter and Eckbert the story of her life. As a child, she had run away from her overly strict parents and had made her way to the home of an old woman living in the forest. Later she also left this woman's home and won Eckbert's love. In the course of her story, she reminds Walter of a forgotten name she had overheard in the old woman's home. Eckbert, becoming mistrustful and jealous, shoots his friend. Berta dies in anguish and psychological torment. Dying, the old woman reveals to Eckbert that his "friend Walter" is none other than she herself and that Berta is Eckbert's sister. Driven mad, Eckbert falls dead.

Here again the author's powerful defense mechanisms express themselves in that the discovery of the unknowingly committed sibling incest ends with insanity and death. By projecting his own psychic complexes onto his protagonist and thus freeing himself from his oppressive sensation of guilt, Tieck not only consistently depicted mental illness and insanity as favored themes, but did so with great mastery. It would be of much psychological interest to trace the highly complex figure of compromise, the old woman, back to its actual levels of significance. Here, though, only a brief discussion is possible. This compound character represents both the parents and the brother of the protagonist. She represents the parents in that she plays their role with respect to Berta, and in that Berta runs away from her home, just as she had run from her parents' home. It is especially her designation as "old woman" that suggests the mother. The mother is also suggested in that the old woman is killed by her "son," an event already noted in *Karl von Berneck*. That in *Karl von Berneck* the father is named Walter, just as is the old woman here transformed into a man, suggests especially the father; in "Abdallah," we have already observed the murder of the father. The designation "friend" suggests the brother (dampening, displacement); the brother is also suggested by Eckbert's jealousy toward Walter on account of his sister. The relationship (displacement) between love for the mother and love for the sister is also suggested here again and seems to point significantly to Tieck's childhood: it is generally supposed that the germ of this story arose from tales told to him by his mother. In the novella *Das Fest zu Kenilworth* [The celebration in Kenilworth] (1824), which depicts an episode from Shakespeare's youth, Tieck employs reminiscences of his own childhood and youth: he depicts the father as a strict puritan, while the boy, who lives in his fantasies, reads storybooks. Like Wieland's protagonists, Tieck's are primarily characterized by an excessive fantasy life; they all suffer from the contradiction between their environment and the expectations of their fantasy. It is clear that Tieck took these problems very seriously, however, for we know from psychoanalysis that these fantasies promote a clearly excessive degree of eroticism, the content of which usually leads to repression and guilt.

Tieck never tired of producing variations on the theme of rivalry with a friend over the common beloved, taken up in "Der blonde Eckbert" and derived from the infantile incest complex. It is appropriate to cite a few examples. In "Der Fremde" [The stranger] (1796), an unsuccessful suitor dies of grief when he is rejected by the woman he loves. In the forest outside the city, he then appears to his successful competitor, who has just returned from a voyage (theme of returning home). Without recognizing his competitor, the bridegroom invites him to the wedding. The former suitor does attend; the bridegroom finally recognizes him and falls dead with fright, while the bride goes mad. This fantasy of marriage thwarted by jealousy at the last minute melds almost indistinguishably the jealous attitude toward the parents and the brothers' rivalry over the sister. This fantasy is especially interesting, since one of Richard Wagner's earliest works of youth, *Die Hochzeit* [The wedding], reveals nearly the same thematic developments, derived from the same complexes. In Tieck's tale "Tannhäuser," the demented protagonist murders his friend's wife, whom he had once loved, and lures the friend into the Venusberg. Further, this theme of depriving the bridegroom of his bride appears in Tieck's later works as well. In the 1840 novella *Waldeinsamkeit* [Forest solitude], a devotee of forest solitude is abducted by means of a sleeping potion. In the end, though, he discovers before it is too late that he is being held in seclusion in order to deprive him of his bride.

The tale "Liebeszauber" [Love magic], which arose fifteen years after "Der blonde Eckbert," is modeled on the same schema as the earlier tale, though the depiction of sibling incest is cut short. A young man happens to notice a young woman of the neighborhood as she ritually sacrifices her young foster daughter; the woman hopes the ceremony will win her his love. Seeing this, he becomes deranged for a time. Later he unwittingly marries her. Eventually, though, he recalls the young woman and the forgotten incident; he stabs his wife to death and plunges [over a balcony] to his death. All the elements of "Der blonde Eckbert" are represented here: marriage to the unrecognized beloved, the reawakening of repressed memories, insanity, and death.

That Tieck was closely concerned with the theme of unwitting sibling marriage is clear not only from "Der blonde Eckbert," but also from his frequent use of the same theme in the defensive form of siblings who manage to recognize one another in time.

In the novel *Peter Leberecht* (1795), the parents of the protagonist hear a sermon on their wedding day praising the virtues of celibacy, whereupon they separate and enter monasteries. Forced by illness to visit the same spa, they meet once again; the fruit of their union is a pair of twins, a boy and a girl, who are raised separated from one another. When he is grown Peter, employed as a steward, falls in love with a governess working in the same household. The day of the wedding is set, but then the bride is abducted. Peter follows her and arrives in his hometown. There he learns about his origins and marries a poor farmer's daughter. When he finally comes across the governess once again, it is revealed that she is his sister. In the unusual fate of the parents we easily recognize a doublet of the fate of the siblings. We note the separation immediately before the marriage of the siblings can be celebrated, their living apart from one another, and their ultimate reunion. Further, in the novel *Franz Sternbalds Wanderungen* [The wanderings of Franz Sternbald] (1798), in which dreams play a major role, the protagonist is separated from his beloved by peculiar twists of fate but is finally reunited with her by his sister. In addition, we note the theme of prevented sibling marriage. This uniting of the lovers by the sister suggests that in *Peter Leberecht* as well, the marriage to the poor farmer's daughter, also encountered elsewhere in Tieck's works, is a substitute for the prohibited marriage with the sister. In "Geschichte von der schönen Magelone" [Tale of the fair Magelone], another Peter falls in love with a farmer's daughter who herself introduces to him the beloved Magelone. Similarly, in the story "Die beiden merkwürdigsten Tage aus Sigmunds Leben" [The most amazing two days of Sigmund's life], the protagonist meets his bride through a prostitute. The prostitution fantasy involving mother and sister is encountered once again in the tale "Eigensinn und Laune" [Obstinacy and whim] (1835). The protagonist, an emancipated woman, finally ends up, after various love affairs, as a prostitute. In her bordello she is able to reveal the relationship before her son can make love to his unrecognized sister. Thereupon the mother takes poison and the son shoots himself.

These citations should suffice to suggest how Tieck's fantasy centers monotonously on the incest theme, which arose from childhood impressions, experiences, and fantasies and grew to play such a major role in his psychic life. We also note the conditioning factors of the environment that act so powerfully to intensify the Oedipus complex. The precociously mature, highly imaginative child is faced with a strict, sober father, while the mother is gentle, tender, and "inclined to fantasies" herself. Here too the fantasies associated with the parents soon undergo intensive repression and are displaced to the sibling complex, which therefore appears to be so strongly emphasized not only in Tieck's literary works, but also in his life. Here we shall not be further concerned with Tieck's brother Friedrich, who later became a sculptor, and who is relevant only as an object of childhood rivalry. But Tieck's relationship to his sister Sophie, for whom he felt a special affection throughout his life, merits at least a brief discussion. The deep affection of the two siblings is clear from their whole association. In 1795 and 1796 Tieck spent time with his sister in a summer home outside the Rosentaler Tor in Berlin. The siblings led a happy life and collected a large circle of cheerful friends, including Tieck's brother Friedrich. The desire to live with the sister has already been noted in the lives of Byron, Schiller, Kleist, and others as a typical expression of incestuous affection. At Tieck's social gatherings, Sophie surely served as the "housewife." Tieck's parents both died during Easter week of 1802, and "owing to the strong emotional upheaval, his beloved sister Sophie, married since 1799 to Bernhardi, became so ill that for a long time there was doubt she would recover" (preface to Klee's edition of Tieck's works). In a child who has already been married for some years, an emotional upheaval of this magnitude upon the parents' death is by no means normal. It is usually associated with the reactivation of repressed hostile impulses derived from the parent complex. Sophie's neurosis, however, was connected with her own marriage and with that of her brother.

Her first husband, her brother's close friend Wackenroder, died shortly after their wedding; she then married Bernhardi. But this marriage was by no means a happy one either. The spouses separated, and in 1805 they were divorced. It was no coincidence that Sophie's marriage was unhappy. Indeed, considering the appearance in neurosis of the same factors, albeit strongly distorted, it must be supposed that the infantile fixation of the libido on related persons necessarily leads in later life to a certain disability or disturbance in the psychic function of love. Since Tieck's sister was in love with her brother, she could never be happy in any marriage. We found the same to be true of Goethe's and Schiller's sisters. Incidentally, Sophie married just one year after her brother, as though having lost hope of possessing her brother himself. For a long while, though, Tieck also hesitated to marry (probably owing to similar unconscious feelings for Sophie); he was engaged to his later wife, Amalie Alberti, for two years before marrying her in 1798.

It is worthy of note that in his brief youthful drama *Der Abschied* [The farewell], Tieck already had a premonition of his sister's unhappy marriage. Psychologically this is easy to understand, for between the siblings, as we have seen, there reigned a sort of unconscious solidarity. Just as his sister, because of her affection for her brother, was necessarily unhappy in her marriage, early in his life Tieck must also have secretly nourished the wish that his sister, if she married at all, should marry a man she did not love, thus saving her love for him. In *Der Abschied* this wish is realized.

The relationship of Luise to her unloved husband fits this interpretation; for Luise, the picture of her beloved, which she claims is that of her brother, functions as a substitute for real love. But just as Tieck wished his sister would marry a man she did not love, we must suppose that the sister herself secretly harbored the same wish for an unhappy marriage. Indeed, she married a man she did not love in order to devote her love further to her brother. Yet it must be noted that because of the fixation of her affections upon her brother, she was incapable of loving any other man, and that therefore of necessity she married a man she did not love. In addition to external considerations, the unconscious hope of escaping from the fruitless psychic struggle for her brother's love may have moved her to marry. Thus she made the wrong choice or left the choice to others. However this occurred, it can be no coincidence that her marriage was unhappy. Owing to a number of conscious and unconscious factors connected with her affection for her brother, her marriage was doomed to unhappiness.

After her separation from her husband, Sophie was once again more strongly attracted to her brother. When she was about to travel to Italy in autumn 1804 to restore her extremely weakened constitution, she overwhelmed her brother with fervent requests that he accompany her and did not depart until he had agreed to do so. In this way she lured him away from his family; she enticed him away from his wife in order to possess him completely for herself. In Munich, however, her condition became so poor that they were forced to remain there for the winter. The psychology of neurosis suggests that the unconscious wish to possess her brother even longer and more completely contributed to the worsening of her nervous ailment. In the spring Tieck took ill himself (perhaps owing to similar factors), and their health seems to have improved only after Tieck's brother Friedrich, who had come to Munich, and Esthlander von Knorring, who later married Sophie, disturbed the siblings' intimate cohabitation. Finally, in summer 1805 they were able to undertake their journey to Italy, where they remained for one year. Thus the siblings lived together for two years, once again attempting to realize, at least in part, the old infantile wish for unimpeded cohabitation and undivided loving possession of one another in a world thoroughly inimical to such desires. His whole life long, this tendency dominated and activated Tieck's artistic fantasy.

Achim von Arnim

Achim von Arnim, whose works exhibit a highly autobiographical character, concerned himself especially with the theme of incest, whether enacted or prevented. In his novel *Ariels Offenbarung* [Ariel's revelation], whose protagonist bears unmistakable similarity to the author, the first episode, the heroic poem *Herrmann und seine Kinder* [Herrmann and his children], entails a tormented presentation of the incest theme. Duke Herrmann, descended from the family of the heroes of Teutoburg, lives in exile as a shepherd under the name Odin. With him live his children Heimdall and Freya; their mother was a shepherdess. A noble stranger arrives with his warrior band and soon wins Freya's love. Driven by jealousy, Heimdall reveals to his father that he is living with his sister in incest. The melancholy old man, who had already been considering the sacrifice of his son, thrusts Heimdall into the Druids' cave, whose vapors immediately prove fatal to all who enter. The mother is quick to follow her son. Thereupon Odin proceeds to the celebration of Freya's wedding to the stranger. It is revealed, however, that the stranger is the young Duke Herrmann, a son whom Odin/Herrmann had once exposed. When, despite this revelation, he still wishes to marry his sister, their father reveals her incestuous relationship with Heimdall. Freya dies, and the young Herrmann carries her into the Druids' cave. The father follows his children, choosing to die as well.

Here the brothers' rivalry over the sister is depicted in an unusual fashion. One brother is permitted knowingly to possess her (wish), while she is denied to the other (defense). This state of affairs is reflected only to an extent in Arnim's real life. His mother died at his birth; he was raised, with his elder brother, by their grandmother, who acted as a mother to them. He also attended university with his brother; their father did not die until Arnim had completed his university education. Given these family circumstances, the fantasy of rivalry with the father seems to have expressed itself in Arnim in the form of passive impulses of repentance. In *Herrmann und seine Kinder*, Herrmann sacrifices his incestuous son. Similarly, in the puppet play *Die Appelmänner* [The Appelmanns] the father's hatred is exhibited in a peculiar defense form. Egged on by the vengeful pastor, Mayor Appelmann of Stargardt has his own son executed as an arsonist, but the executioner, Hämmerling, is able to revive the dead son (defense and repentance).

In form and content, Arnim's tragedy *Der Auerhahn* [The capercaillie] approaches the tragedy of fate. In his old age Asprian, hereditary lord of Thüringen, becomes so infatuated with hunting that his soul is transmuted into the body of a capercaillie. As long as the capercaillie lives, his house will rule. Later Count Heinrich the Ironclad aims his ancestor's enchanted crossbow at his own father, not having seen him clearly. His father banishes him from his sight forever, and hatred reigns between father and son. Heinrich then extends this hatred to his younger half-siblings. In a dispute, he also kills his own son, Heinrich the Pious. He now gives the crossbow to his daring son Otto, who is thus able to win at the shooting match in Cleves. But Otto also employs it to engage in hunting capercaillies, forbidden to his family. A spectral capercaillie lures him to the window of the bedchamber of his bride, Elisabeth of Cleves. He sees her in the embrace of a monk—actually Otto's own sister Jutta in disguise—and wishes to shoot them both. In a deathly fright, Elisabeth vows to enter a convent if she is spared. However, the count forces Otto to abduct Elisabeth from the convent. By night, though, the count mistakes Otto for his stepbrother Otnit, who has shot a capercaillie and has given the feathers to Jutta, betrothed to him by his grandfather. Heinrich and Otto fall by each other's swords; Otnit and Jutta inherit Thüringen. The drama exhibits the incestuous complications typical of the tragedy of fate. These give expression to the complexity of the ambiguous psychic impulses and defense against them.

In his drama *Halle und Jerusalem,* based on Gryphius's *Cardenio und Celinde,* Arnim deals with prevented sibling incest. Cardenio loves Olympia but harbors deadly hatred for his more successful competitor, Lysander. Still, the realization that Olympia loves only Lysander prevents him from committing a jealous murder. The wandering specter of Olympia's mother, strongly suggesting Arnim's own mother, who died young, appears like Grillparzer's ancestress. She is complemented by Ahasverus, the Wandering Jew. It is finally revealed that Cardenio is the son of Ahasverus and Olympia's mother. Thus it is possible to avoid sibling incest in time.

Arnim's drama based on the history of Brandenburg, *Der falsche Waldemar* [The unfaithful Waldemar], depicts an incestuous relationship between father and daughter. The princess Magelone, once seduced and then deserted by Waldemar, reveals to him that his youthful bride Agnes, whom he has just married, is their own daughter. Waldemar has himself sealed alive in a coffin, and he is mourned as dead. Only Agnes knows the secret. Later, in the resurrected son of Mayor Appelmann, we see a similar figure. In the drama *Markgraf Karl Philipp* [Margrave Karl Philipp], the bitter relationship of King Friedrich I to his stepsiblings forms the dark background to a love tragedy ending in doom.

Clemens Brentano

Clemens Brentano deserves discussion at this point not only because he and Arnim belonged to the same literary school, but also because he was Arnim's close friend and, later, brother-in-law; in 1811 Arnim married Brentano's sister Bettina (Elisabeth), and the two men shared a lasting relationship. Clemens Brentano was born in 1778 as the third child; Bettina was the seventh. Five more children were born later. Brentano spent his first two years of life in the home of his grandparents; then he was brought to the home of his Aunt Luise, in Koblenz, where his elder sister Maria Sophie also lived. At the end of 1786 both returned to their parents' home. The father died in 1799 and Sophie in 1800. After the death of his beloved sister, Brentano became even more attached to Bettina, whom he had first met in 1798 when she was already thirteen. This attraction to his sister is of interest, since the infantile motivation appears to be absent. In its suddenness, and considering Brentano's age, this attraction resembles a "first love." However, the infantile motivation is to be found in the displacement of Brentano's attraction to his deceased sister Sophie: it was displaced to his sister Bettina. A "spiritual bond of friendship" soon developed between the siblings, but deeper erotic elements were not lacking. This "spiritual coexistence," as they called it, lasted only until 1803, for in autumn of that year Brentano married the divorced Sophie Mereau; Bettina jealously but correctly felt that her spiritual bond with her brother was threatened by the presence of his spouse. Their earlier close bond was never reestablished.

Toward the end of 1806, Brentano's wife died. The next year he married Auguste, the "mad" niece of the banker Busmann. The marriage was very unhappy. Brentano suffered much from his wife's unstable mood swings. Frequently she feigned suicide. In 1809 she followed her husband to Landhut and Munich, where he was seeking refuge with Bettina, and feigned suicide by poisoning. When Brentano insisted on a divorce, she went to live with her relatives in Frankfurt. The divorce was then completed, and Auguste married again in 1816. In 1832 she drowned herself in the Main. Brentano's incestuous fixation on his sister Sophie, whom he had loved first of all, and with whom he had spent his earliest childhood, is reflected in that soon after her death he fell passionately in love with a woman who bore the same name as his beloved deceased sister and who, because of her destiny, corresponded to Brentano's infantile mother ideal; in the long run, even Bettina proved an inadequate substitute for the deceased sister.

Brentano married Sophie Mereau, eight years older than he was. She was living in an unhappy marriage, and Brentano, always in need of affection, now became attached to her as he had earlier been attached to his mother and to Sophie. He overwhelmed her with protestations of love, but she only rejected him. In a subsequent correspondence, their relations began to improve. Finally, during a brief visit in Weimar, he was able to attain his desired goal. Although he was deeply disappointed with the physical appearance of his beloved, as he confided to his friend Arnim in a letter, he won her over completely. Brentano's letters to her reflect the sensual fire of this first passion. In the depths of his soul, however, he must already have tired of her. He implied in public that it was she who had imposed herself upon him. This lack of tact can be understood only as a projection of his own feelings of defense. After her divorce, she lived with Brentano unmarried but died in 1806 upon the birth of their third child. The ardent, passionate love for an older, unhappy, married wife and mother—accompanied, though, by an inhibition of sensual desire—is typical of fixation on the mother complex.

The fixation of the erotic affections on mother and sister is also revealed in Brentano's literary works, which would be worthy of discussion in a monograph. Here, though, the discussion will be limited to brief mention of certain characteristic traits. His first novel, *Godwi, oder Das steinerne Bild der Mutter* [Godwi, or The stone image of the mother], was published under the pseudonym "Maria," Brentano's middle name and that of his sister Sophie. In this novel Römer falls in love with the beloved of his friend Godwi without realizing that she is his own mother. However, the "image of the mother" played a role not only in Brentano's literary creations and in his psychic life, but also in his real life. Before she succumbed to his entreaties of love, he had given Sophie a portrait of his mother. After her initial abrupt rejection of his suit, he asked his brother to retrieve it from her, for he no longer felt her worthy of his love. Ironically, it was the return of the portrait that brought Brentano and Sophie to express themselves openly in letters, allowing their mutual love to develop. In the novella *Die drei Nüsse* [The three nuts], erotic affection for the sister is presented in the context of the theme of the suspension of sibling relationship. A jealous man finds his wife tenderly embracing another man, whom he immediately kills. The woman declares that it was only her brother, and her husband is executed. Years later it is revealed that the man was not her brother and that the execution had thus been carried out unjustly. The theme of prevented incest is also encountered in Brentano's "Rosenkranzballaden" [Rose garland ballads]. In the second portion of "Geschichte vom braven Kasperl und dem schönen Annerl" [Tale of the good Kasperl and the fair Annerl], the officer commits suicide because he has had to arrest his father and brother for robbery. This suggests intensive defenses against the impulses of father and brother hatred.

Theodor Körner

The literary personality of Theodor Körner is of great interest to us because it demonstrates the importance the family complex has not only for literary production, but also for life. Further, his numerous works are highly valuable for psychological investigation; since Körner died at age twenty-two, all of them can be considered works of youth. A detailed analysis of his destiny reveals a strong dependence on the family complex. On the other hand, his case is informative in a negative sense; it shows his later family relations apparently dissociated from the Oedipus complex. Still, the unusually kind father demonstrates that, given the appropriate predisposition, an Oedipal orientation and fixation in the child cannot be avoided through any action by the parents. Indeed, the later relations of the father and son were unusually intimate and friendly. Although in his letters the son repeatedly characterizes his father as friend and confidant, he does nevertheless reveal a certain rebelliousness toward him; while he was studying in Leipzig, he involved himself in all sorts of wild and dangerous adventures without his father's knowledge or approval. Of course, the father's mild condemnation of some of these did not bring the son to desist. In Vienna, where he soon became a favorite of theater devotees and society, he became engaged without the knowledge of his father. He feared his father's disapproval of his union with the actress Antonie Adamberger, for whom he wrote many of the roles (including men's parts to be played by women) in his dramatic works. Finally, he made the fateful decision to join the Lützow Volunteer Corps without the knowledge and then against the will of his father, who tried in vain to hold his son back: "I repeat my plea that you take no decisive step without first speaking with me in person. . . . Even given the noblest motivations, we are not safe from illusions of fantasy, and if sacrifices must be made, one should at least make them at the right time" (Zipper 1900, 67).

The basis for this constant opposition to his father's probable and even expressed wishes was doubtless established in earliest childhood. The well-meaning, pedagogically inclined father planned, surely with the best intentions, to provide his son with a solid education from the beginning. To the wild and excitable boy, though, these efforts must have seemed a restricting and unwelcome regimen. As soon as he escaped from his father's discipline and entered the free student life of the university, his impetuous personality broke through. In lengthy epistles, his father sought in vain to bring him back to the path of serious study and bourgeois conformity without arousing his hostility: "Is it really impossible for you to interest yourself in any branch of study or occupation, whatever it might be? . . . Besides poetry, one must think of an occupation that will provide a certain solid income" (September 1811).

Like the conditioning factors of the father complex, suggestions of childhood fixation on female relatives are to be found in Körner's biography. Whereas the father wanted first and foremost to make his son a civilized human being, to the female members of the family—his mother, his Aunt Dora, and his sister Emma—Theodor seemed from the beginning to be a remarkable genius. Just as he was pampered by these family members as a child, the handsome youth was spoiled by the friends of his sister, and in Vienna he was treated in like manner on all sides. Thus the conditions for intensification of and fixation on the Oedipus complex were provided, and Körner's literary production reveals the power of this complex so completely that in this light his life's destiny becomes clear. As a dramatist, he exhibited amazing productivity. During his fifteen months in Vienna, he produced six tragedies, five comedies, and five operas. In his works, the theme of rivalry between father and son or between two brothers over the same woman appears repeatedly.

One of the first dramatic productions of the late autumn of 1811 (in Vienna) is the one-act comedy *Die Braut* [The bride], in which father and son appear as suitors of the same woman without realizing one another's identity. In the five-act tragedy *Rosamunde* as well, written in two weeks (September 10–28, 1812), father and son compete for the love of the same woman. The plot was borrowed from an English ballad in Percy's collection. (Wieland had already written an opera based on this ballad.) The marriage of Henry II of England and Eleanor of Poitou is an unhappy one; she has been divorced from Louis VII of France. In secret, Henry marries Rosamunde Clifford. But Richard, the king's second son, falls in love with Rosamunde when he happens to see her. From him she learns that her beloved is the king. Although she is now ready to renounce relations with the king voluntarily, the playwright introduces a tragic solution reminiscent of Grillparzer's *Jüdin von Toledo* [Jewess of Toledo]. Eleanor, conspiring with her four sons, attacks Rosamunde in her hiding place and by threatening to harm her children forces her to drink a goblet of poison. Henry, returning from battle, finds his beloved dying. In the one-act drama *Die Sühne* [The atonement], Körner addressed the incest theme of the husband's return, already familiar to us from the works of Tieck and Christoph Houwald. He was heavily influenced by the romantic drama of fate, coming into full bloom at the time. The typical theme of the hatred between two brothers and their love for the same woman is central to the plot. Associated with this, and derived from the father complex, is the theme of the return of the spouse presumed dead, whose supposed widow has in the interim married her first husband's brother. When the returning husband demands his rights, the brother, disturbed in his possession of his beloved, wishes to eliminate him. Accidentally, though, he kills his beloved and is himself killed by his brother. Given our interpretation of the theme of the husband's return, in the place of the returning first husband, believed (wished) dead and having prior claims to the wife, we can posit the father. Thus it becomes clear that here, as in Körner's other works, conflict between father and son ends either in sentimental reconciliation or in the father's victory over the son.

This all suggests powerful impulses of repentance and defense against an inimical orientation toward the father. Since these impulses found no justification or motivation in the real world, they were transformed into self-reproach toward the playwright himself. However, this guilty perspective proved decisive not only for his literary production, but also for his personal destiny. Like Max Piccolomini, whom Körner took as his example, in the struggle between an affection forbidden by his feelings of guilt and the call of duty, represented by his father, Körner chose a self-sacrificing death for the fatherland as an escape and a punishment. The youth's decision to offer up to certain death his life, blessed so early and bountifully with love, fame, and happiness, can be understood only from the unconscious motivation of the parent complex. It is of special psychological interest that this turning point in his inner life, accompanied by the most intense desire for self-sacrifice, came only after he found himself in a happy, loving relationship approved of by his father. In this period arose his most important work, the tragedy *Zriny,* which glorifies with glowing patriotism the Hungarian hero who, with his men, sacrificed himself for his lord. Körner's last work, *Joseph Heyderich, oder Deutsche Treue* [Joseph Heyderich, or German loyalty] is also characterized by strong sentiments of patriotism; it was the poet-hero's final attempt at an artistic depiction of self-sacrificing loyalty before he decided to transform his fantasy into reality. His personal complex is expressed in that in the one-act drama, Körner places in the mouth of the lieutenant who calls his comrades to battle for the fatherland the very words with which he told his father of his decision to fight the French.

In Körner, the sudden appearance of patriotism can be characterized as a reactive construct. This is suggested not only by his exaggerated emphasis upon it, but also in that at the university, corresponding to his rebelliousness toward his father, he was anything but patriotic. It is highly characteristic of his personal complex that he was able to combine fervent patriotism with opposition to the ruling monarch. Upon joining the Lützow Volunteer Corps, he traveled through Saxony, where he saw his family for the last time and distributed a call to arms to "the people of Saxony" to rise up against Napoleon, with whom the elector was allied at the time. Thus Körner encouraged the elector's subjects to revolt against their own monarch. Accordingly, Körner's ardent patriotism appears to be a reaction to childhood rivalry with the father, associated with a sensation of guilt intensified to an unconscious wish for self-punishment.

The appearance of this repentant impulse after he had fallen in love with Antonie demonstrates the erotic source of this entire complex. We know that the jealous perspective toward the father is fed and powerfully intensified by the sources of repressed love for the mother. Thus, given the theme of sexual rivalry between father and son that constantly appears in Körner's literary output, it is in the incest complex that we must seek the source of this guilt associated with his love life. The playwright approached his love for Antonie as something forbidden; although he described his beloved to his father and to his friend in the most glowing terms, he was unable to realize his love for her. This inhibition derived from the incest complex; as he himself naively admitted in a letter to his father (May 20, 1812), he had found in his beloved an image of his mother: "Father, I love, and if you really know me, then you know how I love!—eternally, infinitely. She bears a close resemblance to my mother, a coincidence that greatly pleases me for my sake and for yours. Therefore I await your arrival this time with especially great anticipation, for I look forward to the unbounded happiness of the moment when you tell me that you are infinitely pleased by Toni. Oh, what a sober word that is! You will tell me that she has earned your love and your blessing! Father, may my certainty that you will be as enthusiastic about her as am I be a guarantee of my love and my choice" (Zipper 1900, 48). In addition to this object selection clearly based on similarity to the mother, the unambiguous wish for rivalry with the father is also expressed in this frank confession, for Körner wished to see his father as enthusiastic about Antonie as he himself was. This is reminiscent of Goethe's novella *Der Mann von fünfzig Jahren* [The man of fifty years] in which the son fears—correctly, as it turns out—that his father will have stronger feelings for his beloved than the son would wish. This also reminds one of Schiller's wish as a bridegroom that someone appear to challenge his possession of the bride so as to lend affairs a tragic twist.

In addition to the superficial resemblance to the mother, a number of psychological motivations were of course also involved in Körner's object selection. Though in the real life of his beloved, who was watched over by a strict aunt, the playwright found no reflection of the typical youthful fantasy that the mother is unfaithful because she has a relationship with the father, seen as a preferred rival, this fantasy nevertheless appears in many of his literary works. This is true of his first serious drama, revealingly entitled *Toni,* the material for which he adapted from Kleist's novella *Die Verlobung in Santo Domingo* [The betrothal in Santo Domingo], which had appeared two years before. Although Körner destroyed the tragic effect of the material, it was probably the fantasy of the suspected unfaithfulness of the beloved, killed by her fiancé, that so attracted him. This conclusion is justified in that the same fantasy reappears in his tragedy of fate *Die Sühne* [The atonement]. Here again the second husband, though unwittingly, kills his unfaithful beloved. In the same way Rosamunde, violating all the rules of tragic guilt, dies as the unfaithful beloved of father and son. Indeed, this jealous murder of the beloved is also found in an episode of *Zriny.* Here the lack of motivation and the crudeness of depiction demonstrate the subjective determinacy of literary fantasy. The lovers Juranitsch and Helena, obviously modeled on Schiller's Max and Thekla, are denied earthly love but given heavenly love in its stead; before undertaking his last battle, Juranitsch murders his beloved in cold blood so that she will never be tempted to be unfaithful. This sacrifice of the lovers derives from the union of lovers in death—the association of death and sexuality—a theme in which Zacharias Werner, Körner's admired idol, also reveled. A letter of May 16, 1812, reveals how far a longing for death was associated in his psyche with the need for love. In this letter Körner describes to a friend in youth his happiness in love: "At last I am totally, totally happy. May death take me when it will! I can ask no more happiness of this earth." Like the unhappy Kleist, Körner was unable to experience the joy of love in reality, but only in association with death. His poems in praise of liberty, which quite clearly are substitutes for love poems, demonstrate how much he sexualized his patriotic and military activity. Honor, liberty, and the fatherland are repeatedly designated as a "bride," battle is described as a celebration of marriage, and in "Das Schwertlied" [The sword song], completed on the day of his death, the day of death is lauded as the day of marriage and the sword, as a bride:

> Now let the beloved sing
> So that bright sparks spring forth!
> The wedding day is dawning.
> Hurrah! The bride of iron!
> Hurrah!

From all this, we can only come to the psychological conclusion that the playwright unconsciously longed for death and indirectly sought it. Thus the premonitions of death that plagued him during his last days and especially on the day of his death can also be explained as an expression of the corresponding unconscious wishes, driving him to his death. If any doubts remain, these should be eliminated by Körner's behavior during his final moments. From the very beginning, he burned with hatred for the enemy and deliberately sought danger. It is characteristic that on August 26, 1813, during a quite insignificant battle, he was killed through his own fault: despite the signal to retreat, he rashly pursued the enemy soldiers withdrawing into a thicket. The various accounts of his death provided in the past have never led to clarity concerning his end, for the unconscious suicidal tendency was not taken into consideration. Since Freud (1907b, 85–88) emphasized such tendencies and demonstrated their presence in several cases, there can no longer be any doubt as to the existence or the possibility of such perspectives. Freud (1907b, 88) also states directly that "the situation of the battlefield is such, for it satisfies the unconscious suicidal wish that still avoids the direct route." He refers to Max Piccolomini, of whom it was said that "he wished to die" and who has always served as an example to the Körners of the world. Freud also emphasizes the tendency for harm to the self as decisive. In Körner this tendency appeared as a reaction to his hostility toward his father. In this context it is highly characteristic that in his last, fanatically patriotic period, he was filled with burning hatred toward Napoleon, in whom he, like so many others, saw an exemplar of tyrannical paternal power. With reference to the Lützow Volunteers, Napoleon stated the intention that "of all those who participated in this insolent venture, as an example to others no man should be spared" (Zipper 1900, 77). Thus Körner's completely unnecessary self-sacrifice in the futile battle against "the lord of Europe" appears to have occurred like a wished-for punishment of the insolent child at the hand of the angry father.

The powerful influence of the parent complex on the child's destiny and death is also exemplified by Karoline von Günderode (1780–1806), whose letters and works were published by Elisabeth Brentano in 1840. Günderode was the daughter of a privy councillor of Baden, who had also written some literary works. After her father's early death, she grew up in the care of her mother, who worked secretly as a journalist. Her love as a young woman for the thirty-four-year-old Kreutzer appears unusual; Kreutzer himself was married to a colleague's widow, thirteen years older than he was. Thus we can suppose that in this love affair with an older, married man, Günderode, orphaned at a young age, sought and found a substitute for her beloved father, who had died so early in her life. Her intense fixation on her father becomes more obvious still when it is noted that in order to be reunited with her beloved father she committed suicide when Kreutzer ended their relationship. Further, that she merely loved her mental image of the men in her life and was easily disappointed by reality suggests that she was influenced by an indelible and thoroughly irreplaceable infantile image. That she was subject to the father complex and in suicide symbolically expressed reunion with her beloved parent is clear from the content of her poems, which deal with the theme of love enduring beyond the grave. It was only in an unconscious sense, however, that Kreutzer served as a father substitute for her (as "father imago" in the Jungian sense). This is clear in that long before this relationship she had already characterized herself as a deserted "Ariadne." She can be understood only with reference to her father. Here again we see the deep connection between experience and literary production. This shows that both expressions derive from a common source—the infantile perspective. Thus, it was not only because Kreutzer left her that she characterized herself as a deserted woman, but also because of her father's departure. She devoted her young heart to an older, married man who could indeed substitute for her father, but she must have sensed that the discrepancy in their ages, as well as his marriage, would bring about an unhappy end to the relationship, just as her relationship to her father had ended unhappily.

Given actual circumstances, in real life emotions can be expressed only in a disguised manner; but in the fantasy of literary creativity they can be expressed more freely. Thus we can take as crucial evidence for our conception of the symbolic meaning of suicide that she derived most of the material for her works from the incest complex.

The dramatic fragment *Hildegund* (1800) concerns the story of the murder of Attila by his bride on their wedding night, reminiscent of the Judith legend. Only four scenes were completed; her work on the fragment broke off after the wedding scene. But the few completed portions clearly illustrate the playwright's personal complex. Hildegund flees back to her father, whom Attila has threatened to conquer in war. Then, despite her love for Walter, she decides to accept Attila's suit in order to save her father and his land. The choice between father and suitor is also observed in the drama *Udohla,* where the theme of incestuous love is briefly taken up as well. The sultan is in love with his supposed sister Nerissa. During the course of the drama, however, it is revealed that she is the daughter of an enemy whom the sultan had executed; she had been raised in place of the true sister. When one of Udohla's brothers appears and reveals this, Udohla rejects the sultan's love, for he has killed her father; she returns with her brother to her homeland. Just as this heroine is bound by love to her dead father, Günderode's other heroines die in prelude to the death of the playwright. In "Immortalita," an oration based on Lucian's example, the beloved woman throws herself between her lover and his competitor and dies by her lover's sword. In the drama *Mahomed* as well, a senseless passion leading to suicide is depicted. Finally, the tragedy *Magie und Schicksal* [Magic and destiny] is reminiscent of Schiller's *Braut von Messina.* The daughter of a sorcerer has been unfaithful to her husband. By her lover, she bears a second son who becomes the rival of her legitimate son. The brothers commit mutual fratricide without realizing each other's identity.

Richard Wagner

In "Schriften zur Angewandten Seelenkunde" [Writings on applied psychology], a series edited by Freud, two monographs (Graf 1911; Rank

1912b) have appeared that independently conclude that the incest complex plays the greatest role in the dramatic production of Richard Wagner. The following brief comments, intended only to touch briefly on the inner creative world of the poet-composer, must therefore suffice, fragmentary though they may be. As we have already noted, in Wagner's dramatic works the fantasy of rivalry with the father is dominant. Its wish form is such that in various guises identified with various legendary figures, the hero is able to abduct his beloved from his competitor. This wish fantasy, which also dominated Wagner's actual love life, has its personal origins in the family circumstances in which the child grew up. His father died six months after the birth of the child, who was then able to enjoy the mother's love undisturbed until she married the actor Geyer a few months later. Wagner's first inimical impulses are probably associated with his stepfather, who intruded as an impediment to the love of mother and son and deprived him of the possibility of realizing his unconscious wishes. The father's prior acquisition of the mother, which ordinarily occurs before the child's birth, and which playwrights are able to project into their own lifetime through the stepmother theme, was in this case really experienced by the son, and the effects of this infantile experience were so great that the expressions of Wagner's reaction to it can be pursued through his entire life, up to his old age. In his literary fantasies the mature playwright continually attempted to provide himself with a substitute for his mother, lost earlier to his stepfather. He also avenged himself because this father deprived him of his mother: through his heroes Wagner deprived others of the beloved woman. Freud has derived this preference for the spouse or the betrothed of another man—for a woman no longer free—from infantile incestuous sources. It is the child's reaction of jealousy toward the father.

This theme already formed the basis for Wagner's first dramatic project, which bore the significant title *Die Hochzeit* [The wedding], written at the age of twenty. In his autobiographical sketch he writes of this attempt: "I no longer recall where I came across the medieval material. A man madly in love with the bride of his friend climbs to the window of her bedchamber. There she is awaiting her husband. She struggles with her wild admirer and thrusts him down into the courtyard, where he expires. At his funeral, the bride casts herself upon his corpse and yields up her soul with a cry." Similarly, the Dutchman deprives the hunter Erik of his beloved, Manfred wishes to seize her from Nurredin, Tannhäuser defeats Wolfram von Eschenbach, and Lohengrin wins Elsa in battle with Telramund. Tristan first wins his beloved from Morold and then takes her from her husband, Marke. Stolzing takes his beloved from Hans Sachs and also plays a trick on the suitor Beckmesser. Siegmund robs his enemy Hunding of his wife, Siegfried wins the Valkyrie from Wotan in battle, and Parsifal frees Kundry from Klingsor's evil power.

However, this theme of competition extends significantly to Wagner's life as well. He offered the strongest and deepest love of his life to an already wedded woman, the wife of his friend Wesendonck, and this inextinguishable condition for love, derived from the mother complex, appears to have achieved a certain degree of external gratification when, through his marriage to the wife of his friend Hans von Bülow, the already mature Wagner was able to realize his long unconscious childhood wish for the wife of another man (the father). But the expression of defense against the theme of the abduction of the bride is also observed in Wagner's works in the typical form of the union of the lovers in death, already familiar to us as a polysemous substitute for prohibited sexual union. This theme is found already fully developed in *Die Hochzeit* and reappears in the same way in *Rienzi, Der fliegende Holländer* [The flying Dutchman], *Tannhäuser, Lohengrin, Tristan und Isolde,* and *Der Ring des Nibelungen.*

Finally, a third typical theme directly from the composer's life found expression in his works in the form of an infantile wish fantasy: the death of the father immediately before or just at the time of the birth of his heroic son. This theme is expressed most clearly in *Tristan, Siegfried,* and *Parsifal;* the mothers of the corresponding heroes also die early. (Cf. the expression of defense in Schiller's *Don Carlos:* "My first act when I saw the light of day was a matricide.") Where this theme of the father who dies shortly after the conception of the son is expressed less clearly—provided he is not left completely without mention (cf. *Tannhäuser*)—something is always slightly amiss with the paternity. In *Der Fall Wagner* [The case of Wagner], Friedrich Nietzsche, who hints that Geyer may have been Wagner's father, misinterprets the vow of chastity made by the knights of the Holy Grail to their king and ironically asks: "Parsifal is Lohengrin's father? how did he manage that?" In any case, Wagner's interest in the theme of making a secret of one's name (Lohengrin) seems to derive from his doubts as to his own descent. In school his name was entered as Richard Geyer. Only later did he once again take on the name Wagner. Therefore the fathers of most of his protagonists die very early, just as his own father did, so they do not know their fathers. Certainly this has the extra personal meaning that Wagner himself did not know his father either. In his boyhood, therefore, childhood sexual speculations—which, as I have demonstrated, are of great significance in the Lohengrin legend—may have played a great role. Through the perspective of the father complex, these speculations may have increased his interest, already proceeding from the mother complex, in the Lohengrin theme.

The situation is more complex in *Der Ring des Nibelungen,* where, especially, the theme of sibling love appears in the form of conscious incest, receiving greater emphasis than the underlying complex of motherly love. Wagner's extremely affectionate relationship with his sisters is well known, and it is described in especially great detail in the comprehensive biography by Glasenapp (1894). He greatly loved his sister Rosalie, who died young, and for whom he not only destroyed but presumably also composed *Die Hochzeit* [The wedding]. In another youthful work, *Das Liebesverbot* [Forbidden love], based on Shakespeare's *Measure for Measure*, the chaste Isabella, who saves her beloved, sinful brother through her entreaties (Tannhäuser theme), bears a close resemblance to Rosalie. Of his other sisters, Wagner was in later years especially partial to Klara, though he had no close relationship at all with his brothers, especially the eldest brother, Albert. In his later life, though, his relationship with his half-sister Cecilie, who had already been tenderly devoted to Wagner as a boy, became the most intimate. A letter Wagner wrote to Cecilie from Zurich (December 30, 1852) suggests the intensity and the enduring effects of this childhood affection. Here the similarity of the attachment to that of Goethe and his sister is evident: "Whenever you turn to me like this, of necessity I always recall our days of youth, when we two really belonged mainly to one another. No recollection from this time comes to me without your being woven into it. You probably have the same feeling, and since one always considers one's youth to be the happier time, you probably also long, as an escape from the repugnance of the present, for the one who was closest to you then."

Earlier, too, especially during the beginning of his period in Dresden, he had repeatedly sought to invite his sister, married and living in Paris, to visit him. He had only recently left her. He invited her to Töplitz and suggested how inexpensive the trip would be, saying: "We'll keep house together. . . . Oh, how nice that would be" (May 3, 1842). Here again we find the typical wish to set up housekeeping with the sister. With Wagner too there are suggestions of the fantasy of a secret correspondence with the sister, already noted in the case of Schiller. This fantasy of taking the beloved sister from the brother-in-law found its most consummate artistic expression in *Die Walküre*. Here Siegmund abducts his beloved sister from his brother-in-law, Hunding, then kills him in battle. We easily recognize this fantasy as a reworking of the older, and more intense, related impulse to eliminate the father and take possession of the mother. As in *Liebesverbot*, the theme of sibling love is addressed in *Rienzi* as well. There Ariadno is unsuccessful in winning Irene. She remains true to her beloved brother and is united with him in death. In the fragment *Die Sarazenin* [The Saracen woman], the theme of unconscious sibling love is fully developed.

Here Manfred loves his sister Fatime without realizing her identity. Dying, she reveals to him their kinship.

Finally, in *Die Walküre,* this theme is treated in a positive light. Here Wagner adopted the incestuous love of Siegmund and Sieglinde from mythology. In Wagner's work, the siblings fall in love without knowing about their kinship. Even after discovering it, though, they still do not wish to separate. Siegmund abducts his sister from her spouse and sires a child, Siegfried, by her. The boy is raised by Mime. In *Der Ring des Nibelungen,* as a full complement to the theme of sibling love, in addition to rivalry with the brother-in-law (Hunding), also evident with Schiller, brother hatred is portrayed in the inimical relationship of Mime and his brother Alberich. But here the incest fantasy is highly complicated through Siegfried's kinship to Wotan and Brünnhilde. Wotan is the father of Siegmund and Sieglinde and therefore Siegfried's grandfather. However, he is also the father of Brünnhilde. Thus Siegfried loves his aunt. Wagner, with an intuitive conception—derived from his personal complexes—of the mythological material, conceived of this relationship as incest with the mother. This is clear in the magnificent scene from *Siegfried* in which the undaunted hero releases Brünnhilde, surrounded by fire, from her deathlike sleep, thus winning her as his wife, while the "wronged third" appears this time in the form of the malevolent "father" Wotan, who associates the winning of his beloved daughter with an impossible condition. The ingenuous youth Siegfried mistakes this woman—won from the father substitute (grandfather) and awakened from her deathlike sleep by his own kiss—for his mother. The image of the sleeping woman awakens in him the memory of his beloved mother, whom he has never seen:

> Mother! Mother!
> Remember me!
>
> . . . . . .
>
> Oh, Mother! Mother!
> Your brave child!
> A woman lies in sleep;
> She has taught him to fear!

And when the awakened one expresses herself in words that in normal circumstances could only be those of a mother, the youth believes that in this woman, who has awakened his senses, he has found his mother.

> *Brünnhilde:* Oh, if you knew, joy of the world,
> How I loved you!
> You were my thought,
> You were my sorrow.

I nourished you, tender one,
Before you were conceived.
Before your birth
My shield protected you.
So long have I loved you, Siegfried!
Siegfried (quietly and shyly): Thus my mother did not die?
Did the beloved one only sleep?
Brünnhilde (smiling): Oh, blessed child,
Your mother will not return to you.

(*Siegfried* 3.3)

Just as Siegfried finds his beloved in his foster mother, Brünnhilde, he kills his foster father, Mime, and fights victoriously the man who wishes to deprive him of the beloved mother. Once again it is clear that the figure of the hated and eliminated foster father derives directly from life and that erotic love for the mother, excessively offensive, is represented by the foster mother and the theme of sibling love. Still, one more wish fantasy of the incest complex finds its most sublime expression in the figure of Brünnhilde. This is the typical wish for the rejuvenation of the mother, which finds expression in the stepmother (foster mother) theme. Thus, on the one hand, the offensive relationship is eliminated, while on the other hand the mother is so rejuvenated that she can be seen as the son's bride. In the saga of Brünnhilde and the legends connected with it (Sleeping Beauty), this fantasy is realized through the sleep of many years, preserving, as it were, the mother imago for the son. Indeed, this occurs in a characteristic manner: before Siegfried's birth, Brünnhilde is put to sleep with the expectation that only Siegfried (the son) can free her from this state.

Siegfried's incestuously tinged relationship to Brünnhilde has its complement in *Parsifal*, where a demonic woman attempts to "awaken" the inexperienced youth to sensual life but is, in the sense of the Phaedra schema, rejected by the hero, made steadfast by his sexual abstinence. In *Siegfried*, on the other hand, before submitting to his suit, the motherlike loved one repels the impetuous youth "with the highest power of anxiety." These feelings of rejection are a specific characteristic of the identification of mother and beloved. In *Parsifal* this is suggested in that Kundry attempts to seduce the "pure fool" through the memory of his mother, Herzeleide:

Know the love
That embraced Gamuret
When Herzeleide's passion
Flowed burning over him.

> She who once
> Gave you body and life,
> Before whom death and simpleness must yield,
> She offers
> You today
> As the last greeting of a mother's blessing
> The first kiss—of love.

After her kiss, "Parsifal springs up suddenly with a gesture of the greatest horror. His bearing expresses a frightful change. He presses his hands violently against his heart as if to master a gripping pain. Finally he cries out:"

> The wound! The wound!
> It burns in my heart.
> . . . .
> Oh! Torment of love!
> How everything shudders, quakes, and trembles
> In sinful desire!

Repeatedly, though, he pushes Kundry back with vehemence. The sexual abstinence he expresses here is motivated by the fixation of his erotic affection upon his mother and corresponds to defense against repressed love for the mother.

In the last artistic confession of the aging Wagner, erotic affection for the mother, arising in earliest childhood, finds its highest expression of defense. In the artistically still immature youth, however, this affection is revealed with naive frankness in a letter written by the twenty-one-year-old Wagner to his mother: "Oh, how the love of a mother still stands above all that! I am probably one of those who cannot always express at the same moment the feelings that lie within the heart. Otherwise you would often have had the chance to know me from a gentler side. Still, my feelings remain the same. You see, Mother, now that I am away from you, I am so overwhelmed by thoughts of thanks for your wonderful love toward your child—which just recently you again exhibited to me so sincerely and warmly—that I should like to write you and tell you this in the tenderest tones of a lover toward his beloved."

Thus we see how the family impressions absorbed and processed by the child in the very earliest periods of life remain indelibly in the unconscious and how, from there, they can decisively influence life and production. We see how the artistic fantasies constructed from the few primitive building blocks of infantile impression continually create and resolve the same wish situation with stubborn uniformity—the situation of the son who, identifying like Hamlet with the mother's second spouse (the stepfather), disturbs a loving relationship and seizes the woman from his rival, more entitled to her than he is, as if to take revenge because in his childhood the mother was taken from him by the stepfather. We see how the playwright never tires of depicting this fantasy and indeed how he continually attempts to realize it. Thus we again observe that artistic activity is not some form of psychic luxury for the individual overly endowed with energy and fantasy but arises from the tormented drive for psychic self-preservation, which can be achieved only with the help of the colossal compensations of fantasy. Wagner, who like every true great artist suffered deeply from life and his own feelings, sensed this connection and repeatedly expressed it in his letters, especially during his period in Zurich. He expressed it most clearly in a letter to Uhlig: "My own thoughts about 'art' often come to me, and usually I cannot help thinking that if we had life, we would need no art. Art begins precisely where life ends. When we have nothing, we cry out through art, 'I wish.' I cannot imagine how it could occur to a truly happy man to produce 'art' [*Kunst*]: it is only in life that one 'can' [*kann*]. Is our art thus nothing more than an admission of our impotence? Surely! Our art is, at least, and so is all art we can imagine, given the perspective of our current dissatisfaction with life! All art is a wish expressed as clearly as possible."

24 The Incest Theme in Modern Literature: A Look into the Past and into the Future

Illness is perhaps the deepest source
Of the whole creative drive.
Creating, I found healing,
Creating, I was cured.

HEINE, "Schöpfungslieder," No. 7

In investigating typical literary themes and their various forms from gray mythical prehistory to the present day, we have seen how writers have occupied themselves in a uniform and unchanging manner with the shared human—and therefore always current—theme of incest. Up to the present, the incest theme has provided the uniformly adopted material for a range of literary works. The inner limitations of the material are clearer still owing to the remarkable conservatism of form. The dramas of Ibsen, for example, demonstrate no significant progress in analytical technique since *Oedipus the King* by Sophocles, written almost two and a half millennia earlier. Given these limitations of the material, it is quite clear how much more value is associated with the "how" in art (technique and depiction) than with the "what" (the material). However, it is not only certain continually repeated themes that have become psychologically comprehensible, given their primitive human sources. We have also learned to consider their treatment and presentation at a given time as the necessary expression of the stage of repression reached at that time and manifested in individual towering personalities. Between these milestones of cultural development representing the consciousness of the time, we find digressions from the line of development, breakthroughs in the line of development, and especially, reactive attempts to stop, interrupt, or reverse the process of repression, which tends toward neurosis. In literature, at the threshold of modern drama, Henrik Ibsen stands as one of the pioneers of "naturalism."

Henrik Ibsen

Ibsen, by far the best known of modern dramatists, also derives his most serious human conflicts almost exclusively from the family complex, apparently intensively emphasized in his own psychic life. But corresponding to the progress of repression, the impulses derived from the incest complex express themselves mainly in subtle ethical and psychic conflicts, which often are presented and dealt with in a psychological manner—dialectically and intellectually. In lieu of incestuous acts, murders, and killings, we find reserved affections, unpronounced relationships, or differences of opinion, debates, and conflicts of will. The characters are doomed not by some external, powerful fate but by their own sufferings—by their neurosis.

Behind the apparent form and technique of presentation we find once again the typical old themes of the incest complex. We have already discussed in detail the depiction of the father conflict in *The Wild Duck* and in *Ghosts* (chap. 5), as well as the son's associated fantasy that the mother suffers from the father's unfaithfulness. In Ibsen's "romantic" works, which arose in his youthful period, the mother complex is still clearly expressed. This is true of the dramatic poem *Peer Gynt*, where mother and beloved merge, and of the youthful work *Fru Inger of Østeraad*, derived technically and thematically from the drama of fate. In this work the mother loves her illegitimate son passionately, while feeling only revulsion toward her daughters:

> My daughters! May God forgive me if I have not a mother's heart for them. The duty of a wife was slavery to me, so how could I love my daughters? But with my son, it was different! He was the child of my soul! He was the only thing that reminded me of the time when I was a woman and nothing but a woman. And they had taken him from me!

Under an assumed name, this son comes into her home, and since she believes he is her son's competitor for rulership, she has him murdered by the loyal Skaktavl. This must be considered an expression of defense against her erotic affection toward her son. Her unconscious struggle between erotic affection and defense against it is also expressed when Olaf Skaktavl enters her son's room to kill him and Fru Inger is left alone.

Fru Inger (pale and trembling): Shall I dare do it?

(Noise is heard in the room.)

Fru Inger (hurrying with a cry toward the door): No, no, this must not be.

(The dull sound of someone falling is heard.)

Fru Inger (hurries back through the room with both hands over her ears and with a desperate expression; after a brief pause she cautiously removes her hands and listens again): Now it is done. It has grown quiet within. You saw it, God: I changed my mind, but Olaf Skaktavl was too fast.

Later, love for her son appears at the same time as the corresponding impulses of defense:

Fru Inger (gasping for breath; more and more wildly): No one saw what happened within. No one can testify against me. (Suddenly, she extends her arms and whispers): My son! My beloved child! Come to me! Here I am! Listen! I want to tell you something. There above, beyond the stars, I am hated because I gave you birth.

Indeed, she still does not know that it is her son whom she has had murdered, but her powerful defense against the underlying suspicion that she has killed him is so overwhelming that the opposing wishes are intensified as hallucinations. She takes her son's funeral procession for his coronation procession and the funeral music for sounds of celebration. While his body is being brought in, she sees her son on the throne. Still, although she has not yet realized that it is the body of her son, at the sight of the coffin she cries out:

The body? (Whispering) Oh, this is a foul dream.

From a ring, though, she at last recognizes the body as that of her son:

(Aghast)The ring? The ring! (She rushes forward and grasps it.) Sten Sture's ring! (With a cry) O Jesus Christ! My son! (She throws herself upon the bier.)

Here again, we find the symbol of shared death.

Fru Inger (with a muted voice; she raises herself up halfway): What I need . . ? Another coffin. A grave beside my son! (Once again, she sinks down exhausted upon the bier.)

In a mature work as well, *John Gabriel Borkman,* the mother's love for her son is suggested. However, the son's need to pass beyond this love in order to develop a normal sexual life is also depicted. Here the inimical brothers, elsewhere in competition over the same woman, are replaced by inimical twin sisters who twice compete for a man. At first Gunhild and Ella struggle for the love of John Gabriel Borkman, who marries Gunhild. They later compete for Gunhild's son Erhard, whom mother and aunt both love passionately.

> *Ella:* I love Erhard. As much as I can love anyone, now, at my age. . . . And therefore, you see, I'm troubled when I see that he is threatened by someone—like this Fru Wilton. At least, that is what I fear.

Both sisters are jealous of this woman, whom Erhard loves passionately. Still, they are not as jealous of her as they are of each other, for they both say: "Better she than you!"

> *Ella:* For the first time in our life, we twin sisters agree.

They now engage in a bitter struggle over Erhard, who nevertheless evades them both in the end.

> *Gunhild* (threateningly): You wish to come between us! Between mother and son. You!
>
> *Ella:* I wish to free him from your influence, from your power, from your domination. (Warmly) I want his loving disposition, his soul, his whole heart.
>
> *Gunhild* (horrified): For all time, that you shall never have again!

However, Ella tells her deranged brother-in-law John Gabriel Borkman, her beloved in youth, what she is unable to tell her sister:

> You have killed all human joy in me, at least all the human joy of a woman. From the time when your image began to fade within me, it became more and more difficult for me to love anyone. . . . Only one person—Erhard, of course. Erhard—your son, Borkman.

In the complementary themes of the recognition of siblings and the dissolution of kinship, with which we are already familiar, the two typical forms of the sibling complex find expression in Ibsen's works. The first theme finds expression in the "family drama" *Ghosts*. Here Osvald Alving falls in love with his father's daughter, his half-sister Regina, without knowing of their blood relationship. He wishes to marry her, for he believes that only she can make him happy. His mother, who knows Regina's origins, hesitates to ruin the happiness of her beloved son, but Pastor Manders is horrified at the thought of such a "shocking union." Thus Fru Alving decides to reveal their kinship to them, whereupon Regina leaves the house. Suggestions of deeper erotic affection between mother and son, such as that underlying the sibling incest complex, are not lacking either. Aversion toward the father is also strongly emphasized.

In *Ghosts,* the lovers discover they are siblings. In *Little Eyolf,* on the other hand, it is revealed that the siblings, who love one another passionately, are actually not related. That they are still separated from one another by sexual rejection even after this revelation clearly reveals the incestuous source of this affection, which because of the high degree of repression can no longer manifest itself, despite the theme of defense. The attempt at defense is only a conscious act, but for the unconscious, the kinship and the incestuous character of the affection remain.

The poor tutor Alfred Allmers marries the sensual Rita, whose wealth enables him to live life in his own way, free from care. They have a child, Eyolf. Once, while Alfred is caring for the child, Rita tempts the man into her room and seduces him. In the meantime the child falls to the floor, seriously injuring himself. From then on Eyolf must use crutches. After this Alfred is despondent. He wishes to make amends for the guilt he feels toward the child; he wants to raise him to be happy despite his affliction, dedicating all his time and energy to this task. He comes to this conclusion during a long journey from which he has just returned at the beginning of the drama. Rita receives him in the evening with all the refinement of a wife in need of love, who has had to endure her husband's absence for several weeks without a substitute. She receives him in a dimly lit room, alone, with her hair down, attractively dressed, and offers him champagne. He fails to react, however, and she is no longer able to seduce him to have sexual relations with her. The next day, she says to him with symbolic significance:

> There was champagne but you just let it stand.

Alfred replies, "almost gruffly":

> Well, yes, I let it stand.

Rita correctly ascribes Alfred's neglect of her to his affection for his "younger half-sister" Asta, with whom Alfred had lived intimately until his marriage. Rita now pronounces aloud her wish that Asta no longer visit them.

> *Alfred* (stares at her amazed): What! You wish to be rid of Asta?
> *Rita:* Yes, Alfred! Yes!
> *Alfred:* But why in the world . . . ?
> *Rita* (passionately throwing her arms around his neck): Because then I could finally have you all to myself.

For the same reason, she tells Alfred she would prefer that the child die or never have been born than that he rob her of her husband's love. When the child really does die, the mother accuses herself of having brought about his death through her wish.

With Alfred, though, this feeling of guilt is associated more deeply with the rejected sexual act, during which the child fell. With deep psychological insight, Alfred's sexual rejection of his wife is derived from the childhood fixation of his libido upon his sister. The association of this attachment with feelings of guilt in connection with the son is brought about through the name "Eyolf." Indeed, while they lived together, Alfred was wont to address his sister by that name. In a private moment, he had revealed this to Rita. This moment surely reminds him unconsciously of his love for his sister, but he rejects conscious recollection of this love.

Rita: Did you not use to call her Eyolf? I believe you told me that once, in a private moment. (Approaching him) Have you forgotten it, this heavenly moment, Alfred?
Alfred (drawing back as though horrified): I know nothing! I wish to know nothing!
Rita: It was at the very same time your other little Eyolf became a cripple!

The unconscious fantasies underlying this whole complex of confusingly related emotions can best be characterized with the words of Pfister, who presents this drama as evidence for the playwright's unconscious psychological knowledge (1912, 72):

> The short sexual encounter is actually associated with the sister. Alfred wishes that the child who bears her name had been borne by her. This also explains why Rita is unable to love the child. In fact, she declares that the aunt has come between herself and her little son. . . . The unhappy woman suspects that her rival and her beloved husband are bound by repressed incestuous love. Alfred's feelings of guilt in fact derive from this incestuous affection. The sibling complex, which also prohibits the sister from loving another man, is derived in Alfred's case from the mother-and-father complex: he wishes to make amends because his father was unkind to his [step]mother and sister. In his efforts to compensate for his father's faults, he actually identifies with him by mistreating his own wife.

Ibsen himself reveals, though unwittingly, that the sexual rejection Alfred exhibits is associated with the childhood fixation of his affections on Asta.

Asta: Go to Rita. I beg you. . . .
Alfred (starting back violently): No, no. Say not a word of that! You see, I cannot. (More quietly) Let me stay here with you. I have loved you.
Asta: Since childhood.

Asta also loves her brother and is therefore unable to marry the engineer Borghejm.

Alfred: Yes, yes. But just tell me why you cannot. . . .
Asta: No! I beg you, don't ask me. You see, it is so painful for me.

Still, she rejects her love for Alfred.

Alfred: Rita and I can no longer live together.
Asta: But you are not a man who can remain alone.
Alfred: Indeed I am. I managed before.
Asta: Before, certainly. But then I was with you.
Alfred: And to you, Asta, I also wish to return now.
Asta (avoiding him): To me! No, no, Alfred! That is quite impossible.
Alfred: Dear, dear sister. I must return to you. I must come home to you to heal and purify myself after living with. . . .
Asta (horrified): Alfred, this is a sin toward Rita!
Alfred: I have sinned toward her, but not because of that. Think back, Asta, to the time when we lived together. Wasn't it like one great celebration from beginning to end?
Asta: It was, Alfred. But such a thing cannot be relived.
Alfred (bitterly): Do you mean that marriage has spoiled me beyond hope?
Asta (quietly): That is not what I mean.
Alfred: Good. Then let us take up our old life once again.
Asta (with determination): We cannot, Alfred!
Alfred: Indeed, we can. For the love of siblings . . .
Asta (tensely): What has that to do with the situation?
Alfred: It is the only relationship not subject to the law of transformation.

Now follows defense against the incestuous sibling love in the form of the revelation that the two are actually not related. Asta has learned this from letters she read the morning after Alfred's arrival. Alfred, however, still does not know the truth. Before she actually reveals the truth, Asta hints that she and Alfred may not share the same father:

Asta (quietly): Mother probably did not always act as she should have.
Alfred: Do you mean toward our father?
Asta: Yes.

The revelation scene, during which Alfred mentions that sibling love is the only relationship not subject to the law of transformation, continues as follows.

Asta (trembling, quietly): But if our relationship is not of that sort? . . . I do not have the right to bear the name of your father. . . . You are not my brother, Alfred.

Here it is also clear that we are dealing with defense against this incestuous attraction. It is not merely revealed that Asta is not Alfred's half-sister. Indeed, it is revealed that they bear no blood relationship whatever, though she is officially his half-sister: she was born during the second marriage of Alfred's father. However, that Alfred's father is not actually her father affects only their blood relationship and not their nominal relationship. Alfred continues to speak of himself as her brother; he still wishes to convince her to remain despite this revelation.

Alfred (mastering his excitement): Stay, and share life with us, Asta. With Rita. With me. With me, your brother.
Rita (withdrawing her hand with determination): No, I cannot.

She then quickly packs her things in preparation for her departure. When she is about to go, the dialogue continues.

Alfred (quietly, nervously): What does this mean, Asta? It seems that you are fleeing.
Asta (quietly, with anxiety): Yes, Alfred, I am fleeing indeed.
Alfred: Fleeing—from me!
Asta (whispering): Fleeing from you—and from myself.
Alfred (drawing back): Ah!

Defense (flight) is stronger than the incestuous impulses. With increasing sexual repression, defense comes more and more strongly to the fore. With Ibsen, sexual repression has almost reached the limit beyond which its mechanisms either lead to neurosis or must become conscious. With Goethe (*Die Geschwister* [The siblings]), wish fulfillment was still possible through the deflection of the conscious from the rejected incestuous union. Here, though, this possibility is eliminated through increased repression.

The Incest Theme in Contemporary Literature

In the relationship of parents with their children the whole cycle of human emotional possibilities, from folly and vice to heavenly glories, comes to completion.

The man inimically disposed toward his mother and sister will never be able to love his spouse with true inner conviction either. All the fruits of love derive their strength from the same root.

GABRIELE REUTER

In apparent contrast to the progress of repression in the totality of human psychic life, repeatedly emphasized and illustrated in our investigation, in modern literature the incest theme, which occurs in all its variations, appears with surprising frequency in its fully conscious manifestations. Thus one investigator can by no means provide anything approaching a comprehensive discussion. We must therefore limit ourselves to a few of the more important examples and attempt at least to characterize the most important types. Beforehand, though, we should attempt to explain the frequency and persistence of the incest theme in modern literature in the context of the progress of repression. It has been claimed "that modern literature tends so noticeably, and so much more than in other times, to sexual themes and their free portrayal" (Eulenburg 1911). Still, even superficially, the claim can be made that in contemporary literature the automatic distinction between works that live on permanently owing to their effective content and works that are soon forgotten has not yet occurred and that the works of other times that have prematurely disappeared from view would perhaps reveal that the situation some wish to claim holds only for contemporary literature held for other literary periods as well. This possibility—which, by the way, should not be taken too seriously—would gain support from the psychologically relevant fact that it is works with undisguised sexual content that are renewed with each generation and disappear most quickly from the literary scene. By contrast, as we have attempted to demonstrate, it is those works derived through the highly valued process of repression and sublimation (cf. *Hamlet*) that remain young and effective for centuries, precisely because they correspond more and more closely to the effects of progressing repression, in which their writers were far ahead of their contemporaries.

However, we do not wish to deny that modern literature tends most strongly to the undisguised depiction of sexual, especially incestuous, themes. Indeed, we believe we have come to appreciate and understand this situation from a psychoanalytical standpoint. In the Introduction, we mentioned that the progress of repression in human psychic life necessarily brings about, in compensation, constantly greater perfection of consciousness so that, given the increased demands of repression, the originally repressed impulses become more and more subject to conscious control. Control of the repressed (incestuous) impulses, which earlier was still possible via unconscious projection and the corresponding reaction in the work of art, is now possible, given the increasing pressure from the tendency for repression, through conscious contemplation and action. In the main, the development of the presentation of the incest theme shows the realization of this practical-psychoanalytical principle. This provides us with evidence that we are on the correct path in our understanding of these phenomena. This "return of the repressed from repression" (Freud) bears a strong resemblance to neurosis and is ultimately in conflict with artistic production. After a brief overview of the incest theme in modern literature, we shall conclude this volume with a discussion of this resemblance, looking both backward and forward.

In the following summary, of course, it will not be possible to discuss in detail the psychic life and total production of individual writers. After illustrating the importance of the incest complex in life and artistic production for a few important writers through a detailed discussion of biographical points and a comparison of literary works, we shall, contrastingly, investigate the popularity and frequency of the incest theme with writers varying widely in their paths of human and artistic development. This will serve as evidence for the importance of the incest complex in general and as indirect evidence for its role with individual literary personalities.

To complete our account of the frequency and manner of treatment of the incest theme in contemporary literature, in addition to numerous references to individual works, we will discuss the modern works dealing with the struggle between father and son or with the love between father and daughter. Further, we will refer to the numerous examples of modern works dealing with the themes of sibling recognition or the dissolution of sibling relationship (cf. chap. 17: Heimann, Kraus, Zahn, Bahr, Heyse, Jensen, Sachs, etc.). We can now turn to a discussion of these forms of the incest theme. First, we should note certain presentations in which incestuous fixation leads, with fine psychological understanding on the part of the writer, to a lack of function in love and sex toward persons outside the family.

In the novella *Untrennbar* [Inseparable] (1885), Adolf Wilbrandt portrays the deep affection of two siblings for each other. Their love is so fixated on one another that each is incapable of transferring it to any other person of the opposite sex. First the sister saves the brother, to whom "her loving heart had been dedicated with a certain wild fervor," from the bonds of a woman and of death. Then the brother, who is "at first jealous of her beloved," frees his sister from this man by killing him in a duel. The dying man confesses that from the beginning he had been planning to kill the brother. The siblings now live beside and for one another, linked to each other. The brother says: "I could only love a woman like Susanne." Later he declines to marry a young woman " 'because she is not of Susanne's kind, for I can live only with a woman of her kind; but I cannot find her. Yes, my dear man,' he continued, facing me with a tragicomic expression, 'that is the strange thing, the deeply troubling thing in my life. This young woman (he pointed to Susanne) always spoils all the other women for me. She makes it impossible for me truly to fall in love with any other woman for life.' " It is characteristic of the mutual "rescue fantasies" of the two siblings that the brother later, through attentive care, saves the life of the sister, who had once saved his life, and finally also rescues her from a burning house (cf. *Nathan der Weise*). In caring for his sister he contracts her fatal affliction, and she resolves to die united with him (death symbolism).

In the novella *Die Schauspielerin* [The actress] (1906), Heinrich Mann portrays with great psychological sensitivity a man's psychic impotence and a woman's frigidity arising from failure to transcend the incest complex. Leonie says to her cousin, who desires her passionately, "bracing herself, with an imperious enthusiasm bearing the overtones of a secret: 'No touch, never! I can give my body to no one, as long as I live!' He thought: 'Does she mean that she is ill?' In this way, it was not he alone who was rejected. She rejected all." She is willing to give herself to one man only, the young Rothaus: "I would let him have me tomorrow." Still, he rejects her, and all other women as well. "In love, he is a sort of monster." His rejection is expressed in a characteristic manner: "Two bodies that have so forgotten all cleanliness and restraint that their whole life long, with each other, they . . . : incomprehensible! Never again to belong to one's self, never to save one's skin from another's touch, never to be able to keep one's breath pure from contamination by another's." In this behavior Leonie's cousin, the orchestral conductor, perceives the abnormal: "I can tell you one thing: whoever finds physical love dirty, whoever wishes to avoid contact with another person's body, for any reason whatsoever, is a blatant egoist." Then Leonie and her cousin converse: " 'Just imagine him! What can be holding him back?' Then the conductor said: 'Is he perhaps lacking the natural means?' 'No, I cannot believe that,' continued Leonie with conviction. 'Or he has . . . other loves about which he wishes to deceive the world by appearing in public with a woman.' 'That has occurred to me as well. But that cannot be it: the state in which we once were—no one would mime that!' 'It would take an idiotic psychological perspective to make someone avoid you.' But how? They conversed further. Did he anticipate everything in fantasy with abnormal sensuality? Such things existed."

Nor does the author's delayed revelation shed much light on the subject, aside from the hint of a psychic impotence whose origins are not clearly stated:

> At the age of twenty he had discovered that he could not love. It had been a half-understood experience involving his first love. Perhaps he would never have approached a woman had he not heard or read of a process known as love. He had thought he had observed it in himself, but the possession of a woman suddenly cut him off from it. He wanted to leave immediately, but he forced himself to remain—through hesitation and with the help of curiosity. Calmly, he observed the dark, unknowing impulses of the other soul. . . . Protesting, his lover sensed his equanimity. . . . Upon their separation, she expressed her disgust and he hid his shame. . . . An opportunity spoiled or wrongly taken. She had been too easy for him, perhaps too young. Then he became familiar with hysterical passion and moral

> degradation through a woman of immense sensuality bordering on the humanly possible. It took ten days before he knew absolutely that he had lied, that he had wanted to creep into the destiny of others and had failed. Behind him lay also a questionable experience with a very young, untouched woman of his own circle who had spent several nights with him, on his bed, in his arms. He had promised to spare her. Why had he broken his word in the end? What had begun with strange overhearings ended, as always, with a repulsed knowledge of everything and nothing. This time he had felt that love was forming, but the shock of the flesh destroyed it brutally. Now he despised it, the flesh. He determined never to be subject to it again. Of his weakness he made a strength; he regarded his abstinence as elevation of the self. The feelings of guilt associated with desire he regarded as the noble timidity of the solitary one. What did not involve him he considered coarse. What he could not fathom he considered obscene. When he began to desire Leonie, the farewell glance of his first beloved and the inquiring horror in her wide eyes returned to him from seven years of shadow. Never again! He could die for a woman without having possessed her, but he could never bear to meet this glance again! He saw it awaiting him in Leonie's loving expression. Each time he was about to take Leonie in his arms, he fled, seeing in her face the expression at the hour of separation when she would have found him out.

As the deepest source of this rejection of sex the novella reveals incestuous fixation, an explanation Leonie considers meaningfully: "But that is not humanly possible: simply because he has taken it into his head that I am his sister?" This conception constantly reappears: "Then he mentioned love and suddenly the word 'sister' was spoken. It fell like a stone into a well. Leonie gazed at him, stunned by such depth." And one evening when her highest hopes had once again been disappointed by him, she asks: " 'I am your sister; is that it?' Time passed. Then he said slowly: 'But do you perhaps know about the king of Egypt? A very lonely man. He never touched the bodies of strange women. He could only marry one woman—his sister.' '. . . It's true,' he said, 'we are no pharaohs!' " In another place it is stated directly that "if she was a woman, she was much more than a lover. She possessed the soul of the sister, and the enchantment of her sex was contained in flesh that seemed to consecrate an unnamed relationship. The thought of touching it filled one with the sacred horror surrounding incest. One withdrew. One loved in one's thoughts without even touching hands. Such was fate. . . . And her sisterly eyes shone large upon him." But her passion, too, has overtones of sisterhood, and her inability in physical love seems incestuously derived through the rejection of her cousin as well: " 'Return and call me "sister" if you wish. I have not the strength to turn away'. . . . She loved him. Her feelings were not sisterly, not sisterly at all. It seemed she had deceived herself." The rejection of this love makes her ill. "Her feminine suffering, which had already left her in an indolent sort of torment after she withdrew from her first involvement, broke out more strongly still and exhausted her."

The author is able to depict the psychic consequences of this imposed abstinence very effectively: "They could not find the strength to renounce their fruitless excitement, now mixed with enmity as well. . . . Only indirectly did they reveal their excessive obsession—their desire to share one life. . . . She became sleepless. . . . In her sleeplessness she became filled with irritating and insufferable anxiety, and in her thoughts she directed her physical anger at anyone at all—a seamstress, a colleague. . . . She was more than ever inclined to compensate for the one great denied passion through many insignificant caresses. She substituted high living for love. As if her senses, denied the one passion, could never have enough of these forgivable substitutes, she became a connoisseur, adopting a certain brand of champagne, a certain cigarette."

In Karl Borromäus Heinrich's story "Menschen von Gottes Gnaden" [Men of God's grace] (1910), Miéville, later Pater Bonaventura, loves Countess Riom, who bears a striking resemblance to him. She marries his friend, Baron Frangart, and Miéville decides to renounce life and the countess who has shown him affection, who turns out to be his half-sister. As in Mann's novella, Lieutenant Miéville's fixation on his sister leads to sexual abstinence: "I have had leave for a week. And today for the seventh time I have invited a lady of the night to my hotel. Every night it's a different one. To each I have given one hundred francs. And to each one I have said: 'You must pray with me for a noble woman!' One of them asked me: 'Is this a new perversion?' " The tale further depicts the solitary life of the young Baron Frangart, who also bears a great resemblance to Miéville and is regarded by him with fatherly love. As a boy, his father having died early, he suspected his mother's relationship and her secret affection for Miéville; he remains lonely his whole life long. Besides his beautiful, gentle mother, whom he treats with refined politeness, he never approaches any woman, although his handsome appearance attracts many to him. In fact, he drives the young wife of his servant from his home because she "repulses" him. Nor is he able to return the faithful attentiveness of his school comrade Schlagintweit. His final, narcissistic attempt to adopt a boy from the orphanage, whom he clothes as he himself was clothed as a boy, and to "displace himself into the boy" is a failure. Rather than developing an internal identity with Miéville's example, Frangart merely copies it adroitly. Thus defense against this orientation is required: "Save me, release me . . . from this echo, from this mirror, from this shifting mask, this chameleon."

Emil Strauss's novella *Schwester Euphemia* [Sister Euphemia] (1909) relates in an English medieval setting and in legendary form the story of the princess Philippa, who loves her own brother but resists this love with all her physical and mental power. She goes abroad, works as a lowly servingwoman, but sees in her young rescuer, who finds in her a substitute for his dead sister, only the image of her beloved brother. She becomes a nun and does penance, but to no avail. The sweet, sinful sensation does not leave her, and she is destroyed by it.

In *Prinz Kuckuck,* by Otto Julius Bierbaum, we find one of the most important motivations for a brother's struggle for his sister. The protagonist, who has been raised since puberty with his brother and sister but considered their cousin and a ward, desires the sister and finally wins her. The brother is fixated on the sister, but true incest does not occur. This fixation makes him impotent with other women (cf. Mann's novella), ultimately leading to homosexuality (cf. Heinrich's tale). The brother attempts to murder his rich and attractive rival, envied and despised for his sexual power, but he is himself killed. The incest theme of the mother plays a lesser role, but in its relation to the family complex, the leitmotiv of the novel, it is also developed in a psychoanalytically accurate manner (as Dr. Federn has kindly informed me). In the story "Somalio Pardulus" by the same author, conscious sibling incest is portrayed.

Thus we can proceed to actual, conscious sibling incest, so often portrayed in modern literature. In the novella *Verstörte Zeit* [A troubled time], the first in the cycle *Frühschein: Geschichten vom Ausgang des grossen Krieges* [Early light: Tales from the end of the Thirty Years' War], the recently deceased Jakob J. David portrays conscious incest between children of the same father by different mothers. Here again we find a typical theme: the brother does not meet the sister until she is grown. He falls in love with her so passionately that he even challenges his father, who threatens him with legal punishment; the siblings feel nothing objectionable in their love, placed by the author in the frightful time of the war. Besides the passionate sibling love, the bitter enmity between father and son is emphasized. Finally this enmity leads the old Hirschvogel to take vengeance on his own children.

A brother's passion for the sister, bordering on insanity, has been portrayed by the Polish writer Stanislaw Przybyszewski in his fantasy *De Profundis,* which he dedicates to his sister and his wife. The protagonist loves his sister Agaj, of whom his wife is jealous with reason: "I fear that you love her more than me. . . . She really loves you not at all like a sister. I have never seen such a thing between siblings!" The author reveals the childhood origins of this passion with great sensitivity: "You were probably twelve years old then—thirteen, perhaps? You were afraid of the storm and came to my bed. You wanted me to tell you stories. You were so spoiled. You stayed to sleep with me. . . . And then suddenly, that fearful crashing and thundering, lasting for a minute, when the lightning struck the poplar near our home! Then you threw yourself trembling upon my breast and pressed so tightly toward me. I can still feel your thin little hands squeezed around me, and your soft legs burning into me with a feverish glow. You did have a fever then. You were always feverish." But he too suffers from such feverish fantasies associated with his sister. To find peace, it is sufficient for him to recreate this childhood experience, to hold his sister's hand and press her body toward his.

> It was strange that he succumbed to this fever each time he left his wife. Now he would have her [the sister] here. He would simply hold her hands and all would be well. He would surely fall directly into slumber. A sickly longing for her hands, a tormenting desire to press her body toward his, to lay his face upon her breast. He clearly felt her hand trembling as it glided and ran over his body. . . . And suddenly, once again, a wild paroxysm of desire and lust for Agaj came over him. And once again he wished to throw himself into the feverish orgy of this incestuous pleasure. . . . She did not leave him. He still saw her close, so close to him. With his eyes, he disrobed her. He reveled in her nakedness, he desired her.

One night, to escape from this fantasy, he goes onto the street and takes home a prostitute, a "child." He falls asleep beside her without making love to her. In Heinrich's and Mann's tales we have noted the same trait—the unconscious association of the prostitute with the sister and the resulting impotence. Here the author directly identifies this association. The protagonist directly refers to the child selected from the street as a substitute for his sister: "I was searching for my Agaj of younger days; do you understand?" Finally the brother openly confesses to his sister his sexual passion for her. Still, though she is passionately devoted to him, she can love him only as a brother. " 'Is this reason? No. no. This is something I am not familiar with. I feel an insane longing for you. How often I have pressed you close to me with these arms at night! See my thin body! How often it has wound itself about yours. And, and,' she stammered confusedly, 'at the last moment, something separates us, tears us apart. It must be our shared blood. Can you not feel it?' " "They sank down, they succumbed to the mute ardor of their blood. Wildly, beyond reason, they plunged into the frightful whirling of sexual ecstasy."

In Kurt Münzer's fervently sensual novel *Der Weg nach Zion* [The way to Zion] (1907), brother and sister are united in conscious incest. From the beginning they feel latent sensuality toward one another. Finally it breaks forth openly in the sister, and all the adventures of the flesh she has experienced seem to her to be only a prelude to the one final spiritual union through which she wishes to conceive by her brother chastely and without sensuality.

> She embraced him when they parted and kissed him like a bride. "Yes, you," she whispered, "if you were not my brother." . . . "Ephra," she whispered, taking her brother's hands and extending his arms, then laying down her head, inhaling, upon his breast. "I love you, brother!" . . . "Rebekka, Rebekka!" he cried, groaning, and pushed her away. . . . She touched him lightly, placed his mouth on her breast, and whispered passionately: "No shame! No shame! We are beautiful." He felt her warm flesh shudder beneath his lips. "Sister, sister!" he said in horror. A fearsome feeling grew within him. Only with difficulty did he recognize and feel the sister in her. . . . But she did not release him. She said, forgetting herself: "Do you not feel that nature brought us forth from the same womb only so that we could finally find one another and become one, just as we were before we lived, when our seeds slept together in the primordial womb? Do you not feel that nature has destined us for one another, brother and sister?" "Rebekka!" he cried in desperation, "Do not touch me; not like this, not like this!" He tore himself loose. . . . "Where has your peace gone, sister?" Suddenly she was embracing him. "You," she whispered passionately, ardent, overflowing, "You, you can give it back to me. Give me the content of my life. My deepest depths are awaiting you. There I am clean and untouched. There I would receive you!" "You are mad! You are mad!" he cried, terrified. "Be still, be still!" She did not release him from her arms. "Nature calls us together," she cried out with ardor. "Before we were, we were one. Brother and sister! It is no sin. It is a triumph. I desire no pleasure from you, Ephraim! Our two lives shall take their spark from each other, shall be consumed in a third that unites us both. We are not succumbing to desire but to a command, the highest command. Do you understand me, brother?"

Finally, invoking the pure and holy purpose of conception, she brings her brother, physically and spiritually broken, to commit incest. Afterward, though, sensual desire for the sister breaks forth in the brother and he kills her. "'*This night must become as though it had never been. Its last trace must be destroyed.*' 'The child, the child!' he cried and laughed harshly. . . . 'You are no longer safe from me. I love you, I love you.' . . . 'What did you just say, you pure and chaste one? Where is your dream of immaculate conception? A man remains a man, a man.' . . . 'Now you must die,' he said hoarsely. 'Do you understand? You as well as I. Shall our child live? The child of incest?' " The dedication of the novel suggests the author's deep personal association with the figures of his fantasy: "To my sister Adele."

In his drama *La città morta* [The dead city] (1898), Gabriele D'Annunzio depicts a sister's conscious love for her brother, who therefore commits suicide. In his last novel as well, *Forse che sì, forse che no* [Maybe yes, maybe no] (1910), brother and sister secretly live together in incest. This is revealed by the jealous younger sister to her elder sister's beloved. The guilty sister goes mad, concealing a deeper meaning from those around her. The doctor says: "She is in such turmoil that her human powers do not suffice to master it. Yet in her wildest attacks she still demonstrates incredible control. I still sense in her an internal effort concerning a hidden clue in her conscience. She concentrates her whole mind upon it, lest it appear and reveal itself." But in clear hints, the "complex" does express itself.

> "For a while, she stared straight ahead. Then, with an unexpected tone, she began to recite a verse from the Bible—this one here." The doctor found the place in 2 Samuel and read: " 'And then Amnon was filled with a great hatred for her so that his hatred was greater than the love he had felt for her. And he spoke to her: "Rise up and go from me!' " I asked her directly: 'Who is Amnon?' She answered: 'The one who has driven me from him and closed the door behind me.' Then she began to fantasize again. She was delirious, constantly obsessed with one overwhelming impression. After a sort of long, incomprehensible monologue she said suddenly, and with a clarity by which she seemed frightened herself: 'But still, as for the guilt you have placed upon me, I am the guilty one and I have no justification!' Then I repeated my question and looked directly into her eyes: 'Who is Amnon?' She smiled in an indescribable way. Then she recited another verse, painfully drawing it out from her memory, as if from a fire: 'And Amnon was in such despair, that he became sick of love for his sister Tamar.' Once again, I repeated my question insistently: 'But who is Amnon?' She sprang up with a swift motion like a whirlwind of ash and glowing fire, crying: 'My brother, my brother!' "

From here on, now that the lover who has rejected her has been identified with the brother (Amnon), we are in a position to obtain a deeper understanding of the work. The lover, for whom the two sisters are rivals, is revealed to be a less objectionable substitute for the brother, beloved by both sisters.

In the Russian novel *Sanin,* by Mikhail Artsybashev (1907), the protagonist desires his sister and argues for free, unhindered sexual activity in every form—apparently so he can justify and carry out without blame his incestuous wishes. The love of two siblings and their hopeless resistance to this inclination are dealt with in the tale "Paula und Fery" by Josef Schneider (1906). Finally, incest between brother and sister is the theme of a novel by Catulle Mendés, for which Eulenburg (1911, 91) does not cite the title.

The unknowing enactment of sibling incest and neurotic defense against it can be illustrated in two dramatic works.

Geschwister: Drei kleine Theaterspiele [Siblings: Three short plays] by Christian Kraus (1909). The first play, *Geschwister* [Siblings] deals with a brother and sister in love without knowing each other's identity. The sister, identifying with the mother, had already sunk to prostitution but had then redeemed herself through honest work. Her lover of the evening proves to be her lost brother. She feels a powerful attraction to him because of his resemblance to her father. "That was what attracted me to you so much last night. It's just that there is something in your face that reminds me of my father. One would think you were the brother of the one in the picture, or even his son." The two siblings, who had been searching for one another since childhood, discover too late that they have committed incest. They nevertheless make the difficult decision to continue with their relationship as it is. "Have they inquired as to our sibling incest laws? Shall we obey their laws? The world has robbed me of you as a sister and you of me as a brother. We were not permitted to become siblings. Now we have found one another as lovers. This is the fault of the world itself. I shall remain with you. We shall live together, just as many others do. No one shall know that we are siblings. I want no woman but you. You are my happiness, and we shall be happy together."

The second play, *Um Mitternacht* [At midnight], depicts the awakening of sensual passion for one another in two adolescent siblings, with special emphasis on childhood sexual curiosity.

The third play, *Liebestod* [Love-death], in many details reminiscent of the first, portrays the flowering of passion between two people who formerly regarded one another only as brother and sister. "We grew up as brother and sister. There is another love between you and me." In this love the protagonist's rival is his elder brother, who has returned unrecognized and finally renounces his sister. That the sister, beloved by both brothers since childhood, bears the name Elisabeth, the name of the brothers' mother, suggests the underlying rivalry for the mother's affections.

Ernst Didring's drama *Hohes Spiel* [High stakes] (1909) deals with the sexual jealousy of a man who bears mortal hatred toward his brother as a competitor, since he is in love with his brother's wife. All the typical themes of the incest complex appear here once again; for example, the denial of kinship with the hated competitor and the fantasy that the beloved is unhappy in his rival's arms.

Signe: Do you mean your brother?
Gunnar: Your husband.

Ivar: You wish to kill your brother?
Gunnar: I wish to kill the stranger who possesses the woman I desire, the woman intended for me. He has robbed me of her.

. . . .

Gunnar: Are you happy?
Signe: Why shouldn't I be happy?
Gunnar: Yes, you are right.

Later, though, Gunnar insistently demands that she follow him. He claims that his brother does not love her, that his brother could never love her as passionately or intimately as he can. The "cure" for this criminal passion is made possible when Ivar lets his brother wonder for an entire night, tormented, whether or not he has killed his envied competitor by shooting at an elk. In the morning he discovers that his brother had only been visiting a sick acquaintance during the night. He breathes a sigh of relief that his murderous impulse toward his brother had been carried out in mind only. Through a psychoanalytical confession of his forbidden passion before his whole family, he is "cured."

Before discussing the presentation of mother incest in modern literature, let us turn to three interesting depictions of the father complex.

In the drama *Mutterschaft* [Motherhood] by Johannes Raff (1911), which bears a striking resemblance to Ibsen's *Lady from the Sea,* a young woman's hysteria is depicted. In childhood she has fixated her libido on her deceased father. She feels revulsion toward her mother as well as toward her newborn child. She is repulsed by sexual relations with her husband and by "animalistic" sexuality in general. She identifies with the unrestrained personality of her father and longs for reunion with him in the beyond, which she therefore pictures in a quite material fashion. Again and again her fantasy concentrates on the ideal, glorified image of her father, which of course she can never find in real life. The merging of this image with that of the Heavenly Father is also remarkable:

> Enlightenment, Father in heaven! Behold, my soul is before you and desires one glance. Release it, oh, my Father, it is ready! Papa, my poor Papa, help me pray! Be near me in this hour and pray for me! Pray that my soul will be released, pray that it may come to you! For it belongs to you! Oh, it belongs to no one else in the world. And it will perish if it is not released. It will sink! (With fearful terror) Oh, Lord God, protect me. It is sinking into the abyss! (She buries her head in her hands and then looks up again. Her expression suddenly becomes serene, as if filled with quiet joy. She sees something and whispers.) Papa! Yes, I know. It is you! I see you. I see you! Oh, my Papa, my Savior, are you near? Thank you, thank you, thank you!

In this vision her father, at whose side she sees the Holy Mother of heaven, brings her her child. Only then, after she has, as it were, conceived the child immaculately by her father, is she able to love it and live for it. Fixation on the father complex is portrayed with psychological accuracy to the last detail.

The theme of the father-in-law's fear of incest with his deceased son's spouse is found intensified by the theme of sexual rivalry (abduction of the bride by the father) between father and son in Ernst Zahn's novel *Lukas Hochstrassers Haus* [The house of Lukas Hochstrasser]. After the death of his son Martin (wish for the elimination of the competitor), Lukas Hochstrasser has taken in his son's wife and her little son. Both are soon seized by passionate love for one another. She rejects a new suitor. " 'I know of only one to whom I can belong,' said Brigitte Fries. With both hands she tightly held Lukas's right hand. Then he was seized by a wondrous feeling." However, the old man chooses to renounce her, apparently because he cannot bring himself to possess the woman who has been his son's.

In Siegfried Trebitsch's drama *Ein Muttersohn* [A son of his mother] (1911), the painter Richard Victorius competes with the count for the love of the painter Laura. Based on a hint from his mother, he concludes that the count is his father. "You have taken from me my belief in my origins. You have taken from me the woman I loved and who felt love for me. You have taken from me everything one can take from a man one still leaves with his life. You have placed the most sacred thing in human life, one's mother, in a twilight where I can no longer see her." Indeed, when Laura is about to choose the count a second time, Richard even attempts to attack his supposed father violently and is restrained only by his actual father, who suddenly appears, just now fully revealing himself. In this scene we see the merging of the two fathers derived from the split in the fantasies associated with the family complex—the father as progenitor and protector, and the father as hated competitor for the mother's love. It is characteristic of this orientation and of the mother nature of the desired object (Laura) that Richard designates Laura's relationship with the count as incestuous. "But surely you can have no relationship with a man who is my father! (Reconsidering) No, no, with a man who could be my father! It is impossible! A relationship with a man of the count's age is always incestuous, for he could be our father—yours just as well as mine."

At this point, hints and disguised presentations of mother incest in modern literature can be discussed in brief.

In Jacobsen's *Nils Lyhne,* the protagonist loves his mother, his Aunt Edele, and his cousin Fennimore, whom he finally wins for himself when she has already become his friend's wife.

In *Die Aufzeichnungen des Malte Laurids Brigge* [The notebooks of

Malte Laurids Brigge] by Rainer Maria Rilke (1910), the neurosis of the protagonist is associated with the childhood Oedipus complex, also clearly presented. The boy is successful in getting his mother to hurry home to him from a party: "Mama entered wearing her long courtly gown, which she seemed not to notice. She almost ran, letting her white fur fall behind her, and took me into her bare arms. Amazed and transported as never before, I felt her hair and her small, well-cared-for face, the cold gems at her ears, the silk beside her shoulders, which bore the scent of flowers. We remained thus and cried and kissed each other until we felt that Father was there and that we would have to part. . . . It was not pleasant to have to explain ourselves whenever someone entered. Toward Father, especially, we expressed ourselves with exaggerated clarity. Only when it grew dusky outside and we were quite sure that we would not be disturbed would we sometimes give ourselves up to memories, common memories that seemed old to both of us, for we had both grown up since then."

In a psychologically interesting novella, "Die Hochzeitsnacht" [The wedding night] (*Osterzeit,* April 7, 1912), Hugo Salus portrays the incestuous fixation of parents on their children. On her daughter's wedding night the sensual mother, still in need of sexual attention and identifying with her daughter's young happiness, attempts in vain to seduce her husband: "He did not wish to think about the fact that his daughter had now become a woman as well. It was torment for him to be reminded of it. It was unpleasant for him to know that his daughter was in the desiring, ardent arms of a man and to imagine his child shuddering beneath the conquering kisses of a man. He bit his lips. It seemed like a desecration to be reminded of it."

Willy Speyer's novel *Ödipus* (1907), which the author dedicates to his mother, is the fine tale of a boy who suffers from the psychological consequences of erotic fixation on the mother. The father of the protagonist, who commits suicide shortly after the boy's birth, had, besides an amazing fondness for prostitutes, "the desire for a woman who resembled his mother, who would redeem him and bear him anew." He finds this woman in Beatrice, "to whom it seemed that the father of her children would be her child himself." Indeed, the father regards his young son as his brother, as though he had produced him, like Oedipus, in incest. It is apparently this disturbance of his own childlike relationship to his wife that drives him to death. "Yes, Beatrice had two children—a perfect son and a perverse one. Was it not natural that she should hate the perverse one?" As he grows up, the boy is disturbed by the origin of children and especially by the fate of the dead—particularly his father. He is redeemed by a young woman whose personality and appearance resemble those of his mother. "Where had he seen Brigitte before? He must have seen her frequently before, with her unique, confident stride and her healthy, beautiful hands. Otfried pondered for days where he could have seen her. 'How beautiful Brigitte is,' he said to himself. 'No, how glorious Brigitte is. No, how calm Brigitte is. No, how. . . .' He found no word that could accurately describe her being." After shyly declining for seven long months even to greet the adored person, he is finally released from the spell by a conversation with a friend. " 'Do you love your mother?' 'Yes, Olaf, I . . . love . . . my . . . mother. . . . Oh!' Otfried suddenly opened his eyes wide. 'What is it then?' 'Oh, Olaf, finally I understand: Brigitte is like my mother!' "

From the standpoint of the mother who longs for youthful love, the erotic passion of the maturing youth for his still youthfully beautiful mother, leading to suicide, is strikingly pictured in Klara Viebig's tale "Frühlingsnot" [Spring need] (Whitsunday supplement to *Die Zeit,* May 26, 1912). During a walk, the mother asks her son, who has returned home after a long absence, having taken his exams and having withdrawn from society: " 'Where do you have your lady?' 'You are my lady.' The mother placed her arm in her son's. How nice of him to visit her! She had felt a bit out of place, faced with so much youth. She grasped his arm more tightly. 'So you have come back to your old mother?' She smiled; she herself found the expression strange: 'Old mother!' 'I know no old mother, nor do I wish to.' And before realizing how emphatically he had said it, he embraced her. She felt a kiss on her soft cheeks—a kiss filled with masculinity. To strangers, they must have seemed a pair of lovers." However, it is clear that they also see themselves as a pair of lovers. This is demonstrated by her immediate loving recollection of her husband and the identification with her son's father: "Once she had taken just such a stroll with Viktor's father. He had drawn her toward his heart and had asked: 'Do you love me?' and she had responded with passion. She still felt the delicious terror that flowed through her then. Dear God, how long, long ago it was! In a delicious recollection, the woman closed her eyes. She let herself be carried along as if in a dream, an enduring, tender smile on her face." And on this stroll, the son "suddenly asked softly (with the same words as his father years before): 'Do you love me?' He asked it almost shyly and without looking at her. 'Of course. You're so queer!' Teasing, she slapped his cheek. He grasped her hand and kissed it. She pressed his hand. 'But come now!' He held her back. 'Let's walk more slowly. Please! I do so enjoy being alone with you. I've never been alone with you. There are always others about. Always. And I. . . .' He stopped short. His voice was deep. She was glad that he so much wanted to be alone with her. She had almost thought that the long separation, his long absence from his parents' home, had alienated him from her. She seemed to feel a tenderness like that she had felt toward him as a small boy. She smoothed his dark lock from his forehead.

'Close your eyes!' A light kiss touched his eyelids—a kiss on the right eye and a kiss on the left; a kiss on the right cheek and then on the left; and then a kiss on the mouth. It was a game she had played with him in childhood. The tall man stood quite still, hardly breathing. He still held his eyelids tightly closed. She cried, 'That's all. That's all. Now there are no more left!' but even then he did not open his eyes. 'Please,' he said softly, but so softly that she did not understand him." In the evening, when the adored mother, having promised the first dance to her son, dances instead with another man, he is overcome by jealousy: "Viktor's face became gloomy. 'Why did you dance with that fellow?' . . . He embraced her hastily." And after the dance, during which "he pressed her close to him," they withdraw together to a quiet niche.

> He groaned, and before she was fully aware of it, sunk down upon her, tightened his arms around her body, and pressed his face against her lap. Was he sobbing? His shuddering body made hers do the same. Was he really feeling so ill!? Shocked, she bent down toward him. Then he raised his face and leaned upward. With both hands he pulled her face down toward him, pressing a wild, desperate kiss upon her mouth: "Do you love me?" He seemed to be crying out. She was thoroughly confused. "Stand up!" The blood rushed to her head. In her sudden, anxious haste, she strove to remove his hand from her body. What could he be thinking, to embrace her so?! Timidly, she looked about. Had anyone seen? She suddenly felt so worried, so . . . so . . . 'Anxious' was not the right expression. Suddenly, he was a stranger to her, thoroughly unfamiliar. How could this be!? With shuddering hands, she pressed him away. "Let me go!" She pressed him away; she stepped away from him, out of the hidden niche, into the bright circle of the light.

Soon afterward he is discovered outside, a bullet through his temple. " 'But why has he done it? Why, why?' His pale lips, pressed tightly together beneath his small mustache, gave no answer. Nor could any other mouth."

A psychologically excellent sketch, "Schicksal spielen" [Playing fate] (*Osterzeit,* April 16, 1911), by Jakob Wassermann, touches on the deep secret of erotic attraction between mother and son. A widow lives in seclusion with her only son. "She cared for the child like the apple of her eye, and it was as though the passionate love she had given her husband had been transferred twice as strong and in pure form to her son." But the "growing youth [also] adored his mother passionately; he had infinite trust in her. The more he became aware of his emotions, the more he was drawn to her, even in his dreams. Given the tender sensitivity of his personality, he was fascinated by art at an early age. He painted and wrote poetry. But whatever image he placed on the canvas, whatever face, it was the image and face of his mother. In his verses, filled with oppressive premonitions of death, in which the world and its inhabitants were mirrored only in a dim, ghostly manner, his mother was also likeness and image." But when he had reached the age of eighteen, he became strangely absent minded and restless. The mother "feared that her son was suffering from the painful emotions of a shameful passion." She "could not even bear to imagine" yielding him to another woman. He always returned to his mother,

> who began to sense that he was doomed once and for all to disappointment, for at the beginning of his life there had been fulfillment and harmony that could never be found in any form in his later life. He returned to her, it is true, but more mutely, more reticently than before. Still unable to speak with others, he saw the wide abyss that stretched between him and the world. Accustomed to beauty and peace, poetry and inner contemplation, he felt boundless anger at the wide, satiated, loud coarseness of everyday life. And when he saw women, when he saw young girls whose glance and voice and face made his heart tremble, when at night his blood rushed and youthful desire seethed in his unconscious, his spirit clung to the image of his mother. Exaggerated expectation and overly refined timidity kept him hovering in conflict between emotional torment and the duty of his heart.

One evening he experiences purely sensual pleasure, finding himself in the arms of a friend's sister. He feels that he has been desecrated and that his pure affection for his mother has been betrayed; this leads him to suicide.

Conscious incest with the mother is encountered in typical guise in three modern tales, with which we shall close this portion of the discussion.

In Adolf Paul's short story "Ödipus im Norden" [Oedipus in the north] (1907), all the emotions of the Oedipus complex appear as if focused together. First published in Swedish in 1892, it is based, according to a comment by the author, on an actual occurrence. To illustrate fully the complete correspondence with the typical forms of the incest complex discovered in our investigation, it would be necessary to reproduce the entire twenty-five pages of the story. Strictly raised and ill-treated by his father, but admired and loved by his mother, the son finally commits incest with his mother and kills his father. Then, identifying with the father in defense against his criminal deeds, he is driven to neurotic penance; he and his mother must finally face earthly justice. This is so masterly a portrayal that we cannot neglect to cite at least the most important passages. The conflict with the father and erotic affection for the mother both burst forth openly when Anders wishes to go to the young woman he loves but is violently held back by his father. He creeps back to his room; from there he is able to observe his parents in secret (theme of eavesdropping).

"Larsson stood at the hearth and gazed gloomily forward. On the edge of the bed sat Stine, wearing only her nightshirt. Anders suddenly noticed that his mother was still beautiful, sitting there like that, curled up like a lustful cat. He could not turn his gaze from her. He stared and stared at her soft, white-clad body, nearly losing his senses. He had never seen anything so beautiful; never, not even Grete."

Then the parents approach each other, whispering softly.

> Anders started and pressed his face more closely against the crack in the floor. He held the white-clad feminine image in his eye's embrace. He heard nothing more; no longer did he see anything definite. What he saw and heard melted together, ran with his blood through his veins, beat like a hammer in his breast and temples; he sweated and shivered at once. . . . His gaze drew in the female figure, literally absorbing it. A strange, creeping feeling in his whole body; a shower of sparks before his eyes. He fell backward; now he had it. He felt it in his arms, her white body. It was she—Grete. He came to himself once again, dragged himself to his room, and fell into a deep sleep. From then on, day and night he dreamed of Grete. And he became depressed.

But the mother also loves the son with more than motherly feelings. She spies on him while he is bathing and "rejoiced at the sight of his white body. 'The boy! How large he was! He is becoming a man already! And he was beautiful, too!' " "Ashamed, she told herself that it was criminal, lustful curiosity on her part. She had felt an excitement she had never known during her whole marriage. And from this hour on, in her thoughts she was always with her son."

She takes advantage of her husband's absence to hide in her son's room, and once again it is the sight of his nakedness that drives her to the extreme: "She could no longer master herself. Without hesitation, she rushed forward, casting herself upon him and kissing him violently, passionately. 'Mother!' She kissed him until she had kissed his shame away, she fondled him until his timidity disappeared and he forgot his mother, feeling only that there was a woman beside him. And then he began to kiss her as well."

After this decisive step, his jealous enmity toward his competitor, his father, becomes more and more difficult to master:

> Anders always suffered terrible torments on hearing the exchange of words below. He would have liked to rush down and grasp her from his father's arms. But he never came farther than the foot of the stairs. There he stood, trembling from cold and jealousy, a witness to his father's abduction of his

> beloved. . . . He hated and despised him like the plague. And this hatred, constantly restrained, was collected and concentrated, growing stronger and stronger. He already knew now that he would not be able to restrain himself much longer from striking, striking without hesitation. His hatred for his father was as unnatural as his love for his mother. . . . When his father came home the next time and began to rage, Anders no longer hesitated. With determination, he went down, flung open the door, and grasped his father by the arm.

But in speaking to his father, he does not use the word "mother," referring to her only by her first name. This angers his father, who has already noticed his wife's coldness toward him. He gives himself over to drinking without worrying further about his wife and son, who become more and more careless. Once, thinking him completely drunk, they believe they can do just as they wish even in his presence but narrowly escape his boundless wrath. He attempts to kill them with an ax but falls down intoxicated. They then strangle him together and claim he has died of apoplexy.

From now on the son begins to drink, like his father before him. He begins to beat his mother, who resists with revulsion, and to take her against her will, just like his father, to whom he also bears a physical resemblance. "Anders was the image of his father. He had the same walk, the same gaze, the same tone of voice when he asked for something." This identification with his father, whose role he has taken on not only in his typical youthful fantasies but also in reality, persecutes him as a morbid idea, a hallucination.

> Was that not his mother who lay there waiting? Indeed, it was his mother. But he was . . . What was he doing here? Naturally, he had just beaten her; of course, he was Larsson. The memory of the first evening when he had lain upstairs on the floor gazing down on his parents suddenly stood clearly before him. He saw her now, in his memory. He lay upstairs, on the floor, and saw how she waited, how he—Larsson—went to her. But was he himself, Anders, not down here also? Could he be down here and up there simultaneously? Was he double? Father and son together?

Following the pronouncement of earthly punishment, the tale ends characteristically with reminiscences of childhood. After his attack, his mother is caring for him: "And she sat beside his bed, remaining awake. Once again she was his mother and he was a little child whom she sang to sleep; everything was good and beautiful again. His whole childhood was encompassed in these few, pitiful tones that appeared through recollection of other things."

In the rustic novel *Nils Tufvesson and His Mother*, Gustaf Geijerstam portrays "the memory of the evil mother who seduced her son and forced him to murder his wife."

> She had gained this power [over him] by seducing him to forbidden love when he was no longer a boy, but not yet a man. This began while the sickly Tufve Tufvesson was still alive. And if the hostile rumors after his death were true, it was this criminal love that caused it. . . . For when Tufve Tufvesson had been buried, Nils took his father's place in the wide bed in the living quarters. There he fell asleep every evening. There he awakened every morning, there the cruel Fates ensnared him more and more each night in the mesh of the net that drew him away from life and separated him from mankind. . . . He was like wax in her hand. For she had captured his senses at such an early age, and love is so powerful, especially when it takes on the deep red, peculiar color of sin. She was also so much stronger than he: all the questions he wanted to ask remained unspoken and were pressed back into his soul by her smile. In his soul they lay in slumber, tormenting him perhaps.

The rumors grow ever louder, and to quell them the mother encourages her son, "who had never turned his thoughts to a woman," to marry, but makes him promise never to touch his wife. "When the mother had received this promise, he sensed for the first time that everything evil and hard would grow worse after the wedding and not better. But he had put his thoughts aside, just as one puts aside what one wishes to forget." Finally, the mother brings him to kill his wife with her aid.

If the incestuous inclination, associated with such momentous psychic and social questions, is fully conscious here, in the following work—the last in our discussion of modern literature—the infantile and psychological conditioning factors of incestuous attraction have themselves become conscious. In the novel *Sündige Seligkeit* [Sinful bliss] by Stefan Vacano (1909), we find the passionate love of a son for his mother. This love resists every attempt at defense, finally leading to the sexual act and to the son's psychic ruin. The boy is enlightened about sex by the homosexual man who raises him. On learning that father and mother have sexual relations, he can no longer believe in God as the loving father. Through this enlightenment, his slumbering sensuality is awakened. He is now jealous of the young man courting his mother. "I felt that he was robbing me of her love. In my fantasies I regarded my mother as my lover." Repeatedly, though, he experiences incestuous dreams. There is an indirectly incestuous dream filled with anxiety; there is a nightmare; in general, defense against the incest wish leads to the release of anxiety. The protagonist reports: "I dreamed, that is I saw, that great white cloud, like a wonderful feminine bosom, suspended as it sank slowly down. It sank farther and farther down toward me and began to take my breath. It grazed my lips, threatening to suffocate me. I attempted to turn away, to repel the frightful vision. In vain. Then I suddenly dreamed I was a little child. I grasped with my little child's hands for my mother's breast and drank from it in long drafts. The tension in my soul subsided. The cloud, so threatening earlier, rose up again, transfigured with a pink glow. I seemed to hear a sigh of relief from those cloudy white breasts. I awakened." One can better understand this defense against the incest wish through disguise in the form of a harmless, infantile act of love, since we are told that the dreamer already exhibited sensuality as an infant.

One day after being enlightened, the boy eavesdrops on his mother while she is making love to her lover. "From this night on, I was no longer able to think of Mother as my mother. 'She is a woman,' my mind seemed to tell me. When I was a child, she was for me the tenderest, most loving, purest thing on earth. Now she was a woman . . . from whom I fled, of whom I dared not think." In a sort of stupor, as can often be observed in young people as a consequence of unsuccessful defense, the youth flees his parents' home. He roams about aimlessly, joins a wandering troupe, and falls in love with an actress—because she resembles his mother. Associated with the love for his mother, he harbors the typical fantasy of a past existence. Here too it was "for us two as if we had known each other always." In the darkness of the barn, he addresses her directly as "Mother," and she wishes to be everything for him—"mother and sister and everything." But he cannot touch her like a woman, "for I recognized with horror that I had only transferred to this dear creature the terrible inclination I felt for my mother." Indeed, in this love, his whole relationship to his mother is repeated. He also eavesdrops on the young woman while she is making love to another man, and he flees from her too.

He now goes to sea, where in his lonely nights he excites and gratifies himself by gazing at his mother's image on a medallion. Finally he struggles to an awareness of the truth that the man who raised him had explained as a universal human experience: "What he predicted has occurred: I love my mother. I recalled his words: 'Every mother is her son's first lover.' My mother will always be my lover. With horror, I now saw this clearly." Strengthened by this realization, he considers himself ready to return home and to carry on with this pure, motherly affection. In the meantime, the father has committed suicide (elimination fantasy of the son). The son wishes to be for the mother "what Father was for you." Indeed, in her son, Speranza has always loved his young father. "When I had grown, she sometimes became strangely excited while regarding me pensively. 'Your father,' she often said to me, 'must have looked like that.' In saying this, she blushed as though ashamed of some thought." Now she fully identifies her grown son with his deceased father and hopes that her son "will substitute for him completely." Thus on both sides the conditions for forbidden love are present.

> I longed for a lover. Then my hot love found her, the only one, the one I should have avoided according to human law. . . . What I had so often seen as a dream image, what had brought me to the border of insanity, sick with desire, . . . all my sinful dreams had now become reality. . . . Like an oracle demanding fulfillment, everything had occurred—everything I had been warned of by the one who raised me, everything I had fled and resisted. Two perverted beings, unable to resist, had found each other in sinful bliss and had fallen back into their atavistic, animal nature.

Finally, defense against sinful passion is suggested in that the protagonist, whose confession the author presents for us, fears that his whole life may have been only a dream: "It was of course painful to think of it—never to have lived. But then my love for the dead woman ⟨mother⟩ too would have been only a dream, and that is truly fortunate."

In the preface, the author comments that he had not intended to publish this confession, but "then I happened to come across a volume by the Viennese doctor, Professor Sigmund Freud, entitled *Drei Abhandlungen zur Sexualtheorie* [Three essays on the theory of sexuality]. When I had finished reading the portion on infantile sexuality, I knew that it was my duty to publish this confession."

We stand here at the border of psychoanalysis and art, and thus at the end of our task. On our long path we have seen that incestuous impulses are by no means to be interpreted in a sexual-pathological manner, but that they belong, rather, to the most primitive expressions of human drives and emotional life. Real gratification becomes impossible to attain, and these impulses become more and more repressed in the individual. They are justified through myths; freedom from guilt is found in religion. Finally these impulses take refuge in literary production. For the individual gifted with stronger drives, literary production becomes the ultimate form of release from this psychic conflict produced by the demands of culture. Thus the creative artist is characterized especially by the strength and intensity of his drives. To dam them in the context of culture, so much repression work is required that abnormally high degrees of sublimation result. Given relatively minor disturbances, though, such sublimation fails to come to fruition. This can easily lead to neurosis, closely related in its conditioning factors and psychic mechanisms. The artist, given his need for more intensive repression, lives out his powerful drive impulses in his fantasy, just as primitive man abreacted these same impulses, when they were first repressed from reality, through myths and religions. Affectively speaking, both ontogenetically and phylogenetically, then, the artist, despite his highly intellectual achievements in sublimation, represents a regressive stage, a failure to pass beyond the infantile level. In his discussions of factors leading to psychoneurosis, Freud has described this as regression to infantilism. However, the study of neurosis and individual cultural-historical observations made from this point of view have revealed that the central problem of psychic (affective) infantilism is manifested in the incest complex. Supported by the results of our investigation, therefore, we can claim that the incest complex with all its diversity, opposing aspects, and derivatives represents the nuclear complex of neuroses and of the literary creative drive as well. In nearly all important writers, we have observed a noticeably uniform childhood development. To this corresponds also the uniformity of a few typical literary fantasies. This course of childhood development results from the oppressive presence of a strict, stern father, whom the son opposes, and a gentle, tender, loving mother who enjoys and permits an intimate connection with a son in need of love and tenderness.

Of course we do not claim that literary talent derives exclusively from powerful incest impulses fixated in childhood. We claim simply to have recognized that the psychic energy (affects) resulting from the repression of these impulses constitutes one of the major driving forces in literary production. In the process of displacement, naturally, literary production can take up other themes. But in an astounding number of cases the selection of material appears to be decisively influenced by a tendency for liberation from repressed complexes. This is most clearly demonstrated by neurotics, a great many of whom engage in writing and lend a strongly subjective, technically insufficient expression to the same primitive complexes the great artist is capable of depicting in a formally sublime and also universal manner. But this technical inadequacy of expression in neurotics or dilettantes results for the most part from insufficient success in sublimating the same complexes that determine the content and affect of the works of great writers. Thus formal talent cannot be separated from the content and intensity of complexes and their repression. And if one hears again and again that powerful repressed complexes, no matter how strong, do not make an artist in the absence of technical talent, there is even more truth in the reverse of this statement: an individual gifted with technical ability, no matter how perfect, will remain nothing but a craftsman unless he has psychological struggles and sufferings to deal with through his technical ability. In no way do we wish, then, to claim that the essence of literary ability is to be found in relating incestuous accounts. We do not underestimate the importance of formal talent, though it too derives from certain typical repression mechanisms and can be easily understood. Nor do we deny that the writer is able to depict people, destinies, conditions, and moods in an appealing and impressive manner. But we are of the opinion that all of this is possible only in the context of a remarkable introspection: the writer expresses all the possibilities of his own being, lying within him, through a sort of neurotic turning away from life. This remarkable state, however, is itself derived from the powerful fixation of infantile complexes and fantasies that has been brought about by his strong drives. From the unconscious, these complexes and fantasies demand release. Our study of the literary depiction of themes has revealed that the writer suffers throughout his life from the significant complexes of his infantile psychosexuality. His social inability, too, is explained by the overly powerful demands his libido continually places on his ego, which he can gratify, at least at times, only through rich wish fantasies and defensive fantasies. The tragic conflicts he continually attempts to resolve in his works simply correspond to his inner conflict between drive and repression. Freud has characterized this as disharmony between the ego and sexuality. Here we cannot discuss in detail the technical means by which the writer masters these tragic conflicts of his psychic life. Nor shall we address why the writer is able to master them through art in the first place, though he is unable to do so in the normal way, yet need not resort to neurotic symptoms of defense. In the Introduction, we emphasized that in our investigation we are dealing with only one aspect of the process of artistic development and creativity. In such a limited discussion, one cannot hope for psychological explanations for specific artistic talents and forms of expression. However (disregarding the continual stimulation of the creative affective powers), to the extent that abnormal fixation on the family complex and the wish and defense fantasies associated with it influence and determine the artistic selection of material and its presentation—and we believe we have demonstrated that this is the usual case—we have also reduced the selection and presentation of material to their basic psychological mechanisms. Most important, we believe we have demonstrated that the writer, like the mythmaker, deals with given material not through external borrowing or assimilation, but from a deep psychic need, insistently demanding release. In this sense, having recognized how the ability to sublimate results from the mastery of powerfully active drives, we can no longer believe in inborn artistic talent. In this light it appears that talent is an expression of psychic need and that the degree of talent may serve as a measure for the tension present in the psyche of the artist. Therefore all great artists have suffered unspeakably from life and from themselves, finding peace and gratification only while engaged in creative activity. Possessed of deep knowledge of the psyche, Flaubert generalized his personal painful experiences, saying: "I feel that the artist is a monster, something outside nature. All the misfortunes providence heaps upon him result because he negates this axiom. He suffers from this and causes others to suffer from it. One need only ask women whom writers have loved or men who love actresses" (cf. Reik 1911). Similarly, Klages (1899a) writes: "How did the artist come to be one? Who can write for us the story of his development? How could natural drives be so much turned inward? Is this an escape, as is, perhaps, everything spiritual? As is, perhaps, social man per se, with his astoundingly unnatural institutions? . . . Perhaps all artistic activity is a psychic escape route for excessive or powerfully restrained life forces. . . . Art warms one with thirst for life and great self-awareness."

We believe that in this volume we have, in fact, written a portion of this story of the development of the artist. We have demonstrated that the writer commences creative activity because of impulses and affects that are effective because of insufficient repression. Their special content regularly includes the infantile Oedipus complex, which also decisively affects the selection and manner of presentation of material. Incestuous impulses per se do not, of course, bring the individual to engage in artistic creativity—any more than the simple relating of incestuous material can be a work of art or a myth. It is only the repression of such overly powerful, intensified impulses and the resulting struggle for defense that can make possible the liberating projection of these conflicts from the unconscious in a communal fantasy, a myth, or a work of art.

However, if artistic production depends to such an extent on the activity of unconscious, repressed drives, then, owing to the expansion of consciousness proceeding parallel to advancing repression, artistic ability to portray these complexes must necessarily suffer. Through the continually increasing need for repression, these complexes enter higher and higher spheres of conscious ability to master them. A review of thematic development extending all the way to contemporary literature has demonstrated how true this is in the case of incest. In this organic process of increasing expansion of consciousness, the psychoanalytical movement, which proceeded from the systematic expansion of consciousness to the therapeutic goal of treating specific individuals who have become neurotic, plays a highly catalytic role. Of course psychoanalysis cannot aim for the complete elimination of these complexes in the individual patient or, prophylactically, in society as a whole. What it aims for, and given appropriate conditions always produces, is the conscious mastery of the impulses to be repressed in the service of culture. As Freud aptly puts it, they are to be subjected not to unconscious repression, which can easily produce pathological effects, but to conscious consideration. Under these conditions, though, artistic liberation from these complexes seems not only unnecessary but also impossible, at least in the forms and means of expression of our contemporary art, which relates to repressed complexes. It seems to be an unavoidable consequence of the advancing expansion of consciousness that the artist, with this increased need for repression, must learn to master himself consciously, thereby teaching us to pass beyond him. Future developments will show whether, and to what extent, an art adapted to a higher level of consciousness is possible and by what means it can be executed. But our psychoanalytical experience with individuals—of whom, of course, society is composed—leaves no doubt whatever that our contemporary literature, which clings with remarkable conservatism to the tragic conflicts and solutions of Sophoclean Athens, will free itself from these primitive complexes as soon as the requisite spheres of consciousness are attained.

In identifying incestuous impulses as one of the most important driving forces in literary production, we have not intended to provide any ethical or intellectual valuation of the artistic personality. Instead, we have attempted only to demonstrate that literary ability, far from being a gift bestowed indiscriminately at birth by benevolent genii, is nothing but the attempt, essential for psychic self-preservation, to escape from the power of unconscious infantile complexes. The normal person is able to master these with relative ease; the neurotic fails but under favorable conditions can learn to master them consciously with the help of psychoanalysis; the artist, under favorable conditions, deals with them through unconscious abreaction.

References

Abraham, Karl. 1909. Die Stellung der Verwandtenehe in der Psychologie der Neurosen [The place of marriage among relatives in the psychology of neuroses]. *Jahrbuch für Psychoanalytische und Psychopathologische Forschungen* 1:110–18.

Adler, Alfred. 1907. *Studie über die Minderwertigkeit von Organen* [Study concerning the inferiority of organs]. Vienna: Urban und Schwartzenberg.

Albrecht von Eyb. 1472. *Ob einem manne sei zu nemen ein elich weibe oder nit* [Whether a man should take a wife or not]. Nürnberg: Creussner.

Alfieri, Vittorio. 1803. *Tragedie*. 6 vols. Paris: Molini.

Amélineau, Emile. 1888. *Contes et romans de l'Egypte chrétienne* [Stories and romances of Christian Egypt]. Paris: Leroux.

Bab, Hans. 1906. Geschlechtsleben, Geburt, und Missgeburt in der asiatischen Mythologie [Sex life, birth, and deformity in Asiatic mythology]. *Zeitschrift für Ethnologie* 38:269–311.

Bachofen, Johann Jakob. 1897. *Das Mutterrecht* [Matriarchy]. 2d ed. Basel: Schwabe.

Behagel, Otto. 1907. *Bewusstes und Unbewusstes im dichterischen Schaffen* [The conscious and the unconscious in literary production]. Leipzig: Freytag.

Bergel, Joseph. 1882–83. *Mythologie der alten Hebräer* [Mythology of the ancient Hebrews]. Leipzig: Friedrich.

Berger, Alfred. 1897. Wahrheit und Irrtum in der Katharsis-Theorie des Aristoteles [Truth and error in Aristotle's theory of catharsis]. In *Aristoteles' Poetik* [Aristotle's poetics], ed. Th. Gomperz. Leipzig.

Berger, Karl. 1905. Schillers Doppelliebe [Schiller's double love]. *Marbacher Schiller-Buch,* vol. 3, ed. Otto Güntter. Stuttgart: Cotta.

Bethe, Erich. 1891. *Thebanische Heldenlieder* [Theban heroic epics]. Leipzig: Hirzel.

Bettelheim, Bruno. 1983. *Freud and man's soul.* New York: Knopf.

Bloch, Iwan. 1904. *Neue Forschungen über den Marquis de Sade und seine Zeit* [New research on the marquis de Sade and his times]. Berlin: Harrwitz.

———. 1906. *Rétif de la Bretonne: Der Mensch, der Schriftsteller, der Reformator* [Rétif de la Bretonne: The man, the author, the reformer]. Berlin: Harrwitz.

———. 1909. *Das Sexualleben unserer Zeit in seinen Beziehungen zur modernen Kultur* [The sexual life of our times in its relation to modern culture]. Berlin: Marcus.

Boas, Franz. 1895. *Indianische Sagen von der nord-pacifischen Küste Amerikas* [Indian legends of the north Pacific Coast of America]. Berlin: Asher.

Bodenstedt, Friedrich M. 1858–60. *Shakespeares Zeitgenossen und ihre Werke* [Shakespeare's contemporaries and their works]. Berlin.

Böklen, Ernst. 1907. *Adam und Qain im Lichte der Vergleiche* [Adam and Cain compared]. Leipzig: Hinrichs.

———. n.d. *Christliches Adambuch des Morgenlandes* [The Oriental Christian book of Adam]. n.p.

Brandes, Georg M. 1895–96. *William Shakespeare.* Copenhagen: Gyldendalske.

Brauns, David. 1885. *Japanische Märchen und Sagen* [Japanese folktales and legends]. Leipzig: Friedrich.

Breuer, Josef, and Sigmund Freud. 1909. *Studien über Hysterie* [Studies on hysteria]. 2d ed. Leipzig: Deuticke. Originally published 1895.

Brevio, Giovanni. 1545. *Rime et prose volgari* [Popular rhymes and prose]. Rome: Blado.

Brugsch, Heinrich K. 1888. *Religion und Mythologie der alten Ägypter* [Religion and mythology of the ancient Egyptians]. Leipzig: Hinrichs.

Brunet, Gustave. 1858. *Le violier des histoires romaines* [The flower of Roman stories (*Gesta Romanorum*)]. Paris: Jannet.

Brunet, Jacques-Charles. 1860–65. *Manuel du libraire et de l'amateur de livres* [Bookseller's and book lover's handbook]. 5th ed. Paris: Firmin Didot.

Buchan, Peter. 1875. *Ancient ballads and songs of the north of Scotland.* Edinburgh. Originally published 1828.

Büdinger, Max. 1866. *Mittelgriechisches Volksepos* [Middle Greek folk epics]. Leipzig: Teubner.

Byron, George Gordon. 1966. *The works of Lord Byron.* Edited by Rowland E. Prothero et al. New York: Octagon.

Campbell, John F. 1890–93. *Popular tales of the West Highlands.* New ed. London: Gardner.

Cholevius, Carl Leo. 1854. *Geschichte der deutschen Poesie nach ihren antiken Elementen* [The history of German poetry with reference to its classical elements]. Leipzig: Brodhaus.

Christ, Wilhelm. 1888. *Geschichte der griechischen Literatur* [History of Greek literature]. Munich: Beck.

Comparetti, Domenico. 1867. *Edipo e la mitologia comparata* [Oedipus and comparative mythology]. Pisa.

Constans, Léopold Eugène. 1881. *La légende d'Oedipe* [The Oedipus legend]. Paris: Maisonneuve.

Creizenach, Wilhelm. 1876. Judas Ischarioth in Legende und Sage des Mittelalters [Judas Iscariot in the legends and myths of the Middle Ages]. *Beiträge zur Geschichte der Deutschen Sprache und Literatur* 2:177–207.

Creuzer, Georg Friedrich. 1841. *Symbolik und Mythologie der alten Völker, besonders der Griechen* [Symbolism and mythology of the ancients, especially the Greeks]. Vol. 2. 3d ed. Leipzig and Darmstadt: Leske.

D'Alméras, Henri. 1908. *Une amoureuse: Pauline Bonaparte* [A woman in love: Pauline Bonaparte]. Paris: Albin Michel.

D'Ancona, Alessandro. 1869. *La leggenda di Vergogna et la leggenda di Giuda*. Bologna.

De Gubernatis, Angelo. 1872. *Zoological mythology*. New York: Macmillan.

———. 1909. Die neue *Phädra* [The new *Phaedra*]. *Deutsche Revue*, June.

Delius, Nicolaus. 1882. Shakespeares Julius Caesar und seine Quellen in Plutarch [Shakespeare's Julius Caesar and his sources in Plutarch]. *Shakespeare-Jahrbuch* 17:67–81.

Detter, Ferdinand. 1892. Die Hamletsage [The legend of Hamlet]. *Altertum und Deutsche Literatur* 36:1–25.

Diederichs, Victor. 1880. Russische Verwandte der Legende von Gregor auf dem Stein und der Sage von Judas Ischariot [Russian versions of the legends of Saint Gregory of the Rock and Judas Iscariot]. *Russische Revue* 17:119–46.

Dilthey, Wilhelm. 1887. Bausteine für eine Poetik [Fundamentals of a theory of poetics]. In *Philosophische Aufsätze, Eduard Zeller gewidmet* [Philosophical essays dedicated to Eduard Zeller]. Leipzig.

———. 1906. *Das Erlebnis und die Dichtung* [Experience and poetry]. Leipzig: Teubner.

Duméril, Edélstand. 1839. *Histoire de la poésie scandinave* [History of Scandinavian poetry]. Paris: Brockhaus et Avenarius.

Duncker, Max. 1855–57. *Geschichte des Alterthums* [Ancient history]. Berlin: Duncker und Humbolt.

Dunlop, John Colin. 1814. *History of fiction*. 3 vols. London: Longman.

Durán, Augustín. 1851. *Romancero general* [General romance collection]. 2 vols. Madrid: Rivadeneyra.

Du Tillet, Jacques. 1894. [Review of Maeterlinck's translation of *'Tis Pity She's a Whore*]. *Revue Bleue* 4:2.

Eckermann, Johann. 1827. *Gespräche mit Goethe in den letzten Jahren seines Lebens* [Conversations with Goethe in the last years of his life]. Leipzig: Brockhaus.

Ehrenreich, Paul. 1910. *Die allgemeine Mythologie und ihre ethnologischen Grundlagen* [General mythology and its ethnological foundations]. Leipzig: Hinrichs.

Ellis, George. 1805. *Specimens of early English metrical romances*. London: Hurst, Rees, Orme, and Brown.

Engel, Eduard, ed. 1904. [*Byrons*] *Tagebücher und Briefe* [The diaries and letters of Lord Byron]. 5th ed. Berlin: Simion.

Erdélyi, János. 1850. *Ungarische Sagen und Märchen* [Hungarian legends and folktales]. Translated by G. Steir. Berlin: Dümmler.

Erman, Johann. 1885. *Ägypten und das Leben im Altertum* [Egypt and life in antiquity]. Vol. 1. Tübingen.

Eulenburg, Albert. 1911. *Sadismus und Masochismus* [Sadism and masochism]. 2d ed. Wiesbaden: Bergmann.

Ferenczi, Sándor. 1909. Introjektion und Übertragung [Introjection and transference]. *Jahrbuch für Psychoanalytische und Psychopathologische Forschungen* 1:423–57.

Freud, Sigmund. 1900. *Die Traumdeutung* [The interpretation of dreams]. Wiesbaden: Bergmann.

———. 1905. *Drei Abhandlungen zur Sexualtheorie* [Three essays on the theory of sexuality]. Vienna: Deuticke. (2d ed., 1910.)

———. 1907a. *Der Wahn und die Träume in W. Jensens "Gradiva"* [Illusion and dreams in W. Jensen's *Gradiva*]. Schriften zur Angewandten Seelenkunde [Writings on applied psychology], vol. 1. Vienna: Deuticke.

———. 1907b. *Zur Psychopathologie des Alltagslebens* [On the psychopathology of everyday life]. 2d ed. Berlin: Karger.

———. 1909a. Analyse der Phobie eines fünfjährigen Knaben [Analysis of phobia in a five-year-old boy]. *Jahrbuch für Psychoanalytische und Psychopathologische Forschungen* 1:1–109.

———. 1909b. Bemerkungen über einen Fall von Zwangsneurose [Remarks on a case of obsessional neurosis]. *Jahrbuch für Psychoanalytische und Psychopathologische Forschungen* 1:357–421.

———. 1909c. Bruchstück einer Hysterienanalyse [Fragment of an analysis of hysteria]. In *Sammlung kleinerer Schriften zur Neurosenlehre* [Collected lesser writings on neurosis], 2:48 ff. Leipzig: Deuticke.

———. 1909d. Der Dichter und das Fantasieren [The poet and fantasy activity]. In *Sammlung kleinerer Schriften zur Neurosenlehre* [Collected lesser writings on neurosis], 2:197 ff. Leipzig: Deuticke.

———. 1909e. *Sammlung kleinerer Schriften zur Neurosenlehre* [Collected lesser writings on neurosis]. Vol. 2. Leipzig: Deuticke.

———. 1909f. *Die Traumdeutung* [The interpretation of dreams]. 2d ed. Leipzig: Deuticke.

———. 1909g. Über infantile Sexualtheorien [On infantile sexual theories]. In *Sammlung kleinerer Schriften zur Neurosenlehre* [Collected lesser writings on neurosis], 2:162 ff. Leipzig: Deuticke.

———. 1909h. Zwangshandlungen und Religionsübung [Obsessional neurosis and religious practice]. In *Sammlung kleinerer Schriften zur Neurosenlehre* [Collected lesser writings on neurosis], vol. 2, Leipzig: Deuticke.

———. 1910. Beiträge zur Psychologie des Liebeslebens. I. Über einen besonderen Typus der Objektwahl beim Manne [Contributions to the psychology of sexual life. I. Concerning a special type of object selection by men]. *Jahrbuch für Psychoanalytische und Psychopathologische Forschungen* 2:389–97.

———. 1911. Formulierungen über die zwei Prinzipien des psychischen Geschehens [Formulations concerning the two principles of psychic activity]. *Jahrbuch für Psychoanalytische und Psychopathologische Forschungen* 3:1–8.

———. 1912a. *Über Psychoanalyse* [On psychoanalysis]. 2d ed. Leipzig: Deuticke.

———. 1912b. *Der Witz und seine Beziehung zum Unbewussten* [Humor and its connection with the unconscious]. 2d ed. Leipzig: Deuticke.

Freytag, Gustav. 1872. *Technik des Dramas* [Dramatic technique]. 2d ed. Leipzig: Hirzel.

Friedjung, Josef K. 1912. Eine sonderbare Rationalisation einer inzestuösen Eifersucht [An unusual rationalization of incestuous jealousy]. *Zentralblatt für Psychoanalyse* 2:293.

Friedrichs, Gustav. 1909. *Grundlage, Entstehung, und genaue Einzeldeutung der bekanntesten germanischen Märchen, Mythen, und Sagen* [The basis, development, and precise individual interpretation of the best-known Germanic folktales, myths, and legends]. Leipzig: Heims.

Frobenius, Leo V. 1904. *Die Zeitalter des Sonnengottes* [The era of the sun-god]. Vol. 1. Berlin: Reimer.

Geiger, Wilhelm, and Ernst Kuhn, eds. 1895–1904. *Grundriss der iranischen Philologie* [Fundamentals of Iranian philology]. 2 vols. Strasbourg: Trübner.

Gercke, Alfred. 1905. Die Entstehung des *Don Carlos* [The origin of *Don Carlos*]. *Deutsche Rundschau* 123:60–84.

Glasenapp, Carl. 1894. *Das Leben Richard Wagners* [The life of Richard Wagner]. Leipzig: Breitkopf und Härtel.

Goldziher, Ignaz. 1876. *Der Mythus bei den Hebräern und seine geschichtliche Entwicklung* [Hebrew mythology and its historical development]. Leipzig.

Gonzenbach, Laura. 1870. *Sicilianische Märchen* [Sicilian folktales]. Leipzig.

Graf, Max. 1911. *Richard Wagner in "Der fliegende Holländer": Ein Beitrag zur Psychologie künstlerischen Schaffens* [Richard Wagner in *The Flying Dutchman:* A contribution to the psychology of artistic creativity]. Schriften zur Angewandten Seelenkunde [Writings on applied psychology], vol. 9. Leipzig: Deuticke.

Grässe, Johann G. T., ed. 1850. *Legenda aurea* [The golden legend], by Jacobus de Varagine. Leipzig: Arnold.

Greith, Karl. 1838. *Spicilegium Vaticanum* [Vatican gleanings]. Frauenfeld: Beyel.

Griesbach, E. 1886. *Die Wanderung der Novelle von der treulosen Witwe durch die Weltliteratur* [The wanderings of the unfaithful widow through world literature]. Berlin.

Grimm, Jakob. 1899. *Deutsche Rechtsalterthümer* [Antiquities of German law]. 4th ed. Vol. 1. Leipzig: Dieterich.

Grimm, Jakob, and Wilhelm Grimm. 1812. *Die beiden ältesten Gedichte aus dem achten Jahrhundert* [The two oldest poems of the eighth century]. Kassel: Thurneisen.

———. 1816. *Deutsche Sagen* [German folktales]. Berlin.

Gruppe, Otto, 1897. *Griechische Mythologie und Religionsgeschichte* [Greek mythology and religious history]. Munich: Beck.

Guessard, François, and L. Larchey, eds. 1860. *Parise la duchesse: Chanson de geste* [Parise the duchess: Romance]. Paris: Vieweg.

Hagen, Friedrich H. 1808. *Deutsche Gedichte des Mittelalters* [German poems of the Middle Ages]. Vol. 1. Berlin.

———. 1850. *Gesamtabenteuer* [Collected tales]. 3 vols. Stuttgart and Tübingen: Cotta.

Hahn, J. G. 1864. *Griechische und albanenische Märchen* [Greek and Albanian folktales]. Leipzig: Engelmann.

Hartung, Johann A. 1865–73. *Religion und Mythologie der Griechen* [Religion and mythology of the Greeks]. 4 vols. Leipzig: Engelmann.

Haupt, Moritz. 1860. [Article]. *Monatsbericht der Akademie zu Berlin,* 141 ff.

Helbing, Franz [pseud.]. 1908. *Geschichte der weiblichen Untreue* [History of adultery by women]. Berlin: Jacobsthal.

Hertz, Wilhelm. 1862. *Poetische Erzählungen nach altbretonischen Liebessagen* [Poetic tales after Old Breton love stories]. Stuttgart.

Hettner, Hermann. 1894–1913. *Literaturgeschichte des achtzehnten Jahrhunderts* [Literary history of the eighteenth century]. 5th ed. Braunschweig: Vieweg.

Heyse, Paul. 1900. *Jugenderinnerungen und Bekenntnisse* [Memoirs and confessions of youth]. Berlin: Hertz.

Hinrichs, Hermann. 1827. *Das Wesen der antiken Tragödie* [The nature of classical tragedy]. Halle: Ruff.

Hoffmeister, Karl. 1838. *Schillers Leben, Geistesentwicklung und Werke im Zusammenhang* [Schiller's life, intellectual development, and works in relation to one another]. Stuttgart: Balz.

Homer. 1961. *Odyssey.* Translated by Robert Fitzgerald. Garden City, N.Y.: Doubleday.

———. 1974. *Iliad.* Translated by Robert Fitzgerald. Garden City, N.Y.: Anchor Press/Doubleday.

Hoogers, P. J. 1910. Théorie et pratique de la piété filiale chez les Chinois [Theory and practice of filial piety among the Chinese]. *Anthropos* 5:1–15, 688–702.

Horstmann, C. 1876. Gregorius auf dem Steine [Saint Gregory of the Rock]. *Archiv für das Studium der Neueren Sprachen und Literatur* 55:407–39.

Hüsing, Georg. 1906. *Beiträge zur Kyros-Sage* [On the Cyrus legend]. Berlin: Peiser.

Jagić, Vatroslav. 1876. Dunav-Dunaj in der slawischen Volkspoesie [The Danube in Slavic folk poetry]. *Archiv für Slawische Philologie* 1:299–333.

Jakob, Franz. 1907. *Die Fabel des Atreus und Thyestes in den wichtigsten Tragödien der englischen, französischen und italienischen Literatur* [The myth of Atreus and Thyestes in the most important tragedies of English, French, and Italian literature]. Leipzig.

Jensen, Wilhelm. 1911. *Fremdlinge unter den Menschen* [Strangers among men]. Dresden: Reissner.

Jeremias, Alfred. 1904. *Das Alte Testament im Licht des alten Orients* [The Old Testament in the light of the ancient East]. Leipzig: Hinrichs.

———. 1905. *Babylonisches im Neuen Testament* [Babylonian elements in the New Testament]. Leipzig: Hinrichs.

Jessen, Jarno, ed. 1906. *Die Briefe Lord Byrons* [The letters of Lord Byron]. Leipzig: Reclam.

Jiriczek, Otto. 1894. *Die deutsche Heldensage* [The German heroic saga]. Stuttgart: Göschen.

Jonas, Fritz, ed. 1892. *Schillers Briefe: Kritische Gesamtausgabe* [Schiller's letters: Critical complete edition]. Stuttgart.

Jonckbloet, W. J. A. 1870. *Geschichte der niederländischen Literatur* [History of Dutch literature]. Leipzig: Vogel.

Jung, Carl G. 1909. Die Bedeutung des Vaters für das Schicksal des Einzelnen [The importance of the father to the destiny of the individual]. *Jahrbuch für Psychoanalytische und Psychopathologische Forschungen* 1:155–73.

———. 1911. [Article]. *Zentralblatt für Psychoanalyse* 1:85.

Kelle, Johann. 1868. Zu den *Gestis Romanorum* [On the *Gesta Romanorum*]. *Serapeum* 29:96–100.

Kersten, Dr. 1904. [Article]. *Archiv für Kriminal-Anthropologie und Kriminalistik* 16:330.

Kirpichnikov, Aleksandr. 1873. *On the comparative theory of the Western and Russian epic: The poems of the Longobardian cycle* (In Russian). Moscow.

Klages, Ludwig. 1899a. Aus einer Seelenlehre des Künstlers [Aspects of the psychology of the artist]. *Blätter für die Kunst* 5, 2. Berlin: Bondi.

———. 1899b. Vom Schaffenden [The creator]. *Blätter für die Kunst,* 4, 1 and 2. Berlin: Bondi.

Knust, Hermann. 1866. [Article]. *Jahrbuch für Romanische und Englische Literatur* 7:398 ff.

Koeppel, Emil. 1895. Quellstudien zu den Dramen Ben Jonsons, John Marstons, und Beaumonts und Fletchers [The sources of the dramas of Ben Jonson, John Marston, and Beaumont and Fletcher]. *Münchener Beiträge zur Romanischen und Englischen Philologie,* vol. 11.

Köhler, Reinhold. 1868. [Article]. *Revue Critique d'Histoire et de Littérature* 2:413 ff.

———. 1870. Zur Legende von Gregorius auf dem Steine [On the legend of Saint Gregory of the Rock] *Germania* 15:284–91.

———. 1899. *Kleinere Schriften* [Lesser writings]. Vol. 2. Edited by Johannes Bolte. Weimar: Felber.

Kossmann, Robby. 1905. *Züchtungspolitik* [The politics of breeding]. Berlin: Renaissance.

Krauss, Friedrich. 1911. *Das Geschlechtsleben in Glauben, Sitte, Brauch, und Gewohnheitsrecht der Japaner* [The sexual life of the Japanese in religion, tradition, practice, and common law]. 2d ed. Leipzig: Ethnologischer Verlag.

Laistner, M. L. W. 1899. *Das Rätsel der Sphinx* [The riddle of the Sphinx]. Berlin.

Landau, Marcus. 1899. *Geschichte der italienischen Literatur im achtzehnten Jahrhundert* [History of Italian literature in the eighteenth century]. Berlin: Felber.

Lenormant, François. 1872. *Lettres assyriologiques et épigraphiques* [Assyriological and epigraphical letters]. Paris.

Lessing, Gotthold E. 1790. *Leben des Sophokles* [Life of Sophocles]. Edited by Johann J. Eschenburg. Berlin: Voss.

Lessmann, Heinrich. 1906. Die Kyros-Sage in Europe [The Cyrus legend in Europe]. Lecture given at the Königliche Realschule zu Charlottenburg.

———. 1908. *Aufgaben und Ziele der vergleichenden Mythenforschung* [Tasks and goals of comparative mythology]. Leipzig: Hinrichs.

Liebrecht, Felix. 1869. [Article]. *Göttinger Gelehrte Anzeigen*, p. 1037.

———. 1879. *Zur Volkskunde: Alte und neue Aufsätze* [Ethnography: Old and new essays]. Heilbronn: Henninger.

Lippold, Friedrich. 1896. Zur Geschichte der Legende [On the history of the legend]. Dissertation, Leipzig.

Löwenfeld, Leopold. 1908. Über sexuelle Träume [On sexual dreams]. *Sexualprobleme* 4:588–601.

———. 1911. Die Libido als geistige Triebkraft [The libido as a source of psychic energy]. In *Über die sexuelle Konstitution und andere Sexualprobleme* [On sexual constitution and other sexual problems]. Wiesbaden: Bergmann.

Luzel, François Marie. 1881. *Légendes chrétiennes de la Basse-Bretagne* [Christian legends of Lower Brittany]. 2 vols. Paris: Maisonneuve.

Mannhardt, Wilhelm. 1858. *Germanische Mythen* [Germanic myths]. Berlin.

Marcuse, Max. 1908. Zur Kritik des Begriffes und der Tat der Blutschande [A critical analysis of the concept and act of incest]. *Sexualprobleme*, March, 129–52.

Matthieu, Pierre. 1606. *Histoire de France et des choses mémorables advenues aux provinces estrangères durant sept années de paix* [History of France and of the memorable events occurring in the foreign provinces during seven years of peace]. Vol. 3. Paris.

Méon, Dominique. 1823. *Nouveau recueil de fabliaux et contes inédites des poètes français des XIIe, XIIIe, XIVe, et XVe siècles* [New collection of unpublished fables and stories by French poets of the twelfth, thirteenth, fourteenth, and fifteenth centuries]. 2 vols. Paris: Chasseriau.

Meyer, Paul. 1868. *Guillaume de la Barre*. Paris.

Meyerfeld, Max. 1908. Byron und seine Schwester. *Die Neue Rundschau*, May.

Miller, Orest. 1869. *Ilya Muromets and Kievan heroism* (in Russian). Saint Petersburg.

Millin, Aubin Louis. 1790–99. *Antiquités nationales* [National antiquities]. 5 vols. Paris: Drouhin.

Minor, Jakob. 1890. *Schiller: Sein Leben und seine Werke* [Schiller: His life and his works]. Berlin.

Mone, Franz Joseph. 1833. [Article]. *Anzeiger für Kunde der Deutschen Vorzeit* 2:238.

Moser, Werner. 1903. Die Kainsage in ihrer ursprünglichen Form [The Cain legend in its original form]. *Nord und Süd*.

Müller, Max. 1869. *Essays*. Leipzig: Engelmann.

Müller, Wilhelm. 1856. Die Sage vom Schwanritter [The legend of the Swan Knight]. *Germania*, n.s., 1:418–40.

Multatuli [Eduard Douwes Dekker]. 1901. *Die Abenteuer des kleinen Walther* [The adventures of little Walter]. Translated by Karl Mischke. Halle: Hendel.

Mundt, Theodor. 1857. *Pariser Kaiser-Skizzen* [Parisian sketches of the emperors]. Vol. 1. Berlin.

Näcke, P. 1902. [Article]. *Archiv für Kriminal-Anthropologie und Kriminalistik*, vol. 20.

Nauck, August. 1889. *Tragicorum graecorum fragmenta* [Fragments of Greek tragedies]. Leipzig: Teubner.

Nodilo, Natko. 1898–1905. *Historija srednjega vijeka za narod hrvatski i srpski*. 3 vols. Zagreb: Jugoslavenska Akademija Znanosti i Umjetnosti.

Nöldeke, Theodore. 1887. *Aufsätze zur persischen Geschichte* [Essays on Persian history]. Leipzig: Weigel.

Novaković, Stojan. 1888. Die Oedipus-Sage in der südslawischen Volksdichtung [The Oedipus legend in south Slavic folk poetry]. *Archiv für Slawische Philologie* 11:321–26.

Paris, Gaston. 1879. Le lay de Doon [The lay of Doon]. In Lais inédits [Unpublished lays]. *Romania* 8:29–72.

Patin, Henri J. G. 1870–73. *Etudes sur les tragiques grecs* [Studies on the Greek tragedies]. 4th ed. 4 vols. Paris: Hachette

Petitot, Emile. 1886. *Traditions indiennes du Canada nord-ouest* [Indian traditions of northwest Canada]. Paris: Maisonneuve.

Pfister, Oskar. 1912. Anwendungen der Psychoanalyse in der Pädagogik und Seelsorge [Applications of psychoanalysis in pedagogy and spiritual instruction]. *Imago* 1:56–82.

Ploss, Hermann H. 1895. *Das Weib in der Natur und Völkerkunde* [Woman in nature and ethnography]. Edited by Max Bartels. Leipzig: Grieben.

Preller, Ludwig. 1854–55. *Griechische Mythologie* [Greek mythology]. Vol. 1. Berlin: Weidmann.

Preuner, August. 1864. *Hestia-Vestia: Ein Cyclus religionsgeschichtlicher Forschungen* [Hestia-Vestia: A cycle of research in the history of religion]. Tübingen: Laupp.

Quélen, Marie. 1868. *Chants populaires de la Basse-Bretagne* [Folk songs of Lower Brittany]. Paris: Duzel.

Rank, Otto. 1907. *Der Künstler: Ansätze zu einer Sexual-Psychologie* [The artist: Preliminaries to a sexual psychology]. Vienna: Heller.

———. 1909. *Der Mythus von der Geburt des Helden* [The myth of the birth of the hero]. Leipzig: Deuticke.

———. 1911a. Beispiel eines verkappten Ödipustraumes [Example of a disguised Oedipal dream]. *Zentralblatt für Psychoanalyse* 1:167–70.

———. 1911b. *Die Lohengrin Sage* [The Lohengrin legend]. Leipzig: Deuticke.

———. 1912a. Völkerpsychologische Parallelen zu den infantilen Sexualtheorien [Ethnopsychological parallels to childhood sexual theories]. *Zentralblatt für Psychoanalyse* 2:372–82, 425–37.

———. 1912b. *Die Lohengrin Sage: Ein Beitrag zu ihrer Motivgestaltung und Deutung* [The Lohengrin legend: A contribution to its thematic form and interpretation]. Schriften zur Angewandten Seelenkunde [Writings on applied psychology], vol. 13. Leipzig: Deuticke.

———. 1913. Die Nacktheit in Sage und Dichtung [Nakedness in legend and literature]. *Imago* 2:267–301, 409–46.

———. 1975. *The Don Juan legend*. Trans. and ed. David G. Winter. Princeton: Princeton University Press.

Reibmayr, Albert. 1908. *Entwicklungsgeschichte des Talents und Genies* [Developmental history of talent and genius]. Munich: Lehmann.

Reik, Theodor. 1911. Die liebende Flaubert [Flaubert in love]. *Pan*, vol. 2, no.4.

———. 1912. *Richard Beer-Hofmann*. Leipzig: Eichler.

Ribbeck, Otto. 1875. *Die römischen Tragödien im Zeitalter der Republik* [The Roman tragedies in the age of the Republic]. Leipzig: Teubner.

Ribot, Théodule-Armand. 1902. *Die Schöpferkraft der Phantasie* [The creative power of fantasy]. Translated by Werner Mecklenburg. Bonn: Strauss.

Richter, Helene. 1887. *Der entfesselte Prometheus* [Prometheus unbound]. Stuttgart.

———. 1898. *Percy Bysshe Shelley*. Weimar: Felber.

Riklin, F. 1908. *Wunscherfüllung und Symbolik im Märchen* [Wish fulfillment and symbolism in the folktale]. Schriften zur Angewandten Seelenkunde [Writings in applied psychology], vol. 2, Leipzig: Deuticke.

Rink, Henry John. 1875. *Tales and traditions of the Eskimo*. Edinburgh: Blackwood.

Rittershaus, Adeline. 1902. *Die neuisländischen Volksmärchen* [Modern Icelandic folktales]. Halle: Niemeyer.

Rochholz, Ernst L. 1856. *Schweizer Sagen aus dem Aargau* [Swiss legends from Aargau]. Vol. 1. Aargau: Sauerländer.

Roscher, Wilhelm Heinrich. 1884–1937. *Ausführliches Lexikon der griechischen und römischen Mythologie* [Detailed lexicon of Greek and Roman mythology]. Leipzig: Teubner.

Rudbeck, Erik. 1852. *Suomen kansan satuja ja tarinoita* [Collection of Finnish folktales]. Helsinki: Salmelainen.

Sachs, Otto. 1898. *Von zwei Geschwistern* [Of two siblings]. Berlin: Schuster und Löffler.

Sadger, Isidor. 1909a. *Aus dem Liebesleben Nikolaus Lenaus* [On the love life of Nikolaus Lenau]. Leipzig: Deuticke.

———. 1909b. Zur Ätiologie der konträren Sexualempfindung [The etiology of contrary sexual response]. *Medizinische Klinik*, no. 2.

Sakellarios, Athanasios. 1868. *Ta Kypriaka* [Cypriot folktales]. Vol. 3. Athens.

Salvá, Vicente. 1826. *A catalogue of Spanish and Portuguese books with occasional literary and bibliographical remarks*. London.

Sánchez, Climente. 1860. *El libro de los exemplos por a.b.c.* [The book of examples for abc]. Madrid: Rivadeneyra.

Sauer, August, ed. 1901. *Die deutschen Säculardichtungen an der Wende des achtzehnten und neunzehnten Jahrhunderts* [German secular literature at the turn of the eighteenth and nineteenth centuries]. Deutsche Literaturdenkmale des Achtzehnten und Neunzehnten Jahrhunderts [German literary monuments of the eighteenth and nineteenth centuries], nos. 91–104. Berlin: Behr.

Schaeffer, Adolf. 1890. *Geschichte des spanischen National-Dramas* [History of Spanish drama]. Leipzig: Brockhaus.

Schanz, Martin. 1907. *Geschichte der römischen Literatur* [History of Roman literature]. Munich: Beck.

Schiefner, Anton. [n.d.] [Article]. In *Mélanges russes,* 2:622. Saint Petersburg: Imperial Academy of Sciences.

Schiller-Tietz, Nikolaus. 1892. *Folgen, Bedeutung, und Wesen der Blutsverwandtschaft im Menschen-, Tier-, und Pflanzenleben* [The consequences, significance, and nature of blood relationship in the life of humans, animals, and plants]. Berlin: Heusers.

Schmidt, Bernhard, ed. and trans. 1877. *Griechische Märchen, Sagen, und Volkslieder* [Greek folktales, legends, and folk songs]. Leipzig: Teubner.

Schmidt, Erich. 1899. *Lessing: Geschichte seines Lebens und seiner Schriften* [Lessing: His life and works]. 2d ed. 2 vols. Berlin: Weidmann.

Schneider, Hermann. 1907. *Kultur und Denken der alten Ägypter* [Culture and thought among the ancient Egyptians]. Leipzig: Voigtländer.

Schneidewin, Friedrich Wilhelm. 1852. *Die Sage vom Ödipus* [The legend of Oedipus]. Göttingen: Dieterich.

Schrader, Otto. 1901. *Reallexikon der indogermanischen Altertumskunde* [Encyclopedia of Indogermanic archaeology]. Strasbourg: Trübner.

Schreck, Emmy. 1887. *Finnische Märchen* [Finnish folktales]. Weimar: Böhlau.

Schultz, Wolfgang. 1909. *Rätsel aus dem hellenischen Kulturkreise* [Riddles of the Hellenic culture area]. Leipzig: Hinrichs.

Schulz, W. 1911. Das Geschlechtliche in gnostischer Lehre und Übung [The sexual in Gnostic doctrine and practice]. *Zeitschrift für Religionspsychologie* 5, no. 3.

Schwartz, Friedrich L. W. 1860. *Der Ursprung der Mythologie dargelegt an griechischer und deutscher Sage* [The origin of mythology exemplified by Greek and German legend]. Berlin: Hertz.

———. 1874. [Article]. *Jahrbuch für Klassische Philologie,* vol. 3.

Seligmann, Siegfried. 1910. *Der böse Blick und Verwandtes* [The evil eye and related themes]. 2 vols. Berlin: Barsdorf.

Siecke, Ernst. 1892. *Die Liebesgeschichte des Himmels* [The story of love among the gods]. Strasbourg: Trübner.

———. 1897. *Die Urreligion der Indogermanen* [The protoreligion of the Indo-Europeans]. Berlin: Mayer und Müller.

———. 1901. *Mythologische Briefe* [Mythological letters]. Berlin.

———. 1908. *Hermes der Mondgott* [Hermes the moon-god]. Leipzig: Hinrichs.

———. 1909. *Götterattribute und sogenannte Symbole* [Attributes of the gods and so-called symbols]. Jena: Costenoble.

Simrock, Karl Joseph. 1864. *Auserlesene Deutsche Volksbücher* [Collected German folktales]. Frankfurt am Main: Winter.

———. 1870. *Die Quellen des Shakespeares in Novellen, Märchen, und Sagen* [Shakespeare's sources in novellas, folktales, and legends]. 2d ed. Bonn: Marcus.

Spitteler, Carl. 1906. [Article]. *Kunstwart* 20:73–79.

Stekel, Wilhelm. 1908. *Nervöse Angstzustände und ihre Behandlung* [Nervous states

of anxiety and their treatment]. Berlin: Urban und Schwarzenberg.
———. 1909. *Dichtung und Neurose: Bausteine zur Psychologie des Künstlers und Kunstwerkes* [Poetry and neurosis: fundamentals of the psychology of the artist and the work of art]. Wiesbaden: Bergmann.
Stoll, Otto. 1908. *Geschlechtsleben in der Völkerpsychologie* [Sexual life in ethnopsychology]. Leipzig: Veit.
Storfer, A. J. 1911. *Zur Sonderstellung des Vatermordes* [The special significance of patricide]. Leipzig: Deuticke.
Streicher, Andreas. 1965. *Schillers Flucht von Stuttgart* [Schiller's flight from Stuttgart]. Stuttgart: Reclam. (Originally published Cotta, 1836.)
Stucken, Eduard. 1896–1907. *Astralmythen der Hebräer, Babylonier, und Ägypter* [Astral myths of the Hebrews, Babylonians, and Egyptians]. 5 vols. Leipzig: Pfeiffer.
———. 1902. [Article]. *Mitteilungen der Vorderasiatischen Gesellschaft* 4:52.
Talvj [Therese Robinson]. 1853. *Volkslieder der Serben* [Folk songs of the Serbians]. 3d ed. Leipzig.
Tressan, Louis Elisabeth de La Vergne, comte de. 1788. Tristan de Léonois. In *Soixante-sept oeuvres choisies du comte de Tressan* [Sixty-seven selected works by the count of Tressan], 7:31. Paris: Romans.
Trollope, Anthony. 1980. *An Autobiography.* Oxford: Oxford University Press.
Uhland, Ludwig. 1865. *Schriften zur Geschichte der Dichtung und Sage* [Writings on the history of poetry and legend], Vol. 1. Stuttgart: Cotta.
Verdier, Antoine du. 1585. *Bibliothèque* [Library]. Lyon.
Virgil. 1950. *Aeneid.* In *Vergil's Works.* Translated by J. W. Mackail. New York: Random House.
Warnke, Karl. 1885. *Die Lais der Marie de France* [The lays of Marie of France]. Halle.
Warrens, Rosa. n.d. *Germanische Volkslieder der Vorzeit* [Ancient Germanic folk songs]. Hamburg.
Weil, Gustav. 1845. *Biblische Legenden der Muselmänner* [Biblical legends of the Moslems]. Frankfurt: Literarische Anstalt.
Welcker, Friedrich G. 1839–41. *Die griechischen Tragödien* [The Greek tragedies]. Bonn: Welcker.
Wesselofsky, Alexander. 1879. Beiträge zur Erklärung des russischen Heldenepos [Contributions to the interpretation of the Russian heroic epic]. *Archiv für Slawische Philologie* 3:549–93.
Westermarck, Edward A. 1908. Gattenwahl, Inzucht, und Mitgift [Spouse selection, endogamy, and the dowry]. *Die Neue Generation,* vol. 1, no. 2.
———. 1909. *Sexualfragen* [Sexual questions]. Leipzig.
White, John. 1887–90. *The ancient history of the Maori.* Wellington: Didsbury.
Wilamowitz-Moellendorff, Ulrich. 1875. *Analecta Euripidea.* Berlin: Borntraeger.
Wilhelmine [consort of Frederick William, margrave of Bayreuth]. 1910. *Eine preussische Königstochter* [A Prussian princess]. Munich: Langewiesche-Brandt.
Winckler, Hugo. 1895–1900. *Geschichte Israels in Einzeldarstellungen* [History of Israel in individual presentations]. 2 vols. Leipzig: Pfeiffer.

———. 1901. Arabisch-Semitisch-Orientalisches. *Mitteilungen der Vorderasiatischen Gesellschaft,* vols. 4–5.

———. 1907. Der alte Orient und die Bibel [The ancient East and the Bible]. In *Ex Oriente lux* [Light from the East], ed. Hugo Winckler, vol. 2. Leipzig: Pfeiffer.

———. 1907. *Die babylonische Geisteskultur in ihren Beziehungen zur Kulturentwicklung der Menschheit* [Babylonian intellectual life and its relationship to the cultural development of mankind]. Leipzig: Quelle und Meyer.

Witkowsi, Georg. 1903. *Cornelia, die Schwester Goethes* [Cornelia, Goethe's sister]. Frankfurt: Rütten und Loening.

Wright, Thomas. 1842. *A selection of Latin stories from manuscripts of the thirteenth and fourteenth centuries.* London: Richards.

Wundt, Wilhelm. 1909. *Völkerpsychologie* [Ethnopsychology]. Vol. 2. Leipzig: Engelmann.

Wurzbach, Alfred Wolfgang. 1899. *Lope de Vega und seine Komödien* [Lope de Vega and his comedias]. Leipzig: Seele.

Zainer, Günther. 1471–72. *Leben der Heiligen* [Lives of the saints]. Augsburg: Winterteil.

Zipper, Albert. 1900. *Theodor Körner.* Leipzig: Reclam.

Zitelmann, Katharina. 1912. [Article]. *Die Zeit,* February 16.

Index

Hochzeit, Die (Wagner), 519, 534, 536; Oedipus theme in, 535

Designed by Martha Farlow

Composed by Graphic Composition, Inc., in Plantin

Printed by The Maple Press Company, Inc., on 50-lb. Glatfelter Eggshell Cream and bound in ICG Arrestox B with Multicolor Elephant Hide endsheets.